BRITISH WARSHIP LOSSES in the Age of Sail
1649–1860

BRITISH WARSHIP LOSSES in the Age of Sail 1649–1860

DAVID HEPPER

Copyright © David Hepper 2023

First published in Great Britain in 2023 by
Seaforth Publishing,
A division of Pen & Sword Books Ltd,
George House, Beevor Street, Barnsley S71 1HN

www.seaforthpublishing.com

British Library Cataloguing in Publication Data
A catalogue record for this book is available from the British Library

ISBN 978 1 3990 3102 8 (Hardback)
ISBN 978 1 3990 3103 5 (EPub)
ISBN 978 1 3990 3104 2 (Kindle)

All rights reserved. No part of this publication may be reproduced or transmitted in any form or by any means, electronic or mechanical, including photocopying, recording, or any information storage and retrieval system, without prior permission in writing of both the copyright owner and the above publisher.

The right of David Hepper to be identified as the author of this work has been asserted by him in accordance with the Copyright, Designs and Patents Act 1988.

Pen & Sword Books Limited incorporates the imprints of Atlas, Archaeology, Aviation, Discovery, Family History, Fiction, History, Maritime, Military, Military Classics, Politics, Select, Transport, True Crime, Air World, Frontline Publishing, Leo Cooper, Remember When, Seaforth Publishing, The Praetorian Press, Wharncliffe Local History, Wharncliffe Transport, Wharncliffe True Crime and White Owl

Typeset in Bembo 9/11pt by Mac Style

Printed and bound in Great Britain by
CPI Group (UK) Ltd,
Croydon, CR0 4YY

Contents

List of Illustrations	vi
Introduction: Losses in the Age of Sail	vii
Ship Types	x
Sea Terminology	xii
1649–1660: The Interregnum: Dutch Wars and Expansion	1
1660–1688: The Restoration: Wars against the Dutch and Barbary Corsairs	9
1689–1714: Invasion, War and Union	32
1715–1739: The Long Peace	78
1739–1748: The War of the Austrian Succession ('The War of Jenkins's Ear')	82
1749–1754: A Brief Peace	97
1755–1763: The Seven Years War	99
1764–1771: Growing Tension in North America	114
1772–1783: American Independence	117
1783–1793: A Period of Peace and Political Agitation	165
1793–1802: Revolution and War	169
1803–1815: World War	219
1816–1859: Empire and Expansion	313
Bibliography	345
Alphabetical Index of Ships Lost	349

List of Illustrations

Between pages 114 and 115
1. 4 March 1653. Battle of Livorno – *Samson* being destroyed. (*Thaliastock/Mary Evans*)
2. June 1666. Dutch ships returning with their prizes after the Four Days' Battle – probably depicting in the background, the *Convertine*, *Swiftsure* and *Loyal George*. (© *National Maritime Museum, Greenwich, London*)
3. June 1667. The Dutch burn English ships in the Medway. (*Mary Evans/The Everett Collection*)
4. May 1692. A fireship burning a flagship (la Hougue). (© *National Maritime Museum, Greenwich, London*)
5. February 1799. Passengers and crew leave the *Proserpine* frigate. (© *National Maritime Museum, Greenwich, London*)
6. March 1800. The sloop *Speedy* with the wreck of the *Queen Charlotte*. (© *National Maritime Museum, Greenwich, London*)
7. 25 March 1804. The loss of the *Magnificent* off Brest. (© *National Maritime Museum, Greenwich, London*)
8. 4 February 1805. *Arrow* sinking after action with two French frigates. (© *National Maritime Museum, Greenwich, London*)
9. 4 March 1807. The loss of the *Blanche* on the coast of Britanny. (© *National Maritime Museum, Greenwich, London*)
10. 28 December 1807. Wreck of the *Anson* frigate at Helston. (© *National Maritime Museum, Greenwich, London*)
11. 24 December 1811. The wreck of the *Hero* in the Texel. (© *National Maritime Museum, Greenwich, London*)
12. 29 December 1812. The destruction of the *Java* after capture. (*Mary Evans/The Everett Collection*)
13. 20 February 1815. Action of the *Cyane* and *Levant* with USS *Constitution*. (*Mary Evans/The Everett Collection*)
14. 26 February 1852. *Birkenhead* sinking in Algoa Bay. (*Mary Evans Picture Library*)
15. 12 May 1854. The *Tiger* aground near Odessa. (*Mary Evans Picture Library*)
16. 14 April 1857. The *Raleigh* salutes the French admiral whilst running onto the beach at Macao. (© *National Maritime Museum, Greenwich, London*)

Between pages 210 and 211
1. 5 October 1744. A ship in distress – the loss of the *Victory*. (© *National Maritime Museum, Greenwich, London*)
2. 10 June 1772. Schooner *Gaspee* being burnt. (*Mary Evans Picture Library*)
3. 23 September 1779. *Serapis* versus the *Bonhomme Richard*. (*Mary Evans/The Everett Collection*)
4. 11 October 1780. The *Andromeda* in a hurricane. (© *National Maritime Museum, Greenwich, London*)
5. 29 August 1782. *Royal George* heeling over. (*Mary Evans Picture Library*)
6. 16 September 1782. *Centaur* in the storm. (© *National Maritime Museum, Greenwich, London*)
7. 28 April 1789. *Bounty* mutineers cast adrift Captain Bligh. (*Mary Evans Picture Library*)
8. 28 August 1791. *Pandora* sinking in the Torres Strait, Great Barrier Reef. (*Mary Evans Picture Library*)
9. 29 August 1794. The burning of the *Impetueux*. (© *National Maritime Museum, Greenwich, London*)
10. 1 May 1795. *Boyne* on fire. (© *National Maritime Museum, Greenwich, London*)
11. 5 November 1799. Wreck of the *Sceptre* in Table Bay. (© *National Maritime Museum, Greenwich, London*)
12. 17 August 1803. Rafts leave the wreck of the *Porpoise*. (© *National Maritime Museum, Greenwich, London*)
13. 8 May 1804. Action between *Vincejo* and a French flotilla. (© *National Maritime Museum, Greenwich, London*)
14. 11 April 1809. *Mediator* in the Basque Roads 1809. (© *National Maritime Museum, Greenwich, London*)
15. 24 August 1810. Battle in the Grand Port, Mauritius. (© *National Maritime Museum, Greenwich, London*)
16. 25 October 1812. Capture of the *Macedonian* by USS *United States*. (*Mary Evans/Classic Stock/H Armstrong Roberts*)
17. 10 September 1813. Battle of Lake Erie. (© *National Maritime Museum, Greenwich, London*)
18. 29 April 1814. USS *Peacock* captures the *Epervier*. (© *National Maritime Museum, Greenwich, London*)
19. 2 October 1817. Wreck of the sloop *Julia* on Tristan da Cunha. (© *National Maritime Museum, Greenwich, London*)
20. 20 December 1847. The loss of the steam frigate *Avenger*. (© *National Maritime Museum, Greenwich, London*)

Introduction: Losses in the Age of Sail

THE AIM OF THIS BOOK is to provide a complete list of those ships of the Royal Navy which were lost at sea during the age of sail. Arranged in chronological order, it includes outline details of each vessel and the name of the commanding officer, as well as the circumstances of the loss.

The listing comes from several years' research using original primary sources in the main. It is hoped that the list is complete, and the details given correct. However, with such a large subject, some errors or omissions are inevitable, but it is to be trusted that these are few.

The choice of commencing the listing from 1649 may be considered as somewhat arbitrary. Medieval monarchs usually maintained a small force of ships, but it was not until the Tudors of the sixteenth century that the Navy became a permanent force, and an administration to support it gradually formed. The civil wars in the early seventeenth century saw a fleet divided, with rival factions. With the death of the King and the withdrawal of Prince Rupert with the last few Royalist ships from British waters in 1649, the Navy began a new phase as an instrument of the State and this seems to be an appropriate starting point. The launch of the iron-hulled, steam-powered *Warrior* in 1860 effectively marked the end of wooden-hulled sailing warships.

During the late seventeenth and early eighteenth centuries, the Government did issue details of losses, and they appear in the Parliamentary Journals. Newspapers of the day often carried reports of maritime misfortunes, but these have to be treated with some caution, as they often relied on third-party reports and were liable to distortion or exaggeration. Later in the eighteenth century, lists of those ships and vessels that had been lost appeared in contemporary publications such as *Naval Chronology* by Isaac Schomberg and William James's *Naval History* whilst Gold's *Naval Chronicle* and Steel's monthly editions of the *Navy List* which appeared during the French Revolutionary and Napoleonic Wars provided readers with regular updates on the progress of the war, detailing both success and disaster.

The nineteenth century saw a number of naval and maritime histories, which included *Narratives of Shipwrecks* in 1857 by William Gilly and culminating in William Laird Clowes' multi-volume *The Royal Navy: A History* which contained a list of casualties.

All of these sources were used to provide an outline listing, but the prime source used for the detail of a loss has been the courts-martial records held in The National Archives. A court martial was usually held on the senior survivors of a loss, to establish the cause. These records are somewhat scattered in the archives: the earliest of these are now in the collection of the State Papers, although from about 1673 some are to be found in the papers of the Navy Board (ADM.106 series). After 1689 they seem to have been kept separate from other documents and are contained in the correspondence directed to the Admiralty (ADM.1 series). They tend to be sparse until 1694, after which the majority of the ship losses, where there were survivors, have a court-martial enquiry.

Perils of the Sea

There were many reasons for a ship being lost: enemy action, fire, grounding, mutiny or foundering at sea. Life at sea was a hazardous pursuit. A correspondent to the *Nautical Magazine* in 1841, using the name 'An Old Tar', stated that the causes for ships being lost '… are more numerous than are generally imagined', and went on to detail fifty reasons for a loss, from being short of men to abandonment without sufficient cause, and included the poor condition of a ship through age and want of repair, incorrectness of charts and poor dead reckoning as well as other, rather odd, reasons such as 'the presence of captain's wives and other women'.

One of the most common reasons for a loss was navigational error. For much of the period, the charts carried onboard were inaccurate, and not only were dangers such as rocks and reefs frequently found to be missing but could be wrongly placed. Even with a reasonably accurate chart, the difficulties of navigation are evident, with the reliance on regular sun-sights and an inability to determine the longitude, which required an accurate chronometer. This forced officers to trust on dead reckoning – calculating how far they believed they had travelled, based on the speed of the ship and course steered. Such estimates were liable to errors and mistakes, often due to the strength of the wind and current. The difficulty of identifying a landmark in poor weather added to the complications. Ships were wrecked simply because they were not aware of being so close to the shore, often being many miles out in their reckoning.

Poor weather was an obvious peril, especially in the Caribbean and the Indian Ocean, where ships were exposed to hurricanes and cyclones. The losses in those regions feature regularly, but storm-force winds in home waters could also cause mass casualties, such as the Great Storm of 1703 or the disaster of the Baltic convoy in late 1811. For many ships, they have the melancholy fate of disappearance – overwhelmed by storm and sea, unseen by anyone. Even if a ship was in harbour, it was not necessarily safe. The force of wind and the sea could put such a strain on hemp cables that they parted, or an anchor could lose purchase and with little room to manoeuvre, ships found themselves driving into shallow water.

Collisions feature occasionally. The difficulties of manoeuvring a vessel dependent on the wind whilst in company with several other ships, often in close company, are evident, and this was made more hazardous at night or in poor weather.

Fire was a constant worry, and despite stringent regulations around the handling of flammable or explosive material, several ships were lost, despite the best efforts of fire-fighting teams. The presence of gun powder with the consequent risk of a magazine explosion also sometimes influenced any assistance from other ships or from shore – this may be seen in the burning of the *Queen Charlotte* in 1800.

A few ships were lost to mutiny – that of the *Bounty* is perhaps the best known, but there were several others, and the uprising that occurred on the *Hermione* was notable for its violence. Some were triggered by excessive discipline, but the co-ordinated action of a disaffected group in a ship's company could also be a factor.

For the ships lost to the enemy, the reasons are more straightforward; when faced with a larger opponent with a heavier armament, it was not a dishonourable action to surrender, to save further casualties.

The number of casualties, where known, is given, but often the figures from contemporary sources are vague. The presence of women aboard should also be noted, although they were not included in any musters or indeed officially noticed or recorded. It was not uncommon for warrant officers, the skilled specialists, such as the Carpenter, Gunner etc, to have wives and families accompany them and other women seemed to have found their way onboard and were a familiar sight.

Details of the Listing

Date of the loss: The date of the loss was usually established by the court, although occasionally, and curiously, the records sometimes fail to record the date. The gap can be filled by consulting surviving logs, contemporary letters and other documents, such as pay books (ADM.32, 33, 34 and 35), although the last-named source may not always be reliable, as a ship's company was frequently paid until the day of the court martial. For dates prior to 1689, letters to the Navy Board (ADM.106) are useful, whilst earlier dates can be established from the Calendar of State Papers (CSPD) or from the volumes of the Navy Records Society.

It should be noted that until 1752 it was the practice to officially commence the new year on 25 March, with the period between 1 January and that date often being written as two years, e.g., 1689/90, but this did not always happen. This has caused some confusion and error in the past, and I have taken the liberty of converting the dates so that they conform to modern practice. Up to 1752 Great Britain used the Julian calendar, whilst much of continental Europe conformed to the Gregorian, which meant that different dates for incidents may be found dependent on the source. In this case I have retained the date cited in British documents and it should be noted that different dates will be found in documents of foreign origin. This is further complicated by the naval practice, common until the early nineteenth century, of not commencing the new day until twelve noon. I have – I hope – shown the correct date of the loss, in spite of these complications.

Ship details: The two volumes of J J College's *Ships of the Royal Navy* provided the original starting point, but these have been since been greatly supplemented and expanded by David Lyons' *Sailing Navy List* and the four volumes by Rif Winfield, *British Warships in the Age of Sail*, which comprehensively cover the period 1603–1863.

Commanding Officers: Usually established from the court-martial records. Where no enquiry record exists, the name can be ascertained from the regularly-compiled lists of ships and officers (ADM.7 and ADM.8 series), supplemented by pay books. Prior to 1660 the publications of the Navy Records Society have proved invaluable.

Circumstances: Courts were established to investigate a loss, but the standard of the enquiries seems to have varied considerably. There was occasionally extensive questioning of the survivors, to examine fully the circumstances of the loss, with the Captain submitting a written report, sometimes accompanied by copies of relevant orders and extracts from journals and logs. Other courts seem to have decided what the cause was before they assembled, and a few leading questions were put to confirm their own suspicions. The records of others are incomplete, with only a single page noting the sentence, or else entirely missing. Ships' logs and Admirals' and Captains' letters have been used to rectify the deficiency where possible, and these sometimes give the details needed. Secondary sources have been resorted to where there are no primary sources apparent, or to supplement a sparse court-martial record.

Each entry follows the following format: date of loss, with name and type of vessel. The origin of the vessel, and, if built for the Navy, the location where the vessel was built with the year of launch or acquisition. Any previous names are noted in brackets; tonnage, measured dimensions, which are usually length of gundeck and beam; rated number of guns carried. The name of the Commanding Officer is shown, and the † marker indicates that he did not survive the loss. The notation after the entry indicates the principal source of information.

Acknowledgements

I gratefully acknowledge the cooperation of the staff at the National Maritime Museum, Greenwich, and Mary Evans Picture Library and for their permission to reproduce the illustrations.

Note

An earlier version of this work appeared several years ago, published by Jean Boudriot in 1994. The passage of time has allowed numerous revisions, corrections and additions to be made to the original text. Although retaining the skeleton of the original, this edition is essentially a new work.

Ship Types

A WIDE VARIETY OF VESSELS are listed, and a brief outline of the different types is shown below.

The Rates

The term was originally introduced into the Navy during the seventeenth century to indicate the different levels of pay for the commanding officers – the larger the ship, the higher the rate of pay. This became connected to the number of guns carried, so the First Rate was always the most powerful ship of the fleet. The precise definitions of each rate shifted over time, with the trend being to an increase in size and number of guns.

First Rate	100 guns or more
Second Rate	Originally more than 80, later from 84 to 90 guns
Third Rate	Originally from 60, later 64 to 80 guns
Fourth Rate	Initially from 40, later 46 to 50 guns
Fifth Rate	Early ships from 30, later standardised as 32 to 44 guns
Sixth Rate	Indicated the smallest ship that could be commanded by a Captain; originally from as few as 8 guns, later established as 24 to 28 guns

Ship of the line – indicated a ship that carried a heavy armament, able to stand in the line of battle. It usually meant a ship of the first three rates.

Frigate – the name originally referred to the build of a ship, 'frigate built' meaning a fast-sailing, fine-lined vessel. From the 1750s it was the term applied to the ships of the Fifth and Sixth Rates

Sloop – Strictly meant a sailing vessel with a single mast, but confusingly the term 'sloop of war' was also applied rather loosely to those warships that were too small to fit into one of the rated classes. By the end of the eighteenth century there were two distinct types of naval sloop – the brig sloop with two masts and the ship sloop with three masts. Both were square rigged.

In addition to the rate, the number of guns carried by a warship became a standard method of reference, with the name being followed by a number, so *Agamemnon*, 64, indicated the number of guns carried by that ship. It should be noted that this became distorted by the introduction, from 1779, of the carronade, a short-barrelled heavy-calibre weapon, as the Royal Navy did not include these weapons in the officially 'rated' force until 1817.

Other Types

Advice Boat – a small vessel used for carrying despatches and orders

Armed ship or vessel – a merchant vessel hired for a particular service, such as guarding a specific area

Bomb – vessel armed with mortars for bombarding shore positions

Brig – a two-masted square-rigged vessel

Buss – a type of broad-beamed fishing vessel with two masts

Cutter – a fast single-masted craft, with a square yard and a mainsail on a boom

Dogger – a North Sea fishing vessel, broad-beamed and usually two-masted

Felucca – an open-decked boat with lateen sails, used in the Mediterranean

Fireship – a vessel fitted out to be packed with flammable material, with the aim of closing and setting fire to enemy craft

Flyboat – a large flat-bottomed trading vessel with a high, broad stern

Galley – a vessel that relied on oars for propulsion

Galliot – a small single-masted vessel, that could also be rowed

Gunboat – a small, lightly-armed vessel used in shallow waters

Gun brig – a term used to identify a small brig commanded by a Lieutenant

Gundalow – a small flat-bottomed barge used in North America

Gunvessel – a term introduced at the end of the eighteenth century to designate small craft that were purchased into service for use in harbours and shallow waters

Hoy – a small coasting vessel, usually single-masted, fore and aft rigged

Hulk – usually referred to an old vessel converted to another purpose, such as floating stores, accommodation or prisons. The sheer hulk was used for lifting out masts

Ketch – denoted a small two-masted vessel: usually square rigged.

Lugger – a small two-masted vessel with lugsails

Packet – vessel used to carry mail. During the early nineteenth century, the Admiralty was responsible for these craft

Pettiauger – also rendered as Periauger and Piragua – a small flat-bottomed schooner-rigged vessel, common in the West Indies

Pink – a small square-rigged vessel with a narrow 'pinched' stern

Pinnace – a ship's boat, that could be rowed or sailed

Polacre – peculiar to the Mediterranean, usually three-masted, with a lateen-rigged foremast and square-rigged main and mizzen.

Prame – also Praam; flat-bottomed craft, usually two- or three-masted, used as gunboats, particularly by the French

Privateer – a privately-owned armed vessel holding a government commission to attack enemy shipping

Radeau – a simple raft or floating platform

Schooner – a fore-and-aft rigged vessel, usually two-masted, often with square-rigged topsails

Schuyt – a Dutch coasting barge

Shallop – a small vessel, often used as a tender to larger ships; often employed lug-sail rig

Ship – a seagoing vessel with three masts, square rigged

Smack – a small vessel usually used for inshore fishing

Snow – two-masted vessel, square-rigged on both masts, with a small mast immediately abaft the mainmast to allow a trysail to be rigged

Tartan – a single-masted lateen-rigged vessel

Tender – a small craft attached to a larger ship, for support purposes

Xebec – a vessel of the Mediterranean, lateen rigged and usually with overhanging bow and stern

Yacht – from the Dutch jacht, a small fast sailing vessel. During the seventeenth century often employed both as tenders to larger ships or as despatch vessels as well as pleasure craft

Sea Terminology

Some of the terms and expressions found within the book may not be familiar to everyone, therefore the following glossary is included

Aback – in a square-rigged ship when the sails are trimmed into the wind, so the sails are pressed against the mast

Abeam – at right angles to the ship; also, on the beam

Athwart – across the ship, from side to side

Bare poles – no sail spread

Beam – a strong piece of timber that went across the ship

Beam-ends – when a vessel is listing so much that her deck beams are almost vertical

Bear away – to change course to run before the wind

Bear down – to approach another ship from windward

Bear up – to sail closer to the wind

Beating – to progress by making a series of tacks

Bilge – the ship's bottom, next to the keel; to be bilged, means that the bottom has been pierced

Bobstay – rope securing the bowsprit to the stem

Boom – a spar used to secure or spread the bottom of a sail

Bow chase – guns located in the bows that could be fired ahead of the ship

Bower anchor – the largest anchors in a ship; the best bower was on the starboard side, the small bower on the port

Bowline – line attached to a side of a square sail, used to trim the sail

Bowsprit – the spar that projects ahead of the ship

Braces – the ropes used to haul the yards round and keep the wind

Bring to – to halt a vessel by turning the head to windward

Breakers – waves with breaking crests indicating shallow water

Broach to – to be brought broadside on to the sea

Broadside – the side of the vessel; *also*, the simultaneous discharge of all guns on one side

By the board – a synonym for overboard

Cable – as a length, 120 fathoms (240 yards)

Careen – to haul a ship over onto its side, usually for repair

Cartel – a ship granted safe conduct for the exchange of prisoners

Case shot – a number of small rounds packed into a metal case; also known as canister shot

Cat – to hoist the anchor to the cat-head

Cat-head – short beams projecting from the bows to allow the anchor to be prepared for letting go, or bringing it inboard

Chains – a projecting ledge from the hull forming the base for the shrouds

Clew up – to furl the sails

Courses – the sails attached to lower yards, usually foresail and mainsail

Cross-jack – lower yard on the mizzen mast

Dead reckoning – in navigation, a position based on estimated course and speed from a determined position

Drive – when the anchor will not hold, and the vessel is taken by the wind and sea

Driver – a fore-and-aft-rigged sail on the aftermost mast

Fathom – a measurement of 6ft

Fore and aft rig – when the sails are not attached to yards, but set on stays in line with the keel

Gaff – spar to which a fore-and-aft sail is attached

Garboard strake – the planking next to the keel

Grapeshot – type of shot, consisting of numerous small rounds separated by iron discs held in a canvas bag

Gunwale – the uppermost plank on the ship's side

Halliard – rope used to raise or lower a sail or yard

Haul the wind – to alter course to sail closer to the wind

Heave to – to bring a vessel to a stop, usually by putting the head to windward

Jib – a triangular sail rigged from the foremast to the bowsprit or jibboom

Jury mast – temporary mast, often a spare yard or spar

Kedge – a small anchor; kedging is the use of a kedge anchor to haul a ship through shallow water

Knee – an angled piece of timber which supported the beams at the ship's side

Langrage – a type of shot; odd bits of ironwork bound together or in a sack

Larboard – the left side of the ship; replaced by the term Port

Lateen – a triangular sail, common in the Mediterranean

Lay or Lie to – to heave to in poor weather

Lead-line – a method of finding depth, a long line and lead weight

Luff – to bring the ships head closer to the wind

Lug sail – a sail that has the forward edge shorter than the after edge

Mizzen or Mizen – the aftermost mast in a ship

Missed stays – when a ship fails to go about from one tack to another

Musket shot – 300 to 400 yards

Orlop – the lowest deck

Pistol shot – 50 yards

Prize – a ship of the enemy that has been captured

Quarter – the aftermost part of the ship, forward of the stern

Rake – when an opponent's guns can sweep the length of another ship, fore and aft, by lying under the bows or stern of an opponent

Reef – to reduce sail area by gathering in part of the sail

Royals – the uppermost part of the mast

Sheathing – a covering over the ship's bottom; from the mid-eighteenth century this was often copper

Sheet anchor – the heaviest anchor carried, usually as a spare or for use in very heavy weather

Shrouds – the ropes supporting the mast, running from the mast to the sides of the ship

Spanker – a fore-and-aft sail rigged on the mizzen mast

Spar – general term for onboard timbers such as yards and booms

Spring – a cable or hawser, usually fastened for the purpose of hauling the ship to bear in a different direction

Sprung – usually refers to a mast or spar which has split

Square rig – where the sails are attached to yards or spars which are horizontal to the mast

Stay – a rope that supports the mast fore and aft

(to) Stay or to put in Stays – means the act of tacking; to miss stays is to fail in the attempt to tack

Staysail – a triangular sail fixed to a stay

Strake – a line of side planking

Stream anchor – a spare anchor

Strike – to lower the flag

Studding sail – an extra sail rigged on an extension of a yardarm

Sweep – a long heavy oar

Tack – to change course, by working the ship's head to windward

Tail – when the bottom touches the ground

Thrum – to push lengths of rope-yarn through a sail to allow it to be used to stop a leak

Topmast – the mast mounted above the lower part of a mast

Topgallant – the mast above the topmast

Trysail – a small fore and aft sail

Warp – to move a ship by pulling on ropes (warps) secured to anchors or the shore

Wear – to change course by turning the stern to windward

Weather – to pass clear of an obstacle

Yard – spar mounted across a mast to carry a sail

1 | 1649–1660: The Interregnum: Dutch Wars and Expansion

FROM 1639 GREAT BRITAIN and Ireland suffered a series of conflicts, with insurrection and rebellion against the religious intolerance and political arrogance of the monarchy. With the execution of King Charles I in January 1649 England effectively became a Republic governed by a Council of State and from 1653 Oliver Cromwell acting as the Lord Protector. The state faced numerous threats: fighting continued in Ireland against the Confederates who resisted English rule and privateers from both Ireland and continental Europe were a constant problem.

The overthrow of the monarchy led to very strained relations with France, which actively supported exiled Royalists. Attacks on British shipping led to open hostilities and war (June 1649–December 1652). Deteriorating relations with the Dutch over trade finally led to the First Dutch War (July 1652–May 1654) and an attempt to challenge Spanish domination of the West Indies led to war with that country (March 1656–September 1660). Because of these constant threats and conflicts, the fleet expanded to meet the various threats to make it the most effective in Europe.

1649

May ROBERT Sixth Rate
Royalist prize 1642 (*Fortune*); 100 tons; 8 guns
Captain William Jennings
Ordered to patrol in the English Channel off the port of Dungeness on the coast of Sussex to give some protection to local shipping from privateers, Admirals Deane and Blake reported on 12 May that she had herself been taken '… off Fairleigh' (i.e., Fairlight) by two Irish privateers.
[*CSPD: Interregnum May 1649*]

(late) June ANTELOPE Third Rate
Rebuilt 1618; 384 tons; 92ft × 31.9ft
The *Antelope* had defected to the Royalists and been taken to Holland in July 1648, and she remained moored in the Hellevoetsluis, disarmed and only partly manned. A boarding party from the *Happy Entrance* and *Dragon* directed by Captain Anthony Young entered the harbour, gained entry and a party led by Lieutenant Stephen Rose took the ship with no bloodshed, the few men on board offering no resistance. She was then set on fire. Lieutenant Rose was later awarded a gold medal and £50 as reward for his part in the attack. James Parker and Thomas Tulley received a medal and £10, whilst another nine men received £5 each.
Note: the date is uncertain; Whitelocke records the attack on 26 June, but this is evidently when the news reached London. The Council of State discussed the attack on the same date.
[*Whitelocke vol 3 p59; CSPD: Interregnum June & October 1649*]

26 September CRESCENT Sixth Rate
Purchased 1642; 167 tons; 14 guns
Captain Jacob Reynolds
In September 1649 Colonel Edward Popham was sent with a small force of ships to search the Channel Islands for the fugitive Prince of Wales and he was joined on 22 September by the *Crescent*, which had been tasked to carry Parliamentary Commissioners to Guernsey. The ships lay at anchor on 'the Guernsey Banks' in poor weather, the wind steadily increasing in strength until it blew a full westerly gale. During the storm the *Crescent* parted from her cables and was driven onto rocks and wrecked. Captain Badiley was later sent on board, but it was clear that she could not be saved, and she was abandoned as a wreck, but her guns and most of her stores were salvaged.
[*HMC: Leybourne-Popham pp30–1; CSPD Interregnum September 1649*]

September TIGER'S WHELP 'frigate'
Prize 1649 (*Mary Antrim*); 120 tons; 14 guns
Captain Anthony Houlding
Part of the force assembled to support the Parliamentarian campaign in Ireland, on 27 September Colonel Richard Deane wrote to the Council of State informing them that *Tiger's Whelp* had been wrecked on the bar of Dublin harbour
[*HMC: Leybourne-Popham p42*]

1650

(February) MARY ROSE Fourth Rate
Deptford 1623; 384 tons; 83ft × 26.9ft; 24 guns
Captain Francis Penrose
A petition was presented to the Council of State in early March from the company of the *Mary Rose* for relief, '… upon certificate from the Generals of the

Fleet, that the ship was cast away in chasing an enemy'. Relief was granted, as the ship had been 'lost on the coast of Flanders'. Some of her guns were later reported to be salvageable. No other details have been found, but it may be connected to an entry in Whitelocke, for 23 February, that letters from (Great) Yarmouth advised that '… a small frigate of the Parliaments of twelve guns maintained fight with two of the enemy's, one of eighteen, the other of twenty-six guns, and at last run herself on shore, and saved her men, guns and tackle.' – the ship is not otherwise identified, but no other losses are noted at this time, and it may refer to the *Mary Rose*.
[Whitelocke vol 3 p153; CSPD Interregnum March 1650]

March INCREASE Sixth Rate
Royalist prize 1645; 133 tons; 12 guns
Captain Robert Wilkinson
On 2 April, the Admiralty Committee of the Council of State ordered that 'some person' should be appointed to look after the remains of the *Increase*, which was reported to have been wrecked near Cardiff.
[CSPD Interregnum April 1650]

14 October LIBERTY Second Rate
Woolwich 1633 (*Charles*); 810 tons; 105.2ft × 35.7ft; 44 guns
Captain Edward Hall
Ordered to proceed to Chatham to be paid off, she ran aground on a sandbank off Harwich '… by carrying too much sail' and was lost. Work to recover her guns and tackle continued for several years, with Robert Willis salvaging several cannon and anchors. In 1655 the wreck was reported to be still visible, lying upright in 15ft at low water, but was going to pieces.
[CSPD Interregnum: (Letters and Papers relating to the Navy) October 1650 & May 1655; Whitelocke vol 3 p249]

1651

30 September CONSTANT REFORMATION Second Rate
Deptford 1619; 742 tons; 106ft × 35.6ft; 42 guns
Captain Robert Fearnes
Flagship of the last remnant of the Royalist squadron that was commanded by Prince Rupert, in July 1651 they assembled in the Azores to take on stores and food intending to make for the West Indies. Any plans they were making were interrupted by a gale which forced them from their anchorage in late September. On 27 September, the *Reformation* was about 10 miles from Terceira, going before the wind, when a leak became evident. It was kept under control by constant pumping, but during the morning of 30 September it suddenly worsened, probably due to timbers giving way forward.

Loose stores were packed into the hole, and a sail slung over the bow, but this had no effect and the water increased. During the afternoon, the yawl was lowered and Prince Rupert with eight others managed to row to the *Honest Seaman*. The main and mizzen masts were cut away and the anchors and upper deck guns were jettisoned in efforts to lighten her. The *Honest Seaman* managed to get close enough to send her boat across, secured by a line. Using this, five more men, including Captain Fearnes, were rescued, but another attempt failed when the boat was swamped. The *Swallow* had also managed to close her, but in the high winds and heavy seas, neither ship could render any assistance. Her light went out at about ten o'clock that night and it was presumed that she had sunk. The position was then about 75 leagues (225 miles) to the south-west of Terceira. About 300 men were lost.
[Mariner's Mirror vol 21 pp72–7]

22 October TRESCO Fifth Rate
Royalist prize 1651 (*Michael*); 24 guns
Captain William Blake
Part of the Parliamentary fleet sent to reduce the Channel Islands, which remained loyal to the Royalist cause. The ships arrived off Jersey during 20 October, and after bombarding shore positions, they moved to attempt a landing in St Aubin's Bay, but *Tresco* found herself too near Elizabeth Castle. In trying to shift her position she struck a submerged rock and foundered with heavy loss of life.
[Powell: Robert Blake p127]

1652

January JOHN Fourth Rate
Purchased 1644; 367 tons; 32 guns
Captain Robert Dennis[†]
In September 1651, the *John* was ordered, in company with the *Guinea* frigate, to proceed with a force of 600 men to Virginia where they were 'To use their best endeavours to reduce all the plantations within the Bay of Chesapeake' to the rule of Parliament. The pair sailed in October and arrived at Barbados in December before proceeding to the coast of America. The *John* was lost en-route, 'on the coast of Virginia', with all hands.
[CSPC America and West Indies September 1651; October & November 1652]

July FORTUNE 'frigate'
Prize 1652 (a 'pirate', probably a Dunkirk privateer)
Captain John Wild
Captured by a Dutch privateer in the North Sea and taken into Flushing; it was reported that the crew '… cried quarter and forced the captain and master to

deliver that frigate, who otherwise would have brought her off'.
[CSPD Interregnum August 1652; Gardiner & Atkinson vol 1 pp96, 126]

13 August HART Sixth Rate
Royalist prize 1643; 120 tons; 12 guns
Captain James Coppin
Captured by a Dutch privateer in the North Sea; Whitelocke records that the *Hart* '...fought with three Dutch ships but was taken by them'.
[Gardiner & Atkinson vol 1 pp96, 126; Whitelocke vol 3 p447]

16 August CHARITY Fireship
Prize 1650 (*Charité*)
Captain Simon Orton
In the first major action of the First Dutch War, Sir George Ayscue with forty ships attacked a Dutch force of about thirty ships under Adrianszoon de Ruyter off Plymouth. The *Charity* went to cover the retreat of the *Bonaventure*, which was being hard-pressed by the Dutch, and after receiving several shots in the hull, she was deliberately set on fire and 'turned among the enemy'. The crew escaped although some were injured when powder prematurely exploded.
[Gardiner & Atkinson vol 2 p180]

28 August PHOENIX Fourth Rate
Woolwich 1647; 414 tons; 96ft x 28.6ft; 38 guns
Captain John Wadsworth
The English had kept a small squadron in the Mediterranean since 1651 to pursue Royalist ships and protect trade. Under the command of Richard Badiley, four of these ships were escorting four merchant vessels from Smyrna (Izmir) to Leghorn (Livorno) when during the afternoon of 27 August, they encountered a Dutch squadron of ten ships commanded by Jan van Galen near the island of Monte Cristo, about 80 miles south of Leghorn. The Dutch attempted to close, but with little wind only an exchange of distant shot was possible. The following day the Dutch again closed from windward, with Badiley placing his ships between the convoy and the enemy. Both sides suffered badly with damaged rigging and masts, and the Dutch lost two of their captains. The *Phoenix* was the only ship lost; astern of the *Paragon*, she attempted to close to render assistance when that ship was hard pressed, but the *Eendracht*, 40 guns, ran alongside and entered a large number of boarders and forced her to surrender.
Note: Retaken by boat attack at Leghorn 20/26 November 1652
[Mariner's Mirror vol 49 pp248–51]

30 September ANTELOPE Second Rate
Woolwich 1652; 828 tons; 120ft x 36ft; 50 guns
Captain Andrew Ball
The *Antelope* was part of a large force of warships sent to Copenhagen to escort home the trade from the Baltic. Arriving on 20 September, several days were spent negotiating with the Danes before Captain Ball sailed for England on 27 September. The weather was poor, and three days later, at 3 o'clock in the morning she ran aground on the Danish coast of Jutland and was lost. Most of the crew were saved.
[Gardiner & Atkinson vol 2 p365]

30 November Battle of Dungeness
Dutch Lieutenant-Admiral Marten Harpetszoon Tromp, having successfully escorted a huge convoy into home waters, turned back into the English Channel to offer battle to a smaller English force under General Robert Blake. The English ships were penned between the shore and the Varne sandbank and were badly mauled by the Dutch and forced back into Dover.

Two ships were lost to the Dutch:

GARLAND (or GUARDLAND) Third Rate
Deptford 1620; 567 tons; 96ft x 33ft; 44 guns
Captain Richard Batten†
As the Dutch approached the English line, Tromp in the *Brederode*, 54 guns, attempted to engage the English flagship *Triumph*, but Blake passed under his bow. As a result, the Dutch flagship rammed the *Garland*, which was astern of Blake, breaking her bowsprit and beakhead as she ran on board. The *Anthony Bonaventure* (see below) was next in line and laid herself alongside the Dutch ship and some desperate hand-to-hand fighting ensued. When the *Hollandia*, 38, joined in the attack the advantage swung to the Dutch and the *Garland* surrendered despite loose gunpowder being ignited by the crew in their efforts to dislodge the Dutch. She suffered about 60 dead from a crew of 200.
[Gardiner & Atkinson vol 3 pp95, 102, 117]

ANTHONY BONAVENTURE Fourth Rate
Hired 1650; 450 tons; 36 guns
Captain Walter Hoxton†
Captain Hoxton attempted to assist the beleaguered *Garland* by boarding the *Brederode* (see above). The intervention of the *Hollandia* commanded by Jan Evertsen led to the capture of both ships after fierce fighting, during which Captain Hoxton 'cleared his decks many times', until he was overwhelmed and killed.
[Gardiner & Atkinson vol 3 pp95, 117]

★ ★ ★

1 December HERCULES Fourth Rate
Hired 1650; 480 tons; 34 guns
Captain Zachary Brown
Proceeding from Portsmouth to the Downs in company with the *Portsmouth* and *Ruby* to join General Blake, the trio found the victorious Dutch fleet commanded by Tromp dominating the eastern Channel. After an engagement with two Dutch warships, they attempted to retrace their course to Portsmouth. The *Hercules* could not get away, so Captain Brown deliberately ran her aground near Dungeness to avoid capture. It was not very well done as the following day the Dutch hauled her off as a prize. It was subsequently ordered that Brown should never serve in the Navy in a position of command again.
[Gardiner & Atkinson vol 3 pp109, 118; Powell: Robert Blake pp190–1]

1653

18 February SAMPSON Fourth Rate
Prize 1652 (*Samson*); 22 guns
Captain Edmund Button
Whilst escorting a large convoy through the English Channel, the Dutch fleet under Tromp and de Ruyter encountered the main English fleet under Blake, Penn and Monck. In the action which followed off Portland the *Sampson* was disabled and so severely damaged that her men were taken out and she was allowed to founder.
[Gardiner & Atkinson vol 4 pp79, 102, 166]

21 March FAIRFAX Second Rate
Deptford 1650; 745 tons; 116ft × 34.9ft; 56 guns
Captain Sir John Lawson
The ship was laying at Chatham, out of commission, when during the morning, a fire broke out on board. It was discovered at about 10 o'clock in the morning from the shore before the ship's company were sensible of it and the blaze spread quickly. With only sixteen men on board, they could do little to tackle the blaze and she was soon burning fiercely. The anchor cable burnt through, and she eventually drifted until she grounded on the west side of the river where she burnt down to the waterline. It was believed that the fire was caused when loose gunpowder in the gunroom had been accidentally ignited by a dropped candle.
[CSPD: Interregnum March 1653; Gardiner & Atkinson vol 4 pp237, 242]

4 March The Battle of Leghorn
In an attempt to link the two English squadrons in the Mediterranean, Richard Badiley with eight ships arrived off Leghorn to await the six ships of Henry Appleton. They were intercepted by a Dutch squadron of sixteen ships under Jan van Galen, which successfully interposed themselves between the groups. The precipitate action of Appleton in attacking van Galen before the other English ships could join led to the destruction of his squadron, with only a single ship surviving.

BONAVENTURE Third Rate
Deptford 1621; 557 tons; 98ft × 32.5ft; 44 guns
Captain Stephen Lyme†
Lost at the very start of the battle; leading the line of Appleton's squadron, she was the first to be attacked. As the action started with an exchange of broadsides between *Bonaventure* and the Dutch flagship *De Zeven Provincien*, a shot apparently entered the powder room, and she blew up with only five survivors from a complement of 180 men.
[Mariner's Mirror vol 49 p260]

SAMSON Third Rate
Hired 1653; 40 guns
Captain Edmund Seaman
Badly mauled by the *Halve Maan*, 40 guns, she was subsequently grappled by a fireship which set her alight and she later blew up. Forty-two men were picked up from a crew of 180.
[Mariner's Mirror vol 49 p261]

LEVANT MERCHANT Fifth Rate
Hired 1653; 28 guns
Captain Stephen Marsh
After driving off one opponent in a sinking condition, she was then attacked and captured after being disabled by the *Maagd van Enkhuisen*, 34 guns.
[Mariner's Mirror vol 49 p261]

PEREGRINE Fourth Rate
Hired 1653; 30 guns
Captain John Wood†
Engaged by two ships, the *Roode Haes* and *Susanna*, she held out for over an hour, despite having her mainmast shot away, and driving off an attempt to board. When a third ship, the *Zwart Arend*, joined the fight, with her mizzen mast shot away she was unable to manoeuvre and surrendered.
[Mariner's Mirror vol 49 p261]

LEOPARD Third Rate
Woolwich 1635; 95ft × 33ft; 516 tons; 40 guns
Captain Henry Appleton
The last ship to surrender, she held out for six hours, holding off two attackers only to have a third enemy join in the assault. With her stern beaten in, her tiller shot away, and 14 guns dismounted she was captured. She suffered 70 dead and 54 wounded from a complement of 200.
[Mariner's Mirror vol 49 p261]

★ ★ ★

14 April BETTY
Hired 1653
Captain James Abelson
Foundered in the North Sea; all twenty-four members of the crew were rescued by the *Amity*.
[CSPD: Interregnum (Letters and Papers relating to the Navy) April 1653]

9 July HARRY BONAVENTURE
Hired 1652
Captain Robert Swanley
The only English warship left in the Mediterranean after van Galen's victory off Leghorn and the subsequent exit of Badiley, Captain Swanley continued to attack Dutch shipping. A Dutch squadron of ships under Cornelis Tromp in *de Zeven Provincien* eventually found the *Harry Bonaventure* anchored in Trapani harbour, Sicily. Tromp entered the harbour and captured his quarry without difficulty.
[Mariner's Mirror vol 49 p263]

31 July The Battle of Scheveningen
In one of the largest fleet actions of the war, General Monck brought Admiral Marten Tromp to battle off Scheveningen, both sides having about 100 ships, with attendant fireships and tenders. The action went decisively in favour of the English, with Tromp killed and several Dutch ships taken. Two of the English fleet were lost:

OAK Fourth Rate
Prize 1652 (*Akerboom?*); 32 guns
Captain John Edwin
During the action, the *Oak* caught fire after a Dutch fireship was laid alongside and was abandoned and allowed to burn, with most of her men being saved.
[Gardiner & Atkinson vol 5 p350, 368; CSPD: Interregnum August 1653]

HUNTER Fireship
Prize 1652 (*la Chasseur*); 10 guns
Captain John Bowrey
Attached to the Blue Squadron, she received several shots in the hull and started to fill with water. With the sails and rigging also damaged, and Captain Bowrey wounded in the leg, she fell away from the squadron, all of the men leaving her as she did so. Subsequently set on fire by the Dutch.
[TNA: SP 46/119; Gardiner & Atkinson vol 5 pp350, 369]

★ ★ ★

7 September LILY Sixth Rate
Purchased 1642; 110 tons; 10 guns
Captain Isaiah Blowfield
In the first week of September off Land's End, *Lily* encountered a Royalist privateer from Brest which she captured after a sharp action and sent her prize into Torbay. The *Lily* anchored off Weymouth to effect repairs in worsening weather, and by 7 September there were storm-force winds from the south-west. The firing of guns brought out a local pilot, and an attempt was made to enter the harbour, but they were unable to do so in the high seas but were able to anchor again. This held until mid-afternoon, when it was found that they were being steadily driven inshore and by 3 o'clock they were dangerously close to the shore. The ship was pounded by waves which washed over her, and to ease the movement, the main and foremasts were cut away. Attempts by local people to reach her by boat failed, but pumping kept the water at bay, until by the early evening the men were exhausted and the water started to gain. At 7 o'clock the anchor cable was cut, and the ship was run onto the shore, about half a mile to the east of the main town. Several of the men managed to scramble over the yards and rigging to the shore, but four men, including the Gunner, Carpenter and Surgeon, were drowned in the attempt, and Captain Blowfield was nearly lost when he tried to follow them, but managed to haul himself back onboard. A little later the wind shifted round to the west, and decreased, which enabled three boats from the town to come alongside and lift off Blowfield, the town pilot and twenty-eight members of the crew.
[TNA: SP 46/115; Whitelocke vol 4 p36; CSPD: Interregnum, September 1653]

13 September SWAN Fifth Rate
Prize 1645 (ex-Royalist); 200 tons; 12 guns
Captain Edward Tarleton
The *Swan* was part of a force that was sent to the island of Mull, to land a force of men under Colonel Ralph Cobbett to attack Duart Castle, a stronghold for local Royalists under the Earl of Glencairn. On 13 September in a strong north-westerly gale, she was driven inshore and wrecked, along with two merchant ships, the *Martha & Margaret* and the *Speedwell*. The remains of the wreck were discovered in 1979, immediately east of Duart Point.
[CSPD: Interregnum (Letters and Papers relating to the Navy) September 1653; Whitelocke vol 4 p39; canmore.org.uk/site/80637]

9 December SUSSEX Fourth Rate
Portsmouth 1652; 600 tons; 46 guns
Captain Roger Cuttance
Laying at anchor at Spithead, at about 3 o'clock in the afternoon, with little warning, the ship was blown apart

by a large explosion. Just five men, including the Master, were subsequently picked up. Captain Cuttance escaped, with about forty of the crew, who were fortunately all ashore. An inspection of the area early the next morning found only wreckage and various timbers and spars came ashore over the next few days, including a large piece of the keel.
[TNA: SP 46/115; Whitelocke vol 4 p54]

1654

11 April RAVEN (or WHITE RAVEN) Fourth Rate
Prize 1652 (*Raaf?*); 38 guns
Captain Henry Southwood
Escorting a convoy from the Firth of Forth to London when attacked by a group of Dutch privateers off St Abbs' Head and captured. The *Weymouth* and *Sparrow* sloops were in sight but could not assist. The crew were set ashore on Holy Island by their captors.
[CSPD: Interregnum (Letters and Papers relating to the Navy) May 1654]

1655

25 May DISCOVERY Fourth Rate
Purchased 1651; 20 guns
Captain John Wills
One of a large squadron under the command of General William Penn sent to attack Spanish possessions in the West Indies, Jamaica being captured on 17 May. Whilst lying off Port Royal in that island, fire broke out after spilled brandy in the steward's cabin ignited. Despite assistance being sent from other ships, the fire spread with thick choking smoke filling the ship. She burnt until midnight when the fire reached the powder room and she blew up with a large explosion, scattering burning debris over a large area.
[Penn vol 2 pp108–09]

13 July PARAGON Second Rate
Deptford 1633 (*Henrietta Maria*); 792 tons; 106ft × 35.9ft; 54 guns
Captain George Dakins
One of General Penn's fleet in the West Indies, the ships were cruising to the north of Cuba in the hope of intercepting the Plate Fleet from Havana. Between 9 and 10 o'clock in the morning a fire broke out in the steward's cabin. The fire spread, with the masts going by the board after an hour. Some three hours after the fire started, she blew up and sank, then being about 11 or 12 leagues (33–36 miles) from Havana. About 100 men died.
[Penn vol 2 p126; Thurloe vol 3: September 1655]

June PORTSMOUTH Shallop
Prize 1655; 4 guns
Captain Jeremy Country
A former French prize fitted out in April, she was captured in the English Channel by a Royalist privateer and taken into Brest.
[CSPD: Interregnum, August 1655]

24 July ISLIP Fifth Rate
Bristol 1654; 22 guns
Captain Edward Tarleton
Based on the west coast of Scotland, under the direction of Colonel Brayne at Inverlochy, the ship sailed from her anchorage off the island of Canna for the Western Isles, but the weather changed, with strong winds and high seas, and it was decided to run for shelter. The embarked pilot, Daniel MacDonald, advised that they make for a sea lough, where they might anchor. As they steered into the mouth of Lough Linnhe the pilot suggested a sheltered bay in which they could anchor in 12 fathoms. As they approached the head of the bay, they discovered rocks ahead of them and despite putting the helm over, and attempting to tack, the ship was carried onto the rocks and bilged, as the current was very strong '... a Tide like unto that running under London Bridge at the time of flood'. The guns and stores were subsequently salvaged and secured at nearby Dunstaffnage Castle. Although an inquiry found they could not blame the officers for the loss, it was believed that the ship could have anchored earlier. As a result, Captain Tarleton and the Master, John Sayers, lost half their pay, for neglect of duty.
[TNA: SP 46/117: CSPD: Interregnum (Letters and Papers relating to the Navy) September 1655]

1 September ADVISER Pink
Prize 1654: 8 guns
Captain Thomas Sankey†
Ordered to patrol the coast in the vicinity of Rye, to protect local vessels, she was attacked and captured by the Royalist privateer *St George* and carried into Boulogne; the Captain and Master were both killed in the engagement.
[CSPD: Interregnum (Letters and Papers relating to the Navy) September 1655]

15 December HARE Ketch
Prize 1649; 12 guns
Captain Francis Cranwell
Whilst escorting a convoy, ran aground on the Whitaker spit, a sandbank in the Thames Estuary and was lost. The thickness of the weather was offered as an excuse, but the Navy Commissioners believed that '... if more circumspection and diligence had been used, she might have been brought off'.
[CSPD: Interregnum (Letters and Papers relating to the Navy) December 1655]

1656

13 February PELICAN Fourth Rate
Wapping 1650; 500 tons; 100ft × 30.8ft; 42 guns
Captain Robert Storey
Whilst laying at anchor off Portsmouth, with Captain Storey ashore, the ship caught fire and was destroyed. The fire was discovered at about 4 o'clock in the afternoon and spread rapidly. Cables were cut and the ship drifted ashore until she grounded, where she continued to burn, blowing up about five hours later. It was found that the Boatswain's Yeoman had failed to properly extinguish a candle in the Boatswain's store which set light to sails and cordage, and the fire spread to the powder room.
[CSPD: Interregnum (Letters and Papers relating to the Navy) February 1656]

13 March PRIMROSE Fifth Rate
Wapping 1651; 287 tons; 86ft × 25.11ft; 26 guns
Captain John Sherwin
Cruising in company with the *Mayflower*, the pair were in the western approaches to the English Channel searching for Spanish frigates reported in the area. They were off Land's End when her consort sprung her main topmast. Captain Sherwin went aboard the *Mayflower* to consult with her captain and in his absence the ship drifted onto the Seven Stones reef. The ship was freed but almost immediately filled with water and foundered. Sixteen men, two women and a child were drowned. Subsequently, Sherwin and Edward Baron, master of the *Primrose*, had half their wages withheld, for neglect of duty.
[CSPD: Interregnum (Letters and Papers relating to the Navy) March 1656]

28 April CAT Pink
Prize 1653; 8 guns
Captain Richard Pittock
Whilst engaged in protecting fishing vessels off the coast of Kent, being stationed between the North Foreland and Brighton, she was off Pevensey when she was closed and attacked by a large Dunkirk privateer. The fight went on for over an hour, until with masts and rigging shattered and several men wounded, she was boarded and surrendered.
[CSPD: Interregnum (Letters and Papers relating to the Navy) April 1656]

18 May CULLEN Fifth Rate
Hired 1652; 26 guns
Captain Thomas Gilbert
Loaded with supplies for Admiral Blake's fleet off Cadiz, they were off Lisbon when they were closed by an Ostend privateer, the *Jésus-Marie-Joseph*. Being suspicious of the approaching vessel, Captain Gilbert fired a shot at the privateer, but received a broadside in reply which killed two men and wounded eight others. The privateer then ran alongside and entered a large number of boarders and captured her. Efforts were later made to cut her out from the harbour at Baiona, but she was found to be secured under the guns of several batteries and the attempt was abandoned.
[CSPD: Interregnum (Letters and Papers relating to the Navy) June 1656]

14 June GREYHOUND Fifth Rate
Woolwich 1636; 168 tons; 60ft × 20.3ft; 12 guns
Captain John Wager†
After escorting a convoy to Leith, the *Greyhound* was en-route to Newcastle for provisions, when she encountered a group of four Dunkirk privateers off the Farne Islands. After a long fight, the enemy closed and entered boarders, but as they did so, she blew up with all but two of her crew perishing.
[CSPD: Interregnum (Letters and Papers relating to the Navy) June 1656]

8 July FOX Fireship
Prize 1650; 22 guns
Captain William Pickering
Burnt in an attack on Spanish shipping in the harbour of Malaga. The *Fox* was successfully laid alongside two ships in the mole and set fire to them. During the assault, several other ships were destroyed, with Captain Pickering leading a party that spiked guns in a fort.
[CSPD; Interregnum November 1656; Powell: The Letters of Robert Blake pp416, 439]

July ARMS OF HOLLAND Fifth Rate
Prize 1652 (*Wapen van Holland*); 32 guns
Captain Samuel Hawkes
One of General Penn's West Indian squadron, she was one of several ships sent to cruise off northern Cuba. Soon after sailing from Jamaica, she caught fire, which apparently started in the powder room, and despite the efforts of the crew, the fire spread and the ship eventually blew up with heavy loss of life, only four men and the Captain being saved.
[Thurloe, vol 5 August 1656; CSPD Interregnum (Letters and Papers relating to the Navy) September 1656]

1657

30 May LAUREL Fourth Rate
Portsmouth 1651; 489 tons; 103ft × 30.11ft; 48 guns
Captain Francis Kirby
Ran aground on the Newarp Banks off Yarmouth Roads, Norfolk and was subsequently lost. It was found

that she had struck the sands during the night, whilst all the senior officers were below, despite being in shallow waters. The Captain, Master, Master's Mate and the embarked pilot all lost the wages due to them, as it was judged there had been great neglect. The ship evidently broke up and wreckage was reported being recovered for several weeks afterwards.
[CSPD: Interregnum (Letters and Papers relating to the Navy) July 1657]

2 July PARROT Ketch
Chatham 1657; 60 tons; 6 guns
Captain Thomas Horne
Bound for the Downs with letters for the Commander-in-Chief, they sighted four ships which they closed, believing them to be English, only to discover that they were Spanish privateers. Two of the enemy, one of 18 guns, the other of 16 guns, then ran alongside the ketch, and hailed, saying they would give no quarter if they resisted, at which she surrendered without resistance and was taken into Flushing. Captain Horne later claimed he would have fought, but the crew, led by the Boatswain Thomas Atwell, refused, claiming '… they had wives and families, why should they destroy themselves when there was no probability of escaping'.
[CSPD: Interregnum July 1657]

1658

8 February PRINCESS MARIA Fourth Rate
Prize 1652 (*Prinses Roijaal Maria*); 442 tons; 114ft × 27ft; 38 guns
Captain John Grimsditch
After the ship sailed from the anchorage in the Downs for Harwich in cold, icy weather, the embarked pilot attempted to steer her through the Goodwin Sands, but she ran aground on the Brake Bank to the east of Ramsgate. Her masts were cut away to lighten her and thick ice prevented her from capsizing, but her timbers gave way and she filled with water. An enquiry found that the wind had dropped away, and she had been carried by a strong tide onto the sands. There was, however, some 'want of duty' in failing to anchor as soon as it was realised that she was drifting. The guns and much of her stores were salvaged.
[CSPD: Interregnum (Letters and Papers relating to the Navy) February 1658]

28 February HAPPY ENTRANCE Third Rate
Deptford 1619; 540 tons; 96ft × 32.2ft; 40 guns
Under repair at Chatham, a dockyard boat with hot pitch was left unattended alongside whilst the workmen went ashore for dinner. The pitch boat caught fire and the blaze spread to the ship, which drifted into shallow water, where she grounded and was burnt out. The Master Caulker of the yard, William Thompson, and two foremen were dismissed for neglect of duty, although Thompson was reinstated later.
[CSPD: Interregnum (Letters and Papers relating to the Navy) September; October 1658]

1659

3 February NONSUCH Ketch
Purchased 1654; 47 tons; 54ft × 15.6ft; 6 guns
Captain Jonathan Waltham
Escorting a ketch through the English Channel from the Downs to St Valery, as they neared the French shore they were chased by two large Ostend privateers. After holding off her opponents for an hour, the pair ran alongside and entered a large number of boarders, who after a short struggle captured her. Sixteen men were wounded in the assault.
  Note: recaptured 5 April by the *Merlin*
[CSPD: Interregnum, March & April 1659]

September ACADIA Sixth Rate
Purchased 1656; 10 guns
Captain Robert Henfield[†]
Ordered to ply in the English Channel between Beachy Head and Chichester, '… to search all vessels passing that way for persons suspected to be enemies to the Commonwealth …', the ship disappeared, and was presumed to have foundered with all hands.
[CSPD: Interregnum (Letters and Papers relating to the Navy) August & November 1659]

2 | 1660–1688: The Restoration: Wars against the Dutch and Barbary Corsairs

IN MAY 1660, THE EXILED King Charles returned to England to assume the throne. He inherited a powerful – and expensive – navy. Despite the financial difficulties, the next years saw the confrontation with the Dutch renewed, which led to a further two conflicts (February 1665 – July 1667 and March 1672 – February 1674). Operations continued against the North African corsairs who remained a constant menace to merchant shipping throughout the period.

1661

(16?) July HUNTER Sixth Rate
Prize 1656; 50 tons; 45ft × 14.6ft; 6 guns
Captain Robert Duck
Stationed in the North Sea between the Thames Estuary and Great Yarmouth, protecting merchant shipping, she is listed by Pepys as being 'cast away at sea' in July, but no further details have been found. Captain Duck is shown as being command of the *Hunter* until 16 July which is suggestive for a date of loss.
[Tanner: Naval Manuscripts in the Pepsyian Library vol 1 p279; TNA: ADM 10/15]

1662

19 September SATISFACTION Fifth Rate
Purchased 1646; 284 tons; 89ft × 24.6ft; 26 guns
Captain Robert Mohun
Ordered to the coast of Holland, to take on board some goods for Jamaica on behalf of Sir William Davidson, a wealthy merchant resident in Amsterdam, she was run ashore on the island of Schouwen, where she broke up, thirty men being drowned. The loss was blamed on the neglect of the pilot, John Lewis.
[Clarendon vol 5 p274; CSPD Charles II October 1662]

1664

August WESTERGATE Fourth Rate
Prize 1653 (*Westergo*); 273 tons; 86ft × 24.6ft; 24 guns
Captain Samuel Titsell†
After sailing from Port Royal, Jamaica, in company with the *Swallow*, the area was swept by an intense tropical storm on 18 August. The ships became separated, and the *Swallow* survived although she was beaten down into the Bay of Campeche, but the *Westergate* was not seen again and was presumed to have foundered with all hands.
[CSPC, America and West Indies: February 1665]

August GRIFFIN Sixth Rate
Prize 1656; 121 tons; 60ft × 19.6ft; 12 guns
Captain Adrian van Diemen Swarts†
Sailed from Jamaica in July for Barbados, but she disappeared and was presumed lost with all hands. Her fate was uncertain – it is likely that she was lost in the same mid-August storm that saw the loss of the *Westergate* (see above), but various reports (or rather rumours) from the West Indies variously claimed that she had been either captured or sunk by the Dutch or the Spanish, but none of these were substantiated.
[CSPC, America and West Indies February 1665]

19 October ELIAS Fourth Rate
Prize 1653; 406 tons; 101ft × 27.6ft; 36 guns
Captain William Hill
One of Colonel Richard Nicholls' squadron which captured New Amsterdam (New York) in August 1664, the *Elias* foundered on the return voyage, about 420 miles to the east of the New England coast. Captain Hill and twenty others survived, being rescued by the *Martin*, but eighty-six men were lost. The survivors claimed she was poorly caulked.
[CSPC, America and West Indies November 1664; Latham: Samuel Pepys and the Second Dutch War pp93, 108]

3 December NONSUCH Fourth Rate
Deptford 1646; 418 tons; 98ft × 28.4ft; 34 guns
Captain Philip Bacon
One of a squadron under Vice Admiral Thomas Allin which attempted to pass through the Straits of Gibraltar

to the Atlantic, the weather was extremely poor, with constant rain and strong winds. The ships stood over to the Barbary shore, being 'puzzled' by the contrary currents and winds on the first attempt but in the early hours of the morning, judging themselves well over to the North African shore, they tacked and made another attempt. They suddenly saw the land and surf breaking close ahead and the leading ship, *Plymouth*, went ashore on the eastern side of Gibraltar and several others followed. The *Plymouth, Portsmouth* and *Bonaventure* all hauled themselves off, but at daybreak the *Nonsuch* was seen to be 'sunk and all the masts by the board'.
[Anderson: The Journals of Sir Thomas Allin vol 1 pp184–5]

3 December PHOENIX Fourth Rate
Woolwich 1647; 414 tons; 96ft × 28.6ft; 38 guns
Captain John Chicheley

Wrecked at Gibraltar with the *Nonsuch* in similar circumstances (see above). She had followed the others, and only sighted land just before running onshore, and was wrecked. 'Of so many ancient masters and officers never was such an oversight committed. They at first never considered their currents and steered away S.S.E. and lay by and then S.S.W. and were all ashore by one or two in the morning, they saying they could not see my lights, although I put as many candles as there was pockets ... but the night was so dark and rainy that we could not see a ship's length ...' (Allin's Journal).
[Anderson: The Journals of Sir Thomas Allin vol 1 pp184–5]

1665

7 March LONDON Second Rate
Chatham 1656; 1,104 tons; 123.6ft × 41ft; 76 guns
Vice Admiral Sir John Lawson

The ship was being taken from Chatham to the Hope reach in the Thames Estuary to complete fitting out when, being a little to the west of the buoy of the Nore, she suffered a massive internal explosion and rapidly sank. Sir John Lawson was not on board at the time, but about 300 people died, although several people, variously quoted as 12, 19 or 24, who were in the roundhouse survived. The wreck was located during 2005, apparently broken into two parts.
[Pepys' Diary: 8 March 1665; Anderson: The Journal of Edward Montagu p171; CSPD: Charles II March 1665; Historic England Site 1000088]

20 May GOOD HOPE Fourth Rate
Hired 1664; 272 tons; 89.6ft × 23.1 1ft; 34 guns
Captain Anthony Archer

Whilst escorting a fleet of store ships from Hamburg through the North Sea, they were intercepted by a squadron of Dutch warships, part of the fleet commanded by Lieutenant-Admiral Jacob van Wassenaer. The *Good Hope* evidently mistook them for the English fleet and did not realise her error until too late. She, along with eight vessels of the convoy loaded with valuable supplies of hemp, tar, cables and plank, was captured. The Dutch later claimed that they found Captain Archer was very drunk when taken.
[CSPD: Charles II May 1665; Fox p107]

3 June: The Battle of Lowestoft
The Dutch, with about 111 ships commanded by van Wassenaer Obdam, arrived off the East Anglian coast during 1 June to find the English fleet, commanded by the Duke of York, with about 102 ships, at anchor off the coast of Suffolk, in Southwold Bay. The Duke weighed and stood out to the south-east to gain sea room, the lateness of the hour and the scattered situation of the Dutch fleet preventing them from immediately attacking. After two days of manoeuvring to gain the weather gage, the English fleet attacked the Dutch in the early hours of 3 June, when about 14 miles NNE of Lowestoft.

Three English ships were lost:

CHARITY Fourth Rate
Prize 1653 (*Groote Liefde*); 453 tons; 106ft × 28.4ft; 46 guns
Captain Robert Wilkinson

During the ensuing battle, the fleets initially passed on opposite tacks, and the *Charity*, along with a hired ship, the *John and Abigail*, found themselves to leeward of the Dutch and effectively cut off. The hired ship, despite being much battered, eventually passed to the rear of the Dutch line and safety. Captain Wilkinson attempted to re-join the English line but found that he could not pass through the Dutch line and was consequently surrounded by the Dutch fleet and badly battered. The *Stad en Lande* ran alongside and forced her to surrender. About eighty men were killed or wounded.
[Anderson: The Journal of Edward Montagu p224; Fox p110]

DOLPHIN Fireship
Prize 1655 (Royalist *Wexford*); 149 tons; 70ft × 20ft; 4 guns
Captain William Gregory

At about 6 o'clock in the evening, three Dutch ships, the *Maarseveen*, 78 guns, the *Ter Goes*, 34, and the *Zwanenburg*, 30, all with damaged rigging, fell astern of the main Dutch fleet and ran aboard one another. Unable to manoeuvre, the three ships, after exchanging shots with the closing English ships, struck their flags in surrender. Despite this, Captain Gregory laid his fireship alongside them and burned all three. This attack on a defeated enemy who had surrendered was held in contempt by others; '... this cruel act was much detested by us, as not beseeming Christians'.
[Anderson: The Journal of Edward Montagu p228]

FAME Fireship
Prize 1655 (*la Renomée*); 208 tons; 68ft × 24ft; 8 guns
Captain John Gethings
Towards the end of the day the Dutch fell into confusion and the Dutch ships, *Koevorden*, 56 guns, the *Prins Maurits*, 50, and the *Utrecht*, 38, were seen to be foul of each other. Before they could free themselves, the Duke of York ordered a fireship to burn them; the task was successfully completed by Captain Gethings.
[Anderson: The Journal of Edward Montagu p227]

★ ★ ★

4 June BRAMBLE Fireship
Prize 1657; 125 tons; 59ft × 20ft; 12 guns
Captain Napthali Ball
In the aftermath of the action off Lowestoft (see above), the Dutch retreated to their own coast, and could stretch ahead when the English shortened sail during the night. The following morning several Dutch stragglers were attacked and captured. The *Bramble* was expended in an attempt to destroy the *Hilversum*, 60 guns. The Dutch ship managed to free herself but was then captured by the *Bristol*.
[Fox p122]

3 September HECTOR Fifth Rate
Prize 1657 (Royalist *Three Kings*); 111 tons; 71ft × 17.2ft; 22 guns
Captain John Cuttle
Part of an English squadron under the Earl of Sandwich which intercepted a homeward-bound Dutch East India fleet in the North Sea. In the action that followed the *Hector* foundered, either by a shot or by water flooding into the lee ports. About eighty men died.
[Anderson: The Journal of Edward Montagu p277; CSPD: Charles II September 1665]

13 October MERLIN Sixth Rate
Chatham 1652; 129 tons; 75ft × 18ft; 12 guns
Captain Charles Hayward
The *Merlin* sailed from Plymouth 28 September in company with the *Fox* to escort several merchant vessels to ports in North Africa. The ships were off Cape Spartel when the *Fox* and a merchant ship separated to make their own way. A gun salute fired as they left evidently attracted the attention of a nearby squadron of Dutch ships which closed and commenced an attack on the rear of the convoy. The *Merlin* was at the head of the ships and Captain Hayward tacked to place himself between the enemy and the merchant ships, but three of his charges were taken before he could engage. There followed a long running battle, with the *Merlin* finally running alongside one of the Dutch ships. With the rigging badly cut up and most of his men casualties, Hayward, wounded in the shoulder by a musket ball, finally surrendered. His actions meant that most of the convoy escaped.
[London Gazette issue no.1: 8 January 1665/66]

A clarification on an obscure ending:

CHESTNUT Ketch
Portsmouth 1656; 81 tons; 45ft × 18.6ft; 8 guns
Captain John Stephens
One of a squadron of five ships sent to the East Indies in March 1662 as part of the fleet under the Earl of Marlborough to take possession of Bombay, ceded to England under the marriage agreement of King Charles and Catherine of Braganza. The ketch is often listed as being wrecked, which follows the entry by Pepys in his Catalogue of Ships as having being 'cast away' in November 1665, but no further detail on this has been found. Elsewhere Pepys notes that the '*Chesnut*' had been 'cast in the Indies', meaning being cast aside, rather than having foundered. After their arrival in India, the *Chestnut* was kept on station, as it was felt she would never be fit for a return to England, and in March 1665 the Court of Committees of the East India Company advised that following a meeting with the Principal Officers of the Navy, that they had agreed to bring home the King's men, but the *Chestnut Pink* would be retained and used locally by the company. Captain Stephens evidently died in September 1665. The *Chestnut*, variously referred to as a pink, a pinnace and a ketch, remained in East India Company service until 1669, when she was 'worn out and would be sold'.
[Tanner: Naval Manuscripts in the Pepysian Library vol 1 p293; Latham p165; CSPD: January 1668; Sainsbury: Calendar 1664-1667 pp132, 136; and Calendar 1668-1670 p13; Foster pp52, 200]

1666

22 January GEORGE OF BRISTOL 'frigate'
Hired 1665; 20 guns
Captain William Davis
Driven ashore in storm-force winds and heavy seas and wrecked '… after many extremities', near Padstow, though without loss of life. Her guns and much of the stores were saved.
[CSPD: Charles II January 1666; TNA: ADM.10/15; London Gazette 1 February 1665/66]

17 February PRINCE WILLIAM Flyboat
Prize 1665 (*Prins Willem*); 253 tons; 90ft × 23ft; 4 guns
Captain John Totty
Reported to have been captured by the Dutch in the North Sea, but no further details known
[CSPD: Charles II February 1666]

20 February HARE Fireship
Prize 1665; 180 tons; 67ft × 22.6ft; 6 guns
Whilst lying at Harwich, she was burnt out after the accidental dropping of a candle. The burning wreck threatened other ships in the harbour, and it took some effort by the dockyard personnel to save them.
[CSPD: Charles II February 1666]

1–4 June: The Four Days' Battle: Day One
At the beginning of the protracted fleet action known as the Four Days' Battle in the southern North Sea, the English fleet under the Duke of Albemarle, inferior in numbers to the Dutch under de Ruyter, found the enemy at anchor about 15 miles to the east of North Foreland and immediately attacked. After about three hours' action on a south-easterly course, the English put about to avoid the approaching shoals and steered to the north-west, the Dutch following.

SWIFTSURE Second Rate
Woolwich 1653; 898 tons; 118ft × 37.10ft; 66 guns
Captain Sir William Berkeley†
With the close of the initial action, the fleet put about, but the *Swiftsure* with several other ships failed to tack and continued their course for some time, being closely engaged with the *Liefde*, 68 guns, and *Hollandia*, 80, which had fouled each other. Berkeley broke off action as other enemy ships came up, but the main yard was shot away and the rigging was shattered, and he was consequently surrounded by the enemy. Two large Dutch ships, the *Calantsoog*, 72 and *Reiger*, 72, laid themselves close alongside but Berkeley continued to fight until fatally wounded, and the ship was boarded and captured. The body of Berkeley was found in his cabin, covered in blood.
[Fox: pp242–4]

LOYAL GEORGE Fourth Rate
Hired 1665; 406 tons; 91.6ft × 28.11ft; 42 guns
Captain John Earle
In the van of the English fleet at the start of the battle, she supported the *Swiftsure* after the main fleet tacked away to the north-east and like her was surrounded and battered by several large Dutch warships, losing her main and mizzen masts. Eventually the *Deventer*, 66 guns, sent boarders on board and she surrendered.
[Fox: p250]

SEVEN OAKS Fourth Rate
Prize 1665 (*Zevenwolden*); 684 tons; 105ft × 35ft; 52 guns
Captain James Jennifer
Another ship of Berkeley's squadron, she also held her course when the main fleet tacked away, supporting the *Swiftsure*. After exchanging broadsides with the *Vrijheid*, 60 guns, when the *Swiftsure* struck her flag she attempted to make her way clear, but was then engaged by the *Beschermer*, 54, which ran alongside and entered boarders to take her surrender.
[Fox: p248]

2 June: The Four Days' Battle: Day Two
By 10 o'clock on the first night, both fleets had fallen apart, but the English renewed the action the following morning. The fighting went on for most of the day, until in the afternoon Albemarle turned the fleet for the English coast.

BLACK (SPREAD) EAGLE Fourth Rate
Prize 1665 (*Groningen*); 367 tons; 86ft × 28.4ft; 44 guns
Captain John Silver
As the fleets drew apart, the *Black Eagle*, severely damaged in the action, could not maintain her station and fell behind, with water gaining on the pumps. Her men were removed to other ships, and she was set on fire and allowed to founder.
[Fox: p273]

SAINT PAUL Fourth Rate
Prize (*Sint Paulus*); 291 tons; 84ft × 25.6ft; 48 guns
Captain John Holmes
Disabled during the fighting and making water, she was unable to keep up with the fleet and was abandoned and burnt to avoid capture.
[Fox: p275]

SPREAD EAGLE Fireship
Prize 1665; 240 tons; 74.8ft × 24.8ft; 6 guns
Captain William Searle
During the afternoon, part of the Dutch fleet under Lieutenant-Admiral Tromp were seen to be in some confusion and two fireships were sent in. Captain Seale attempted to set fire to a large Dutch ship believed to be a Vice-Admiral's ship. Although the fireship managed to run alongside, the Dutch ship managed to disengage herself and the fireship drifted away, to burn out and eventually founder.
[Fox: p265]

YOUNG PRINCE Fireship
Prize 1666 (*Jonge Prins*); 375 tons; 90ft × 28ft; 8 guns
Captain William Bustowe
The second of the fireships sent to attack Tromp's beleaguered squadron, Captain Bustowe successfully grappled the *Liefde* and set her on fire
[Fox: p265]

3 June: The Four Days' Battle: Day Three
The third day saw the English fleet heading towards the Thames, conducting a fighting retreat, followed by the Dutch

ROYAL PRINCE First Rate
Chatham 1663; 1,432 tons; 132ft × 45.2ft; 92 guns
Captain Sir George Ayscue

As the English retreated, pursued by the Dutch, several of the English ships ran aground on the Galloper Sand. All but the *Royal Prince* were successfully refloated, but the larger ship found herself stuck fast. She soon found herself surrounded by the Dutch fleet and surrendered to the *Gouda*, 72, '... when she had not herself shot ten guns in defence or received ten shots from the enemy'. At about 7.30pm she floated free on the rising tide, but it was found that her rudder was damaged and as the English fleet was still nearby and it was feared that they might attempt to retake her, her Dutch captors set her on fire. She burned until midnight when the powder magazine exploded, marking her end.
[Fox: pp281–3; Powell & Timings: Rupert & Monck pp253–4]

4 June: The Four Days' Battle: Day Four

The final day saw the squadron of Prince Rupert joining the English fleet during the morning. The fighting was renewed until the fleets finally parted during the afternoon, a fog cloaking the scene.

CLOVE TREE Third Rate
Prize 1665 (*Nagelboom*); 596 tons; 103ft × 33ft; 62 guns
Captain John Chappell†

With her rigging badly damaged, she straggled from the main fleet and fell behind, and with her captain dead, when the *Groningen*, 72, ran alongside she surrendered.
[Fox: p309]

ESSEX Third Rate
Deptford 1653; 652 tons; 118ft × 32.2ft; 56 guns
Captain William Reeves

During the fighting the *Essex*, already damaged by enemy fire, suffered further after colliding with the *Black Bull*. Unable to manoeuvre and with Captain Reeves gravely wounded, she was surrounded by Dutch ships and captured.
[Fox: p309]

BLACK BULL Fourth Rate
Prize 1665 (*Wapen van Edam*); 480 tons; 103ft × 30ft; 40 guns
Captain John Gethings†

With sails and rigging cut up by enemy fire, she was effectively disabled, and fell aboard the *Essex*, and both were surrounded and captured. The *Black Bull* was so severely damaged that she foundered soon after her capture, with many men, including Captain Gethings, being drowned.
[Fox: pp309–11]

CONVERTINE Fourth Rate
Prize 1650; 493 tons; 103ft × 30ft; 52 guns
Captain John Pearce

The *Convertine* had become separated from the main fleet during the fighting, her slow sailing qualities being further hampered by battle damage. When the *Wassenaar*, 56, closed her she immediately yielded.
[Fox: p312; Powell & Timings: Rupert & Monck p255]

Four fireships were expended during the last day:

HOUND Fireship
Prize 1656; 206 tons; 80ft × 22ft; 6 guns
Captain James Coleman

When part of the Dutch fleet became separated and cut off, a fireship was sent in to take advantage of the confusion and successfully laid herself alongside the *Landman*, 46 guns, setting her on fire. It is believed that the *Hound* was the ship responsible for this action.
[Fox: p300]

LITTLE UNICORN Fireship
Prize 1665 (*Eenhoorn*); 185 tons; 72ft × 22ft; 8 guns
Captain John Kelsey

During the intense fighting in the morning the Dutch *Ridderschap*, 66, was seen to have drifted out of line, disabled. A fireship was sent to destroy her and did lay herself alongside to set her opponent on fire, but the Dutch managed to haul her clear and extinguish the flames. A little later a Dutch *brander* (fireship) was seen making for the *Royal James*, but an English fireship intervened and placed herself in the way, saving the flagship but being burnt herself. The fireships involved in these actions were not identified but must have been either the *Little Unicorn* and *Greyhound*, although it is uncertain which vessel was responsible for which action.
[Fox: pp298–9]

GREYHOUND Fireship
Prize 1657; 145 tons; 62ft × 21ft; 6 guns
Captain William Flawes

See *Little Unicorn* above; the *Greyhound* was either used to attack the *Ridderschap* or tackle an approaching Dutch fireship.
[Fox: pp298–9]

HAPPY ENTRANCE Fireship
Prize 1658 (*Lichfield*); 233 tons; 76ft × 24ft; 6 guns
Captain Andrew Ball

Despatched to set fire to a large enemy warship – probably the *Eendracht*, 76 – Captain Ball did succeed in closing and setting the larger ship on fire, but the Dutch managed to extinguish the flames and survived the attack.
[Fox: p305]

★ ★ ★

25 July: Saint James's Day Battle

The re-formed Dutch fleet of about eighty-eight ships, still commanded by de Ruyter, sought out the English fleet under Albermarle and found him, with eighty-one ships, in the Thames Estuary. The English commenced the action in mid-morning and the fighting went on until about 2 o'clock in the afternoon when the Dutch formation broke up and retreated towards their own coast. One English capital ship was lost:

RESOLUTION Third Rate
Ratcliffe 1652 (*Tredagh*); 771 tons; 117.3ft × 35.2ft; 58 guns
Captain Willoughby Hannam

During the action she was damaged, with the foretopmast shot away, and being disabled, she drifted out of line. She was grappled by a Dutch fireship which set her on fire. Captain Hannam managed to clear the fireship, but the fire had taken hold and she was abandoned to burn out. She blew up at about 3 o'clock in the afternoon.
[Anderson: The Journals of Sir Thomas Allin vol 1 pp275–6]

Six fireships were burned in the action, without success – '... our fireships lost very foolishly, they going on without order were torn a-pieces and then forced to burn themselves without doing any execution'.
[Anderson: The Journals of Sir Thomas Allin vol 1 p278]

ABIGAIL Fireship
Purchased 1666; 143 tons; 63ft × 20.8ft; 4 guns
Captain Thomas Willshaw

BLESSING Fireship
Purchased 1666; 173 tons; 63ft × 22.9ft; 4 guns
Captain William Maiden

FORTUNE Fireship
Prize 1666; 392 tons; 94ft × 28ft; 4 guns
Captain William Lee

GREAT GIFT Fireship
Prize 1652 (*le Don de Dieu*); 490 tons; 98ft × 30.8ft; 4 guns
Captain John Kelsey

LAND OF PROMISE Fireship
Prize 1665; 191 tons; 68ft × 23ft; 4 guns
Captain William Minterne

Attempted to close the Dutch flagship *de Zeven Provincien*, which manned boats to tow her away. However, the fireworks were set on ablaze prematurely by a shot from the Dutch ship, causing the crew to abandon her, and she was towed away clear of her target by the Dutch.
[Perrin: Naval Miscellany vol III p13]

PROVIDENCE Fireship
Purchased 1665; 150 tons; 60ft × 21.8ft; 4 guns
Captain John Wood

★ ★ ★

25 July COVENTRY Fifth Rate
Prize 1658 (*San Miguel*); 191 tons; 68ft × 23ft; 20 guns
Captain William Hill

During an expedition mounted from Jamaica against French possessions in the West Indies, the *Coventry* was sent to the Iles des Saintes, Guadeloupe (also known as Todos los Santos), where they attacked a French convoy, burning one ship and capturing another, with Hill anchoring after the action. On 25 July in strong winds and a rising sea the anchor cables parted, and she was driven onshore. Efforts were made to free her, but the arrival of substantial French land forces forced their surrender. The ship was subsequently hauled off by the French as a prize.
[CSPC: America and West Indies 1661-1668]

25 July HOPE Fourth Rate
Prize 1665 (*Hoop*); 493 tons; 103ft × 30.6ft; 40 guns
Captain Jacob Reynolds†

Part of the small squadron assembled in the West Indies that was intended to attack French possessions, she was driven from her anchorage off the Iles des Saintes in hurricane-force winds, along with the merchant transports, and not seen again. Only two of the ten merchant vessels survived, and both of those lost masts. It was presumed that all were lost with all hands in the storm. Lord Willoughby of Parham, the governor of Barbados, was on board the *Hope* and was lost with her.
[CSPC: America and West Indies August 1666]

9 August: Sir Robert Holmes's Bonfire

Following the battles in the North Sea (see above), which left the English fleet dominant, it was decided to exploit the situation by attacking a Dutch port. With a small force of warships and fireships, Sir Robert Holmes was sent to attack shipping gathered off the islands of Vlie and Schelling. During the attack two small Dutch warships and over 100 merchant vessels were destroyed. Four fireships were expended in the action:

FOX Fireship
Prize (*le St Antoine*); 203 tons; 72ft × 23ft; 12 guns
Captain John Elliott

LIZARD Fireship
Prize 1653; 165 tons; 60ft × 22.9ft; 6 guns
Captain Joseph Harris

RICHARD Fireship
Purchased 1666; 198 tons; 62ft × 24.6ft; 4 guns
Captain Henry Browne
Successfully laid alongside the frigate *Vollenhove*, '… with the advantage of the wind laid him aboard and so fired him'.
[Perrin: The Naval Miscellany volume III p20]

SAMUEL Fireship
Purchased 1666; 121 tons; 54ft × 20.6ft; 4 guns
Captain William Seale
[London Gazette 13 August 1666; CSPD: Charles II August 1666]

* * *

15 August BREDA Fourth Rate
Bristol 1655 (*Nantwich*); 511 tons; 100ft × 31ft; 46 guns
Captain Thomas Page
Part of an escort to a convoy of ships carrying stores to the fleet, they sailed on 13 August from the anchorage on the Rowling (or Rolling) Grounds off Harwich, in a strong westerly gale. As night fell, they initially lay-to with their heads to the south and then bore away on a westerly wind to the north-east. By 8pm that night they judged themselves to be about 11 leagues (33 miles) off the Texel and altered course to the east, the convoy following, but at 1 o'clock in the morning, with little warning, she ran aground, with four of the store ships following her. Sail was taken in, and water barrels emptied and masts cut away in efforts to lighten her, but she would not come free, and water was reported to be entering. All the victualing ships were able to free themselves, but the *Breda* remained stuck fast. During the morning, several Dutch vessels closed and took off most of the crew as prisoners, after which the *Little Mary* closed and set her on fire.
[TNA: SP 29/129; Perrin: The Naval Miscellany vol III p26; London Gazette 16 August 1666]

1 September CHARLES MERCHANT Fourth Rate
Hired 1666 (*Royal Charles*); 588 tons; 103ft × 32.9ft; 54 guns
Captain John North
There was a partial engagement with the Dutch fleet off the Long Sand Head, Thames Estuary, during 31 August, the action being continued the following day in strong winds and heavy seas between North Foreland and the coast of France. The *Charles*, having lost her foremast, drifted apart from the main English fleet and was taken and later burnt by the Dutch.
[Perrin: The Naval Miscellany vol III p31]

13 October LITTLE MARY Sixth Rate
Prize 1654 (*Maria*); 109 tons; 60ft × 18.6ft; 12 guns
Captain John Brooks
Whilst guarding the herring fishery off Great Yarmouth, a group of Dutch fishing vessels and their escort came in sight. She closed to tackle the enemy, exchanging three or four broadsides with the leading opponent, before two other Dutch ships came up and forced her surrender.
[CSPD: Charles II October 1666]

24 November SAINT ANDREW Second Rate
Deptford 1622; 891 tons; 116ft × 38ft; 66 guns
Captain Valentine Pyne
After an engagement between the Dutch and English fleets on 31 August/1 September in the southern North Sea, the fleets parted, the weather being poor, with gale-force winds and high seas. The English fleet steered west, making for the shelter of the Isle of Wight. During the gale, on 3 September the *St Andrew* ran aground near Rye. She was freed and came to anchor off the town to repair damages, but they proved to be extensive, and when surveyed the hull was found to be in such an extremely poor state that the ship was in danger of sinking in the harbour. On 24 November she was run into shallow water until she grounded. When the tide left her, her seams opened, and she filled with water. She settled into the sand and fell over onto her side. Work went on to remove the guns and stores for several weeks after.
[CSPD: Charles II September & November 1666]

1667

5 February SAINT PATRICK Fourth Rate
Bristol 1666; 621 tons; 102ft × 33.10ft; 48 guns
Captain Robert Saunders[†]
In company with the *Malaga Merchant* fireship, the pair fell in with two Dutch warships, the *Schakerlo*, 30 guns, and the *Delft*, 34, off North Foreland. The *St Patrick* steered towards the enemy, despite being short-handed, and maintained the fight alone for some time, the fireship keeping clear, with Lieutenant Samuel Linzee assuming command after Captain Saunders had been killed. She ran alongside one of her opponents and attempted to board, but the other Dutch ship boarded on the other side, and she was forced to surrender with a loss of nine killed and sixteen wounded. The subsequent court martial ruled that the loss was due to the lack of men. The captain of the *Malaga Merchant*, William Sealey, was court-martialled for deserting the *St Patrick* and failing to support her. He was executed by firing squad on the quarterdeck of his own ship on 5 November.
[London Gazette 7 February 1666/7; Clowes vol 2 p434; CSPD: Charles II February 1667]

24 March COLCHESTER Fifth Rate
Great Yarmouth 1654; 287 tons; 83ft × 25.6ft; 28 guns
Captain Arthur Laugharne†
Having sailed from Barbados to scout ahead of a small squadron which was intending to attack French and Dutch colonies in the West Indies, she was off St Kitts when she sighted and chased a French warship. She overhauled her after nightfall, and after firing a broadside ran alongside and entered boarders. They met with strong resistance, as her opponent, *les Armes d'Angleterre*, formerly the British *Coventry*, had a large contingent of soldiers on board. As the fighting went on, the French ship continued to fire musketry at point-blank range into the British ship. The French ship cleared her decks of the boarders, and watched the *Colchester* drift away, having lost her mainmast, and evidently in distress. She sank during the night.
[CSPC: America and West Indies May 1667; Information from Frank Fox]

28 March WILLIAM Fireship
Purchased 1667; 6 guns
Captain William Rosewell
A member of Captain John Berry's small fleet in the West Indies, she was expended at Basse-Terre, St Kitts, destroying a large Dutch merchantman which had been mistaken for a 30-gun warship.
[Clarendon vol 5 p598]

10 May PEMBROKE Fifth Rate
Woolwich 1655; 269 tons; 81ft × 25ft; 28 guns
Captain George Legge
Foundered in Tor Bay after the *Fairfax*, 52 guns, had collided with her in the night, driving her anchor into the hull, causing the *Pembroke* to rapidly fill with water.
[London Gazette 13 May 1667; CSPD: Charles II May 1667]

10 May COMPANION Fourth Rate
Hired 1667; 30 guns
Captain John Thompson†
A member of the small fleet assembled under Captain John Berry which was despatched to attack Franco-Dutch forces in the Leeward Islands, the ships met the combined squadron of the enemy off the island of Nevis. As they were approaching, the *Companion* was blown up, apparently by the ignition of her own powder, after firing a gun. In addition to her nominal complement of 150 men, she had embarked 30 soldiers at Nevis, so as many as 180 men may have been killed.
[CSPC: America and West Indies May 1667, Charnock vol I, pp147–9]

5 June ELIZABETH Fifth Rate
Deptford 1647; 475 tons; 101.6ft × 29.8ft; 32 guns
Captain John Lightfoot
She was lying in the Penobscot River, off James Town, Virginia with a large number of merchant ships assembled for a convoy, when four Dutch warships with two fireships under the command of Abraham Crijnssen entered the bay. They were taken completely by surprise, with most of the officers and men ashore. Only token resistance could be organised before the Dutch boarded and burnt her. Eighteen merchant ships were subsequently burnt or captured by the Dutch. Captain Lightfoot was later court-martialled and found guilty of negligence, imprisoned for one year and dismissed the service.
[The London Gazette 15 August; 19 December 1667; CSPC: America and West Indies June 1667]

10–13 June: The Dutch in the Medway
With peace talks underway, as an economy measure the majority of the English fleet was laid up for the summer of 1667. The Dutch seized the opportunity and a large fleet under de Ruyter and de Witt advanced into the rivers Thames and Medway to attack the English in their own harbours. On 10 June they attacked the fort at Sheerness, driving off the small garrison and landing troops. The following day the Dutch advanced up the Medway to the protective chain across the river at Upnor, with the English scuttling ships in front of them in an attempt to block their passage.

11 June
The Dutch steadily advanced and the following ships were scuttled in the Long Reach off Mussell Bank in the Medway as blockships. In the event this tactic failed, as the Dutch were able to haul one of the scuttled vessels clear, allowing them to proceed. The upper works of the ships remained visible above the water and were set fire to by the Dutch as they left. The remains of most the vessels were sold in October 1669.
[HCJ 31 October 1667; Rogers p86; CSPD: Charles II June 1667]

Three fireships were scuttled under the direction of Captain William Rand at the Mussell Bank during the morning:

CONSTANT JOHN Fireship
Purchased 1665; 180 tons; 67ft × 22.6ft

JOHN and SARAH Fireship
Purchased 1666; 132 tons; 59ft × 20.6ft

UNICORN Fireship
Purchased 1666; 180 tons; 64ft × 23ft

After this was complete, it was evident that a passage was still clear, so more vessels were scuttled at the Mussell Bank.

BARBADOS MERCHANT Fireship
Purchased 1666; 223 tons; 76ft × 23.6ft

DOLPHIN Fireship
Purchased 1666; 143 tons; 64ft × 20.6ft

GOOD FORTUNE dogger
Prize 1665; 73 tons

Note: a further two vessels – the *Edward and Eve* ketch and *Hind* ketch – were reported to have been scuttled at the same time on the Mussel Bank but appear to have been merchant vessels. The Dutch found the *Edward and Eve* in shallow water, and were able to haul her clear, and open the channel.

12 June
During the early morning a further three ships were towed from Chatham to Upnor and were scuttled near the protective chain. Later that day the Dutch were able to sweep aside what resistance the disorganised English could offer and advanced past the protective chain and blockships at Upnor to attack the ships at anchor at Chatham.

MARMADUKE Fourth Rate
Prize 1652 (*Royalist Revenge*); 457 tons; 87ft × 31.5ft; 34 guns
Deliberately sunk at about 8am next to the chain, with a cable also fastened to a large merchant flyboat, the *Norway Merchant*, which was scuttled nearby. Despite these efforts, the Dutch were able to pass the blockships without difficulty. Later efforts to raise her failed and the salvaged timbers that had been recovered were ordered on 6 July 1669 to be used in repairs to the dock at Chatham, the remains of the wreck being sold on 22 September 1669 to Mr Boys.
[Rogers pp89–90, p158]

CHARLES V Fourth Rate
Prize 1665 (*Carolus Quintus*); 555 tons; 102ft × 32ft; 54 guns
Captain John Fortescue
Stationed at the northern end of the chain across the river at Upnor, she was attacked by two Dutch fireships. The *Charles* sank one by gunfire, but the second came alongside and set her on fire. Simultaneously she was boarded by boats' crews who drove off or captured the small crew on board. After removing the prisoners, the Dutch allowed the ship to burn out.
[Rogers p96]

MATTHIAS Fourth Rate
Prize 1653 (*Sint Mattheus*); 588 tons; 108ft × 32ft; 52 guns
Captain Henry Millett
Moored at the southern end of the chain in the river Medway, she was attacked by the Dutch fireship *Pro Patria* which set her on fire. She burnt fiercely before blowing up and sinking.
[Rogers pp95–6]

UNITY Fourth Rate
Prize 1665 (*Eendracht*); 303 tons; 95ft × 24.6ft; 42 guns
Captain Thomas Trafford
Stationed off the fort at Sheerness, with a small crew, to act as a guardship, but on the approach of the Dutch, fired one broadside and was then moved further upriver to take up position next to the chain barrier. She was attacked by the *Vrede* which gave her a broadside, ran alongside and boarded, driving off her crew, which were mainly pressed River Thames watermen. The Dutch took their prize back to Hellevoetsluis.
[Rogers pp95–7]

MARIA SANCTA Fourth Rate
Prize 1664 (*Sancta Maria*); 396 tons; 106ft × 26.6ft; 50 guns
Ordered to be scuttled as a blockship near the chain, whilst under the direction of the Master Attendant, John Brookes, she ran aground on a sandbank between Gillingham and Upnor before she reached her position and was abandoned. The Dutch yacht *de Brak* sent a party on board and set her on fire.
[Rogers pp90, 99]

PROSPEROUS Hoy
Chatham 1665; 68 tons; 50ft × 16ft
A dockyard craft, she was found by the Dutch moored near the chain and was set on fire by them.
[Rogers p155]

ROYAL CHARLES First Rate
Woolwich 1655 (*Naseby*); 1,258 tons; 131ft × 42.6ft; 82 guns
Laying off Gillingham, the *Royal Charles*, the pride of the English fleet, was captured. Orders had been given for her to be burnt, but this was not done, and the small party of men on board made off when a boat from the *Bescherming* came alongside. 'The Dutch did take her with a boat of nine men, who found not a man aboard her, and … presently a man went up and struck her flag and jack.' On 18 June her captors sailed out of the Medway, past the wrecks and barriers '… they did carry her down at a time when both for wind and tide, when the best pilot in Chatham would not have undertaken it, they heeling her on one side to make her draw little water'.
[Pepys' diary 22 June 1667]

13 June
As the Dutch advanced past the chain, the Duke of Albermarle gave orders for ships to be cut adrift from their moorings and scuttled; most were later successfully refloated to re-enter service, but one of the great ships was too severely damaged:

VANGUARD Second Rate
Woolwich 1631; 860 tons; 112ft × 38ft; 60 guns
Scuttled in the river Medway near the bridge at Rochester, all subsequent efforts to raise her failed, and she was broken up where she lay, explosive charges being used as late as 1669 to disperse the remains.
[Rogers p152]

On the same day, the following ships were scuttled in the River Thames at Woolwich as blockships, along with several merchant ships. They were ordered to be raised in August 1667 and broken up:
[Tanner: Naval Manuscripts in the Pepsyian Library]

HOUSE OF SWEEDS Third Rate
Prize 1665 (*Huis te Zwieten*); 786 tons; 111ft × 36.6ft; 70 guns

GOLDEN PHOENIX Third Rate
Prize 1665 (*Vergulde Phenix*); 113ft × 36ft; 60 guns

FORTUNE Flyboat
Prize 1666; 180 tons; 64ft × 23ft

HORSEMAN Flyboat
Prize 1665 (*de Ruiter*); 192 tons; 68ft × 23ft

WELCOME Fourth Rate
Prize 1652; 366 tons; 82ft × 29ft; 36 guns
Scuttled in the Thames at Woolwich, she was raised in October 1667 but found to be fit only for use as a fireship.

LEICESTER Sixth Rate
Purchased 1667; 257 tons; 84ft × 24ft; 24 guns
Scuttled in the Thames at Blackwall as a blockship

14 June
The final day of the raid on the Medway ports saw the Dutch consolidating their triumph. Those great ships they could not take away were destroyed.

ROYAL JAMES Second Rate
Woolwich 1658 (*Richard*); 1,108 tons; 124ft × 41ft; 82 guns
Found by the Dutch lying below Chatham partly sunk in shallow water, she was set on fire and burnt to the waterline. Her remains were ordered to be raised and taken to Woolwich, but little could be salvaged, and the wreck was broken up in August 1670.

LOYAL LONDON Second Rate
Deptford 1666; 1,134 tons; 127ft × 41.9ft; 80 guns
Also scuttled in shallow water at Chatham, she was set on fire by the fireship *Rotterdam* and burnt to the waterline. The remains were ordered to be salvaged on 15 July 1667 and rebuilt at Deptford, although it is doubtful whether anything more than a few timbers could have been used.

ROYAL OAK Second Rate
Portsmouth 1664; 1,021 tons; 121ft × 39.10ft; 76 guns
Like the *Loyal London*, she lay below Chatham scuttled in shallow water and was burnt by the Dutch. The remains were ordered 15 July 1667 to be raised and broken up.
[Rogers passim; HCJ: 31 October 1667; London Gazette 13 June 1667]

* * *

June MARY Fireship
Purchased 1667; 108 tons; 56ft × 19ft; 4 guns
Captain John Swayne
Apparently expended during the actions against the Dutch in the Medway, exact date, time and circumstances uncertain.
[Tanner: Naval Manuscripts in the Pepsyian Library vol 1 p284]

26 June JOSEPH Fireship
Purchased 1665; 101 tons; 55ft × 18.6ft; 4 guns
Captain John Wyborne
A British squadron under Admiral Sir John Harman attacked the French West Indian colony in Martinique. After three days of engagement with shore batteries and anchored shipping, the *Joseph* was sent in to burn the French vessels. The *Joseph* ran alongside the enemy flagship *Lis-Couronneé* and set her on fire, the blaze spreading to another three ships. The French scuttled the rest the next day when Harman appeared to be renewing the attack.
[London Gazette 9 September 1667]

23–26 July: Actions in the Thames Estuary
Following their successful raid on the Medway, a Dutch squadron under Lieutenant-Admiral van Nes blockaded the Thames. To counter them, a force of fireships under Sir Joseph Jordan and Sir Edward Spragge was assembled at Harwich and the Hope anchorage in the River Thames, respectively. On 23 July, the Dutch attacked the squadron off Tilbury, both sides expending fireships with little success. This was followed three days later by Jordan taking his force towards the Dutch vessels anchored off the Isle of Sheppey. This action was not successful, as several of the fireships failed to reach their targets and others were abandoned too soon to be effective. This resulted in several of the Captains being court-martialled for misconduct in action.

23 July: Action off Tilbury
The following were expended:

ALBEMARLE Fireship
Purchased 1667; 165 tons; 64ft × 22ft; 6 guns
Captain John Shelley

CAMEL Fireship
Prize 1667; 130 tons; 62ft × 10.10ft; 4 guns
Captain William Maiden

STAR Fireship
Purchased 1667; 121 tons; 54ft × 20.6ft; 4 guns
Captain Hugh Ridley

26 July: Action off the Isle of Sheppey
The following were expended:

OWNER'S ENDEAVOUR Fireship
Purchased 1667
Captain John Ward

SAINT JACOB Fireship
Purchased 1667; 276 tons; 90ft × 24ft; 4 guns
Captain George Colt

SWAN Fireship
Purchased 1667; 71 tons; 52ft × 16ft; 4 guns
Captain John Votier

VIRGINIA Fireship
Purchased 1666; 148 tons; 64ft × 20.10ft; 4 guns
Captain William Howes
Captain Howe was later court-martialled for cowardice and 'non-performance' of his duties, by failing to bring his ship into action properly and abandoning his ship too soon. He was found guilty and ordered to be executed, although later reprieved.
Note: This ship is variously listed as *Virgin*, *Virginia* and *Virginee*
[*London Gazette* 22 July, 25 July; 11 November 1667; *CSPD: Charles II July 1667*]

* * *

22 July HELVERSTON Third Rate
Prize 1665 (*Hilversum*); 597 tons; 103ft × 33ft; 54 guns
Having survived the attack on Chatham, she was being taken to Sheerness to act as an accommodation hulk, when she ran onto the submerged wreck of the *Norway Merchant*, which had been scuttled near the Medway chain and the stump of the mast ran through her bottom and she sank.
[*CSPD: Charles II July 1667*]

2 September ALLEPINE Fireship
Purchased 1666; 233 tons; 76ft × 24ft; 6 guns
Captain Andrew Ball
Ordered to Kinsale in Ireland, Captain Cowdray of the *Hardereen* reported that the *Allepine* had foundered in poor weather.
[*CSPD: Charles II September 1667; TNA: ADM 10/15*]

15 November SORLINGS Fifth Rate
Prize 1654 (*Royal James*); 321 tons; 86ft × 26.6ft; 22 guns
Captain Stephen Akerman
Ran aground on the Woolpack Sand off Reculver and wrecked. The *Enquiry* smack went to her aid and lifted off all 120 men onboard. By 22 November it was reported that she had broken up in the poor weather. The court-martial in December cleared the officers and crew of all blame, the 'miscarriage being solely attributed to the wilfulness, ignorance and ill grounded confidence of Aaron Johnson the pilot'.
[*CSPD: Charles II November & December 1667; London Gazette 19 December 1667*]

11 December HIND Ketch
Wivenhoe 1656; 56 tons; 41ft × 16ft; 8 guns
Captain John Withers
Returning to England from Corunna, the weather was poor which prevented any sun or star observations being made. During the night of 10 December, in strong south-east winds, fearing they were close inshore she wore round to the south. The lead-line was used constantly, but despite this precaution in the early hours went ashore on rocks to the south-west of the Scilly Isles.
[*TNA: SP 29/237*]

1668

March COLCHESTER Ketch
Colchester 1664; 72 tons; 48ft × 16.10ft; 8 guns
Listed by Pepys has having been 'Taken by the French; she being bound to the North-West Passage' in March 1667, which I presume to mean March 1667/1668. I can find no other reference to this. It is possible that she was intended to be part of the expedition to Hudson Bay under Pierre Esprit Radisson and Médard des Grosselliers which was sponsored by Prince Rupert in early 1668 and was given to them, rather than taken as a prize, but if so, then she was never used. She apparently became the *Petit Anglais* in French service.
[*Tanner: Naval Manuscripts in the Pepsyian Library vol 1 p291; Demerliac vol 1 p72*]

21 October PROVIDENCE Fireship
Bermondsey 1637; 304 tons; 90ft x 26ft; 6 guns
Captain Hugh Ridley
Part of the squadron under Sir Thomas Allin in the Mediterranean, she was sent to Tangier carrying released prisoners from Algiers. Unfortunately, she ran aground near Old Tangier, and being unable to be freed, she was abandoned and set on fire to prevent her being captured.
[London Gazette 3 December 1668]

6 December DEFIANCE Third Rate
Deptford 1666; 863 tons; 117ft x 37.3ft; 64 guns
The ship was lying 'in Ordinary' – out of commission – at Chatham when at 5 o'clock in the afternoon a fire was discovered in the steerage compartment on the lower deck, which spread rapidly and largely destroyed the ship. The Gunner, Robert Waymouth, was the senior officer in her, living on board with his wife and daughter. An enquiry found that he had allowed unguarded candles to be used below decks, which was believed to be the source of the blaze, 'trusting a girl to carry fire into his cabin'. Waymouth was subsequently ordered to be rowed from Upnor Castle to the *Charles* and then to stand for three hours on the upper deck of that ship 'with a halter around his neck and his fault writ upon his breast'. The remains of the ship were ordered on 2 March 1672 to be used as a hulk.
[TNA: SP 46/137; CSPD: Charles II December 1668; Pepys' Diary 25 March 1669]

1669

2 January OXFORD Fifth Rate
Deptford 1656; 220 tons; 72ft x 24ft; 26 guns
Captain Edward Collier
Under the control of the Governor of Jamaica, Sir Thomas Modyford, who placed the *Oxford* under the command of a privateer captain, at the disposal of Henry Morgan, who would lead a buccaneer attack on Cartagena. The ships intended for the expedition assembled in a bay at the western end of the Île à Vache off Hispaniola and a conference of war was held on board by Morgan with the captains. While they were at dinner on the quarterdeck, the *Oxford* blew up, and about 200 men were lost, with only six men and four boys being saved. The accident is supposed to have been caused by the negligence of the gunner.
[CSPC: America and West Indies January 1669]

1670

22 March ROE Ketch
Wivenhoe 1665; 91 tons; 50ft x 18.6ft; 8 guns
Captain Thomas Foulis
Attached to Admiral Allin's fleet in the Mediterranean, she was driven ashore and wrecked in the Canary Isles near Tenerife.
[Tanner: Naval Manuscripts in the Pepsyian Library vol 1 p291]

31 March SAPPHIRE Fourth Rate
Ratcliffe 1651; 442 tons; 100ft x 28.10ft; 36 guns
Captain John Pearce
Whilst cruising in the Western Mediterranean, the ship was off Cape Passero, Sicily, when a group of four ships were sighted, apparently closing, which Captain Pearce was convinced were Algerine corsairs. Despite the crew evidently being willing to fight, Pearce took the ship close inshore to avoid an engagement and then deliberately ran her aground on the coast of Sicily to the south of Messina, where she was wrecked. Pearce and his Lieutenant, Andrew Logan, were court-martialled for cowardice, and were found guilty of '... being possest with a pannick fear'. On 26 September both were executed by firing squad on board the *Dragon* at Deptford.
[London Gazette 15 September & 26 September 1670; CSPD Charles II May 1670]

22 December ORANGE Fifth Rate
Prize 1665 (*Oranjeboom*); 250 tons; 74ft x 25.3ft; 32 guns
Captain Andrew Ball†
Sailed from Leghorn (Livorno) in company with the *Dartmouth* on 15 December, to escort home a number of merchant ships, but during the night of 21/22 December, when to the north-east of Minorca, they encountered a very fierce storm during which the *Orange* disappeared. She was last seen at about 3 or 4 o'clock in the morning when she was heard firing guns before she put before the wind and was lost to sight and was presumed lost with all hands.
[CSPD: Charles II April 1671]

1671

3 May EAGLE Fireship
Prize 1670; 54 tons; 56ft x 13.6ft; 6 guns
Lieutenant Dominic Nugent
Part of a squadron under Sir Edward Spragge sent to the Mediterranean to tackle the continuing problem of North African corsairs. Discovering a number of Algerine ships at anchor off Bugia (modern Béjaïa)

and determined to attack them, during the night of 2/3 May Lieutenant Nugent led two fireships into the bay. Nugent left the *Eagle* to row into the harbour to discover the position of the enemy ships. The ship was fired by the crew in his absence and burned in the harbour to no effect.
[CSPD: Charles II May 1671; Charnock vol 1 p326]

3 May ROSE Fireship
Prize 1670; 112 tons; 65.6ft × 18ft; 4 guns
Masters Mate Henry Williams
The second of the fireships which were prepared to attack the Algerines at Bugia (see *Eagle* above); the vessel was prematurely burnt, apparently when a drunken gunner fired a pistol, setting off a powder explosion.
[CSPD: Charles II May 1671]

8 May LITTLE VICTORY Fireship
Chatham 1665; 245 tons; 80ft × 24ft; 6 guns
Captain Leonard Harris
In a repeat of the attack on the corsairs' harbour at Bugia, Sir Edward Spragge sent in his last remaining fireship, the *Little Victory*, which had been lightened so that she drew only 8ft of water. During the afternoon supported by the fire of the *Mary*, the *Dragon* and *Revenge*, the boats of the squadron cut through a boom laid across the harbour's mouth and the *Little Victory* was successfully laid alongside the tightly-packed Algerine ships, seven of which were burnt. Harris was severely wounded in the action.
[HMC Dartmouth 3 pp5–6; CSPD: Charles II May 1671]

7 July MILFORD Fifth Rate
Wivenhoe 1654 (*Fagons*); 262 tons; 82ft × 24.6ft; 28 guns
Captain John Shelley
Lying at Port Mahon, Menorca, it was decided to dry the bread room, and lighted coals were placed in in a copper kettle or container and were left unattended in the compartment. Within 30 minutes smoke was filling the lower deck and despite managing to remove the kettle and a lighted candle, the smoke became thicker, and it was clear that the bread room had caught fire. Efforts to tackle the fire failed and eventually cables were cut, and she was carried before the wind until she ran aground where she was allowed to burn out. Several explosions completed her end, scattering debris, with three of her guns being blown ashore. A court martial cleared the Captain of any responsibility for the loss, which was blamed on the lack of tinning in the bread room and the carelessness of those lighting the coals. They were ordered to be flogged around the fleet, each man receiving three lashes by the side of every ship riding in the harbour.
  Note: Pepys' Register of Ships wrongly places the loss in July 1673, an error copied by others.
[CSPD: Charles II July 1671]

1672

5 May FRENCH VICTORY Fifth Rate
Prize 1666 (*la Victoire*); 393 tons; 88ft × 29ft; 38 guns
Captain John Fletcher
Sailed from the Nore on 2 May to join the fleet, having been delayed by the absence of Captain Fletcher, and then loitered to await her longboat to rejoin, which had been sent away to collect the wives of Captain Fletcher and other officers. They then sailed, making for the Downs, and during the evening of 4 May saw a number of ships which they assumed were the English fleet. They brought to under mainsail and in the early morning found themselves close to the ships, which were then discovered to be Dutch. They hastily made sail but was pursued by three large Dutch warships. One of them, the *Zeelandia*, 44 guns, soon overhauled her, firing 10 or so shots, at which the *French Victory* surrendered without offering any resistance. Pepys noted that Fletcher had '… lost his ship and fled his trial'.
[CSPD: Charles II May 1672; Tanner: Naval Manuscripts in the Pepsyian Library vol 1 p350]

28 May: The Battle of Solebay
The combined Anglo-French fleets commanded by the Duke of York were at anchor in Sole Bay, off Southwold, taking in stores and water, when the Dutch fleet under de Ruyter approached and attacked, taking them by surprise. Fortunately for the allies, the winds were light, which prevented the Dutch from fully pressing home their attack and enabled the combined fleets to leave the anchorage, albeit in separate bodies. The consequent battle was a close and confused action which lasted until the wind shifted to give the English the weather gage, at which the Dutch retired.

ROYAL JAMES First Rate
Portsmouth 1671; 1,416 tons; 132.6ft× 44.10ft; 100 guns
Captain Richard Haddock
Flagship of the Earl of Sandwich during the action, the *Royal James* became fiercely engaged with the Dutch, who sent two fireships to close her, but the first was sunk, the other disabled. About 30 minutes after this incident the *Groot Hollandia*, 60 guns, ran aboard her, to lay athwart the bows, where she could rake the *James* with impunity and casualties steadily mounted from the constant fire. Seeing that she was unable to manoeuvre, other Dutch ships took the opportunity to close and fire into the *Royal James*. The *Dolfijn*, 80, flagship of Lieutenant-Admiral van Ghent, ranged along her starboard side and fired with such ferocity that most of *Royal James*'s upper deck guns were disabled and gun crews killed or wounded. Realising that she was being carried by the tide, in order to free herself, Captain Haddock ordered the ship to be

anchored by the stern. This had the desired effect and the *Groot Hollandia* drifted away on the current. However, before Haddock could get underway again, the ship was attacked by a third Dutch ship, the *Olifant*, 82, which covered the approach of a fireship. The *Royal James* could not clear the fireship which successfully grappled her and set her alight. Boats were sent to rescue the survivors but many of her complement, including the Earl of Sandwich, died.
[Anderson: Journals and Narratives pp165–7; CSPD: Charles II May 1672]

The following fireships were lost during the action:

ALICE and FRANCIS Fireship
Purchased 1672; 266 tons; 76ft × 25.8ft; 6 guns
Captain Ezekiel Yennis†
The fireship had stood by the *Royal James* until Captain Yennis was killed and she then bore away into the Dutch fleet and was lost.
[Anderson: Journals and Narratives pp167–8]

ANN and JUDITH Fireship
Purchased 1672; 264 tons; 76.6ft × 25.6ft; 6 guns
Captain Joseph Harris
Captain Harris attempted to attack the Dutch flagship, *de Zeven Provincien*, and despite a fierce barrage managed to lay his ship alongside, despite his fore yard and rigging being shot to pieces. Unfortunately, they could not secure a hold and Dutch boats cut the ship free before it could damage her opponent, and she drifted away to burn out. Five men were killed.
[Anderson: Journals and Narratives p175]

BANTAM Fireship
Purchased 1672; 276 tons; 75ft × 26.3ft; 6 guns
Captain Henry Pattison†
The *Bantam* attempted to close the enemy, but the Dutch, '… perceiving what she was, paid her so, that she sank'.
[Anderson: Journals and Narratives p180]

FOUNTAIN Fireship
Prize 1664; 371 tons; 88ft × 28.2ft; 8 guns
Captain Robert Stout
Ordered to close the enemy fleet, as she did so, she came under heavy fire and was burnt prematurely after being repeatedly hit before she could reach her target.
[Anderson: Journals and Narratives p180]

KATHERINE Fireship
Purchased 1672; 230 tons; 73ft × 24.4ft; 6 guns
Captain Thomas Andrews
Directed to attack the *Eendracht*, 76 guns, she managed to run alongside but under constant heavy fire she sank by the side of the Dutch ship without being able to set her on fire.
[Anderson: Journals and Narratives p300]

★ ★ ★

June HOPE Hoy
Prize 1666; 46 tons; 41ft × 14.6ft; 4 guns
Listed by Pepys as being recaptured by the Dutch in this month – no further details found.
[Tanner: Naval Manuscripts in the Pepsyian Library vol 1 p288]

28 July PORTSMOUTH Sloop
Portsmouth 1667; 42 tons; 40ft × 14ft; 4 guns
Captain Edward Pearce
Detached from the main fleet on 24 July to proceed to the Thames Estuary, they made little progress due to contrary winds and fog, and then encountered the main Dutch fleet. Steering south to escape this threat, they soon sighted the spires of Ostend and anchored in shallow water. On seeing two strange ships approaching, the sloop weighed and made sail to the west, pursued by the strangers. They soon overhauled her, and the sloop surrendered after they fired a volley of small shot and were preparing to board. Her captors were privateers from Flushing, one of 28 guns, the other of 16.
[CSPD: Charles II September 1672]

16 September TULIP Sloop
Deptford 1672; 22 tons; 43ft × 10ft; 2 guns
Master Thomas Frizell
Sailed from Great Yarmouth with despatches for the fleet, she worked her way southward and it was after nightfall, when she was off Orford Ness, that she became aware of a ship approaching. Mr Frizell hailed her but received no reply until the stranger fired a broadside into her. The sloop returned fire with muskets, but the stranger ran alongside and entered a large number of boarders. After a brief struggle, the sloop surrendered. Her captor was a Dutch privateer from Zeeland.
[CSPD: Charles II September 1672]

5 October THOMAS and GEORGE Fireship
Purchased 1672; 245 tons; 72ft × 25.3ft; 6 guns
Captain Theophilus Scott
Listed by Pepys as having been 'cast away' in this month, but no further details have been found. Her pay book was closed on 5 October, which is indicative of a date.
[Tanner: Naval Manuscripts in the Pepsyian Library vol 1 p286; TNA: ADM 33/128]

15 October KENT Fourth Rate
Deptford 1652 (*Kentish*); 601 tons; 107ft × 32.6ft; 46 guns
Captain John Wood
In thick weather at about 10 o'clock in the morning she ran aground on the Leman and Ower sandbank off the north Norfolk coast. The rudder was unshipped, and the constant pounding on the ground in the surf broke her back. During the evening she started to break up and with the water up to the gun deck, the crew started leaving her. Captain Wood was one of the first to leave. Abandoning nearly 200 men, he took the pinnace with 10 men and successfully reached the shore in Lincolnshire. Some of those left behind built rafts, one of which was picked up by the *Antelope* and another two were washed ashore near Winterton. Wreckage came ashore over a wide distance along the north Norfolk and Lincolnshire coasts. Six days after she ran aground the last survivors were taken off the wreck by Captain Direchst of the Dutch privateer *Geeldseer*, who intended to put them ashore at Yarmouth, but on his way was captured, but he was rewarded with a payment of £140. Captain Wood and the pilot were deemed responsible and were ordered to be committed to the Marshalsea Prison, the pilot protesting that he had only been engaged to negotiate the Thames Estuary whilst Captain Wood was accused of overriding the advice of the pilot and master and had ignored their warnings.
[*CSPD: Charles II October & November 1672*]

18 November FORESTER Fifth Rate
Lydney 1657; 266 tons; 80ft × 25ft; 28 guns
Captain Robert Stout
Laying at anchor off Leghorn (Livorno), Captain Stout went ashore to supervise the loading of provisions. He had hardly landed when the town was shaken by a massive explosion and the ship could be seen to be on fire. Boats quickly went to the scene and picked up several survivors, including the Lieutenant and Gunner. No cause was found for the disaster.
[*CSPD: Charles II January 1673*]

November (?) SWALLOW Sloop
Deptford 1672; 68 tons; 50ft × 16ft; 2 guns
Captain Isaac Gilding (?)
Vaguely listed by Pepys as being 'cast away at sea 1673', but no details have been found. Captain Gilding was certainly in command in October 1672, but was appointed to a new command in February 1673, which perhaps indicates that she had already been lost by then. The *Swallow*'s pay book was closed 18 November 1672 which is suggestive of a date, and I can find no mention of her after this.
[*Tanner: Naval Manuscripts in the Pepsyian Library vol 1 p292; TNA: ADM.33/128*]

1673

17 February SUCCESS Fireship
Purchased 1672; 127 tons; 51ft × 21.8ft; 6 guns
Captain John Rice
Driven from her anchorage off Sheerness in a strong south-westerly gale and stranded on a sandbank. In efforts to keep her upright, the mainmast was cut away, and as it fell it carried away her mizzen mast. Several holes were cut in the bilges to allow the water to escape, but she settled, and soon the water was '… as high within as without'. She lay on the bank for two days before she was refloated but on survey was found to be damaged so badly, that she was condemned on 23 March.
[*CSPD: Charles II February 1673*]

17 April EAGLE Fireship
Purchased 1672; 208 tons; 74ft × 23ft; 6 guns
Captain Richard Keigwin
Part of a small squadron that sailed from the Downs 15 January under the command of Captain Richard Munden bound for the island of St Helena, she foundered in the Atlantic.
[*Tanner: Naval Manuscripts in the Pepsyian Library vol 1 p282*]

11 May ORANGE TREE Fireship
Purchased 1672; 159 tons; 68ft × 21ft; 6 guns
Captain John Johnson
Accidentally caught fire and burnt out in the early hours of the morning, whilst lying at anchor with the fleet off Rye.
[*CSPD Charles II May 1673*]

28 May: First Battle of Schooneveld
The Dutch fleet under de Ruyter clashed with the combined Anglo-French fleets off the Dutch coast amongst the sandbanks in the Schooneveld channel off Walcheren. The allies closed on the anchored Dutch who weighed and prepared to meet them but with only part of the allied fleet getting into action, the resulting battle was indecisive.
[*London Gazette 29 May 1673; Tanner: Naval Manuscripts in the Pepsyian Library vol 1 pp284, 286*]

The following were burnt in action against the Dutch fleet, but without achieving success:

PROVIDENCE Fireship
Purchased 1672; 180 tons; 67ft × 22.6ft; 6 guns
Captain William Andrews

RACHEL Fireship
Purchased 1672; 134 tons; 60ft × 20.6ft; 6 guns
Captain John Kelsey

SAMUEL and ANNE Fireship
Purchased 1672; 243 tons; 73.3ft × 25ft; 6 guns
Captain Richard Haddock
On closing with the Dutch fleet, '… they shot his masts around his ears' before he could tackle his target.
[Thompson p19]

4 June: Second Battle of Schooneveld
After the inconclusive fighting of 28 May, the rival fleets remained close to each other, and after the weather cleared the Dutch closed to renew the action. The battle again proved indecisive, with the allies coming into action in a confused manner, the Dutch keeping at long range.

Two ships were burnt in action:

ORANGE PRIZE Fireship
Prize 1672; 194 tons; 69ft × 23ft; 6 guns
Captain Francis Turner

WELCOME Fireship
Prize 1652; 366 tons; 82ft × 29ft; 6 guns
Captain Abraham Goodhart†
[Tanner: Naval Manuscripts in the Pepsyian Library vol 1 pp284, 286]

★ ★ ★

17 July ALGIER Fifth Rate
Prize 1670; 344 tons; 82.6ft × 28ft; 26 guns
Captain Thomas Knevitt
Steering along the Swin channel in the Thames Estuary, she was under the command of Captain Knevitt for the passage, as no river pilot was available. Knevitt took her close to visible shallows and then ordered a course which, combined with the tide and wind, took her onto the Black Tail bank at the Nore, despite the *Emsworth* sloop being stationed nearby to warn ships of dangerous waters. The subsequent pounding that she took as she lay on the bank broke her back and she was lost. At a court martial Knevitt was found guilty of negligence and was dismissed the service and ordered to serve one year in the Marshalsea Prison. The Master, Richard Kingston, who had left the deck and failed to order the constant use of the lead-line, was sentenced to six months in prison and loss of half his pay. Seaman George Trist, who had taken the opportunity to desert, was ordered to be ducked three times from the main yard of the *Phoenix*.
[TNA: ADM.106/283; ADM.106/284]

26 July HART Dogger
Prize 1672; 73 tons; 45ft × 17.6ft; 6 guns
Captain John Norwood
Cruising in the North Sea, she stood over to the Texel to gain intelligence of the strength and position of any Dutch warships. On 25 July she ran along the shore and sighted four large ships, but when one of them was seen to be getting underway in pursuit she was forced to stand off, heaving some ballast overboard to lighten the ship and cutting away her boat to escape. The dogger outpaced her pursuer, but then sighted a further two ships closing from seaward, forcing another change of course, but with nightfall she again lost her pursuers. The following day 'a small frigatt' was seen to windward and Norwood determined to engage. Unfortunately, as they altered course the topmast was carried away, which caused some confusion with the sail and rigging coming down onto the deck. When this was cleared the stranger was close by them and there was an exchange of broadsides, before the enemy ran under their lee quarter and fired repeatedly into them with small arms, causing several casualties. They tried to make sail away but were pursued and surrendered when a boat full of the enemy came alongside, the men refusing to fight anymore, running down into the hold.
[TNA: ADM.106/285]

7 August GOLDEN HAND Fireship
Prize 1665; 287 tons; 90ft × 24.6ft; 6 guns
Captain William Mather
Attached to the main fleet, she foundered in poor weather whilst laying at anchor off Terschelling
[TNA: ADM.8/1; Tanner: Journals and Narratives of the Third Dutch War p330]

8 August HARD BARGAIN Dogger
Prize 1672; 73 tons; 45ft × 17.6ft; 6 guns
Captain Thomas White
Listed as being recaptured by the Dutch in the North Sea; no further details found.
[TNA: ADM.8/1; Tanner: Naval Manuscripts in the Pepsyian Library vol 1 p280; vol 2 p28]

10 August MARIGOLD Fireship
Purchased 1673; 109 tons; 57ft × 19ft; 4 guns
Captain John Rice
Part of the fleet under Prince Rupert, she was abandoned during the forenoon as unseaworthy and allowed to sink in the North Sea off Texel.
[Anderson: Journals and Narratives p353]

11 August: The Battle of the Texel
The final fleet battle of the Dutch Wars was fought in the shallow waters off the Dutch coast. The Dutch under de Ruyter outmanoeuvred the Anglo-French

fleet to gain the weather gage and then closed to start the fighting. The allies came about to regain the wind and the fighting became general and fierce, with the squadrons separating, the French contingent hardly participating. The fleets eventually fell apart with the allies steering for home, leaving the scene to de Ruyter.

The following were either sunk or foundered during the action:

DOLPHIN Sloop
Deptford 1673; 60 tons; 54ft × 14.6ft; 2 guns
Captain William Orchard
[Tanner: Naval Manuscripts in the Pepsyian Library vol 1 p292]

HENRIETTA Yacht
Woolwich 1663; 104 tons; 52ft × 19.5ft; 8 guns
Captain Thomas Guy
During the morning she was struck by two shots, one forward, the other abaft, under the waterline, and she soon filled and sank, all the crew managing to escape to the *John's Advice*.
[CSPD: Charles II August 1673]

ROE Dogger
Prize 1672; 73 tons; 45ft × 17.6ft; 6 guns
Captain Joseph Symonds
Hit by several shots and sank, the crew being rescued by the *St Andrew*.
[TNA: ADM.106/285]

ROSE Dogger
Prize 1672; 73 tons; 45ft × 17.6ft; 6 guns
Captain Ralph Wrenn
[Tanner: Naval Manuscripts in the Pepsyian Library vol 1 p280]

Both sides expended numerous fireships in efforts to disrupt the enemy, but with little success, the Dutch claimed that '… the enemy spent 9 or 10, several of which our shallops took or forced them to set themselves on fire' (*London Gazette 18 August 1673*).

BLESSING Fireship
Purchased 1673; 109 tons; 57ft × 19ft; 4 guns
Captain William Andrews†

FRIENDSHIP Fireship
Purchased 1673; 180 tons; 64ft × 23ft; 4 guns
Captain John Kelsey†

HOPEWELL Fireship
Purchased 1672; 242 tons; 70ft × 25.6ft; 4 guns
Captain Henry Fitton

KATHERINE Fireship
Purchased 1672; 294 tons; 76ft × 27ft; 4 guns
Captain John Votier

(Saint) LAWRENCE Fireship
Purchased 1672; 154 tons; 60ft × 22ft; 4 guns
Captain John Cooke

LEOPARD Fireship
Purchased 1672; 220 tons; 68ft × 25ft; 4 guns
Captain Matthias Bird
Attended the *Triumph*, she was disabled after having her main topmast and foremast shot away and having several shot in the hull. She drifted out of the allied line and was then boarded from two Dutch pinnaces. The crew were removed, and she was then set on fire.
[TNA: ADM.106/285]

PEARL Fireship
Purchased 1673; 162 tons; 63ft × 22ft; 4 guns
Captain William Booth

PRUDENT MARY Fireship
Purchased 1673; 295 tons; 76ft × 27ft; 4 guns
Captain Christopher Billop
Attempted to close the *Olifant*, 82 guns, but was intercepted by a Dutch fireship and the pair burnt together.
[Anderson: Journals and Narratives p360]

SOCIETY Fireship
Purchased 1673; 318 tons; 82ft × 27ft; 4 guns
Captain Robert Washburne

SUPPLY Fireship
Purchased 1672; 230 tons; 73ft × 24.4ft; 4 guns
Captain Henry Williams

TRUELOVE Fireship
Prize 1647 (Royalist *Katherine*); 102 tons; 59ft × 18ft; 4 guns
Captain Peter Bonamy
Attended the *Charles* in the engagement, her masts were shot away and after several shot struck her below the waterline, she foundered.
[TNA: ADM.106/285]

★ ★ ★

17 August KATHERINE Yacht
Deptford 1661; 94 tons; 49ft × 19ft; 8 guns
Captain Thomas Lovell
Ordered to join the main fleet in the North Sea, she sailed from the Thames Estuary on 14 August and steered north towards Great Yarmouth. The weather

was poor with regular rain squalls, and she spent some time laid-to. During the evening of 16 August, she spied a large number of ships, but realising that they were the enemy, she quickly made sail to escape. The following morning with the wind to the north-west, a ship was seen to be in pursuit, and she made sail away, and initially made for another ship that was in sight, believed to be English, but as they closed, they saw 'a Hollands insignia' and were forced to alter away, steering as close to the wind as they could. The pursuers continued the chase. Water butts were emptied, and the anchor cut away in efforts to lighten her, but she could not shake off her pursuers and at 4 o'clock in the afternoon, land was seen ahead. She tried tacking round to the northeast but was forced further inshore until they were in 8 fathoms of water, and she surrendered to the *Schiedam*, 24 guns, and was taken into Amsterdam.
[TNA: ADM.106/284; ADM.106/287; London Gazette 25 August 1673]

22 August BENJAMIN Fireship
Purchased 1673; 130 tons; 57ft × 20.9ft; 4 guns
Captain John Polea
The fireship was forced from her anchors off Great Yarmouth in poor weather when the *Swiftsure* drove on board her, and she lay-to under her main course as the wind increased from the south-west. The wind shifted round to the north in the early hours and morning found her detached from the fleet. At noon, an 18-gun Dutch privateer closed, and she surrendered without resistance, and was taken into Rotterdam.
[TNA: ADM.106/285]

19 September FAIRFAX Third Rate
Chatham 1653; 785 tons; 120ft × 35.2ft; 72 guns
Captain Dominic Nugent
With the ship underway in the Thames Estuary, as she altered course, she ran hard aground on the north shore of the river, about 1½ miles from Grays. Men from the dockyard at Woolwich attended the scene but could do little as the tide left her and although she heeled over, she was reported as remaining dry and stable. At the next high tide, she righted herself but efforts to free her failed. At the next low tide, it was clear that she was suffering from the weight of guns and stores on board, as several planks and timbers gave way. Work started to lighten her, taking off guns and stores and striking yards and topmasts, but with the next high tide she filled with water, and this became worse with every tide. Despite the difficulties the salvage efforts continued and eventually on 5 October she was floated off and taken to the dockyard, but on survey was found to be so irreparably damaged that she was not put back into service but converted to a hulk. At a court martial held in November 1673 it was found that the commanding officer was not on board, having left the ship in charge of the lesser officers. Nugent was found guilty of being absent without permission and was dismissed his ship.
[TNA: ADM.106/286; ADM.106/290]

21 September CUTTER Sloop
Portsmouth 1673; 46 tons; 60ft × 12ft; 2 guns
Captain John Harris
Riding at anchor off Dover, on 16 September she was driven from her moorings in strong winds, but she managed to re-anchor off Deal. The weather remained poor, with limited visibility, the nearby land often being obscured. During the night of the 21st the wind increased to a full gale and when the anchor cable parted, she was driven onto the shore near Sandown castle. Sir John Holmes, commander of ships in the Downs, made efforts to haul her off, but failed, the weather remaining poor, and she was written off as a wreck on 26 September.
[TNA: ADM.106/286; ADM.106/287]

(26) September FLY Dogger
Prize 1672; 73 tons; 45ft × 17.6ft; 6 guns
Master Edmund Whiteside
Listed by Pepys as being 'Cast away, September' but with no further details. Her books were closed on 26 September, which is suggestive of a date.
[Tanner: Naval Manuscripts in the Pepsyian Library vol 1 p280; TNA: ADM.33/91]

16 October PORTSMOUTH Pink
Portsmouth 1667; 42 tons; 40ft × 14ft; 4 guns
Captain Thomas Binning
Whilst engaged in fishery protection duties off Great Yarmouth, she was captured by a Dutch privateer and taken into Amsterdam.
[TNA: ADM.106/288; Tanner: Naval Manuscripts in the Pepsyian Library vol 1 p292; CSPD: Charles II December 1675]

29 October SWAN Smack
Harwich 1666; 24 tons; 36ft × 11.3ft
Master Isaac Patten
After joining a westbound convoy through the English Channel bound for Portsmouth, she had difficulty in keeping up with the other ships, and in bearing sail to keep company, the crossjack yard broke and the smack fell astern. They were off Shoreham when at 8 o'clock in the morning a Dutch privateer ran alongside and captured them. The convoy escort, the *Falcon*, 36 guns, pursued the pair, but was forced to give over the chase after she lost her foretopmast.
[TNA: ADM.106/289; ADM.106/290]

2 December ANN Third Rate
Deptford 1653 (*Bridgwater*); 743 tons; 116.9ft × 34.7ft; 50 guns
Captain Thomas Elliott†
Lying at Sheerness, a party from the dockyard arrived during the afternoon to carry out work in the powder room. Shortly after they started, a massive explosion occurred. The forward part of the ship was ripped apart, with the foremast and bowsprit being blown clear, the after part remaining afloat for some time before sinking. The Gunner, John Adams, was ashore at the time and initially insisted that no gunpowder was on board, but enquiries revealed that he was embezzling powder and had kept back a quantity after entering harbour instead of landing it. He was ordered to be confined in the Marshalsea Prison. About 120 of the crew were killed along with five dockyard workers. Twenty men were picked up alive, although five subsequently died of their injuries. The remains of the wreck were ordered to be destroyed 1 August 1674, 'by such means for blowing her to pieces as may be found most effectual'. The final pieces of the wreck were not removed until March 1675.
[TNA: ADM.106/291; ADM.106/293]

2 December HESTOR Fireship
Purchased 1673; 101 tons; 50ft; 19.6ft; 6 guns
Captain Edward Harvey
In the process of shifting berth at Sheerness, she was close to the *Ann* when she blew up. An eyewitness said the fireship was blown about 30 yards and 'entirely shaken to pieces'. Three men were killed from the thirteen on board.
[TNA: ADM.106/291]

1673? SAINT KATHERINE Dogger
Prize 1672; 73 tons; 45ft × 17.6ft; 6 guns
Listed by Pepys as having been 'cast away at sea – 1673' – no details found
[Tanner: Naval Manuscripts in the Pepsyian Library vol 1 p280]

1674

16 January NIGHTINGALE Fifth Rate
Horsleydown 1651; 290 tons; 86ft × 25.2ft; 28 guns
Captain Edward Pearce†
Driven from her anchorage in the Downs during a strong gale, along with a Dutch prize that she had taken the day before, the pair were carried onto the Goodwin Sands and wrecked. She was seen to be in difficulties by the *Stavoreen* who sent their Boatswain and eleven men to their assistance, but despite this, the ship was carried away and lost. About thirty men were saved by Margate fishing vessels.
[Charnock vol 1 p327; TNA: ADM.106/307]

15 February SAINT PETER Galliot
Prize 1672; 73 tons; 45ft × 17.6ft; 6 guns
Captain William Cotton
Ordered to the French port of Le Havre to collect a cargo of wine for the royal household, she was captured in the Channel by a Dutch privateer.
[Tanner: Naval Manuscripts in the Pepsyian Library vol 2 pp204, 261; TNA: ADM.106/299]

24 February DOVE Dogger
Prize 1672; 73 tons; 45ft × 17.6ft; 6 guns
Captain Abraham Hyatt
Sailed 20 July in company with the *Cambridge* and *Crown* from the Thames, heading northwards for Scotland, but the following night lost contact with her consorts. She continued north independently, the weather worsening all the time, with high seas and regular snow squalls on a strong easterly wind. She lay-to under reefed mainsail and mizzen but was carried inshore and at 4 o'clock in the morning she drove onshore at Boulmer, near Alnmouth on the Northumberland coast. She was driven further onto the shore during the day as the gale continued and was wrecked. Much effort was made to save as much of her guns and stores as possible.
[TNA: ADM.106/299]

26 February LIZARD Sloop
Deptford 1673; 39 tons; 47ft × 12.6ft; 4 guns
Captain John Nicholson
Attached to the fleet in the Channel, when they sailed from the anchorage in the Downs to the west she lost contact in a strong easterly gale and regular snow showers. She attempted to make Plymouth Sound but was unable to do so because of the high seas and anchored off Berry Head. Sailing when the weather had moderated, she again made for Plymouth, but soon after they had weighed, they found a Dutch privateer in chase of them. When off Start Point the enemy came alongside and after several broadsides were exchanged, which cut up her sails and rigging, and unable to manoeuvre with one killed and one man wounded, she surrendered.
[TNA: ADM.106/301]

(26?) February HIND Dogger
Prize 1672; 73 tons; 45ft × 17.6ft; 6 guns
Captain Thomas Marshall
Listed by Pepys as being retaken by the Dutch in this month. No details found but the ship's books were closed on 26 February, which may suggest a date.
[Tanner: Naval Manuscripts in the Pepsyian Library vol 1 p280; TNA; ADM.33/98]

(31) March LILLY Sloop
Deptford 1672; 58 tons; 52ft × 14.6ft; 6 guns
Captain William Sherwin
Listed by Pepys as being 'cast away at sea', but no details found. The ship's books were closed on 31 March which is perhaps indicative of a date of loss.
[Tanner: Naval Manuscripts in the Pepsyian Library vol 1 p292; TNA: ADM.33/106]

(10) August OLIVE BRANCH PRIZE Fireship
Prize 1672; 199 tons; 65.6ft × 24ft; 6 guns
Captain William Lee†
Vaguely listed as 'Lost at sea' by Pepys, but no further details given. She had been ordered to sail from Plymouth to Deptford in late July 1674, so it was presumably during this passage. Pepys dated the loss in 1673, but correspondence and the pay book clearly shows the following year, with the book being closed on 10 August, which indicates a likely date.
[TNA: ADM.33/102; Tanner: Naval Manuscripts in the Pepsyian Library vol 1 p284; vol 2 p329]

1675

25 March MARY Yacht
Gift 1660; 92 tons; 50ft × 18.6ft; 6 guns
Captain William Bustowe†
Coming from Ireland, at about 2 o'clock in the morning, in thick fog, she touched a rock to the south-west corner of the Skerries reef in Holyhead Bay, Anglesey. After initially freeing herself, she again struck hard on rocks and was held fast with the sea beating over her. The mast went overboard at about noon and a group of men used this to scramble ashore, but the Earl of Meath and Captain Bustowe were among the thirty-four men drowned as the yacht broke up. The survivors, which included fifteen passengers, were forced to stay on the rocks, managing to make a fire from timbers from the wreck, for three days until rescued by a boat from Beaumaris.
[London Gazette 5 April 1675; CSPD: Charles I March 1675]

31 August VULTURE Sloop
Deptford 1673; 68 tons; 50ft × 16ft; 4 guns
Captain George Colt†
Lost at Barbados when the island was struck by a hurricane. 'Never was seen such prodigious ruin in three hours; there are three churches, 1,000 houses, and most of the mills to Leeward thrown down, 200 people killed ... The King's frigate *Foresight* saved herself by standing out to sea, perceiving the storm coming.'
  Note: Pepys' *Register of Ships* wrongly shows the *Woolwich* sloop as being lost on this occasion, a mistake copied by others
[Tanner: Naval Manuscripts in the Pepsyian Library vol 3 p192; vol 4 p313; CSPC: America and West Indies: October 1675]

1676

9 April EUROPA Hulk
Prize 1674; 406 tons; 113ft × 26ft
Captain William Betts
Stationed at Malta to support the squadron in the Mediterranean, she was burnt, apparently by an act of arson. Some seamen were later executed for the deed.
[Tanner: Naval Manuscripts in the Pepsyian Library vol 3 p352; vol 4 pp380, 385]

29 June SPEEDWELL Fifth Rate
Deptford 1654 (*Cheriton*); 1656; 233 tons; 76ft × 24ft; 26 guns
Captain John Wood
In the spring of 1676 the *Speedwell*, in company with the *Prosperous* pink, was despatched on a voyage of Arctic exploration in an attempt to find a north-east passage. At about 11pm her consort made signals for seeing breakers ahead. The *Speedwell* attempted to tack, but failed to do so in time, and she ran aground on a ledge of rocks on the island of Novaya Zemlya. The following day the ship went to pieces in the pounding surf and the crew escaped to the island, two men drowning when a boat capsized. The survivors remained on the island '... a most dreary, cold and uncomfortable region', until 8 July, when the *Prosperous* could return and rescue them.
[Mariner's Mirror vol 56 p88; Charnock vol 1 pp378–80]

1678

10 February CHATHAM Sloop
Chatham 1673; 50 tons; 57.6ft × 12.10ft; 4 guns
Captain William Tennant
Laying at Tangier, having embarked a number of slaves, Captain Tennant went ashore to receive his orders prior to sailing for Cadiz. Whilst he was absent the slaves overpowered the men on board and deliberately ran the ship aground where it was wrecked. It was ruled that no wages were to be paid to the crew apart from Captain Tennant and his boat's crew, because of their negligence.
[TNA: ADM.106/330; ADM.106/346]

27 November CHARLES Yacht
Rotherhithe 1675; 120 tons; 54ft × 20.6ft; 6 guns
Captain William Faseby
Driven ashore and wrecked on the Dutch coast near Brill during a storm.
[Tanner: Naval Manuscripts in the Pepsyian Library vol 4 p638]

1679

31 January MARIGOLD Fourth Rate
Prize 1677; 495 tons; 100ft × 30.6ft; 38 guns
Captain James Dunbar
Part of the squadron maintained in The Straights (the western Mediterranean), under Vice Admiral Herbert, the *Marigold*, in company with the *Bonaventure* and *Charles Galley*, anchored off Tangier during 30 January. Captain Dunbar went ashore, leaving the ship's Lieutenant, James Morris, in charge. A strong easterly wind, or Levanter, was blowing, and this steadily increased, until by that evening it was a full gale, preventing Dunbar from returning. The gale continued the next day, and she started to drag her anchors, but Morris refused to put to sea, until the ship drove so near the shore that it was too late to do so. The ship was driven onshore to the westward of the Old Parade and broke up. Morris and fifty-two men were drowned in the disaster.
[Mariner's Mirror vol 14 p215 quoting TNA:ADM.7/688; ADM.106/341]

13 October DATE TREE Fifth Rate
Prize 1677; 265 tons; 28 guns
Captain Matthew Aylmer
A former Algerine prize, she was hauled into shallow water at Cadiz to be heeled for cleaning, but when this was done, despite being well shored, several of her floor timbers broke and her seams opened, and she sank until '… the water was as high within board as without'. On examination, her timbers were found to be quite rotten and 'iron sick', and the senior officer, Admiral Herbert, had little choice but to condemn her as unseaworthy. All the stores were removed, and the hull sold off locally.
[Mariner's Mirror vol 68 p75]

2 December SUCCESS Fifth Rate
Chatham 1658 (Bradford); 294 tons; 85ft × 25.6ft; 32 guns
Lieutenant Thomas Johnson
Having arrived at Jamaica in September, her commanding officer Captain George Tyte died soon after, and Lieutenant Johnson took command. She was employed in cruising against Spanish privateers and pirates and had some success, capturing the pirate Captain Richard Sawkins in November and sending him into Port Royal. She was ordered to search for another pirate, Harris, reported to be in the cays off Southern Cuba. However, as she searched amongst the islands she got into shallow water and then ran onto the flukes of her own anchor whilst attempting to anchor, filled with water and sank, although her upper works remained above water. A boat was sent to Port Royal and the *Hunter* soon arrived on scene, finding her lying on her larboard side on Scotch Key. Considerable efforts were made to save her stores, and anchors were laid out in preparation to salvage her. By February 1680 she was largely cleared, and by heaving on cables she was brought to an upright position, but divers reported that her hull was in a poor state, with three planks out of four damaged. It was clear that she was irrecoverable, and the wreck was finally abandoned on 2 February 1680. The pilot was tried by court martial and ordered to be flogged, being whipped on board five different ships and then imprisoned for 12 months.
[TNA:ADM.106/350; ADM.51/3870; CSPC:America and West Indies December 1679]

1682

6 May GLOUCESTER Third Rate
Limehouse 1654; 755 tons; 117ft × 34.10ft; 62 guns
Captain Sir John Berry
Bound for Leith, Scotland, with the Duke of York on board, who was accompanied by several gentlemen of his suite, the *Gloucester* sailed from the Downs anchorage on 4 May in company with four other ships and two yachts. During the evening of 5 May the squadron was off the coast of Norfolk, and there was a debate over the proposed course for the night, the extensive sand banks in the area leading some to urge that the ships should stand out to sea to ensure that they weathered the shallow waters, but Captain James Aire (or Ayre), who was acting as pilot, insisted that they could easily continue. The Duke proposed a compromise; that the ships should alter away until the early hours of the morning and then resume their northerly course. In the event the ships only headed east for about two hours until they again altered, to initially steer to the north-east and at about 2 o'clock in the morning to the north on a strong easterly breeze. At about 5.30am *Gloucester* ran hard aground on the western edge of the Leman and Ower sandbank off the north Norfolk coast. The ship beat on the sand for some time until the rudder was lost, and several planks were beaten in at the quarters. After this the ship started to fill rapidly with water. The ship eventually came free of the sand and anchored in 15 fathoms, but the water was entering at an uncontrollable rate, and she sank very quickly. The Duke, along with a few of his retinue, left the ship through the stern windows to gain safety in a boat and went off to the *Mary* yacht. One boat was put into the water, but something of a panic ensued as the ship settled, and several men jumped into it and it was only with great difficulty that it could get away and reach the yacht *Charlotte*. Others jumped into the water to be picked up by the other ships, but about 130 men died, including the Earl of Roxburgh, Lord Donough

O'Brien and Lord Hopton. Captain Aire, who had been entrusted with the navigation and had urged the ship to continue the fatal course, was court-martialled and sentenced to be dismissed the service and imprisoned. Captain Christopher Gunman of the *Mary* yacht was also court-martialled, accused of failing to give warning of shallow water, the yacht being ahead of the *Gloucester*. He was sentenced to be imprisoned and dismissed his ship; however, he was pardoned just a few days later by the Duke of York and re-instated.
[London Gazette 11 May 1682; Mariner's Mirror vol 42 pp113–26, 219–29]

16 May HENRY Second Rate
Deptford 1656 (*Dunbar*); 1,082 tons; 124ft × 40.6ft;
82 guns
Laid up 'in Ordinary' at anchor in the river Medway with a small crew of about thirty men on board headed by James Hawes, the Boatswain, she caught fire during the night of 15/16 May. It later emerged that an elderly seaman, Richard Wallis, was using a cabin in the middle deck, which was also used to store about 20 pounds of oakum, as a sleeping berth. On going to bed he dropped a lighted candle which fell into the oakum and set it on fire. He failed in his efforts to extinguish the blaze, burning his hands and face as he did so, but did raise the alarm with loud shouts. A chain of buckets was established to bring water to the fire, but it was not enough, and the men were driven back by thick smoke and the ship was consumed by the blaze. At a court martial Wallis was found guilty of negligence and sentenced to forfeit all pay due and to stand for 90 minutes with a halter about his neck on board the hulk at Chatham, the rope reeved to a gibbet. The Boatswain was found guilty of negligence by failing to ensure that all naked lights were properly extinguished – he was dismissed from the service and sent to prison 'during His Majesty's pleasure'.
[TNA:ADM.1/5253]

19 June NORWICH Fifth Rate
Chatham 1655; 266 tons; 80ft × 25ft; 30 guns
Captain Peter Heywood
Stationed in the West Indies, she had escorted a ship from Jamaica to Cartagena, and was on her return voyage when she encountered poor weather, with strong winds and high seas. When they calculated that they were to the leeward of Port Royal, they bore up for that port, believing they were well clear of the land. On 17 June land was sighted, but she spent the next two days beating against strong contrary winds, and it was not until the 19th that she was able to shape a course for the harbour of Port Royal. During the afternoon as she was steering for the entrance channel, she struck a reef off the south-east cay. Work went on through the night to free her, with twenty guns being thrown overboard and merchant's stores that she had embarked being taken off and an anchor being laid out astern to try and haul her off. She was eventually freed during the following afternoon and taken into harbour, pumping and bailing constantly. On 21 June she was run into shallow water, with stores and ballast being taken out by parties of slaves. The work to save her went on for another week, until on 25 June as carpenters were preparing a patch, she sprang another leak, the water flooding in at so fast a rate that it was clear that she could not be saved. The following day she was surveyed and condemned. The subsequent locally-held court martial acquitted the officers of the loss, which was blamed on the strength of the currents. Evidence was also produced which showed that the ship was in a poor state before the loss, with several knees found to be rotten or split and the hull in poor condition. The case caused something of a stir when the news of the wreck reached London. Captain Heywood came in for criticism for taking on board unauthorised cargo, and it was questioned whether the Governor of Jamaica, Sir Thomas Lynch, had the legal authority to convene a court martial. Heywood was ordered to return to London, but it would not appear that he ever did so; he effectively retired from the Navy and settled in Jamaica.
[TNA:ADM.51/3926;ADM.106/361; CSPC:America and West Indies November 1682]

1683

(7) October FRANCIS Sixth Rate
Harwich 1666; 140 tons; 66ft × 20ft; 16 guns
Captain Charles Carlisle†
Disappeared, and believed lost with all hands in a hurricane in the Leeward Islands. Sir William Stapleton, the Governor of the Leeward Islands, first raised his concern for her safety in November, as he had heard that she '… was in the hurricane of 7th October in Barbados', after which nothing had been seen of her. There were reports in March 1684 that she may have been blown off station and taken shelter in Jamaica, but by May this was found to be untrue, and with no news of her, she was given up for lost. Her books were officially closed on 31 October 1684.
[CSPC:America and West Indies November 1683; March 1684;TNA:ADM.33/108]

1684

4 April SHEDAM Sixth Rate
Prize 1683 (*Schiedam*)
Captain Gregory Fish

A former Dutch fly boat, she was a prize captured in the Mediterranean from North African corsairs and was returning to England from Tangier loaded with horses, timber and stores. During the night, she drove ashore in Dollar Cove, near Gunwalloe in Mounts Bay, apparently due to Captain Fish being unaware that he was so close to land, despite being warned by a Dutch vessel they encountered that they were steering towards the shore. Most of the guns were salvaged, but much of her rigging, sails and stores were plundered by the local populace.
[HMC: Dartmouth 1 p115; TNA: ADM.106/371]

1686

28 September HALF MOON PRIZE Fourth Rate
Prize 1681; 556 tons; 113.11 x 34.1ft; 44 guns

Laid up 'in Ordinary' at Chatham, parties of men from the dockyard were working on board when during the morning, smoke was seen rising from below decks. On investigation, it was found that the cook's cabin was on fire. Buckets of water were called for and the bell rung as an alarm. John Miller, carpenter of the *Centurion*, who was working on board, went through the smoke and managed to pull the unconscious cook out of his cabin, but was forced by the heat and smoke to leave him lying on the deck. Despite the firefighting efforts the ship was burnt. No surviving person was found to blame; the most likely cause being judged to be a candle falling over in the cook's cabin. The only casualty was the cook.
[TNA: ADM. 1/5253]

1688

17 November HELDERENBURG Hospital ship
Prize 1685; 243 tons; 74ft x 24.10ft
Captain Albion Howell†

Part of the fleet under Lord Dartmouth that was attempting to intercept the Dutch fleet carrying the Prince of Orange to England, the ships sailed from the anchorage in the Downs during the afternoon of 16 November. By the evening of the following day, they were approaching the Isle of Wight, and at about 7pm the Admiral made the signal to tack. The night was very dark, and the signal was evidently not seen by *Helderenburg*. As the *Bonaventure*, 48 guns, came about, before they could trim their sails, they collided with the hospital ship. The larger ship lost her bowsprit and foremast, but the *Helderenburg* was damaged so badly that she foundered. Thirteen men, the only survivors, were picked up in her long boat by the *Defiance*.
[TNA: ADM.52/9; HMC: Dartmouth 3 pp58, 67–8]

3 | 1689–1714: Invasion, War and Union

IN OCTOBER 1688 A DUTCH FLEET had avoided the English fleet and taken an army though the Channel to land the Prince of Orange in Torbay. Support for the Catholic King James evaporated to allow the invader to take the throne with little difficulty. French support for the deposed king and the determination of King William to join the Grand Alliance and limit the power of France led to war (May 1689–September 1697). The war was initially dominated by the operations in Ireland, but the gathering of the French fleet off the Normandy ports in 1692 for a planned invasion of England led to the decisive battles of Barfleur and la Hougue in which the French suffered heavily. There were to be no more fleet actions, and the Royal Navy found itself engaged in tackling the problem of the rising numbers of privateers, which frequently acted in concert to great effect. As part of the effort to curb the problem, several attacks were made on the northern French ports, with St Malo, Brest, Dieppe, Le Havre, Calais and Dunkerque all being bombarded, some more than once, in efforts to destroy the bases for the privateers and cruisers. Colonial expeditions were limited to the West Indies and Canada, featuring some minor actions with some losses on both sides. The Act of Union of 1707 merged England and Scotland into a single state, with the small Scottish Navy being incorporated into the Royal Navy.

1689

2 January SEDGEMORE Fourth Rate
Chatham 1687; 692 tons; 123ft × 34.6ft; 50 guns
Captain David Lloyd
Ordered by Lord Dartmouth to close the harbour at Dover to take on provisions and stores for the fleet, Lieutenant Thomas Bulkeley was in charge of the ship, Captain Lloyd being ashore on duty. The ship anchored, but when a stores hoy attempted to come alongside, the poor weather prevented this. With the weather worsening it was decided to weigh and bear away for the Downs, the pilot assuring Bulkeley that he could guide the ship to a safe anchorage. The ship steered to the north-east, regularly sounding with the lead-line, the wind increasing with flurries of snow, but they could see the glimmer of lights which they believed to be North Foreland. Just after sounding in five fathoms, they ran aground in St Margaret's Bay. All sail was taken in, and water and beer casks were emptied to lighten her, but she would not move. The pinnace was hoisted out and sent away to reach the shore, and two hawsers were placed in the longboat to take out an anchor for an attempt to kedge her off. The longboat went to the starboard bow to take on the stream anchor, but the high seas would not allow it to stay alongside, and the boat was taken away and eventually steered for the shore. Water was now reported to be entering and she was carried further onto the ground and wrecked. At a court martial, although the ship's officers were cleared of any fault, the weather being so bad that the landmarks were obscured, it was found that the overconfidence of the pilot was a major factor, and he was ordered to lose all pay due and never to pilot any of His Majesty's ships again. When later inspected by officers from Chatham dockyard, the ship was found to be in a poor state, having been driven over rocks and lying on her larboard side with her head to the west. They recommended that she be broken up in situ. Some of her timbers were evidently salvaged as in March 1690 any usable material from the ship was ordered to be used in the building of a new Fourth Rate ship at Chatham.
[TNA: ADM.1/5253; ADM.106/388]

21 June ALEXANDER Fireship
Prize 1689; 150 tons; 6 guns
Captain Thomas Jennings
Newly fitted out at Portsmouth, she joined the main fleet under Admiral Lord Torrington, which headed west from Spithead to cruise in the western approaches to the Channel. During the afternoon, when six leagues (18 miles) south-west of Lizard Point, the *Alexander* 'took fire by accident', and subsequently blew up, with the loss of three men.
[TNA: ADM.106/3120; ADM.51/4180; HMC: Finch 2 p220]

9 August PORTSMOUTH Fourth Rate
Portsmouth 1650; 463 tons; 100ft × 29.6ft; 46 guns
Captain George St Loe
Ordered to sail from Plymouth 8 August with urgent despatches for the Earl of Torrington, the following day she fell in with *le Marquise*, 58 guns, which had been detached from the main French fleet to find the combined Anglo-Dutch fleet, believed to be in the vicinity of the Scillies. The pair closed and exchanged broadsides and in the exchanges of fire the *Portsmouth* suffered in her rigging, being dismasted. The fight continued with volleys of musketry, during which

Captain St Loe was severely wounded, shot through the body and arm, although he managed to throw the despatches overboard. With about sixty men killed or wounded, she surrendered. The French captain, the Chevalier du Mené, lost his leg to a cannon ball in the action and died the following day.
[CSPD: William and Mary August 1689, Sevin de Quincy Tome II p230; HMC: Finch vol 2 p235]

26 August DEPTFORD Ketch
Deptford 1665; 89 tons; 52ft × 18ft; 10 guns
Captain Thomas Berry†

Whilst lying at anchor in Nominy Bay, in the Potomac River, Virginia, mid-afternoon she was struck by a sudden violent squall from the south-west which capsized her. Captain Berry, who was lying sick in his cabin, and eight men were drowned. Survivors managed to cling to wreckage and the mast, which remained above water, to be picked up by their own boat which happened to be inshore at the time. The *Dunbarton* went to the scene, but attempts to raise the ketch failed, although much of her rigging and gear was later salvaged.
[TNA: ADM.106/391; CSPC: America and West Indies October 1689; London Gazette 25 November 1689]

24 September RICHARD and MARTHA Ketch
Hired 1689; 10 guns
Master Arthur Condose

On 22 September, then being at anchor off Hoylake, she received orders to proceed with urgent letters for Ireland, and despite the weather being poor, she sailed the following day. As she arrived in sight of the coast of Ireland the conditions worsened, with storm-force winds, and she was driven onto the shore near Lambay Island. With much difficulty, the men were landed and over the next few days the great guns and some stores were salvaged.
[TNA: ADM.106/388]

4 October LIVELY PRIZE Fifth Rate
Prize 1689 (l'Éveille); 309 tons; 78.4ft × 27.3ft; 30 guns
Captain William Tichborne

The *Lively* sailed from Plymouth to cruise to the south-west of the Scilly Isles, in company with the *Foresight* and *Mordant*, when at 10 o'clock in the forenoon they sighted a squadron of about twelve ships with their heads to the south-west. They initially stood towards them, but when the English ships hoisted their colours, the strangers hoisted French, and could be seen to be men of war, from 40 to 70 guns. The English squadron immediately bore away, the enemy pursuing them. Her companions stretched away, firing stern chase guns, and escaped, but the *Lively Prize* fell astern, and was overhauled at about 3pm by two large French warships. A short engagement took place in which she lost her main topmast and much of her rigging was cut up, and she surrendered.
[TNA: ADM.51/364; London Gazette 14 October 1689]

26 October PENDENNIS Third Rate
Chatham 1679; 1,051 tons; 150.10ft × 40.3ft; 70 guns
Captain George Churchill

En-route to Chatham from the Downs anchorage, the ship was under the guidance of a pilot, Thomas Whiterow, with the *Quaker* ketch in company. Despite the waters being familiar to all on board, the ship ran aground on the Kentish Knock sands and efforts to free her failed, and with planks and timbers giving way as she settled, the ship filled with water and was lost. Whiterow claimed that he had set a true course and blamed a faulty compass. It was proved that the compass was indeed not true, but it was not the main cause of the loss, as it was found that Whiterow had advised the use of too much sail which had carried them further to the north than calculated, and the lead-line had not been used. He was ordered to be imprisoned during His Majesty's pleasure. Captain Churchill had hailed the *Quaker* and ordered them to stand by his ship and assist, but the ketch had stood away. Captain Austin Birch of the *Quaker* was disciplined, being dismissed from his ship and imprisoned during His Majesty's pleasure.
[TNA: ADM.1/5253]

12 November FIREDRAKE Bomb
Deptford 1688; 203 tons; 85.2ft × 24.1ft; 12 guns, 2 mortars
Captain John Votier (or Votear)

Listed as being captured by the French, but little further detail found. The *Firedrake* had been part of the fleet off the south coast of Ireland and was en-route to Plymouth when she was captured and taken into St Malo.
[TNA: ADM.106/3120; CSPD: William and Mary March 1690]

29 November CHARLES and HENRY Fireship
Purchased 1688; 120 tons; 6 guns
Captain William Stone

Lying at anchor in Plymouth Sound, the wind steadily increased until it reached gale force and the strength of the wind was such that it was decided to shift to a safer position. She weighed and ran into the Cattewater, where she managed to re-anchor. However soon after this, the *Dover* frigate, also attempting to reach safer waters, was driven down onto her and the anchor cable parted. With little room to manoeuvre, she was driven into shallow water and grounded on rocks at Cattedown, where she capsized and broke up.
[TNA: ADM.106/392; ADM.106/385; Laughton: Memoirs relating to the Lord Torrington p41]

25 December HENRIETTA Third Rate
Horsleydown 1654 (*Langport*); 781 tons; 116ft × 35.7ft; 60 guns
Captain John Neville

One of several ships that were sheltering in Plymouth Sound from the weather, which was a hard wind from the south-west and heavy seas. During the day, the wind steadily increased until by nightfall it was blowing a violent storm. Despite the sheet and bower anchors being laid out, she was driven across the Sound ('the sea making free passage over us …') until she struck the ground heavily, first off St Nicholas' Island and then under the Citadel, breaking the sternpost. The masts were cut away, and despite pumping and bailing she was filling with water. She eventually drove off the rocks and finally went aground in the Cattewater where she sank. About sixty men were lost. The remains continued to be a problem for some time and were ordered to be broken up on 11 April 1690 with the sound timbers 'to be used to repair the graving place' but it was not until August 1692 that she was finally weighed.
[TNA: ADM.1/391; ADM.1/5253; ADM.106/385; ADM.106/418; London Gazette 30 December 1689]

25 December CENTURION Fourth Rate
Ratcliffe 1650; 532 tons; 104ft × 31ft; 50 guns
Captain Bazil Beaumont

Laying at anchor in Plymouth Sound when the storm struck (above); the Dutch warship *Unity* parted her cable and fell onboard the *Centurion*. Her cables parted and both ships were driven across the Sound until they went ashore on Mount Batten and went to pieces. About 150 men lost their lives.
[TNA: ADM.106/385; London Gazette 30 December 1689]

Two other ships, both prizes that were not fully manned, were also driven from their anchors and wrecked in Plymouth Sound during the same storm:

25 December BLADE OF WHEAT Fireship
Prize 1689 (*Fleur de Blé*); 150 tons; 76ft × 18.2ft; 10 guns
Driven into Millbay where she went ashore and was wrecked.
[TNA: ADM.106/385]

25 December DOVER'S PRIZE
Prize 1689; 329 tons; 86ft × 26.2ft
A privateer brought in by the *Dover*, she was taken by the storm into the Cattewater and wrecked
[TNA: ADM.106/385; London Gazette 30 December 1689]

1690

12 January SUPPLY Fifth Rate
Hired 1688; 308 tons; 34 guns
Captain William Harding

Having sailed from the river Clyde with a convoy of merchant ships on 22 December, they collected more vessels at Carrickfergus before heading south to Chester. The weather worsened as they progressed, and when they approached Hoylake on 11 January it was blowing a strong gale from the north-west, with regular flurries of snow. Several attempts were made to enter, but she was forced to anchor, with topmasts and yards struck. Despite the precautions, the following day she dragged her anchor and was driven further inshore until she tailed onto a sandbank, striking the ground heavily, which beat the rudder off and broke the tiller. By mid-morning the water had left her, and she was abandoned as a wreck. No blame was attached to the crew.
[TNA: ADM.1/5253; ADM.51/3981]

12 January DRAGON PRIZE Sloop
Prize 1689 (*le Dragon-Volant*); 57 tons; 8 guns
Captain Frederick Weighman

Ships laying at anchor in the Downs were affected by a gale, with high winds and heavy seas which scattered ships, several being forced from their anchors. The *Antelope* lost all her masts, and the *Dragon* was driven from the anchorage in storm-force winds and wrecked at Kingsgate, Thanet.
[TNA: ADM.106/3120; ADM.106/400]

18 March MARY Sloop
Hired 1689; 105 tons; 12 guns
Captain Abraham Wise†

The *Mary* sailed from Plymouth on 7 March, in company with the *Dartmouth, Lark* and *Smyrna Merchant* to escort several smaller vessels, which were carrying supplies for the army in Northern Ireland. The weather was poor, and they were forced to shelter in the Scilly Isles for some days, before resuming their voyage on 16 March. After initially making good progress, the ships were scattered the following day by gale force winds, and the *Mary* was driven ashore and wrecked at Wicklow, Ireland
[TNA: ADM.106/3120; ADM.106/398]

23 March KING'S-FISHER Ketch
Purchased 1689; 61 tons; 47.9ft × 15.6ft; 4 guns
Captain Robert Audley

Reported to have been captured by the French in the English Channel, no further details have been found.
[TNA: ADM.106/3120; HCJ 1695]

3 June HOPEWELL Fireship

Shoreham 1690; 253 tons; 93.3ft × 24.10ft; 8 guns
Captain Thomas Warren

Laying at anchor in the Downs with the main body of the fleet, a fire was discovered in the hold, which rapidly spread to the fireship's combustible material. The *Royal Sovereign* sent boats to her aid, and they succeeded in heaving grapnels into her head and securing a hawser, by which means they towed the burning ship away from the other ships into the shore, where she grounded in shallow water and burned out. A subsequent court martial found that she had been lost through negligence and lack of care by the ship's officers.
[TNA: ADM.1/5253; ADM.106/399]

6 July ANN Third Rate

Chatham 1678; 1,051 tons; 150ft × 40.3ft; 70 guns
Captain John Tyrell

A large French fleet under the Comte de Tourville assembled in the western Channel and stood to the east, to meet the smaller Anglo-Dutch fleet under Admiral Lord Torrington on 25 June which declined action and withdrew before them. The fleets' manoeuvring continued in light breezes for several days until 30 June when a general action took place off Beachy Head. The French had the best of the encounter, with the allied Blue Squadron, of which the *Ann* was part, being pressed hard by the superior numbers of the French division under Comte d'Estrées. During the action *Ann* suffered about 100 casualties killed or wounded, the Boatswain being killed in the first broadside. Her foremast was shot away, and the mainmast, mizzen mast and bowsprit were all shattered, and she received more than sixty shots in the hull. During the afternoon, the English fleet anchored, and on the strong ebb tide the French were carried out of gunshot to end the battle. After the action, the allied fleet retired from the Channel towards the Thames Estuary. Onboard the *Ann*, a spare topmast was rigged as a jury foremast, but she was unable to carry much sail and could make no progress and the *Swallow*, 40 guns, took them in tow but could make little headway. The next day the *York*, 50, took the tow, but it was found that they were losing ground rather than gaining. With the French fleet now in command of the Channel her position was precarious, and it was feared that she would be captured. With the agreement of all the officers, she was steered inshore and with the incoming tide she was deliberately run into shallow water about eight miles to the west of Rye, Sussex. The French, seeing her plight, sent fireships inshore to ensure her destruction, but Captain Tyrell forestalled them by setting her on fire as he left.
[TNA: ADM.106/401; CSPD: William and Mary July 1690].

9 October DARTMOUTH Fifth Rate

Portsmouth 1655; 261 tons; 80ft × 24.9ft; 28 guns
Captain Edward Pottinger†

Stationed off the western coast of Scotland to prevent supplies reaching the sympathisers of the ousted King James, she anchored in Scallastle Bay off the Isle of Mull. The weather worsened until there were storm-force winds and heavy seas. The masts were cut away in an attempt to ease the ship, but she was driven from her anchors and wrecked with a heavy loss of life, just five men and a boy surviving the wreck. When the *Lark* arrived on scene, they found she had been 'splitt to pieces' and little of the wreck could be salvaged. Her remains were found in August 1973 close to the small islet of Rubha an Ridire, on the Movern side of the south-east entrance to the Sound of Mull.
[TNA: ADM.106/396; https://canmore.org.uk/site/102424/dartmouth-eilean-rubha-an-ridire-sound-of-mull]

12 October BREDAH Third Rate

Harwich 1679; 1,022 tons; 151.3ft × 39.11ft; 70 guns
Captain Matthew Tennant†

Part of a force assembled to lay siege to the city of Cork, Ireland. After the surrender of the city on 29 September, the bulk of the fleet returned to England, but the *Bredah* remained on scene, with Captain Tennant acting as the senior officer. Whilst lying at anchor off Spike Island in Cork harbour, she was seen to be on fire and soon after was blown apart by a massive internal explosion with the loss of most of her crew and several Irish prisoners being held on board. Captain Tennant was picked up alive but died of his wounds within an hour.
[London Gazette 23 October 1690; HMC: Finch vol 2 p476; Charnock vol 2 p58]

16 October DREADNOUGHT Third Rate

Blackwall 1654 (Torrington); 734 tons; 116ft × 34.6ft; 62 guns
Captain Robert Willmott

Ordered to Woolwich to be refitted, she sailed from Spithead in company with the *Foresight* and *Portsmouth* store ship on 10 October. During the passage, water was found to be entering the hold and it became clear that she had several leaks, which could not be stopped. She had difficulty in weathering the Goodwin Sands, and when it became apparent that the pumps were being overwhelmed, she was abandoned and allowed to founder about five leagues (15 miles) from North Foreland. Captain Willmott was cleared of any blame at a subsequent court martial.
[London Gazette 20 October 1690; TNA: ADM.1/5253; ADM.106/400]

11 November SAINT DAVID Fourth Rate
Lydney 1667; 687 tons; 107ft × 34.9ft; 54 guns
Captain John Graydon

At Portsmouth, *St David* was ordered to be careened, to clean and 'pay' her bottom. By about 11 o'clock in the morning, all was ready; the ship had been positioned alongside the hulk, guns had been run across to the starboard side, some ballast shifted, and men stationed on the yards to mark the angle of the heel. She was slowly hauled over, but as the heel increased water was found to be entering the ship with increasing force, apparently entering through unsecured ports. She quickly settled and sank on her starboard side in seven fathoms of water, still lashed to the hulk and the masts showing above the water. Lighters were brought up and successfully secured to the starboard side and efforts began to initially bring her upright. The efforts succeeded and by 17 November the heel had been reduced and her trim restored, but she was not finally raised until July 1691, and was subsequently employed as a hulk. A court martial found that the sinking was due to the great neglect of the officers, particularly the First Lieutenant, Henry Lumley, and the ship's Carpenter, Peter Chamberlain. Not only had they failed to properly supervise the operation, but they allowed the ballast and guns to be moved without ensuring that the ports were both closed and sealed and had failed to keep Captain Graydon informed. Lumley was ordered to forfeit all pay and serve six months in prison. The Carpenter lost all his pay and was imprisoned for a year. The Master, William Parker, was fined four months' pay.
[TNA:ADM.106/390;ADM.1/5253]

1691

12 July MARY ROSE Fourth Rate
Woodbridge 1653 (*Maidstone*); 527 tons; 100ft × 31.6ft; 42 guns
Captain John Bounty

Escorting an outward-bound West India convoy that departed from Falmouth on 9 July, over the next two days distant sightings were made of a number of large ships and the convoy was still in the western approaches to the Channel when at first light a group of ships were again sighted on the horizon. Another of the escorts, the *Constant Warwick*, was ordered to investigate and signalled that many ships were in sight. They were presumed to be hostile, and the convoy was ordered to make all sail to the south and the escorts cleared for action. The strangers steadily closed and could soon be seen to be French. By noon the leading French ship, a large warship of 70 guns, part of the fleet under the Comte de Tourville, was close and the action began by *Mary Rose* firing her stern chase guns. A running battle then started, with a constant exchange of fire, the *Mary Rose* and *Constant Warwick* firing stern chase guns, the French ship her bow guns. By 7 o'clock that evening another two French warships were within gunshot and joined the action. Soon after this, with her rigging disabled and over twenty killed and wounded, she struck her flag in surrender. Captain Bounty was found guilty at a subsequent court martial of ill conduct, in steering too southerly a course, and then wasting time by sending the *Constant Warwick* to close the enemy instead of immediately bearing away. He was dismissed the service.
[TNA:ADM.1/5253]

12 July CONSTANT WARWICK Fourth Rate
Portsmouth 1666; 379 tons; 90ft × 28.2ft; 42 guns
Captain James Moody

The second of the escorts to the West India convoy that was intercepted by a powerful French force under the Comte de Tourville. She placed herself between the oncoming threat and the convoy, and like her consort, maintained a running fight through the afternoon. After the *Mary Rose* was taken, she continued the action until 10 o'clock at night with two ships which were within gunshot. One then fired a broadside which carried away her mizzen and fore yards, and Captain Moody called all his officers together and they mutually agreed that further resistance was futile, and a lamp was hung in the mizzen shrouds to signify her surrender.
[TNA:ADM.1/5253]

12 July TALBOT Ketch
Rotherhithe 1691; 94 tons; 62ft × 51.2ft; 10 guns
Captain Charles Staggins

Third of the escorts to the ill-fated West India convoy, when the *Mary Rose* and *Constant Warwick* engaged the enemy, she stood away to stay close to the merchant ships. When the French ships overhauled him later that night Captain Staggins struck his flag on being hailed. A court martial found him guilty of failing to offer any resistance, and he was dismissed the service and ordered to be imprisoned during His Majesty's pleasure.

Note: The ketch was retaken in October 1693.
[TNA:ADM.1/5253]

24 July PETER Ketch Tender
Hired 1691; 2 guns
Lieutenant Elias Waffe

Tender to the *Suffolk*, 70 guns, the pair sailed on 20 July to join the fleet in the western Channel but became separated in the night. The ketch was to the south-west of Ushant when at first light a sail was seen which they closed, believing it to be a merchant vessel. However, they discovered the stranger to be a French privateer and hastily made sail away, with the privateer

in pursuit. She was soon overhauled and struck her flag in surrender without offering any resistance. At a subsequent court martial Lieutenant Waffe claimed that he had little powder or shot, and that to have fought would only have caused unnecessary casualties. The Gunner denied this, stating that there was no want of ammunition, but Waffe had discouraged his small crew from fighting and gave up the ketch. Waffe was ordered to lose 12 months' pay.
[TNA: ADM.1/5253]

3 September CORONATION Second Rate
Portsmouth 1685; 1,346 tons; 160.4ft × 44.9ft; 90 guns
Captain Charles Skelton†
In August, the *Coronation* was part of the fleet under Admiral Russell in the English Channel, and with the weather deteriorating, the ships took shelter in Torbay. During a respite in the weather the fleet sailed, but the weather again worsened, and the ships tried to take shelter in Plymouth Sound. Most of the ships were unable to make the Sound in the storm-force southerly winds and chose to anchor off Rame Head, including the *Coronation*. Shortly after she had veered out of the anchor cable, water was reported to be entering the ship at a fast rate, and it was believed that several planks and butt joints had given way. She steadily filled and driven by the storm she eventually capsized about 1½ miles offshore, the hulk being driven ashore to the west of Penlee Point. About 600 men lost their lives. The wreck has been found and is now a protected site.
[TNA: ADM.1/5253; http://www.promare.co.uk/ships/Wrecks/Wk_Coronation.html]

3 September HARWICH Third Rate
Harwich 1674; 993 tons; 123.9ft × 38.10ft; 64 guns
Captain Henry Robinson
In the same storm that wrecked the *Coronation*, the *Harwich* made the shelter of Plymouth Sound and anchored. The storm-force winds made this very unsafe, and she attempted to run into the shelter of the Hamoaze, but the wind proved too strong, and she anchored further inshore. Pumping and bailing went on constantly, but the combination of gale-force winds and an ebb tide led her to drag her anchors and she was forced ashore at Barn Pool and wrecked. The remains were sold to a Mr Joseph Bingham for breaking up on 20 February 1693.
[TNA: ADM.1/5253]

4 November HAPPY RETURN Fourth Rate
Great Yarmouth 1654 (*Winsby*); 608 tons; 104ft × 33.2ft; 48 guns
Captain Peter Pickard
Cruising in the English Channel when she was advised of a number of French ships nearby, believed to be merchants with no convoy. On sighting a number of ships, she closed, but discovered them to be a squadron of French warships. In the engagement which followed, her rigging and masts were severely damaged, and several shots in the hull led her to have 5ft of water in the hold. With the men quitting their quarters, and more enemy ships in sight, she surrendered, being taken into Brest.
[TNA: ADM.1/5253; ADM.106/418]

18 December JERSEY Fourth Rate
Maldon 1654; 560 tons; 101.10ft × 32.2ft; 42 guns
Captain John Bomstead
Cruising off Guadeloupe when she fell in with two French warships, one of 40 guns, and a smaller vessel of 16 guns. She entered the action in an unprepared state and after a brief exchange of shots the French closed and eventually boarded from both sides. In the fighting, the First Lieutenant was severely wounded, and the Second Lieutenant and the Master killed. At this, Captain Bomstead threw down his sword and cried out for quarter, but the Gunner picked up the weapon and struck Bomstead with it, at which he fled below. After a further 15 minutes of fighting, she surrendered. Captain Bomstead was later court-martialled and found guilty of negligence, ill-conduct and cowardice, and sentenced to be shot, although he was later pardoned.
[TNA: ADM.1/5253; CSPC: North America & West Indies January 1692]

1692

9 February SWALLOW Fourth Rate
Wapping 1653 (*Gainsborough*); 543 tons; 100.10ft × 31.10ft; 42 guns
Captain William Bridges
Attempting to enter the harbour at Kinsale in poor weather, she found a transport ship blocking the main channel and was forced toward shallow water to anchor. As she did so, she ran over a buoy rope, which became snagged under her rudder, and she steered out of control until she struck the bar. She rested quietly at high water, but as the tide ebbed, she bumped heavily on the ground and several planks gave way and water started to enter. Despite pumping and bailing, they could not free her and when the chain pump broke, she filled with water, after which she heeled over onto her broadside and sank. No blame was attached to the ship's officers, the poor state of the hull being to blame, the ship '… not being well repaired'.
[TNA: ADM.106/421; ADM.1/5253]

9 February CROWN'S PRIZE Sixth Rate
Prize 1690 (la Friponne); 223 tons; 84ft x 24.10ft; 26 guns
Captain William Tichborne†

Sailed from Spithead on 3 February and within three hours, water was reported to be entering the hold. The wind was then blowing hard from the south-east and it was decided to take shelter in Portland Roads. The crew worked hard to clear the hold of water, but the pumps became choked with ballast, and it was three days before they could control the level of water and could get under sail again. She eventually anchored off Dartmouth, intending to raise men locally, as they were under-manned. The weather remained poor, and the wind increased and by the morning it was blowing a strong gale with heavy seas and the pumps were again being worked constantly to clear water in the hold. Despite firing guns of distress, no help could reach the ship from the town because of the high seas and strong winds. They were anchored uncomfortably close to the Blackstone Rock, and fearing they may be driven onto the Rock and certain that they would be unable to weather Start Point if they went to seaward, they determined to get into Dartmouth. Using a spring on the anchor cable, they hauled the head of the ship round and spread the mainsail, but this forced her to heel over until the gunwale was under water, forcing them to take in sail and abandon the attempt. The pump was now reported to have been choked again and they resorted to bailing by hand. The main and mizzen masts were cut away, but she was eventually forced to cut her cables and under a spritsail drove into the shore in the early hours and was wrecked. Captain Tichborne, the Gunner, Carpenter and about twenty men were drowned.
[TNA: ADM.106/415; ADM.106/425; London Gazette 18 February 1691]

12 April PORTLAND Fourth Rate
Wapping 1653; 605 tons; 105ft x 32.11ft; 48 guns
Captain Thomas Ley

Having successfully escorted a convoy from England to Cadiz, *Portland* sailed from that port in company with the *Phoenix*, to escort a small number of ships to Malaga. At first light as they approached the port, several ships could be seen coming out of the harbour. A small boat then closed them, bringing a message from the British Consul, warning that the ships in sight were the French Toulon squadron, under the Comte d'Estrées. Captain Ley ordered the convoy to make all sail and attempt to run to windward. The French pursued them, and by that evening it was clear that they would not be able to escape, as they were being outpaced. The convoy was ordered to steer toward the shore, and they came to anchor off Fuengirola, where some of the merchant ships ran themselves aground. Preparations were made to defend the ships, but the French held off until the following morning, when a number of ships, armed from 60 to 90 guns, closed and anchored in a line near the British ships, and commenced a heavy fire. The fire was returned from both *Portland* and *Phoenix* and a small battery ashore, but after an hour, clearly outmatched, the ships were ordered to be abandoned, and were set on fire.
[London Gazette 9 May & 12 May 1692; TNA: ADM.1/5253; ADM 106/421]

12 April PHOENIX Fourth Rate
Portsmouth 1671; 367 tons; 89ft x 27.10ft; 42 guns
Captain Jacob Banks

Consort to the *Portland* acting as escort to a small convoy bound for Malaga (see above), which was intercepted by the Toulon squadron. Along with the other ships, she was run into shallow water off Fuengirola, and was subjected to a bombardment from several ships of the line, before being abandoned and set on fire. The French squadron managed to capture two or three of the merchant ships and set fire to another six that could not be hauled off.
[London Gazette 9 May & 12 May 1692; TNA: ADM.1/5253; ADM.106/415; ADM.106/421]

19 May: The Battle of Barfleur
At daybreak on 19 May the combined Anglo-Dutch fleet under Admiral Edward Russell successfully intercepted a smaller French force under the Comte de Tourville off Cap Barfleur, Normandy. The ensuing battle lasted for most of the daylight hours, until, at about 6 o'clock in the evening, the French, who despite the disparity in numbers had not lost any ships, commenced anchoring in drifting patches of thick fog, surrounded by the allied fleet. The following morning the French weighed and headed for ports in Normandy.

One of the Allied fleet was lost to enemy action:

EXTRAVAGANT Fireship
Prize 1691 (l'Extravagant); 263 tons; 88.6ft x 26ft; 10 guns
Captain Fleetwood Emes

Attached to the Red Squadron, or centre division of the fleet, she was struck by a shot from a French ship early in the action and set on fire.
[Aubrey p104]

The following were expended during the evening in an effort to burn the French ships at anchor, but without success:

CADIZ MERCHANT Fireship
Purchased 1688; 320 tons; 93.6ft x 25ft; 12 guns
Captain Robert Wynn

FOX Fireship
Shoreham 1690; 263 tons; 93.4ft x 25.1ft; 8 guns
Captain Thomas Killingworth

HOPEWELL Fireship
Purchased 1690; 157 tons; 8 guns
Captain William Jumper

PHAETON Fireship
Deptford 1691; 263 tons; 91.5ft × 25.7ft; 8 guns
Captain Robert Hancock
[Aubrey passim; London Gazette 19 May; 23 May and 2 June 1692]

22 May: The Attack on Cherbourg

Following the fleet action off Cap Barfleur, the French fleet scattered to take shelter in various northern French ports and bays. The flagship, *Soleil Royal*, 102 guns, along with two smaller ships, ran into Cherbourg. They anchored in shallow water under the guns of a small fort and prepared to defend themselves. A detachment of the allied pursuers under Admiral Ralph Delavall stood off with his larger ships to batter the stranded French ships and then sent in fireships:
[London Gazette 23 May 1692]

BLAZE Fireship
Deptford 1691; 260 tons; 76.1ft × 25.4ft; 8 guns
Captain Thomas Heath
The ship was laid alongside the enemy flagship, *Soleil Royal*, and set her on fire.

HOUND Fireship
Limehouse 1690; 271 tons; 93.8ft × 25ft; 8 guns
Captain Thomas Foulis
Set on fire by enemy shot as they attempted to lay alongside the *Soleil Royal*.

WOLF Fireship
Deptford 1690; 270 tons; 93.1ft × 24.11ft; 8 guns
Captain James Greenway
Successfully taken alongside the *Triomphant*, 74, and set her on fire.
[Aubrey passim; TNA: ADM.106/420; London Gazette 2 June 1692]

24 May: The Attack on La Hougue

A further twelve French ships had taken shelter in the port of St Vaast la Hougue, usually called la Hogue in contemporary British accounts, hauling themselves close inshore. The main body of the allied fleet under Admiral Edward Russell attacked them on 23 May, battering them with cannon fire and sending in armed parties in boats to board and set fire to several ships. The action continued the next day, with another successful boat attack on the remaining grounded ships. The work was completed when Vice Admiral George Rooke led a combined boat and fireship attack on the harbour, to set fire to the assembled transports.

Two fireships were used in the attack on the transports, although both ran aground close under Fort St Vaast, where they burned out before they could reach their targets:

HALF MOON Fireship
Prize 1685; 214 tons; 67.4ft × 25ft; 16 guns
Captain John Knapp

THOMAS and ELIZABETH Fireship
Purchased 1688; 184 tons; 10 guns
Captain Edward Littleton
[Aubrey; London Gazette 2 June 1692]

* * *

9 June HART Pink
Rotherhithe 1691; 96 tons; 62.6ft × 18.11ft; 10 guns
Captain David Condon
Escorting a group of coastal craft through the English Channel, they were off St Ives, Cornwall, when at first light they discovered that they were being chased by two French privateers, which proved to be the *Coëtquen*, 18 guns, and *Saint-Aaron*, 18, from St Malo. Lieutenant Sackville Webb assumed command after Captain Condon was wounded, but after maintaining a fight for 90 minutes, the *Hart* surrendered, suffering fourteen men killed and six wounded. The corsairs were subsequently able to pursue the convoy and twelve vessels were captured.
[TNA: ADM.1/5253; ADM 106/414]

15 June SWAN PRIZE Fifth Rate
Prize 1673; 246 tons; 74ft × 25ft; 28 guns
Captain Hon. Edward Neville
On 7 June, the island of Jamaica was struck by a massive earthquake, which in 10 minutes demolished all the churches, dwelling houses and sugar works and two-thirds of Port Royal was swallowed up by the sea. The *Swan* was alongside the careening wharf and was swept ashore by a tsunami wave that followed the earthquake and was '… suckt amongst the houses'. At a subsequent inspection, it was found that her keel was broken, and the ship so severely damaged, with all her guns, rigging, cables and anchors lost, that she was condemned as a wreck, and paid off.
[TNA: ADM.106/420]

4 July RUZEE PRIZE Fireship
Prize 1692 (le Rusé); 135 tons; 6 guns
Captain Charles Wager
Sailed from Spithead in company with the *St Vincent* fireship, at about 4pm, then being about two leagues (six miles) off Culver Cliff, Isle of Wight, the quarterdeck guns were exercised. They had fired two guns when

it was reported that the hold was on fire. The blaze spread rapidly through the stored combustible materials, and she was soon completely ablaze. The crew hastily abandoned her, but twenty-four men died.
[TNA: ADM.106/425]

6 October NORWICH Fourth Rate
Portsmouth 1691; 616 tons; 125.7ft × 33.8ft; 50 guns
Captain Richard Pugh†
Blown away from her anchors off the island of St Christopher's in the Leeward Islands during a tropical storm on this date, and not seen again; presumed lost with all hands.
[CSPC: Colonial, America and West Indies February & March 1693]

1693

12 January SCARBOROUGH Ketch
Scarborough 1691; 94 tons; 10 guns
Captain Thomas Taylor
Captured in the Irish Sea by two French privateers from Nantes, the *Saint-Antoine*, 20 guns, and the *Marianne*, 18, after a two-hour fight in which all her rigging was reduced to a shattered condition. She was retaken on 27 January by the *York*.
[TNA: ADM.1/5253; London Gazette 30 January 1692/93]

13 January SPY Fireship
Rotherhithe 1690; 253 tons; 91.6ft × 25.3ft; 8 guns
Captain John Norris
In a winter storm, she was blown from her moorings at Portsmouth and driven onto a mud bank. Lighters were used to take off cables and guns, and she was refloated on 13 January, and taken alongside the *Exeter* hulk for repairs. She had been there for about four hours when it was discovered that she was on fire, which quickly took hold, and she was destroyed, being cut adrift and allowed to burn out in shallow water. The cause of the blaze was uncertain, although men from the dockyard were working on board at the time. The Gunner and Carpenter were adjudged to have been negligent; both were ashore without leave whilst works were in progress in the firerooms. Thomas Kew, the Gunner, was fined all his pay and Thomas Cranaway, the Carpenter, lost six months' pay.
[TNA: ADM.1/5253; ADM.106/437]

13 January TARTAN PRIZE Advice Boat
Prize 1692 (*la Tartane*); 49 tons; 36ft × 16ft; 4 guns
Captain John Tancred
Sailed from Plymouth with orders to cruise to gain intelligence on the French coast, she was captured by a privateer in the western approaches to the Channel and taken into St Malo.
[TNA: ADM.106/3120; HCJ 1695]

26 February MERMAID PRIZE Fireship
Prize 1692 (*la Sirène*); 174 tons; 78ft × 23ft; 8 guns
Captain Edward Rigby
Whilst laying in the Cattewater at Plymouth, fitting out for sea, the Captain's servant, who was carrying a hamper of bottles to the Captain's store-room, dropped an unguarded candle into some straw and shavings, starting a fire, which spread rapidly. With no buckets and insufficient hands on board to tackle the blaze, she was burnt to the waterline
[TNA: ADM.106/432; ADM.106/438; London Gazette 27 February 1692/93]

28 April WINDSOR CASTLE Second Rate
Woolwich 1679; 1,326 tons; 162ft × 44.6ft; 90 guns
Captain Daniel Jones
With several other ships of the fleet, sailed from the Nore on 23 April into the North Sea, and during the afternoon of 28 April headed towards the Downs anchorage. Although the weather was clear and fine, she ran aground on the South Sand Head of the Goodwin Sands, '... through the unskilfulness of the pilot.' Other ships sent boats to her aid, and the sheet anchor was carried out astern for an attempt to kedge her free. At high tide the following morning, an effort was made to heave in on the cable, but she would not move. Several local ketches and smacks went to her assistance and stores and men were taken off to lighten her, and water and beer casks emptied but she remained firmly aground. Work went on for several days to free her, and although a large proportion of the stores and provisions were removed. it became clear that she had broken her back, and she was finally abandoned on 6 May. The subsequent court martial found the pilot, John Harris, guilty of negligence and sentenced him to seven years' imprisonment.
[TNA: ADM.51/4009; ADM.106/442; London Gazette 24 April and 1 May 1693]

22 May EAGLET Ketch
Rotherhithe 1691; 95 tons; 62.2ft × 18.10ft; 10 guns
Captain David Greenhill
Ordered to New England, the ketch sailed from off Galloway on 17 May, in company with a ketch which was bound for North America and a local trading vessel. They headed north into the Firth of Clyde but became separated. The *Eaglet* made for the Isle of Arran where she was held up by contrary winds, so anchored and Captain Greenhill went ashore. During the evening two ships were seen approaching, and thinking they were her missing companions, Greenhill sent his boat to row out and speak to them. The pair were actually French privateers, the *Phélypeaux*, 40 guns, and the *Grenédan*, 30, which detained the boat with its crew. Greenhill, annoyed with the delay in the return of his boat, went out himself in a boat from the shore, but was captured

after the French fired into his boat. The privateers then closed and attacked the *Eaglet*, which was now under the command of the Gunner, John Hoare, who had realised the danger and got the ketch underway but was unable to escape due to the lack of wind. The French landed a party of armed men onshore, and the ketch found herself caught between several fires but managed to hold out for six hours until she was forced to surrender. Captain Greenhill was later found to be guilty of ill conduct in failing to get the ketch underway rather than sending a boat, and then compounding it by going out himself. He was ordered to lose a year's pay and serve time as a volunteer.
[TNA: ADM.1/5254]

17 June HARP Ketch
Scarborough 1691; 94 tons; 10 guns
Captain John Ward
In company with the *Sun Prize*, the pair were employed in protecting fishery smacks in the North Sea, and the ketch was off North Foreland, when she was reported to have been attacked and captured by two privateers from Dunkirk; no further details found.
[TNA: ADM.106/432; HCJ 1695]

17 June SUN PRIZE Sixth Rate
Prize 1692 (*le Soleil*); 214 tons; 90.9ft × 24ft; 22 guns
Captain Francis Manley†
Stationed in the southern North Sea with the *Harp* ketch for the protection of the Mackerel fishery (see above), she was attacked and captured off North Foreland by '… John Dubart with two ships', i.e., Jean Bart.
Note: Recaptured 8 October 1696.
[TNA: ADM.106/432; HCJ 1695]

20 September DIAMOND Fourth Rate
Deptford 1652; 548 tons; 127.6ft × 31.3ft; 48 guns
Captain Henry Wickham
Escorting a convoy from the West Indies, they were about 50 miles to the south-west of Cape Clear, Ireland, when two ships were seen to windward. They were initially believed to be ships that had become detached from the convoy, but as they closed, they could be seen to be two large French privateers. The *Diamond* placed herself between the strangers and the convoy, and by late morning fire was being exchanged, firing broadsides and small shot, until one of the privateers, the *Grenédan*, 30 guns, closed to lay on her larboard quarter, whilst the other, the *Phélypeaux*, 40, ran close alongside the starboard side and entered a large number of boarders. The French gained the quarterdeck and great cabin, and fighting went on for some time, until the French cleared away the defenders by throwing grenades and stink-pots, which filled the ship with foul black smoke. After this Captain Wickham ordered the Bosun to call for quarter and they surrendered. The privateers went on to take six ships of the convoy. Despite being short-handed and making a stout defence, suffering about fifty men killed or wounded, Captain Wickham was found guilty at a court-martial of 'wanting in his conduct'. The court believed he could have taken men from the merchants and had surrendered despite being urged by his Lieutenant to continue fighting. He was fined and imprisoned for 10 years.
[TNA: ADM.1/5254; London Gazette 2 October 1693; De la Roncière vol 6 pp 176–7]

20 September CYGNET Fireship
Purchased 1688; 100 tons; 8 guns
Captain John Perry
In company with the *Diamond* (see above), acting as convoy escort when attacked by two French privateers, the *Phélypeaux*, 40, and *Grenédan*, 30, off south-west Ireland. Initially she stayed aloof from the fight, but when they saw the privateers run close alongside the *Diamond*, the Master suggested they could close and set fire to them, but Captain Perry refused saying 'Let us not be foolhardy'. Far too late, she finally attempted to close and assist, but after the larger ship surrendered, the *Cygnet* surrendered without firing a shot. Captain Perry was found guilty of failing in his duty to support the *Diamond* and failing to take the opportunity of 'doing execution on the enemy,' when they boarded. He was fined and imprisoned for 10 years.
[TNA: ADM.1/5254; London Gazette 2 October 1693]

19 November VESUVIUS Fireship
Rotherhithe 1691; 269 tons; 92ft × 25.2ft; 24 guns
Captain John Guy
As part of a campaign to attack the French Channel ports, a force under Captain John Benbow bombarded the port of St Malo. After three days of firing shot and shell at the town, the attack concluded with the sending into the harbour of the specially-equipped *Vesuvius*, filled with 100 barrels of gunpowder, covered with pitch, tar and other combustible materials. Above this was a layer of 230 mortar carcasses, grenades, cannon and musket balls. At about 8 o'clock in the evening she was taken close inshore but ran aground on rocks owing to the tide being on the ebb. Captain Guy lit the fuses and left the ship which exploded with great violence, although it would seem that some of the carcasses were damp and failed to explode. The detonation was such that the whole town was covered in the debris of the ship; it '… shook every house in the Town, and overthrew the Roofs of above Three Hundred, which were nearest. The Capstan of the Vessel, which weighed above a Tun Weight, was thrown over the Wall, on Top of the House which it beat down.'
[TNA: ADM.51/3926; London Gazette 23 November 1693; Lediard vol 2 p681]

22 November MORDAUNT Fourth Rate
Deptford 1682; 567 tons; 122.6ft × 32.4ft; 46 guns
Captain Francis Maynard

Stationed in the West Indies, she sailed from Jamaica on 8 November to escort several homeward-bound merchant vessels from Jamaica clear of the island. Having seen the ships out in safety, she parted from them, then being to the north-east of Cuba and steered back towards Jamaica. On 18 November it was estimated that Cape Antonio, the western point of Cuba, was to the south-east and the ship continued to stand to the south-west to clear the land, but in the early morning breakers were seen ahead. The helm was put over and they tried to wear ship, but the ship ran onto rocks. The impact was heavy, and she was immediately bilged and started to fill with water. The masts and anchors were cut away, but she was held fast, and the water soon overcame the pumps. Rafts were made and boats put into the water, and she was abandoned. It was found that she had been wrecked on the Colorados shoals, 20 miles from the coast of Cuba. The court of enquiry was satisfied that the strong and uncertain currents had taken her further inshore that was expected, and her officers were acquitted of any blame.
[TNA: ADM.1/5254]

1 December MILFORD Fifth Rate
Woolwich 1690; 355 tons; 105.2ft × 27.6ft; 32 guns
Captain Roger Vaughan

The *Milford* sailed from Norway escorting a convoy of seven ships bound for the Medway ports, laden with naval stores and they were about 20 miles to the east of Lowestoft, when in the grey of the early morning four ships were seen on the horizon. By 8 o'clock they could clearly be seen to be closing, and were showing Dutch colours, but Captain Vaughan believed them to be French, and so ordered the merchant ships to make all sail away and placed himself and his consort, the *Warrington*, between the oncoming French and their convoy. At 10 o'clock the leading enemy ship, *l'Adroit*, 48 guns, was within pistol-shot and the engagement began. The dispute lasted for over an hour, with another French ship astern firing chase guns into her. Her rigging was shattered, with the mainmast and main topmast being shot through. A third ship, believed to be *la Fortuné*, ran alongside her starboard quarter and soon after this her mizzen mast went overboard, and when a large number of boarders entered, she surrendered. Sixteen men were killed in the engagement. Four ships of the convoy were also taken by the French Dunkirk squadron, which was commanded by Jean Bart.
[TNA: ADM.1/5254; ADM 106/438; London Gazette 14 December 1693]

1 December WARRINGTON Sixth Rate
Hired 1692; 212 tons; 70.2ft × 23.9ft; 30 guns
Captain John Oake

In company with the *Milford* in the North Sea, when the convoy they were escorting was attacked by a squadron of four large French warships from Dunkirk commanded by Jean Bart. One large ship closed and fired a broadside followed by a volley of musketry into the *Warrington*, before moving on to tackle the *Milford*. The *Warrington* was then tackled by a second warship for nearly two hours, her enemy laying on her weather bow for much of this time. When another ship came up and lay on her starboard quarter, she could not resist any longer and surrendered. Both Captains Oake and Vaughan were cleared by a court martial and praised for showing great resolution.
[TNA: ADM.1/5254; ADM 106/438; London Gazette 14 December 1693]

9 December SAINT ALBANS Fourth Rate
Deptford 1687; 615 tons; 128.4ft × 32.10ft; 50 guns
Captain Thomas Gillam†

In company with the *Virgin Prize* and *Sheerness*, the three ships sought shelter from poor weather, with high winds and frequent showers of snow, at Kinsale, Ireland. After they had anchored Captain Gillam took the opportunity to go ashore with Captain Hailes of the *Virgin*. In their absence the wind freshened, shifted to the east, and was soon gusting to gale force. The officers attempted to return on board their ships in the *St Alban*'s pinnace, but unfortunately, as the boat reached Gillam's ship, it was thrown against the bows, capsized and sank, drowning both captains and eleven men, only two seamen surviving. Soon after this, finding they were being driven across the harbour, and fearing for the ship's safety, they shortened cable, but they continued to drive until they went ashore at Sandy Cove and bilged. The guns, anchors and stores were subsequently salvaged.
[TNA: ADM.52/107; ADM 106/435; London Gazette 18 December 1693]

22 December LUCAS GALLEY Sloop
Hired 1693; 120 tons; 16 guns
Captain Jonathan Hardham

A former privateer hired into service, she had been ordered to cruise in the North Sea, between Great Yarmouth and Tynemouth, but was reported to have been cast away on the coast of Holland in poor weather; no further details found
[TNA: ADM.7/655; ADM.33/165; ADM 106/434; HCJ 1695]

1694

19 February SUSSEX Third Rate
Chatham 1693; 1,203 tons; 157.2ft × 41.4ft; 80 guns
Captain Charles Hawkins†

Flagship of Rear Admiral Sir Francis Wheeler, Commander-in-Chief of an Anglo-Dutch squadron ordered to the Mediterranean, the ships sailed from the Bay of Cadiz on 10 February. After several abortive attempts over the next few days to pass through the Straits, all frustrated by strong contrary winds and regular rain squalls, the squadron took shelter in the Bay of Gibraltar. During the afternoon of 17 February, they sailed with a north-west wind, but were again baffled the following morning, when the wind veered round to the east and increased in strength and the ships were forced to lay-to under courses, in dark, heavy weather. At about 5pm the weather briefly cleared to reveal the fleet spread across the Straits of Gibraltar, with several clearly having suffered, having lost sails and damaged rigging. The Admiral signalled that land was in sight and spread more sail, making the signal to tack, to pass clear of the Straits and gain open water. Some ships were quite close inshore, and with the weather closing in again and the light failing, sight of the land was lost. During the night, it would seem that some ships mistook the Bay of Gibraltar for the Straits and found themselves embayed, others were taken inshore and were unable to come about. The *Sussex* was one of these, and at 5 o'clock in the morning she ran aground on the Spanish coast near Gibraltar, the ship breaking up very quickly. There were only two survivors from a complement of 550.
[TNA: ADM.1/5254; London Gazette 26 March 1694; Lediard vol 2 p684]

Other ships of the squadron lost were:

CAMBRIDGE Third Rate
Deptford 1666; 881 tons; 121ft × 37ft; 70 guns
Captain John Ward

One of the leading ships of the squadron, in the continuing strong winds and rain, she could make little progress, and lay-to for some time under a balanced mizzen sail, her head to the south. At about 4 o'clock in the morning, a flash of lightning revealed land and breakers close to her, and despite an attempt to come about she was driven onto the Spanish shore about nine miles to the east of Gibraltar. One hundred men were lost.

LUMLEY CASTLE Fourth Rate
Hired 1692; 56 guns
Captain George Meester

Close inshore when she followed the Admiral's order to stand to the east. She found herself close to the shore at about 10 o'clock in the evening and let go the sheet and bower anchors in four fathoms. They would not hold, however, and during the night she was driven ashore, swinging broadside on to the sea and was wrecked about three miles to the east of Gibraltar. One hundred and thirty men were lost.

SERPENT Bomb
Chatham 1693; 260 tons; 86ft × 26.6ft; 12 guns
Captain Abraham Colfe

The bomb vessel followed the *Sussex* close inshore during the storm and became embayed. Unable to come about she ran aground and was wrecked with no survivors.

MARY Ketch Tender
Hired 1693
Master John Layton†
Wrecked on the Spanish shore near Gibraltar.
[TNA: ADM 33/165]

WILLIAM Ketch Tender
Hired 1693
Master Charles Cricket
Wrecked on the Spanish shore near Gibraltar; all six men on board survived the loss.
[TNA: ADM.33/153]

In addition to the warships lost, six merchant vessels were also wrecked.

★ ★ ★

24 February PEMBROKE Fifth Rate
Deptford 1690; 356 tons; 105.6ft × 27.2ft; 32 guns
Captain Roger Bellwood

Part of a squadron cruising in the western approaches to the English Channel under Admiral Mitchell, she became separated from the other ships during the night of 17/18 February but remained on station. During the afternoon of 23 February, a sail was seen to leeward, and they closed to investigate, and discovered it to be a large French privateer, the *Ville de St Malo*, 40 guns. In a fresh gale with a large swell the pair opened fire at each other, and a running fight began which went on through the afternoon, with the British ship suffering badly in her rigging, losing her mainmast and mizzen topmast, with all the sails shot through. Captain Bellwood was shot and wounded but stayed at his post. The pair separated in late afternoon, and the crew was busily engaged clearing the wreckage and repairing the rigging. Exchanges of fire went on through the evening and into the night, but the next morning the French ship stood away, leaving the *Pembroke* to continue repairing her rigging. At about 11 o'clock a sail was seen approaching

which proved to be another large French privateer, the *St Louis*, 40 guns, which soon came up with them to start another engagement. After two hours the foremast of the *Pembroke* went by the board, which carried away the bowsprit. Having lost control of the ship, several guns dismounted and making water, she surrendered. The crew was removed but the French found that she was so severely damaged that they could not keep her afloat. A small party was put aboard to set her on fire, but before they could do so she was carried further inshore and was run onshore about three miles to the west of Lizard Point.
[TNA: ADM.1/5254; London Gazette 1 March 1693/94]

1 May FALCON Fourth Rate
Woolwich 1666; 349 tons; 88ft x 27.4ft; 36 guns
Captain Thomas Bryant
Ordered to cruise to the east of Jamaica to find privateers reported in the area, she gave chase to a corvette, but when a further three ships came into sight, clearly large warships, she made off. She was overhauled by the *Solide*, 44 guns, and maintained a running fight for some time, until with fifteen of his men killed, many wounded, and others deserting the guns, and two more ships, the *Temeraire*, 54, and *Envieux*, 44, closing, Captain Bryant was forced to surrender. The ship was carried into Petit-Goâve, Hispaniola.
[CSPC: North America West Indies June 1694; de la Roncière vol 6 p249]

17 May PEARL PRIZE Sixth Rate
Prize 1693 (*la Suffisante*); 195 tons; 69.10ft x 22.11ft; 12 guns
Captain Francis Dove
Sailed from Goeree, Holland, in the morning, in fine weather, in company with the *Lizard*, two yachts and a ketch, but during the afternoon the weather steadily deteriorated, with approaching black clouds, thunder and lightning. At about 4pm the group was hit by a violent squall, in which the *Lizard* and the *Aldboro* ketch lost all their topmasts, and the *Mary* yacht was dismasted. The *Pearl* had reduced sail to clewed-up topsails, but when the squall hit, she was laid over onto her beam ends. She hung like this for about five minutes, before she capsized and sank. Captain Dove and twenty men were saved.
[TNA: ADM.1/5254; ADM.51/4256; London Gazette 24 May 1694]

18 June WILD PRIZE Sixth Rate
Prize 1692 (*la Farouche*); 70 tons; 51.3ft x 16ft; 12 guns
Captain Thomas Smith
Coming home from the West Indies, she was about 350 miles to the south-west of Land's End when two large ships were seen. The strangers closed under English colours until they were within gunshot, when the closest of them fired a gun, and hoisted French colours. The pair stationed themselves on each quarter and called on her to strike. Being unable to carry any sail on her foremast, which was in poor condition and clearly outgunned, she surrendered. Her captors proved to be St Malo privateers, the *Diamant*, 50, and '*Counterlewis*' (perhaps *Comte de Toulouse*?).
[TNA: ADM.1/5254]

5 July BASING GALLEY Sixth Rate
Hired 1693; 121 tons; 18 guns
Captain John Pointon†
Engaged in chasing French fishing vessels off the Sussex coast, they had made a capture at about 8 o'clock in the morning and then saw two more sails towards Dieppe, to which they gave chase. She presumed they were merchant ships but as she closed, discovered them to be privateers, one of 12 guns, the other of 8. She fired at the smaller of the two, and then tacked to put her head to the east, to maintain a running fight with both. The *Basing* maintained the combat for over an hour, driving one of them off by hurling hand grenades when they attempted to board, until with the Captain and nine others killed and fifteen wounded, she surrendered and was taken into Calais.
[TNA: ADM.1/5255]

12 July SAINT NICHOLAS Machine Vessel
Purchased 1693; 107 tons; 57ft x 18.10ft
Master and Commander Robert Dunbar
The machine or 'Infernal Machine' was a variant of the fireship, being designed for use against shore defences. Filled with gunpowder, mortar shells and a variety of other combustible material, the idea had been first attempted with the *Vesuvius* in November 1693 (*q.v.*). Several small merchant vessels were taken up and so converted, to be used in the campaign of attacks on northern French ports. The *St Nicholas* was taken into Dieppe harbour after an all-day bombardment. After setting the fuses, the crew abandoned the vessel, but it became clear that they had gone out, so Captain Dunbar returned on board and relit them. The vessel drifted against the pier-head at Dieppe, where it exploded, causing some limited local damage, but not with the great success that had been hoped for.
[CSPD: William and Mary July 1694]

16 July GRENADA Bomb
Rotherhithe 1693; 279 tons; 87ft x 26.10ft; 12 guns
Captain Thomas Willshaw
Part of the force assembled to bombard the French port of Le Havre; several fires were started by the shells fired into the town. Whilst laying off the town, the *Grenada* was struck by a bomb-shell fired from the shore, which

exploded on impact causing her to be '... entirely blown to pieces'. Thirteen men were killed
[London Gazette 19 July 1694; CSPD: William and Mary July 1694]

18 July SCARBOROUGH Fifth Rate
Woolwich 1694; 374 tons; 104.10ft × 28.10ft; 32 guns
Captain Thomas Killingworth†

Ordered to cruise off the northern Irish coast in search of privateers, she was off Tory Island when two ships were seen to windward in the early hours of the morning, which proved to be the *Comte de Revel*, 36 guns, and *l'Etoile*, 22. They bore down on her and the *Revel* came under the lee quarter and fired a broadside, which commenced the engagement which went on for over an hour. The Captain was killed, and the Master mortally wounded, at which Lieutenant Peter Fountaine assumed command. He ordered the flag struck in surrender, against the protests of Richard Scott, the Gunner. A court martial judged that she was lost through the cowardice of Lieutenant Fountaine, but I have not found any resulting sentence; the circumstances may have been complicated as Fountaine was a refugee French Huguenot.
[TNA: ADM.1/5255]

12 September ABRAM'S OFFERING Machine Vessel
Purchased 1693; 63 tons; 43.6ft × 16.7ft
Master and Commander Edward Cox

Intended to be blown up in Dunkirk harbour at the completion of an all-day bombardment, at nightfall the fuses were lit before the crew left and she was allowed to drift inshore. As she came near the mole head, she was taken aback, and eventually drove ashore about 200 yards from the head, where she blew up. The resulting explosion, however, occurred too far away from the shore to do any great damage.
[CSPD: William and Mary September 1694]

12 September WILLIAM and MARY Machine Vessel
Purchased 1693; 23 tons; 24ft × 13.6ft
Master and Commander Thomas Robinson

Taken into Dunkirk harbour, to follow the *Abram's Offering*, to destroy the shore defences, but when Captain Robinson spotted two boats coming towards him from the harbour, evidently with the intention of boarding, he lit the fuses and left her to drift in. She exploded about 100 yards from the pier, causing little or no damage.
[CSPD: William and Mary September 1694]

1 October POSTBOY Advice Boat
Portsmouth 1694; 73 tons; 53ft × 16.1ft; 4 guns
Master and Commander Anthony Philips

Sailed from the Downs anchorage in the early hours of the morning to look into Dunkirk for intelligence, she had been out for just three hours when a ship was sighted to the north-east. The stranger steadily closed until it could be seen to be a French privateer of 22 guns. The *Postboy* altered away and made all sail, but she was overhauled off Calais. The privateer fired two guns at her, but *Postboy* was unable to reply, due to the heavy swell with water regularly washing over the upper deck, and she surrendered.
[TNA: ADM.1/5255]

26 November JAMES GALLEY Fifth Rate
Blackwall 1676; 436 tons; 112ft × 28.11ft; 30 guns
Captain Joseph Soames

Sailed from Ostend during the afternoon of 25 November, to carry several Army officers and their equipment to Leith, Scotland, but during the night Captain Soames argued with the Pilot, John Potter, over the course to be taken. Soames feared that the ship was steering too much to the west, and eventually ordered the Mate to stay by the compass all night and ensure they did not go more to the west. At midnight, the lead-line was cast which found that they were in 17 fathoms, and they continued, and were running at about six knots when at 2am they ran hard aground on the Longsands, at the entrance to the Thames Estuary. The ship was held fast, and water was found to be entering. Pumping and bailing started but by first light it was clear that she was beyond recovery. The boats were hoisted out, but there was some chaos, with Captain Soames leaving in the pinnace and not returning, the passengers and remaining crew relying on several hoys and local fishing boats which came to their assistance. She could not be moved, steadily filled with water and was lost. At a subsequent court martial, Captain Soames was found to have been negligent and ordered to lose all pay due, and to pay a fine of £300, being imprisoned until the money had been paid; John Potter the Pilot was reckoned to be most at fault, by taking the ship too far to the west. He was sentenced to five years' imprisonment. Prior to this he was to be carried around all the ships moored at Blackstakes, a halter around his neck and his sentence read out. The Master, who had given little or no assistance, was disrated and ordered to forfeit all pay due.
[TNA: ADM.1/5255; ADM.106/448]

15 December TALBOT Ketch
Rotherhithe 1691; 94 tons; 62ft × 18.9ft; 10 guns
Master and Commander Anthony Tollat

Searching for privateers off the Irish coast, they were steering north along the Wexford coast under the guidance of a pilot, the lead-line being used regularly. The pilot insisted that the course they were taking was safe, as they were sounding in eight to ten fathoms. However, at about 11 o'clock in the morning there

was a sounding of two fathoms, and Captain Tollat promptly ordered the helm to starboard, but the pilot countermanded the order, putting the helm to port. A few minutes later they ran hard aground on the Glassgorman bank off Arklow. Strenuous efforts were made to free her, heaving overboard ballast and guns, and about an hour later she did float free, but it was found that the ship was not answering the tiller, and she was carried by the wind onto the bank again. She heeled over and an attempt to haul her off by use of a kedge anchor failed. By late afternoon she was filling with water, and she was abandoned as a wreck. At a court martial Captain Tollat was cleared of any blame, the pilot, William Jones, was found to be responsible for the wreck, through his 'negligence and ignorance'. However, the court was lenient towards him, as it was explained that he was '... ancient, dark-sighted and only a fisherman'. He was ordered to be taken from ship to ship at the Nore, with a halter around his neck and his offence read out. After this he was to be taken back to his home port of Dublin and his punishment repeated, but he should never serve as a pilot again.
[TNA: ADM.1/5255]

December DRAKE Sixth Rate
Rotherhithe 1694; 253 tons; 93ft × 24.9ft; 24 guns
Captain John Stapleton†
The exact date and circumstances of the loss of the *Drake* are obscure. Newly built and fitted out, it was reported in February 1695 that she had been ordered to 'attend on the Commissioners of Ireland' but had never arrived at Dublin and was must subsequently be presumed to have foundered in her passage with all hands. An Admiralty Order of 27 March 1696 ordered that, not being heard of, she officially be paid off, with the pay books being made up to 20 December 1694.
[HCJ 1695 p351; TNA: ADM.33/181; CSPD: William and Mary April 1695]

1695

4 January NONSUCH Fourth Rate
Portsmouth 1668; 359 tons; 88.3ft × 27.8ft; 40 guns
Captain Thomas Taylor†
Convoying home five merchant ships from New England laden with mast timber, they were scattered by a strong gale when about 200 miles to the west of Scilly, but all but one had re-joined by the morning of 3 January, when a large French privateer, the *François*, 48 guns, approached. After initially engaging the *Falkland*, one of the mast ships, the privateer moved on to engage the *Nonsuch*. A running fight was maintained through the afternoon, both ships lying-to during the night to repair damages. The following day the engagement was renewed, but during the morning the *Nonsuch* lost both her main and mizzen masts, and Captain Taylor was killed. Crippled and unable to use her lower tier of guns due to the high seas, she surrendered. At the subsequent court martial, some blame fell on the late Captain Taylor, who had failed to put his ship into a full state of readiness for the engagement, thereby exposing his ship and convoy to hazard. Lieutenant Abraham Howard was found guilty of ill conduct, by failing to take command after the death of Captain Taylor, having retired below claiming he was wounded; he was dismissed the service and ordered to serve six months in prison. In addition, the Master, Gunner and Boatswain, who had surrendered the ship when more might have been done, were all dismissed the service for 'ignorance and ill conduct'.
[TNA: ADM.1/5255; London Gazette 4 February 1694/95]

4 February DARTMOUTH Fourth Rate
Rotherhithe 1693; 603 tons; 122ft × 33.8ft; 50 guns
Captain Roger Vaughan†
On 1 February, then cruising about 100 miles to the south-west of Scilly, two ships were sighted during the afternoon. She bore down on them, but discovering them to be large French privateers, stood away to the south-west, the strangers in pursuit. She lost them during the night, but two days later sighted them again in the late afternoon and was again forced to stand away with the pair in chase. The pursuit went on through the night until at 6 o'clock the next morning, the *Saint-Esprit*, 38 guns, began the engagement. The fight went on through the morning, the other ship of 40 guns also joining the battle. At noon, the mainmast went by the board and an hour later the mizzen mast was also lost. With her rigging shattered, water washing in through her lower ports, rendering her lower tier of guns useless, and having taken forty casualties, including her Captain and Lieutenant Jackson who lost a leg, she surrendered and was taken into St Malo.
Note: recaptured in October 1702.
[TNA: ADM.1/5255; London Gazette 14 February 1694/95]

16 February ENGLAND Fifth Rate
Hired 1693; 406 tons; 93ft × 28ft; 42 guns
Captain William Cooper†
Escorting a large convoy of merchant ships, on 15 February they were about 100 miles to the south-west of Cape Clear in Ireland, when a ship was sighted during the afternoon. The *England* gave chase for a while, but as the stranger was able to keep their distance, she returned to her convoy. That night she made ordered the convoy to make the best of their way independently and placed herself in the way of the threat. The next morning the stranger was still in sight and closing, and it was clear that it was a French man of war. At 10 o'clock the ship,

which was the *Fortuné*, 54 guns, came up with them, and in the first exchange of broadsides, the rudder and sternpost of the *England* were shattered, preventing her from manoeuvring. They continued to exchange fire for some time until the French ship ran alongside and entered a large number of men. By this time, they had received numerous shots in the hull and with only Lieutenant Richard Ryder and twenty-three of the men not wounded, they surrendered. The ship was so badly damaged that she foundered soon after.
[TNA: ADM.1/5255]

23 February GOODWIN PRIZE Sixth Rate
Prize 1692; 72 tons; 58.10ft × 16ft; 6 guns
Captain John Martin

Lying at anchor in the Downs, the Captain and several of the crew were ashore, leaving only the Master, Peter Wallis and twenty men on board. During the day, the wind steadily increased to gale force and a second anchor had to be laid out after a cable parted. Soon after she had done so, a French privateer was seen approaching the anchorage, at which the Master ordered the cables to be cut and an attempt to be made to gain the refuge of Dover harbour. The privateer manoeuvred to force her further inshore until she ran aground in Langdon Bay, about two miles from Dover Castle and was wrecked, the privateer giving her a broadside before standing off. Captain Martin was found guilty of an offence under the 32nd Article of War, in that he had negligently performed his duty and forsaken his station. As a penalty he was ordered to serve in a line of battle ship for three months in the summer, with the status of a Volunteer.
[TNA: ADM.1/5255; ADM.106/476]

16 April HOPE Third Rate
Deptford 1678; 1,052 tons; 151.5ft × 40.4ft; 70 guns
Captain Henry Robinson

In charge of a large convoy from the Mediterranean, when on 14 April in the early hours of the morning, they became separated from the convoy, only two other escorts, the *Anglesey* and *Roebuck*, remaining in company. A senior Mate, Edward Thompson, who had the watch when sight of the convoy was lost, had not signalled a course change and had failed to inform Captain Robinson when it was discovered that they had parted, causing the Captain to exclaim when he found out '… if you were not so old a man, I would kick you off the quarter-deck'. At about 2 o'clock in the afternoon of 16 April, when about 180 miles south-west of the Lizard, a squadron of five large French warships under the command of the Marquis de Nesmond was sighted. Captain Robinson was unwell, and the ship undermanned, but he maintained a very brave fight for over seven hours. Initially the *St Antoine*, 40 guns, exchanged broadsides, before the French ship stretched ahead to engage the *Anglesey*. Her place was taken by the *François*, 48, which stationed herself on her quarter, with the other ships astern and keeping up a constant fire of great and small shot. When Captain Taylor was shot and wounded in the neck, Lieutenant Foulis took command. They lost the mainmast, fore and mizzen topmasts and the sails were shot to pieces. The *St Antoine* meanwhile had lost her fore topmast in her fight with the *Anglesey*, and she then fell back to join the combat with the *Hope*. With 7ft of water in the hold and surrounded, they were forced to surrender. Both other British ships escaped. For his incompetence, Mr Thompson was ordered to forfeit all pay due and to be taken around the fleet in the Medway with a halter around his neck and his crime read out, and then dismissed the service.
[TNA: ADM.1/5256]

10 June FALCON Sixth Rate
Shoreham 1694; 240 tons; 91.6ft × 24.6ft; 24 guns
Captain Henry Middleton

Cruising in the English Channel, she was off Dodman Point when at first light she sighted three ships, which were evidently in chase of her. She attempted to out sail them, but by 7am, she had been overhauled by one of them, which was the *St Antoine*, 40 guns. An engagement began, which lasted for an hour, when a second French ship, the *Tigre*, 24, joined in the engagement. The *Falcon* had her rigging torn to pieces and yards damaged, and with ten killed or wounded, she surrendered, then being off the Manacles rocks near Lizard Point. Captain Middleton was adjudged to have been guilty of an error of judgement by failing to run the vessel ashore rather than allow her to be captured and was ordered to forfeit three months' pay.
[TNA: ADM.1/5256]

3 July POSTBOY Advice Boat
Portsmouth 1695; 77 tons; 56.6ft × 16ft; 4 guns
Master and Commander Wagden Baker

Detached from the main fleet off the Channel Islands to proceed to Plymouth with letters, she made landfall off Portland in the early morning of 2 July and altered course to the west. During the following morning as they approached Start Point, she was chased by two French privateers. They came up with her at about 8 o'clock, one running onto her larboard quarter and firing a volley of small shot. They returned fire, but by now the second privateer was closing on her starboard quarter, and fired a broadside which shot away her ensign, and then ran alongside. The men on the upper deck called for quarter and she surrendered.
[TNA: ADM.1/5626]

5 July CHARLES Fireship
Purchased 1688; 90 tons; 6 guns
Captain Edward Durley
The French port of St Malo became the target for an intense bombardment and attack from the English fleet from 4 July. After a day of firing shot and shell into the town, at 8 o'clock in the morning of the second day the *Charles*, along with a Dutch fireship, were sent inshore where they ran onto rocks and then set on fire, the smoke providing a screen for the bombarding ships offshore.
[CSPD: William and Mary July 1695, London Gazette 11 July 1695]

6 July DREADFUL Fireship
Limehouse 1695; 147 tons; 66.10ft × 23.6ft; 4 guns
Master and Commander John Carleton
Part of the bombarding force off St Malo, she was hit repeatedly by fire from a shore battery. When a signal was made to break off action, they weighed anchor, but found they could not work her, as the rudder had been shot away. They managed to rig a capstan bar for a rudder and got underway, but manoeuvring was still difficult and to alter course, had to anchor, allow the head to come around and then cut the cable. She had taken several shots in the hull which caused her to make water, until it reached 5ft in the hold, defeating the pumps. The approach of several enemy boats led Mr Carleton to order the *Dreadful* to be abandoned and set on fire.
[TNA: ADM.1/5255; London Gazette 11 July 1695; CSPD: William and Mary July 1695]

1 August: Attack on Dunkirk
Dunkirk became the object of the fleet's attention on 1 August and an attack by fifteen machine vessels on the several forts and gun batteries was planned. They were fitted out either as explosive ships or 'smoke vessels' and would be escorted inshore by supporting sloops and small frigates. The attack was poorly co-ordinated, with the escorts not being in position and in the event only four of the smoke vessels were used, and the explosive ships never got into position before the attack was abandoned. Of the vessels that were expended, two ran onto the shore where they burnt out, and two were intercepted by boats from the shore, towed clear and allowed to burn out.

The four machines expended were:

EPHRAIM Machine Vessel
Purchased 1695; 170 tons
Master and Commander John Carleton

HAPPY RETURN Machine Vessel
Purchased 1695; 84 tons
Master and Commander Robert Isaac

MAYFLOWER Machine Vessel
Purchased 1695; 109 tons
Master and Commander John Dixon

WILLIAM and ELIZABETH Machine Vessel
Purchased 1695; 46 tons
Master and Commander William Carleton
[CSPD: William and Mary August 1695]

★ ★ ★

22 August FLY Advice Boat
Portsmouth 1694; 73 tons; 61.6ft × 16.1ft; 4 guns
Master and Commander Cornelius Willmore†
Reported to have capsized and foundered off Toulon with no survivors.
[TNA: ADM.106/473; ADM.106/3120; HCJ 1695]

14 September BETTY Fifth Rate
Purchased 1695; 372 tons; 103ft × 28.6ft; 36 guns
Captain John Popwell†
Convoying twenty merchant ships from the West Indies in company with the *Tiger* hired armed ship, the convoy was joined during the night of 13/14 September, when about 200 miles south-west of Cape Clear, Ireland, by a large 30-gun French privateer. The privateer was seen to board one of the ships of the convoy, then made sail with the *Betty* in chase. As she neared, the privateer initially stretched away, but then tacked to get to windward and bore down on the *Betty*. They passed ahead, with a mutual exchange of broadsides then backed their sails. After a further exchange of gunfire, the privateer filled her sails and laid her athwart the bows and raked her with great and small shot, without the *Betty* being able to reply. The privateer then boarded her opponent, and with the Captain and seventeen others killed and fourteen wounded, she surrendered. The surviving officers of the *Betty* were cleared of blame, but Captain Henry Tottendale of the *Tiger* was found guilty at a court martial of failing to go to the assistance of the *Betty*. He was ordered to be dismissed from the service, fined £500 and sent to prison for seven years.
 Note: *Betty* was recaptured on 15 February 1696.
[TNA: ADM.1/5256; ADM.106/483]

24 September WINCHESTER Fourth Rate
Bursledon 1693; 942 tons; 146.2ft × 38.2ft; 60 guns
Captain John Soales (or Soule)
Sailed from Jamaica in company with five other ships, bound for Virginia, Cape Florida was raised at 6 o'clock in the evening of 23 September, the ships steering north on an easterly wind. At midnight, the wind shifted to the north-east, and the senior officer in the *Dunkirk* signalled for the ships to go about. The *Winchester* struggled to comply with the order, as she

was both short-handed and had many men sick. With only eight men on deck, she fell astern of the others as she tried to put the helm over, and when breakers were seen close by, she could do little and went aground on a reef to the north of Cape Florida. The yawl was hoisted out and sounded around her, but she was held fast in the rocks, and soon after this water was found to be entering. Unable to free her, and filling with water, she was abandoned. A brigantine which had been with the squadron bore down to their aid and took off all the men. Her wreck was found in 1938, about 1½ miles to the south-west of Carysfort Reef, Florida.
[TNA: ADM.1/5256; ADM.52/120]

6 November FRIENDS ADVENTURE Ketch
Hired 1694
Master John Masters
Tender to the *Albemarle*, she kept company with the *Unity* ketch tender, after being separated from the fleet in poor weather. The pair anchored off Dungeness for the night, but on seeing two French privateers approaching, she cut her cables and ran herself onshore between Rye and Dungeness. The French privateers followed and burnt her where she lay.
[TNA: ADM.1/5256]

6 November UNITY Ketch
Hired 1695
Master Francis Philpott
Tender to the *Britannia*, and manned by only nine men and boys, she anchored off Dungeness in company with the *Friends Adventure* tender after becoming separated from the fleet. When two French privateers from Calais approached them, the *Unity* managed to weigh and attempted to outsail them, but the French ships used sweeps to come up with her. The little *Unity* bravely held them off for an hour, before the privateers came up, boarded after a 'great volley of small shot' and captured her, the small crew taking to the boat to escape.
Note: retaken by the *Maidstone* the next day.
[TNA: ADM.1/5256; ADM.51/571]

1696

27 January ROYAL SOVEREIGN First Rate
Chatham 1685; 1,606 tons; 167.1ft x 48ft; 100 guns
The ship was laid up 'in Ordinary' (out of commission) at moorings in the river Medway at Chatham, with just the standing officers and a small number of men on board. One of them, an old seaman called Thomas Couch, left a lighted candle in a cabin near the entering port when going on watch at 4 o'clock in the morning. About an hour later, smoke was seen pouring from the cabin and the fire was found to have spread to new tarpaulin stored nearby. Thick smoke soon filled the ship, and the reduced crew were unable to contain the blaze, which destroyed the ship. The subsequent courts martial established that all the standing warrant officers were sleeping onshore at the time, with only a small number of watch keepers on board. Couch was ordered to be flogged, '31 lashes on his bare back' and then to suffer life imprisonment. The Carpenter, Thomas Everden, was found guilty of negligence; he had claimed to be ashore sick but had not reported himself as such. He was imprisoned for a year and lost all pay due.
[TNA: ADM.1/5256; ADM.106/481]

28 January CARLISLE Fourth Rate
Limehouse 1693; 913 tons; 145ft x 38ft; 60 guns
Captain John Norris
Sailed from the Downs anchorage for the Nore in the early hours of 27 January, and stood to the north-east, and by late afternoon the pilot reckoned that they had passed around the Long Sand and could haul round to the west. The lead-line was used constantly, and this showed steadily shallowing water, and then the Master, in the main-top, called out that sand was visible to leeward. Captain Norris prepared to go about, but the pilot, Mr Mumbray, insisted they were clear and in no danger. The next cast of the lead showed five fathoms and then she ran aground. Sails were put aback, but she would not move. The water steadily left them as the tide went out, but she lay quietly, and at the next high tide she floated free, but in doing so she lost her rudder and it was found that water was entering, so they anchored and started pumping and bailing. Despite this the water gained so fast that she weighed anchor and could drift onto the sands again to prevent her sinking. At first light a vessel from Harwich came up and stood by them. The foremast and mizzen masts were cut away to prevent her capsizing, but during the afternoon at high tide she filled with water and was abandoned as a wreck. It was found that she had run aground on the Shipwash Sand, the pilot having mistaken the distinguishing marks and tide times. Because of his previous good character, he was acquitted of any blame.
[TNA: ADM.1/5256; ADM.52/14]

9 February ALDBOROUGH Ketch
Aldborough 1691; 99 tons; 52.9ft x 18.10ft; 10 guns
Master and Commander Thomas Mitchell
Sailed from Portsmouth on 7 February with stores and personal chests belonging to men standing by the *Orford*, fitting out at Shoreham. She anchored the following day off Brighton, to land the stores, and the captain took the opportunity to go ashore to arrange transport. He had not returned on board when at noon there was a massive explosion, which blew the ketch apart and she quickly sank. The cause was never discovered. Ten

men were picked up from the sea, but twenty-one men were killed.
[TNA: ADM.1/5256; ADM 106/485; ADM.106/492]

22 February SWALLOW PRIZE Sixth Rate
Prize 1692 (la Hirondelle); 119 tons; 68ft × 20.4ft; 16 guns
Captain William Urry
Ordered to take the Lieutenant-Governor of Guernsey and a small convoy of ships to the Channel Isles, she sailed from Portsmouth on 21 February. At first light the following morning, Portland then being about 20 miles to the north, several ships were seen on the horizon to the eastward and as the haze cleared another group of three ships could be seen closer by. She immediately made sail to the north with the strangers in pursuit. By 9.30am the nearest ship, a large armed vessel of 38 guns, passed ahead and then shortened sail, as another warship closed from astern. They were showing English colours and responded in English when hailed by Captain Urry. The ship ahead then fell alongside, struck his flag to hoist French colours and fired a broadside. They returned fire and made all sail they could, conducting a running fight for nearly an hour. By this time her sails and rigging were badly cut up and a larger, 48-gun ship had come up with her, and when she went onto her larboard bow, Captain Urry surrendered.
[TNA: ADM.1/5256]

23 February SAUDADOES Sixth Rate
Portsmouth 1669; 181 tons; 74ft × 21.6ft; 16 guns
Captain Thomas Day
Cruising off the coast of northern France in company with the *Charles Galley*, 30 guns, the pair was off Cape Barfleur when daybreak revealed two large ships, carrying 48 and 38 guns, closing them. The pair altered to the north and spread more sail in an effort to outpace them. The *Charles Galley* slowly stretched away and escaped, but the *Saudadoes* found herself in a running fight, firing guns whenever a gun would bear. With her main-topmast shot away and rigging shattered, she could not get away, despite using sweeps when the wind dropped away, and she surrendered. The French found her in such poor condition, they burnt her.
[TNA: ADM.1/5256]

(23/24) March LIZARD Sixth Rate
Chatham 1694; 250 tons; 94.3ft × 24.4ft; 24 guns
Captain Joseph Welby†
On 20 March, having joined company with the *Romney* in the western Mediterranean, the pair were ordered to cruise between Majorca and Toulon to gain intelligence of the French fleet. The weather was poor and deteriorated further, and by 22 March it was blowing a strong westerly gale with lightning and frequent squalls of hail and snow, accompanied by high seas. The following day the pair bore up to run before the wind under reefed courses, and the *Lizard* was seen at about 6 o'clock in the evening about a mile distant from her companion, but parted company during the night and was not seen again. They were then about 30 leagues (90 miles) north-east of Minorca. She was presumed to have foundered with all hands during the night. With no news of her, her books were closed 31 May.
[TNA: ADM.106/3120; ADM.51/4313]

6 April THUNDER Bomb
Limehouse 1695; 147 tons; 65.6ft × 23.5ft; 4 guns
Master and Commander Thomas Symonds
Whilst on passage from the Downs anchorage to bombard Calais, she became separated from the main English force and was captured by two French privateers when off the Dutch coast.
[TNA: ADM.1/5257]

5 July NEWPORT Sixth Rate
Portsmouth 1694; 253 tons; 94.3ft × 24.7ft; 24 guns
Captain Wentworth Paxton
In company with the *Sorlings*, 30 guns, she was cruising off the coast of Newfoundland, when during the early afternoon as the fog cleared, two ships were sighted to the north-east, off the entrance to the St John River in the Bay of Fundy. They bore down on the strangers, which were lying under topsails, and one could be seen to be showing English colours. Despite that, Captain Emes of the *Sorlings* hailed the *Newport*, saying that he feared they were enemy vessels, believing them to be a French man of war and a prize. The ships cleared for action, and as they got within gunshot the strangers, which were the *Envieux*, 50, and *Profond*, 40, replaced the English flag with French and ran out their guns. At 3pm the leading French ship fired a broadside, at which the English pair returned fire and then altered away and made sail, pursued by the French. The wind was now so strong that Captain Paxton could not spread topsails, and she was overhauled by the *Envieux*, which commenced firing broadsides into her opponent. At least two shots struck her on the waterline, causing bad leaks. By 6 o'clock she had 5ft of water in the hold, her main topmast had been shot way and her rigging was badly torn. When the *Profond* came up close by her stern and fired a broadside and a volley of small shot, she struck her flag in surrender. The ship was clearly in danger of sinking, and her captors ran her onshore. The *Sorlings* escaped.
[TNA: ADM.1/5257; ADM.106/485; ADM.51/3975]

August SWIFT Brigantine
Chatham 1695; 80 tons; 63ft × 17ft; 6 guns
Master and Commander Edward Baker†
Sailed from Plymouth on a cruise in the western approaches to the English Channel but disappeared –

'Supposed overset in a storm in the Soundings, as not since heard of'. With no news, her books were closed on 17 August 1696.
[TNA: ADM.106/3120; ADM.33/189]

5 September SAINT JOHN PRIZE Advice Boat
Prize 1695 (*St Jean*); 71 tons; 59ft x 16.4ft; 4 guns
Master and Commander Thomas Williams
Returning to England after delivering despatches to St Helena for the East India Company, she was chased and captured by a French privateer when to the south of Ireland and taken into St Malo.
[TNA: ADM.1/5257]

11 September SAPPHIRE Fifth Rate
Harwich 1675; 341 tons; 105.8ft x 26.10ft; 32 guns
Captain Thomas Cleasby
The *Sapphire* was laying at anchor in the Bay of Bulls, Newfoundland, when a large squadron of ships under the command of the Marquis de Nesmond arrived. Despite being outnumbered Captain Cleasby attempted to defend his ship and the port by engaging them, but as more ships closed, he ran his ship inshore until she grounded and then set her on fire to prevent capture.
[TNA: ADM.1/5257; ADM.106/486]

29 September PORTSMOUTH'S PRIZE Sixth Rate
Prize 1694 (*la Joyeuse*); 106 tons; 68ft x 18.9ft; 10 guns
Master and Commander George Ramsey
Ordered to carry letters from Vice Admiral Aylmer to Vice Admiral Benbow, who was cruising in the southern North Sea, the *Portsmouth's Prize* sighted a group of five ships at 8 o'clock in the morning and closed them, believing them to be Benbow's squadron. It was not until they were close, that they realised they were a squadron of French ships. She immediately bore away but was quickly overhauled and after firing a broadside at her pursuer, she struck her flag in surrender.
[TNA: ADM.1/5257]

11 October PORTSMOUTH Fifth Rate
Portsmouth 1690; 412 tons; 106.3ft x 29.6ft; 32 guns
Captain Gabriel Milleson
Cruising in the English Channel she went in chase of a snow off Pevensey until she saw four ships standing towards her from the south, which she recognised as French privateers, the largest of which had 30 guns. She attempted to outsail them, cutting away her boat and anchors, but they caught her off Romsey. In the initial exchange of fire, she lost her main topmast, and she subsequently lost her fore topmast and spritsail topmast. Unable to escape, and with some of her men quitting their quarters, she surrendered. Captain Milleson and other officers were found to have failed to make sufficient resistance and given her up too easily. All were ordered to forfeit all pay due.
[TNA: ADM.1/5257]

1697

7 January MILFORD Fifth Rate
Ipswich 1695; 386 tons; 107.10ft x 28.4ft; 32 guns
Captain Thomas Lyell
Escorting a group of merchantmen from Yarmouth to Rotterdam, soon after sailed they were attacked by two French 24-gun privateers. *Milford* engaged them for two hours until they ran close alongside and entered boarders, but the crew continued to resist, being driven to shelter behind close-quarter barriers. When a gun split which killed or wounded several men and shattered the bulkhead, the ship was surrendered, to be carried into Dunkirk. Several ships of the convoy were also taken.
[London Gazette 14 January 1696/97; TNA: ADM.1/5257; ADM.106/489]

15 January HIND Pink
Wapping 1691; 96 tons; 63ft x 18.8ft; 10 guns
Master and Commander Walter Riddell
Laying off Folkestone harbour to take in water and provisions, when she saw a strange ship loitering offshore, which she initially believed to be another English cruiser. She made sail and closed, and it could be seen to be larger than expected and was showing Ostend colours. The *Hind* continued to close until within gunshot, when a single gun was ordered to be fired, to bring the stranger to. At this the stranger hauled down the Ostend colours, hoisted French and ran alongside to attempt to enter boarders. This failed and the stranger, now seen to be a 14-gun privateer, fell astern, but quickly made sail and ran alongside and successfully entered boarders who gained control of the upper deck. Hand grenades and smoke bombs were then thrown below to force the surrender. At a court martial it was found that the ship had not been put into a proper state for action, and Riddell was ordered to forfeit three months' pay.
[TNA: ADM.1/5257]

29 March WREN Pink
Redbridge 1695; 105 tons; 53.7ft x 19.2ft; 10 guns
Master and Commander Thomas Dennett
Whilst on fishery protection duties off the south coast of England, she anchored off Rye, Sussex, to oversee the local fishing smacks. In the early morning, a squadron of eight large ships could be seen approaching, which were identified as French privateers, and they ignored the fishing fleet to attack the *Wren*. She cut her cables

and attempted to make the open sea, but two of the nearest privateers, the *Portsmouth* (ex-British) and *Demi-Lune*, 16 guns, fired on the pink several times and then ran alongside, forcing her surrender.
[TNA: ADM.1/5257]

18 April ETNA Fireship
Hessle 1691; 284 tons; 90.11ft x 25.7ft; 24 guns
Master and Commander Kendrick Anderson
Cruising off the south Devon coast, they were off Berry Head when a large French privateer came into sight, clearly in pursuit of the fireship. The *Etna* made all sail away but was overhauled by the privateer who lay on her quarter and opened fire with cannon and small shot. A Dutch 60-gun ship was in sight and the fireship attempted to get up to her but was dismayed when the warship tacked and stood away. Captain Anderson kept up a running fight for over an hour until he was shot and wounded in the arm, and the rigging badly cut up. The privateer then ran close alongside, and a volley of musketry cleared the upper deck, men quitting the guns to go below. The colours were shot away, and when they attempted to hoist them again, the privateer hailed and warned that no quarter would be given if they were replaced, and so they surrendered.
[TNA: ADM.1/5257]

30 April LOOE Fifth Rate
Plymouth 1696; 385 tons; 110ft x 28ft; 32 guns
Captain Richard Paul
Sailed from Plymouth 3 April to cruise in the western approaches to the English Channel, but she suffered from hard gales and rain for most of the time. On 24 April, it was decided to bear away for Kinsale, her provisions being poor, the bread particularly bad. The following evening, she anchored in Baltimore Bay, as it remained 'dirty, blowing weather'. The weather cleared by 30 April and with the wind at the south-west, she weighed to move closer into the shore. As she steered through the narrows the wind fell away and then shifted, which took her aback. She was carried into shallow water and tailed onto rocks. An anchor and cable were taken out to heave her free, but the cable parted and further attempts during the day failed to move her. As the tide left her, she settled and was bilged.
[TNA: ADM.1/5257]

1 May HOPEWELL Smack Tender
Hired 1696
Master Peter Taylor
Tender to the *Kingston*, fitting out at Hull, she was ordered to sail to Bridlington to embark some men. On her return she fell in with a French privateer from Dunkirk off Spurn Head and was captured.
[TNA: ADM.1/5257; ADM.106/512]

5 May SEAFORD Sixth Rate
Purchased 1695; 293 tons; 98.5ft x 26.1ft; 28 guns
Captain George Walton
One of a squadron of five warships escorting an outward-bound convoy for the West Indies, they were about 180 miles to the south-west of Ireland when in the early morning four large French warships were sighted. The Commodore, Captain Symonds in the *Norwich*, made the signal for the ships to form line of battle, and spread more sail, but in light winds the ships never achieved this. The *Seaford* became detached from the other ships and, with the *Blaze* fireship, found herself cut off. Captain Walton kept up a fight for four hours, initially against a 50-gun ship, but having got clear of her, faced another opponent of 70 guns. Her foretopsail yard and main yard were shot away, and eventually her mainmast went by the board. With 4ft of water in the hold, her rigging shattered and several killed and wounded, she surrendered. The French found her so badly damaged that they burnt her. Two of the convoy were also taken.
[TNA: ADM.1/5258; London Gazette 13 May & 24 May 1697]

5 May BLAZE Fireship
Purchased 1694; 253 tons; 93ft x 24.9ft; 8 guns
Captain John Wooden
In company with the *Seaford* when they were attacked by the Brest Squadron commanded by the Sieur d'Ardennes (see above). When the *Norwich* made the signal to form line of battle and spread sail, she soon fell astern, and became detached. Two of the French warships passed by her, without firing, to attack the *Seaford*, and Captain Wooden determined to send his men away and burn his ship, but only half of his men had been placed into nearby merchant ships before two French warships closed and placed themselves on each quarter. After an exchange of fire, in which Captain Wooden was wounded, and seeing no prospect of escaping, she surrendered.
[TNA: ADM.1/5258; London Gazette 13 May & 24 May 1697]

19 June MERCURY Advice Boat
Portsmouth 1694; 73 tons; 61.6ft x 16.1ft; 4 guns
Captain Thomas Warren
Ordered to look into Brest for intelligence, she spent three days loitering close off the French shoreline, and having obtained some good information, she made her way to seaward on a fresh north-easterly wind. On the morning of 19 June, with Ushant in sight, two ships were seen to be in chase of her, but she initially outstretched them. By afternoon, the wind was increasing, and a high sea was running, and the pair started to gain. The boat was heaved overboard, and the lee anchor cut away

to lighten her, but the pursuers steadily gained. By 6 o'clock in the afternoon they were within gunshot, and after several shots had been fired, unable to escape, she surrendered. Her captors were the St Malo privateers *le Comte de Frise*, 30 guns and *le Succès*, 12.
[TNA: ADM.1/5258]

28 July OWNER'S LOVE Fireship
Purchased 1688; 200 tons; 71.2ft × 22.6ft; 10 guns
Master and Commander Robert Lloyd†
Part of a small force ordered to Hudson's Bay to resupply the outposts at Fort Nelson and Fort York, she became detached from the group and was crushed by ice. At least ten men were lost
[TNA: ADM.106/3120; ADM.33/195; CTB July 1698; HCJ 1699]

22 August FLAME Fireship
Rotherhithe 1691; 273 tons; 91.7ft × 25.4ft; 8 guns
Captain Henry Searle
Sailed from Jamaica on 15 August in company with the *Southampton* to escort a convoy of five merchant ships to England and very soon after sailing, several leaks became evident, which required the pumps to be employed constantly. By 21 August she had 3ft of water in the hold and asked for assistance from the ships in company. The Master and Carpenter of the *Colchester* came on board and after a survey agreed that she was unable to proceed with the voyage to England and doubted that she could make Jamaica. A party of men from the *Southampton* was sent to relieve the men on the pumps and stores were transferred to other ships. During the next afternoon she was abandoned, having over 7ft of water in the hold. She sank at about 5.30 that afternoon, then being to the south-west of Cape St Nicholas, Hispaniola.
[TNA: ADM.52/33; ADM 106/483; London Gazette 14 October 1697]

26 August HAMPSHIRE Fourth Rate
Deptford 1686; 489 tons; 118ft × 30.2ft; 46 guns
Captain John Fletcher†
Tasked to convoy two ships of the Hudson's Bay Company to re-supply Fort York, as they neared the outpost on the south eastern shore of the Bay, they encountered the *Pélican*, 44 guns, commanded by Lemoyne d'Iberville. A prolonged three-hour engagement ensued, until the *Hampshire* foundered with a heavy loss of life. The *Pélican* then captured one of the supply ships but had been so severely damaged in her encounter with *Hampshire* that she was run into shallow water and lost. The French went on to capture the outpost.
[TNA: ADM.106/3120; Dictionary of Canadian Biography – entry for d'Iberville]

30 August ROE Ketch
Limehouse 1691; 92 tons; 62.2ft × 18.8ft; 10 guns
Master and Commander Robert Hawkins
Bound for the York River, Virginia, she approached the shore under the guidance of a local pilot, William Minsen. At about 4 o'clock in the afternoon she struck a sandbank about six miles from the river's mouth. She set out anchors to hold her fast until high tide, in hopes that she would float free, but she failed to do so, several leaks becoming apparent. Efforts to free her failed, and when she started to break up, she was abandoned. Mr Minsen the pilot was ordered to be secured, but apparently escaped before he could be tried for the loss.
[TNA: ADM.1/5260]

15 September SOUTHSEA CASTLE Fifth Rate
Redbridge 1696; 373 tons; 106.6ft × 28.2ft; 32 guns
Captain Thomas Legge
Caught in Liverpool Bay in poor weather, she attempted to take shelter in the Dee estuary. As she did so the main-topsail clew blew out, forcing Captain Legge to anchor amongst the sandbanks off Hoylake. During the evening, the wind increased, with heavy rain, and she struck yards and topmasts. By 11pm it was blowing a violent storm and she dragged her anchor and struck the ground and started bumping heavily. In an effort to ease her, the main and foremasts were cut away, but the following morning with the wind veering to the north-west, she was forced to cut her cables and under mizzen sail tried to run into Hoylake, but she struck the ground again. Her head swung round, and she lay on the sands with the sea beating over her until she started to break up.
[TNA: ADM.1/5259]

10/11 December HASTINGS Fifth Rate
Shoreham 1695; 384 tons; 108.8ft × 28.2ft; 32 guns
Captain John Draper†
The ship came to an anchor at Waterford in poor weather, but during the night the wind increased to gale force, and she was driven ashore and wrecked, with all the men drowned except for the Purser and four or five men.
[London Gazette 23 December 1697; HCJ 1699]

1698

24 January SWIFT Advice Boat
Arundel 1697; 154 tons; 76.11ft × 21.4ft; 10 guns
Master and Commander Nathaniel Bostock
Laying at anchor off Point Comfort, Virginia, the Commanding Officer and all senior warrant officers were onshore on various tasks. During the afternoon, the weather deteriorated, and large amounts of ice came

drifting downriver, surrounding the *Swift*, to such an extent that it 'sent her on the careen' and threatened to sink her. The senior officer on board was the surgeon, Richard Walton, who ordered the cables to be cut which allowed the vessel to drift free of the ice. The *Swift* grounded on sands near Point Comfort where the crew gained the shore. Overnight the wind steadily increased and the *Swift*, with no one on board, was blown out to sea. Several days later she was discovered on sandbanks off Currituck, North Carolina, but efforts to free her failed, and after removing what stores could be saved, she was abandoned as a wreck. Bostock was later found to have been negligent, in being absent ashore longer than his business required; he was fined four months' pay. The warrant officers were all cleared of any blame except for the Master, Christopher Potter, absent without authority. He was ordered to lose all pay due and dismissed the service.
[TNA:ADM.1/5260; CSPC:America and West Indies May 1698]

4 July FORESIGHT Fourth Rate
Deptford 1650; 522 tons; 102ft × 31.1ft; 52 guns
Captain Charles Richards
Escorting a brig with a cargo of slaves bound for Veracruz, Mexico, from Jamaica, the pair steered to the north-west, and at night continued under easy sail. At 2 o'clock in the morning the brig, which was ahead of the *Foresight*, was heard to fire a gun as a warning signal but then ran aground soon afterwards. An attempt was made to tack, but before the ship would come around the *Foresight* also ran aground. The longboat was hoisted out which carried out an anchor to haul themselves off, but this failed, and she filled with water. The crews of both ships managed to get ashore and survived for six weeks before a party in a small boat managed to reach a settlement on the island of Cuba and organised a rescue. It was found that the ships had been wrecked on the western edge of the Jardines de la Reina, 50 miles to the south of Cuba. It was believed that strong currents had set them further north than calculated.
[TNA:ADM.1/5260]

1699

12 November SOUTHSEA CASTLE Fifth Rate
Deptford 1697; 387 tons; 108ft × 28.6ft; 32 guns
Captain Thomas Stepney
Bound for Jamaica in company with the *Bideford*, the pair saw land on the beam during the evening of 11 November, which they believed to be the Île à Vache off the southern coast of Hispaniola. They steered west before altering to the north-west when they believed that they were clear of the island. The night was very dark and with regular rain squalls, and at about 2am breakers were seen close ahead, but before they could alter away the ship ran hard aground on the Île à Vache. Warning guns were fired to alert her consort, but little could be done for the ship, which soon filled with water and was abandoned as a wreck. The ship's officers were cleared of any blame for the loss, which was due to the uncertainty of the currents, coupled with the poor charts held on board and the darkness of the night.
[TNA:ADM.1/5261]

12 November BIDEFORD Sixth Rate
Harwich 1695; 256 tons; 93.1ft × 24.9ft; 24 guns
Captain Henry Searle
Companion to the *Southsea Castle* (see above), she followed her movements. The *Bideford* was first alerted to danger by the signal guns fired by the *Southsea Castle* after running aground on the Île à Vache. The *Bideford* attempted to tack but missed stays. Finding herself close to the shore she attempted to anchor, but the anchor became fouled in the chains, and she went ashore and was wrecked.
[TNA:ADM.1/5261]

2 December FOX Sloop
Sheerness 1699; 65 tons; 58.6ft × 16.4ft; 2 guns
Master and Commander Henry Gore
Caught in a storm off southern Ireland, the ship laboured in a strong south-easterly gale. They struck the topmast and lay to under reefed mainsail until about 8.30pm, when they were struck by a series of large waves which heeled the sloop over onto her beam-ends. She recovered but it was decided to run for the shelter of land, and the yard was struck and under bare poles the sloop drove into Castlehaven Bay. She anchored, but with the gale still blowing hard, the mast was cut away to ease the ship's movement. This proved only a temporary solution, as the anchor cables parted, and she was driven onto the rocks known as the Stags and wrecked. Eighteen men were drowned.
[TNA:ADM.1/5261]

1700

3 February INTELLIGENCE Brigantine
Woolwich 1696; 75 tons; 52ft × 16.6ft; 6 guns
Master and Commander John Clifton
Having sailed from Dublin to cruise in the Irish Sea, the weather worsened until by 2 February it was blowing hard, with heavy seas, and it was decided to take shelter and she anchored in Douglas Bay, Isle of Man. The wind continued to increase, and a further two anchors were let go, but the seas were constantly washing over her. The mainmast was cut away to ease her movement, but

4 July GERMOON PRIZE Sixth Rate
Prize 1691 (le Gramon); 103 tons; 68ft × 18ft; 6 guns
Master and Commander Philip Boys

Sailing from Jamaica on 17 May to cruise along the coastline of Panama in search of pirates, it became clear that the ship's bottom needed cleaning, and so Commander Boys initially took the ship inshore to heel and scrub the ship, but on doing so found that the lead sheathing on the bottom was damaged. They sailed on to Porto Bello (modern Portobelo), where they were able to careen her, hauling her over onto her side. The starboard side was successfully cleaned and repaired, and on 4 July she was hauled over onto her other side, but as they were doing so, the harbour was struck by a strong squall, and she rolled completely over to lay on her beam-ends and was wrecked.
[TNA: ADM.1/5261; ADM.1/1462]

19 September CARLISLE Fourth Rate
Plymouth 1698; 709 tons; 132ft × 34ft; 50 guns
Captain Francis Dove

The ship was lying at anchor in the Downs, with Captain Dove and several of the senior warrant officers ashore, when the ship was destroyed by a massive internal explosion which occurred at about 9 o'clock in the morning. The Master and seven others on board were saved, but 124 men were lost. The reason for the detonation was uncertain, but Mr Simon Flew, the Master, believed that gunpowder was being brought up to charge the guns for salutes, and carelessly spilled powder may have been the cause.
[TNA: ADM.1/5261]

6 October HARWICH Fourth Rate
Deptford 1695; 683 tons; 130.2ft × 34.4ft; 50 guns
Captain William Cock

One of the squadron sent to the Indian Ocean under Captain Littleton to suppress piracy, the *Harwich* was detached to the South China Sea, after reports of an active pirate in the area. After a fruitless search, in August she put into Amoy (modern Xiamen), China, to obtain provisions. The Carpenter reported that a bottom clean was necessary, and it was also feared that several planks and timbers needed to be replaced. After negotiating with the shore authorities, she was initially directed to a bay about two leagues (six miles) to the east of the harbour, where at the end of August she commenced offloading guns and stores and was then permitted to return to the outer harbour, where she was prepared for cleaning and repair. This was achieved by hauling her close to the shoreline and careening her, with anchors laid out to secure her, as well as lines to the shore. This allowed her to be heeled over onto her side to be breamed and defective timbers replaced. By early October this was complete and on 5 October work started to haul her off the shore. As they heaved on the cables, one of the shore securing lines became fouled and passed under the hull, which led to her swinging onto nearby rocks. Efforts to free her failed, and she began to take in water, her hull evidently having been pierced. Pumps were manned, and shores set up, but as the tide left her, she broke her lashings and capsized over onto her beam-ends. Work went on for some days to recover stores and rigging, and she was abandoned as a wreck on 13 October.
[TNA: ADM.1/5262; ADM.51/4215]

15 December FORTUNE Store ship
Purchased 1699
Master and Commander Unton Deering

A ship with a somewhat chequered history, apparently having been used by Dutch merchants in New York to bring slaves from Africa, but in 1698 she was seized by the colonial government in New York when it was found that she had been associated with piratical activities in the Indian Ocean. Lord Bellomont, the Governor of New York, then purchased her for the King and sent her to England loaded with timber for the royal dockyards. They sailed from Sandy Hook on 29 October, but the next day found that the lower rudder irons had given way. An attempt was made to bear up for New York, but little progress was made in strong contrary winds, so they decided to continue to England. Later, in mid-Atlantic, the rudder broke away completely. On 14 December land was sighted, which was identified as the Scilly Isles, and on a strong south-westerly gale they cleared the islands, to sight land they identified as Cape Cornwall the next morning. It was decided to head for St Ives Bay and anchor, and during the afternoon they ran close inshore and let go the best bower anchor in 9 fathoms but did not have enough cable to bring her up and it was found that she was driving. Despite letting go the small bower anchor as well, they continued to be carried inshore on a strong wind and tide. She eventually struck rocks and was wrecked near Holywell, on the coast of north Cornwall. Six men were drowned when a boat capsized. Much of the timber was subsequently salvaged.
[TNA: ADM.1/5261; ADM.106/547; CSPC: North America West Indies October 1700]

1701

24 February ROEBUCK Sixth Rate
Wapping 1690; 292 tons; 96ft × 25.6ft; 6 guns
Captain William Dampier

Returning to England after a voyage of exploration to Australia and New Guinea, as she approached the island of Ascension on 22 February, a bad leak became evident in the larboard bow. The *Roebuck* anchored in the north-west bay of the island in 10 fathoms about half a mile from the shore, while efforts were made to stop the leak. Some of the internal planking was taken up, but it seemed that a plank in the Gunner's storeroom, about four strakes up from the keel, was completely rotten. Despite pumping and bailing she was filling with water, so in the evening of 23 February she was warped inshore, and the boats hoisted out. The following day she was run further inshore until she ran aground, which allowed the crew to land before she foundered. The crew spent some time onshore before they attracted the attention of an East Indiaman to take them off the island. Dampier was cleared by court martial in September 1701 of any blame for the loss, but a further court martial followed in 1702 for his actions on board the *Roebuck*, when he was accused of cruelty to another officer. He was found guilty and was ordered to forfeit all pay due and not to be employed again.
[TNA:ADM.1/5262]

7 April LOYALTY Hulk
Purchased 1694; 400 tons

Since her purchase, the *Loyalty* had served at Cadiz, where she supported the British squadron on the Spanish coast and Mediterranean, both as a store ship and also in careening and cleaning. Fears that a war might break out with Spain led to the decision to withdraw the ships based at Cadiz. Captain Mark Noble in the Sixth Rate *Dunwich* was sent to prepare the hulks for sea and after arriving on 5 March spent much time and effort in getting up masts and rigging. By the first week in April strong rumours were circulating that war was imminent, and nearby Spanish warships were seen to be getting up topmasts and bending sails. It was decided to leave, although the ships were not complete. Taking advantage of the presence of a convoy under the protection of the *Tilbury*, the hulks were taken out the harbour, to anchor in the Bay of Bulls. The weather, however, turned against them, and strong winds and high seas forced most of the convoy back into the shelter of Cadiz harbour, one of the hulks doing the same. The *Loyalty* managed to ride out the storm but was seen to be making signals of distress. It was found that she was leaking badly, and the small party of men on board were exhausted by constant pumping and bailing. It was clear that she was unfit for a sea voyage, so Noble ordered as much of the stores as could be saved to be taken out of her, and she was then abandoned, the Carpenter aiding her end by cutting a hole in the bottom. She foundered just before midnight.
[TNA:ADM.1/2215; ADM.51/3825]

11 April ASIA Hulk
River Thames 1683, purchased 1694; 460 tons

As with the *Loyalty* (above), she was based at Cadiz to support the British squadron. After much work by the crew of the *Dunwich* to prepare her for sea, she was taken to the Bay of Bulls, opposite Cadiz harbour. Stormy weather proved too much for her, and she ran back into the anchorage. When the weather had moderated, on 10 April she sailed, in company with the *Dunwich*, but she could make little headway in the strong 'levanter' winds, and clearly in distress was forced inshore to anchor off Rota. She was rolling so heavily in the sea that it was difficult to work her, so the decision was made to abandon her. The sails were cut from the yards and all the men removed. The carpenter then cut holes in the bottom, and she was abandoned, to sink two hours later.
[TNA:ADM.1/2215; ADM.51/3825]

November MESSENGER Advice Boat
Plymouth 1694; 73 tons; 50.11ft × 16.5ft; 4 guns
Master and Commander Peter Coode† (or Coade)

Disappeared on passage from Maryland to England during this month and presumed to have foundered with all hands. With no news of her the books were closed by Admiralty Order of 15 October 1702 with pay up to 30 November 1701.
[CSPC: North America West Indies November: 1702; TNA: ADM.33/209]

1702–1715: War of the Spanish Succession

The disputed claims over the throne in Spain led to England joining in another war against France and Spain between May 1702 and March 1713. The main seat of the war was the Mediterranean, with districts and cities in Spain being persuaded or occasionally coerced into support for the appropriate candidate for the throne, with the naval forces assisting the army and interrupting enemy supplies. In home waters, commerce protection became increasingly important, and there were small-scale actions in the West Indies, with expeditions to Canadian waters to disrupt the French settlements. In 1707 the Kingdoms of England and Scotland, already a united monarchy, were linked by a single government, the small Scots Navy being absorbed into the British Navy.

1702

30 May POSTBOY Brigantine
Deptford 1696; 76 tons; 51.6ft × 16.8ft; 4 guns
Master and Commander Gilbert Frankland
Sailed with the fleet from the Nore bound for Spithead on 29 May, but in poor weather she fell astern and lay-to under reefed topsails for the night. The following day she tried to re-join but was still three leagues (nine miles) astern when, at about 7 o'clock in the evening, she decided to anchor off Beachy Head, but as she did so, two French ships closed under British colours. As they neared, they were recognised as being enemy ships, so the cable was cut, but one of them ran across her bows, fired a broadside and then a volley of small shot, killing one man. Several more volleys of fire followed, driving the men below, and unable to continue she surrendered.
[TNA: ADM.1/1777]

28 July OTTER Sloop
Deptford 1700; 83 tons; 61ft × 17.8ft; 4 guns
Captain Isaac Andrews†
Based in the West Indies, she was captured by a French privateer soon after sailing from Barbados and carried into Martinique.
[CSPC: North America West Indies November 1702; TNA: ADM.106/3120]

14 August PROHIBITION Sloop
Woolwich 1699; 68 tons; 48.4ft × 16.4ft; 2 guns
Master and Commander John Barter
Chased by a large 18-gun French privateer as she headed for Portsmouth from Liverpool, the *Prohibition* was overhauled south of the Scilly Isles. After a brief exchange of shots, in which one of the crew was wounded, the sloop surrendered.
[TNA: ADM.1/5264]

18 August SWIFT Sloop
Portsmouth 1699; 65 tons; 58.6ft × 16.6ft; 2 guns
Boatswain John Brookes (acting Commander)
Having carried despatches to Boston, Massachusetts, the commanding officer of the *Swift*, Commander Robert Jackson, was involved in a serious incident with the shore authorities. After pressing several seamen from ships in the harbour without authority, he was then verbally and physically abusive when challenged about his actions. An attempt to sail from the harbour was halted when the sloop was fired on from the shore, killing one man, and Commander Jackson was subsequently arrested. The Lieutenant-Governor then placed the Boatswain in command for the voyage back to England. When about 500 miles to the south-west of Lizard Point, a ship was sighted at first light, and fearing that it was an enemy, Brookes tacked and stood to the west. The stranger was clearly in pursuit, so the sloop was put before the wind to outrun her but found that she could not outpace her pursuer. By mid-morning the ship, which was the French privateer *Duc de Bourgogne*, 18 guns, was within gunshot and fired into the *Swift*, shooting away the topmast and cutting up the rigging. Unable to out sail her opponent, and outgunned, the *Swift* surrendered.
[TNA: ADM.1/5264; CSPC: America and West Indies July 1702]

30 August MARTIN Ketch
Southampton 1694; 99 tons; 52.7ft × 19ft; 6 guns
Master and Commander Thomas Warren
Cruising in the English Channel, she was chased by two French privateers off Jersey. The ketch attempted to outrun them, but finding herself unable to do so, the crew decided to resist, even though Warren was confined to his cabin with sickness. The ketch kept her opponents at bay for some time, until with rigging damaged and unable to get clear, she surrendered.
[TNA: ADM.1/5264]

1703

16 January LUDLOW Fifth Rate
Woodbridge 1698; 382 tons; 108ft × 28.3ft; 32 guns
Captain William Cock
On passage to Holland, with a ketch in tow, two ships were sighted that were clearly in chase, and as they closed it could be seen that they were French warships. The ketch was cut away and all sail was made to escape, but they steadily overhauled her, and she was caught by the largest of them, *l'Adroit*, 40 guns. Captain Cock kept up a running fight for four hours, before the second ship, *le Milford*, 30, came up and laid herself across the quarter of the *Ludlow*. At this, having thirty killed or wounded, she surrendered.
[TNA: ADM.1/5264]

(27/28) January LINCOLN Fourth Rate
Woolwich 1695; 676 tons; 130.7ft × 34.3ft; 50 guns
Captain Henry Middleton†
Sailed on 17 January from Spithead in company with the *Ipswich* and *Chester*, to escort a convoy of over thirty merchant ships clear of the Channel. The weather was good, with clear skies and a freshening wind. By 25 January, the weather was worsening, the wind steadily increasing in strength, and the following day, the ships were forced to lay-to under reduced sail in a hard gale and constant rain. They were then about 285 miles to the south-west of Lizard Point. During the night, the ships became separated, and the *Lincoln* was not seen again and was presumed to have foundered with all

hands soon after this. The ship was ordered to be paid off by Admiralty Order of 30 June 1703, with pay book closed on 29 January.
[TNA:ADM.106/3120;ADM.51/479;ADM.33/212]

30 March SHARK Sloop
Deptford 1699; 66 tons; 58.2ft × 16.1ft; 2 guns
Master and Commander George Fisher

Whilst chasing a French merchant snow in the English Channel, to the south of the Isle of Wight, a French warship of 40 guns came into view, which bore down on her. She stood away with the French ship in pursuit, but after a chase in misty weather, the French ship overtook her and stationed herself on the weather quarter of the sloop, taking the wind from her sails. Unable to escape her larger opponent, the *Shark* surrendered. Fisher was later court-martialled for having his wife on board during the engagement. He confessed that it was true, she was taking passage from Dover to Portsmouth, but the court acquitted him of any wrongdoing, as it was judged that '… her presence was not any hindrance to the service'.
[TNA:ADM. 1/5264]

10 April SALISBURY Fourth Rate
Baileys Hard 1698; 682 tons; 134.4ft × 34.2ft; 50 guns
Captain Richard Cotton

Sailed from the anchorage off the River Maes (Maas), on 9 April in company with the *Adventure* and *Muscovia Merchant*, to act as escorts to a large convoy of about sixty merchant ships and six yachts, bound for the Thames and east coast ports. The ships were about 50 miles off the Dutch coast, when at about 2pm they were approached by a squadron of seven French ships, led by the Chevalier de Saint-Pol Hécourt in *l'Adroit*, 40 guns. The *Salisbury* initially stood toward them, putting out her colours, but when it became clear that they were French, she tacked and stood inshore. She was overhauled and was engaged by both the *Adroit* and *Dryade*, 46, for two hours, until with masts, sails and rigging shattered, another two ships coming up to place themselves on her quarters, and having suffered seventeen dead and thirty-four wounded, she surrendered. The *Adventure* was unable to render any assistance as the French ships got between her and the *Salisbury*. She engaged with one privateer, driving it off in a sinking condition, and shepherded the yachts and other ships away, but the French went on to capture eight ships of the convoy.
[TNA:ADM.1/5264;ADM.51/11; de la Roncière vol 6 pp413–14]

10 April MUSCOVIA MERCHANT Store Ship
Hired 1702; 324 tons; 94.8ft × 25.4ft; 24 guns
Captain Daniel Parsons

One of the ships in the convoy being escorted by the *Salisbury* (see above), as the French ships came up, the *Muscovia* surrendered without offering any resistance, and was taken into Dunkirk. The ship's officers were criticised for failing to fight and were judged to have been wanting in their duties. However, it was recognised that she had been hired for service as a store vessel, and as Captain Parsons did not hold a commission from the Admiralty, he was referred to Prince George of Denmark as Lord High Admiral, to be punished 'as His Majesty thinks fit'.
[TNA:ADM.1/5264;ADM.106/577]

19 April SWALLOW Sloop
Chatham 1699; 66 tons; 59.2ft × 16ft; 2 guns
Master and Commander Henry Cremer

Chased by two large French privateers off Goeree, Holland, Cremer tried everything to escape, throwing stores overboard to lighten her. Despite this, she was overhauled and after a brief exchange of shots, the *Swallow* surrendered.
[TNA:ADM.1/5264]

21 September SQUIRREL Sixth Rate
Portsmouth 1703; 259 tons; 93.6ft × 24.8ft; 24 guns
Master and Commander Gilbert Talbot

Having sailed from the Downs anchorage to cruise off the coast of Kent between Rye and Folkestone, during the late morning a group of five ships were seen approaching from seaward. They were showing Dutch colours, and Commander Talbot had no concern until they were very close when it was realised that it was a ruse, and that they were French privateers. On realising his mistake, he wore round and stood out to sea, suffering a broadside from each of them as he did so. A chase developed and finding that he could not outrun them, an attempt was made to get under the guns of Sandhurst Castle, but this failed and with her main yard shot away, she was captured. Talbot was found guilty by court martial of 'want of judgement and ill conduct' in failing to have his ship in a fit posture for the engagement. He was ordered to forfeit all pay due, serve a year in prison and not to be given a position of command again. The Boatswain, Thomas Roberts, was found guilty of neglect in failing to provide extra rope slings for the main yard and failing to show the character expected of a warrant officer. He was dismissed from the Navy.
[TNA:ADM/1/5264]

12 October FIREDRAKE Bomb
Deptford 1693; 279 tons; 85.2ft × 24.1ft; 12 guns
Master and Commander Edward Rainey†

The *Firedrake* was part of the fleet under Admiral Shovell in the Mediterranean, which sailed from Leghorn (Livorno) on 2 October to return to England. When they were about eight leagues (24 miles) from

Minorca they were struck by a violent storm, which split the sails and damaged yards of the ships. The *Firedrake* disappeared at this time and was presumed lost with all hands.
[TNA: ADM.106/3120; Laughton: Torrington Memoirs p109]

15 October SERPENT Bomb
Chatham 1693; 261 tons; 86ft × 26.6ft; 12 guns
Master and Commander John Williams
In company with Admiral Graydon on his return from Canada, the bomb vessel lost contact with the squadron during the night of 12 September after the main topmast went by the board. Her misfortunes continued when the mainsail split, forcing the main yard to be lowered, and she continued independently under staysails. On the morning of the 15th, then in the western approaches to the English Channel, several ships were seen to the south-east, one of which was seen to detach and steer towards the bomb. They were quite unable to escape, and very soon a large 24-gun privateer was within gunshot. They resisted for as long as they could, but after firing four broadsides, the privateer ran close alongside at which they surrendered. Their captor was the *Comte de Revel* of St Malo.
[TNA: ADM.1/2642; ADM.1/5264]

22 November YORK Fourth Rate
Blackwall 1653 (*Marston Moor*); 749 tons; 139ft × 35ft; 60 guns
Captain John Smith
On passage to the Nore from the Downs anchorage, the ship was under the guidance of a pilot from Deal, Marmaduke Farrer (or Ferrar). The weather was hazy, and as they steered to the north-north-west Farrer had difficulty in seeing landmarks but believed he could identify Bawdsey church on the Suffolk coast. Soon after, the ship was found to be coming into shallow water, and the main topsail was put aback, but her stern struck the ground. Boats were hoisted out and anchors laid out in efforts to haul her free, but this failed. Stores were heaved overboard and water butts emptied in efforts to lighten her, but it was no use, and as she bumped on the sands, water was reported entering the ship. She steadily filled with water and was finally abandoned as a wreck. Four men were lost when leaving the ship. The subsequent court martial found that the ship had run onto the south-west part of the Shipwash Sand off Harwich through the 'ignorance and negligence' of the pilot. In his defence, he claimed that the compass was defective, and the crew had missed stays in their attempts to come about. Both latter charges were denied by the ship's officers. Farrer was ordered to be imprisoned for a year and never to pilot one of HM ships again.
[TNA: ADM.1/5264]

27 November: The Great Storm
The night of 26/27 November 1703 saw one of the greatest storms ever to strike the southern half of England. The weather had been poor for several days, with strong winds and rain, but during the evening of the 26th the winds became increasingly strong and reached hurricane force in the early hours of the morning. The storm moved rapidly across southern England in a line from the Bristol Channel to the Thames Estuary, leaving a trail of destruction. The damage caused was extensive, the Eddystone lighthouse was demolished, and it '... Blew down a Multitude of Chimneys, Tops of Houses, and even whole buildings ... beat down spires of churches, Roll'd up great quantities of Lead, like Scrolls of Parchment'. Not surprisingly, shipping suffered greatly – '... a great Number of Vessels, Barges and Boats were sunk in the River Thames, and the Arches of London Bridge were stop'd with the Wrecks of them'.
[TNA: ADM.106/575; Lediard's Naval History vol 2 p779; London Gazette 29 November and 2 December 1703]

The following men of war were lost:

VANGUARD Second Rate
Portsmouth 1678; 1,357 tons; 160ft × 44.10ft; 90 guns
The *Vanguard* was out of commission, lying at moorings in the river Medway at Chatham when the storm broke. At about 4am, the swivel of the mooring parted, and she drove across the harbour endangering other ships. A party of dockyard officers and shipwrights led by Robert Shortis, Master Shipwright, with his assistant Jacob Acworth and Sampson Bourne the Master Attendant, managed to get aboard and cut a hole in the bottom, which effectively sank her. During 1704 she was successfully raised, and she was ordered on 21 March 1705 to be taken into a dock at Chatham and rebuilt.
[TNA: ADM.1/5264]

NORTHUMBERLAND Third Rate
Chatham 1702; 1,096 tons; 152ft × 40.4ft; 70 guns
Captain James Greenaway[†]
At anchor in the Downs, she was blown from the anchorage in the early hours of the 27th and driven onto the Goodwin Sands where she was wrecked. There were no survivors from a crew of 220 men.
[TNA: ADM.106/575; various secondary]

RESOLUTION Third Rate
Chatham 1698; 902 tons; 148.2ft × 37.6ft; 70 guns
Captain Thomas Lyell
The *Resolution* was at anchor in St Helens roads, off the Isle of Wight, with topmasts and yards struck when the storm broke. After the bower anchor cable parted,

an attempt was made to weigh, but this failed as the anchor cable could not be brought home. At just after midnight, the small bower cable parted, and the sheet and stream anchors were let go, but no sooner had they brought up the ship than they parted. An attempt was then made to set sail, but the sails were immediately blown out. Driving before the hurricane, she grounded on a mud bank, but drove over the obstruction, heavily striking several times as she did. The *Resolution* was now driven up Channel, in an increasingly poor condition, with the pumps unable to cope. During the morning, when it became clear that she could not survive for much longer, she was run ashore on the coast near Pevensey. All 221 men on board survived.
[TNA: ADM.1/5264]

RESTORATION Third Rate
Portsmouth 1702; 1,045 tons; 150.9ft x 40ft; 70 guns
Captain Fleetwood Emes†
Like the *Northumberland* (see above), she was driven from her anchorage in the Downs and onto the Goodwin Sands, where she was wrecked, with no survivors; 391 men drowned.
[Various secondary]

STIRLING CASTLE Third Rate
Chatham 1699; 1,087 tons; 151.2ft x 40.6ft; 70 guns
Captain John Johnson
Wrecked on the Goodwin Sands after being blown from the anchorage in the Downs, with 206 men drowned. Four officers and seventy men were saved from the wreck the following day by the efforts of boats from Deal
[Various secondary]

MARY Fourth Rate
Woolwich 1688; 829 tons; 143ft x 36.8ft; 60 guns
Captain Edward Hopson
Flagship of Admiral Basil Beaumont, she was the senior ship in the Downs. Captain Hopson was ashore when the storm broke and was unable to return on board. The ship was driven from the anchorage and onto the Goodwin Sands, where she was wrecked. The Admiral, with 269 men, were drowned. One man was saved. Having been swept off the *Mary*, he was carried down to the wreck of the *Stirling Castle* and rescued the following day
[Various secondary]

NEWCASTLE Fourth Rate
Rotherhithe 1692; 642 tons; 131ft x 33.4ft; 50 guns
Captain William Carter†
Lying at anchor off Portsmouth at Spithead, she was driven from her anchors and foundered, the ship breaking up, with the wreckage being strewn along the shore near Chichester '... the most doleful spectacle that ever mortal eye behold it is covered with wreck to which a man cannot set a foot clear'. One hundred and ninety-three men were lost, forty men being saved from the wreck.
[TNA: ADM.106/570; Various secondary]

RESERVE Fourth Rate
Deptford 1701; 580 tons; 117.6ft x 33.7ft; 50 guns
Captain John Anderson
At anchor off Gorleston, Norfolk, the Captain and several crew members were onshore and unable to return in the rising storm. Despite cutting away the masts and bowsprit, she was overwhelmed by the storm, filled with water and foundered at her anchors. One hundred and seventy-four men died, but the Surgeon, clerk and forty-four others were saved.
[TNA: ADM.1/5264; ADM.106/577]

VIGO Fourth Rate
Rotherhithe 1693 (*Dartmouth*); 605 tons; 122ft x 33.6ft; 50 guns
Captain Thomas Long
At anchor off Hellevoetsluys, Holland, when the hurricane struck, as the storm increased, she put out another anchor, but despite this, by 6 o'clock in the morning she was dragging her anchors. Other ships were constantly threatening her by driving across the anchorage. She struck the ground a little later, shattering the rudder and driving the tiller up into the great cabin. The ship heeled over '... the seas making free passage over her, so that there was no standing on the deck'. She then drove onto some piles near the shore which stove her quarter in, and she rapidly filled and sank. Most of the crew survived.
[TNA: ADM.1/5265]

PORTSMOUTH Bomb
Deptford 1674; 143 tons; 71ft x 21.4ft; 10 guns
Master and Commander George Hawes†
Foundered at the buoy of the Nore and lost with all hands. Fifty men, including four 'fireworkers and bombardiers,' were lost.
[TNA: ADM.106/3120; ADM.33/221]

VESUVIUS Fireship
Shoreham 1693; 270 tons; 92ft x 25.7ft; 24 guns
Master and Commander George Paddon
At anchor at Spithead when the storm broke, and despite cutting away the masts, her cables parted, and she drove ashore with the sea beating over her. The *Expedition*, also riding at Spithead, rode out the storm and seeing the men clinging to the shrouds and rigging of the fireship, successfully launched a boat which managed to save them all. Her commanding officer had

been ashore in Cowes and was unable to return before the storm – he found her stranded under Southsea Castle. During 1704 she was successfully re-floated, but the damage was such that she was not recommissioned and was ordered on 7 September 1705 to be broken up in Portsmouth Dockyard.
[TNA: ADM.1/2278; ADM.51/327]

EAGLE Advice Boat
Arundel 1697; 154 tons; 76ft × 21.4ft; 10 guns
Master and Commander Nathaniel Bostock
Lying in St Helen's Bay, Isle of Wight, when the storm struck, at about 1 o'clock in the morning one of the anchor cables parted and the other was cut, as '… she lay her gunnels underwater'. The mainmast was cut away, the mizzen following shortly after, to stabilise the vessel. She drove before the wind and at 4 o'clock in the morning ran onto the Sussex shore near Selsey and rapidly broke up.
[TNA: ADM.1/5264]

CANTERBURY Store Ship
Purchased 1692; 367 tons; 96ft × 28.11ft; 8 guns
Captain Thomas Blake†
At anchor off Bristol with other store ships and merchant vessels, they were driven from their anchors onto the shore, the *Canterbury* being grounded about four miles from King Road. The sea beat over her for several hours before the survivors managed to get ashore, but the Captain and about twenty men had died by then. The tide was reported to flow over her at high tide, her rudder beaten off and the half deck collapsed. Work went on for some time to clear the ship of its lading and the wreck was eventually hauled off the shore and taken into Bristol on 9 February 1704 but was found to be so badly damaged that the remains were sold on 29 February.
[TNA: ADM.106/567; London Gazette 10 February 1704]

* * *

2 December MORTAR Bomb
Chatham 1693; 260 tons; 69.9ft × 26.6ft; 12 guns
Captain Baymont Raymond
During the Great Storm of 26/27 November, she was laying at anchor in the Downs, and in the early hours of the morning the bower anchor cable parted and despite letting the sheet anchor go, she started dragging. Both main and mizzen masts were cut away, and she drove out to sea. After being driven across the North Sea, she successfully anchored off the Dutch coast near Goeree. She remained there for two days until it was found that the anchor cable was about to part. With no anchors left and her masts gone, she was allowed to go onto a sandbank, where her crew left the vessel in safety. She broke up shortly afterwards.
[TNA: ADM.1/5264]

1704

16 January COLCHESTER Fourth Rate
Blackwall 1694; 697 tons; 131.4ft × 34.3ft; 50 guns
Captain David Wavell†
On her passage from Kinsale in Ireland to Plymouth, she was driven ashore and wrecked in Whitesand Bay near Land's End during a strong westerly gale. Only eighteen men were subsequently mustered after the disaster, with the Purser and the Master, Henry Anderson, being the only officers to survive. The wreck site attracted people from a wide area to plunder the remains. When Commissioner William Wright arrived some days after the wreck, he reported that although some guns, with an anchor and cable had been saved, the site had been '… pillaged and pilfered by the country people' and that despite the presence of officers to prevent this, '… they carry it away before his face'. Notices were placed on church doors in several parishes, urging people to surrender what they had, but these yielded no results.
[TNA: ADM.106/581; ADM.106/594; ADM.106/3120]

14 March SEAHORSE Sixth Rate
Limehouse 1694; 256 tons; 93.10ft × 24.9ft; 24 guns
Captain William Jones
Sailed from Port Royal, Jamaica, intending to get intelligence of the Spanish forces, but soon after sailing, she sighted and chased a French privateer. The chase went on for some time until the privateer steered inshore and eventually ran into Manchioneal Bay. The *Seahorse* followed, with the Boatswain acting as pilot to guide her in. However, as they closed, they came under fire from parties of men that had landed from the privateer and then ran onto a rock and settled, rapidly filling with water. Captain Jones landed with a large party of men from the *Seahorse* and after driving off the enemy, boarded and captured the privateer. All the guns and most of her sails and stores were subsequently salvaged from the *Seahorse*, but the hull was found to be in poor condition, badly affected by the ship worm or *teredo* and she was abandoned as a wreck.
[TNA: ADM.1/5265; CSPC: North America West Indies May 1704]

24 June WOLF Sloop
Portsmouth 1699; 65 tons; 58.6ft × 16.6ft; 10 guns
Master and Commander Wagden Baker†
Chased, overhauled and boarded by a large French privateer in the North Sea off the Humber Estuary, she continued to resist after the commanding officer was

killed, but surrendered when the enemy ran alongside and entered a number of boarders.

Note: The sloop was recaptured by the Dutch in December and restored to the Royal Navy.
[TNA: ADM.1/5265]

24 July COVENTRY Fourth Rate
Deptford 1695; 670 tons; 106ft × 34.5ft; 50 guns
Captain Henry Lawrence
Escorting an outward-bound convoy for Newfoundland, they were about 200 miles south-west of the Scilly Isles, when several ships were sighted at first light, which proved to be a squadron under the command of Duguay-Trouin. The French closed and whilst *l'Auguste*, 50 guns, made for the main body of the convoy, Duguay-Trouin in *le Jason*, 50, engaged the *Coventry*. An initial attempt by the French to board was driven off, but after only a short exchange of fire, the *Coventry* surrendered, the whole action taking less than 45 minutes. The French squadron went on to capture several ships of the convoy. Captain Lawrence was later judged to have been 'highly wanting' in his conduct; he was ordered to forfeit all pay due to him and to be imprisoned for seven years. The First Lieutenant, Lionel Lee, also forfeited all pay due and the Master, Jonathan Booth, was dismissed the service and lost all pay due.

Note: The ship was re-taken in May 1709 but not recommissioned.
[TNA: ADM.1/5266]

1 August FOWEY Fifth Rate
Shoreham 1696; 377 tons; 108ft × 28.2ft; 32 guns
Captain Richard Brown
Part of the escort to a large homeward-bound convoy from New England, they were to the south of the Scilly Isles when she was ordered to investigate a strange sail. She stretched away, but lost sight of the convoy in patches of thick fog. As the mist lifted, she found herself close to a squadron of seven French warships commanded by the Chevalier Saint-Pol-Hécourt in *le Salisbury*, 50 guns. She altered away and tried to outrun them, but failing in this, she maintained a running fight for some time, until her rigging and sails were so shattered that she could no longer manoeuvre, and with an attempt to run herself ashore blocked, she surrendered.
[TNA: ADM.1/5266]

4 August FALMOUTH Fourth Rate
Limehouse 1693; 611 tons; 611 tons; 124ft × 33.7ft; 50 guns
Captain Thomas Kenny†
Sailed from Plymouth on 20 July in company with the *Revenge* to cruise in the western approaches to the Channel, and initially had some success, capturing the corvette *la Mouche*, which had become detached from Duguay-Trouin's squadron. They encountered the main French squadron on 27 July, but as the enemy were superior, the British pair manoeuvred to stay clear and escape. They were about 150 miles to the west of the Lizard, when at 8 o'clock in the morning, eight ships were sighted to windward. Fearing that they were the French squadron they had escaped from earlier, the *Revenge* made the signal for an enemy in sight and the pair made sail away, hoping to join two ships seen to the northward, which they believed were British, the *Falmouth* being astern of her companion. The strangers, which were the Dunkirk squadron commanded by Saint-Pol-Hécourt in the *Salisbury*, came down on the wind and soon came within gunshot. A running fight developed with the *Falmouth* being engaged by *l'Amphitrite*, 50 guns, and *l'Héroïne*, 20. Captain Kenny was killed during the engagement, but Lieutenant Robert Johnson continued to fight her until she was in such a disabled condition, and with a further two French ships, both ex-British, the *Salisbury* and *Jersey*, coming up, that at about 11am, she surrendered. The *Revenge* continued to fight for another two hours, until with wind freshening, the French gave up the chase and she managed to escape.
[TNA: ADM.1/5265; ADM.51/4310]

22 September HENRY and JANE Smack Tender
Hired 1704; 4 guns
Master Henry Roote
Tender to the *Namur*, she lost touch with the fleet as it returned to England from the Mediterranean, the smack splitting her sails attempting to keep up. A squadron of three French ships under the command of Saint-Pol-Hécourt in the ex-British *Salisbury* overhauled her in the approaches to the Channel and forced her to surrender. The tender was burnt by her captors.
[TNA: ADM.1/5265]

22 September SAINT GEORGE Smack Tender
Hired 1704; 4 guns
Master John Green
Tender to the *Royal Katherine*, she kept company with the *Henry and Jane* tender (see above), after losing touch with the main fleet as it returned from the Mediterranean. On being overhauled by three French warships to the west of Ushant, she surrendered without a fight when the former British *Salisbury* came alongside. The men were taken out and the smack was then burnt.
[TNA: ADM.1/5265]

17 October TERROR Bomb
Limehouse 1696; 149 tons; 65.8ft × 23.6ft; 4 guns
Master and Commander Isaac Cooke
Moored at the Old Mole at Gibraltar when she was attacked, at just after midnight, by eleven French rowing

boats, which were towing a tartane, a lateen-rigged trading craft. The detachment of soldiers on board fired a volley of musketry into the approaching enemy, but before they could reload, the boats came alongside and boarded and soon took command. The tartane, which had been fitted out as a fireship, was then brought alongside the *Terror* and set her alight, burning both vessels.
[TNA: ADM. 1/5265]

12 November ELIZABETH Third Rate
Portsmouth 1704; 1,153 tons; 153.3ft × 41.5ft; 70 guns
Captain William Crosse
Sailed from Cork on 8 November in company with the *Chatham*, 54 guns, to convoy a number of ships to England, but being short-handed and with a sickly crew, it was decided to bear away for Plymouth. At 10 o'clock, when 30 miles to the south of the Scilly Isles, four ships were sighted ahead of them, which was Duguay-Trouin's squadron, with the *l'Auguste*, 50, *le Jason*, 50 and *la Valeur*, 30, with a prize. The *Elizabeth* stood on, '... running at ten knots', Crosse insisting that the strangers were Dutch. Not until they were within pistol shot was the ship cleared for action, and then lost their main and mizzen topmasts as they brought to, with the *Jason* on their quarter, the *Chatham* still being some way astern. They fought for about 30 minutes until with the *Jason* now ahead and raking her, and preparing to board, the *Elizabeth* struck her flag in surrender. The *Chatham* meanwhile fought off the *Auguste* and escaped to the north. At his court-martial, Captain Crosse was found guilty of '... notorious management and ill-conduct', in that he had entered action ill-prepared, failed to animate the seamen under his command or behave himself as he ought. In his defence, Crosse claimed that his ship was ill-manned, his crew untrained, there were nearly 100 men on the sick list and the ship had suffered 52 killed and wounded in the action. Nevertheless, he was ordered to suffer life imprisonment, forfeit all pay due and never be employed again. The prison sentence was later lifted, but he never served again.
[TNA: ADM. 1/5266; ADM.5 1/1190]

1705

11 August PLYMOUTH Third Rate
Blackwall 1705; 897 tons; 140.5ft × 38.3ft; 60 guns
Captain Hercules Mitchell†
The night of 10/11 August saw a particularly violent storm affect the southern half of the country, with ships being driven from their anchors and losing masts and yards. The *Plymouth* disappeared in the Channel at this time and was presumed to have foundered with the loss of all hands.
[London Gazette 13 August 1705]

10 October FLAMBOROUGH Sixth Rate
Chatham 1697; 252 tons; 94ft × 24.8ft; 24 guns
Master and Commander Joseph Winder
Stationed at Gibraltar for the support of the garrison there, she was cruising in the Straits when chased and captured by the French *Jason*, 54 guns, off Cape Spartel, after an engagement which lasted 45 minutes. After the action, her captors found that the ship was so severely damaged that it was scuttled.
[De La Roncière vol 6 p383]

20 October BLACKWALL Fourth Rate
Blackwall 1696; 678 tons; 131.1ft × 34.2ft; 54 guns
Captain Samuel Martin
One of three escorts to a homeward-bound Baltic trade convoy of twelve ships, they were off the Dogger Bank in the North Sea, when they sighted the Dunkirk Squadron of five warships and six privateers under the command of the Chevalier Saint-Pol-Hécourt. The escorts placed themselves between the oncoming enemy and the convoy. The *Blackwall* was engaged by the *Protée*, 50 guns, which ran alongside and attempted to board. This was fiercely resisted and the *Pendennis* came to her aid and fired into the French ship's unengaged side. The fight continued for some time until *le Triton*, 50, arrived to assist and with *le Salisbury* coming up, the *Blackwall* gave up the unequal fight and surrendered.
[TNA: ADM. 1/5266]

20 October PENDENNIS Fourth Rate
Deptford 1695; 682 tons; 130.2ft × 34.3ft; 54 guns
Captain John Foljambe†
One of the Baltic trade escorts engaged by the Dunkirk Squadron under Saint-Pol-Hécourt in the North Sea, she fought the ex-British *Salisbury* for some time, with some success, as the French ship fell away after Saint-Pol had been shot and mortally wounded. Foljambe then pushed forward to come to the support of the *Blackwall*, until the *Triton*, 50, arrived, at which *Blackwall* surrendered. With *le Salisbury* closing, the *Pendennis* was now faced with three ships, and she surrendered.
[TNA: ADM. 1/5266]

20 October SORLINGS Fifth Rate
Shoreham 1694; 362 tons; 102.8ft × 28.2ft; 32 guns
Captain William Coney
The third of the ill-fated Baltic convoy escort taken by the French squadron of Saint-Pol-Hécourt, she engaged and held off *Jersey*, 30 guns, until the French ship ran her on board and entered a large number of men. After a brief fight, the *Sorlings* surrendered. The French squadron went on to capture ten ships of the convoy, laden with tar, pitch and hemp.
[TNA: ADM. 1/5266]

5 December OWNER'S ADVENTURE Smack Tender
Hired 1704
Master Thomas Teer

Tender to the *Devonshire*, she was on passage from Gibraltar to England, but lost contact with the fleet in bad weather. When in the western approaches to the Channel, to the west of Ushant, she was chased and captured by a large French privateer, *Jarret*, 28 guns. The tender was subsequently released for a ransom of £100. A seaman, Anthony Gibson of Barking, was taken hostage until the money was paid. Unfortunately, the owners of the smack were reluctant to pay the ransom, and it was not until the mother and sister of Gibson pleaded with one Josiah Greene of Wapping to pay the money that the hostage was released after a year in France.
[TNA: ADM.1/5270]

10 December LAUREL Stores Ketch
Hired 1705; 4 guns
Master Thomas Merryman

After delivering her cargo of pitch and tar to Plymouth Dockyard, she was returning to the Nore when foul weather took her onto the French coast. She took shelter in Havre de Grace Bay, but when she got underway, she was chased and captured by a French 18-gun privateer.
[TNA: ADM.1/5266]

12 December LOOE Fifth Rate
Portsmouth 1697; 357 tons; 108.1ft × 27.8ft; 32 guns
Captain Timothy Bridges

Having sailed from Newfoundland with a homeward-bound convoy, she parted company in poor weather, and was on her own as she approached the western end of the Isle of Wight on a strong south-westerly wind. Captain Bridges asked the Master if they could safely pass by the Needles, the Master believing they could. However, as they approached the rocks the wind shifted to the west-north-west with squalls of rain. They tried to tack, but missed stays, so quickly let go an anchor to bring her head round. This done, the cable was cut, but she was too close to the land and went ashore in Scratchwell Bay. With the wind steadily increased and in rising seas, the masts were cut away to try and ease her, but it was clear that she was a wreck. A raft was constructed which made the shore, despite some men being washed off, and others were hauled up the cliffs. Eight men were drowned.
[TNA: ADM.1/5266; ADM.1/1467]

19 December FALKLAND'S PRIZE Fifth Rate
Prize 1704 (*la Seine*); 732 tons; 132.6ft × 35ft; 46 guns
Captain William Fairborne

Having escorted a convoy from North America, the *Falkland's Prize* anchored in the Downs on 15 December in poor weather, with strong winds and rain. During 18 December she parted her cables but let go the sheet anchor which brought her up and was later able to lay out the small bower anchor. The winds continued to increase and the following day it was a hard gale from the south-east and at nine o'clock in the evening the bower anchor cable parted, and she started to drag. The sheet anchor cable could be seen to be parting at the bitts, so Captain Fairborne decided to cut the cable, and the ship was rapidly carried inshore until she grounded in shallow water in Sandwich Bay a little to the south of the town. The Master Attendant came on board with a small team from the Dockyards on 22 December, and believed that the ship could be saved, but all the guns and stores must be removed first. Work went on raising sheers to lift out the heavy items, but their efforts were hampered by the continued poor weather and lack of men – most of the crew had been put ashore and many promptly disappeared. Parties of men were sent from Deal and other ships, but they struggled to cope. On 29 December, an examination showed that she had settled further into the sand, but they continued to get stores out of her. The ship was examined by local ship owners and pilots on 5 January and found to have 12ft of water in the hold, several timbers and joints were destroyed and '… water is flowing as fast within board as without' and she was abandoned on 12 January. Some remains of the ship were salved, but the wreck was ordered to be sold 11 March 1706.
[TNA: ADM.1/5266; ADM.1/1777; ADM.51/376]

21 December BENJAMIN Store Ketch
Hired 1705; 4 guns
Master Henry Gyles

Bound for Rotterdam from the Downs with a convoy to embark a cargo of pitch and tar for the dockyards, she became separated during night from the other ships. In the morning two ships were sighted closing, and she made sail away but was quickly overhauled and when hailed surrendered, her captors being privateers from Ostend.
[TNA: ADM.1/5266]

1706

2 March PRECIOUS Sloop Tender
Hired 1705; 2 guns
Master Thomas Dewstowe

Tender to the *Swiftsure*, with Lieutenant John Ripley aboard, the sloop was sailing to Lyme Bay to press men, when she was chased by a French 6-gun privateer. Lieutenant Ripley and the small crew kept the privateer at bay for two hours, until with the rigging badly damaged and several shots in the hull, the Master ran her ashore to prevent capture.
[TNA: ADM.1/5266]

4 March JOHN and SARAH Hoy Tender
Hired 1705; 4 guns
Master Richard Green

Tender to the *Dorsetshire*, she lost contact with the larger ship in thick weather south of the Isle of Wight whilst on passage to Portsmouth. In a break in the gloomy weather, she sighted a group of ships under Dutch colours, which she allowed to approach, until she realised that they were French privateers. After a 14-gun privateer had come alongside and fired two shots accompanied by a volley of musketry into her, she surrendered when hailed. The Master took some blame for the loss, as he had tacked to the west, against his orders.
[TNA: ADM.1/5266]

23 May FERRET Sloop
Blackwall 1704; 128 tons; 72ft × 20ft; 10 guns
Master and Commander Nicholas Smith

Ordered to gain intelligence of the enemy, she sailed from the Downs and made towards the French coast. The next morning, she found herself off Calais, and steered north along the coast to Gravelines. Several fishing boats could be seen ahead, and after a short chase, she overhauled and captured one, the intention being to interrogate the skipper. She was now about five miles from Dunkirk, and six galleys could be seen lying off that port. Her actions had clearly gained their attention, as they quickly put to sea in pursuit of her. She headed away from the coast, but the wind fell away to a dead calm, and she was forced to use sweeps (long oars) to maintain headway. The galleys however, seen to be rowing with fifty-two oars each, approached quickly, and just an hour after capturing the fishing boat, she was forced to release her prize. Any hopes that this might detain her pursuers proved to be in vain, as they pressed on. After a three-hour chase the leading galley was close in her wake and started the engagement by firing a shot into her stern. The sloop returned fire when she could, but the galley manoeuvred to keep clear. When another two galleys joined in the dispute, they joined to run close alongside, and unable to defend herself, with the hull holed, her rigging torn and several killed and wounded, she surrendered.
[TNA: ADM.1/5266]

6 June WINCHELSEY Fifth Rate
Redbridge 1694; 365 tons; 103.5ft × 28.4ft; 36 guns
Captain John Castle†

Chased by a squadron of five French privateers when off Hastings, the *Winchelsey* engaged the first to come up with her, but the initial exchange of fire killed Captain Castle. Lieutenant Thomas Ashton continued the fight, but as other ships closed, found he was engaged on both sides, and when boarded by a 32-gun ship, he surrendered.
[TNA: ADM.1/5266]

3 July DEAL CASTLE Sixth Rate
Deptford 1697; 240 tons; 91.11ft × 24.1ft; 24 guns
Master and Commander Chaloner Ogle

Chased by three large privateers, she was overhauled by the largest of them, a ship of 26 guns, when about 20 miles north of Ostend. She maintained a fight for about an hour until her helm was shot away, killing the two men stationed there. This caused her to fly up into the wind, throwing her sails aback. The French ship shot ahead to take station across the bows and raked her. The other privateers could be seen closing, and with the rigging badly cut up and unable to defend herself, the *Deal Castle* surrendered. Seven men were killed in the engagement.
[TNA: ADM.1/5266; ADM.1/2241]

7 July SQUIRREL Sixth Rate
Portsmouth 1704; 259 tons; 93.6ft × 24.8ft; 24 guns
Master and Commander Daniel Butler†

Chased by several French privateers off Dover, she was unable to get away and forced to engage them. Captain Butler was killed soon after the action started, but Lieutenant Ellis Brand continued to fight her, until surrounded and captured.

Note: recaptured but foundered 15 March 1708.
[TNA: ADM 1/5266]

28 July GOSPORT Fifth Rate
Shoreham 1696; 377 tons; 107.9ft × 28.11ft; 32 guns
Captain Edward St Loe

Bound for Jamaica with a large convoy under her charge, she was about 400 miles to the south-west of the Lizard when two ships were sighted closing. By noon, the largest of them, the *Jason*, 54 guns, was close enough to hoist French colours, fire a broadside and a volley of small arms and run alongside and attempt to board. This was initially driven off and firing continued between the pair for over 30 minutes before the *Jason* again ran alongside and entered a large number of boarders. Fierce hand-to-hand fighting went on for some time, until with twenty men killed and forty wounded, the *Gosport* surrendered.
[TNA: ADM.1/5266]

28 August FOX PRIZE Sixth Rate
Prize 1705 (*Le Beringhen*); 273 tons; 76ft × 26ft; 24 guns
Master and Commander Henry Roche†

In storm-force winds, she attempted to anchor off Holyhead, Anglesey, but one anchor broke and the cable of the second parted. This led her to be driven ashore and wrecked with heavy loss of life.
[TNA: ADM.1/5266]

10 October COMET Bomb
Blackwall 1695; 143 tons; 66.1ft × 23.2ft; 4 guns
Master and Commander Francis Gregory†
Captured after being chased by a force of three large French privateers off Dunkirk, she finally surrendered when a 30-gun ship ran close alongside. Captain Gregory died of his wounds later.
[TNA: ADM.1/5266]

23 October SARAH Ketch Tender
Hired 1706; 145 tons; 4 guns
Master William Richardson
Tender to the *Prince George*, she lost contact with the fleet in poor weather when in the western Channel. When she was to the south of the Lizard, she was overhauled by two French privateers and surrendered without a fight.
[TNA: ADM.1/5266]

30 October NASSAU Third Rate
Portsmouth 1699; 1,081 tons; 150.9ft × 40ft; 70 guns
Captain John Edwards
Attempting to come to anchor at Spithead, the manoeuvre was delayed for so long that she was in shallow water before she could be brought up, and consequently the ship ran aground on the Bembridge Ledge, between the Dean and Horse Sands. Much effort was made to haul her free and over the next few days guns and stores were hoisted out, although hampered by poor weather, to lighten her. All failed, and she was given up as a wreck at the end of November, the hull being stripped of usable stores. Captain Edwards was subsequently found to have been 'wanting in his behaviour' and was fined £123 4s 6d – the equivalent of a year's pay – and the Master, Bartholomew Orde was also found to have been negligent, in failing to take soundings. He was committed to prison for six months and fined six months' pay.
[TNA: ADM.1/5266; ADM.106/614]

19 November HAZARDOUS PRIZE Fourth Rate
Prize 1703 (*le Hasardeux*); 876 tons; 137ft × 38ft; 50 guns
Lieutenant John Hare (temporary)
Part of the escort to a homeward-bound convoy from Virginia, Captain Richard Brown had died on 12 November, and the First Lieutenant assumed command. With the weather deteriorating, it was decided to take shelter in St Helens Roads, Isle of Wight, but in the failing light and strong winds, the ship missed stays twice, and then the anchor failed to come home. She was carried inshore, striking the bottom several times before going aground on a sandbank in Bracklesham Bay, between Selsey Bill and East Wittering and was wrecked. No blame was placed on Lieutenant Hare, but Captain John Lowen of the *Advice*, senior ship in company, was found to have been negligent; he had failed to take the opportunity to anchor earlier, in Plymouth Sound, when the wind was favourable, and then had chosen not to sail directly for the Downs but had attempted to take them into Spithead. In doing so he had failed to make signals indicating the presence of shallow water to the *Hazardous Prize*. Lowen was dismissed the service, although he was restored four years later.
[TNA: ADM.1/5266]

1707

10 February HASTINGS Fifth Rate
Woodbridge 1698; 381 tons; 108.4ft × 28.3ft; 30 guns
Captain Francis Vaughan†
At Great Yarmouth in company with the *Margate* to escort a fleet of about 100 merchant ships across the North Sea to Holland, she made the signal to unmoor during the early hours of 8 February, but the wind shifted during the day, so little progress was made, and the fleet anchored. As the weather worsened, with strong winds, and frequent rain squalls, after lying at anchor for two days it was decided to return to the shelter of the roads and at 1pm the *Hastings* made the signal for the ships to bear away for the roads. Having seen all their charges to safety the escorts made their way inshore, but in the gathering gloom, the pilot mistook the marks and confused the lights on shore and took them through the wrong channel and both ships ran onto the Knowle Sand. The *Margate* managed to free herself and anchor nearby, cutting away her mainmast to ride out the gale, but the *Hastings* remained aground, and as the tide left her, she capsized. She filled with water and within 30 minutes was lost. There were only 24 survivors from a complement of about 200.
[TNA: ADM.1/5266; ADM.51/574; London Gazette 10 February 1706/07]

21 March RESOLUTION Third Rate
Woolwich 1705; 1,103 tons; 150.10ft × 40.11ft; 70 guns
Captain Henry Mordaunt
En-route to Genoa from Barcelona in company with the *Enterprise* and *Milford*, with the Earl of Peterborough embarked, they fell in with a squadron of six French warships. The *Resolution* stood away on a wind, with the French in pursuit, with some exchanges of distant fire, and the Earl was put aboard the *Enterprise* and successfully made his escape, accompanied by the *Milford*. The French continued to chase and at daybreak on the 20th the *Toulouse*, 70 guns, and *Ruby*, 50, overhauled the *Resolution* and a running action commenced, which was maintained for eight hours. With her rigging damaged, main topsail yard shot away and seeing no prospect of escaping, during

the afternoon, at about 3 o'clock, she was run ashore near the castle at Ventimiglia, northern Italy. The French ships closed to continue the attack whilst she lay stranded, the *Resolution* kept up her resistance, driving off several boats which attempted to close her. The following morning a large 70-gun ship approached, clearly with the intention of continuing the action. With her powder either spent or wet, little resistance could be offered, so it was decided that, to prevent her capture, she should be destroyed. At 11am, after all the crew and some of the ship's stores had been landed, she was set on fire, continuing to burn through the day. Captain Mordaunt, son of the Earl of Peterborough, was gravely wounded in the action and never served at sea again.
[TNA: ADM.1/5267]

30 March **THOMAS and KATHERINE** Smack Tender
Hired 1706; 4 guns
Master Thomas Smith
Tender to the *Severn*, she had Lieutenant Youlden Collier of that ship on board when she sailed from the Downs for Portsmouth. Chased and overtaken by a large French privateer off Margate, she held her off for some time, until the French vessel ran alongside and cleared the smack's decks with small-arms fire and hand grenades, boarded and captured her.
[TNA: ADM 1/5267]

2 April **THOMAS and MARY** Hoy Tender
Hired 1706; 4 guns
Master Peter Halfknight
Tender to the *London*, she was laying at anchor in the Downs, with only the Master, Master's Mate, one seaman and three boys on board. A French privateer boldly entered the anchorage and running alongside, boarded and forced the hoy to surrender after a brief struggle, during which the Master was wounded in the knee. The hoy was to be taken to Calais, but their captors agreed to ransom the vessel, with a member of the crew being held hostage until paid. The Master was found to have been 'wanting in his duty' by being at anchor with so few hands on board. He was ordered to forfeit six weeks' pay. The Master's Mate, James Horsenail, had failed to keep a good lookout, was found guilty of neglect and imprisoned for four months.
[TNA: ADM.1/5266; ADM 106/623]

2 May **GRAFTON** Third Rate
Rotherhithe 1700; 1,103 tons; 150.8ft × 40.10ft; 70 guns
Captain Edward Acton†
One of three escorts to a convoy of over fifty ships, a mix of transports and merchant ships, which sailed from the Downs on 1 May bound for Lisbon and the West Indies. The following morning, when the ships were abreast Beachy Head, a powerful French squadron of twelve warships under the command of Chevalier Claude de Forbin approached. Captain Clements in the *Hampton Court* was the senior officer and ordered the escorts to place themselves in line of battle, between the oncoming enemy and the convoy. At noon, having worked to windward, the French attacked, with the *Grafton*, the sternmost ship of the line, being first engaged; *le Blackwall*, 54 guns, attempted to board, but was driven off with heavy casualties, but was followed by *le Griffon*, 44, and *la Dauphine*, 54, which closed and engaged. Following a close engagement, and after clearing the upper deck with musketry and hand grenades, a large number of boarders were entered, and the *Grafton* surrendered.
[TNA: ADM.1/5267; London Gazette 24 June 1707; Owen pp195–7]

2 May **HAMPTON COURT** Third Rate
Blackwall 1701; 1,073 tons; 150.6ft × 40.4ft; 70 guns
Captain George Clements†
Senior officer of the escorts to the large westbound convoy attacked by Forbin off Beachy Head, Captain Clements ordered the ships into line, taking the centre, between *Grafton* and *Royal Oak*. She was initially attacked by Forbin in the *Mars*, 60 guns, which succeeded in laying herself alongside and entering a large number of boarders, but this attack was driven off with heavy casualties amongst the French. Two more French ships, *le Fidèle*, 56, and *la Protée*, 54, came up to join the fight, and *le Blackwall*, 54, after being driven off by the *Grafton* (see above) also fired into her. In a short time, her mainmast, fore-topmast and the tiller were shot away. With about 200 casualties, unable to escape, the *Hampton Court* surrendered after two hours of fighting. Captain Clements was severely wounded in the action, and unseen by his captors, was put into a boat, which escaped into Rye, but he died before reaching shore. The *Royal Oak* managed to fight off her attackers and escape, although badly damaged.
[TNA: ADM.1/5267; London Gazette 24 June 1707; Owen pp195–8; Charnock vol 3 p65]

(17?) August **SWAN** Sixth Rate
Deptford 1694; 249 tons; 93.3ft × 24.6ft; 24 guns
Master and Commander Charles Howard†
Disappeared in a tropical storm in the West Indies and presumed lost with all hands, on or about this time. Her books were closed on this date.
[TNA: ADM.33/256]

25 August **NIGHTINGALE** Sixth Rate
Chatham 1702; 251 tons; 93ft × 24.6ft; 24 guns
Captain Seth Jermy
Escort to a convoy of Newcastle colliers bound for London, which became the target for an attack by

a squadron of six galleys which had recently been established at Dunkirk under the command of the Chevalier de Langeron, who led the force in *la Palme*. The *Nightingale* placed herself between her charges and the advancing enemy, and commenced the action, to give them time to escape. She initially drove one galley off with heavy casualties and put up such a vigorous resistance that she engaged all the galleys, continuing to fight even when large numbers of boarders were entered. The action continued for most of the day, in one of the most protracted actions of the war. Only when he was sure that all his convoy had escaped, did Jermy surrender, being taken into Dunkirk.

Note: The ship was recaptured in December 1707 and taken back into service as *Fox*.
[TNA: ADM.1/5267; de la Roncière vol 6 p457]

29 August WINCHESLEY Fifth Rate
Blackwall 1706; 422 tons; 105.6ft × 30.5ft; 30 guns
Captain William Jones†

During late August the Leeward Islands were struck by a strong hurricane '... that has not left any fruit, or hardly a green leaf on the Island, not a house or a mill is standing without great damage'. The *Winchelsey* had been sent to escort some merchant vessels and was last seen during the evening of 29 August off St Kitts and was presumed to have foundered with the loss of all hands. Wreckage and a body were later washed ashore at St Barthélémy which was identified as being from the *Winchelsey*.
[CSPC: North America West Indies October; November 1707]

30 August CHILD'S PLAY Sixth Rate
Prize 1706 (*Jeux*); 373 tons; 103ft × 29.6ft; 24 guns
Captain George D'Oyley

Stationed in the Leeward Islands, she was also affected by the hurricane (see *Winchelsey* above) which swept through the islands. During the storm she was driven ashore near Palmetto Point, St Kitts and wrecked. All the men were saved, and over the next few weeks the guns and much of the stores were saved.
[TNA: ADM.1/1693; CSPC: North America West Indies October; November 1707]

9 October MARGATE Sixth Rate
Deptford 1694 (*Jersey*); 262 tons; 94.6ft × 24.8ft; 24 guns
Master and Commander Samuel Meade

In company with the *Hector*, the pair was cruising off the coast of Colombia, and gave chase to a Spanish sloop off Punta Canoas. When the sloop steered inshore the *Hector* stood off and ordered the *Margate* to continue the chase. The pursuit went on for some time, until she successfully overhauled the Spaniard and sent a boat on board. Whilst awaiting its return, the *Margate* drifted onto a reef and stuck fast. Despite a two-hour fight to save her, she filled with water and sank, her position then being 12 miles east-north-east of the Sambay or Zamba banks.
[TNA: ADM.1/5266]

10 October: The attack on the Lisbon Convoy
In the autumn of 1707, a large number of ships were at Spithead awaiting convoy; ships bound for Virginia were joined by vessels bound for the Mediterranean and several transports loaded with horses bound for the Portuguese army. Two ships, the *Chester*, 54 guns, and the *Ruby*, 50, were detailed to escort all the ships to Lisbon, and then take the Virginia trade on to North America. As an extra precaution three great ships, *Cumberland*, *Devonshire* and *Royal Oak*, were ordered to provide an escort '... forty or fifty leagues beyond Scilly'. The convoy, consisting of about 120 ships, sailed on 7 October. Three days later, when to the south of the Lizard, the combined squadrons of Duguay-Trouin and Forbin, consisting of twelve warships, armed from 32 to 70 guns, which had been joined by two large privateers, came into sight. In the subsequent action four out the five escorts were lost, and twelve of the merchant ships were captured. The *Royal Oak* escaped, and this led to her commanding officer, Captain Baron Wylde, to be court-martialled. It was ruled that he had failed to observe signals and failed keep his station in the line of battle; he was dismissed the service, although this was reversed some years later.
[TNA: ADM.1/5267; Owen pp220–34]

CUMBERLAND Third Rate
Bursledon 1695; 1,220 tons; 156ft × 42ft; 80 guns
Captain Richard Edwards

Captain Edwards, as the senior officer, ordered his ships to form up in line of battle between the approaching French and the convoy, which did its best to escape, which they did, heads to the south, although the *Royal Oak* remained to leeward of the line and some way distant. Duguay-Trouin in the *Lis*, 70 guns, ran close along the port side of *Cumberland* and then attempted to cross her stem. Captain Edwards put his helm over, but the *Cumberland* struck the French ship amidships, with the main shrouds of the *Lis* fouling the bowsprit of the *Cumberland*. This exposed the British ship to a punishing raking fire, to which she could not effectively reply. Then a second ship, *la Gloire*, 40, came up to the port side of the *Cumberland* and fired into her and under the combined fire of both ships she was dismasted. The French then boarded from both the *Lis* and *Gloire*, covered by volleys of musketry and a hail of grenades and stink-pots, which covered the ship in thick, choking smoke. After a short, fierce fight the *Cumberland* surrendered, having suffered 60 killed and 120 wounded, including Captain Edwards. The First

Lieutenant, John Gaches, who had assumed command on Edwards being taken below, was rather harshly ordered to be dismissed the service for ordering the flag to be struck, although this does seem to have been reversed later.
[TNA: ADM.1/5267]

DEVONSHIRE Third Rate
Woolwich 1704; 1,220 tons; 156ft x 42.1ft; 80 guns
Captain John Watkins†
The *Devonshire* led the small line of battle which faced the combined French squadrons in their attack on the Lisbon Convoy and as the line astern of her was engaged, she was free of the action for some time. She was then engaged by two of the enemy, both former British ships, *le Blackwall*, 50 guns, and *le Salisbury*, 50, which she was able to hold at bay for some time, until the *Lis*, 70, joined after her battle with the *Cumberland*. The fighting continued through the afternoon, with other French ships firing at her when they could, until the stern galleries caught fire. The flames spread, until she was covered in smoke and finally, she blew up and sank. There were only three survivors from the crew of 500 men.
[TNA: ADM.1/5267; Owen p233]

CHESTER Fourth Rate
Woolwich 1691; 663 tons; 125.1ft x 34.4ft; 50 guns
Captain John Balchen
Bringing up the rear of the line of battle which attempted to protect the Lisbon Convoy, attacked in the western Channel, the *Chester* was engaged by *le Jason*, 54 guns, and held her own for some time, driving off an attempt to board. A second French ship, *l'Amazone*, 40, then joined the action. Captain Balchen continued to hold out until the *Jason* ran alongside and entered a large number of men who captured her.
[TNA: ADM.1/5267; Owen pp230–1]

RUBY Fourth Rate
Deptford 1706; 675 tons; 128.4ft x 34.8ft; 50 guns
Captain Peregrine Bertie
Ahead of the *Cumberland* in the line which resisted the combined French squadrons off the Lizard, she was engaged by *le Mars*, 54, and *le Maure*, 50. Bertie held the pair at bay, but other French ships approached to fire into her, Eventually the *Maure* came alongside, boarded and carried the *Ruby*. Captain Bertie was severely wounded in the action and died in France whilst still a prisoner.
[TNA: ADM.1/5267; Owen p232]

12 October ENTERPRISE Sixth Rate
Prize 1705 (*Entrepenante*) 320 tons; 93ft x 27.6ft; 24 guns
Captain William Davenport†
Wrecked with the loss of all the crew, near Toulon, in the western Mediterranean.
[TNA: ADM.106/3120; ADM.33/257]

22 October ASSOCIATION Second Rate
Portsmouth 1697; 1,459 tons; 165ft x 45.5ft; 90 guns
Captain Edmund Loades†
Flagship of Admiral Sir Cloudesley Shovell, returning from the Mediterranean in company with a fleet of twenty-one ships, which sailed from Gibraltar on 29 September, the ships arrived off the south-west coast of England on the morning of 22 October, the position being assessed by soundings. The Admiral ordered the fleet to lay to: until the evening, until at 6pm, although it was now dark, he made sail again on a fresh south-westerly breeze, steering to the north-east, evidently believing that he had the English Channel open before him. The *Association* was leading the fleet, when at about 7.45pm breakers were seen ahead, and despite trying to stand away, and firing signal guns to warn the other ships of the danger, she ran onto the Gilstone Rock at the south-western edge of the Scilly Isles. The ship broke up and sank rapidly, with the loss of the Admiral and the crew of about 800 men.
[London Gazette 24 February 1707/08; Harris p331-353]

22 October EAGLE Third Rate
Chatham 1699; 1,099 tons; 156.6ft x 40.8ft; 70 guns
Captain Robert Hancock†
In company with the *Association* when the fleet ran into the rocks of the Scilly Isles and was wrecked, there were no survivors from her crew of over 500. The exact site of the wreck is somewhat uncertain – it was generally believed that she was lost on the Crim Rocks, to the north of the Bishop and Clerk rocks, but is now believed to have been wrecked a little further to the south-east, on the Crebinicks.
[Harris p346]

22 October ROMNEY Fourth Rate
Blackwall 1694; 683 tons; 130ft x 34.4ft; 50 guns
Captain William Coney†
Along with the *Association*, she followed the Admiral until she was wrecked, with no survivors on the rocks to the west of the Scilly Isles. The exact site of the wreck is unknown but may be either on the Crim Rocks or Crebinicks.
[Harris p346]

* * *

22 October FIREBRAND fireship
Limehouse 1694; 268 tons; 92.3ft × 25.5ft; 8 guns
Master and Commander Francis Piercey
The fireship was close to the *Association* when that ship ran onto the Gilstone Rock, and she followed her onto the rocks, but came free and Piercey steered east, along the southern edge of the chain of rocky islands. The ship was making a large amount of water, despite pumping and bailing. Seeing the light on St Agnes the ship was steered towards this, but foundered in 10 fathoms, near the Menglow Rock. There were twenty-four survivors from the wreck.
[TNA: ADM.1/5266; Harris pp345–6]

1708

9 January LION Stores Hoy
Purchased 1703; 99 tons; 54ft × 19.9ft; 4 guns
Master Jacob Wayman
After sailing from Spithead, in company with several warships bound for the Downs, the *Lion* became separated in the night. Chased in the morning by a 26-gun French privateer, she was caught off Beachy Head and forced to surrender.
Note: Recaptured during 1708.
[TNA: ADM.1/5267]

17 January SUN PRIZE Sixth Rate
Prize 1704 (*Soleil*); 215 tons; 82.8ft × 24.2ft; 20 guns
Master and Commander Andrew Ley
Sailed from the Solent to escort two small merchant vessels to Weymouth Bay, she was off St Albans Head when at 2pm she was sighted and chased by the Dunkirk privateer *Duc de Vendome*, 28 guns. Overhauled, a three-hour running fight was maintained until with all standing and running rigging disabled, masts, yards and sails shot through, the privateer ran alongside and boarded, forcing her to surrender. She suffered two killed and ten wounded, one of whom died later.
[TNA: ADM.1/2035; ADM.1/5267]

26 April DUMBARTON CASTLE Sixth Rate
Acquired 1707 (ex-Scots Navy, built London 1696); 24 guns
Captain Matthew Campbell
Sailed from Kinsale bound for Waterford and Dublin escorting a small convoy of six merchant ships, when during the afternoon a strange ship was seen closing from seaward. Captain Campbell placed himself between the convoy and the stranger which proved to be the French *le Jersey*, 44 guns. By late afternoon, the *Jersey* had come up with her and a short engagement took place, during which the smaller ship had her main-topmast shot away and the rigging cut up. Clearly outclassed, Captain Campbell surrendered. All the convoy escaped into Waterford.
[TNA: ADM.1/1593; ADM.1/5267]

27 May WORCESTER'S PRIZE Sixth Rate
Prize 1705 (*Catherine*); 140 tons; 72.10ft × 20.10ft; 14 guns
Captain Clempson Cave
Weighed and sailed from St Ives during the morning, to escort a small convoy of eleven merchant vessels eastward through the English Channel. Ships were seen in the offing, which seemed to be closing, and it was feared that they were enemy warships. Captain Cave ordered his convoy to spread sail and distance themselves, whilst he steered towards the strangers. As they neared it was clear that they were French privateers and she commenced a running fight with the largest of them, *la Providence* of Morlaix, 16 guns. The engagement continued for three hours until a second privateer, *le Dauphin* of Roscoff, 12 guns, came up and fired into her from astern. Cave attempted to put his ship across the bows of the *Dauphin*, but his rigging was so badly cut up the manoeuvre failed, and unable to escape he struck his flag. She was then in sight of the island of Lundy.
Note: Recaptured in June 1708 by a Dutch privateer.
[TNA: ADM.1/1593; ADM.1/5267]

19 June WOLF sloop
Portsmouth 1699; 66 tons; 58.6ft × 16.6ft; 12 guns
Master and Commander James Milleson
Cruising in the Irish Sea in company with the *Speedwell*, on 18 June the pair escorted four merchant ships into Milford and then stood over towards the Irish Coast. The following morning at 8 o'clock, then being about eight leagues (24 miles) to the west-south-west of the Smalls, two ships were seen, and they altered course and stood towards them. They continued to close until within gunshot, when it became clear that they were French, the larger being the *Jersey*, 40 guns, with the *Providence*, a 16-gun Morlaix privateer. All sail was then made away, the pair steering different courses, the *Speedwell* bearing away before the wind soon outpaced everyone. The *Wolf* was chased by the *Providence* which came up under her stern and ran her bowsprit over her quarter and commenced the fight. Unable to escape, and with the *Jersey* closing, she surrendered.
Note: recaptured two days later by the *Speedwell*.
[TNA: ADM.1/2094; ADM.1/5267; ADM.51/837]

6 October WORCESTER'S PRIZE Sixth Rate
Prize 1705 (*Catherine*); 140 tons; 72.8ft × 20.10ft; 14 guns
Master and Commander Finch Reddall
Ordered to cruise to the west of the Scilly Isles and escort merchant ships bound for Bristol to safety, *Worcester's Prize* had three vessels under convoy, steering north-east in the Bristol Channel. When they were

to the north of St Ives, a strange ship could be seen standing towards them. Ordering the merchants to close the shore, Captain Reddall tacked towards the stranger, which proved to be a large, 24-gun privateer from St Malo. Sail was made away, but she was overhauled after a chase of about an hour, and the French ship came alongside to fire a broadside and a hail of small shot. The exchange of fire went on for some time, until with rigging and sails cut up, she struck her flag. All of the merchant ships were also taken.
[TNA:ADM.1/2377]

18 October DUNKIRK'S PRIZE Sixth Rate
Prize 1705 (*Hocquart*); 291 tons; 70.8ft × 27.10ft; 24 guns
Master and Commander George Purvis
Cruising off Hispaniola in company with the *Severn*, the pair sighted a ship and gave chase, but the *Dunkirk's Prize* stretched ahead and soon lost sight of her consort. The chase went on through the afternoon and night, and the following morning the stranger was seen standing into Cap Francois. The pursuit continued until both pursuer and chase ran aground. *Dunkirk's Prize* found herself on a ledge of rocks which pierced the bottom, and held fast, she filled with water. Purvis urged the crew to man the boats and capture the chase, which could be seen to be a large French merchant ship, which was aground on a sandbank. This was achieved, and they successfully warped her off the sand and used her to return to Jamaica. Some of the seamen had refused to follow the Captain in this venture and two seamen, Samuel Darby and Ebenezer Williams, were later found guilty of mutinous conduct and ordered to be flogged around the fleet '… receiving ten lashes on the bare back alongside every ship at Port Royal, Jamaica'.
[TNA:ADM.1/5267; CSPC: North America West Indies October 1708]

10 December VULTURE Fireship
Deptford 1690; 270 tons; 93.1ft × 24.10ft; 8 guns
Master and Command William Lloyd
On passage to England from Jamaica, she fell with a French squadron of eleven warships to the west of Ushant; she was chased, but was unable to escape, and when overhauled she surrendered when hailed.
[TNA:ADM.1/5267]

15 December CRUIZER Sixth Rate
Prize 1705 (*Meric*); 280 tons; 75ft × 26.6ft; 24 guns
Master and Commander William Cawley
Bound for England from the West Indies, she was in a poor condition, and several leaks became evident, and the pumps were continuously in use. When she sighted the Azores, course was steered to take her inshore of the island of Terceira. She remained off the island for two weeks in attempts to keep her afloat, but the leaks could not be stopped and as the weather worsened, she was run ashore on the island, where she broke up.
[TNA:ADM.1/5267]

1709

5 January ARROGANT Fourth Rate
Prize 1705 (*Arrogant*); 928 tons; 137.8ft × 39.6ft; 60 guns
Captain George Nicholls†
Loaded with timber and naval stores, she had sailed from Lisbon for the Mediterranean, but failed to arrive as expected at Port Mahon. The western Mediterranean was affected by strong gales in early January, with a storm on 5 January, with high winds and driving snow, which had separated the British squadron and it was presumed that she was lost with all hands on or about this date
[Tunstall vol 2 pp319, 325]

6 February BURCHETT Sloop
Hired 1708; 50 tons; 6 guns
Master and Commander William Smith
Whilst endeavouring to gain intelligence of the enemy by reconnoitring northern French ports, she was chased by a French privateer off Calais. The *Burchett*, short of complement, could not maintain the engagement, especially when several of the crew quit their stations when the French ship opened fire, forcing Commander Smith to surrender.
[TNA:ADM.1/5267]

8 February WINCHELSEY Fifth Rate
Purchased 1708; 415 tons; 108.2ft × 29.10ft; 36 guns
Captain Francis Percey
In company with the *Medway's Prize*, she was escorting a convoy from the Mediterranean; they were to the north-west of the Burlings, when a large ship, which appeared to be a warship of about 50 guns was sighted, making towards the fleet. The weather was poor, with strong winds and high seas, and this seems to have prevented the ship from closing. During the evening of 6 February, it was decided to evade the stranger; a boat was sent around the convoy ordering them to make their best way to Viana, whilst the *Medway's Prize* would put lights in the rigging and poop whilst *Winchelsey* would be darkened. This seemed to succeed, as the following morning the *Winchelsey* was on her own. She made her way south, towards Viana, but the following day sighted a French 40-gun ship, which chased and soon overhauled her. The pair fought for some time, until with disabled rigging, she was forced to surrender. Some of the crew had quit their guns during the action, and subsequently two warrant officers, the Gunner, William Orchard and the Mate, Richard Pallaster, were

found guilty at a court martial of discouraging the men to fight. They were both dismissed from the service and forfeited all pay due.

Note: recaptured 24 February 1709 by the *Chester*.
[TNA: ADM.1/2280; ADM.1/5267]

1 March ADVENTURE Fifth Rate
Chatham 1691; 438 tons; 117ft x 29ft; 44 guns
Captain Robert Clarke†
Cruising between Montserrat and Martinique, she sighted and chased two French ships, and came up with one of them, finding it to be *la Valeur*, 36 guns. She was engaged for some time, until the steering gear was shot away, which, with her rigging severely damaged, left her unmanageable. The *Valeur* then laid her across the bows, raked her, and entered a large number of boarders, and after a brief struggle, with the Captain and Lieutenant killed, she surrendered, the crew refusing to fight anymore. She suffered twenty-nine killed and seventy-six wounded.
[TNA: ADM.1/5267]

14 April FOWEY Fifth Rate
Chatham 1705; 412 tons; 108ft x 29.6ft; 32 guns
Captain Richard Lestock
On passage from Alicante to Lisbon with despatches, during the afternoon of 12 April she saw two ships to the south-east, which chased her, using sweeps in efforts to close when the wind dropped. The chase went on through the night, and although Lestock made all sail away, she was overhauled during the afternoon by a ship that came up on her larboard quarter, hoisted French colours and opened fire. The second ship came up under her stern, yawed, and fired a broadside. This manoeuvre was repeated several times, cutting up her sails and rigging. The *Fowey* continued to maintain the fight until by 3am, when the wind shifted to the south-east she was taken aback and with all the running rigging cut they could not work the ship. Several shots had penetrated the hull and the pumps were disabled, which led to her making water. With a ship on each quarter, she could no longer defend herself and surrendered. Her captors proved to be a warship, *la Vestale*, 40 guns, and a privateer, *le Phenix*, 42 guns.
[TNA: ADM.1/2036; ADM.1/5267]

16 April SWEEPSTAKES Fifth Rate
Woolwich 1708; 416 tons; 108.5ft x 29.6ft; 32 guns
Captain Samuel Meade
Ordered to convoy some merchant ships into Falmouth, and then to cruise 15–20 leagues (45–60 miles) to the south-west of the Scilly Isles, at first light she sighted four ships, which gave chase. They soon overhauled her, and proved to be *l'Amazone*, 40 guns and *l'Astrée*, 24 guns, with two merchant-ship prizes. A running fight commenced, but unable to get clear, outnumbered and outgunned, she surrendered, Captain Meade consulting his officers before he did so. The *Amazone* took charge of the prize to escort her back to Brest. At a subsequent court martial, both Captain Meade and the Master, John Tomlinson, were found to have been 'very remiss' in failing to defend the ship for as long as they might have. Both were dismissed the service, although Meade was reinstated in 1713.
[TNA: ADM.1/2094; ADM.1/5267]

24 April BRISTOL Fourth Rate
Deptford 1693; 671 tons; 130ft x 34.3ft; 50 guns
Captain Henry Gore
After sailing from Plymouth on 23 April, bound for Lisbon, the *Bristol* encountered two French warships, the *Achille*, 66 guns, and the *Gloire*, 40. A sporadic running fight developed, but after nightfall Captain Gore tacked, lightened ship and got before the wind, hoping to escape the pair, but at first light they were seen to be still in chase. At 6am the *Achille* came up with her, but Gore backed his sails which allowed him to pass under her stern, taking the wind from her opponents' sails, then put the helm over and successfully ran across the bows of his opponent. However, this initial success was checked by the constant small-arms fire from the French ship, which caused many casualties amongst the upper-deck crew and attempts to board were driven back. On being informed there was 6ft of water in the hold, having taken seventy killed and wounded and some of the crew quitting their quarters, Captain Gore surrendered. The ship was recaptured the following day by Lord Dursley's squadron, but she was full of water, and was abandoned about three hours after being captured and foundered.
[TNA: ADM.1/5267; London Gazette 12 May 1709]

6 May PEMBROKE Stores Hoy
Hired 1709
Master Giles Wiggoner
On passage from Plymouth to Portsmouth, she was laden with provisions for the fleet and was escorted by a Dutch warship. When approaching the Isle of Wight, she left the escort to enter the Solent. A French privateer intercepted her when abreast Hurst Castle and forced her to surrender. Wiggoner was blamed for the loss because he had prematurely left his escort. He was ordered to forfeit all pay due.
[TNA: ADM.1/5267]

7 May POSTILLION PRIZE Sixth Rate
Prize 1702 (*Postillon*); 105 tons; 65.4ft x 19.4ft; 10 guns
Master and Commander Thomas Dennett
Sailed from the Downs escorting a convoy of thirty merchant vessels to Ostend, they arrived without

incident, and she led the ships into the harbour at high tide. As she did so she struck heavily on a submerged object, which turned out to be a line of wooden piles. The hull was pierced, and the ship quickly filled with water, and within 15 minutes the upper deck was awash. The other ships sent help, and an attempt was made to weigh her, but the tackles broke, and she swung into deeper water and sank.
[TNA: ADM.1/5267]

27 May ORFORD'S PRIZE Sixth Rate
Prize 1708 (*Gaillarde*); 283 tons; 74.11ft × 26.9ft; 24 guns
Master and Commander William Collier
Cruising in the Bristol Channel, tasked to escort homeward-bound merchant vessels into harbour, she was off Lundy Island, when at first light four ships were seen to windward. Believing them to be merchant vessels heading for Bristol, she stood towards them, as she did so, two of the strangers stretched ahead of their companions to meet her to the south of the island. They were both showing British colours and appeared to be British-built and rigged. *Orford's Prize* shortened sail as they neared, and when within gunshot hailed them. They replied, shouting that they were English ships of war with prizes. This was not believed, especially when there was no reply when hailed again to ask their name. The strangers then hauled down their colours to replace them with French and fired a broadside. The *Orford* replied as she could, and made sail away, pursued by the French ships which could be seen to be 30-gun ships. She maintained a fight for 'five glasses' (2½ hours), until with masts, yards, sails and rigging disabled she could no longer manoeuvre, and surrendered. Four men were killed in the engagement; the crew (except the officers) were landed on Lundy.
[TNA: ADM.1/5267]

13 September SUCCESS Sloop
Purchased 1709 (*Swift*); 111 tons; 56.2ft × 19.3ft; 10 guns
Master and Commander Charles Boyle
Chased by several enemy privateers when about 40 miles south-east of the Scilly Isles, the sloop used every endeavour to escape, including the use of sweeps, the chase going on for several days. Eventually one large ship overhauled her, fired a broadside and a volley of small arms into the sloop, whose men were exhausted after rowing all day, and she surrendered.
[TNA: ADM.1/5267]

16 September HIND Sixth Rate
Purchased 1709; 161 tons; 78.4ft × 21.10ft; 12 guns
Master and Commander Robert Cremer
On being informed that a French privateer was loitering off Christchurch, the *Hind* sailed from Yarmouth, Isle of Wight to search for the intruder. Cremer attempted to steer through the north channel of the Solent, between Hurst Castle and the Shingles, on the last of the ebb tide. Unsure of the currents and in a fresh south-westerly breeze, it was found that she would not answer the helm and then the ship ran aground as the tide left her. It was found that she would still not move on the flood tide, despite anchors being carried out in an attempt to kedge her free, and she filled with water and became a wreck. Cremer was found guilty of negligence and ordered to lose all pay due.
[TNA: ADM.1/5267]

26 October GLOUCESTER Fourth Rate
Rotherhithe 1709; 923 tons; 143.8ft × 38.3ft; 60 guns
Captain John Balchen
Sailed from Spithead in company with the *Falmouth* on 9 October to screen the passage of a convoy through the western approaches to the English Channel. The pair were to the south of Ireland when, on 24 October they became separated after the *Gloucester* lost her main topmast when they were detached to chase a strange sail. Two days later, she was sighted and chased by a squadron under the command of Duguay-Trouin. Overhauled, the *Gloucester* was engaged by the *Lis*, 70 guns, for two hours, and despite having her foreyard shot away, and the sails and rigging reduced to shreds, she successfully held off the French ship until the *Achille*, 66, came up at which the *Gloucester* surrendered.
[TNA: ADM.1/5267; ADM.51/341]

29 November GARLAND Fifth Rate
Woolwich 1703; 496 tons; 115.6ft × 31.2ft; 40 guns
Captain Isaac Cooke
Having been cruising locally, she was intending to return to the shelter of Chesapeake Bay, and confidently stood in for the shore during the evening, expecting to raise Cape Henry in the morning. It was therefore a surprise when at 1 o'clock in the morning breakers were seen ahead. An attempt was made to come about, but it was too late, and she struck a sand bank a little to the south of Currituck Inlet, North Carolina, her stern tailing onto the shore. The ship subsequently sank, and all but fifteen of the men were saved, and most of the stores and rigging were able to be salvaged. The loss was blamed on the current being considerably more to the southward than had been expected.
[TNA: ADM.1/5268; CSPC: North America West Indies January 1710]

21 December PLYMOUTH'S PRIZE Sixth Rate
Prize 1709 (*Dryade*); 134 tons; 56.6ft × 21.2ft; 16 guns
Master and Commander James Hanway
Chased by a large 30-gun French privateer in the western approaches to the Channel, she was outsailed

and overhauled. Unable to escape and faced with a superior force, she surrendered when hailed.
[TNA: ADM.1/5267]

25 December SOLEBAY Sixth Rate
Redhouse 1694; 256 tons; 92.1ft x 24.11ft; 24 guns
Master and Commander George Stidson†
In poor weather, whilst convoying eight merchant ships to King's Lynn, she ran hard aground on the Boston Knock sands, Lincolnshire and was wrecked, only two boats of survivors escaping. The weather remained poor, but efforts were made to recover the stores from the wreck, although it was reported that it was being plundered – a Newcastle collier reportedly taking some of her sails, and a man from Boston had recovered the cooking cauldron.
[TNA: ADM.106/653; Clowes vol 2 p522]

29 December PEMBROKE Fourth Rate
Limehouse 1694; 908 tons; 145ft x 37.7ft; 60 guns
Captain Edward Rumsey†
On a cruise between Toulon and Corsica in company with the *Falcon* when three large warships were sighted, which were initially believed to be British, but as they closed, they could be seen to be French. All sail was made, and they attempted to escape, but were overhauled by the French squadron, which were the *Parfait*, 70 guns, *Sérieux*, 60 and the *Phénix*, 52, under the command of Jacques Cassard. A three-hour fight followed, with *Pembroke* initially being engaged by the *Parfait* on the starboard side, which was joined by the *Sérieux* on the larboard. Captain Rumsey was killed after an hour, Lieutenant John Berkeley assuming command. With the sails and rigging reduced to shreds, the mizzen mast having gone by the board, and with sixty killed and wounded she surrendered.
[TNA: ADM.1/5267]

29 December FALCON Fifth Rate
Deptford 1704; 411 tons; 106.5ft x 29.7ft; 32 guns
Captain Charles Constable
In company with the *Pembroke* in the western Mediterranean, they were overhauled after a short chase by three large French warships under the command of Admiral Cassard (see above). The *Falcon* was fired into by the *Parfait*, 70, and then both other ships engaged her. They effectively destroyed her sails and rigging, and her fore topmast was shot away, despite which she maintained the fight for over an hour, until with only sixteen of the crew unwounded, she surrendered.
[TNA: ADM.1/5267]

1710

11 April SUCCESS Sloop
Purchased 1709 (*Swift Galley*); 111 tons; 56.2ft x 19.3ft; 10 guns
Master and Commander Robert Cremer
Steering north along the coast of Portugal, the sloop was about 200 miles to the north-west of Lisbon when on 10 April, two ships were sighted, which steadily closed, despite Cremer heaving overboard the boat, an anchor and some stores to lighten the sloop and keep her distance. By nightfall they were within hailing distance, and shouted in good English, that they were from the West Indies, bound for England and they would be 'glad of our company'. The weather was not good, with a strong south-west wind and high seas, obliging them to lower the main yard and reef the foresail. The strangers kept in company all night, and at first light hoisted French colours, closed and fired a volley of small shot. The seas were running so high that with water continually washing over the decks she could not effectively reply and so surrendered.
[TNA: ADM.1/5267]

6 September VALEUR Sixth Rate
Prize 1705 (*la Valeur*); 321 tons; 100.9ft x 27.4ft; 24 guns
Master and Commander John Hare
Lying at anchor in Carbonnear Harbour, Newfoundland, when at about 2am, a body of French seamen and troops approached in three fishing shallops. They had a captive English seaman held at pistol-point with them, who answered the hail from the deck of the *Valeur*, to assure them they were innocent fishermen. The boats then ran alongside and quickly boarded. The Carpenter, senior officer on the deck, was shot dead in the first moments of the attack, and the Captain shot five times as he emerged from his cabin, but he survived. The crew below resisted the boarders for nearly two hours, until with twenty-eight men killed or wounded, they surrendered.
Note: recaptured 12 September by the *Essex*.
[TNA: ADM.1/5268]

20 September TERRIBLE Fifth Rate
Shoreham 1694; 252 tons; 92.3ft x 25ft; 28 guns
Captain Thomas Mabbutt
Returning to England from Gibraltar, she became separated from the main fleet in poor weather and continued independently. When off Cape St Maria, Portugal, she encountered the French *Faucon*, 36 guns. A fight was maintained for over an hour, until with her rigging and sails cut up, four men killed and sixteen wounded, she surrendered and was taken into Cadiz.
[TNA: ADM.1/5268]

21 September FAME Sixth Rate
Prize 1709 (la Renomée); 316 tons; 106ft × 26ft; 24 guns
Captain Ambrose Cole
On passage from Port Mahon to Barcelona with despatches for General Stanhope, they were chased by three French warships, the *Toulouse*, 56 guns, *Vestale*, 40 and *Méduse*, 30, which she attempted to outrun. She was unable to do so and was steadily overhauled, and faced with superior force, she surrendered, being taken into Cartagena.
[TNA: ADM.1/5268; SP.42/67]

23 September HUNTER Sixth Rate
Rotherhithe 1690; 277 tons; 93.6ft × 24.10ft; 28 guns
Captain Francis Drake
Ordered to proceed to Lisbon to obtain supplies and stores for the garrison at Gibraltar, she was off Cadiz when she was chased by two large ships. Drake made all sail he could to escape, but could not get clear, and one of the strangers came up with them during the night, and at first light stretched ahead. She could now be seen to be a large French man-of-war, and during the morning a running fight began, which lasted for two hours, until the second ship, which was the former British 70-gun ship *Hampton Court*, came within gunshot. With the rigging and sails cut up, and with seventeen men killed, she surrendered to *l'Adelaide*, 42 guns.
[TNA: ADM.1/1693: ADM.1/5268]

1 November SCARBOROUGH Fifth Rate
Southampton 1696; 391 tons; 108ft × 28.7ft; 32 guns
Captain Edward Holland
Engaged in visiting the various trading outposts of the Royal African Company, the *Scarborough* was in the Gulf of Guinea, to the north of Cape Lopos (or Lopez), when two ships were seen closing from windward. Unsure of their identity, she spread sail and stretched away to the south-east and hoped that during the night she would escape, but in bright moonlight one of the strangers, which was the largest, could be seen to be not only in pursuit, but closing. At daybreak, the stranger showed a British ensign, and fired a gun, evidently as a signal. The *Scarborough* replied in a similar manner, and then several more, in an attempt to bring the stranger to, but no notice was taken. The ship, which seemed to have 30 guns, continued to close, until the British flag was hauled down to be replaced with French, at which the *Scarborough* attempted to weather his opponent and get across his bows. This failed, and the French ship ran her bows alongside the starboard cathead, from where she raked her with great guns and small-arms fire. Boarders were then entered from the French ship, which were initially repulsed with heavy losses, but the privateer continued to rake her with cannon fire and cleared the upper deck with concentrated volleys of small-arms fire. A second attempt at boarding was successful and the *Scarborough* surrendered, finding her captor was the *Saint François* privateer of Rochelle. She suffered thirty-two killed and over forty wounded.
Note: recaptured 31 March 1712 by *Anglesey*.
[TNA: ADM.1/1878; ADM.1/5268]

1711

5 January POMPEY Stores Hoy
Hired 1710
Master John Beacham
Bound for the anchorage in the Downs from Portsmouth, she joined company with the homecoming Virginia fleet, which came under attack from several French privateers. The *Pompey* found herself being chased by a dogger of 2 guns and attempted to run onshore on the Sussex coast but was cut off and captured.
[TNA: ADM.1/5268]

10 January RESOLUTION Third Rate
Deptford 1708; 1,118 tons; 150.1ft × 41.3ft; 70 guns
Captain Richard Haddock
Part of the fleet in the western Mediterranean under the command of Sir John Norris, they arrived off Barcelona on 10 January, and *Resolution* anchored in 25 fathoms with the other ships. The wind was blowing a fresh gale from the east, and during the day it steadily increased until it was a full gale. At about midnight the anchor cables parted, and she drove across the anchorage until she grounded in shallow water near Fort Montjuich. Efforts were made over several days to save her, but the pumps could make no headway against the water which flooded into her as she broke up.
[TNA: ADM.1/5268; ADM.51/4307]

27 June ADVICE Fifth Rate
Woolwich 1698; 551 tons; 118ft × 32.4ft; 50 guns
Captain Kenneth, Lord Duffus
Having sailed from the Downs on 26 June for Leith, she was off Great Yarmouth when she was chased by a squadron of six French privateers that closed under Dutch colours, until they were within pistol shot. The two largest ships, both of 28 guns, lay on her quarters and another pair with 20 and 18 guns, lay alongside her, the *Advice* finding it impossible to use her lower tier of guns due to the high seas. Despite this, she maintained the fight for two hours, suffering sixty men killed and wounded, until with sails and rigging quite disabled, braces, bowlines and sheets all shot away, she surrendered. The Carpenter, Christopher Gabriel, who quitted the deck during the engagement, was dismissed the service.
[TNA: ADM.1/5269]

29 July SWALLOW'S PRIZE Fifth Rate
Prize 1704 (*l'Etoile*); 200 tons; 32 guns
Captain John Shales

Based in the western Mediterranean, she successfully chased and captured a Spanish merchant ship on 23 July off Corsica and took the prize into Ajaccio. She sailed on 29 July, but the weather was stormy and turned to a hard gale from the north, so decided to return to the anchorage, reducing sail as she did. Quite unexpectedly at 4 o'clock in the afternoon, as she approached the anchorage she struck hard on an underwater object and was held fast. A boat was lowered, and the Master sounded, finding 13–14 fathoms of water around her, and it was clear that she had struck a submerged pinnacle of rock. Boats came to her assistance from the shore and took out anchors in an attempt to haul her free, but she was stuck fast. The guns were run from fore to aft to lighten her forward, but this failed, and water was reported to be entering the hold, which the pumps could not control. When the water flooded the cockpit, the Captain ordered her to be abandoned, and all the hands were taken off by boats from the shore, the ship steadily settling until only her masts were showing above the water. No blame was placed on the ship's officers, as they were unfamiliar with the harbour and had no reliable charts. Despite using the lead-line continuously on entering, they failed to discover the rock until they struck.
[TNA: ADM.1/5268; ADM.52/282]

26 August GREYHOUND Fourth Rate
Ipswich 1703; 494 tons; 114.3ft x 31.3ft; 40 guns
Captain James Stuart

Employed in protecting east-coast shipping, she arrived at Tynemouth on 1 August and was warped into Tynemouth Haven to refit and re-provision. On 26 August, with several merchant ships ready to proceed, at 6 o'clock in the morning the local pilot came on board and took charge of the ship as she spread topsails and fired a gun as a signal to get underway. Just 30 minutes after weighing she ran hard aground on the Hind Sand and was wrecked. The subsequent court martial placed the blame on the pilot, Timothy Hogg, who had attempted to take the ship over the bar with insufficient water under the keel. The court took into consideration the fact that he was a very aged man and ordered that he not serve as a pilot in the Royal Navy again.
[TNA: ADM.1/5268; ADM.52/180]

7 October FEVERSHAM Fifth Rate
Shoreham 1696; 372 tons; 107ft x 28.1ft; 32 guns
Captain Robert Paston

Escorting three provisions ships from New York to Nova Scotia, in support of the expedition against the French colony of Quebec, they sighted the land and stood inshore during the day, before altering course for the night to take them clear of Cape Breton. During the early hours of the morning, however, they found that they were being taken further inshore and attempted to tack away, but were unable to do so, and went ashore, broadside on, near the Cape and broke up in the surf. The merchant transports also went ashore and were lost. The strong currents were blamed for taking them unexpectedly close inshore. Ninety men drowned, forty-five were saved.
[TNA: ADM.1/5269]

15 October EDGAR Third Rate
Rotherhithe 1709; 1,120 tons; 149.8ft x 41.6ft; 70 guns
Captain George Paddon

Having taken part in the expedition to Canada, *Edgar* returned to England, and anchored in St Helen's Roads off the Isle of Wight on 10 October. Whilst still lying at anchor, with the Captain and all commissioned officers ashore, she was blown up at about midday by a massive internal detonation and destroyed, with heavy loss of life. The cause of the explosion was not positively identified, but gunpowder was being shifted from aft to forward magazines that morning, and despite the First Lieutenant testifying that the decks were ordered to be swabbed afterwards, an accidental spillage was possible. Lieutenant Brooke, who should have remained on board, was reprimanded and forfeited all pay due.
[TNA: ADM.1/5268]

9 November RESTORATION Third Rate
Deptford 1706; 1,106 tons; 151ft x 41ft; 70 guns
Captain John Hartnoll

Stationed in the western Mediterranean, she arrived at Leghorn (Livorno) on 9 October, as part of the squadron commanded by Sir John Jennings which escorted the King of Spain from Barcelona. The ships anchored in fresh winds, and over the next few days the weather was poor, with strong gale-force winds from the south-west. Under orders to proceed to Port Mahon, the fleet weighed anchor on 27 October, but the strong winds continued, and unable to clear the anchorage they were forced to anchor again. On 2 November they again unmoored, and on a north-west wind stood out to sea, but the *Restoration* lost contact with the other ships during the night. As the winds picked up to gale force, she stood inshore and anchored again before she again attempted to clear the coast, but during 8 November the winds again shifted to the south-west and increased to gale force. During the night, the mainsail and topsail were ripped apart and yet again she stood inshore to anchor. When the bower anchor cable parted, she dropped the sheet anchor, but this cable also parted,

and she was driven onto the Malora (Meloria) shoals and wrecked.
[TNA: ADM.1/5269; ADM.51/812]

29 November HIND Sixth Rate
Prize 1709 (la Diane); 190 tons; 78ft × 23.3ft; 16 guns
Master and Commander Robert Jennings
Running into Poolbeg harbour, Dublin, under the command of a local pilot, as they passed over the bar the ship unexpectedly struck several times on a submerged object. Water was reported entering rapidly, and very soon there was 4ft of water in the hold. The flow of water could not be stemmed, and she was warped into shallow water before she sank to the upper deck. The guns and cables were salvaged, and the ship prepared for weighing. Several attempts were made to lift her, but the swell proved to be too great, and the bridles broke. On 12 December she was found to have settled deeper into the sand and was abandoned. The exact cause was not discovered but an unmarked discarded anchor was the prime suspect.
[TNA: ADM.1/1981; ADM.1/5269]

29 November SEAHORSE Sixth Rate
Limehouse 1709; 161 tons; 76ft × 22.1ft; 14 guns
Captain Humphrey Blowers
Lying at anchor off Dartmouth when the weather deteriorated, with rain and gusts of strong wind from the north-east, and it was decided to warp her further upstream. However, the wind shifted further to the east and strengthened, blowing in 'great gusts', and this led her to tail onto the rocks on the west side of the haven, below Dartmouth Castle. She let go anchors, but this failed to bring her up in time and she was beaten to a wreck on the rocks.
[TNA: ADM.1/5269]

1712

26 March DRAGON Fourth Rate
Rotherhithe 1707; 719 tons; 131.8ft × 35.5ft; 50 guns
Captain George Martin
Sailed from Guernsey, in company with several merchant ships, bound for England. The ships initially steered safely through the Great Russel passage between Herm and Sark, before turning to the north. It was found that the strong currents in the area were setting them towards the Casquets rocks, near Alderney, and being aware of the danger, topsails and foresail were set and she was put in stays to tack away. A merchant ship was following close astern and unfortunately collided with the *Dragon* during the manoeuvre, and she consequently failed to come about and struck the rocks and was wrecked. An anonymous letter to the Admiralty accused the Captain and officers of '... drinking and dancing to excess with several females' at the time of the disaster, but despite several advertisements in newspapers, no one came forward to substantiate the claims, which were dismissed as malicious at the subsequent court martial.
[TNA: ADM.1/5269; London Gazette 24 April 1712]

29 May STAR Bomb
Purchased 1694; 117 tons; 53.11ft × 20.2ft; 8 guns
Master and Commander Thomas Smart
In company with *Jersey*, the bomb sailed from Jamaica to escort several merchant ships on passage to England, but the *Star* lost contact in thick weather. She continued independently, steering through the Windward Passage until the island of Heneago (Inagua) was sighted. She tacked away and stood to the north-west to clear the land. The strong current set further to the east than she realised, and she ran onto a ledge of rocks about a league (three miles) to the west-south-west of Inagua and was wrecked.
[TNA: ADM.1/5269]

12 June SEAFORD'S PRIZE Sloop
Prize 1708 (la Marie-Anne); 86 tons; 62.7ft × 17.10ft; 12 guns
Lieutenant George Rawlings (or Rawlins)
Commanded by the ship's Lieutenant as Commander Benjamin Wilshaw was ashore sick, the *Seaford's Prize* sailed from Greenock, Scotland, to convoy five merchant ships to ports in Ireland. When off the island of Islay, a large ship was sighted approaching, and the sloop altered to close the stranger, until she discovered her to be a French 30-gun privateer. Rawlings used every effort to escape, using sweeps to row away, but she was overhauled by the French vessel. A fight was kept up for an hour, until with the sails and rigging shattered, she surrendered.
  Note: recaptured in August 1712.
[TNA: ADM.1/5269]

1714

12 November HAZARD Sloop
Woolwich 1711; 113 tons; 62.7ft × 20.8ft; 6 guns
Master and Commander Roger Green[†]
Bound for Boston with mail and despatches from England, she was driven ashore and wrecked in dark, blowing weather in Massachusetts Bay, about 10 leagues (30 miles) from Boston, with the loss of all hands. Much wreckage was washed ashore, and some of the mail was salvaged.
[CSPC: North America West Indies November 1714]

4 | 1715–1739: The Long Peace

THE PERIOD WAS MARKED BY a long period of peace, which was broken by a brief outbreak of hostilities with Spain in 1718–19 over the occupation of Sardinia, the British fleet in the Mediterranean both protecting British interests and supporting the Austrian emperor.

1715

9 October JAMAICA Sloop
Deptford 1710; 114 tons; 64.7ft × 20.8ft; 10 guns
Master and Commander Francis Knighton
Cruising to the west of Jamaica when the area was hit by a tropical storm. On 3 October, as the weather worsened, the sloop took in all canvas and scudded before the wind under bare poles, with the seas continually washing over her, so when the tiller broke, she broached-to and lay with her hatches in the water. To ease her, the mast, boats and booms were cut away and the guns and fire hearth were jettisoned overboard. This enabled her to survive the storm and, using a spare yard for a jury rig, slowly made her way back towards Jamaica. On 7 October, a merchant sloop came to her aid, which took her in tow, and it was decided to make for the nearest island of Grand Cayman. Unfortunately, the pilot took the sloop through the wrong channel, and she ran hard aground onto a reef and started beating on the rocks. This unseated the rudder and started leaks. Undeterred, the crew re-hung the rudder, commenced bailing and took aboard extra pumps from the assisting merchant ship. Despite all their efforts, the water could not be held back. A diver reported that the sloop's forefoot was beaten back into the powder room and the larboard bilge was pierced by rocks. The sloop was abandoned and allowed to settle and sink.
[TNA: ADM.1/5271; ADM.51/4225]

1716

10 November AUGUSTE Fourth Rate
Prize 1705 (l'Auguste); 932 tons; 141.6ft × 39ft; 60 guns
Captain Robert Johnson
Part of the Anglo-Dutch squadron sent to the Baltic to protect British trade during the Swedish-Russian war, she sailed from Copenhagen on 4 November with a large convoy. The weather worsened, and the convoy, with escorts were forced to anchor off Læsø Island on 8 November. During the following day the wind increased to a strong south-westerly gale, the ships riding with yards and topmasts struck. At about noon the *Auguste*'s anchor cable parted, and she made signals of distress as she was driven out of the anchorage. With the wind veering to the north-west, she managed to spread a mizzen sail, and hoisted yards and topmasts, but later that night she went ashore on the island of Anholt and was wrecked. The foremast and mainmasts were cut away to ease her movement and the barge and longboat were both despatched to summon help, but the crews took the opportunity to abscond. Local craft went to her assistance, and the *Oxford* and *Deal Castle* were despatched to the scene, but nothing could be done, and she was abandoned as a wreck.
[TNA: ADM.1/2; ADM.1/1596; ADM.1/1982]

1717

17 December SORLINGS Fifth Rate
Sheerness 1706; 506 tons; 116.6ft × 31.8ft; 44 guns
Captain John Goodall
Part of a squadron that had escorted British merchant vessels to ports in the Baltic, she sailed from Copenhagen on 23 November in company with the *Valeur* and *Rye* to return to England. They battled against strong westerly gale-force winds as they steered into the North Sea, and on 7 December sighted land. Signals for danger were made, but *Sorlings* broke her foreyard, so when her companions tacked and stood away to the north-west, she came to anchor in 12 fathoms. She remained at anchor and after repairing the yard weighed and sailed on 10 December but made little progress against strong westerly winds. On 14 December, they twice shipped heavy seas which washed the spare anchor and fittings off the upper deck and that night they anchored again, in 16 fathoms. They unrigged topmasts and hoped to ride out the storm, but with water constantly breaking over them, the crew became exhausted from constantly pumping and bailing. Late on the 16th the anchor cable parted when she was hit by another big wave and she was driven before the wind, until in the early hours of the next morning she struck a sandbank, beating off her rudder. The small bower anchor was let go and the mainmast cut away to stabilise her. During the morning it was decided to run the ship on shore, so the cable was cut to allow the ship to drive, but the ebbing tide took her down onto another

sandbank and she grounded. Land could be seen nearby and during the afternoon the pinnace was launched, and Captain Goodall left to summon aid from the shore. The boat spent a miserable night at sea, before landing the next morning on the island of Borkum. One small sloop was all that was available, and this, accompanied by the pinnace, returned to the ship, but found that she had broken up and sunk into the sand. One raft with 21 men was saved from the wreck, but 142 men died.
[TNA:ADM.1/1826]

1718

1 September FERRET Sloop
Deptford 1711; 114 tons; 64.7ft x 20.8ft; 10 guns
Master and Commander John Yeo
Following the engagement between Sir George Byng and the Spanish fleet under Gastañeta off Cape Passaro, with no formal declaration of war, the Spanish retaliated by seizing British shipping in Spanish ports. The *Ferret* had been sent to Cadiz to collect monies for the garrison at Gibraltar, and soon after anchoring, a squadron under Admiral Guevara entered the harbour, with five warships anchoring very close to her. Apprehensive of their intentions, Commander Yeo decided to weigh immediately, but her way was blocked by the Spanish 50-gun ship '*Armiñona*' (probably *Hermiona*), who forced her to surrender without a fight.
[TNA:ADM.1/5271]

5 September GREYHOUND Sixth Rate
Woolwich 1712; 276 tons; 94ft x 26ft; 20 guns
Master and Commander John Cundett
Whilst lying at anchor in St Jerome's Bay, near Cape Spartel, Morocco, five Spanish warships approached, entered the bay and commenced anchoring around her. Unaware of the recent battle between Byng and Gastañeta, but apprehensive of Spanish intentions, that evening the *Greyhound* attempted to cut her anchor cable and run out of the bay. She was foiled by contrary winds and a large Spanish warship fired into her, shooting away her main topsail yard. Clearly unable to escape, she surrendered.
Note: retaken 16 September 1719 by *Weymouth* and *Antelope* and burnt.
[TNA:ADM.1/5271]

1719

29 January CROWN Fourth Rate
Deptford 1704; 653 tons; 126.8ft x 34.5ft; 50 guns
Captain John Roberts
The *Crown* escorted a small fleet of store ships and victualling ships from England to Lisbon, arriving off the port in the late afternoon. A pilot came onboard and assured Captain Roberts that the ship could be taken into harbour, despite Roberts' concerns that the tide was on the turn, assuring the ship's officers that there would be water enough for the ship. Boats were hoisted out and the anchors prepared for release as the ship proceeded. As they came abreast St Julian's fort the wind fell away to a calm, and the ship was taken by the strong tidal current inshore. The boats were hailed and ordered to close and prepare to tow her, and an anchor was let go, but to little purpose, as before it could bring her up, she struck the ground. She swung to the northward into a small sandy bay, one of the boats being capsized with the loss of the crew as they attempted to assist. She struck the ground heavily and as the tide ebbed, she was left high and dry. Her guns, sails, anchors and much of the stores were saved from the wreck before she broke up.
[TNA:ADM.1/5271;ADM.1/2378]

14 February BURFORD Third Rate
Deptford 1698; 1,113 tons; 152.9ft x 40.8ft; 70 guns
Captain Charles Vanburgh
Part of the squadron in the Mediterranean under Admiral Byng, she anchored in Pentemelia Bay, near Reggio, Italy, on 6 February about 200 yards from shore. The weather was poor and worsened, with winds rising and on the 13th it increased to storm force. The lower yards were lowered to the gunwales, topmasts struck, and topsail yards trimmed fore and aft. Despite all the precautions, at the height of the gale, about 7 o'clock in the evening, the best bower cable parted. The sheet anchor was dropped but it would not hold, and the ship started dragging. She tailed onto the shore on the southern side of the bay and ran aground. An attempt was made to rig sheers on one side, but these failed due to the motion of the ship. By 8 o'clock in the morning there was 5ft of water in the hold, and it was clear that she had bilged, bottom planks having been broken and pushed up. The guns and much of her stores were subsequently saved over the next few days. A Spanish prize and two local trading vessels went ashore at the same time.
[TNA:ADM.1/5271;ADM.51/4133]

28 March BLANDFORD Sixth Rate
Woolwich 1711; 276 tons; 94ft x 26ft; 20 guns
Captain Erasmus Philips†
Sailed from Plymouth on 14 March in company with the *Seahorse* to escort a small convoy to St Jean de Luz in south-west France. The ships arrived off the port on 27 March, in poor weather, and all anchored in the roads and prepared to ride out an oncoming storm, unrigging topmasts and trimming lower yards as the wind increased to gale force, with regular squalls of rain

and hail. A boat from the shore managed to reach the *Seahorse* to give assistance and warned that they feared for the safety of *Blandford*, as her chosen anchorage was on foul ground, with numerous sharp rocks, and despite the urgings of Captain Martin of the *Seahorse*, no boat could reach her. At about 9.30 in the evening, she was seen to be making signals of distress, and these were repeated through the night, until, with her anchor cables parting, at 5.30am the ship was driven on shore and wrecked. Both the Captain and Lieutenant were drowned, with forty-three others, but forty-two men were saved.
[TNA: ADM.51/881; ADM 106/729]

1720

18 June MILFORD Fifth Rate
Deptford 1705; 421 tons; 108.7ft × 29.10ft; 36 guns
Captain Peter Chamberlain†
Sailed from Jamaica to escort a convoy of eleven ships to England, they were joined by two American sloops for the first part of the voyage. The *Milford* and every ship of the convoy went ashore in poor weather on Cape Corrientes, Cuba, with heavy loss of life. Only the Purser and thirty men survived from the warship, who had to spend several uncomfortable days existing on a reef, before they were found by a sloop engaged in catching turtles. They alerted the *Mermaid*, which closed the wreck site on 3 July and rescued the survivors.
[www.britishnewspaperarchive.co.uk: Caledonian Mercury 18 August 1720 pp4 & 22 August 1720 p4; TNA ADM.51/605]

21 November SPEEDWELL Bomb
Deptford 1716; 274 tons; 95.5ft × 25.6ft; 12 guns
Master and Commander Edward Brookes
Part of the squadron under Sir John Norris deployed to the Baltic, the ships weighed from Elsinore on 3 November to return to England. The weather was poor, and deteriorated, the ships being scattered by hard gales and driving rain. By the 21st the *Speedwell* was labouring in the high seas, and it was found that the head had been damaged, the rails having been washed away. The Carpenter lashed a block to the knee of the head to support it, but it was found that the ship was making water. She was forced to lay with her head into the wind for much of the time, but during that afternoon the wind shifted to the north-west and seemed to increase in strength with the seas washing over her. It was agreed by all the officers that she was close to sinking, and so to save the men, she was put before the wind, with the yards lowered to the gunnels. At about 3.30am she drove onshore at Wyk-Op-Zee (modern Wijkaan Zee). The mainmast was cut away, which also carried away the mizzen topmast. This allowed all the men to escape onto the shore.
[TNA: ADM.1/1472; ADM.1/5271]

24 November MONCK Fourth Rate
Rotherhithe 1701; 808 tons; 137.6ft × 36.5ft; 64 guns
Captain George Clinton
Returning to England from the Baltic, she was caught in the North Sea in the mid-November storms and anchored off the Suffolk coast to ride out the gale. The storm not abating, the mainmast was cut away to ease the ship, but this was unskilfully done, and it brought down the mizzen mast as well. She was eventually forced to cut her cables and run out to sea, pumping and bailing constantly. After initially attempting to make Goeree in the Netherlands, jury masts were rigged and she turned back for the English coast, raising the land near Great Yarmouth on 24 November. Attempting to run into the roads, she ran hard aground on the Corton Sands, and started beating heavily. A local fisherman came alongside and recommended that they abandon ship until high tide the next day, which was done. The following day, with the weather moderating, the Captain and officers returned to the ship with some of the crew, although a large number had mutinously refused to return, saying that '… they did not intend to return to a sinking ship to drown'. Strenuous efforts were made to pump the ship out and assistance was sought from the Mayor of Great Yarmouth. After two days of constant pumping, little headway was being made and it was decided that as the crew were '… entirely jaded and unable to keep up the pumping' that she could not be saved, and she was run ashore about a mile to the south of Gorleston, where she broke up. The Trinity House pilot on board, George Long, was blamed for running her onto the sands, as had not '… for thirty years past piloted any ship of consequence into Yarmouth roads …'. He was ordered to lose all pay due and never serve as a pilot for the Navy again.
[TNA: ADM.1/5271]

1721

10 November ROYAL ANNE GALLEY Fifth Rate
Woolwich 1709; 511 tons; 127ft × 31ft; 40 guns
Captain Francis Willis
Sailed from Portsmouth on 28 October for Barbados with the new Governor, Lord Belhaven and his retinue embarked and anchored in Plymouth Sound on 31 October. They sailed on 7 November in light winds and tacked south and west over the next two days against westerly winds. During the afternoon of 9 November land was sighted which was identified as the Lizard. With the wind freshening, she lay-to for some time but as the

weather was clearly worsening, it was decided to bear away for Plymouth, and at midnight, stood to the north-east under reefed topsails. At 3 o'clock in the morning breakers were seen ahead, and an attempt was made to wear ship and the helm was put over, but she struck the ground hard, 'about a pistol-shot' from the land, on the Stag Rocks off Lizard Point. The ship was pounded by the waves and quickly broke up in the surf. Bodies and wreckage were scattered over a large area of the coast. There were only three survivors from those onboard.
[London Gazette 25 November 1721]

7 December HIND Sixth Rate
Woolwich 1711; 276 tons; 94ft × 26ft; 20 guns
Captain John Furzer†

With some passengers and despatches for the island, the ship approached St Aubin's Bay, Jersey under the guidance of Peter Askipo, acting as pilot. Approaching on a strong south-easterly wind, they were to the south of Elizabeth Castle when they struck a rock with some force, which pierced the hull under the larboard bow. A few moments later they struck hard again, and water entered so rapidly that within 10 minutes she had foundered. Twenty-one men were drowned. It was found that she had struck a known hazard, the Hinguette reef, the blame being placed entirely on the '... ignorance and negligence' of the pilot who had failed to calculate the tides accurately. He was sentenced to lose all pay due and to serve three years in the Marshalsea Prison.
[TNA: ADM.1/5271; ADM.106/742]

1722

19 April GREYHOUND Sixth Rate
Deptford 1720; 371 tons; 105ft × 28.5ft; 20 guns
Captain John Waldron†

Stationed at New York, she was sent to Port Maria, Cuba, to assist with trade, and after anchoring on 29 March, parties were sent ashore to embark water and provisions. Captain Waldron invited a party of Spaniards to dine onboard and about eighteen people, 'merchants, attendants and friends' arrived and whilst six or eight went into the cabin, the remainder stayed on deck. When the ship's company were piped to dinner, the Spanish on deck attacked and overpowered the watch, whilst those below produced pistols. In a short fight Captain Waldron, along with the Surgeon, was shot dead whilst Lieutenant Edward Smith was wounded. The Spanish, having taken the vessel, proceeded to plunder it of money and stores. She was recaptured later that night by the *Greyhound's* tender, which, manned by about thirty hands, returned alongside, the Spanish leaving as they did so.
[www.britishnewspaperarchive.co.uk: Newcastle Courant 7 July 1722 pp9–10]

1736

18 March BIDEFORD Sixth Rate
Chatham 1727; 372 tons; 106ft × 28.4ft; 20 guns
Captain Matthew Consett

About an hour after sailing from Bridlington Bay, Yorkshire, where she had been lying at anchor, the steward came on deck to say that his store was filling with water. On investigation it was discovered that the fish-room, under the steward's room, was also full of water. Soon after this, water came up through the fore-hold and flooded the galley, putting out the fire. Captain Consett immediately stood for shore and ran the ship aground on Steel Point, near Flamborough Head, where the men scrambled ashore. The exact cause of the leaks could not be discovered. The hawse plugs had been left out after weighing, but this would not account for the amount of water in her. The Carpenter claimed that it was poor caulking, but this was dismissed as the ship had been inspected in Sheerness Dockyard in June of the previous year and no faults found.
[TNA: ADM.1/5273; ADM.106/888]

29 December PRINCESS LOUISA Fifth Rate
Woolwich 1728; 602 tons; 124.2ft × 33.4ft; 40 guns
Captain Thomas Bradley

Ordered to Hellevoetsluis, Holland to escort the Royal Yacht and 'attend the passage of the King', she sailed from the Downs anchorage on 28 December. The following evening, they sighted the Dutch coast at Schouwen, and with a stiff south-westerly wind, the pilot James Stuart assured the Captain that there would be sufficient water to take the ship in that night. However, at about 10.30pm she grounded on the flats off Goeree about a mile from the shore. The boats were hoisted out and on sounding it was found that she had only three fathoms of water around her. The ship started to beat hard, and despite the masts being cut away to ease her, the rudder was beaten off and she then broached-to, and water was reported entering. Several boats from the shore approached and the bulk of the crew was ordered to leave, although one boat overset, by which fifteen men were drowned, the only casualties. Captain Bradley remained onboard overnight with a small number of men, but the following morning in poor weather, with strong winds and the sea breaking over her, the ship was abandoned, the men being rescued by local craft. The pilot's decision to enter that day was blamed for the wreck, although this was tempered by the testimony of other pilots, including that of the Royal Yacht, who backed his claim that there should have been sufficient water. In consequence no prison sentence was awarded, but he was ordered not to serve as a pilot in Royal Navy ships again.
[TNA: ADM.1/5273]

5 | 1739–1748: The War of the Austrian Succession ('The War of Jenkins's Ear')

THE PEACE WHICH HAD LASTED since 1719 was broken 20 years later with a clash with Spain. The South Sea Company had been granted the *Asiento do Negros* by Spain in 1713, allowing them to transport slaves from Africa to Spain's American colonies. The British were accused by the Spanish of abusing this agreement by trading in other goods not allowed under the contract and British ships were stopped and searched. There was already growing tension with continental Europe over British expansion into North America, and the demands that the Spanish stop interrupting trade heading for North America, and the perceived failure of the Spanish to promptly compensate for confiscation of British goods, was a convenient excuse for a declaration of war in October 1739. The following year continental Europe found itself going to war over the disputed succession to the Austrian throne. This alone would probably have brought about a war with France, which was already supporting Spain both financially and tactically. The war later acquired its popular name of 'Jenkins's Ear', due to an incident in which a British sea captain had an ear severed during a search of his vessel by the Spanish, an event seized upon by proponents of a war against Spain.

The support given by Louis XV to the claims of Charles Stuart (the 'Young Pretender') to the British throne gave the French another reason to open hostilities. War was finally declared against France in March 1744. The conflict continued against the Bourbon powers until the treaty of Aix-la-Chappelle in 1748.

The war started well for the British with a successful expedition to the Caribbean although later operations in this region were not so well conducted, with a series of failed expeditions. Actions in the Mediterranean were marred by the hostility between the senior British officers, Admirals Mathews and Lestock, which resulted in court martials for both after the poorly-conducted fleet action off Toulon in 1744. The French backing for the Stuart cause led to a rebellion in Scotland in 1745, which in turn saw several minor naval actions. Expeditions were mounted against the French settlements in Canada and actions also took place in Indian waters where both powers had established trading posts.

1739

September OWNER'S GOODWILL Sloop Tender
Hired 1739
Master John Perry†
Sailed from Yarmouth, Isle of Wight, 17 September, with Lieutenant Hugh Fortescue on board, and not seen again, so presumed foundered in the Channel with all hands.
[TNA: ADM.106/2179; NMM ADM 354/115/66]

October HAWK Sloop
Chatham 1721; 100 tons; 62ft x 19.10ft; 8 guns
Master and Commander John Nevison†
Sailed from Charleston, South Carolina, on 16 October bound from England and never seen again, she was presumed to have foundered in the Atlantic with all hands. With nothing being heard, she was officially paid off on 31 January 1740.
[TNA: ADM 33/360]

1740

January TRIUMPH Sixth Rate
Prize 1739 (*Triunfo or San Cristobal*); 500 tons; 24 guns
Lieutenant Charles Wimbleton
A Spanish frigate captured at Portobello (Portobelo), by Admiral Vernon's squadron, she was manned from the British ships and ordered to Jamaica. However, in her passage she sprang a leak which could not be stopped, and she was deliberately run aground on the Samballas Keys (modern San Blas), off the coast of Panama, and then burnt to avoid capture. Lieutenant Wimbleton and his men walked through the jungle to the settlement of Bastimentos, where they were rescued by an American privateer.
[Ranft p85]

1741

2 March WOLF Sloop
Deptford 1731; 244 tons; 87ft x 25ft; 8 guns
Master and Commander John Draper
Weighed from her anchorage in Irish Bay, Hispaniola, on 24 February and steered north to head for the

Caicos Passage between Mayaguana and Caicos Island. At about 3 o'clock in the morning she struck the ground heavily and found herself held fast. Despite heaving guns overboard and emptying the water butts, she could not be moved, and steadily filled with water and sank. The crew took shelter on the reef and were eventually taken off by a French squadron. At the time of the wreck, Draper thought himself to be over 20 miles from the nearest land and blamed a strong current for setting the ship further to the north, onto a reef near Mayaguana. The court martial decided that Draper must take part of the blame, believing that he could have tacked earlier to avoid the rocks, and sentenced him 'to be broke' from his rank. That he was not and was promoted to Captain in September 1741 would indicate that this was overruled. The ship's Carpenter, who had been insulting to Draper during the episode, was dismissed from the Navy.
[TNA: ADM.1/5274]

14 May WAGER Sixth Rate
Rotherhithe 1734, purchased 1740; 559 tons; 123ft × 32.2ft; 22 guns
Captain David Cheap
One of the ships in the squadron under Commodore Anson sent to the raid the Spanish settlements on the western coast of South America, the ships had battled against storm-force winds for two months in their attempts to round Cape Horn. Separated from the other ships, and badly affected with sickness, Captain Cheap attempted to steer for one of the designated rendezvous, the island of Socorro off the coast of Chile. On 13 May the *Wager* found herself embayed in the Golfo de Peñas, and with only 13 men fit for duty from a crew of 130, and the sails and rigging in a very poor condition, they could not tack the ship, and Cheap was injured when he fell down the quarterdeck ladder. They could do nothing when the ship was taken inshore. At 4.30 in the morning, she struck a rock on the eastern side of a small island and unshipped her tiller. She was taken further inshore and finally ran aground, where she quickly filled with water and settled. Many of the sick were drowned, but the Captain and most of the crew got ashore to set up camp on the island now known as Wager Island. The crew survived on the shore for some time in an increasing state of indiscipline, which resulted in Captain Cheap shooting dead one of the crew for mutiny. The crew spilt into factions, with the majority abandoning Cheap and returned around Cape Horn in the long boat which had been rebuilt and lengthened to reach the Portuguese settlement of Rio Grande, from where several successfully returned to England. Captain Cheap with a smaller part of the crew that had remained loyal to him, after an incredible series of hardships, eventually reached the Spanish settlement of Chiloe. At the court martial for the loss, not held until 1746 when Cheap had finally returned to England, the survivors were acquitted of any wrongdoing, except for Lieutenant Robert Baynes, who was admonished for failing to report a sighting of land the day before the wreck.
[TNA: ADM.1/5288; Walter pp137–44]

20 August ANNA Pink
Hired 1740; 200 tons; 8 guns
Master – Gerrard
One of the store ships hired to support Anson's voyage to the South Pacific, like the *Wager* she became separated from the squadron in poor weather and found herself close to the Chilean coastline. Unlike the unfortunate *Wager*, however, the *Anna* successfully found a safe haven in a sheltered bay, where the ship rode out the storms and the crew recovered from sickness. The bay is now known as Bahia Anna Pink. The store ship was able to rejoin Anson at the island of Juan Fernandez on 17 August, where the last of her stores were offloaded to the other ships, although much of the foodstuffs had been ruined by water damage. Mr Gerrard requested a survey of the pink, and it was found that she was in poor condition, with broken knees and beams, timbers rotten and ironwork decayed. The vessel was therefore purchased by Anson, and the vessel then stripped to provide spare parts for the other ships. The remains were then scuttled.
[Walter p147–8]

4 October TRYALL Sloop
Deptford 1732; 200 tons; 84ft × 23.6ft; 8 guns
Master and Commander Charles Saunders
The smallest of the squadron under Commodore George Anson to enter the South Pacific to attack Spanish settlements and shipping on the Pacific coast of South America, the little vessel successfully rounded Cape Horn in the teeth of fierce storms to reach the island of Juan Fernandez. After this the sloop had successfully chased and captured a Spanish merchant ship off the coast of Chile. This had badly strained the vessel, and she lost her main topmast and strained the mainmast during the chase. She also leaked constantly, the seams opening all the time in the sea, and the rigging was in a terrible condition. As it was feared that at the next tropical storm, she would probably founder, the men and stores were transferred to other ships and she was scuttled, then being to the west of Valparaiso.
[Walter pp161–3]

1742

13 January TIGER Fourth Rate
Sheerness 1722; 712 tons; 130ft × 35.5ft; 50 guns
Captain Edward Herbert

Ordered to cruise between Grand Cayman and Cape Corrientes, she left her station to proceed to the north-west of Cuba, in search of prizes. During 13 January she chased and overhauled a sloop, which proved to be from Barbados, the crew of which wrongly advised them they were near the Bahama Banks. That evening, sighting low-lying islands, they mistakenly believed that it must be the Reques Reef. The lead-line was ordered to be used constantly and this showed the water to be steadily shallowing, but when they attempted to tack, they missed stays. They managed to wear ship, but the ship was now close to the rocks, and at 5.30pm they struck the ground. All sail was thrown aback and she initially floated free, but before they could drop anchor, she again struck the ground, and this time would not move. All boats were hoisted out to lay out kedge anchors, but she would not shift. The wind picked up during the night and the ship started to bump heavily, and it was reported that water was entering. She lay on the reef for two days, until it became clear that she could not get off. After this the ship was abandoned and over the next few weeks was stripped of stores and the crew moved ashore where they set up a defended camp, which included the ship's guns. On 19 January, the longboat was despatched to New Providence in the Bahamas, but when that did not return, the yawl was sent away on 7 February, but this returned on the 15th, having been chased by Spanish ships. On 22 February when a Spanish sloop approached the camp, the wreck was burned, and the camp prepared for an assault. However, the Spanish did not attack, and under a flag of truce, advised them that the crew of the longboat had been captured. When the sloop returned a few days later, an attempt was made to capture it, but this failed. On 19 March, the camp was abandoned, and all embarked in a variety of small boats to sail to Jamaica. Herbert finally arrived at Port Royal on 10 May 1742. It was subsequently found that the ship had been wrecked on Garden Key in the Dry Tortugas. The subsequent court martial reprimanded Captain Herbert for leaving his station and his pay was mulcted, but any criticism was tempered with praise for his actions after the wreck.
[TNA: ADM.1/5273; ADM.51/1000]

14 January OTTER Sloop
Deptford 1721; 91 tons; 64.6ft × 18.3ft; 6 guns
Master and Commander Alexander Gordon†

Sailed from Harwich on 13 January to convoy ships to Bremen but was driven onto the Sizewell bank off Aldborough the next day in high winds and driving snow and wrecked. All the crew were lost except eighteen men and a boy.
[TNA: ADM.106/950; www.britishnewspaperarchive.co.uk: Ipswich Journal 16 January 1742 p3]

18 April SALTASH Sloop
Deptford 1741; 221 tons; 89ft × 24.1ft; 8 guns
Master and Commander Arthur Upton

Cruising between Gibraltar and Faro, Portugal, on 16 April she sighted and chased a Spanish polacre which attempted to escape by running inshore, to the northern side of the Gulf of Cadiz. The *Saltash* steered in between the chase and the shore and successfully cut her off, sending a boat to board her. Whilst she awaited the return of the boat, she sounded with the lead-line and discovered only three fathoms of water under the keel. She attempted to tack, but missed stays, fell off before the wind and with her head to the shore, touched and then ran hard aground. Attempts were made to warp her off using anchors carried out by boats, but without success. The following day the efforts continued, but with the seas beginning to rise, she commenced pounding and the rudder separated. On the morning of 18 April, she was leaking badly and the arrival of three Spanish schooners from Ayamonte which commenced firing decided her fate. The crew took to the boats, after setting fire to the sloop, and all were rescued by a schooner.
[TNA: ADM.1/5273]

16 June DUKE Fireship
Purchased 1739; 199 tons; 83.1ft × 23.9ft; 8 guns
Master and Commander Smith Callis

A small British squadron commanded by Captain Richard Norris was cruising off the coast of southern France to intercept Spanish supplies for their army in Italy. During 16 June, five Spanish galleys were observed to sail from their anchorage off Île Sainte-Marguerite. The British squadron chased, and the galleys ran into the harbour of Saint Tropez to seek shelter in a neutral port. Captain Norris sent a message to the governor requesting that the Spanish vessels be ordered to sea but was refused. At this he ordered the fireship *Duke* to burn the galleys. That night the British ships warped in to close the enemy, and at 1 o'clock in the morning, the fireship, accompanied by the boats of the squadron, successfully burnt all five galleys. Commander Callis did this with some skill and 'great coolness and effectiveness' and was awarded a gold chain for his courage.
[London Gazette 6 July 1742; TNA: ADM. 43/4 – 43/7]

16 August GLOUCESTER Fourth Rate
Sheerness 1737; 866 tons; 134ft x 38.8ft; 50 guns
Captain Matthew Mitchell

Part of Commodore Anson's squadron in the Pacific Ocean, the ships had been at sea for two years, had travelled half way around the world, and the little expedition was now reduced to just two ships, the *Centurion* and *Gloucester*. After leaving the coast of South America, where they had attacked Spanish shipping and settlements, the pair headed across the Pacific, bound for the Philippines. The *Gloucester* became increasingly leaky, and the much-spliced rigging and rotten masts were in a dangerous state. Scurvy was affecting the crew badly, with men dying at the rate of five a day. On 26 July, the fore topmast collapsed and the foreyard broke in the slings. This impeded her sailing even further and the ship springing a serious leak only added to her misery. By 14 August, despite constant pumping she had over 9ft of water in the hold. The following day a survey showed that she had no usable masts or spars, had at least two leaks and '… was extremely decayed in every part'. She was therefore stripped of anything usable, the men transferred to the *Centurion*, and she was then set on fire. She burned through the night, with the cannons firing as the flames reached them, until at about 6 o'clock in the morning of 16 August she blew up with '… an exceeding black pillar of smoke, which shot up into the air to a very considerable height'. The position was noted as 15.08N 216.35W (*i.e.*, 144.25E).
[Walter pp277–82]

21 September TILBURY Fourth Rate
Chatham 1733; 963 tons; 144.2ft x 39.2ft; 60 guns
Captain Peter Lawrence

Whilst cruising off the island of Hispaniola, West Indies, she caught fire and was lost, reportedly following an accidental spillage of rum. It emerged that a marine, Robert Meads, had attempted to take a bottle of rum from the Purser's boy, Francisco Bianco. A struggle ensued '… the Marine asked for a dram, but [the boy] would give him none, and he shook the boy'. The bottle was dropped, and smashed, and the lamp the boy was holding was also thrown to the deck in the scuffle and the spilled rum ignited. The fire spread rapidly to the other rum casks in the hold and soon became uncontrollable, forcing the crew into the boats. Marine Meads did not survive, but young Bianco did.
[TNA: ADM.1/5273]

[10] October GRAMPUS Sloop
Woolwich 1731; 160 tons; 70ft x 23.2ft; 6 guns
Master and Commander Alexander Stewart†

Missing, presumed foundered in gale-force winds, in the English Channel, in the vicinity of the Channel Islands, with all hands. The pay book was closed on this date.
[TNA: ADM.33/373; www.britishnewspaperarchive.co.uk: Newcastle Courant 4 December 1742 p2]

27 November DRAKE Sloop
Wapping 1741; 207 tons; 85.1ft x 23.6ft; 8 guns
Master and Commander John Stringer

Laying at Gibraltar, Commander Stringer was sent ashore, sick with rheumatic fever, so Lieutenant Nathaniel Stephens assumed command when the *Drake* was ordered to sail to Faro. Having weighed, she used sweeps to manoeuvre out of the bay, but then anchored and struck topmasts and yards as the weather looked increasingly threatening. At about 8.30pm the best bower anchor cable parted and the sheet anchor was let go, but just 30 minutes later the small bower cable also parted. A Dutch merchant ship then drove down onto them, fouling the sheet anchor cable, which the Dutch crew then cut, to free themselves. After this the *Drake* drove before the wind and went ashore near the Ragged Staff Steps, the mainmast and foremast both going overboard soon after.
[TNA: ADM.1/5276]

1743

18 September BRIDGEWATER Sixth Rate
King's Lynn 1740; 437 tons; 106.3ft x 30.7ft; 20 guns
Captain William Fielding

Having successfully escorted a convoy to North American waters, she was approaching the coast of Newfoundland, when the watch on deck were surprised at about 2.30 in the morning to see breakers close ahead, as they believed themselves to be several miles from land. An attempt was made to tack, but the ship missed stays and struck the rocks. The ship hung on the reef for some time, pounding heavily, until by noon the rudder was broken and the quarters beaten in. The crew then took to the boats and were rescued by a merchant ship. The cause was believed to be the extraordinarily strong currents which had set the ship further to the north than expected and embayed her in St Mary's Bay, Newfoundland, near St Shotts.
[TNA: ADM.1/5283]

1744

17 January ASTRAEA Store Ship
Prize 1739; 522 tons; 100ft x 31.4ft; 20 guns
Captain Robert Swanton

Accidentally caught fire at about 2 o'clock in the morning, when laying at anchor in the river Piscataqua, New Hampshire, loaded with timber and masts for Jamaica. The alarm was raised when smoke was seen in the fore-hold, but the fire spread rapidly. The crew's efforts to fight the blaze were hampered by the water alongside being frozen, and the fire was fanned by a

strong northerly wind. The crew were eventually forced to abandon the ship at 7am, and the ship burnt to the waterline.
[TNA: ADM.1/5283; NMM: ADM 354/124]

5 February LOOE Fifth Rate
Limehouse 1741; 685 tons; 124.4ft x 35.8ft; 40 guns
Captain Ashby Utting
Cruising to the north of Cuba, during 4 February she sighted, chased and stopped a snow, which claimed to be French, but which was suspected to be Spanish, so it was decided to tow the prize to Charleston for adjudication. Believing themselves to be about seven leagues (21 miles) to the north-west of the Pan of Matanzas, they steered to the north-north-west until they were clear of the Double-Headed Shot Cays, and then altered to the north-east to raise Cape Florida. At just after 2 o'clock in the morning they ran onto a small sandy key on the edge of the Martyr's sandbank, Florida, together with the prize and was wrecked. The court-martial investigation decided that the probable cause was a strong current, unknown to the officers. Modern investigation suggests that it was more likely that the departure point was mistaken, and they were much further to the north than they believed. The cay is now known as Looe Cay.
[TNA: ADM.1/5283; Mariner's Mirror vol 47 pp139–42]

11 February ANN GALLEY Fireship
Purchased 1739; 302 tons; 97.9ft x 26.7ft; 8 guns
Master and Commander James Macky†
The combined Franco-Spanish fleet under Admiral Navaro and Chef d'Escadre Gabaret were engaged off Toulon by the British fleet under Admiral Thomas Mathews. During the battle, the Spanish flagship *Real Felipe* had been badly mauled by several British ships and became somewhat separated from the main body of the fleet in a disabled condition. Admiral Mathews ordered the *Ann Galley* fireship to close and burn her. As the fireship approached her quarry she came under fire from several Spanish ships, and it was also seen that boats were being launched to tow her away. Commander Macky and a small number of the crew stayed onboard as long as they could. When a Spanish launch approached Macky fired into it, initially with a blunderbuss and then by a gun in the waist. As there would have been loose powder scattered around the upper deck this set off a powder explosion and with '... Hatches unlaid, Skuttles open, Funnels uncapt', it triggered a larger explosion and fire, and she sank by the head before reaching her target. Commander Macky, Lieutenant Somerset Stillier, a mate, a gunner and two quartermasters who had stayed onboard were killed.
[London Gazette 20 March 1743/44; Matthews: A Narrative ... pp79–81]

4 March INDUSTRY Snow Tender
Hired 1741
Master William Johnson
In company with several other tenders and store vessels, she joined a convoy at Spithead under escort of the *Terror* bomb vessel, en-route to the Downs anchorage. The little convoy sailed during morning of 3 March and made slow progress eastwards in hazy weather. During the day, the weather steadily deteriorated into dank, drizzling weather, with strong gusts of wind. The *Terror* had ordered one of the tenders, *Amsterdam Packet*, to go ahead and show a light as a guide, and to fire a gun when she could see the light at Dungeness, but in the dark, they lost sight of the light, but continued the same course.

At about 10.30pm the *Terror*, followed by four of the tenders, ran hard aground on to the Sussex shore at the Burling Gap near Beachy Head. Two of the tenders were re-floated, but the *Industry* capsized and was lost. The *Terror* bomb lay on the shore for a month before being hauled free.
[TNA: ADM.1/5283; ADM.51/1009]

4 March NEPTUNE Tender
Hired 1744
Master Zachary Romaine
As with the *Industry* (above), one of the little convoy to the Downs that ran aground on the Sussex shore near Beachy Head. The *Neptune* could not be refloated and was abandoned as a wreck. Both the captains of the escorting *Terror* bomb vessel and the masters of the tenders were criticised for failing to keep a good look out, complacency and neglect.
[TNA: ADM.1/5283]

8 May NORTHUMBERLAND Third Rate
Woolwich 1743; 1,300 tons; 154.1ft x 44.2ft; 64 guns
Captain Thomas Watson†
One of a British squadron under Admiral Sir Charles Hardy cruising off Ushant, the *Northumberland* was detached at 5 o'clock in the morning to investigate strange sails to the north-east. They found that they could not gain on the chase and at 2pm she was recalled, by signal and gun. Despite this Captain Watson continued to press on over the horizon. Soon after this a hard shower of rain obscured visibility for some time, and on clearing it was found that two large warships were in sight about a league (three miles) distant. The strangers were the French *Content*, 64 guns, and the *Mars*, 64, and Watson continued to press on, evidently believing that as they were some distance apart from each other he could engage one before the other could assist. Despite the warnings of his officers, he did not clear for action until the last minute, consequently the ship went into action largely unprepared. Watson then

compounded his error by passing the *Content* to engage the *Mars* and soon found himself fighting both. The helm was shot away causing her to fly up into the wind, allowing the enemy to rake them. The unequal combat was maintained for three hours, until Watson was taken below, mortally wounded, and the Master surrendered the ship. The subsequent court martial found that the loss was directly due to the 'rash and inconsiderate' actions of Captain Watson. Some explanation of his behaviour may be found in the fighting at Port Belo in 1739 when he had suffered a fractured skull, which seemed to affect his mind. The Master, James Dixon, was found guilty of calling for quarter and surrendering the ship and was sentenced to be imprisoned in the Marshalsea Prison for life.
[TNA: ADM.1/5284]

6 August SOLEBAY Sixth Rate
Plymouth 1742; 429 tons; 106ft x 30.5ft; 20 guns
Captain Thomas Bury
Ordered to cruise between Gibraltar and Cape St Vincent to gain intelligence of the enemy and then return to Lisbon, she sighted the squadron under de Rochambeau during 5 August and made sail away. She was chased by the enemy throughout the day and into the night, the French steadily gaining. During the night she attempted to evade the French by tacking and passing by them. The manoeuvre was seen and the *Saint Michel*, 64 guns, came alongside, forcing her to surrender. Captain Bury was later mulcted a month's pay for giving up his ship without offering a fight.
  Note: retaken 20 April 1746 by privateer *Alexander*.
[TNA: ADM.1/5284]

30 September GRAMPUS Sloop
Blackwall 1743; 249 tons; 87.10ft x 25.1ft; 14 guns
Master and Commander Hugh Littleton
Sailed from Spithead on 25 September for Lisbon, she was chased, overhauled and captured by a French squadron under de Rochambeau and carried into Brest.
[Lloyd's List no 937 13 November 1744; Troude vol I p297]

(4/5) October VICTORY First Rate
Portsmouth 1737; 1,921 tons; 174.9ft x 50.6ft; 100 guns
Captain Samuel Faulkner†
The flagship of Admiral Sir John Balchen, the *Victory* had led the squadron that successfully raised the blockade of Lisbon by the French and escorted a convoy to Gibraltar. Returning to England, the ships were overtaken and dispersed by a storm when off Ushant. The *Victory* was separated from the other ships during 4 October, when about 30 leagues (90 miles) south-west of Scilly and was not seen again. During the early hours of 5 October signal guns of distress were heard by the inhabitants of Alderney in the Channel Islands, but the night was so dark and stormy with violent winds, that no one could discover the cause. Sometime later wreckage was reported to have been washed ashore in the Channel Islands that was associated with the *Victory*, and it was presumed that she had been wrecked, with the loss of all hands (some 880 men), on the Casquets rocks. However, in 2008 her remains were found in the western approaches to the Channel, north of the Hurd Deep, some 60 miles to the west of the Casquets. This would suggest that she was overwhelmed soon after she parted company on 4 October.
[TNA: ADM.106/1007; ADM.106/1012; Gentleman's Magazine vol XIV pp562, 563, 616. http://www.shipwreck.net/pdf/OMEPapers2-HMS_Victory.pdf; Various secondary]

October: Jamaica Hurricane
In October, Jamaica was struck by a powerful hurricane, which caused widespread damage. *The Gentleman's Magazine* published an account, taken from the *Kingston Gazette*: 'On the 20th instant, happened as dreadful a storm as ever was known in this part of the world. It began about six o'clock in the evening and lasted till 6 o'clock in the morning; the wind was all that time due south. By this hurricane, the new fort at Mosquito Point was demolished, many houses were blown down, roofs and piazas' blown off, and the wharfs of this town, Port Royal and Passage Fort destroyed, and a great part of the goods thereon washed away.' [*Gentleman's Magazine* vol XV p163]

20/21 October GREENWICH Fourth Rate
Chatham 1730; 759 tons; 134.2ft x 36ft; 50 guns
Captain Edward Allen†
The victim of a hurricane which struck Jamaica, the *Greenwich* was in a partly-rigged condition alongside the *Lark* sheer hulk (see below). The storm began during the afternoon of 20 October and by early evening the hurricane was blowing at full force across the island, reaching its peak between midnight and 1am. There was widespread damage ashore, and over ninety merchant vessels either wrecked or driven ashore. During the hurricane, the *Greenwich* capsized, drowning the Captain, First Lieutenant and seventy men.
[TNA: ADM 1/5284; London Gazette 6 April 1745; www.britishnewspaperarchive.co.uk; Scots Magazine 1 March 1745 p45]

20/21 October SAINT ALBANS Fourth Rate
Plymouth 1737; 854 tons; 134ft x 38.6ft; 50 guns
Captain William Knight†
Laying at anchor in Port Royal, Jamaica, preparations had been made for a storm, with topmasts struck and yards trimmed fore and aft, but despite this it was found that she was driving. The sheet anchor was let go, but during the evening the anchor cables parted,

and when the sheet cable parted, she was driven across the anchorage and was wrecked on the Lee Spit near Mosquito Point.
[TNA:ADM.1/5284;ADM.52/328]

20/21 October BONETTA Sloop
Woolwich 1732; 201 tons; 81.4ft × 24ft; 8 guns
Master and Commander William Lea†
During the hurricane-force winds which crossed Jamaica, she was swept from the anchorage at Port Royal and driven onto Salt Pan Hill where she was wrecked.
[TNA:ADM.1/5284]

20/21 October THUNDER Bomb
Rotherhithe 1740; 272 tons; 91.3ft × 26.3ft; 8 guns
Master and Commander Thomas Gregory
The hurricane which hit Jamaica forced the *Thunder* from her anchors, and she, like the *Bonetta*, was driven out of the anchorage and onto the shore near Salt Pan Hill, Port Royal, where she was wrecked.
[TNA:ADM.1/5284]

20/21 October LARK Sheer hulk
Woolwich 1726; 598 tons; 124.2ft × 33.3ft
The hulk was based at Port Royal, Jamaica when that island was struck by a powerful hurricane. The *Greenwich* was alongside the *Lark* undergoing maintenance, when the storm struck. The *Greenwich* was capsized by the force of the wind and sea and carried away part of the hulk's side timbers, which also sank. One hundred and ten men, ninety of them black slaves and workers, were drowned.
[www.britishnewspaperarchive.co.uk: Scots Magazine 1 March 1745 p45]

* * *

21 October COLCHESTER Fourth Rate
Harwich 1744; 976 tons; 140.1ft × 40.2ft; 50 guns
Captain Frederick Cornwall
Sailed from the Nore anchorage on 20 September to convoy two ordnance ships to the Downs, they anchored that same night. Weighing anchor at first light the little group continued, but it was decided to anchor again for the night near the Longsands sandbank. At about 7 o'clock in the evening as the ship manoeuvred near the sands, she struck the ground heavily. Unable to get free, a boat was sent into Harwich for assistance, signal guns were fired and lights hung out. Several fishing vessels came to her assistance the following day, but she could not be shifted. She was therefore stripped and abandoned on 23 September as a wreck; twenty-nine men were lost when a boat capsized. The embarked pilot, John Benger, was subsequently sentenced to serve two years in the Marshalsea Prison, for neglect and carelessness. He had failed to order the constant use of the lead-line, despite signals for danger being made by one of the ordnance ships.
[TNA:ADM.1/5284; Gentleman's Magazine vol XIV p564]

28 November RYE Sixth Rate
Rotherhithe 1740; 447 tons; 106.7ft × 30.11ft; 10 × guns
Captain Ormond Thompson
Having sailed from the river Humber, she was escorting two merchant ships along the east coast in poor weather, with thick fog being replaced by constant drizzle. At 4.30 in the morning the anchor was ordered to be let go as soundings showed only five fathoms of water, but before it could take hold she ran aground. The ship swung broadside-on to the shore, which could now be seen as a line of breakers. She fired guns as signals to the other ships and then lowered a boat which carried a rope to the shore, but the boat capsized as it beached, and the rope parted. People soon came to the shore, and eventually a heaving line was passed to them, and this was used to establish a rope line, along which the boat was hauled, carrying the men to the land. During the day, as the tide left the ship she heeled over onto her side and settled into the sand. By 29 November it was found that she was sinking deeper into the sand and was full of water at every high tide. Work went on to remove all the stores and guns and she was finally abandoned as a wreck when the ship started breaking up in December. She had run aground at Weybourne, near Salthouse, Norfolk. The blame for the loss was placed on the pilot, John Weller, who mistook the rate of the setting of the flood tides into the Lynn and Boston Deeps, which was then compounded by altering course inshore, instead of hauling off to seaward. He was condemned to lose a year's pay and serve three months in the Marshalsea Prison. However, the court, hearing representations that he was elderly and blind in one eye, recommended that the prison sentence be relented. The ship's Master, John Feast, was also criticised for failing to object to any of the pilot's actions or inform the Captain of the fatal course change. He was ordered to be mulcted three months' pay.
[TNA:ADM.1/5284;ADM.1/2580;ADM.51/807]

(12/13) December MERCURY Fireship
Purchased 1739; 217 tons; 89.11ft × 23.10ft; 8 guns
Master and Commander Moses Peadle†
Disappeared whilst on passage from Spithead to Deptford, she was last seen on 12 December, when at anchor off Margate. That day saw storm-force winds from the north-west with heavy snow affect the south-east of England, forcing several ships out of the safety of the Downs anchorage, and it was presumed that one of these was the *Mercury*, which must have foundered soon afterwards, with the loss of all on board. Pay Book closed 12 December.
[TNA:ADM.180/3;ADM.33/379; Lloyd's List no.946 14 December 1744]

24 December SWALLOW Sloop
Deptford 1744; 272 tons; 91.4ft x 26.3ft; 10 guns
Master and Commander Andrew Jelfe

En-route to New Providence in the Bahamas, the sloop steered between Sale Key and Abaco Island and believed that she was well clear of land. It was a surprise when at 9.30pm breakers were seen ahead and despite an effort to come about, the sloop ran aground on a reef on the Bahama Bank shortly afterwards. The foremast, main topmast and the anchors were all cut away in efforts to ease the vessel, which was beating heavily on the rocks. She could not be freed and started filling with water; boats were hoisted out and rafts ordered to be made from the yards and rigging. The following morning the sloop was abandoned, and the crew took refuge on the reef, from where they were rescued by sloops from New Providence. The current was blamed for setting the vessel further to the east than calculated.
[TNA:ADM.1/5285]

1745

7 February PEMBROKE Fourth Rate
Woolwich 1733; 956 tons; 144.2ft x 39.1ft; 60 guns
Captain George Balchen

Having been refitted and re-rigged at Chatham, she sailed from her moorings in the River Medway to take in guns and stores at Blackstakes, when she was hit by a squall when in Kethole Reach which heeled her over. She failed to recover and continued to slowly roll over and capsized. About 100 men, including five ship's officers, together with seven dockyard officers and several women, were drowned. The ship lay on her side, partly submerged, until she was successfully hauled upright and salvaged on 22 February and taken to Chatham to be refitted.
[TNA:ADM.51/4286;ADM.106/1005;ADM.106/1016; NMM:ADM.354/128]

14 February ORFORD Third Rate
Limehouse 1713; 1,099 tons; 151.1ft x 41.3ft; 70 guns
Captain Perry Mayne

Sailed from Jamaica on 4 February with a convoy bound for England, but during the night of 13/14 February she lost company with them. They continued independently during the next day, with the island of Great Inagua being sighted during the late afternoon. At 9.30pm, without warning, they suddenly struck the ground. All sail was thrown aback, but she was held fast. The small bower anchor was let go and boats were hoisted out, which sounded around them, but could find only shallow water. The swell was making the ship pound on the rocks and the rudder became unshipped, and soon water was reported entering the hold. The masts were cut away to try and ease her movement and upper-deck guns heaved overboard to lighten her. The pumps were manned, but by midnight they had 7ft of water in the hold. By the morning it could be seen that they were hard aground on the Hogsty Reef, surrounded by rocks. The boats found a passage through them to a cay, and with the water now above the orlop deck, work started to ferry men and stores to the island where a tented camp was made. On 19 February, a sloop was seen, which closed when signals were made. It proved to be the *Margaretta* of New York, bound for Jamaica, and a Lieutenant and small party on men were sent onboard to bring help. Over the next few days, other schooners and sloops also managed to close, and they took off some of the men, but on 9 March the *Rippon* arrived to rescue the remainder. After salvaging most of the guns, stores and provisions, the wreck was abandoned on 14 March. On his return to England, any disappointment Mayne may have had was tempered by the news that he had been advanced to Rear Admiral of the Blue in his absence abroad.
[TNA:ADM.1/5284;ADM.51/655]

16 February WEYMOUTH Fourth Rate
Plymouth 1736; 1,065 tons; 144ft x 41.5ft; 60 guns
Captain Warwick Calmady

The *Weymouth* arrived in English Harbour, Antigua on 10 February, having escorted three store ships from England. Three days' later gunfire was heard from seaward, and it was learned that the bomb vessel *Comet* was in action with a large Spanish privateer. The warships in the harbour were sailed that evening, to search the area. The *Weymouth* steered around the island of Montserrat, headed north to Nevis and finally north to seaward, but having failed to find the enemy, decided to return to Antigua. On the evening of 16 February, she fixed her position from observations of Antigua and Montserrat. Just before midnight land was sighted ahead, and the ship tacked to steer away, but soon after this, breakers were seen ahead. There was a frantic effort to wear the ship, but before this could be done, she ran hard aground on a reef in the approaches to English Harbour, Antigua. A kedge anchor was carried out by boat to allow an attempt to haul her off, but she failed to move. At first light other ships closed to render assistance, but further efforts to haul her free failed. The mizzen mast was cut away, with all the topmasts, and boats commenced removing stores, to lighten her, but she was held firmly on the rocks and water entered steadily and she settled further into the water. Over the next few days her stores and guns were removed, and the ship was then abandoned as a wreck. In the consequent court martial, the officer of the watch, Lieutenant John Crispo, was found guilty of neglect, in failing to keep a good look out and failing

to use the lead-line; he was mulcted six months' pay and severely reprimanded. The ship's Master, James Whitwood, was also found guilty of neglect on similar charges, and was dismissed from the service. The pilot, Robert Sharpe, was found guilty of neglect; he had advised Captain Calmady to continue to stand into the land and had then told Lieutenant Crispo not to call the Captain when land was sighted. He was sent to England for confinement in the Marshalsea Prison for two years. Modern research has suggested that the likely cause of the wreck was an error in identification, mistaking Antigua for Montserrat when taking bearings.
[TNA: ADM.1/5284; Mariner's Mirror vol 48 pp207–15]

29 March ANGLESEA Fifth Rate
Hull 1742; 712 tons; 126ft x 36.2ft; 40 guns
Captain Jacob Elton†

Having just sailed from Kinsale, where she had landed several sick members of the crew, including the First Lieutenant, a ship was sighted approaching them. It was the French *Apollon*, 54 guns, but Captain Elton believed her to be the British *August*, known to be cruising in the area. Not until the French ship was almost alongside was the mistake discovered. Captain Elton then ordered the ship to be cleared for action and the foresail to be set to give him some manoeuvrability. These actions were far too late, however, and the ship was never properly cleared for action, moreover, the setting of the foresail only served to bury the ship's head. The *Apollon* ran close under the stern of the *Anglesea* and lay on her port quarter raking her with broadsides and volleys of small-arms fire. Both Captain Elton and the Master were killed in the first few minutes of the engagement. The command then fell on the young Second Lieutenant, Baker Philips, who left the upper deck to briefly confer with John Taafe, the Third Lieutenant. Now the ship was being raked by their opponent, with the *Anglesea* unable to properly reply, casualties were mounting, the ship was in confusion and water was washing in through the lower deck ports. Philips therefore surrendered the ship to save further casualties. In the subsequent court martial, the blame for the ship's loss was placed on the late Captain Elton, for failing to have his ship in a proper posture for defending itself, nor did he behave '… like an officer or seaman, which was the cause of the ship being left to Lieutenant Philips in such distress and confusion'. Lieutenant John Taafe was ordered to be cashiered; the Boatswain, Abraham Hall, to be disrated and in future to serve before the mast, whilst poor Philips was sentenced to be shot for failing to encourage the common men to fight, leaving the deck and surrendering the ship. Despite the court recommending that he be shown mercy as he was young and inexperienced, the Admiralty ordered that the sentence to be carried out. He was executed on the fo'c'sle of the *Duke* on 19 July.
[TNA: ADM.1/5285]

14 April MERCURY Brig Sloop
Purchased 1744 (*Poulteney*); 16 guns
Master and Commander Robert Wellard

En-route to Plymouth carrying despatches, two ships were sighted which were evidently closing, which Commander Wellard initially believed to be British, but as they continued to close it was feared that they may be French, and the *Mercury* was ordered to steer away. A three hour chase ensued, until off the Lizard, when the largest of the ships, which was the privateer *Grand-Turc*, 32 guns, of St Malo, ranged alongside and a mutual exchange of broadsides and small arms commenced. The French aimed at the rigging, and in successive broadsides shot away the main brace, fore braces and foremast backstay. The second vessel, a large brig of 20 guns, then came up and stationed herself on the lee quarter. With no prospect of escape, Commander Wellard surrendered his ship.
[TNA: ADM.1/5285]

3 June MEDIATOR Sloop
Purchased 1745; 105 tons; 61.4ft x 21.2ft; 10 guns
Master and Commander George Hamilton

Having sailed from Spithead that morning, she was off the western end of the Isle of Wight when a French snow-rigged privateer was seen approaching, and all preparations were made for a fight. The sloop was overhauled after a short chase, and after a broadside and volley of small shot from the French ship, which was the *Naïade*, 16 guns, the *Mediator* surrendered without further resistance. The Master, David Coulton, who had advised the Captain not to resist and to strike the flag was ordered to lose all pay due and never to serve as a warrant officer again.

Note: retaken the following day by *Assistance*.
[TNA: ADM.1/5285]

22 July FAME Sloop
Purchased 1745; 272 tons; 12 guns
Master and Commander James Campbell

Weighed and sailed on 15 July from Basse Terre, St Kitts, in company with the *Otter*, *Lynn* and *Deal Castle* to escort a large fleet of homeward-bound merchant ships. By 19 July, a leak had become evident, and the pumps were having to be continually worked to clear the water. Despite all their efforts the water was clearly gaining, and the Carpenter finally discovered the leak, which was under the magazine, within a strake or two of the keel. They fell astern of the convoy but were kept company by a Rhode Island privateer and the sloop *Otter*. All the powder was cleared from the magazine as efforts were made to stem the flood, by forcing oakum into the gap,

but to no purpose. A bucket chain was established to help keep the water under control. During 21 July it was clear that they were fighting a losing battle and stood towards the island of St Martin and by that evening she could anchor in Plum Bay (Baie aux Prunes). The Carpenter of the *Otter* came onboard to assist, but by now she had over 4ft of water in the hold. The boats were hoisted out and the men taken ashore, and the ship was hauled further inshore until she grounded. At 5 o'clock in the morning she capsized, putting paid to any hopes of saving her. The next two days were spent in salvaging what stores could be found, and she was then abandoned.
[TNA: ADM.1/5285; ADM.51/358]

29 July MEDIATOR Sloop
Purchased 1745; 105 tons; 61.4ft x 21.2ft; 10 x guns
Master and Commander Charles Brown
Ordered to Ostend to collect despatches for England, the sloop was in a poor state; the Carpenter reported that the bows and breast hooks were weak and allowed water to enter, the bowsprit worked so much that it lifted deck planking and Commander Brown complained that she was crank, constantly heeling so far to leeward that the hatches were under water. It was no surprise when, soon after entering Ostend harbour, that she foundered in shallow water. On 31 July, Commodore Smith ordered the sloop to be abandoned and all the stores and provisions that could be saved being landed for the use of the garrison ashore.
[TNA: ADM.1/481]

28 September FALCON Brig Sloop
Harwich 1744; 272 tons; 91.3ft x 26.2ft; 10 guns
Master and Commander Richard Cartaret
Captured in the western approaches to the English Channel by a large French privateer, the *Deux Couronnes*, 22 guns. The French ship had closed under British colours, but the *Falcon*, suspecting her to be an enemy, had steered away and an all-night chase developed. Not until 3 o'clock in the afternoon of the following day did the privateer catch her. With her rigging shot to pieces and unable to use her lee ports as the water washed in, the sloop surrendered.
Note: retaken on 19 March 1746 by *Captain* and re-entered service as *Fortune*.
[TNA: ADM.1/5285]

September SAPPHIRE'S PRIZE Sloop
Prize 1745 (*Sovervio*); 164 tons; 78.6ft x 22.1ft; 10 guns
Master and Commander Matthew Squire†
Disappeared off the Irish coast in a storm after sailing from Dublin in late September and presumed foundered with all hands. Nothing having been heard of her, she was officially ordered to be paid off on 25 October 1746.
[TNA: ADM.180/3; ADM.33/394]

19 October BLAST Bomb
Deptford 1740; 271 tons; 90.9ft x 26.3ft; 8 guns
Master and Commander Molyneaux Shuldham
Fitted out as a cruising sloop, the *Blast* was cruising to the south of Jamaica, when in the early hours of the morning she sighted and chased two suspicious vessels. They proved to be large Spanish xebec-rigged vessels, carrying 14 and 12 guns. A three-hour fight developed in light and fitful winds, until one of the xebecs successfully ran across the bows of the *Blast* and entered a large number of boarders, the other xebec stationing herself on the bomb's stern. The fighting went on for another 30 minutes, until with forty dead and wounded and confusion caused by exploding powder cartridges, Commander Shuldham surrendered.
[TNA: ADM.1/5288]

29 October WOLF Brig Sloop
Deptford 1742; 246 tons; 89.6ft x 25ft; 14 guns
Master and Commander John Hughes†
When in mid-Channel to the north of the Channel Islands, the *Wolf* found herself being chased by a large French privateer. After a chase of three hours the privateer *Lys* came within gunshot, and with the sloop still heading northwards, a running fight commenced. The privateer concentrated on the rigging, reducing it to tatters, which was accompanied by regular volleys of small-arms fire. Commander Hughes was shot and mortally wounded soon after the action started, but Lieutenant Lobb continued the fight, until with two killed, three wounded and the ship unable to manoeuvre, he surrendered.
Note: recaptured on 1 March 1746 by the *Amazon*.
[TNA: ADM.1/5285]

14 November FOX Sixth Rate
Rotherhithe 1740; 440 tons; 106.8ft x 30.8ft; 20 guns
Captain Edmund Beavor†
Part of the squadron in the North Sea preventing French attempts to supply rebel forces in Scotland, she was driven ashore near Dunbar in poor weather, grounding to the west of the town at low water and breaking up overnight. There were reported to be only nine survivors from the crew of 140 men or the Scottish rebel prisoners on board.
[www.britishnewspaperarchive.co.uk: Derby Mercury 22 November 1745 p2; Stamford Mercury 5 December p2]

15 November BALTIMORE Armed Vessel
Hired 1744
Master and Commander Christopher Hill
Having sailed from Hoylake, as they steered along the coast of North Wales, they found themselves close under the land in dark, heavy weather, with strong winds and frequent squalls with snow. A vain attempt to

tack was made, but she could not clear the land and ran hard aground near Point Lynas, Anglesey. The foremast, bowsprit and main topmast all went by the board soon after striking the ground and she was abandoned as a wreck. Nineteen men were reported lost. Wrongly calculating the tides was blamed for the loss.
[TNA: ADM.1/5285]

25 November HAZARD Brig Sloop
Rotherhithe 1744; 273 tons; 92.3ft × 26.2ft; 10 guns
Master and Commander Thomas Hill
Lying at anchor in Montrose harbour, Scotland, when large numbers of Highlanders, supporters of Prince Charles Edward Stuart, the 'Young Pretender', were seen coming into the town. The previous day Commander Hill had seized arms from ships in the harbour, and, intending to do the same again, boats had been sent inshore. However, the longboat was fired on as it approached the shore, killing one crew member and bringing a halt to the action. The sloop was unable to leave the harbour due to the contrary winds, and the following morning it was seen that batteries had been set up on both sides of the river, and these commenced firing at her. Several shots struck the hull, and the rigging was cut up, which restricted her movements further. The following day a messenger called on them to surrender, or they would sink the ship with its crew. Commander Hill, supported by Lieutenant Michael Burgess, then negotiated the surrender of the sloop, in return for the safe passage out of the harbour of the crew, with stores, in the merchant vessel *Owner's Goodwill*. In the event, the merchant vessel was also unable to leave due to the wind continually blowing into the harbour, and all the crew were eventually taken prisoner. The subsequent court martial took a very dim view of the surrender and believed that the sloop could have been warped out or scuttled, rather than given up to the rebels. Both Hill and Burgess were dismissed from the service.
Note: retaken on 25 March 1746 by *Sheerness*.
[TNA: ADM.1/5288; Gentleman's Magazine vol XV p694]

1746

30 May NACTON Cutter
Hired 1745
Taken up for service at Harwich, she was employed as an advice boat, and was en-route to the Downs with despatches when she was captured by a French galley privateer from Calais.
Note: recaptured in December 1746 by the *Shark*.
[TNA: ADM.106/1031; ADM.106/2181]

16 June LIGHTNING Bomb
Rotherhithe 1740; 275 tons; 90.10ft × 26.5ft; 8 guns
Master and Commander William Martin
Cruising off the Italian coast in company with the *Nonsuch*, the pair was off the island of Gorgona, near Livorno, when the weather deteriorated, with regular squalls of rain and thunder. The *Nonsuch*, seeing the weather worsening, shortened sail, but the *Lightning*, with the Captain sick in his cabin, was slow to respond and still with unreefed topsails spread, she was struck by a strong squall which made her heel over. A quarterdeck gun broke loose, entangling the helmsman, which added to the confusion. Her topsails were loosed, but the vessel slowly rolled onto her beam-ends, and she filled and sank. About forty-five men were lost, the survivors being picked up by the *Nonsuch*.
[TNA: ADM.1/5289]

16 June ROCHESTER Cutter
Hired 1746
Master John Bond
Employed as an advice boat, she sailed from Plymouth bound up-Channel with despatches, when she was chased in the early morning by a French privateer, the *Comtesse de Mark*, 4 guns, an ex-Irish Customs House vessel. A running fight developed between the pair, with the rigging of the cutter being badly cut up by shot. Eventually the privateer ran alongside and forced her to surrender, taking their prize into Morlaix.
[TNA: ADM.1/5289]

24 June SALTASH Brig Sloop
Rotherhithe 1742; 249 tons; 87.10ft × 25.1ft; 14 guns
Master and Commander John Pitman†
During the afternoon, the southern counties of England were struck by a particularly violent storm, with strong winds accompanied by rain, thunder and lightning, with buildings being damaged and dozens of trees being uprooted; '… for 15 minutes there was one continued Thunder, without Intermission of Strokes, and a continual Torrent of Hail, Rain and Flame'. The *Saltash* was caught in the storm and was capsized in a strong squall off Beachy Head and sank.
[TNA: ADM.180/3; ADM 33/390; www.britishnewspaperarchive.co.uk: Derby Mercury 27 June p2]

19 July ALBANY Sloop
Purchased 1746; 10 guns
Master and Commander Stephen Colby
Sailed from Louisburg for Chedabucto Bay, Nova Scotia, the sloop was entering the bay when a ship was sighted closing from seaward. It was initially believed to be a British warship, but as it steadily approached it was suspected that it was French, and the *Albany* prepared for action, using sweeps to try and keep her distance.

After a short chase, the enemy vessel, the *Castor*, 28 guns, commenced the action, concentrating her fire on her opponent's rigging. The fore topmast was soon shot away and after two hours, the mainmast was shot through and all the bowlines and braces carried away. Unable to manoeuvre or escape, the *Albany* surrendered. With the French ship continually firing high, one man was killed, the only casualty.
[TNA: ADM.1/5289]

19 October SEVERN Fourth Rate
Plymouth 1739; 853 tons; 134ft x 38.6ft; 50 guns
Captain William Lisle

One of the escorts to a convoy of fifty-one ships bound for England from the Leeward Islands, which was intercepted when in latitude 46.30N, about 160 leagues (480 miles) south-west of Scilly, by three French warships commanded by the Comte de Conflans. The enemy was sighted at first light, and they started the action by attacking and taking several stragglers from the convoy. Led by the *Woolwich*, the convoy was ordered to scatter and make their own way, whilst the escorts joined and stretched ahead of the largest of the French warships. At about 8 o'clock, the *Terrible,* 70 guns, came up and commenced the action, and was joined by the *Neptune*, 70, the pair positioning themselves on either quarter of the *Severn*. The mizzen mast was shot away and the rigging and sails reduced to tatters, and unable to escape or resist further against two larger opponents, she surrendered. Because of the French practice of firing high, the casualties were relatively light, three killed and nine wounded. The *Woolwich* and most of the convoy managed to escape.
[TNA: ADM.1/5289]

21 October POSTBOY Snow
Hired 1746; 12 guns
Master Levi Young

Employed as an advice boat, she was carrying letters from the fleet off Quiberon Bay to Plymouth, when she was chased by a French privateer, the *Revanche*, 24 guns, off Ushant. The *Postboy* tried to outrun the privateer but was overhauled and captured without difficulty and taken into Granville. The Master was subsequently criticised for failing to let the reefs out of his topsails earlier in the chase, although in his defence he claimed that the snow had constantly buried her head and lee ports into the sea.
[TNA: ADM.1/5289]

8 November PANTHER Tender
Hired 1746
Lieutenant George Bromfield

After sailing from Spithead, bound for the Yorkshire ports to press men for the Navy, at 3 o'clock in the morning she ran hard aground on the Sussex coast near Newhaven. Despite efforts to save her, she could not be freed and started to break up in the surf. Lieutenant Bromfield organised the crew to land and take off the stores, to prevent local 'wreckers' from stripping the vessel. The blame for the loss was placed on a defective compass, compounded by the action of the Master, John Bulkeley, who had ordered a course change without informing Lieutenant Bromfield; he forfeited all pay due to him.
[TNA: ADM.1/5289]

4 December LOUISBURG Fireship
Prize 1746 (*St Francis Xavier*); 250 tons; 10 guns
Lieutenant Philip Delamot†

On passage to England from Canada, she was chased by a large French privateer, the *Revanche*, 24 guns, when in latitude 49.30N, about 100 miles to the south-west of the Lizard, Cornwall. The privateer came up on the lee quarter and fired a broadside to open the action, and the fighting went on for another hour, the fireship having her rigging reduced to shreds, the Captain shot and mortally wounded and the Lieutenant having his legs shot away. The Master, Robert Hughes, continued fighting until the *Revanche* went ahead, raked her opponent and prepared for boarding, at which point Hughes surrendered. Three men were killed and five wounded.
[TNA: ADM.1/5289]

10 December HINCHINBROOK Brig Sloop
Bursledon 1745; 271 tons; 91.4ft x 26.1ft; 14 guns
Master and Commander Edmund Townsley

On passage to England from Canada in late November, she suffered during a storm, and was forced to rig jury masts. On 9 December Scilly was sighted, and the following morning she raised Berry Head, but during the afternoon a French privateer was sighted closing her. The privateer, proved to be the *Marie-Madeleine*, 22 guns, of St Malo, which then ran under the stern of the *Hinchinbrook* and fired a broadside. She then stood off, firing at will, destroying the temporary rigging – the mizzen mast, jury topmast and foreyard were all shot away – before the privateer closed and prepared for boarding, at which the *Hinchinbrook* surrendered.
[TNA: ADM.1/5289]

1747

26 January HORNET Brig Sloop
Chichester 1745; 272 tons; 91ft x 26.4ft; 14 guns
Master and Commander Edward Keller

Sailed from Torbay to escort the *King William* store ship, bound for the West Indies, clear of the coast, but her charge, which was laden with ordnance stores, including cannon, proved to be a sluggish sailer, and little progress had been made before a large French privateer was sighted closing from seaward. The French ship closed under British colours and when close enough for hailing, claimed to be the *Blandford*. This was not believed, and the sloop stood away, but was pursued by the privateer, and an exchange of shots preceded an attempt to board. This was foiled, and the privateer stood off to concentrate on firing at the rigging of the *Hornet*. This proved effective and the fore brace, bobstay and most of the fore-shrouds were shot away. The Master and helmsman were killed, which led the sloop to fly up into the wind. The privateer then closed and boarded, but a stiff fight then developed, which continued for some time on the upper deck of the *Hornet* before she surrendered. She suffered five killed and seventeen wounded. Her captor, which was the *Marie-Madeleine*, 22 guns of St Malo, then went on to capture the *King William*.

Note: retaken in October 1747 by the *Triton*.
[TNA:ADM.1/5289]

7 June SHOREHAM'S PRIZE Sloop
Prize 1746 (*Mount Carmel*); 10 guns
Master and Commander William Browne

The *Shoreham's Prize* had arrived at Oporto in November 1746 to refit following an action with a Spanish ship, and soon afterwards a verbal altercation occurred between some of the crew and men from a Spanish privateer moored nearby. This led to a musket being fired into a Spanish boat, killing a man. The Portuguese authorities investigated this as a possible case of murder and ordered the ship to be moored in a secure place, close to the shore, with an armed guard on the shoreline at all times. The sloop was cut off from other ships and the matter dragged on for months, with Captain Browne, the British Consul and the Portuguese government involved in endless arguments and representations. The crew, understandably, did not like this and there was a trickle of desertions and finally a mass desertion in March 1747 when a large number went ashore, only to find themselves arrested and confined in prison. On 1 June 1747, during the night, the stern hawser was let go from the shore which led to the sloop to swing onto nearby rocks. With some difficulty she was re-secured, but the exercise was repeated the following night, and this time the rocks holed the vessel, and she could not be freed. This led to another round of calls by the Captain on the Consul and Portuguese Chancellor, who eventually refused any assistance. By 7 June, the reduced crew was exhausted by continual pumping and their own efforts to free the sloop, and when fresh leaks occurred, they could not be stemmed, and the sloop filled and sank. After further representations most of the crew were then finally released to British ships in the harbour, but seven sailors remained confined in prison until 1750.
[TNA:ADM.1/5290; ADM.51/947; ADM.106/1040]

27 June MAIDSTONE Fourth Rate
Deptford 1744; 979 tons; 140.6ft × 40.2ft; 50 guns
Captain Augustus Keppel

Operating with a British squadron in the Bay of Biscay, the *Maidstone* was busily employed on the French coast in attacking French merchant ships. Having taken two ships in the forenoon, she sighted and chased a group of three ships which were further inshore, near the port of Nantes. Concentrating on the largest, she pursued her quarry close to the shoreline, and seeing the enemy ship pass though patches of surf felt confident to follow, but as she did so she ran hard aground on a ridge of submerged rocks off the Île de Noirmoutier. Efforts to free her went on for the next two days, but on 29 June, unable to get free and with the ship filling with water, the masts were cut away and the crew went ashore in boats and rafts to be made prisoners.
[TNA:ADM.1/5290]

9 July MESSENGER Dogger
Hired 1747
Master William Bellamy

Employed as an advice boat with the fleet, she was on passage from Gibraltar to England in company with the *Falkland* and the *Grand Turk*, when water was reported to be entering the hold. Both pumps were kept going continuously, but she could not be cleared of water. A party of carpenters from the ships in company came on board, but despite taking up large amounts of planking, they could not find the source of the leak, which was believed to be near the keel. The dogger was abandoned in latitude 42.56N, about 95 miles west of Cape Finisterre, and allowed to founder.
[TNA:ADM.1/5290]

8 August WHITEHAVEN Armed Vessel
Hired 1745 (*Adventure*); 14 guns
Master and Commander Carr Scrope

Hired to serve as an armed ship to patrol St George's Strait, and to protect merchant shipping in the area, the *Whitehaven* was off Tory Island when at just before 9 o'clock in the forenoon a fire developed in the Carpenter's storeroom. The fire spread rapidly, and within 30 minutes had taken a firm hold, with flames coming out of the main hatchway. The boats were hoisted out and the ship was abandoned to burn out. The blame for the fire was placed on the position of the galley fireplace, which was only 3ft from the storeroom, with the coals and firewood being stowed underneath the galley and storeroom.
[TNA:ADM.1/5290]

1 September HIND Brig Sloop
Blackwall 1744; 273 tons; 91.6ft × 26.1ft; 10 guns
Master and Commander Peter Robinson†
Missing, believed foundered off Nova Scotia, in a storm during her passage from Baie Verte to Louisburg, with no survivors. Pay Book closed 1 September.
[TNA: ADM.180/3; ADM.33/401]

15/16 September LYME Sixth Rate
Rotherhithe 1740; 447 tons; 106.6ft × 31ft; 20 guns
Master and Commander James Buchan†
Part of the escort to a fleet of homeward-bound merchant ships from the Leeward Islands, the ships sailed from St Kitts on 26 August. During 15 September, when in latitude 38 North, about 150 leagues (450 miles) east of Bermuda, the convoy encountered poor weather, with strong winds and heavy seas. The fleet became scattered by the storm, the ships suffering with lost spars, ripped sails and torn rigging. During the night, the *Lyme* was capsized and sank, with the loss of all but four men who were found in the morning clinging to a hen coop and rescued by the *Esther* merchant ship.
[www.britishnewspaperarchive.co.uk: Derby Mercury 16 October 1747 p3]

8 October DARTMOUTH Fourth Rate
Woolwich 1741; 857 tons; 134ft × 38.7ft; 50 guns
Captain James Hamilton†
The large Spanish warship *Glorioso*, 74 guns, had successfully crossed the Atlantic from the West Indies with a cargo of treasure, having fought off the attentions of a British squadron off the Azores. Landing the treasure at Ferrol, she was making her way to Cadiz when she was intercepted by a squadron of British privateers led by Captain George Walker. Two of the privateers, *King George* and *Prince Frederick*, bravely attacked the Spanish ship and kept up an uneven combat for three hours until they fell away with disabled rigging. Seeing a large ship in the offing, and suspecting it to be a British warship, a boat was sent away to advise them of the situation. The stranger was the *Russell*, 80 guns, which made all sail toward the scene. Before it could come up however, a second British warship, the *Dartmouth*, which was to seaward of the action, had closed on hearing the sound of gunfire to join the privateers and had renewed the combat. The *Dartmouth* began the engagement at about 1 o'clock in the afternoon. A close action ensued during which she suffered much damage to her rigging, with most of the shrouds and stays shot away. At 3.30pm she was blown apart by a massive explosion, evidently after her magazine was hit by a shot. The *Prince Frederick* privateer picked up Lieutenant Lucius O'Brien and about fifteen or sixteen other survivors, but about 300 men died. The *Russell* continued the chase and captured the *Glorioso* the following day.
[London Gazette 3 November 1747; Walker pp173–80; London Magazine 1748 pp172–3]

3 December PORTSMOUTH Store Ship
Southampton 1742; 694 tons; 124ft × 36ft; 24 guns
Master and Commander Joseph Soanes
Having sailed from the Nore, the *Portsmouth*, with the weather worsening, anchored off North Foreland on 29 November. With yards and topmasts struck, she rode out the gales until on 2 December it was found that the ship was dragging her anchor. At about 6 o'clock in the evening the tiller broke, and the rudder was torn away. This led to her filling rapidly with water at the stern, but quick action in using hammocks and bedding to block the hole stopped the main leak. However, water continued entering at a slow but steady rate, probably from a leak at the weakened sternpost, and the following day she was abandoned and allowed to founder, the crew being taken off by merchant ships.
[TNA: ADM.1/5291]

7 December FOGO Fireship
Purchased 1746
Master and Commander John Falkingham
Laying at anchor off Fort St David, Cuddalore, the weather became threatening, so yards and topmasts were ordered to be struck, and all made ready for a gale. Commander Falkingham was ashore at the time and could not return due to the heavy surf running, so the command therefore devolved onto Lieutenant John Strachan. At about 4.30 in the afternoon of 6 December the anchor cable parted, the small bower anchor was immediately let go, but the ship drove for some time before she brought up. She was now dangerously near the shore, and the surf regularly broke over her. The following morning the anchor cable was seen to be chafing itself into strands and it soon parted. After being driven by the wind and water for some distance she went ashore, just before noon, with the surf breaking over her constantly. By mid-afternoon she had gone to pieces.
[TNA: ADM.1/5291]

1748

31 January ACHILLES Schooner
Purchased 1747; 14 guns
Acting Lieutenant (Arthur?) Lowther
Newly purchased at Boston, New England, she was en-route to Jamaica, when she was intercepted off Cape Tiburon, at the western end of Hispaniola by two Spanish xebecs. The initial attack by the pair was beaten

off, and the *Achilles* then made all sail away, yawing regularly to fire at her pursuers. The Spaniards fired at her rigging and after a four-hour chase all the sails were holed, no braces left and the foreyard shot away. The pair then closed and boarded, and after a short fight, captured the schooner. She suffered three killed and fifteen wounded.
[TNA: ADM.1/5291]

18 January HUNTER Dogger
Hired 1747; 100 tons; 12 guns
Master John Beart
Employed as an advice boat, she was ordered to take despatches from Plymouth to Admiral Mostyn on the coast of France. When about 90 miles to the west of Ushant she was closed by the French privateer *Grande Biche*, 22 guns. A long chase developed with stern- and bow-chase guns being employed. When the mizzen-yard of the *Hunter* was shot away, the privateer came up under the lee quarter of the dogger and forced her to surrender.
[TNA: ADM.1/5292]

27 February LIZARD Brig Sloop
Bursledon 1744; 272 tons; 91.5ft x 26.1ft; 10 guns
Master and Commander Alexander Campbell†
Ran aground and wrecked, with no survivors, in the Scilly Isles, apparently on rocks in Broad Sound.
[Lloyd's List 4 March 1748/No.1281; www.britishnewspaperarchive.co.uk: Caledonian Mercury 14 March 1748 p2]

27 June FOWEY Fifth Rate
Hull 1744; 703 tons; 126.9ft x 36.1ft; 40 guns
Captain Francis Drake
On completion of a cruise to the north-west of Cuba, the *Fowey* headed north for Virginia with a small group of merchant vessels in convoy, one prize vessel being in tow. They took their departure from a fix on the western edge of Cay Sal Bank and headed north through the Florida Strait, sounding regularly. During the middle watch a merchant brig was heard to make distress signals, and the *Fowey*, realising that the shore must be close, cut free the tow and attempted to tack away, but could not come around in time and went aground in the Florida Keys in latitude 25.25N. Captain Drake made strenuous efforts to free the ship – laying out cables and anchors to warp her off, moving the forward cannon aft. When this failed, upper-deck guns were thrown overboard, and Spanish prisoners onboard used to pump and bail to stem the water that was entering. As it became clear that she could not be saved, and the water continued to gain, Drake ordered the guns spiked, stores taken out and the ship abandoned. The stern cable was then cut, which led her to swing onto rocks and then holes were cut into the bottom to effectively sink her. The crew were taken off by the merchant ships in company, the *Jane* of New York and *Brigg* of Rhode Island. An 'unaccountable current' was blamed for her being to the west of her planned course, but modern research has suggested that it is likely that the true reason was the incorrect position of Cay Sal on charts. Her wreck was found in 1975, in Legare anchorage, Biscayne Bay.
[TNA: ADM.1/5292; Mariner's Mirror vol 44 pp320–4]

1 September SERPENT Bomb
Limehouse 1742; 275 tons; 92.9ft x 26.1ft; 8 guns
Master and Commander Thomas Hanbury
Heading for Barbados, the crew were startled at about 11 o'clock in the evening to see land looming out of the darkness close ahead of them, as they believed themselves some distance from land. Before any action could be taken, she ran hard aground on a reef close to the island. She remained hanging on the rocks all night, pounding constantly. The mast was cut away to ease her, but the water started to gain on the pumps. The boats were hoisted out and rafts made from the wreckage of the mast, the crew being ferried ashore over a three day period. Seven men were drowned when one of the boats capsized. The subsequent court martial blamed the strong currents which had deceived the officers and set them closer to the land than they had appreciated.
[TNA: ADM.1/5292]

31 December WOLF Brig Sloop
Deptford 1742; 246 tons; 89.6ft x 25.2ft; 14 guns
Master and Commander George Vachell†
Overtaken by a severe storm in the Irish Sea, despite reducing sail to a reefed foresail, it proved difficult to steer her and she was constantly being swamped. Her great cabin was flooded as they were struck by a large wave as they attempted to set the mainsail, and she 'lay like a log' until driven ashore in Dundrum Bay, Ireland, near St Johns Point. She struck the ground at about 7 o'clock in the evening with a great shock 'splitting every knee in her'. The masts were ordered to be cut away but one of the masts in its fall stove in the longboat. The yawl was successfully launched and made it to the shore and raised the alarm, but although the local people came to the shore, there was little they could do. She pounded heavily on the rocks and at the flood tide she filled with water and broke up. There were just 16 survivors from a crew of 125, with the Gunner being the senior, who stated his belief that the ship had been over-masted and was incapable of carrying sufficient sail in high winds, which meant that she could not claw off the land.
[TNA: ADM.1/5292; www.britishnewspaperarchive.co.uk: Newcastle Courant 28 January 1749 p1]

6 | 1749–1754: A Brief Peace

1749

13 April NAMUR Third Rate
Deptford 1729; 1,567 tons; 164ft x 47.2ft; 74 guns
Captain Samuel Marshall
Part of the British naval force assembled in the East Indies, the *Namur* was the flagship of Rear Admiral Boscawen, which was lying at anchor off Fort St David, Cuddalore, when that port was struck by a tropical cyclone. Both the Admiral and Captain Marshall were ashore at the time and unable to return on board. With the wind steadily increasing through the day, her position became increasingly precarious, with the sea breaking over her. At 7 o'clock in the evening the *Namur* was forced to cut her cables and attempt to make the open sea. Little headway was made, and within 30 minutes she had 6ft of water in the hold. The upper-deck and quarterdeck guns were heaved overboard to ease her rolling, but the water still gained on the pumps, until at 8.45pm, when all the masts were cut away which helped to bring the ship upright and some headway was made against the water. On sounding, at just after 9pm, the ship found herself in nine fathoms of water, and the sheet anchor was let go, but the cable almost immediately parted. After this, nothing could be done to save the ship. She filled rapidly and became a waterlogged wreck which drove ashore on a sandy bank to the southward of Porto Novo under the constant pounding of the sea, with the crew clinging to yards, booms and spars. Only two officers and 24 men were saved from a crew of 500.
[Schomberg vol I pp259–60; TNA: ADM.1/5292]

13 April PEMBROKE Third Rate
Woolwich 1733; 956 tons; 144.2ft x 39.1ft; 60 guns
Captain Thomas Fincher†
Lost in the cyclone which struck the eastern coast of India, the *Pembroke* lay at anchor close to the *Namur* (see above), with Captain Fincher sick in his cabin. As the wind increased, preparations were made to ride out the gale, but by 3 o'clock in the afternoon the storm was blowing at full strength and the ship was straining at her cables and taking in water as seas broke over her. The Master urged the Captain to stand out to sea, but Fincher, confined to his cabin and probably not fully appreciating the situation, refused to slip or even veer out any more cable, unless ordered to do so by Admiral Boscawen. At just after 5pm, the cable parted, and the ship hastily set staysails, mainsail and foresail and put her head to seaward. Despite this, little headway was made, and the square sails blew out, and the tiller and rudder chains broke. At about 9 o'clock both the mizzen and mainmast went overboard, followed shortly afterwards by the foremast. The small bower anchor was then let go, which brought her up, but the boats and booms were swept away, and the cable soon parted. The sheet anchor was then let go but the cable immediately parted, and the ship was driven onshore near Point Colderoon where she capsized and lay broadside-on to the sea, with surf beating over her constantly. The ship broke up over the next two days. There were only 12 survivors from a crew of 330.
[Charnock vol V pp376–80]

13 April APOLLO Store Ship
Prize 1747 (*Apollon*); 744 tons; 127.2ft x 36.5ft; 20 guns
Master and Commander Robert Wilson†
One of the ships anchored off Fort St David, Cuddalore, in support of the army in their operations against the French. When the area was hit by a tropical cyclone the *Apollo* was driven from her anchors, and was last seen off the coast, without masts, before being driven onshore and wrecked with heavy loss of life.
[www.britishnewspaperarchive.co.uk: Caledonian Mercury 6 February 1750 p1]

1751

11 September FOX Sixth Rate
Bursledon 1746; 503 tons; 112.2ft x 32.1ft; 24 guns
Captain Samuel Faulknor
Jamaica was hit by a tremendous tropical storm, which began in the early hours of the morning. The wind shifted to the east at about 8.30am and increased to hurricane strength. There was widespread damage on the island, with crops destroyed and buildings demolished. The *Fox*, recently arrived from Havana with passengers and cargo, was obliged to cut away all her masts and was driven from her anchors onto rocks at Negro Head Key, east of Portland Point, where she was wrecked. All the crew were saved.
[www.britishnewspaperarchive.co.uk: The Scots Magazine 1 November 1751 p40; TNA: ADM.1/5294]

1752

26 August FORESTER Stores Hoy
Portsmouth 1693; 125 tons; 2 guns
Master John Sier†
Loaded with timber from Gatcombe Park and destined for Plymouth Dockyard, the *Forester* anchored in company with two other dockyard stores craft off Port Isaac, Cornwall. During the evening of 25 August, the wind shifted to the north and increased to gale force. The *Forester* disappeared in the night and was believed to have foundered at her anchor.
[TNA: ADM 106/1106]

26 August LION Stores Hoy
Deptford 1709; 108 tons; 63.11ft x 20ft; 4 guns
Master Samuel Wakerell
Along with the *Forester* (see above), she was lying at anchor off Port Isaac when hit by a storm; she was driven ashore under the cliff and beaten to a wreck. The people on shore saved the lives of the crew and a portion of the cargo of timber was recovered.
[TNA: ADM 106/1107]

26 August SALTASH Stores Hoy
Chichester 1748; 110 tons; 64.1ft x 20.2ft.
Master John Delamott
The third of the store vessels caught by a storm off Port Isaac, she was driven ashore and wrecked, with the loss of seven men and a boy. The disaster attracted local people from a wide area to the scene to plunder the wrecks; two men were later found in possession of timber marked with the King's arrow from the wreck, being sent for trial at Bodmin.
[TNA: ADM 106/1106]

1753

24 April ASSURANCE Fifth Rate
Bursledon 1747; 823 tons; 133.1ft x 38ft; 40 guns
Captain Carr Scrope
Arriving off the Isle of Wight from the West Indies with Edward Trelawny, the former Governor of Jamaica, onboard, bound for Spithead, Captain Scrope decided to take the western passage and proceed up the Solent. The pilot steered the ship close to the Needles rocks, and when passing about a cable's length from them, struck a submerged rock, which pierced the hull, the ship rapidly filling with water. The ship was held fast, and boats were despatched to Portsmouth Dockyard for assistance, but she steadily settled until the decks were awash. The ship broke up and sank two days later, with wreckage being washed up over a large area. The Captain, crew and passengers were all saved, along with the sum of nearly £60,000 in specie brought home in the ship; one bag only, containing nearly £500 was lost, believed stolen out of a boat. The pilot, David Patterson, was blamed, and in his defence pleaded that the ship had struck a rock which was uncharted. He called local Isle of Wight pilots to back his claim, which they did – but also said that they would not have taken the ship so close to the Needles, which rather negated his argument. He was sentenced to serve three months in the Marshalsea Prison.
[TNA: ADM.1/5294; Charnock vol VI pp101–02]

7 | 1755–1763: The Seven Years War

THE WAR OF 1739–48 HAD LEFT several crucial points of argument between the British and French governments unsettled, particularly in North America, where the French were extending their influence by establishing new trading posts along the Mississippi and Ohio rivers, which had resulted in armed clashes with British colonists. Both the British and French governments responded during 1754–5 by sending forces to the continent. In April 1755, a squadron under Admiral Boscawen sailed for Canada with orders to protect the colonies and, if encountering any of the French expedition, to take possession of them, by force if necessary. This led to a clash off the Newfoundland Banks in June, in which two French ships were captured. In July 1755 orders were issued permitting the detention of French warships and this was extended in August to seize merchant vessels entering the Channel. Although war was not formally declared until May 1756, skirmishing and open fighting between the powers commenced. Following a treaty agreement between France and Spain in August 1761, the expansion of the war became inevitable, and in January 1762 war was declared against Spain. The naval campaign saw several fleet actions, including for the first time in the Indian Ocean. Successful combined operations were mounted with expeditions against Gorée, Quebec, Belle Isle, Havana and Manila.

1755

24 July MARS Third Rate
Prize 1746; 1,374 tons; 159.3ft × 44.9ft; 64 guns
Captain John Amherst
Attempting to enter Halifax, Nova Scotia, the Captain and crew were all unfamiliar with the harbour and so stopped a local fishing vessel to take on board the skipper to act as a pilot. This man, William Leeworthy, although not a pilot, indicated that he was familiar with the approaches and was entrusted with the piloting of the ship. At about 7 o'clock in the evening, the *Mars* ran straight onto a sandbank, despite it being marked and seen by the crew. The sails were set aback, boats hoisted out to carry out anchors in efforts to kedge her off, and water butts were started to lighten her. Despite all their efforts, she could not be moved, and the falling tide made her position increasingly dangerous. Spare yards were used as shores to prevent her from capsizing, but shortly after one in the morning, the starboard shores broke, and she fell over onto her side and filled with water. Leeworthy claimed that he was not a qualified pilot and should never have been given the responsibility for entering the harbour; further the buoy on the sandbank was wrongly placed, being on the centre of the bank, rather than marking the edge which he had assumed. Despite his pleas, Leeworthy was sentenced to be carried to England and serve six months in the Marshalsea Prison.
[TNA:ADM.1/5295]

13 August BLANDFORD Sixth Rate
Deptford 1741; 455 tons; 109ft × 30.10ft; 24 guns
Captain Richard Watkins
Having sailed from Portsmouth on 2 August with Governor William Lyttleton embarked for South Carolina, she was to the west of Ushant, when at 9 o'clock in the evening a squadron of six ships was sighted approaching. Apprehensive of their identity and intentions, the ship prepared for action at the same time as shortening sail to allow them to close. At the time Britain was officially at peace with France, but considerable tension existed, and a French squadron had been attacked by Admiral Boscawen in June. One of the squadron came alongside, hailed her, and on establishing that she was a King's ship, fired into her. The *Blandford* made all sail away that she could, but the French ships soon overhauled her and by 10 o'clock she found that one ship was on her port bow, another on her port quarter, whilst the original vessel which had hailed her was close under her stern. Unable to properly reply, as there was considerable confusion below decks, and faced with a superior force, the *Blandford* struck her flag and surrendered to the *Fleur-de-Lys*, 32 guns. The French Government made it clear that the squadron had captured the British ship as retaliation for the attack on French ships in June. Having made the point, the *Blandford* was restored in September.
[TNA:ADM.1/5295]

1756

11 March WARWICK Fourth Rate
Plymouth 1733; 952 tons; 144ft × 39ft; 60 guns
Captain Molyneaux Shuldham
Cruising to the west of Martinique, at daybreak several strange sails were seen approaching. Believing them to

be an expected merchant convoy, she initially closed, but as she neared, she grew more suspicious as they had the appearance of French warships. When they failed to answer private signals the *Warwick* came about, made all sail away and cleared for action. A long chase then developed with three of the enemy gradually closing her. The closest, the *Atalante,* 34 guns, bravely engaged the *Warwick* on her own, keeping astern of the British ship, which could not properly reply, being confined to the stern-chasers on the quarterdeck. After about 30 minutes, both ships were taken aback by a squall of wind and this enabled the other ships – the *Prudent,* 74, and the *Zephyr,* 32, to close. The *Warwick* now attempted to engage all of them but was quite unable to use her lower-deck armament as water poured into the ports every time they were opened, with gun crews up to their waists in water. The French concentrated on her rigging and within an hour had reduced it to tatters, with the main topmast shot away. Unable to escape or properly resist the *Warwick* surrendered. One killed and three wounded.

Note: she was recaptured on 24 January 1761 by the *Minerva,* but not taken back into service.
[TNA:ADM.1/5297]

27 June PROSERPINE Fireship
Purchased 1756
Master and Commander Paul Ourry
A small local vessel taken up for the defence of the harbour of Port Mahon, Minorca, she was abandoned at the surrender of the port to the French army under Marshal Richelieu.
[TNA:ADM.1/80/20; Erskine: Hervey's Journal pp195, 317]

27 June BLAST Fireship
Purchased 1756
Master and Commander Henry Philips
Like the *Proserpine* (see above), she was a small local vessel taken up for the defence of Port Mahon, Minorca. Not thereafter mentioned, and presumed to have been abandoned at the surrender of the port to the French army under Marshal Richelieu.
[Erskine: Hervey's Journal pp195, 317]

27 June MINORCA LIGHTER Stores Smack
Deptford 1740; 105 tons; 62.6ft x 19.4ft; 2 guns
Employed in the harbour at Port Mahon, Minorca, she disappears from the records at this time, and is presumed to have been lost when the French army occupied the island.
[Sigwart p52]

14 August ONTARIO Brig
Oswego, Lake Ontario 1755; 70 tons; 6 guns
Master and Commander John Laforey
The small Canadian Lakes squadron, based at Fort Oswego, Lake Ontario, was being put into service by parties of seamen from ships at Halifax, under the direction of Commanders Laforey and Broadley. The pair had little chance to organise much, however, as soon after their arrival, the French-Canadian army under General Montcalm surrounded the fort. The British, totally outnumbered, quickly surrendered and all the vessels at the fort were included in the surrender. Laforey and Broadley had prepared their craft for destruction but were not consulted over the terms of the surrender and were obliged to turn them over to the French.
[TNA:ADM.1/5296]

Under the terms of the surrender, the following vessels at Fort Oswego were surrendered to the French at the same time as the Ontario:

OSWEGO Brig
Oswego, Lake Ontario 1755; 70 tons; 6 guns
Master and Commander Houseman Broadley

HALIFAX Snow
Oswego, Lake Ontario 1756; 172 tons; 80ft x 22ft; 18 guns
Master and Commander Archibald Kennedy
[TNA:ADM.1/80/20]

LONDON Brig
Oswego, Lake Ontario 1755; c100 tons; 60ft x 21ft; 14 guns
Master and Commander Joshua Loring
[TNA:ADM1/80/20]

MOHAWK Sloop
Oswego, Lake Ontario 1755; c60 tons; 45ft x 18ft; 12 guns
Master and Commander William Harris

GEORGE Schooner
Oswego, Lake Ontario 1755; 20 tons; swivel guns

VIGILANT Schooner
Oswego, Lake Ontario 1755; 20 tons; swivel guns
[Malcomson pp10–13]

★ ★ ★

17 September ADVENTURE Brig tender
Hired 1756; 10 guns
Lieutenant James Orrock
Newly hired to serve as a press tender, she was off Berwick, bound from Leith to the Medway, when she sighted and chased a strange sail. By noon she had overhauled the vessel, which was found to be a French 14-gun snow-rigged privateer *l'Infernal*. The tender then tried to make off, but the wind by now had dropped to a calm, which meant that the *Adventure* could not

escape, and a hard-fought action started which lasted for over an hour when she ran out of gunpowder. At this the privateer ran close alongside, grappled and boarded. The crew of the *Adventure* continued to fight on, pelting the boarders with shot and other objects thrown by hand, until forced to surrender. Two killed and seventeen wounded. Lieutenant Orrock was promoted to Master and Commander in recognition of his bravery in this action.
[TNA: ADM.1/5296]

October SWIFT Brig Sloop
Limehouse 1741; 203 tons; 85ft × 23.7ft; 10 guns
Master and Commander Walker Farr†
Weighed and sailed from her anchorage at the Nore on 3 October in company with the *Diligence* sloop bound for the Baltic to escort homeward-bound trade, but her consort ran aground the same afternoon. She was eventually freed after being lightened, but *Swift* continued alone rather than be delayed. She was never seen again. The North Sea was swept by strong gales over the next few days, and she was presumed to have foundered with all hands.
[TNA: ADM.180/3; ADM.51/246]

1757

18 March GREENWICH Fourth Rate
Lepe 1748; 1,053 tons; 144.6ft × 41.3ft; 50 guns
Captain Robert Roddam
Cruising off Cape Cabron, San Domingo, when she sighted several ships and being uncertain of their identity, the *Greenwich* edged away, and then found herself being chased by two of the largest ships, which proved to be French ships of the line, *Diadéme*, 74 guns, and the *Éveillé*, 64. A long chase developed with the French firing at long range, attempting to cripple her rigging and sails. The *Greenwich* maintained her distance for most of the day, steering closer inshore, until she was eventually forced to tack away from the land, the French still pursuing her. That night, with her pursuers gaining on her, Captain Roddam attempted to escape by coming about and passing them, but the manoeuvre was seen and the *Éveillé* fired into her, foiling the move. Finding himself surrounded and unable to escape, Captain Roddam surrendered.
[TNA: ADM.1/5297]

22 March EARL of LOUDON Sloop
Fort William Henry, Lake George 1755; c30 tons; swivel guns
Built for service on Lake George, Canada, she was at Fort William Henry when that place came under attack from the French. At about 7 o'clock in the evening the enemy tried to attack the sloop but were driven off by fire from the fort. Undeterred, a second attempt was made later that night, this time successfully, and the sloop was set on fire at about midnight.
[Malcolmson p14; Various secondary]

19 April MERLIN Brig Sloop
Rotherhithe 1756; 224 tons; 86.2ft × 24.5ft; 10 guns
Master and Commander John Cleland
Outward bound from Falmouth in company with the *Arundel* as escorts to a large convoy, she became separated in poor weather. On 19 April, the weather worsened, with high seas, which continually washed over the upper deck, accompanied by frequent rain showers. The guns were all secured fore and aft and the sails reduced to foresail and mizzen sail. At about 11.30 in the forenoon the weather cleared sufficiently for another vessel to be revealed, the large French privateer *Machault*, 30 guns, which promptly chased the *Merlin*. The sloop spread topsails to escape, but this only buried her head into the sea even further and increased the amount of water over the deck. The bowsprit was now frequently submerged, and men were unable to keep on the fo'c'sle. The water came in at such a rate that the row-ports were opened so that they could act as scuttles and take some of the water away. When the *Machault* came alongside and fired a volley of small-arms into the sloop, she had little choice but to surrender.
Note: retaken on 13 July 1757 by the *Lancaster* and recommissioned as *Zephyr*.
[TNA: ADM.1/5296]

9 September GEORGE Sloop
Fort William Henry 1755; c30 tons
Built for service on Lake George, Canada, she was based at Fort William Henry, which was captured by a force of French and Native Americans under General Montcalm on this date. This sloop disappears from the record at about this time and is presumed to have been destroyed by the captors.
[Malcolmson p14; Various secondary]

20 September ANN Cutter
Hired 1756
Master Richard Keys
Hired for service as an advice boat, she sailed from Plymouth, carrying Lieutenant Charles Garencieres with despatches and letters for Portsmouth. She was almost immediately chased by a privateer, but successfully escaped. The following day a second French privateer, schooner-rigged and armed with 6 guns, was sighted and another chase was started, with the privateer using oars to come up with her quarry, firing occasionally with bow-chasers. By mid-afternoon, the French ship was alongside the *Ann* and fired into her. The cutter,

armed only with half-pound swivel guns, could not effectively reply and surrendered, the despatches being thrown overboard.
[TNA: ADM.1/5297]

24/25 September FERRET Ship Sloop
Purchased 1743; 255 tons; 88.4ft × 25.3ft; 14 guns
Master and Commander Arthur Upton†
One of a fleet of ships under Admiral Francis Holburne stationed off Nova Scotia, blockading the French fleet in Louisburg. On the evening of 24 September, the winds picked up from the east and steadily increased in strength. At about midnight the wind veered round to the south and the storm was blowing 'a perfect hurricane'. The British squadron was scattered, and the *Ferret* disappeared during the night and was presumed to have foundered with all hands.
[Beatson vol 2 pp55–7]

25 September TILBURY Fourth Rate
Portsmouth 1745; 1,124 tons; 147ft × 42ft; 60 guns
Captain Henry Barnsley†
One of Admiral Holburne's blockading squadron off Nova Scotia which was struck by the terrible storm of 24/25 September, '... the oldest seaman in the fleet had never seen such a dreadful tempest' (Beatson). The *Tilbury* cut away her foremast, mizzen mast and main topmast in efforts to ease the ship's rolling, which seemed to succeed. On the morning of the 25th, finding herself close to the land at Cape Breton, she anchored with both best and small bower anchors, but within 30 minutes both cables had parted, and she commenced driving before the wind. Shortly before noon she went ashore and started pounding heavily on the rocks. The sternpost gave way and the ship filled from aft very rapidly and sank. The Captain and most of the crew perished, the senior surviving officer being the Second Lieutenant, James Townsend.
[TNA: ADM.1/5297; Beatson vol 2 pp55–7]

4 October HAWKE Cutter
Hired 1756; 80 tons; 10 guns
Master Isaac Gruzelius
Hired for use as an advice boat, she was heading for Plymouth when she was closed off Lizard Point by a French 8-gun privateer. The privateer ran alongside and rapidly reduced the rigging of the cutter to shreds – splitting the mainsail and shooting away the boom and topping lift, which effectively crippled her. The wreckage of the sails and spars fell over the engaged side, preventing her from returning fire. The cutter, weakly manned and having suffered two killed and six wounded, surrendered.
[TNA: ADM.1/5296]

1758

19 February INVINCIBLE Third Rate
Prize 1747; 1,794 tons; 171.3ft × 49.3ft; 74 guns
Captain John Bentley
Part of the squadron under Admiral Boscawen that was anchored off St Helens, Isle of Wight, bound for Canada. At 2.30am the signal was made to weigh, but it was found that on heaving in, her anchor was apparently fouled, as it would not lift. Some time was taken attempting to clear the anchor from the bottom and even after it had been freed, it could not be brought to the head to be catted (secured and stowed). The ship manoeuvred slowly to the north-east in a strong easterly breeze under topsails to clear the restricted anchorage, but when the ship attempted to tack to the south, as the water shallowed, the helm jammed, so the ship's head was taken by the wind to the north. The jam was cleared, and an attempt was then made to wear ship, putting the stern to the wind. The water was now very shallow, and it became clear that the manoeuvre could not be successfully completed. Orders were given to let go an anchor, but this was not done before she went aground on the Dean Sands. Sail was taken in and anchors were taken out in boats to kedge her free, but in a steadily freshening wind the ship was driven further onto the sandbank. During the morning, the ship was lightened by heaving overboard some guns, and water butts emptied, and more sail was spread to drive her over the bank, but all failed. The following day much work went on to remove stores and guns, but water was reported entering. On the morning of 21 February, the weather worsened, and she started to pound heavily on the sandbank and later that day capsized, filled with water and was abandoned.
[TNA: ADM.1/5297]

13 April PRINCE GEORGE Second Rate
Deptford 1723; 1,586 tons; 164ft × 47.6ft; 90 guns
Captain Joseph Peyton
The flagship of Rear Admiral Thomas Broderick, bound for the Mediterranean in company with a large number of merchant ships and two frigates, they had sailed from Spithead on 1 April. At about 1.30 in the afternoon, then being in the Bay of Biscay, a cry of fire was raised, smoke having been seen coming from the Boatswain's store. Despite strenuous efforts by the officers and crew, the fire took a firm hold and spread rapidly. The firefighters were constantly beaten back by thick choking smoke and were unable to get to the seat of the fire. Holes were cut in the deck and the lower deck ports opened to allow water in, but all was in vain. By 5pm it was clear that the ship could not be saved, and the crew commenced leaving in a disorderly and chaotic

manner. The barge was hoisted out and manned for the Admiral, but about forty men attempted to crowd into it, putting it in danger of capsizing. Admiral Broderick then jumped into the water and supported himself for nearly an hour until picked up by a merchant ship. By 6 o'clock the sails and masts were alight and a little after the ship could be seen to be burning from end to end. She rolled over onto her side about an hour later, but did not immediately sink, burning wreckage spreading over the water. Although 260 were saved, about 485 perished.
[TNA: ADM. 1/5297; Charnock vol V pp72–6; Gentleman's Magazine 1758 pp228–30]

28 April BRIDGEWATER Sixth Rate
Northam 1744; 500 tons; 112.2ft × 32ft; 20 guns
Captain Thomas Manning

One of a small British squadron in the East Indies, the *Bridgewater*, in company with the *Triton*, was anchored off Fort St David, Cuddalore, when a merchant ship came in, bringing a report of sighting several strange warships off the coast. The pair sailed to gain intelligence, but after a fruitless day's searching returned to the anchorage off Madras. At about 4am, several ships were seen to be approaching, which soon proved to be the combined squadrons of Comte d'Aché and M. Bouvet. The British pair hastily weighed and attempted to stand out to sea, but their passage was blocked by the French ships. Unable to escape, the *Bridgewater* was deliberately run ashore and then set alight to prevent capture.
[TNA: ADM. 1/5298]

28 April TRITON Sixth Rate
Bursledon 1745; 501 tons; 112.7ft × 32.1ft; 20 guns
Captain John Stanton

As with the *Bridgewater* (see above), the *Triton* spent a day searching off Fort St David, Cuddalore, for the strange warships reported by a merchant ship. The *Triton* sprung her main topmast, and this led to an early return to the anchorage. On the approach of several ships of the French squadron, she cut cables and attempted to escape in company with the *Bridgewater*. Unable to do so, being blocked by the French, she was deliberately run ashore and the burnt to avoid capture.
[TNA: ADM. 1/5298]

14 August PORTSMOUTH Stores Buss
Purchased 1756 (*Beckford*); 80 tons; 63.6ft × 16.7ft; 6 guns
Master and Commander James Orrock

Laying in the River Senegal off Fort Louis, the weather deteriorated, with strong winds and the surf crashing over the nearby bar at the mouth of the river. In the early hours of the morning the anchor cable parted, and in the narrow channel she quickly went aground on the side of the river and was wrecked.
[TNA: ADM. 1/5297]

16 August STORK Ship Sloop
Shoreham 1756; 233 tons; 88.7ft × 24.7ft; 10 guns
Master and Commander Peter Carteret

During the middle watch, whilst cruising to the north-east of Cape St Nicholas, Hispaniola, a ship was discovered closing the sloop. The crew were promptly turned out and the sloop prepared for action. By first light the vessel could be seen to be a large French warship, which was clearly in chase. The *Stork* used every endeavour to escape, employing sweeps in her efforts, but the French ship continued to gain, and by 5.30am the first shots were fired from her bow-chase guns. At 7 o'clock the 74-gun *Palmier* was in range to use her main armament and the *Stork* surrendered.
[TNA: ADM. 1/5297]

23 September MEDITERRANEAN Xebec Sloop
Prize 1756; 200 tons; 92.6ft × 20.6ft; 12 guns
Master and Commander Charles Grant

Heading for the port of Livorno, Italy, the xebec had raised the island of Gorgona at nightfall. The weather was stormy, with hazy visibility, but the officers felt confident enough to stand on under easy sail, using the lead-line constantly. When an object was sighted ahead through the gloom, it was believed to be a sail and this added to their confidence. In the early hours of the morning the ground started shoaling rapidly and then breakers were seen ahead. An effort to tack was too late and she ran hard aground on the Mallora Sand and was wrecked. It later transpired that the 'sail' seen had in fact been a tower on the sands.
[TNA: ADM. 1/5297]

10 October WINCHELSEA Sixth Rate
Limehouse 1740; 441 tons; 105.10ft × 30.9ft; 20 guns
Captain John Hale

Escort to a homeward-bound convoy from South Carolina, which was attacked when to the south-west of Ireland by the French *Bizarre*, 60 guns and *Mignonne*, 28. The *Winchelsea* had seen the lights of the approaching ships in the early morning and altered course to investigate. They ignored her signals of recognition and proceeded to stop and board a merchant ship nearby. Captain Hale continued to steer closer and did not appreciate the full size of his opponents, until the *Bizarre* ran out her lower tier of guns. The *Winchelsea* then attempted to get away but could not outrun her large opponent especially as she had a jury-rigged mainmast. There was a brief exchange of fire before she surrendered. The French went on to capture thirty-four ships of the convoy.

Note: recaptured on 27 October by the Bristol privateer *Duke of Cornwall*.
[TNA: ADM. 1/5298]

29 November LITCHFIELD Fourth Rate
Harwich 1746; 979 tons; 140.2ft × 40.2ft; 50 guns
Captain Matthew Barton

One of a squadron under the command of Commodore Augustus Keppel bound for the West African coast and an intended attack on the French colony of Gorée. During the night of 28 November, the weather was squally, with frequent heavy showers of rain, and sail was reduced to the courses. The night was very dark, and sight was lost of the other ships, but a small light was seen ahead, believed to be the Commodore's. They continued steering south, believing themselves to be well clear of land and it was a shock when at 6 o'clock in the morning the ship ran hard aground. In the early morning gloom, a rocky shore could be seen and in a noticeably short time the ship swung broadside-on to the rocks and all the masts went by the board. Despite a high surf running, which was constantly breaking over the ship, an attempt was made to launch a boat to make the shore, but it was instantly capsized and all eight men drowned. By the afternoon, the seas had abated sufficiently for the survivors to use spars and planks lashed together into crude rafts to make the shore, where large numbers of people were seen to be gathering. Over the next three days survivors continued to struggle ashore through the surf from the wreck, which broke up in the constant pounding of the waves. The local inhabitants seemed to be more interested in salvaging attractive items from the ship than offering help to the crew and busied themselves stripping the bodies and then robbing the survivors. By the morning of 1 December, the ship had gone entirely to pieces and a muster revealed that 220 men had survived, 130 drowned. Help was provided by two local merchants, Mr Andrews and Mr Butler, who organised food and the attendance of a French surgeon. The party were marched to the city of Morocco where they were confined until April 1759, when they were taken to Salé and put aboard a ship which took them to Gibraltar. The subsequent court martial blamed an uncertain current which had set them further to the east than calculated, the ship being wrecked about six leagues (18 miles) north of Cape Cantin.
[TNA:ADM.1/5299; Charnock vol VI pp18–26]

1759

1 April ANSON Cutter
Hired 1758
Lieutenant John Henshaw

Chased, overhauled and captured in the English Channel by the *Gentille* privateer, 14 guns, of Bayonne. The Lieutenant, Master and other officers were taken out, leaving twenty-eight men and boys onboard, who were confined below. They managed to free themselves and overpowered the French prize crew and arrived back at Plymouth on 11 April.
[NMM:ADM 354/163/27; www.britishnewspaperarchive.co.uk: Oxford Journal 21 April 1759 p1]

19 April FALCON Bomb
Rotherhithe 1745; 270 tons; 91.7ft × 26.1ft; 8 guns
Master and Commander Mark Robinson

Fitted out as a cruiser, the *Falcon* was off Guadeloupe when she steered to investigate a schooner seen to be at anchor near les Saintes. As she approached and attempted to tack, she missed stays. The vessel was taken towards the land by the current and despite letting go the best bower anchor, before it could bring her up she struck the ground. Bilged, she filled and sank very quickly. The crew made the shore and was taken off by HM schooner *Fort Louis*. The unexpectedly strong current was blamed for taking her closer inshore than she had intended.
[TNA:ADM.1/5298]

20 November RESOLUTION Third Rate
Northam 1758; 1,569 tons; 165.6ft × 4.10ft; 74 guns
Captain Henry Speake

On 20 November, the English fleet under Admiral Hawke had successfully chased the French fleet under the Comte de Conflans into Quiberon Bay, western France, with a full westerly gale blowing. In the battle that followed in the restricted waters the French were scattered, with the loss of two ships sunk, four wrecked and one captured. The *Resolution* had been engaged throughout the battle and had suffered damaged rigging. She attempted to tack in very restricted waters to leave the bay, but missed stays and ran onto the Fours sandbank, the position of which she was unsure. The weather remained poor, with gale-force winds and high seas. Early in the morning she floated off at high water but could not get free of the sandbanks and grounded again at the ebb tide. The timbers had been badly strained, and the ship filled, settled and sank. A party of seamen disobeyed Captain Speke and left the ship on a raft but were swept away. The remainder of the crew were taken off by the other ships.
[TNA:ADM.1/5298]

21 November ESSEX Third Rate
Woolwich 1741; 1,226 tons; 151ft × 43.6ft; 70 guns
Captain Lucius O'Brien

One of Admiral Hawke's victorious fleet which took part in the battle of Quiberon Bay, at daybreak several French ships could be seen in the bay, with the flagship *Soleil Royal*, at anchor at some distance from the others. Hawke ordered the *Essex* to close the French Admiral and Captain O'Brien slipped his cable and

stood into the bay to do so. The French ship, seeing her approach, cut her cables and ran herself inshore until she grounded. With her quarry gone, the *Essex* was then ordered to stand by the grounded *Resolution* (see above). As she approached, she struck a ridge of rocks of which she was unaware. She anchored but almost immediately the cable parted, and the ship swung onto the rocks and pounded violently. On the second stroke the rudder was unshipped. The ship slid on and off the rocks for some time and attempted to anchor to steady herself but again the cable parted. The foremast was cut away to ease the ship, but she was hard aground, and water poured in from the damaged stern and she steadily filled and sank, all the crew leaving as she did.
[TNA: ADM.1/5298]

6 December MERMAID Sixth Rate
Buckler's Hard 1749; 533 tons; 114.10ft × 32.2ft; 20 guns
Captain James Hackman
The *Mermaid* sailed on 1 December from Charleston, South Carolina, to carry William Shirley to the Bahamas, where he was to take up his new position as the Governor of the colony. The ship headed out in thick, cloudy weather and having no observations to trust, had to rely on dead reckoning to estimate their position. During the early hours of 5 December land was suddenly seen ahead, and they tacked away to the north-west, but more breakers were seen ahead. They came to anchor in shallow water with the best and small bower anchors and lowered a boat to take soundings, but no deep water could be found. Yards and topmasts were struck as the wind steadily increased. At 9 o'clock that night the small bower cable parted, and the sheet anchor was let go. By now the wind was at gale force, and there was a heavy swell, with water breaking on rocks all round the ship. Just after midnight the best bower anchor cable parted, cut by chafing on rocks, and the ship drove a little and struck the ground a few times before the spare anchor was let go and brought her up. The ship was lightened, with guns being heaved overboard and at first light a spring was placed on the cable to haul her round to seaward. At the same time the yawl was launched to take Governor Shirley ashore, as he was '... desirous to take his chance that way'. At 8am the cable was cut as she attempted to run into open water, but almost immediately struck the ground, swung broadside on to a reef and commenced beating heavily. The rudder was unshipped, and they cut away the mizzen mast to ease her. She then beat over the reef to float in open water but with rocks close by, and she brought herself up by using the stream anchor. It was clear that she could not be extricated and when the wind abated efforts were concentrated on clearing stores from the ship to the shore nearby and raising tents as a camp. On 14 December, the yawl was sent away to New Providence and two days later a schooner arrived to remove the crew to safety. The ship was finally abandoned on 6 January, having filled with water, with some of the stores being sold off locally for the hire of local vessels to assist. The subsequent court martial found that the ship had been wrecked on Walker's Key, Abaco, due to a strong current and lack of observations. The ship's Master, Robert Powell, was judged to have been disobedient and negligent during the period and was sentenced to be dismissed from his rank and to serve before the mast.
[TNA: ADM.1/5299; ADM.51/3908]

9 December HAWK Brig Sloop
Limehouse 1756; 225 tons; 88.10ft × 24.1ft; 8 guns
Master and Commander Thomas Elliott
Cruising in the English Channel in stormy weather, when a strange sail was sighted which seemed to be closing at a steady pace. No answer was made to private recognition signals and the *Hawk* rightly suspected that it was a French privateer and made all sail away. The privateer overhauled the sloop and began the engagement with a volley of small-arms fire. This was followed by a broadside, to which the sloop could not effectively reply, as water was washing over the upper deck, preventing her from using her guns. The unequal struggle continued for a while, until, with three men killed, the *Hawk* surrendered to the *Duc de Choiseul*, 24 guns.
[TNA: ADM.1/5299]

December MISSISSAUGA Sloop
Prize 1759; 25 tons
Stationed in Lake Ontario, Canada, she was wrecked by ice about 30 miles west of Oswego.
[Malcolmson p19]

December FARQUHAR Schooner
Prize 1759; 15 tons
As with the *Mississauga* (above), she was wrecked by ice 30 miles west of Oswego, Lake Ontario.
[Malcolmson p19]

1760

15 February RAMILLIES Second Rate
Portsmouth 1749; 1,686 tons; 168ft × 48.1ft; 90 guns
Captain Witteronge Taylor†
Part of a squadron under Admiral Boscawen cruising in the western approaches to the English Channel, the weather was poor and worsened, the wind steadily increasing in strength until it was blowing a gale. The Admiral ordered the squadron to return to Plymouth Sound, the ships becoming separated in the storm.

When the *Ramillies*, now on her own, in thick and hazy weather, sighted land ahead, it was believed to be Rame Head at the entrance to the sound and the ship headed for the landfall. As they approached it was realised that the land was Bolt Head, further to the east. The mistake was not discovered until close to the land and the best bower anchor was ordered to be let go, followed by the small bower. Unfortunately, because of a delay in the release of the best bower, both were let go simultaneously, and the cables then became fouled, and the ship not immediately brought up. By the time the anchors had taken hold she was dangerously near the rocks. All the masts were cut away to ease the movement of the ship, which rode at anchor until about 5 o'clock in the evening, when both cables parted. The ship was driven onto the rocks and pounded heavily in the surf. She broke up very quickly, giving little chance for the crew to escape. One midshipman and 25 seamen survived; about 700 others drowned.
[Charnock vol VI pp151–2]

2 March TARTAR'S PRIZE Fifth Rate
Prize 1757 (*la Marie-Victoire*); 425 tons; 117.3ft × 28.4ft; 24 guns
Captain Thomas Baillie

In the early hours of the morning, the ship then being about 20 leagues (60 miles) north-east of Cagliari, Sardinia, a leak was discovered. The pumps were worked but the water gained, despite an additional hand pump being rigged and worked briskly. They were hampered when the main pump became blocked, and buckets were employed. By 7am it was clear that the water was gaining, and some guns and stores were heaved overboard to lighten the ship. A Danish snow was in sight and a boat was sent to ask that they stand by her, and it was hoped that a tow could be rigged. By late morning it was clear that the leak was so great that they could not succeed in keeping her afloat. The boats were hoisted out and the men were transferred to the snow. When this was complete, Captain Baillie organised parties to return to salvage stores and provisions, although this was difficult as the ship continued to settle lower in the water and it was reported that barrels were floating in the hold. The work went on until the evening when smoke was seen rising from the wreck and within 15 minutes, fire had taken firm hold and she was abandoned.
[TNA:ADM.1/5299;ADM.1/491]

28 March PENGUIN Sixth Rate
Deptford 1732 (*Dolphin*); 428 tons; 106ft × 30.5ft; 20 guns
Captain William Harris

Cruising off the coast of Portugal she was about eight leagues (24 miles) off Viana, when two French warships, the *Malicieuse*, 36 guns, and *Opale*, 32, were sighted, which bore up in chase. The pursuit went on for some time until the *Penguin* lost her main topgallant mast, after which the French pair overhauled her. Unable to use her lee guns, as the ports were under water, she could not properly reply when they came alongside. A volley of small-arms fire and two well-aimed shots which shredded the main shrouds decided the fate of the *Penguin*, which surrendered. Her French captors took the crew off and then burnt her.
[TNA:ADM.1/5299]

17 May VIRGIN Sloop
Purchased 1760; 12 guns
Master and Commander Edward St Loe†

Acting as an escort to a merchant schooner in the West Indies when three vessels were sighted approaching, which she correctly guessed were French privateers. Placing herself between the enemy and her charge, she prepared to take on of the pursuers, which consisted of an 8-gun schooner with a sloop and periagua, both carrying 4 guns. The *Virgin* fought for about 30 minutes until her mainsail boom was shot away and this event, coupled with mounting casualties, led to several of the crew deserting their guns. Forced back at the point of the officers' swords, the fight continued until the largest of the privateers ran the *Virgin* onboard, putting her bowsprit over the main hatchway. The other privateers placed themselves on the sloop's quarters and swept her decks with swivel and small-arms fire, and then entered boarders. Hand-to-hand fighting lasted for about five minutes, during which time Commander St Loe was killed, at which Lieutenant Cotton, the senior officer, surrendered. Six killed and eleven wounded.

Note: retaken in September 1760 by the *Temple*.
[TNA:ADM.1/5301]

19 May LOWESTOFFE Sixth Rate
Limehouse 1756; 594 tons; 118.3ft × 33.10ft; 28 guns
Captain Joseph Deane

One of a squadron assembled in the St Lawrence River supporting the operations of the army in Canada under General Murray against the French-Canadian army. Anchored above Quebec, near the Pointe aux Trembles, in the early hours of the morning she was ordered to weigh and attack French troops that were attempting to cross the river nearby. As she did so the anchor broke off in the shank and whilst attempting to sort out the confusion in the restricted waterway, she swung onto a sandbank. Efforts were made to lighten her, and the masts were cut away, but she could not be freed, and filling with water she was abandoned as a wreck.
[TNA:ADM.1/5299]

26 June EURUS Sixth Rate
Prize 1757 (le Dragon); 547 tons; 121.9ft x 31.10ft; 24 guns
Captain Nathaniel Bateman

After sailing from Quebec, she steered north along the St Lawrence River, in company with the *Prince of Orange* and *Rochester*, but in light airs the ships made only slow progress, anchoring every evening. Their progress was hampered further by thick fog, and she lost contact with her consorts. She lay-to for the night, but with little warning, at about 1.30am, she grounded a little to the west of Cape Chat. Efforts were made to get her off the ground, by throwing all the sails aback and then shifting the guns aft and boats were hoisted out with anchors to kedge her off. She could not be freed and later the main and mizzen masts were cut away, with the fore-topmast and yards struck in attempts to lighten her. All failed, and unable to free her and with water filling the ship, she was abandoned, a camp being set up on shore. The cause was established as an unexpectedly strong current which set her further inshore than expected, but the ship's Master, George Teer, was judged to have been negligent in failing to order the use of the lead-line when in shallow waters and was mulcted six months' pay.
[TNA:ADM.1/5299; ADM.51/316]

24 July PRINCE OF WALES Cutter
Hired 1759; 10 guns
Lieutenant Andrew Barkley

Cruising in the western approaches to the English Channel when a sail was sighted closing her. At first thought to be the *Dispatch* sloop, known to be in the area, as the strange vessel continued to close it was realised that it must be an enemy privateer. A short chase followed, until the French snow-rigged privateer *Renomée*, 20 guns, came within range. An exchange of broadsides followed, with the cutter's rigging suffering – the first shots cut away the square sail halliards, which forced Lieutenant Barkley to let the sail go overboard. A short while after the mainsail boom was shot away, effectively crippling the cutter, at which she surrendered.
[TNA:ADM.1/5299]

23 August ONONDAGA Snow
Fort Niagara 1760 (*Apollo*); c150 tons; 18 guns
Captain Joshua Loring

One of a small force on Lake Ontario, Canada, which escorted several galleys carrying troops to attack French positions in the St Lawrence River. Fort Lévis on Île Royale in the river blocked the advance of the British from the lake towards Montreal and was the subject of an attack by land and water. The British vessels bombarded the fort but met with a strong return fire. The *Onondaga* in her approach to the fort ran aground and when the other two supporting vessels were forced to withdraw, she bore the brunt of the shore fire. Unable to free herself and with several casualties, she struck her flag and sent the Master to the fort to confirm the surrender. The French then went aboard to take possession but found themselves the target of fire from British batteries. A party of soldiers and seamen from the *Williamson* sloop under the command of Lieutenant Sinclair then successfully boarded the snow and regained possession. That night, unable to free her from the mud and facing another shore bombardment in the morning, they abandoned the vessel, allowing her to settle in the water.
[Beatson vol II pp390–1]

4 October HARWICH Fourth Rate
Harwich 1743; 976 tons; 140.2ft x 40.2ft; 50 guns
Captain William Marsh

Cruising to the north-west of Jamaica when caught in a tropical storm, the weather steadily worsening and after 30 September the ship suffered three days of high winds and heavy seas, with regular squalls of rain accompanied by thunder and lightning. During the evening of 3 October, white water was seen ahead, and she promptly wore ship, losing the main-topmast as she did so. The weather continued to be extremely poor, with frequent squalls. At about 2 o'clock the following morning breakers were seen close ahead. She soon after struck the rocks and swung broadside-on, the rudder being beaten off in only a few minutes. Anchors were let go and the mizzen mast cut away to stabilise the ship. Guns, shot and stores were heaved overboard in attempts to lighten her, but she would not move and beat on the rocks constantly, starting several leaks. At daybreak she was finally shifted by cutting the cable and goose-winging the foresail and spritsail to take her into free water. She anchored and found herself surrounded by the reef and with the water gaining on the pumps all the time. Unable to escape and filling rapidly, the crew went to the nearby Isle of Pines, south-east of Cape Corrientes, Cuba, from where they were taken off by the Spanish, who burnt the remains of the wreck.
[TNA:ADM.1/5299]

18 October LYME Sixth Rate
Deptford 1748; 587 tons; 117.10ft x 33.10ft; 28 guns
Captain Edward Vernon

Attempting to leave the Baltic, she was battered by storm-force north-westerly winds as she tried to beat past the Skaw (Skagen). During the morning of 18 October, she was hit by a particularly hard squall which rolled her onto her beam-ends and water poured into the ship. Topsails were let fly, but she hung for some time, until the mizzen mast was cut away, at which she righted herself. The ship was now waterlogged, would bear no sail and was difficult to manoeuvre. Running

before the wind under bare poles, the guns were heaved overboard, and the pumps were manned constantly, the ship being taken towards the Swedish coast. The mainmast was cut away in a further attempt to ease her, but the troubles continued, with the tiller breaking. Now close to the shore, she anchored and cut away the foremast, pumping and bailing all the time. At about 5 o'clock in the evening the cables parted, and she was driven onto the Swedish shore near the village of Holm and wrecked. The Carpenter and twenty-two men were lost.
[TNA: ADM.1/5299]

25 October WILLIAMSON Armed Brig
Prize 1760 (*Outaouaise*); c160 tons; 10 guns
(*Probably*) Master Nathan Tibbols
Employed on Lake Ontario, she was taking stores to Fort Niagara, and anchored during 22 October about a mile from the settlement, the wind and current being against her. Whilst laying at anchor, a serious leak became evident and despite assistance being sent from shore, the water gained and to save the stores, the brig was run aground about five miles to the east of the fort. Over the next few days most of the stores were salvaged, but the vessel buried herself in the sand and was abandoned as a wreck.
[*Northern Mariner* XIV No.3]

26 October CONQUEROR Third Rate
Harwich 1758; 1,432 tons; 160ft × 45.2ft; 74 guns
Captain William Lloyd
After bringing the ship to anchor in Plymouth Sound, although the *Conqueror* was under orders to be taken up to the Hamoaze, Captain Lloyd did not think that the weather would allow this and went ashore. Later that evening, with the weather seemingly moderating, on the advice of a local pilot, Henry Harris, the ship weighed, but whilst manoeuvring in a strong tidal current with a fresh gale from the sea, she ran onto rocks at the south-eastern end of St Nicholas' Island. Attempts to free her failed and the masts were cut away to ease the movement. Hawsers were rigged to prevent her from falling over but rocks had pierced the bottom and she steadily filled with water and fell over onto her side. The crew were all taken off onto the island and over the next few days all the stores and guns were salvaged. The blame was placed on the 'misconduct of the pilot', who was sentenced to 18 months' imprisonment.
[TNA: ADM.1/2049; NMM: ADM 354/165/311]

3 November CUMBERLAND Third Rate
Woolwich 1739; 1,401 tons; 158ft × 45.5ft; 80 guns
Captain Robert Kirk
Laying at anchor in Mormugao Roads, Goa, India, the weather was poor, and deteriorated, as the area was swept by a series of strong gales accompanied by heavy rain. During 1 November, the topmasts were struck, and yards lowered or trimmed fore and aft. During the early hours of the following morning, water was found to be entering the hold and despite pumping and bailing, the water steadily gained. At first light, it was found that the mainmast had sprung, so it was cut away, but the wreckage partly fell across the boom, damaging the boats. The ship was labouring in the heavy swell and high winds, and the rudder and tiller was damaged by some of the wreckage. Distress guns were fired, and a boat managed to get to the shore to appeal for assistance, but none was available. By the evening the hold was filling with water, and gaining on the pumps, so manual bailing was employed. During the early morning of the 3rd, it was clear that the ship was settling by the head and a further appeal for assistance brought a local boat to her aid, which was brought alongside, and at 7 o'clock, the men started to be evacuated, the last of the men abandoning the pumps a little later and leaving her. She then had 10ft of water in the hold. Work went on through the morning to salvage as much of her gear and stores as possible, but by the afternoon she had sunk, with only the poop exposed. No blame was attached to the officers, as the ship was reported to have been in an extremely poor condition, being '… entirely decayed and in no condition to go to sea'.
[TNA: ADM.1/5301; ADM.51/4154]

28 November CAESAR Tender
Hired 1757
Lieutenant James Gaborian
The tender sailed from the anchorage off the Mumbles, Swansea Bay, in company with another tender in poor weather. The weather worsened, and by late afternoon the visibility had been reduced considerably by thick fog, and both decided to return to the anchorage. The *Caesar* approached the shoreline cautiously, using the lead-line constantly, as all the landmarks were obscured by the fog. Breakers were seen looming ahead and attempts were made to wear ship, but the manoeuvre was not completed before she struck the rocks. She beat several times on the rocks and filled with water, leading to her abandonment. The poor weather combined with uncertain currents were blamed.
[TNA: ADM.1/5300]

1761

1 January DUC D'ACQUITAINE Third Rate
Prize 1757; 1,358 tons; 159.5ft × 44.4ft; 64 guns
Captain Sir William Hewitt†
One of the British squadron in India, the ships were at anchor off Pondicherry (Puducherry), supporting

operations against the French. The wind increased during the morning, with strong winds from the north-east, with regular squalls of rain. After falling calm for a while, the wind again picked up, and blew with great force from the south-east. Rear Admiral Stevens, in the *Norfolk*, cut his cable and stood out to sea, and ordered all ships to do the same, but the visibility was so poor that not all ships saw or heard the signals. The *Duc d'Acquitaine* made her way out of the anchorage, but the force of the storm was such that no headway could be made, and she was forced to anchor in very shoal water off Pondicherry. During the night she was overset by the force of the weather and foundered. There were only 19 survivors from a complement of 400.
[Beatson vol II pp364–7]

Three other ships were also lost in the storm:

SUNDERLAND Fourth Rate
Portsmouth 1744; 1,124 tons; 147ft x 42ft; 60 guns
Captain Honourable James Colville†
As with the *Duc* (see above), anchored off Pondicherry (Puducherry) when the anchorage was struck by a tropical cyclone, she attempted to obey Admiral Stevens' orders to make her way into open water, but was unable to do so and re-anchored. She was overwhelmed by the storm about 6 miles north of the anchorage. There were only 17 survivors from a crew of 393.
[Beatson vol II pp364–7]

NEWCASTLE Fourth Rate
Portsmouth 1750; 1,053 tons; 144ft x 41ft; 50 guns
Captain Richard Collins
Another of the squadron off the coast of India forced out of their anchorage by a cyclone, the *Newcastle* successfully left the harbour, but found that she could make little headway out to sea as the wind shifted and blew with great intensity. She was driven ashore about 2 miles south of Pondicherry and broke up rapidly.
[TNA:ADM.1/5300]

QUEENBOROUGH Sixth Rate
Rotherhithe 1747; 519 tons; 113.3ft x 32.4ft; 20 guns
Master and Commander Thomas Daniell
Anchored off Pondicherry she followed the *Newcastle* out of the anchorage and like her, was unable to make her way out to clear water. She was driven ashore about 2 miles south of Pondicherry and wrecked.
[TNA:ADM.1/5300]

Note: Accounts of the disaster also mention the *Protector* fireship being wrecked; she appears to have been a vessel of the Bombay Marine, rather than the Royal Navy.

* * *

5 April SPEEDWELL Cutter
Hired 1760; 8 guns
Lieutenant James Allen
Hired for service on the coast of Spain and Portugal, as the cutter left Vigo in northern Spain, three vessels could be seen off Bayona, evidently making their way towards the harbour. Discovering them to be French warships, Lieutenant Allen decided to return to the anchorage. The French ships chased and overhauled the cutter, firing as they did so. When about 1½ miles from the fort of Vigo the *Achille*, 64 guns, came alongside and forced her to surrender. Britain later protested to the Spanish Government over what was seen as a breach of neutrality, as the capture had occurred inside Spanish territorial waters.
[TNA:ADM.1/5300]

10 October PHEASANT Sloop
Prize 1761 (*la Tourterelle*); 291 tons; 106.7ft x 24.7ft; 14 guns
Master and Commander Thomas Nielson†
Missing, presumed foundered, on or about this date in a storm in the English Channel. Some wreckage was later washed ashore near Weymouth, including the backboard of her barge bearing the name.
[TNA:ADM.1 80/3; www.britishnewspaperarchive.co.uk: Newcastle Courant 17 October 1761 p2]

23 October ANSON Armed Schooner
Prize 1760 (*Iroquoise*); c160 tons; 10 guns
Lieutenant William Deering (Canadian Provincial Marine)
One of the small flotilla of vessels on Lake Ontario, she was bound for Oswego loaded with stores from Fort William Augustus, when at about 10 o'clock in the morning in a fresh northerly gale they ran onto a rocky ledge known as the Niagara Shoal. She struck hard, and within 15 minutes was filling with water and was lost.
[Northern Mariner XIV No 3]

27 October GRIFFIN Sixth Rate
Bursledon 1758; 599 tons; 118.4ft x 33.11ft; 28 guns
Captain Thomas Taylor
Cruising amongst the Leeward Islands, for most of the day the frigate had been in pursuit of two French privateers. By nightfall they had evaded her, but she continued on the same course, believing herself to be well clear of land. At about 9pm, breakers were unexpectedly seen ahead, and an attempt was made to tack but the ship refused to answer the helm. The small bower anchor was immediately let go, but before half a cable had been veered out it parted, and she swung broadside-on to a reef off the north-east part of the island of Barbuda. The ship beat on the rocks all night and broke up into a wreck.
[TNA:ADM.1/5301]

31 December BIDEFORD Sixth Rate
Deptford 1756; 403 tons; 105ft × 29.9ft; 20 guns
Captain Thomas Gordon†

Heading for Great Yarmouth, the ship was being guided by the pilot for the Outer Dowsing light when just before 9 o'clock on the evening of 30 December she struck the ground and found herself on the Happisburgh (or Hazeborough) Sands off the north Norfolk coast. She beat on the sands for about half an hour, the rudder being knocked off, before she freed herself, anchored and struck yards and topmasts. The following morning, having spent a bitterly cold night riding at anchor and pumping constantly, she again went aground and commenced pounding heavily. Despite all their efforts, the ship could not be freed from the sands and the pumps would not clear the water, which soon filled the ship. She started breaking up, with the sea washing over her at frequent intervals. The *Lynx* sloop arrived that evening and took off the survivors, although several of the crew, including Captain Gordon, died of exposure. At the subsequent court martial of the survivors, the pilot, Taft Bailey, was found to have been 'in liquor' at the time of the tragedy and had mistaken lights onshore for those marking the Outer Dowsing.
[TNA: ADM.1/5301]

1762

January PEREGRINE GALLEY Sloop
Deptford 1733 (*Royal Caroline*); 216 tons; 86.6ft × 24ft; 12 guns
Master and Commander Edward Knowles†

The sloop sailed from Plymouth in December with news of the outbreak of war with Spain, and after passing the news to ships off Belle Île, sailed to carry despatches to Lisbon but disappeared and was presumed lost with all hands. The ship's pay books were closed on 31 January 1762.
[TNA: ADM.180/3; ADM.32/265; Gold: Naval Chronicle vol I p97]

7 January RAISONNABLE Third Rate
Prize 1758; 1,326 tons; 159.2ft × 43.10ft; 64 guns
Captain Molyneaux Shuldham

One of a powerful squadron under Admiral Rodney in the West Indies, which was assembled for an attack on the French colony on the island of Martinique, the ships arriving off the island on 7 January. The island's waters were not known with any accuracy and reliance was placed on the knowledge of local pilots, the *Raisonnable* taking on board John Panmure, who was highly thought of. Captain Shuldham was ordered to engage the batteries at Pointe de Jardin and the ship confidently stood in to the shoreline. As they steered along the coast, Captain Shuldham became anxious, as the bottom could clearly be seen from the deck. When about a mile to the east of Pointe de Jardin, white water was seen ahead, at which the sails were thrown aback, the helm put over and the foresail set to prevent her grounding. All was in vain however, and she struck the ground and ran onto a reef. Water butts were emptied to lighten her, and the boats were lowered to lay out anchors in attempts to kedge her free. The work went on throughout the afternoon, but she would not shift. By 6 o'clock in the evening the water was gaining on the pumps, and with the ship clearly settling, she was abandoned as a wreck. Much of the stores and guns were later salvaged. At a subsequent court martial, the pilot admitted that it was 30 years since he had been to Martinique, and then only in a sloop of war. In his defence he claimed that he was a local ship's master who had volunteered to act as a pilot, to serve his King and country. He was cleared of any neglect on his part, but it was ruled that he should not serve as a pilot in a Royal Navy ship again.
[TNA: ADM.1/5301]

23 May HUSSAR Sixth Rate
Chatham 1757; 586 tons; 118.3ft × 33.8ft; 28 guns
Captain Robert Carkett

Ordered to watch the motions of a French squadron off Cape François, Hispaniola, the frigate was cruising about eight miles to the west of the point, when Captain Carkett retired for the evening, stressing to the Master and Pilot that the ship should tack away from the land after 10 o'clock that night. At just after midnight the Captain was awakened to be told that the ship was close to land and would not tack. Soon after Carkett came on deck, the ship struck rocks and went hard aground. Efforts were made to free her – the foremast was cut away, the ship lightened, and kedge anchors used to try and haul her off – but all failed to move her. Being unable to save her, a boat was sent to the French squadron to ask for their assistance, which they promptly provided, taking off all the crew. It transpired at the court-martial proceedings later, that neither the Master, Isaac Deke, nor the pilot Joseph Hitchins, had obeyed Carkett's orders to tack away from the land at 10 o'clock, saying that '… there was time enough'. Both clearly realised that they would take the blame for the loss and disappeared before the enquiry. It was claimed that the Pilot had entered the French service and the Master remained on Hispaniola '… claiming the protection of that island'.
[TNA: ADM.1/5302]

27 June GRAMONT Ship Sloop
Prize 1757 (la Comtesse de Gramont); 324 tons; 98.1ft × 27.6ft; 18 guns
Master and Commander Patrick Mouatt
Stationed at St John's, Newfoundland, she was refitting when news arrived of a French force landing nearby at Pretty Harbour. The garrison ashore in Fort William was weak and requested that as the sloop was not immediately ready to sail, her stores and men be landed to assist them. This was complied with, and the ship's supply of powder and shot was landed, the guns spiked, and preparations made to scuttle her. On the arrival of the French the sloop's cable was cut, which allowed her to drift onto the rocks where she bilged.
[TNA: ADM.1/5302]

30 June SWIFT Cutter
Prize 1761 (le Comte de Valence); 83 tons; 53.10ft × 19.7ft; 10 guns
Master and Commander George Bowyer
When off Ushant on passage from Spithead to Belle Île, carrying despatches for Admiral Hawke, a ship was sighted approaching. Initially the vessels passed on opposite tacks, but then the strange vessel tacked and pursued the cutter. Realising that it was a French privateer, Commander Bowyer made all sail away. The chase went on throughout the day and it was nearly midnight when the 22-gun privateer (*Maney*?) finally overhauled her quarry. Placing herself under the lee quarter of the cutter and firing a volley of small-arms fire into her, Commander Bowyer had little choice but to surrender.
[TNA: ADM.1/5301]

25 July CHESTERFIELD Fifth Rate
Rotherhithe 1745; 719 tons; 127.5ft × 36.3ft; 40 guns
Captain John Scaife
Sailed from New York on 12 June in company with the *Intrepid* as escort to a convoy of fourteen transports carrying troops and stores to the British forces besieging Havana, Cuba. Land around Cape Quibanico was raised during 20 July, and they steered north-west to use the Old Bahama Channel, a narrow and intricate passage close to the northern shore of Cuba. One of the transports ran aground that same day, but after leaving another transport ship to stand by the wreck, the force carried on. During the night of 24/25 July, the ships were brought to, mainsails against the mast. At a little before 4 o'clock in the morning breakers were seen close ahead. The best bower anchor was let go, but before it could bring her up, she struck rocks. Guns were fired as a warning, the boats were hoisted out and topmasts struck. Water came into the ship at a fast rate, and it was clear that she was bilged. Daylight revealed that they were on a reef near Cayo Confites and four transports were also aground nearby. The mizzen mast was cut away and work started to move stores ashore, where a tented camp was set up. Satisfied that little more could be done, the *Intrepid* and the remaining transports left them that afternoon. The work to clear the wrecked ships went on for the next several days, being briefly interrupted by a Spanish schooner which closed and fired on them but made off after the ships replied with volleys of small-arms fire. Several ships were sent to their aid, and on 4 August, with most of the stores and guns having been salvaged, the wreck was set on fire, all the men being taken off by the *Enterprise*, *Lizard* and *Porcupine*.
[TNA: ADM.1/1237; ADM.1/5301; ADM.51/4147]

14 September STIRLING CASTLE Third Rate
Chatham 1742; 1,225 tons; 151ft × 43.6ft; 70 guns
Captain Charles Napier
Part of the fleet assembled under Admiral Sir George Pocock to attack Havana, Cuba. Captain Napier assumed command in late July after the fleet had arrived at Havana and her previous commander, Captain James Campbell, was relieved of his command after failing to support the bombardment as expected. The ship was in a poor state of repair, with several rotten planks and timbers. She had so many defects that after the surrender of Havana a survey was ordered by the Admiral. This confirmed that she could hardly float and could never put to sea, so Pocock ordered all stores and guns to be taken out. When that was complete, on 11 September she was hauled inshore until she grounded in the upper reaches of Havana harbour and was abandoned three days later.
[TNA: ADM.1/1237; ADM.51/934]

18 September HUMBER Fifth Rate
Buckler's Hard 1749; 825 tons; 133.6ft × 37.9ft; 40 guns
Captain Richard Onslow
Acting as an escort to a homeward-bound convoy of sixty ships from the Baltic, they were standing in for the harbour of Great Yarmouth under the guidance of the pilot, when at 10 o'clock in the morning, on a clear day, she ran aground onto the Happisburgh (or Hazeborough) Sands, with four of the merchant ships following her also grounding. The weather was clear and marks visible – when Captain Onslow discovered what had happened, he was incensed. Cursing the pilot, Thomas Ansdale, he cried 'By God, none but you could have run a ship ashore with the marks before your eyes!' All the efforts to kedge her off failed, and on the falling tide she fell over onto her beam-ends and was wrecked. One of the merchant vessels was also lost. Ansdale was sentenced to lose a year's pay and be confined in the Marshalsea Prison for 12 months.
[TNA: ADM.1/5301]

23 September SCORPION Sloop
Buckler's Hard 1746; 276 tons; 91.2ft x 26.4ft; 14 guns
Master and Commander John Henshaw†
Driven ashore on the Isle of Man in storm-force winds and wrecked with no survivors. Much wreckage was washed ashore on the island and seventy-three bodies were recovered.
[TNA: ADM. 1/80/20; www.britishnewspaperarchive.co.uk: Derby Mercury 8 October 1762 p2]

24 September BADGER Sloop
Bursledon 1745; 274 tons; 91.6ft x 26.3ft; 14 guns
Master and Commander Henry Scott†
Sailed from Deer Sound Bay, Orkney, on 20 September in company with the *Flamborough*, as escorts to a small convoy, the weather was poor and worsened after they sailed. By the evening of 23 September, it was blowing a full gale and during the early hours of the following morning increased in strength to storm force, with high seas and driving rain. The *Flamborough* was forced to heave her guns overboard as the ship pitched and rolled heavily, shipping large quantities of water. The *Badger* disappeared during this time, and was presumed lost, with all hands.
[TNA: ADM.1/80/3; ADM.51/4190; www.britishnewspaperarchive.co.uk: Derby Mercury 19 November 1762 p2]

1 October SOUTHSEA CASTLE Store Ship
Liverpool 1745; 711 tons; 126.1ft x 36ft; 28 guns
Captain William Sherwood
Supporting the expedition against the Spanish colony at Manila, Philippines, she had not long arrived, and anchored during 30 September in worsening weather. As the storm increased in strength, she struck topmasts and laid out a second anchor. She rode secure until 10 o'clock in the evening when she found that she was driving and shortly afterwards the best bower cable parted. The sheet anchor was let go which brought her up, but she was now dangerously near the shore. When the small bower cable parted, she again drove, struck the ground by the stern and swung broadside-on to the shore, where the surf broke over her and she was wrecked. It was not an entire disaster, however, since the position of the wreck was such that the guns could be used against some shore positions, and all the stores were saved.
[TNA: ADM.1/5301]

29 October BASILISK Bomb
Deptford 1759; 312 tons; 91.7ft x 28.1ft; 12 guns
Master and Commander William Lowfield†
Sailed from Havana on 12 October with despatches, she was in latitude 41, to the west of Nantucket, when a sail was sighted, which she closed to investigate. It soon became clear that it was a large French privateer and Commander Lowfield made all sail away. The chase went on through the morning, the chasing privateer using bow-chase guns to some effect. The cross-jack yard was shot away and soon after the mizzen mast itself went by the board. This enabled the French ship to come alongside, and a mutual exchange of broadsides commenced. After a short time, the privateer successfully manoeuvred under the bomb's weather quarter, from which position she could rake her opponent and then enter boarders. With the Captain and eight men killed and six wounded, Lieutenant Scott surrendered to *l'Audacieuse*, 18 guns, from Bayonne.
[TNA: ADM.1/5302]

17 November THREE BROTHERS Tender
Hired 1756
Master Richard Pardon
Chased, overhauled and captured off the Île de Groix by a French privateer.
[TNA: ADM.1/5302]

29 November MARLBOROUGH Third Rate
Chatham 1732; 1,567 tons; 164ft x 47.2ft; 80 guns
Captain Thomas Burnett
One of Admiral Pocock's fleet at the siege of Havana, the ship was in a poor condition, with several leaks, when she sailed from Cuba for England at the start of November. The situation worsened as the voyage progressed, with men continuously at the pumps, extra men being drafted on board from ships in company to assist. The weather worsened, and Captain Burnett decided to bear away for Lisbon as he doubted that the ship would make it to England. Now alone, the crew worked around the clock to keep her afloat, bailing as well as pumping. An old sail was thrummed and hung over the bows to stem the leaks but achieved only limited success. The ship was lightened by throwing overboard all the upper-deck guns, but she was clearly foundering. By good chance, the *Antelope*, 50 guns, was sighted, which came to her aid, taking off all the crew, and the *Marlborough* foundered that same night. The ship's Carpenter, John Parlby, was singled out for praise by the court martial enquiring into the loss. It was due to his 'indefatigable efforts' that the ship had survived for as long as she had.
[TNA: ADM.1/5302]

18 December TEMPLE Third Rate
Hull 1758; 1,429 tons; 159.11ft x 45.1ft; 70 guns
Captain Thomas Collingwood
Having taken part in the Havana expedition, the *Temple* sailed for England at the end of October. The ship was not in good condition, and several leaks were evident, although they were able to be controlled with the ship's pumps. As the weather deteriorated the leaks

worsened, and on 15 December she was forced to make distress signals and ask for ships to stand by her. The upper-deck guns were heaved overboard, and a sail was thrummed and hung over the side to stop the leaks. On 17 December all the sick were taken off by other ships in the fleet and the following day, when about 300 miles south of Cape Clear, the remainder of the crew were removed and she was abandoned and allowed to founder.
[TNA:ADM.1/5302]

19 December CATHERINE Sloop
Hired 1762; 8 guns
Lieutenant John McLellan
Stationed in the West Indies, she was lying at anchor near the Saintes rocks off Guadeloupe, having just stopped and examined a periagua. Having completed this task, she weighed and made sail, steering between the Saintes, but shortly after this she struck a submerged rock. The sails were thrown aback, which successfully freed her, but she commenced filling with water. Lieutenant McLellan ordered the sloop to be run ashore on the nearest island, which was quickly performed, sweeps being used to speed her passage. All the crew went ashore from where they were picked up by the *Virgin* sloop. No pilot was onboard, but the enquiry was satisfied that the passage taken had been used before, with the rock the sloop had struck not being marked on any chart.
[TNA:ADM.1/5302]

1763

28 August MICHIGAN Sloop
Navy Island Niagara 1762; 100 tons; 6 guns
Based on Lake Erie, Canada, she was sent to carry provisions to Fort Detroit, under threat from an Indian uprising, but was wrecked on Presque Island, although the cargo was saved.
[Malcomson p23]

8 | 1764–1771: Growing Tension in North America

THE END OF THE WAR IN 1763 had left Great Britain with a huge national debt, and inevitably led to attempts to raise revenue through increased taxes. This was coupled with efforts to tighten controls in the North American colonies which caused resentment and the distance from London added to the growing feeling of independence.

1764

March ÉPREUVE Ship Sloop
Prize 1760; 261 tons; 92.9ft x 25.9ft; 14 guns
Master and Commander Peter Blake†
Disappeared in the North Atlantic coming from Georgia, North America, and presumed foundered with all hands. The pay books were officially closed on 31 March 1764.
[TNA: ADM.180/3; ADM 33/609; www.britishnewspaperarchive.co.uk: Caledonian Mercury 28 July 1764 p2]

October LAPWING Cutter
Broadstairs 1764; 83 tons; 47.9ft x 21.1ft; 6 guns
Lieutenant John Birt†
Based in Lough Swilly, Ireland, she disappeared at sea during this month and was presumed to have foundered with the loss of all hands. With no news of her, she was officially paid off by Admiralty Order of 23 October 1765, the pay book being made up to 31 October 1764.
[TNA: ADM.32/245]

Unknown MOHAWK Snow
Fort Niagara 1759; 140 tons
On Lake Ontario, she is reported to have been lost during the year, but date and circumstances are uncertain.
[Malcomson p23]

Unknown JOHNSON Snow
Pointe au Baril, Lake Ontario 1759; 150 tons
As with the *Mohawk* (above), on Lake Ontario, she is shown as being lost during the year, date and circumstances uncertain.
[Malcomson p23]

1765

6 February KING OF PRUSSIA Cutter
Purchased 1763; 90 tons; 50.10ft x 21.3ft; 6 guns
Lieutenant Henry Prettie
The cutter sailed from the Nore bound for the Downs anchorage in poor weather, with fresh gales and regular flurries of snow. At about 3.30 in the afternoon, she was struck by a fierce snowstorm which obscured all the landmarks, and in the gloom, she ran aground on the Cross Ledge bank off Ramsgate. Attempts were made to kedge her off, but these failed. At high tide, instead of floating off as hoped, she filled with water and then capsized. The following morning the local population descended on the wreck and plundered anything they could find.
[TNA: ADM.1/5303; ADM.51/3961; NMM: ADM.354/176/54]

1766

26 June SAINT LAWRENCE Schooner
Purchased 1764; 115 tons; 50.6ft x 20.8ft; 6 guns
Lieutenant Adam Dundas
The schooner was lying at anchor in Niginish Bay, Cape Breton Island, when the anchorage was hit by a fierce thunderstorm. At about 3 o'clock in the afternoon the *St Lawrence* was struck by a bolt of lightning, which seemed to strike the foremast and pass straight down to the magazine. A massive explosion took place, demolishing the forward part of the vessel and in less than a minute she had foundered. Several people were blown overboard or up through the deck. In all three men were killed, three were missing and nine men were wounded. Efforts were made to raise the wreck, but without success.
[TNA: ADM.1/5303]

August PITT Cutter
Purchased 1763; 100 tons; 58.8ft x 20.8ft; 6 guns
Lieutenant Philip Orsbridge†
Sailed to Guinea in January with despatches but during her return voyage disappeared and was presumed to have foundered with all hands.
[TNA: ADM.32/248; ADM.180/21]

4 March 1653. Battle of Livorno – *Samson* being destroyed. (*Thaliastock/Mary Evans*)

June 1666. Dutch ships returning with their prizes after the Four Days' Battle – probably depicting in the background, the *Convertine*, *Swiftsure* and *Loyal George*. (© *National Maritime Museum, Greenwich, London*)

June 1667. The Dutch burn English ships in the Medway. (*Mary Evans/The Everett Collection*)

May 1692. A fireship burning a flagship (la Hougue). (© *National Maritime Museum, Greenwich, London*)

February 1799. Passengers and crew leave the *Proserpine* frigate. (© *National Maritime Museum, Greenwich, London*)

March 1800. The sloop *Speedy* with the wreck of the *Queen Charlotte*. (© *National Maritime Museum, Greenwich, London*)

25 March 1804. The loss of the *Magnificent* off Brest. (© *National Maritime Museum, Greenwich, London*)

4 February 1805. *Arrow* sinking after action with two French frigates. (© *National Maritime Museum, Greenwich, London*)

4 March 1807. The loss of the *Blanche* on the coast of Britanny. (© *National Maritime Museum, Greenwich, London*)

28 December 1807. Wreck of the *Anson* frigate at Helston. (© *National Maritime Museum, Greenwich, London*)

24 December 1811. The wreck of the *Hero* in the Texel. (© *National Maritime Museum, Greenwich, London*)

29 December 1812. The destruction of the *Java* after capture. (*Mary Evans/The Everett Collection*)

20 February 1815. Action of the *Cyane* and *Levant* with USS *Constitution*. (*Mary Evans/The Everett Collection*)

26 February 1852. *Birkenhead* sinking in Algoa Bay. (*Mary Evans Picture Library*)

12 May 1854. The *Tiger* aground near Odessa. (*Mary Evans Picture Library*)

14 April 1857. The *Raleigh* salutes the French admiral whilst running onto the beach at Macao. (© *National Maritime Museum, Greenwich, London*)

14 September HAPPY Ketch Sloop
Woolwich 1754; 141 tons; 75.6ft × 20.7ft; 8 guns
Master and Commander Hugh Bromedge
Bound for Great Yarmouth, she anchored off Winterton for the evening. The following morning, she weighed and whilst manoeuvring past Scroby Sands, she was hit by a squall which carried her closer to the sandbank. Attempting to tack away, she missed stays, fell off before the wind and struck the ground. She anchored to await the high tide, when all sail was spread, and she successfully drove over the sands, although striking extremely hard several times as she did so. The sloop was now making water quite fast, so she was steered inshore and deliberately run onto the beach at Winterton near the lighthouse. Attempts were made to haul her further onshore to discover the leaks, but the bottom had become firmly buried in the beach sand and the efforts only served to break up the upper works; she was abandoned as a wreck.
[TNA: ADM.1/5303]

30 November VICTORY Sloop
Navy Island 1761 (*Huron*); 80 tons
One of the small squadron maintained on Lake Erie, she was laid up for the winter off Navy Island, Niagara, when she was destroyed by an accidental fire.
[Malcomson p23]

1768

5 October DUKE WILLIAM Schooner
Purchased 1763; 65 tons; 45.8ft × 19.6ft; 4 guns
Lieutenant John Field†
Sailed from Scilly to return to Plymouth, but disappeared, and was presumed lost with all hands. Pay Book closed on this date.
[TNA: ADM.1 80/4; ADM.33/444; www.britishnewspaperarchive.co.uk: Oxford Journal 10 December 1768 p1]

November BOSTON Schooner
Navy Island 1764; 60 tons
One of the small squadron on Lake Erie, she caught fire and was destroyed when laid up at anchor on the Niagara River near Fort Erie.
[Malcolmson p23]

1770

January (?) AURORA Fifth Rate
Chatham 1766; 683 tons; 125ft × 35.5ft; 32 guns
Captain Thomas Lee†
Sailed from Spithead on 2 October 1769 with supervisors from the East India Company – Henry Vansittart, Luke Scrafton and John Ford – for India, where they were due to 'make enquiries into abuses', calling first at the Cape of Good Hope. The ship left the Cape on 23 December 1769 but no positive news of the ship or the crew were ever received again. It was presumed that the ship was overwhelmed in the Indian Ocean by either storm or fire. The pay books were ordered to be made up to 31 December 1769.
[TNA: ADM.33/473; DNB: entries for Vansittart and Scrafton]

27 January JAMAICA Brig Sloop
Deptford 1744; 273 tons; 91.5ft × 26.1ft; 14 guns
Master and Commander George Talbot
Bound for Jamaica from Pensacola, land was raised during the afternoon, identified as Cuba, and the sloop continued under easy sail, having altered course to take her clear of the shore. At about 7 o'clock that evening, breakers were seen ahead and before any action could be taken, she ran hard aground on a reef. The masts were cut away and efforts were made to get off the reef, but she filled with water very rapidly. Rafts were made, and boats lowered to take the crew to a small cay, visible some three miles off. Over the next few days all the stores and provisions were taken off the wreck and a boat despatched to the mainland, where all were rescued by a schooner. The court martial decided that a strong current was responsible for setting her further inshore that anticipated, taking her onto the Colorados reef at the north-west end of Cuba.
[TNA: ADM.1/5304]

13 March SWIFT Ship Sloop
Limehouse 1763; 271 tons; 91.5ft × 26.2ft; 14 guns
Master and Commander George Farmer
One of three sloops supporting the British settlement in the Falkland Islands, the *Swift* sailed from Port Egmont on 7 March to conduct a survey of the islands, but she was caught in a particularly strong storm which drove her off station, towards the South American mainland. With the sloop needing repairs following the storm and the crew being sickly, Commander Farmer decided to steer for the sheltered waters of Port Desire in Patagonia. As the sloop worked in, she struck a submerged rock, from which they successfully kedged themselves off, only to run onto another uncharted rock. By now the tide was ebbing and the sloop found herself balanced precariously, with her bows on a flat rock and the stern

dipping with the ebbing tide. After three hours in this situation, the sloop slipped off the rock stern first, capsized and sank. The crew struggled onto the rocks and the nearby shore, although three men drowned in the attempt. The cutter which had survived was manned and sailed for the Falklands to bring rescue, which, after a perilous 400-mile voyage, was accomplished, the sloop *Favourite* taking off the survivors, who had lived on seabirds and seals, four weeks later.
[TNA: ADM. 1/5304]

20 December PEGGY Brig Sloop
Deptford 1749; 141 tons; 74.6ft x 20.9ft; 8 guns
Master and Commander Richard Toby
On passage for Great Yarmouth from South Shields with freshly-raised men, the sloop anchored for the night off Cromer. The following morning, on getting under way, she carried away her trysail mast. The wind steadily increased during the day until it was blowing a full northerly gale, accompanied by flurries of snow. She anchored again, but soon after found that she was dragging her anchor, and the small bower anchor was also let go, which brought her up, although dangerously close to the land. The mainmast was cut away to ease the ship, but she soon began driving again and within minutes was amongst the breakers and went ashore on the north Norfolk shore near Happisburgh (or Hazeborough). The sloop lay all night on the beach, being pounded constantly by the surf which broke right over her. At first light the local people came down to the wreck and helped the survivors to safety, but forty men died from exposure or drowning.
[TNA: ADM. 1/5304]

1771

30 January JOSEPH and BETSY Brig Tender
Hired 1770; 100 tons
Lieutenant Isaac Vaillant
Employed as a press tender, she had sailed from Fowey, bound for Glasgow, to raise men for the Navy, and put into St Mary's in the Scilly Isles. On sailing she was guided out by local pilots who, when about two miles clear of the harbour, assured the crew that they were now clear of any danger. Shortly after this she struck a submerged, uncharted rock, which she drove over, ripping out the bottom. She sank very quickly all sail standing; all the crew, except one man, were rescued by another tender.
[TNA: ADM. 1/5304]

9 | 1772–1783: American Independence

THE RELATIONSHIP BETWEEN Great Britain and her American colonies had steadily deteriorated since the end of the war in 1763. The war had left the British government with a huge war debt and this, coupled with the need to maintain a sizeable British force in America, led to a perceived need to extend taxes and enforce the collection of existing duties in the colonies. To administer the law in American waters the Royal Navy was employed to both give support to customs collectors and to implement the collection of taxes. This led to widespread resentment amongst the colonists and led to some sporadic violence – in July 1769, the customs sloop *Liberty* was boarded by several men whilst at Newport, Rhode Island, the men put ashore and the vessel scuttled. In November 1771, a similar incident occurred at Philadelphia, when a revenue schooner was seized, the crew imprisoned and the prize she had taken released. The most serious incident of all occurred at Providence, Rhode Island in June 1772, when the Royal Navy sloop *Gaspée* was attacked. In December 1774 news reached America that the importation of gunpowder and warlike stores was being prohibited. This led to the colonists accumulating powder and shot and the consequent British attempts to find and destroy such stores led to the fighting at Lexington and Concord in April 1775. The resulting siege of Boston effectively marks the start of the War of American Independence.

Initially the role of the Royal Navy was to support the garrison at Boston, but by late summer 1775 they had to tackle the problem of armed vessels, initially privateers and from 1776 American warships. In February 1778, the French agreed a treaty of amity and commerce with the Americans, which the British saw as making war inevitable. The dispatch of a powerful French fleet to North American waters under the Comte d'Estaing added to the fears and war was declared. It was almost inevitable that the Spanish should be drawn into the war – the close alliance of Spain with France coupled with a desire to regain the losses in America and the Mediterranean led to hostilities in June 1779. The formation of an Armed Neutrality by the neutral nations of Europe was perceived in London as an anti-British coalition, advocating as it did the continuance of trade with the Americans. The Dutch, as the leading neutral power, became the focus of British hostility and a declaration of war in December 1780.

The war developed from the attempts to control unruly and hostile colonists into a world war, which saw fleet actions in the Atlantic, West Indies and the Indian Ocean, fighting on the North American lakes and rivers, in addition to the numerous inevitable clashes between individual ships.

1772

10 June GASPÉE Schooner
Purchased 1764; 102 tons; 49ft x 19.10ft; 6 guns
Lieutenant William Dudingston

The *Gaspée* was one of several sloops and schooners employed after 1768 to enforce the Acts requiring tax to be paid on various goods entering the American colonies. This involved the stopping of vessels in coastal waters and searching them for illegal or undeclared goods. Both the taxes and the acts of the cruisers thoroughly annoyed the colonists. The *Gaspée* was particularly vigorous and was the subject of several complaints of being overzealous and searching everything that moved, often with armed men. On 9 June, she stopped and searched the local Rhode Island packet boat *Hannah* off Providence, but in doing so grounded in shallow water off Namquit Point, about seven miles from the town. At just before 1 o'clock in the morning the sentinel on the upper deck sighted about eight or nine boats approaching the schooner, which ignored his shouted challenges. Alarmed, the man roused Lieutenant Dudingston, who came on deck in his shirt to find them almost alongside. He shouted a warning to keep clear, but the boats pressed on with a cry of 'God damn your blood, we have you now!' As the attackers came on board, Dudingston slashed at them with his hangar and the sentinel fired his musket. The return fire hit the Lieutenant in two places. The crew were quickly overwhelmed and sent ashore. The schooner was then burnt.
[TNA: ADM.1/5305]

20 October DISPATCH Schooner
Purchased 1771; 14 guns
Lieutenant Michael John Everitt

On passage from Jamaica to England, she was hit by a fierce storm in the North Atlantic. On 19 October, she shipped a particularly heavy sea which swamped her and laid her on her beam-ends. With some difficulty,

the mainmast and foresail were cut away, which righted her, although soon after she was struck by another wave which unshipped the tiller. The schooner drove before the wind all night and it was fortunate that the following morning they fell in with the merchant brig *Josepha* of Dartmouth, which took off the crew, the schooner being quite waterlogged. Some of the crew had done little to assist Lieutenant Everitt in his struggles to save the vessel, indeed, he accused a few of being resentful, mutinous and drunk. Three seamen – David Bryant, Henry Fitzgerald and Matthew Sullivan – were subsequently ordered to receive 200 lashes each for their conduct.
[TNA:ADM.1/5305]

1775

15 February HALIFAX Schooner
Purchased 1768; 83 tons; 58.3ft × 18.3ft; 6 guns
Lieutenant Joseph Nunn
The schooner sailed from Cranberry Harbour, Maine, on 13 February bound for Passamaquody Bay, and steered for Machias, to embark a new pilot, the man embarked not being acquainted with the coast beyond Machias. At 12.30 in the afternoon, ' … the pilot being deceived in the Land', she struck a rocky ledge off Sheep Island (modern Halifax Island) at the entrance to Englishman Bay. She drove over the rocks then swung broadside-on to a small reef, knocking the rudder off. Sails were furled and an attempt was made to kedge her off using anchors taken out by the ship's boats, but this failed. That evening the tide left her dry on the rocks, and later the weather worsened, and soon the sea was beating over the schooner. The crew landed on nearby Sheep Island, whilst the Master and pilot were despatched in one of the boats to bring help. During the night, the schooner was beaten to pieces on the rocks, and morning showed only the masts appearing above the water. The boat's crew eventually gained the assistance of a local man, Mr Beale, who returned with his own vessel and took the crew to Boston. The court martial placed the blame on the ignorance of the pilot – who, foreseeing the outcome, had already taken the opportunity to slip away, whilst the Master was talking to Mr Beale, and disappear.
[TNA:ADM.1/485;ADM.1/5307]

18 May BETSEY Sloop
St Jean 1771; 70 tons; 2 guns
In the spring of 1775, the American rebels made a series of raids on weakly-manned British outposts on Lake Champlain. Led by Benedict Arnold, they captured Fort Ticonderoga and Crown Point, and followed these successes when, with a force of fifty men, Arnold surprised the harbour at St Jean. The small garrison was quickly overrun and a small vessel, described as 'the King's sloop', with just seven men on board was captured. The Americans fitted out the prize as the *Enterprise*. The identity of this vessel is somewhat uncertain, but it may be the government vessel *Betsey*.
[NDAR vol 1:367;503; Malcolmson p26]

28 May DIANA Armed Schooner
Purchased 1775; 120 tons; 4 guns
Lieutenant Thomas Graves
As tension between the American colonists and the British turned to open fighting, the Americans did their utmost to cut off the town of Boston and its occupying forces. During 27 May the small islands known as Noddle and Hog in Boston harbour were raided by the Americans, who took off or killed the livestock and burnt the crops. The *Diana* was ordered to attack the rebels on the islands, and the schooner closed to fire repeatedly on the enemy positions, driving them off the islands. As she returned to her anchorage, she was engaged by more rebel forces at Winisimet Ferry. By now it was dusk, and the wind fell away to a calm, so boats were sent down to tow the schooner away. At the same time troops were landed to engage the rebels. A fierce fight was now under way, with the rebel forces using field guns as well as small arms. At about 11 o'clock that night the *Diana* was taken inshore by the strong tidal current and grounded on the ferry ways. Despite all the efforts of the boats to tow her off and the use of kedge anchors, she could not be moved. All this time she was under fire from the shore, the rebels taking shelter behind hedges, walls and the ferry house. Later, as the tide fell, the schooner capsized, and the crew was taken off by the *Britannia* tender. Later that night the Americans approached the vessel and set her on fire.
[TNA:ADM.1/5307]

12 June MARGUERITTA Schooner Tender
Hired 1775; swivel guns
Midshipman James Moore†
Arriving in the Machias River, Maine, having escorted two vessels from Boston to Machias to get wood and to recover the guns from the *Halifax* schooner (above), she anchored and lay in the river below the town. During 11 June, there was a determined effort by rebel forces to take possession of the vessels, and a sharp fight developed. Outnumbered, the small crew of the schooner slipped her cable and moved out of range, alongside one of the merchant sloops. The following morning a sloop and a schooner could be seen approaching, apparently full of armed men, so the *Margueritta* weighed and stood out to sea, pursued by the Americans. They were overhauled, and the enemy vessels ran alongside, the sloop *Unity* on the starboard quarter, the schooner *Falmouth* on the

port bow, firing swivels and muskets. With one man killed and five wounded, one of them Midshipman Moore, the tender surrendered. Mr Moore died of his injuries the following day.
[TNA: ADM.1/485]

16 June DIANA Brig tender
Prize 1775; swivel guns
Master Savage Gardner
Tender to the *Rose*, she was despatched under the command of the Master and twelve men to reconnoitre the various passages and inlets in Rhode Island harbour. At about 6.30pm, she was approached by an armed sloop, the *Katy*, 6 guns, which hailed the tender and called on her to bring-to. Mr Gardner refused and when the *Katy* opened fire on her, he returned the fire with swivels and small arms, and then made off, the American following, firing constantly. When another ship appeared, to place the tender between fires, Mr Gardner ran the tender ashore at the northern end of Conanicut Island and abandoned her. Two men were wounded in the engagement.
[TNA: ADM.1/485; ADM.52/7743]

15 July DILIGENT Schooner
Purchased 1775 (Byfield); 6 guns
Lieutenant John Knight
Sent to Machias, Maine, to attempt to recover the prisoners taken from the recently-captured tender *Margueritta* (see above), Lieutenant Knight seems not to have been fully aware of the extent of the conflict between the colonists and the British and believed that the tender and its crew had been detained ' ... because of some misunderstanding'. He therefore took the schooner into Machias harbour, anchored and went ashore, where he was met by an apprehensive party of armed local people, headed by a Captain Smith. Assuring them he meant no harm, but came to recover the captured seamen, he was allowed ashore and met the local council. After an initial cautious welcome, the mood changed during the day and he found himself detained as a prisoner – Knight placing much of the blame for this on a 'villainous, dissenting preacher', who stirred up the people. Early the next morning, a sloop, a schooner and a boat approached the *Diligent* and the small crew were easily overpowered by the large number of armed men who boarded her, led by Captain Jeremiah O'Brien.
[TNA: ADM.1/5307]

(26?) August FERRET Ship Sloop
Rotherhithe 1760; 300 tons; 95.6ft × 26.8ft; 14 guns
Master and Commander James Rodney†
Stationed at Jamaica, she disappeared in the West Indies, last being seen on 22 August 1775 off Havana, after which nothing was seen or heard of her. A tropical storm passed through the area on 26 August, and it was presumed that she was lost with all hands in this storm.
Note: her name was not struck from the list until mid-1776, and this had led several publications to mistakenly place her loss in that year.
[TNA: ADM.1/240]

2 September LIBERTY Sloop Tender
Prize 1775; swivel guns
Tender to the *Otter*, she was at anchor, unmanned, in the Elizabeth River, Virginia when the area was struck by a violent storm. In the gale, she was driven from her anchor and went ashore in Back River, when the local inhabitants of Hampton stripped her of all valuable stores and then set her on fire
[TNA: ADM.51/663]

11 September QUEBEC Schooner
Purchased 1775; 6 guns
Lieutenant Sampson Edwards
Heading for Notre Dame Bay, Newfoundland in poor weather, with drifting banks of thick fog, Lieutenant Edwards decided to put into Lassie Harbour and anchor until the weather cleared. That afternoon the fog cleared, to be replaced by squalls and incessant rain. The schooner shortened cable and attempted to strike the topmasts and yards, but this proved difficult, as 'the people could not keep at the masthead' due to the very heavy showers of hail. A merchant brig drove down onto them, carrying away the schooner's bowsprit and fouling her cables. Both vessels were then carried down onto another merchant ship. At this, the anchor cables were cut, and the foresail spread, which freed her. She successfully tacked away from the nearby shoreline, but unfortunately ran onto a reef of submerged rocks. She filled with water very quickly and eventually broke in two before sinking.
[TNA: ADM.1/5307]

14 September PLACENTIA Schooner
Purchased 1775; 6 guns
Lieutenant Lewis Robertson
Cruising off Cape Race, Newfoundland, when caught in the storm which affected the area on 11–13 September, she reduced sail and struck yards to ride out the gale. In the early morning of the 13th, she was struck by a particularly large sea, which shifted the ballast in the hold, carried away the boats, main-hatch cover, binnacle, compass and anything moveable on the upper deck. Two members of the crew were washed overboard and drowned. The mainmast was cut away, which took the foretopmast in its fall. Sails were rigged over the hatchway and under a jury rig she drove before the wind, pumping constantly. The following morning

a merchant schooner was sighted, which took the crew off, and the *Placentia* was abandoned and allowed to founder.
[TNA: ADM.1/5307]

11 October ROYAL SAVAGE Schooner
St Jean; 70 tons; 14 guns
Lieutenant William Hunter
Hastily constructed at Fort St Jean (or St John) on Lake Champlain to provide some means of defence at the fort against the advancing American army, Lieutenant Hunter was sent from Quebec to take charge of her fitting-out. From mid-September, onwards the Americans commenced a siege of the fort, supported by gundalows and galleys. On 11 September, they opened a battery on the riverbank opposite the fort and the sloop. The subsequent bombardment sank the sloop in shallow water and the fort finally surrendered on 3 November. The sloop was later raised and pressed into service by the Americans.
[Gold: Naval Chronicle vol 13 pp39–40]

November CHIPPEWA Sloop
Detroit 1769; 50 tons.
Master Richard Cornwall
Former merchant vessel on Lake Erie, she was used by the Provincial Marine to carry stores, but was reported to have been driven ashore and wrecked at Long Point.
[Malcolmson p25; http://images.maritimehistoryofthegreatlakes.ca/61691/data?n=1]

1776

22 March GENERAL CLINTON Sloop Tender
Prize 1775 (*Hetty*); swivel guns
Fitted out as a tender to the *Falcon*, she had only twelve men on board when overhauled off the coast of North Carolina by the American armed brig *Comet*, 16 guns, which forced her surrender.
[NDAR vol 4 p654]

4 April HAWK(E) Schooner Tender
Purchased 1776; 6 guns
Lieutenant John Wallace
Tender to the *Rose*, she was ordered to cruise off Block Island, but off the eastern end of Long Island fell in with an American squadron of six ships, returning from a raid on the Bahamas. Unable to escape, and faced with a superior force, the schooner surrendered to the *Alfred*, 24 guns, and the *Columbus*, 24.
[NDAR vol 4 p735]

5 April BOLTON Bomb Brig
Purchased 1775; 96 tons; 8 guns
Lieutenant Edward Sneyd
Cruising off the American shore between Block Island and Martha's Vineyard, at first light she sighted several ships, which she presumed to be British. She closed until she found them to be an American squadron, and when she realised her mistake made off. She was pursued, and a running fight developed, until she was overhauled by several of the enemy. When the *Alfred*, 24 guns, ran under her stern and hailed her, she surrendered.
[TNA: ADM.1/5308; Mariner's Mirror vol 44 p241]

17 April EDWARD Sloop Tender
Purchased 1776; 50 tons; 6 guns
Lieutenant Richard Boger
Tender to the *Liverpool*, she was ordered to cruise off the coast of Virginia, when at about 1 o'clock in the afternoon she was chased and overhauled by the American sloop *Lexington*, 14 guns. A sharp fight developed, which lasted for over an hour before she surrendered. One man was killed.
[NDAR vol 4 pp702, 772]

29 June ACTAEON Sixth Rate
Woolwich 1775; 594 tons; 120.6ft × 33.6ft; 28 guns
Captain Christopher Atkins
Part of a British force which mounted an abortive attack on Charleston, South Carolina, the naval force advanced in divisions to attack a fort on Sullivan's Island at the entrance to the harbour. The *Actaeon*, along with the frigates *Sphinx* and *Siren*, were ordered to bombard the western side of the fort, the *Sphinx* leading. As they proceeded up-river, the leading ship ran aground on the middle ground shoal. Warned of the danger the *Actaeon* attempted to tack, but the *Siren*, being close astern, collided with her and carried her down onto the sands, where she became entangled with the already-grounded *Sphinx*, the bowsprit of the latter going through her main-shrouds. After clearing the wreckage away, the frigates then worked to free themselves from the sands. The *Siren* was able to free herself and the *Sphinx* successfully drove over the sandbank. The *Actaeon*, however, remained firmly aground. All attempts to free her, by lightening the ship, taking out kedge anchors and sailing over the sand at high water failed. With no prospect of freeing her and under a constant annoying fire from the fort, she was abandoned and set on fire.
[TNA: ADM.1/5307]

12 July EGMONT Schooner
Purchased 1764; 99 tons; 62ft × 19.7ft; 10 guns
Lieutenant Alexander Christie
Sailed 9 July from St Johns, Newfoundland, bound for Trepassy with despatches, she encountered very thick

banks of fog. Extra lookouts were posted, and the lead-line ordered to be used constantly, but despite these precautions, as she attempted to tack, she missed stays and ran aground. She started beating on the rocks so violently that it was difficult for men to stand on the fo'c'sle. Boats could not be hoisted out because of the movement of the ship and the high seas. Unable to free her and with the schooner starting to break up, the crew clambered onto the nearby rocks. Over the next two days the sea continued to batter the schooner until she broke up.
[TNA: ADM.1/5307]

14 July DISPATCH Schooner
Purchased 1776 (*Sally*); 114 tons; 8 guns
Lieutenant John Goodridge†
Sailed from Halifax, Nova Scotia, to act as escort to twenty-two transports carrying Hessian troops to New York, she became separated from the convoy during a gale on 12 July but continued to stand on to the south-west. When to the east of Long Island, New York, a sloop was sighted closing under all sail. Suspecting her to be an enemy privateer, she cleared for action and when in range fired a shot at the stranger to make her show her identity. The ship, which was the American privateer *Tyrannicide*, 14 guns, hoisted a flag depicting a pine tree and shortly afterwards, at about 3.30pm, the action began with a mutual exchange of broadsides. The privateer appeared to make sail away but Goodridge, although in a smaller vessel, chased and recommenced the action about an hour later. The fighting became intense and lasted for a further two hours, until with the schooner's main topmast and crossjack yard shot away and all the rigging reduced to tatters, the privateer could move under quarter of the *Dispatch* and rake her. At this she surrendered. Lieutenant Goodridge and two seamen were killed, five wounded in the action. One of the latter was the Master, John Consett Peers, who had continued the fight after the Lieutenant's death, despite having his arm shattered by shot. The court martial investigating the loss praised his actions and recommended him to the Admiralty as deserving of encouragement. He received his reward in November 1778 by being promoted to Lieutenant.
[TNA: ADM.1/5309]

16 August CHARLOTTE Schooner Tender
Purchased 1775; 4 guns
Tender to the *Rose*, she was lying at anchor in the Hudson River, New York, just astern of that ship, when at about 11 o'clock that night they came under attack by a pair of fire vessels. One of them fell on board the tender and set her on fire. She burned fiercely and she quickly burnt to the water's edge. The Americans later managed to tow the wreck to the shore and recovered her guns and some stores.
[TNA: ADM.51/805]

(6/7) September POMONA Ship Sloop
Prize 1761 (*Chevert*); 364 tons; 108ft × 27.4ft; 18 guns
Master and Commander Thomas Eastwood†
Ordered to cruise between the islands of Martinique and St Lucia, she failed to return to English Harbour, Antigua as expected. The area was swept by a tropical storm during 6–7 September, and it was presumed that she was lost at this time with all hands. Pay book closed on 7 September.
[TNA: ADM.1/309; ADM.34/563]

16 September SAVAGE Brig Sloop
Woolwich 1750; 144 tons; 73.6ft × 21ft; 8 guns
Master and Commander Hugh Bromedge
At anchor off Scatarie Island, Nova Scotia, she started dragging her anchors in gale-force winds. An attempt was made to stand out to sea, but she was unable to weather the western point of the island, so it was decided to anchor and ride out the storm. Yards and topmasts were struck, and the foresail cut away when it proved impossible to furl. Despite all the precautions, she again started dragging and drove dangerously near the shoreline. Cables were cut and another attempt made to make open water, but she struck rocks, swung broadside-on to a small reef and commenced beating. In half an hour, the sloop had been battered to pieces. All the crew gained the shore through the surf.
[TNA: ADM.1/5308]

2 October CRUISER Ship Sloop
Deptford 1752; 141 tons; 75.6ft × 20.7ft; 8 guns
Master and Commander Francis Parry
Stationed on the east coast of America, several persistent leaks were evident, and Commander Parry complained that that she was in a poor condition. At anchor off Fort Johnston, Cape Fear, North Carolina, Vice Admiral Lord Howe ordered that a survey be conducted, which found that she was incapable of going to sea, and that it was '... not possible to keep her longer above water'. She was ordered to be stripped of all stores and when that was complete, on 2 October the ship was hauled into shallow water near Bald Head and burnt.
[TNA: ADM.51/218; ADM.1/487]

6 December RACEHORSE Sloop
Purchased 1776 (*Polly*); 98 tons; 59ft × 20.6ft; 10 guns
Lieutenant William Jones
Having escorted a homeward-bound convoy from Jamaica as far as latitude 31 North, she was heading for the Turks and Caicos Islands to cruise, when she encountered the American brig *Andrew Doria*, 14 guns,

to the north of Puerto Rico. A sharp engagement ensued which lasted for over two hours, until with three shots through her mast, sails shot to pieces and several men killed or wounded, including Lieutenant Jones, the sloop surrendered.
[TNA: ADM.1/240]

26 December GEORGE Schooner Tender
Prize 1776 (*Warren*); 80 tons; 8 guns
Midshipman Richard Willis
Tender to the *Milford*, based on the east coast of America, she had sailed from Halifax on 8 December with stores and provisions for the *Milford*. On 20 December, she sighted, chased and captured an American sloop and after taking out the crew, set her on fire. The weather was poor and worsened, with regular snow squalls. Fearing that they would be wrecked, the Master of the captured sloop, Mr Pinkham, was asked to take the schooner into a safe haven, and he successfully piloted her into Little Harbor, Portsmouth, New Hampshire, where she was run into shallow water and grounded.
[NDAR vol 7 pp603–04, 618, 845]

December REPULSE Fifth Rate
Prize 1759 (*Bellone*); 677 tons; 122.7ft × 34.11ft; 32 guns
Captain Henry Davis†
Ordered to cruise between Bermuda and the American east coast and then proceed to Jamaica, she was last seen on 16 December, when she was separated from the *Galatea* and *Nautilus* in a gale. Nothing more was seen or heard of her, and it was presumed that she was lost with all hands soon after this. Pay book closed on 31 December.
[TNA: ADM.1/487; ADM.34/632]

1777

14 February TRYAL Schooner
Prize 1775; 88 tons; 2 guns
Lieutenant John Brown
Stationed in Narragansett Bay, Rhode Island, she was ordered to go to the northern end of Prudence Island and cover the passage of a cutter from the *Diamond* frigate, which was going in search of some deserters. Having waited for most of the day at anchor, the wind shifted, and she started dragging her anchor. At the same time, some shots were fired at her from the mainland and a rebel sloop could be seen approaching. Cables were cut and she attempted to make open water but ran aground. Whilst trying to free herself, a false fire was started from waste material to give the impression of being abandoned and this seemed to have some effect in making the enemy sloop keep clear. The efforts to free her failed and that evening she was set on fire and abandoned.
[TNA: ADM.1/5308]

17 May DILIGENT Schooner
Prize 1775 (*Byfield*); 6 guns
Lieutenant Edmund Dod
Acting as a convoy escort, she was leading the vessels toward the Bay of Fundy, Newfoundland in poor weather, thick fog giving way to heavy drizzling rain, with visibility down to only a few yards. During the middle watch breakers were suddenly seen ahead and moments later she ran aground on the Gannet Rock ledge. All sails were thrown aback, but she was stuck fast and started beating on the rocks. The mainmast was cut away to ease her, but she was already filling with water. At low water, she fell over onto her beam-ends, the crew clinging to the upturned hull all night. The following morning the *Berry* transport took off the crew, all of whom survived.
[TNA: ADM.1/5308]

7 June FOX Sixth Rate
Northam 1773; 600 tons; 120.6ft × 33.8ft; 28 guns
Captain Patrick Fotheringham
Cruising on the Newfoundland Banks, when at 6 o'clock in the morning two ships were seen to windward, one a good way ahead of the other. The *Fox* tacked to close, suspecting that they were both enemy frigates. After 30 minutes, they were in hailing distance of the first of the strangers, which was the American *Hancock*, 32 guns, and after a mutual exchange of calls, there was an exchange of broadsides. This led to a close action between the pair for about 30 minutes, when the second American frigate, the *Boston*, 24 guns, was seen to be approaching. The *Fox* made sail away, but with damaged rigging and only light breezes, the *Hancock* easily overhauled her, and the action recommenced. After about an hour the *Boston* came up to join the fight, and stationing herself on the British frigate's starboard quarter, fired a raking broadside into her. With the main yard shot away, all the masts and rigging damaged and unable to escape, the *Fox* surrendered. She suffered four killed and eight wounded.
[TNA: ADM.1/5309; ADM.1/471]

23 October AUGUSTA Third Rate
Rotherhithe 1763; 1,381 tons; 159ft × 44.7ft; 64 guns
Captain Francis Reynolds
Part of the force besieging Philadelphia, she was supporting operations by Hessian troops by leading an attack on a fort on the small island in the River Delaware known as Mud Island. During the evening of 22 October, just as they came to anchor, the *Augusta* ran aground on a previously unknown sandbank – the river's

currents probably having been disturbed by the laying of several large obstructions in the river. She lay quietly, and attempts were made to free her by starting water butts and an anchor was laid out. However, attempts at high tide to haul her off by heaving on the anchor cable failed to move her, and she sent for assistance from other ships. During the following morning, she became the focus of a sustained enemy attack from the shore and several enemy galleys which approached, returning fire when she could. At about 11 o'clock a fire was reported in the stern, and despite the fire being tackled it spread rapidly and soon became uncontrollable. Unable to escape or put out the fire, the crew was evacuated and the ship given up to the flames. Some hours later she blew up with a tremendous explosion. The exact cause of the fire was never ascertained, but the most popular theory was burning wadding landing in stowed hammocks.
[TNA: ADM.1/5308]

23 October MERLIN Ship Sloop
Rotherhithe 1757; 303 tons; 100.2ft × 26.1ft; 18 guns
Master and Commander Samuel Reeve
Another of the vessels ordered to attack the fort on Mud Island in the River Delaware below Philadelphia in support of the Hessian troops. As with the *Augusta*, as she manoeuvred to get into position during the evening of 22 October, she found that she had run aground on a new bank which had only recently appeared. Various attempts were made through the day to shift her during the night, lightening the sloop and taking out kedge anchors making little difference. The morning saw the shore batteries and enemy galleys make several attacks on the grounded pair, which could not free themselves. When the *Augusta* caught fire, the *Merlin* was ordered to be abandoned, as it was feared that the explosion from the powder magazine would seriously damage the sloop. She was therefore abandoned and set on fire.
[TNA: ADM.1/5308]

October PEGASUS Ship Sloop
Chatham 1776; 302 tons; 96.7ft × 26.10ft; 14 guns
Master and Commander Hamilton Gore†
Sailed from Waterford on 18 July to escort a convoy to Newfoundland and after her arrival in September she was ordered to cruise off that island but subsequently disappeared. It was presumed that she was lost in the Atlantic with all hands. Her pay books were closed on 31 October.
[Beatson vol 4 p283; TNA: ADM 34/818]

October VESTAL Sixth Rate
Plymouth 1777; 432 tons; 108ft × 30.1ft; 20 guns
Captain James Shirley†
As with the *Pegasus* (above), she arrived in Newfoundland after escorting a convoy, having sailed from Plymouth on 20 July. She was also then given orders to cruise nearby but disappeared and was presumed lost in the Atlantic with all hands. Pay books closed on 31 October.
[Beatson vol 4 p283; TNA: ADM.34/789]

6 November SIREN Sixth Rate
Chatham 1773; 603 tons; 120.10ft × 33.9ft; 28 guns
Captain Tobias Furneaux
Sailed from her anchorage off Rhode Island in the early hours of the morning as escort to a small convoy to Sag Harbour, the weather was thick, with a constant drizzle. At about 5 o'clock in the morning she ran hard aground a little to the north of Point Judith, the transport *Sisters* and a schooner following her. The ship was lightened, and attempts commenced to heave her off. The schooner which had grounded was freed and she prepared to assist in hauling off the frigate. This was frustrated by rebel forces ashore, who, seeing the ships aground, brought up several field pieces and commenced firing. The schooner had her halyards shot away and ran aground again. The fire now concentrated on the *Siren* and became increasingly accurate. Unable to free herself or effectively return fire, she was abandoned, the crew making their way ashore where they were taken prisoner. Two men were killed and five wounded in the action. Two nights later the *Flora* and *Lark* closed the wreck and sent in armed boats which set her on fire, and she burned to the waterline, although the Americans had already salvaged the guns. The ship's pilot, Thomas Smith, and the Master, William Edwards, were blamed for the wreck, through ignorance and negligence. Smith lost all pay due and was ordered never to serve as a pilot in a Royal Navy ship again. Edwards was dismissed the service.
[TNA: ADM.1/5309]

November THUNDERER Radeau Ketch
St Jean, Lake Champlain 1776; 422 tons; 90.9ft × 33.4ft; 14 guns
Part of the Lake Champlain squadron, she sailed from Ticonderoga, reportedly carrying sick and wounded from the battle of Saratoga, but foundered off Windmill Point, near Alburgh, Vermont.
[Malcolmson p29]

3 December BUTE Armed Ship
Hired 1776; 26 guns
Master and Commander Benjamin Hill
Sailed from Jamaica on 27 October, in company with the frigate *Pallas* and a small convoy of merchant ships bound for England, but soon after leaving, it was evident that they had a leak. The pumps were used regularly to clear the water, but it steadily increased. By 25 November it was found to be entering at 16in an hour and the Carpenter had found the source of the leak

to be in the after hold, behind a timber. The aftermost guns were shifted forward, and stores were moved to try and alter the trim of the ship, but it was clear that they were fighting a losing battle. When the Carpenter of the *Pallas* came on board, he agreed that it was impossible to save the ship. The leak was a substantial one and could not be stopped as the planking was quite rotten: it could be broken up with the fingers and oakum was coming out from the seams. On 1 December work started to transfer the crew and as much of the stores that could be saved to the *Pallas*. Two days later they had to stop as there was 9ft of water in the hold. Commander Hill was the last to leave the ship that night, and she was abandoned and allowed to sink. She was then about four leagues (12 miles) from the Double Headed Shot Cays to the north of Cuba.
[TNA: ADM.52/1622]

December SPRIGHTLY Cutter
Dover 1777; 153 tons; 65.7ft × 24.3ft; 12 guns
Lieutenant William Hills†
Sailed from the Downs anchorage on 15 November, to cruise in the English Channel in the vicinity of the Channel Islands, she disappeared and was presumed to have foundered with all hands. Some wreckage, including a gun carriage, identified as being from the cutter, was washed ashore in Guernsey during the first week of January.
[TNA: ADM.180/4; www.britishnewspaperarchive.co.uk: Stamford Mercury 15 Jan 1778 p1]

24 December MERCURY Sixth Rate
Harwich 1756; 433 tons; 107.8ft × 30.4ft; 20 guns
Captain James Montagu
At anchor off Spuyten Duyvil Creek, in the North or Hudson River, she weighed anchor during the morning to join the main British fleet. When abreast Fort Knyphausen she struck a submerged object, which pierced her bottom. This was almost certainly a *chevaux de frise*, a device constructed of heavy timbers bound together by stout chains, used by the Americans to block rivers. The pumps were quickly manned, but she was filling with water quite rapidly, and by 12.30pm it was clear that she was sinking fast by the head. She was run inshore and grounded, and attempts were made to shore her up using spare yards and spars and a cable was carried ashore and made fast. These efforts failed to save her, mainly because the frigate was full of water, and she capsized. The following day the stores and guns were taken off and the vessel abandoned. Three men who had taken the opportunity to get very drunk were drowned in the ship.
[TNA: ADM.51/600; ADM.1/5309]

December SWALLOW Ship Sloop
Deptford 1769; 309 tons; 95ft × 27.2ft; 14 guns
Master and Commander Charles Warre†
The sloop sailed from Madras for England in September 1777 with several passengers embarked, including Lauchlin Macleane, agent for the Nawab of Arcot. She called at the Cape of Good Hope in November, but after sailing for England in December, the sloop was not seen again and was presumed lost with all hands. With no news of her, the ship was officially paid off 4 September 1778, with the pay books being closed on 31 December 1777.
[TNA: ADM.180/9; ADM.34/681; www.britishnewspaperarchive.co.uk: Hampshire Chronicle 18 May 1778 p1; Saunders' News Letter 17 November 1778 p1; DNB Entry for Macleane]

1778

11 February LIVERPOOL Sixth Rate
Liverpool 1758; 590 tons; 118.4ft × 33.8ft; 28 guns
Captain Henry Bellew
Sailed from on Philadelphia on 7 February, escorting several ships to New York, and as she approached the anchorage at Sandy Hook, New Jersey, land was seen just before nightfall. The ship continued steering along the coast, in poor weather, sounding regularly. At about 3 o'clock in the morning the water was noted to be shallowing, and she shortened sail, but two hours later, having shown 15 fathoms of water only 30 minutes before, she was felt to touch the ground. An attempt was made to tack, but she would not come around, and all sails were then thrown aback in an attempt to free her, but this had no effect. She started beating on the ground in heavy surf and this soon unshipped the rudder, which tore up the cabin deck and broke the transom. Guns were fired as signals of distress and boats were hoisted out, the longboat managing to get through the surf to the shore. During the day the main- and mizzen masts were cut away to ease her, but she could not be freed and by the next evening she was found to have bedded herself deep in the sand. Over the next few days stores and guns were removed, and work on the wreck continued until the end of April when she was finally abandoned. Strong currents were blamed for taking her further inland than calculated, stranding her in Jamaica Bay, Long Island, near Old Rockaway.
[TNA: ADM.1/5309; ADM.51/548]

19 April HINCHINBROOK Armed Brig
Prize 1777 (*Defence*); 144 tons; 16 guns
Lieutenant William Merrick
The *Hinchinbrook*, along with a brig tender and the *Rebecca* provincial sloop, were anchored in Frederica

Sound, Georgia, the crews being provided by the frigate *Galatea*. The Master of the *Hinchinbrook*, James Murray, was joined by Lieutenant Merrick on 18 April. At daybreak, three enemy galleys – the *Lee*, *Bullock* and *Washington* – could be seen rowing towards them. With almost no wind, the British trio could do little, and the galleys took full advantage of this, rowing into position and distance where they could commence a bombardment with no reply from their opponents. The British ships slipped cables and the provincial sloop and brig tender commenced towing the *Hinchinbrook* into mid-channel to engage the galleys. Unfortunately, they all grounded in mid-stream. Finding themselves unable to get free, with the galleys able to manoeuvre and fire at will, the *Hinchinbrook* and her two small associates were abandoned to the Americans, who took possession.
[TNA: ADM.1/5310]

25 April **DRAKE** Ship Sloop
Purchased 1777 (*Resolution*); 275 tons; 91.5ft × 26.1ft; 14 guns
Master and Commander George Burdon†
Whilst lying at anchor in Carrickfergus Bay, Ireland, the *Drake* was alerted to the presence of a stranger when a ship was seen to enter the anchorage, but then promptly cut cables and stand out. Two days later the *Drake*, which had entered several local men to serve as landsmen as she was poorly manned, sailed to investigate reports of the strange ship still being on the coast. After she sailed Lieutenant William Dobbs joined from the shore and volunteered to assist. Sighting a vessel closing the anchorage and thinking it to be a merchant vessel, a boat with a midshipman aboard was despatched to the stranger to press some seamen. The stranger was in fact the American ship sloop *Ranger*, 18 guns, and they promptly detained the boat's crew. Baffled by contrary winds, the *Drake* tacked slowly towards the *Ranger*, and it was late in the afternoon before she was within range to hail. The *Ranger*, which was now displaying American colours, responded by running across the bows of the *Drake* and raked her with an effective broadside. The third broadside mortally wounded Dobbs and after about an hour Burdon was shot through the head by a musket ball and killed. By now the British sloop, poorly equipped, was running low on ammunition and with the officers out of action, the jib, main topsail-yard and mizzen-gaff shot away, John Walsh, the Master surrendered. Five killed and twenty wounded.
[TNA: ADM.1/5314]

16 June **SPY** Ship Sloop
Limehouse 1776; 306 tons; 96.9ft × 26.1 1ft; 14 guns
Master and Commander Thomas Lenox Frederick
Approaching the Newfoundland coast in poor weather, she raised Cape Race just before nightfall, but shortly after this a thick fog descended. At about 11 o'clock at night land loomed out of the darkness and fog and despite a desperate attempt to tack, she ran aground. She found herself lying in a small cove, wedged between rocks which held her at the starboard quarter and larboard beam. The wind and sea steadily increased during the night, baffling all efforts to free her. The main- and mizzen masts were cut away and the night was spent in clearing the wreckage and pumping. By daybreak it could be seen that she was in a helpless condition, and she was left as a wreck, foundering later that same day. The poor weather was blamed for the loss, the ship going ashore just to the east of Cape Pine.
[TNA; ADM.1/5310]

24 June **FOLKESTONE** Cutter
Folkestone 1764; 89 tons; 48.2ft × 21.5ft; 6 guns
Lieutenant William Smith
The relationship between the British and French Governments had steadily deteriorated since the start of the American War, and this had led to a clash in the Channel early in June, resulting in the capture of some French ships. This led to counteraction by a squadron of French frigates that fell in with the *Folkestone*. Having sailed from the river Thames with despatches for Admiral Keppel off Ushant, she was chased by the French squadron in the western approaches to the Channel. She managed to maintain her distance for some time, but with the wind dying out, she was steadily overhauled by the larger ships. The *Surveillante*, 32 guns, closed, and after firing bow-chase guns at the cutter, ran alongside, giving the *Folkestone* little choice but to surrender. She was then about 11 leagues (33 miles) to the north of Ushant.
[TNA: ADM.1/5315]

8 July **MERMAID** Sixth Rate
Hull 1761; 614 tons; 124ft × 33.6ft; 28 guns
Captain James Hawker
Laying at anchor in Delaware Bay, at first light on 7 July a large number of ships were seen in the offing, which she rightly suspected were the French fleet under Comte d'Estaing. Weighing, she attempted to get into open water, but was cut off with the whole of the fleet in pursuit. She attempted to run along the coast but was forced to make a series of short tacks, being driven further and further inshore. The chase went on through the night until early the next morning she went aground off Phoenix Island. With all sail set, she drove over the obstruction, and the chase continued with two French ships, the *Fantasque*, 64 guns, and *Chimere*, 32, still in pursuit. All the guns were heaved overboard, along with the small bower anchor, and the water butts were emptied in efforts to lighten the ship. The French steadily overhauled her, and as it was clear that she

could not escape, Captain Hawker ran her ashore, at about 10 o'clock in the morning, a little to the south of Sinepuxent Inlet where several American ships were lying, and after destroying the signals and charts, struck his flag. The Americans boarded the wreck and salvaged what they could before she settled.
[TNA: ADM.1/5310; ADM.1/904]

9 July LIVELY Sixth Rate
Bursledon 1756; 438 tons; 108ft x 30.5ft; 22 guns
Captain Robert Biggs
Having successfully escorted an ordnance sloop to Guernsey, she was bound for Admiral Keppel's fleet off Ushant, when at first light, as the early morning mist cleared, she found herself close to several ships, evidently the French fleet. She made all sail away, with the fleet in chase. She was overhauled by the cutter *Curieuse*, 10 guns, and ordered to lie-to. Refusing to do so, she continued until overhauled by the frigate *Iphigénie*, 32, who hailed her and ordered her to go down to the French Admiral. Captain Biggs refused and was still standing in the mizzen-chains in full uniform, talking, when the *Iphigénie* fired a broadside into her. Unable to escape, she surrendered. Twelve men were killed by the fire.

Note: recaptured on 29 July 1781 by the *Perseverance*.
[TNA: ADM.1/5314; www.britishnewspaperarchive.co.uk: Derby Mercury 24 July 1778 p1]

10 July YORK Armed Sloop
Purchased 1777 (*Betsey*); 100 tons; 12 guns
Lieutenant Thomas Walbeoff
The sloop was cruising off Little Egg Bay, Delaware, when several ships were sighted to seaward, which the sloop closed to investigate, but soon discovered that it was the French fleet. Making all sail away, she was pursued by a frigate and a ship of the line. After an all-day chase, she was eventually overhauled by the *Languedoc*, 90 guns, and *Engageante*, 32, and when called upon to surrender, she did so, without resistance.

Note: recaptured on 23 August 1778.
[TNA: ADM.1/5310]

17 July ALERT Sloop
Dover 1777; 183 tons; 69.2ft x 25.11ft; 12 guns
Master and Commander William Fairfax
Cruising in the English Channel, the weather was squally with occasional drizzle, but at first light the weather cleared, and three large ships could be seen. The sloop promptly made sail, running before the wind, with the strangers in chase of her. The guns were thrown overboard in an effort to lighten her, but it had little effect and by 6 o'clock the French frigate *Junon*, 32 guns, was alongside, and fired two shots into her, at which the sloop surrendered.
[TNA: ADM.1/5315]

19 July STANLEY Brig Tender
From 1777; 12 guns
Lieutenant Richard Whitworth
Originally fitted out as a tender to the *Roebuck*, she was acting as an escort to some small prizes off New York, when during the night she fell in with the French fleet under d'Estaing. She was chased, overhauled and captured by the *César*.
[NDAR vol 13 p437; www.britishnewspaperarchive.co.uk: Stamford Mercury 24 September 1778 p1]

30 July: The Attack on Rhode Island
The French fleet under Comte d'Estaing arrived off Rhode Island on 29 July to cooperate with the American army under General Washington. The British naval force of frigates and sloops was outnumbered and outgunned. The following morning French ships of the line entered the main channels into Narragansett Bay, the Sakonnet and the Narragansett. As they advanced, Captain John Brisbane, senior naval officer, gave orders for the threatened ships to be destroyed.

KINGSFISHER Ship Sloop
Chatham 1770; 302 tons; 96.8ft x 26.10ft; 14 guns
Lieutenant Hugh Christian
The *Kingsfisher*, anchored in the Sakonnet Passage, sighted the French ships advancing, led by two frigates, so weighed anchor and ran into Foglands Bay as they approached. All the stores and guns were landed. On the morning of the 30th, with no hope of escape and the French manoeuvring to close her, she was abandoned and set on fire.
[TNA: ADM.1/5310]

ALARM Galley
Purchased 1777 (*Mountfield*); 8 guns
Lieutenant Philip d'Auvergne
At anchor near the *Kingfisher* sloop in the Sakonnet Passage, Rhode Island, as the French proceeded up the waterway, the galley was run into shallow water near the sloop and set on fire.
[TNA: ADM.1/5310]

SPITFIRE Galley
Prize 1778; 8 guns
Lieutenant James Saumarez
Along with the *Alarm* and *Kingfisher*, she was taken inshore to Fogland Ferry in the Sakonnet Passage. On the arrival of the French fleet, she was run ashore on North Sandy Point and set on fire.
[TNA: ADM.1/5310]

5 August: The Attack on Rhode Island
The French consolidated their grip on Rhode Island, taking possession of Conanicut Island and deploying

troops. The American army was meanwhile moving from the mainland in a concerted effort to cut off the British garrison at Newport. On 5 August, four French ships of the line passed up the Narragansett passage to take station at the north of Conanicut Island to complete this manoeuvre.

FLORA Fifth Rate
Prize 1761 (*Vestale*); 699 tons; 131.7ft × 34.6ft; 32 guns
Captain John Brisbane
Captain Brisbane was the senior naval officer at Rhode Island and as the French fleet manoeuvred in the waterways, he ordered the British ships to land men, guns and stores ashore to assist the garrison. The *Flora*, in the inner harbour at Newport, was then scuttled, sinking in shallow water. Some considerable time later, when the Americans finally gained control of the town and area, the ship was raised, refitted and sold in July 1784 to the French as *Flore*.
Note: recaptured in July 1798 but not recommissioned.
[TNA: ADM.1/5310]

JUNO Fifth Rate
Rotherhithe 1757; 668 tons; 127.10ft × 34.3ft; 32 guns
Captain Hugh Dalrymple
Taken into Eddington Creek, the *Juno* was stripped of stores and guns for the defence of the garrison. On receiving the orders to destroy the ship from Captain Brisbane, the remaining guns were spiked and the ship set on fire.
[TNA: ADM.1/5310]

LARK Fifth Rate
Rotherhithe 1762; 680 tons; 127.2ft × 34.5ft; 32 guns
Captain Richard Smith
Lying off Newport, the *Lark* was stripped of stores and then set on fire, her cables being cut, which allowed her to drift onto the shore where she burnt out.
[TNA: ADM.1/5310]

ORPHEUS Fifth Rate
Harwich 1773; 708 tons; 130ft × 35.1ft; 32 guns
Captain Charles Hudson
In the inner harbour at Newport, her cables were cut, and she was set on fire. The ship drifted ashore a little to the east of Dyer's Island, where she burnt out.
[TNA: ADM.1/5310]

CERBERUS Sixth Rate
Cowes 1758; 593 tons; 118.7ft × 33.10ft; 28 guns
Captain John Simmonds
After the guns and stores had been landed, her cables were cut, and she was set on fire, slowly drifting onto the Rhode Island shore near Potter's House, where she burnt out.
[TNA: ADM.1/5310]

FALCON Ship Sloop
Portsmouth 1771; 305 tons; 95ft × 27.1ft; 14 guns
Master and Commander Harry Harmood
In the inner harbour at Newport, as with the other ships present, her stores were landed and she was then scuttled, sinking in shallow water. When the siege was lifted in September the sloop was successfully raised and recommissioned during 1779.
[TNA: ADM.1/5310]

PIGOT Galley
Prize 1777 (*Spitfire*); 4 guns
Lieutenant Henry Stanhope
Lying at anchor off Arnold's Point, Rhode Island, she was run into shallow water and set on fire.
[TNA: ADM.1/5310]

★ ★ ★

12 / 13 August FERRET Armed Galley
Philadelphia 1778; 4 guns
Lieutenant John O'Bryen
Part of a small flotilla of galleys that were attached to Lord Howe's squadron that had sailed 6 August from Sandy Hook, New Jersey, to tackle the French fleet under d'Estaing. They were severely affected by a severe storm during 11–13 August, and during this time the *Ferret* was driven onshore near Shrewsbury to the south of Sandy Hook. All the crew was taken prisoner.
[*Royal Gazette* (New York) 26 August 1778; *London Gazette* 24 October 1778]

14 August THUNDER Bomb
Prize 1757 (*Marquise de Vaudreuil*); 386 tons; 96.7ft × 30.8ft; 8 guns
Master and Commander James Gambier
In company with the *Senegal* sloop about 35 leagues (105 miles) to the south-east of Sandy Hook, when two large ships came in sight. The strangers gave chase to the bomb vessel, which was unable to escape, being under jury-rig following the loss of her main- and mizzen masts in a storm a few days before. Easily overhauled by the pair, which proved to be French ships of the line, the *Hector*, 74 guns, and *Vaillant*, 64, she surrendered when hailed.
[TNA: ADM.1/5310]

15 August SENEGAL Ship Sloop
Rotherhithe 1760; 292 tons; 97ft × 26.1ft; 14 guns
Master and Commander John Inglis
Cruising to the south-east of Sandy Hook in company with the *Thunder* bomb vessel, when two large ships were sighted (see above). The *Senegal* initially believed them to be British, and closed, thinking that although they did not answer private signals, they must be part

of Admiral Byron's squadron from England. As they neared, Commander Inglis realised that the pair were French ships of the line and hastily retired, making all sail away. The French pair meanwhile concentrated on chasing and capturing the *Thunder* bomb. The following morning the sloop found the French still in sight and she was chased and overhauled by the *Hector*, 74 guns. A brief exchange of shots took place, with the sloop's main yard being shot away before she surrendered.

Note: retaken on 2 November 1780 by the *Zephyr*.
[TNA: ADM.1/5310]

22 August **MINERVA** Fifth Rate
Rotherhithe 1759; 664 tons; 124.4ft × 34.11ft; 32 guns
Captain John Stott

Cruising off Puerto Plata, on the northern side of the island of Hispaniola, they were unaware that war had broken out with France. On sighting a strange sail, she closed, thinking it to be a merchant ship. The stranger was the French frigate *Concorde*, 32 guns, which was fully prepared for action. The British frigate came within gunshot and was hauling up her courses to hail the stranger when the *Concorde* fired a broadside into her. *Minerva* hastily started clearing for action, but suffered another broadside before she could reply, and in the confusion a powder cask blew up below decks, which dismounted three guns and caused several casualties. Some panic ensued, and some of the crew attempted to flee from the guns and had to be forced back at the point of the officers' swords. In the subsequent action, which lasted nearly two hours, the mizzen mast and the wheel were shot away and both Captain Stott and the First Lieutenant, William Bartholomew, were severely wounded. Unable to manoeuvre and with fourteen dead and thirty men wounded, she surrendered. Both Stott and Bartholomew later died of their injuries.

Note: retaken on 4 January 1781 by the *Courageux*.
[TNA: ADM.1/5314]

23 August **ZEPHYR** Brig Sloop
Rotherhithe 1756 (*Merlin*); 223 tons; 86.6ft × 24.5ft; 10 guns
Master and Commander Thomas West

The sloop was cruising in the western Mediterranean, when at daybreak she sighted two ships closing her. After initially closing to investigate, she discovered the pair were French frigates. All sail was made away, with the French in pursuit. Despite setting all sail possible, she was steadily overhauled, her pursuers occasionally firing bow-chase guns. On being hailed by the *Gracieuse*, 26 guns, she had little choice but to surrender.

Note: retaken by the *Fame* privateer in August 1780 and burnt.
[TNA: ADM.1/5314]

25 August **OTTER** Ship Sloop
Deptford 1767; 305 tons; 95ft × 27.2ft; 14 guns
Lieutenant John Wright

The sloop weighed and sailed from Fort Augustine, Florida, on 20 August, in search of an American privateer which had been reported in the area. As she searched along the Florida coast the weather deteriorated, and by 24 August she was in a tropical storm, with a heavy swell and rain, and hurricane-force winds. She lay to under a balanced mizzen sail but was taken by the wind towards the land and at about 6 o'clock the next morning sighted land near Cape Canaveral. About an hour later she struck the ground extremely hard and immediately started beating heavily. This combined with the heavy surf constantly breaking over her led to the sloop breaking up during the day. The crew managed to struggle ashore without loss.
[Perrin: Keith Papers vol 1 pp130–1]

1 September **ACTIVE** Sixth Rate
Rotherhithe 1758; 595 tons; 118.4ft × 33.10ft; 28 guns
Captain William Williams

Whilst off Cape San Nicola Mole, Hispaniola, bound for Jamaica from Bermuda, at 9 o'clock in the morning she sighted two ships closing, which proved to be the French frigates *Charmante*, 32 guns, and *Dédaigneuse*, 32. Having just gone through a storm in which she had lost all her topmasts and thrown overboard eleven of her guns, she was in no fit state to fight an action. On being overhauled, she surrendered after the second broadside was fired at her. two men were killed. Captain Williams died soon after, 'of mortification'.
[TNA: ADM.1/5314]

10 September **DOLPHIN** Schooner Tender
Hired 1778.
Lieutenant Bartholomew James

Ordered to cruise the approaches to Port Royal, Jamaica, and warn ships of being at war with France, she was off Little Caicos when three ships were sighted. Believing them to be British, she closed until the nearest ship hoisted French colours and fired a shot. A short chase ensued before she was overhauled at which she struck her flag. Her captors proved to be the *Charmante* 32, *Dédaigneuse*, 32 and the prize *Active* (see above).
[Laughton pp54–5]

11 September **FOX** Sixth Rate
Northam 1773; 600 tons; 120.6ft × 33.8ft; 28 guns
Captain Hon. Thomas Windsor

Tasked to search for the French fleet, she was off the approaches to Brest when she sighted a ship and a sloop and bore up in chase, the weather being dark and rainy, with frequent squalls obscuring the chase. The poor visibility masked the approach of the frigate

Junon, 32 guns, which closed the *Fox*. On seeing the new opponent, the *Fox* shortened sail and prepared for action. Manoeuvring for the best position went on for some time, with the French ship trying to rake their opponent from a position on the British frigate's quarter. Foiled in these moves, the pair eventually steered alongside, and broadsides were mutually commenced. The French ship fired into the hull of the *Fox* rather than following the usual French practice of firing at the rigging, and the heavier armament soon began to take its toll. All the masts were shot away, and the casualties mounted, Captain Windsor being seriously wounded, with a musket ball in the arm. Unable to sustain the fight longer, the ship surrendered. Fourteen killed and thirty-two wounded.
[TNA: ADM.1/5314; Troude vol 2 pp26–7]

16 September HELENA Schooner
Purchased 1778; 215 tons; 76.1ft × 26.9ft; 14 guns
Lieutenant Thomas Hicks
Having sailed from Spithead on 13 September, bound for Gibraltar, she suffered poor weather and carried away her bowsprit. The weather cleared sufficiently in the afternoon of the 16th to reveal a large number of ships close by, which she realised was the main French fleet. She made sail away, but was chased by three frigates, and when the *Sensible*, 28 guns, hailed her to surrender, she had no choice but to strike her flag.
[TNA: ADM.1/5314]

10 October HOTHAM Sloop Tender
From 1777
Lieutenant Christopher Hele
Tender to the *Preston*, she was sent under a flag of truce to Philadelphia, with copies of a Manifesto and Proclamation lately issued by his Majesty's Commissioners, offering pardons and a repeal of taxation, but was wrecked on Brigantine Beach, New Jersey. Two men were drowned in the incident, but the despatches were preserved.
[www.britishnewspaperarchive.co.uk: Derby Mercury 8 January 1779 p2]

18 October ZEBRA Ship Sloop
Ipswich 1777; 306 tons; 97ft × 26.1ft; 14 guns
Master and Commander Henry Collins
During early October, the *Zebra* led an attack on the harbour at Little Egg, Delaware, burning several ships and shore facilities. When attempting to leave, she struck the bar at the entrance to the harbour and grounded. Shortly after grounding she was struck by 'a remarkable heavy sea', which swung her broadside-on to the sandbank. Attempts to force her over the bank failed, as did efforts to kedge her off. Pieces of the false keel were seen floating to the surface and the steadily rising water in the hold confirmed the presence of a serious leak. Unable to free the sloop or control the leak she was abandoned, the crew being taken off by HM Armed Ship *Vigilant*, the wreck being set on fire during the night of 21/22 October.
[TNA: ADM.1/5310]

29 October PIGOT Galley
Purchased 1778 (*Spitfire*?); 200 tons; 8 guns
Lieutenant William Dunlop
The galley was lying at anchor in the Sakonnet passage, Rhode Island, when Lieutenant Dunlop was woken at 2.30am to be told that a strange vessel was approaching. By the time he arrived on deck, the vessel, which was the American privateer *Hawk*, was almost on top of them. He was horrified to discover that only the Quartermaster and three men were on deck and the guns were not primed as he had ordered. The *Hawk* ran her bowsprit through the galley's main shrouds and fired a volley of small arms. Total confusion reigned in the galley – apart from small arms, no weapons were available and most of the crew were asleep below. On being boarded Dunlop had little choice but to surrender. Subsequently the Master, John Lanadale, who should have had the watch-on-deck, but was in his hammock, was dismissed the service and imprisoned in the Marshalsea for one year. Midshipman William Allen, who had left the deck without being properly relieved, was severely reprimanded.
[TNA: ADM.1/5310]

31 October MARY Hoy
Plymouth 1728; 52 tons; 49.2ft × 16ft
A dockyard craft, used for carrying stores and provisions, she foundered when returning to harbour from Plymouth Sound
[Burns p81]

2 November SOMERSET Third Rate
Chatham 1748; 1,436 tons; 160ft × 45.4ft; 64 guns
Captain George Ourry
One of the squadron under Admiral Byron which sailed 18 October from Sandy Hook, New Jersey, in search of the French fleet under the Comte d'Estaing. Byron had the unfortunate nickname of 'Foul Weather Jack', as he seemed to attract storms. This occasion was no exception, as on 2 November the ships were hit by a storm in which the *Somerset* was separated from the fleet. The wind blew so strong that the sails were blown out – foresail, fore staysail and mizzen staysail all going in a few minutes. Driving before the wind under bare poles, breakers were seen ahead at about 6 o'clock in the evening and shortly afterwards she went ashore. She struck the ground violently several times, knocking off the rudder and starting several leaks. The masts were

cut away and the upper-deck guns heaved overboard to ease her movement. Daylight revealed that were ashore near Cape Cod and over the next two days the crew struggled ashore through the surf, but one marine officer and twenty men were drowned in the attempt.
[TNA:ADM.1/5311]

3 November PENGUIN Armed Sloop
Purchased 1776; 100 tons; 10 guns
Lieutenant Thomas Shivers

The sloop was attempting to leave the anchorage in the Bay of Bulls, Newfoundland, when the wind shifted. The helm was put over and she attempted to tack but missed stays. The anchor was let go and she brought up close to the shoreline. During the afternoon, the wind steadily increased, and the Master of the *Postilion* sloop nearby came aboard and advised taking the crew off, as he could see no possibility of saving the ship from the rocks in her present position. Most the crew were then landed with a skeleton crew remaining on board. By the evening, a full gale was blowing, and she commenced dragging her anchor with sea breaking over her. The small number left on board then abandoned the sloop, which went ashore and broke up soon after.
[TNA:ADM.1/5311]

22 November SWIFT Ship Sloop
Portsmouth 1777; 303 tons; 96.7ft × 26.10ft; 14 guns
Master and Commander Joseph Tathwell

Having successfully escorted a valuable merchant ship clear of the American coast, the sloop was returning to Sandy Hook, when a sail was sighted and chased. That night she lost the chase, but the following morning it was sighted again, and the pursuit recommenced, the enemy ship heading for the Chesapeake. Cape Henry was raised in the afternoon and the sloop gradually overhauled the stranger, which was rightly identified as an American privateer. When close enough, bow-chase guns were used, but without any visible effect, and eventually the *Swift* came close enough to hail her, calling on her to strike her flag; the response was a defiant cry that Captain Tathwell '... might be damned, for he would not surrender'. By now it was getting dark, and as the pair was running close to the shore it was decided to fire a broadside, yaw and fire the other and then haul off and anchor. One broadside was successfully discharged, but as she yawed to fire again, she struck the ground, the chase was also seen to go ashore at the same time. The following morning yards and topmasts were struck, but efforts to launch boats to carry out anchors were foiled by the strong winds and high seas. The sloop did have the satisfaction to see her opponent, which was the Pennsylvania privateer *Rattlesnake*, 18 guns, roll over onto her beam-ends. That afternoon the weather had moderated sufficiently for a small party to get ashore, where they were detained by the local militia, who sent a message to the sloop that two field pieces were being brought up, a large body of militia was on shore, and finally two American frigates were on their way to the scene. Most the crew were then landed and taken prisoner, the Captain and a few others coming ashore at 7 o'clock the next morning, having set the sloop ablaze.
[TNA:ADM.1/5318]

8 December DISPATCH Ship Sloop
Deptford 1777; 300 tons; 96.7ft × 26.9ft; 14 guns
Master and Commander John Botham†

Reported to have capsized and foundered in poor weather in the Gulf of St Lawrence, with no survivors.
[Schomberg vol 5 p47; TNA:ADM.1/80/9; ADM 34/226]

17 December CERES Ship Sloop
Woolwich 1777; 361 tons; 108ft × 27.4ft; 18 guns
Master and Commander James Dacres

Whilst off Dominica, West Indies, acting as an escort for a group of transports bound for the Cul-de-Sac, St Lucia, a large group of ships were sighted approaching. The strangers continued to close, and it became clear that two of the ships, a frigate and a 50-gun ship, had been detached from a squadron and were in chase of the *Ceres* and her convoy. Captain Dacres ordered the transports to proceed independently to St Lucia and then bore away with the French warships in pursuit. After a long, five hour chase, the frigate *Iphigénie*, 32 guns, came alongside and with the *Sagittaire*, 50, then about three miles astern and closing, the *Ceres* was forced to surrender.

Note: re-taken on 9 February 1782 by a squadron, she was recommissioned as *Raven*.
[TNA:ADM.1/5311]

28 December CUPID Ship Sloop
Purchased 1777; 290 tons; 92.1ft × 27ft; 14 guns
Master and Commander William Carlyon

Sailed from Jamaica on 21 November as escort for a large convoy bound for London, they were on the Newfoundland Banks when a leak was discovered which steadily gained on the pumps. On 27 December, rolling deeply, she sprung her mainmast, and during the afternoon signalled the *Nabob* store ship to close and stand by her. That night it became clear that the water was gaining, and in the early hours of the morning she fired guns and showed lights at the mastheads as signals of distress. The *Nabob* hoisted out her boats and started to take off the crew, and by that evening all had been removed. Boats returned over the next day to take out as much of her stores as they could, but she was then abandoned and allowed to founder. The source of the leak was not discovered but was believed to be in the fish room.
[TNA:ADM.1/5311; ADM.51/617]

1779

13 January WEAZLE Ship Sloop
Purchased 1745; 308 tons; 94.6ft × 27.6ft; 14 guns
Master and Commander Lewis Robertson

Ordered to England with despatches from St Lucia, the sloop was off St Eustatius when a sail was sighted. The *Weazle* closed and made private signals, to which the stranger did not reply, which made the sloop suspicious. When the vessel shaped course to go between her and the land, Commander Robertson decided to stand away and crowded all sail to the south, the stranger following her. The chase continued under all sail for some time, with the pursuer firing her bow-chase guns occasionally and yawing to fire a full broadside before overhauling the *Weazle*. A further broadside was fired before the sloop surrendered, the enemy proving to be the French frigate *Boudeuse*, 32 guns.
[TNA: ADM.1/5311]

19 March ARETHUSA Fifth Rate
Prize 1759 (*Aréthuse*); 700 tons; 132.2ft × 34.5ft; 32 guns
Captain Charles Everitt

Having sailed from Cork to cover the outward passage of a convoy bound for the West Indies, she then stood by a disabled brig until she safely made Baltimore, Ireland. The *Arethusa* then headed back into the approaches to the Channel where a privateer informed her of the presence of some French warships to the east. Deciding to investigate, she stood towards the French coast. On the afternoon of 18 March, the French frigate *Aigrette*, 28 guns, was sighted which closed the *Arethusa,* apparently not realising that she was British. On discovering her mistake, she tacked away, but was pursued and engaged by Captain Everitt. The French ship made all sail away and when two larger ships came into sight, the *Arethusa* gave over the chase. When night fell, the *Arethusa* made towards the last known position of the French frigate, hoping to find her again. A light was seen, which they believed could be their opponent. Too late they discovered it to be a fixed light onshore and with breakers close to it. They tacked, but at 3.30am struck a rock and found themselves aground. The guns were heaved overboard and after a short while she floated free. A sail was slung under the hull to stop the water, but it was of little use and the water soon gained on the pumps. Unable to keep afloat, the *Arethusa* was run inshore until she ran onto mud flats off the Île Molène, western Brittany where she broke up. All the crew made the shore, to be taken prisoner.
[TNA: ADM.1/5315]

1 May MONTREAL Fifth Rate
Sheerness 1761; 682 tons; 125ft × 35.2ft; 32 guns
Captain Stair Douglas

Cruising to the east of the Straits of Gibraltar in company with the *Thetis* frigate, two large ships were sighted which approached under Dutch colours. Rightly suspecting them to be French, the pair bore away under all sail. The *Thetis* successfully escaped but by 9 o'clock that night the *Victoire*, 74 guns, was within gunshot, with the *Bourgogne*, 74. They hailed the frigate and ordered the *Montreal* to send a boat to them. This was done, Lieutenant John Douglas going aboard. The French demanded their surrender and Lieutenant Douglas was made to hail the *Montreal* and call on them to strike the flag. This was refused and Captain Douglas attempted to make sail away. The French ships fired several broadsides into the frigate before she surrendered.

Note: recaptured and destroyed at Toulon in December 1793.
[TNA: ADM. 1/5314]

7 May DILIGENT Armed Brig
Prize 1777 (*Nancy*); 108 tons; 12 guns
Lieutenant Thomas Walbeoff

Ordered to cruise off the Delaware coast and search for American privateers, she had made one capture when at daybreak on the 7th she saw a sail which she closed. She soon ascertained it to be a rebel brig and prepared for action. As she closed the enemy, which was the *Providence*, 14 guns, the American met her with a broadside and a volley of small-arms fire. This was returned in kind and a close action commenced which lasted for almost three hours, until with the rigging shattered, eleven dead and nineteen wounded, the *Diligent* surrendered. The court praised the conduct of Lieutenant Walbeoff and recommended him to the favour of the Admiralty and the Commander-in-Chief. Despite this, Walbeoff had to wait three years for promotion.
[TNA: ADM.1/5311]

8 May ELEPHANT Store Ship
Purchased 1776 (*Union*); 382 tons; 103.3ft × 29.1ft; 10 guns
Lieutenant Robert Long[†]

Part of a convoy bound for England from America and the West Indies, she became separated from the other ships in poor weather off the Newfoundland Banks but continued independently. At daybreak, she saw the American privateer *General Mifflin*, 20 guns, which was rapidly closing on them. Despite the difference in force, Lieutenant Long refused to surrender and resisted the privateer for an hour, until with five killed, including Lieutenant Long, and ten wounded, the ship was surrendered.

Note: retaken 10 days later by the *Hero* letter of marque of Greenock.
[TNA: ADM.1/5314]

22 May GREENWICH Armed Sloop
Prize 1778; 80 tons; 12 guns
Lieutenant Thomas Spry

Attempting to enter Stono Inlet, South Carolina, despite having a pilot on board she ran hard aground on a sandbank. Water butts were emptied to lighten her, and a kedge anchor taken out for an attempt to haul her off, but she could not be moved. The following morning it was clear that she had attracted the attention of the enemy, who sent up two galleys to fire on her. Unable to free herself, she was abandoned and set on fire. The pilot was ordered to be confined on board the *Scourge* galley but contrived to escape prior to the court martial.
[TNA: ADM.1/5311]

2 June GLASGOW Sixth Rate
Hull 1757; 451 tons; 109.4ft × 30.6ft; 20 guns
Captain Thomas Lloyd

During the afternoon, the ship entered Montego Bay, Jamaica, but soon after coming to an anchor, smoke was seen pouring from the Purser's storeroom. The fire spread rapidly and within two hours the ship was completely ablaze. Another frigate moored nearby, the *Badger*, Captain Horatio Nelson, sent assistance, but as the fire increased and fearing that other ships were in danger, Nelson ordered that the cables be cut, allowing the *Glasgow* to drift ashore where she burned out. It was subsequently established that Richard Brace, the Purser's Steward, was drawing rum and had dropped a lighted, unguarded candle onto the barrel which ignited spilled rum. Brace was ordered to be flogged around the fleet, receiving 100 lashes on his bare back.
[TNA: ADM.1/5311]

14 June SUPPLY Store Ship
Purchased 1777 (*Prince of Wales*); 716 tons; 26 guns
Master and Commander John Nasmith

Lying at anchor in Basse Terre roads, St Kitts, the Captain was ashore whilst the ship took on stores, including several barrels of rum. When striking down the barrels, one dropped into the hold and smashed, spilling rum everywhere, and this caught fire. The fire burnt fiercely, and when the cables burnt through, she drifted across the anchorage, causing several ships to hastily slip and stand out to sea, before she went ashore at Bluff Point where she burnt out, the magazine eventually blowing up, scattering debris over a wide area
[TNA: ADM.1/5311]

4 July YORK Armed Sloop
Purchased 1777 (*Betsey*); 100 tons; 12 guns
Lieutenant Daniel Dobree

On 2 July, a large French force under the Comte d'Estaing appeared off the island of Grenada and commenced landing troops. The *York* was the only naval vessel at the island, laying at anchor in the Careenage. During 3 July, the enemy advanced in three columns on the British positions. One of the columns, which attacked the Careenage, was cannonaded with some effect by the *York*. The following morning the outnumbered British garrison, including the sloop, surrendered to the French.
[Beatson vol 4 pp461–3]

16 July HAERLEM Armed Sloop
Prize 1777 (*Harlequin*); 110 tons; 14 guns
Lieutenant Josias Rogers

Cruising off the Delaware coast in company with the *Rainbow* and *Solebay*, she became separated from the others in poor weather. At daybreak, she saw several vessels approaching and soon counted thirteen, a mixture of brigs, sloops and schooners, all of them American. The *Haerlem* made for the shore, intending to run aground if possible, but despite heaving the guns overboard to lighten her, she was overhauled by the brig *Impertinent*, 8 guns, with two others close astern. Lieutenant Rogers left the sloop by boat to go ashore to acquaint the British forces with the intelligence of the American squadron, the Master, Thomas Sproule, being left to surrender the vessel.
[TNA: ADM.1/5314]

7 August PINSON Armed Ship
Hired 1779; 130 tons; 14 guns
Lieutenant Isaac Coffin

Hired at Bristol to take stores to Labrador, and thence to be employed as an armed ship, command was given to Lieutenant Coffin on her arrival in Canada. On her first voyage under his command, she was ordered to join the sloops *Martin* and *Cygnet* in Pitts Harbour, Labrador, and then cruise off the coast. The ships weighed at just after noon and commenced working out of Chateau Bay. The winds were fitful and then shifted to the south-west, meaning the ships were forced to make a series of short tacks to pass between Whale Island and Castle Island. At 4pm the *Pinson* ran onto a ledge of rocks. The sloops in company closed and sent boats to assist, but she could not be moved. Stores were removed and she was abandoned as a wreck on 16 August. The wreck was deemed to have been caused through the negligence of the Master.
[TNA: ADM.1/471; ADM.51/581]

17 August ARDENT Third Rate
Hull 1764; 1,379 tons; 160ft × 44.4ft; 64 guns
Captain Philip Boteler

In the summer of 1779, the combined fleets of France and Spain cruised in the English Channel under the command of Comte d'Orvilliers, with a weak British fleet under Admiral Hardy unable to challenge them. Several ships under repair were ordered to be prepared for sea, the *Ardent* being one of these. With works hastily completed and a crew, largely inexperienced, gathered, she was ready for sea by early August. She sailed from Spithead on 12 August and escorted several merchant vessels to Torbay, where they anchored. During the early hours of 16 August, they weighed with the intention of joining Admiral Hardy, unaware of just how close or powerful the enemy fleet was. During the morning of 17 August, when off Rame Head, several ships were sighted, which were recognised as ships of the line, and presumed to be the British fleet. At the same time a frigate was sighted on the starboard quarter, which was evidently closing her, which seemed to be showing British colours. Now convinced that they were joining Hardy, there was no sense of alarm, and as they closed, some of the larger ships could be seen to have guns run out, so Captain Boteler ordered the larboard lower deck guns to be run out, as it was presumed that Admiral Hardy had ordered this. The closing frigate was the *Gentille*, 32 guns, and the ships the combined Franco-Spanish fleet. A second frigate, the *Junon*, 32, which was re-joining the fleet from a chase also made her way towards the unsuspecting *Ardent*, which was now in the process of reefing main courses and preparing to hail the oncoming frigates for orders. At 10.30am the *Junon* hoisted French colours and fired a shot, which was the first clue that she had joined the enemy fleet, rather than the British. Boteler gave orders to wear ship, and stand away for the shore, the *Junon* firing two broadsides into her as she did so, and the *Gentille* then joined the action by firing into her. All was now confusion on the *Ardent*, which the enemy frigates took full advantage of, firing repeatedly into her as she made sail away, with no reply as she desperately tried to clear for action. By now other enemy ships were crowding sail to join the action, with another two frigates, *Bellone* and *Gloire*, joining the chase, with the *Couronne*, 80, and *St. Michel*, 64. The *Ardent* managed to fire a single broadside before the flag was struck at about noon – this action was also confused, the ensign being hauled down by Marines, apparently without orders, and to the bewilderment of some. She suffered five killed and eight wounded. Captain Boteler was blamed for the loss, as it was judged that the ship had suffered little damage from the fire of the frigates, and there was a good possibility of her escaping. Despite his defence of having a large percentage of raw landsmen on board and no intelligence of the presence of the French fleet, it was found that he had '… failed to do his utmost to prevent the ship from falling into the enemy hands' and was dismissed the service.

Note: retaken on 12 April 1781 by the fleet.
[TNA: ADM.1/5315; Mariner's Mirror vol 27 pp106–30]

25 August THORN Ship Sloop
Mistleythorn 1779; 305 tons; 96.7ft × 26.11ft; 14 guns
Master and Commander William Wardlaw

Inward-bound to New York with despatches from England, two ships were sighted in late afternoon, and the *Thorn* altered course to investigate. Making private recognition signals as she neared the pair, as they were not answered she rightly suspected that the strangers were Americans, and she put about and made all sail away with the strangers in pursuit. By 10 o'clock that night the first of the enemy vessels, the *Deane*, 32 guns, was within gunshot and fired three times at the sloop to bring her to, which she ignored. The chase continued until 2am when the *Deane* was joined by the *Boston*, 24. Unable to escape, the sloop surrendered.

Note: retaken in August 1782 by the *Arethusa*.
[TNA: ADM.1/5316]

27/28 August FALCON Brig Sloop
Portsmouth 1771; 305 tons; 95ft × 27.1ft; 14 guns
Master and Commander Richard Lock†

Having sailed on 22 August from Halifax, Nova Scotia, in company with the *Robust* and *Licorne* and several provision ships, bound for the Penobscot River, during 27 August the wind increased until by that evening it was blowing a strong south-easterly gale, with a heavy sea. Several ships lost sails and spars during the night, and morning showed no sign of the *Falcon*. Wreckage, including chests and oars, were seen, which were thought to be from the sloop, which was presumed to have foundered with all hands.
[TNA: ADM 1/486]

10 September ARIEL Sixth Rate
Blackwall 1777; 435 tons; 108ft × 30.3ft; 20 guns
Captain Thomas MacKenzie

Late in August the French fleet under d'Estaing returned to the American coast, this time to support operations in Georgia and South Carolina. The arrival of the fleet was a surprise to the British and when the *Ariel* sighted a strange sail, she closed to investigate, being unaware of the presence of the French. As she closed to identify the stranger, private signals were made which were unanswered, raising Captain Mackenzie's suspicions. When close, it could be seen to be a large frigate, with two brigs and a schooner in company. She therefore tacked away and stood for the Georgia shore, about 60 miles away. The enemy frigate was the *Amazone*, 26 guns, which bore up in chase. As the French vessel

was steadily overhauling the *Ariel*, Captain MacKenzie decided to stand and fight, so took in sail and waited for the *Amazone* to come up. The resulting fight went on for 90 minutes, until with the mizzen mast shot away and all the rigging cut to pieces, four killed and twenty wounded, the *Ariel* surrendered. The mainmast went overboard after surrendering.
[TNA: ADM.1/5315]

10 September SPHINX Sixth Rate
Portsmouth 1775; 431 tons; 108ft × 30.1ft; 20 guns
Captain Robert Sutton
Sailed from St Lucia on 5 September in company with the *Carcass* bomb vessel and a tender, carrying troops of the 5th Regiment of Foot and some seamen for the fleet in Barbados. During the morning of 10 September, then being to the south-east of Martinique, a sail was sighted closing the little group from the island. At 10 o'clock the ships cleared for action and stood to the north-east, the ship appearing to be a French frigate. By 11.30 the stranger was within gunshot of the *Sphinx* and hoisted a British ensign and fired a shot to leeward. The British ships were not deceived, however, and continued to stand on and a few minutes later the French ensign was hoisted by the stranger, which commenced the action by firing a shot into the *Sphinx*. A close action then followed in light winds, but at 12.30 the main topmast of the *Sphinx* was shot away, and with the rigging torn to pieces and being overpowered by the French ship's heavier armament, she struck her flag, her captor proving to be the *Amphitrite*, 32 guns. The *Carcass* and the tender, which were some way off during the engagement, made off at this point, but the French frigate fired accurately into the tender, bringing down her main topsail and shattering her rigging, after which she also surrendered. The bomb vessel successfully escaped.

Note: recaptured on 29 December 1779 by the *Proserpine*.
[TNA: ADM.1/5314; ADM.51/167]

10 September WEST FLORIDA Sloop
Purchased 1776; 66 tons; 56ft × 17.6ft; 6 guns
Acting Lieutenant John Payne†
Stationed in Lake Ponchartrain, British West Florida, she sent a boat into Manchac on 27 August to contact British land forces, but by the morning of 10 September had given up hopes of its return, so resumed their cruise. On sighting a sail, chase was given, and they soon overhauled the stranger, which seemed to be under British colours. On hailing, they received the reply 'From Pensacola to Manchac', but then hauled down the flag, ran on board the sloop, grappled her and attempted to enter boarders. Despite having only fifteen men on board, Payne resisted the attempted boarding and drove them back. A further attempt was made to board, which was again repulsed but the third time the enemy was successful. Their opponent was the American schooner *Morris*, 8 guns. Two were killed, including Lieutenant Payne, and one wounded.
[TNA: ADM.1/242]

20 September ROSE Sixth Rate
Hull 1757; 449 tons; 108.11ft × 30.6ft; 20 guns
Captain John Brown
The French fleet arrived off the coast of Georgia on 1 September and landed troops to lay siege to Savannah. The British naval forces in the area were taken upriver to help defend the town, with guns and men being landed from the ships to bolster the defences. It was decided to block the River Savannah to prevent the passage of enemy ships, and the *Rose* was selected to be one of the blockships. She was in poor condition, with her bottom timbers severely affected by Teredo shipworm and the stern and rudder quite rotten, and '… she could not swim above two months'. During the afternoon, she was taken to a position about a mile below Savannah, and that evening she was scuttled, with her masts still above water. The following day parties returned to remove rigging and the sails before cutting away the masts, and she was then abandoned.
[TNA: ADM.52/1969; London Gazette 18 December 1779; 21 December 1779]

20 September SAVANNAH Armed Ship
Purchased 1779; 270 tons; 14 guns
Master and Commander Richard Fisher
Purchased for the service by Captain Sir James Wallace of the *Experiment*, she was still fitting out and was not armed when the French forces arrived off Georgia, so, as with the *Rose* (above), she was ordered to be scuttled in the River Savannah to act as a blockship, to impede the entrance of the enemy into that river.
[London Gazette 18 December 1779; 21 December 1779; TNA: ADM 106/1246/169]

21 September HOPE Brig Sloop
Prize 1775 (*Sea Nymph*); 105 tons; 45ft × 20.2ft; 14 guns
Lieutenant Michael Hindman
When returning to the anchorage at Sandy Hook, New Jersey, after a cruise in local waters, she sighted two ships which altered course in chase of her. The *Hope* made private signals, which were not answered, and fearing they were enemy ships she ran under all sail to the south. The larger of the strangers, the American privateer *General Pickering*, 16 guns, overtook the sloop, hoisted British colours and hailed her, claiming to be a Liverpool privateer. Now uncertain of her identity, when the privateer hailed and ordered that they send a boat to them, Hindman promptly complied, Lieutenant

Samuel Dale going on board. On his arrival on the American, he was promptly taken prisoner and sent below. The American colours were now substituted for British, and the sloop was hailed and ordered to surrender. Although the guns of the *Hope* had been cast off, they could not bear on the *Pickering* and ship had not beaten to quarters. As she could neither resist nor escape, Lieutenant Hindman ordered the flag to be struck without offering any resistance. Hindman was subsequently reprimanded for his conduct.

Note: recaptured in May 1781 by the *Assistance* and recommissioned as the *Recovery*.
[TNA: ADM.1/5316]

23 September SERAPIS Fifth Rate
Rotherhithe 1779; 888 tons; 140.2ft × 38ft; 44 guns
Captain Richard Pearson

Escort to the homeward-bound Baltic trade convoy, the *Serapis* had a large number of merchant ships under her charge, in company with the armed ship *Countess of Scarborough*. During the morning of 23 September, then being off Scarborough, a boat from the shore came alongside to warn them of the presence of a squadron of enemy ships. The convoy stretched away towards Flamborough Head, when four strange ships were sighted approaching. Rightly suspecting them to be the enemy squadron, Captain Pearson ordered the convoy to act independently and placed himself between the convoy and the approaching ships. By early evening, the largest of the enemy ships, the American *Bonhomme Richard*, 42 guns, was within gunshot and Captain Pearson hailed them. The reply was that they were a British ship, the *Princess Royal*, which was not believed, and this was followed by the American opening fire, which was followed immediately by a broadside by the *Serapis*. The subsequent fight last for over three hours and was one of the fiercest single-ship actions in history. After exchanging two or three broadsides, the American ran close alongside her opponent, and the pair became locked together, head to stern, with the anchor of the *Serapis* hooked into the quarter of the *Bonhomme Richard*. In this position, they engaged for two hours, and the British ship's heavier armament initially proved highly effective, riddling the hull of the American with holes and causing many casualties. At about 9.30pm, with the American pouring destructive small-arms fire into the *Serapis* and pitching hand grenades on board, one of the latter dropped down the main hatchway and blew up several powder cartridges which dismounted five guns and starting a fire. Despite this, the British recovered, and the fight went on and at about 10 o'clock a shout for quarter was heard from the American. This led to an attempt to board by the *Serapis*, but this was beaten back. The fight continued for another 30 minutes or so, until the French frigate *Alliance*, 36 guns, which had already been firing indiscriminately into the pair, came up and fired a raking broadside into *Serapis*, and positioned herself under her stern. The mainmast of the *Serapis* came down and the casualties were such that she could not continue the fight against both opponents, and Captain Pearson surrendered. The *Serapis* suffered fifty-four men killed and seventy-five wounded. The *Bonhomme Richard* had been so severely damaged that she sank the following day. All the convoy escaped. For his gallantry, Captain Pearson was knighted, and he received a gift of plate worth 100 guineas from the grateful members of the Royal Exchange Assurance Company.
[TNA: ADM.1/5315; Annual Register 1779 pp309–12]

23 September COUNTESS OF SCARBOROUGH Armed Ship
Hired 1777; 500 tons; 22 guns
Master and Commander Thomas Piercy

The second escort to the Baltic convoy attacked by the Franco-American squadron commanded by John Paul Jones in the *Bonhomme Richard* (see above). As the enemy advanced towards them, the *Countess of Scarborough* initially shepherded some of the merchant ships inshore and then stood back to join the *Serapis*. She was initially tackled by the *Alliance*, 36 guns, and after a mutual exchange of broadsides a close engagement ensued for about 20 minutes when the frigate dropped astern. The *Scarborough* attempted to close and assist the *Serapis*, but found the pair locked together, covered in smoke, and was unable to distinguish one from another. A second enemy frigate now closed – this was the *Pallas*, 32, which came up on her starboard quarter and fired a broadside, which opened a new action. Commander Piercy fought his opponent for two hours, until the *Alliance* was again seen to be closing, and with all the braces, most of the running rigging and sheets shot away, several guns dismounted, four men killed and twenty wounded, she surrendered. Commander Piercy was rewarded for his bravery by promotion to Captain and was awarded plate worth £50.
[TNA: ADM.1/5315]

24 September EXPERIMENT Fourth Rate
Deptford 1774; 922 tons; 140.9ft × 38.9ft; 50 guns
Captain Sir James Wallace

Sailed from New York on 12 September with General George Garth embarked, bound for Savannah to take command of the army in Georgia, and a large sum of money as payment for the troops. During the late afternoon, several ships were seen to the westward, and it was correctly surmised that they were the French fleet under d'Estaing. She attempted to make ground away, but as she had previously suffered in a storm and been partially dismasted, she was unable to escape, and they

steadily overhauled her. At about 8pm the *Sagitairre*, 50 guns, came alongside and after a short exchange of fire, with other ships of the line coming up, the *Experiment* was forced to surrender.
[ADM.1/5315]

6 October QUEBEC Fifth Rate
Harwich 1760; 686 tons; 125ft × 35.4ft; 32 guns
Captain George Farmer†

In company with the *Rambler* cutter off Ushant, when at daybreak a ship and a cutter were seen to the south-west, and the British pair gave chase. It soon became clear that they were French and were quite prepared for the fight and waited for the British to come down. As they advanced, the French frigate, the *Surveillante*, 32 guns, fired repeatedly at the *Quebec* as she closed, although with little effect, Captain Farmer reserving his fire until alongside his opponent. The pair then lay close by each other, exchanging broadsides and small-arms fire. The *Rambler* meanwhile stood towards the enemy cutter, which was the *Expédition*, 16 guns, and commenced a close engagement. After about three hours' combat, during which both ships had taken numerous casualties, the *Quebec* successfully shot away all the French ship's masts, which fell clear of the ship. Soon after this, the *Quebec* suffered in a similar manner, all her masts going by the board. Unfortunately, the sails and rigging of the British ship fell over the upper deck and the engaged side. Within moments the sails had been set alight by the firing of the guns and the flames started spreading. The French ship now had her bowsprit over the upper deck of the *Quebec*, entangled in the rigging, and an attempt was made to board, but the smoke and flames beat them back. The engagement ceased, as men jumped overboard, the crew of the *Surveillante* throwing ropes, oars and spars into the water. The *Rambler*, which had been engaging the enemy cutter, had already fallen away from her opponent with damaged rigging and sails, but sent her boat to assist. Captain Farmer and his First Lieutenant, Francis Roberts, were both severely wounded, but directed efforts to try and quell the flames, but little could be done and at about 6 o'clock in the evening the *Quebec* blew up. There were sixty-eight survivors, who did not include Captain Farmer: 127 men died.
[TNA: ADM.1/5314; Annual Register 1779 pp312–14; London Gazette 9 October 1779; Troude vol 2 pp55–8]

4 November TORTOISE Store Ship
Purchased 1777 (*Grenville*); 705 tons; 110.10ft × 34.7ft; 26 guns
Master and Commander John Frodsham

On passage from St Kitts to England in company with a large convoy, she was clearly in poor condition, the pumps having to be employed constantly after sailing. By 30 October the leaks were worsening and with the crew becoming exhausted from the constant pumping, she made signals of distress. Little could be done by the other ships as the weather was poor and that night the *Tortoise* fell behind and parted from the convoy. The following day the weather deteriorated further, and the main topmast was rolled away. To ease the ship, the guns were heaved overboard and a merchant brig that had appeared was asked to stand by her. By the morning of 4 November, the weather had moderated sufficiently for boats to be hoisted out and with the ship full of water the crew were transferred to the brig and other merchant vessels which had arrived on scene, and the *Tortoise* was allowed to founder.
[TNA: ADM.1/5314]

11 November GRAMPUS Store Ship
Deptford 1751 (*Buckingham*); 1,436 tons; 160ft × 45.4ft; 30 guns
Master and Commander Thomas Bennett

The former 70-gun ship was employed as a store ship and sailed from St Kitts on 3 October in company with a large convoy to return to England (see *Tortoise* above). The weather worsened as the ships headed north, and as various leaks became evident, on 30 October she made signals of distress, but in the storm-force winds, no assistance could be sent. The ship struggled on, with the water steadily overcoming the pumps, and she was finally abandoned and allowed to founder, her crew being taken off by a merchant ship.
[TNA: ADM.1/5315]

November PENELOPE Sixth Rate
Liverpool 1778; 522 tons; 114.7ft × 32.2ft; 24 guns
Captain James Jones†

Disappeared in the West Indies and presumed lost with all hands. She had captured a Spanish *guarda-costa* in the Mona Passage between Hispaniola and Puerto Rico, on 14 November and was supposed lost soon after this. Pay books were closed at the end of the month.
[TNA: ADM.1/242; ADM.34/582]

5 December JACKAL Cutter
Purchased 1778; 187 tons; 72.10ft × 25.4ft; 10 guns
Lieutenant John Gibson

Lying at anchor off Deal, both Lieutenant Gibson and the Master were ashore on duty, with Midshipman Garvine being the senior officer on board. In the early hours of the morning a small number of the crew, sixteen in all, mutinously took over the vessel. They quickly detained the loyal members of the crew that were on deck, then weighed anchor and setting foresail and jib, quietly sailed out of the anchorage. The noise roused some of those sleeping below, but when the pilot, Humphrey Holbrook, tried to go on deck, he was confronted by an armed seaman who pointed a pistol at his head, warning him to stay still or ' I will blow your brains out'. The hatches were then blocked by putting the boat and shot boxes on it, effectively imprisoning those below. The ringleaders were a group of smugglers recently ordered on board with some five or six men who were Irish, some having been pressed. Having successfully cleared the port, the mutineers became quite elated, with shouts of 'Its liberty we want and liberty we've got' and 'Huzzah for Captain Love' – referring to Larry Love, one of their number. When some of the confined crew tried to reason with the mutineers they were threatened, with the cook being menaced with a cutlass and told 'Quiet you old bugger, if you open your mouth, you are a dead man'. Early the next morning the pilot was allowed on deck to guide them into Calais harbour, where she was taken alongside, and the mutineers turned her over to the French. Lieutenant Gibson was reprimanded for the loss, 'being answerable' in some degree, in that he had left the cutter when the Master was already ashore. Some of the mutineers seem to have entered French service, but most took the opportunity to enter merchant vessels and disappear. Three years later, Thomas Bushell, Daniel Pain and Thomas Malone – all of whom used other names – were convicted of mutiny; two were hanged, but Bushell was later pardoned.

Note: retaken on 23 July 1781 by the *Prudente*.
[TNA: ADM.1/5314; ADM.1/5322]

12 December NORTH Armed Sloop
Purchased 1778 (*Liverpool*); 16 guns
Master and Commander Jerrard Selby†
Soon after sailing from Sydney, Nova Scotia, with several transport ships, she parted company in poor weather, but managed to take shelter in Beaver Harbour. She sailed again on 10 December, in company with the *St Helena* store ship, and two smaller vessels. The weather continued poor, and as a storm seemed to be approaching it was decided to head for the safety of Halifax. At about 7pm they sighted the lighthouse at Sambro, but as they could not weather Sambro Head they anchored. At about 1.30 in the morning the *North* was heard to fire distress guns, and it was seen that she had gone onto the rocks. Other ships were unable to render assistance as she was beaten to pieces. The number of survivors is unclear, with reports from none to five.
[*Collections of the Nova Scotia Historical Society*, vol 20 (1921) pp41–2]

15 December VIPER Brig Sloop
Deptford 1756; 228 tons; 88.7ft × 24.3ft; 10 guns
Master and Commander Lord John Hervey
Escorting a convoy to Quebec, she closed the land in poor weather – thick cloud with frequent snow squalls. When breakers were suddenly seen ahead, she wore ship, but found she was still close to the shore, which was about 18 miles from Cap Chat in the St Lawrence. She attempted to tack but missed stays and drove onto a rocky ridge. The rudder was knocked off and the sloop started filling with water. The guns shot and spare booms and yards were heaved overboard in efforts to lighten her, but she could not be freed and was abandoned as a wreck.
[TNA: ADM.1/5315]

15 December DUC DE LA VAUGIGNON Cutter
Prize 1779; 164 tons; 68.1ft × 24.5ft; 14 guns
Lieutenant Charles Jordan†
Stationed in the southern North Sea, she disappeared in a strong gale. On this day, a cutter was seen to drive ashore on the island of Vlieland and break up during the night with the loss of all hands. A recovered board identified the wreck as being the *Vaugignon*.
[TNA: ADM.180/4; NMM: ADM 354/200/322]

15/16 December BELLONA Armed Ship
Hired 1779; 18 guns
Master and Commander Francis Tinsley
Escorting ships from Hull to Hamburg, the weather was poor with strong winds and frequent squalls of hail which obscured the sea and landmarks. In a hard squall, she ran onto a sandbank in the approaches to the River Elbe and started filling with water very rapidly. Unable to free herself from the sands or clear the ship of water she was abandoned as a wreck.
[TNA: ADM.1/5315; *Lloyd's List* 21 Dec 1779; www.britishnewspaperarchive.co.uk: *Bath Chronicle* 6 Jan 1780 p2, reporting a letter from Hamburg of 17 Dec]

1780

6 February HOPE Tender
Hired 1778; 6 guns
Lieutenant John Gauntlett
Caught in a storm off Guernsey, she shipped a particularly heavy sea which swept the upper deck clear of anything moveable and poured down the hatches. She spent the next few hours pumping the vessel free of water but was in no fit state to resist when a French privateer came in sight the next day. The French ship came alongside and fired a swivel into the tender, at which she surrendered.
[TNA: ADM.1/5316]

15 February DEFIANCE Third Rate
Woolwich 1772; 1,375 tons; 19.6ft × 44.5ft; 64 guns
Captain Maximillian Jacobs
Arriving off Tybee, Georgia, to enter the river Savannah, the Captain was anxious to enter as soon as possible.

A local pilot, William Scott, came aboard and initially advised against a move that day, but Captain Jacobs was insistent. As they manoeuvred into the river the *Defiance* struck the northern end of the bar. Attempts were made to drive her over the obstruction, but to no avail, so efforts were directed towards kedging her off. She eventually floated free at high tide but was found to be making water. After five days of attempting to pump her free and moving her failed, she was abandoned, the water then being over the orlop deck. The Captain was found to have been partly to blame for her loss, having directed the pilot to take her in, even though warned there was insufficient water. He was dismissed the service. The pilot was also partly to blame, in being poorly prepared for his task and doing little or nothing to help after she struck the bar. He was ordered not to be allowed to serve as a pilot for the Navy again.
[TNA: ADM.1/5315]

27 February LEVIATHAN Store Ship
Plymouth 1750 (*Northumberland*); 1,415 tons; 160ft × 45ft; 30 guns
Captain Robert Lambert
Sailed from Jamaica 24 January in a large convoy of about fifty ships, under the escort of the *Charon*, 44 guns, bound for England. She had been at sea for two weeks when several leaks became apparent. Despite constant pumping the water increased, and in the North Atlantic swell the ship became increasingly frail. The upper deck guns and anchors were heaved overboard in attempts to lighten her, and ropes were frapped around the hull to stop the timbers working. Eventually all the lower deck guns were heaved overboard, as well as some of the stores, and more frapping employed. By 25 February it was clear that a losing battle was being fought, and the crew started transferring to ships in company. The last members left on the 27th when the ship was abandoned, with 11ft of water in the hold.
[TNA: ADM.1/5315]

22/23 March TAPAGEUR Cutter
Prize 1779; 225 tons; 73.6ft × 27.9ft; 14 guns
Lieutenant Lord Charles Fitzgerald
Attached to Rear Admiral Parker's squadron off St Lucia, when the French fleet was sighted on 21 March, the cutter was sent to find Admiral Rodney with the news. During the evening, she lost her mast and the sloop *Barbados* had to tow her into Careenage Bay, St Lucia. Later that night, whilst attempting to warp further into the bay, she ran onto a submerged rock and subsequently foundered during the night.
[TNA: ADM.1/5315; Rodney Letter Books vol 2 p416]

10 April ACTIVE Armed Brig
Purchased 1779 (*Rosebud*); 109 tons; 71ft × 20.2ft; 16 guns
Lieutenant William Quarme
The *Active* was returning to the anchorage at Sandy Hook, New Jersey, having battled her way through a storm, during which the anchors, boats and seven guns had been heaved overboard, and the pumps were working constantly to free her from the water she had shipped. As she headed towards the coastline, at first light a ship was seen which altered course towards her. The brig was in no fit condition to resist an enemy, and all sail was made away from her pursuer and a course steered to close the land, running along the coastline. The ship steadily overhauled her and was seen to be showing British colours. As soon as she was within distance, she hailed and claimed to be an English privateer from Bristol. Lieutenant Quarme was still uncertain as to her identity when the ship altered course to pass under her stern and station herself on the sloop's lee quarter. As she did so the British colours were replaced by American and the *Active* was called on to surrender. Unable to escape or offer effective resistance, the sloop surrendered, finding her captor to be the *General Pickering*, 20 guns.
[TNA: ADM.1/5316]

11 April ADMIRAL SPRY Tender
Hired 1776; 200 tons; 8 guns
Master Humphrey Bunsford
Sailed from Waterford for Plymouth with over 100 men for the Navy, but when off the Scilly Isles she was chased and taken by the *Dunkerquoise* privateer. She had altered course away when the privateer was sighted but was overhauled between 7 and 8 o'clock that evening and surrendered without any resistance.
Note: retaken two days later by the *Ambuscade*.
[TNA: HCA 32/261/111]

26 April FORTUNE Ship Sloop
Woolwich 1778; 300 tons; 96.7ft × 26.9ft; 14 guns
Master and Commander Lewis Robertson
Cruising to the south-east of Barbuda, Leeward Islands, at first light several ships were sighted. The sloop approached cautiously, making private recognition signals which were not answered. When the ships were seen to make signals which could not be understood by the sloop and when two ships detached from the group to close, she rightly guessed that it was the French fleet. All sail was made away with two frigates in chase. The pursuit went on for most of the day with the *Fortune* steadily outpacing her French rivals. Late in the afternoon the wind dropped away, and the frigates slowly started to catch her. As night fell the breeze again picked up and studding sails were set in a further effort to escape. The frigates followed her manoeuvres

and continued to overhaul. By 8.30 o'clock in the evening the *Gentille*, 32 guns, was within pistol-shot and fired intermittently for the next 20 minutes, until the second frigate, the *Iphigénie*, 32, came up at which the sloop surrendered.
[TNA: ADM.1/5317]

21 June COUREUR Schooner
Prize 1778; 138 tons; 68.10ft × 22.3ft; 8 guns
Lieutenant Christopher Major

The schooner sailed from St John's, Newfoundland, on 16 June to gain intelligence on enemy shipping in the area. During 18 June she sighted two brigs, which she closed to within gunshot range and when both showed American colours, she altered away to steer for Bonavista, with the brigs, which were both privateers, the *Fortune*, 16 guns, and *Griffin*, 14, in pursuit. Outpacing the brigs she anchored in Bonavista harbour, putting a spring on the cable and rigging a hawser to the shore, so that by hauling on the cables, she would always present her broadside. The American pair entered the harbour, and a 30-minute exchange of fire took place, after which the attackers withdrew. The following day the pair had disappeared, and it seemed that they had left the area. On the morning of 21 June, the *Coureur* sailed and very soon after clearing Bonavista, saw the two brigs close to the shoreline. They immediately made sail, one steering to cut her off from the harbour, the other to seaward. The engagement started soon after, with the first of the privateers. Lieutenant Major cut away the mizzen mast to allow the boom of the mainmast to swing freely, allowing him to manoeuvre. The schooner suffered in her rigging, the mainstay being shot away, and the mainmast was damaged, but she held her own against the brig until the second privateer came up. She raked the schooner, the mainmast going by the board. Unable to escape and faced with two large opponents, the schooner surrendered. Three killed and four wounded.
[TNA: ADM.1/5316]

30 June CORNWALL Third Rate
Deptford 1761; 1,614 tons; 168.3ft × 47.4ft; 74 guns
Captain Timothy Edwards

Stationed in the West Indies, the *Cornwall* was in a poor condition, and in February Rear Admiral Parker had represented that she was unfit for service and should be sent home. With every ship needed in the area, this was rejected, and she took part in the fleet actions under Admiral Rodney against the French under de Guichen. In the action of 17 April off Martinique she suffered badly, with twenty-one men killed and fifty-nine wounded. The subsequent engagements off Martinique on 15 and 19 May saw her damaged again with a further seven killed, including Lieutenant William Law, the First Lieutenant. She was ordered to proceed to St Lucia for repairs and she anchored in the Careenage during 23 May, now having 6ft of water in the hold. Parties were sent from the shore and other ships to assist with pumping and over the following days the guns were taken out and work started to remove her stores. The leaks could not be stemmed, and on 12 June she was ordered to be taken further inshore and was hauled into shallow water in the Little Careenage, as she was in danger of foundering, and after she took the ground her yards and spars were used as shores, whilst work continued to remove stores. On 15 June one of the larboard shores gave way and she heeled over. Eventually a cable was rigged from the shore to the mainmast to prevent her capsizing. The struggle to save her proved impossible, and on 27 June she was ordered to be abandoned as a wreck and the ship was paid off on 30 June. Work went on for some time removing the last of the stores and the remains were finally burnt.
[Rodney: Letter Books vol 2 p596; TNA: ADM.1/311; ADM.51/211]

30 July WOLF(E) Armed ship
Hired 1779 (*Peggy*); 8 guns

Sailed on 11 July from Halifax to cruise off the southern coastline of Newfoundland in company with the *Hind* sloop, they encountered drifting banks of fog. During 29 July, they entered a particularly thick bank, with little or no wind, the ships becoming separated as they were carried on a strong easterly current. During the early hours, the *Wolfe* went ashore on southern end of the island of St Pierre. Guns were fired at regular intervals, and efforts made to free her. The *Hind* found her during the morning of 31 July, and it was agreed that she could not be moved, so work commenced on transferring stores to the sloop. By 4 August, this work was complete, and the *Wolfe* was abandoned and set on fire.
[TNA: ADM.1/471; ADM.51/457]

4 September UNICORN Sixth Rate
Rotherhithe 1776; 433 tons; 108ft × 30.2ft; 20 guns
Captain Thomas Lenox Frederick

At 2.30 in the afternoon, then being off Tortuga, a sail was sighted on the starboard beam. The *Unicorn* altered to investigate and very soon more ships came into sight over the horizon, and it became clear that she was in contact with the main French fleet. She stood away before the wind, with a large frigate and two line of battle ships in chase. After a two-hour long chase, the frigate *Andromaque*, 32 guns, had caught the *Unicorn* and fired a single shot across her bows, to which she replied with a full broadside. The action continued for over an hour, by which time all the rigging and sails were reduced to tatters with the main topgallant mast and all bowlines and braces shot away, two guns and two carronades were dismounted, and she had suffered four killed and thirteen wounded. When two line of battle ships came up, and one of them, the *Palmier*, opened fire, she surrendered.

Note: retaken on 20 April 1781 by the *Resource*.
[TNA: ADM.1/5317]

13 September ROVER Ship Sloop
Prize 1779 (*Cumberland*); 209 tons; 90ft x 22.8ft; 18 guns
Master and Commander Henry Savage

Cruising off Trinidad, the *Rover* had taken some small prizes when she was informed of the presence nearby of a large French frigate, the *Junon*, 40 guns. Deciding to clear the area, she made ground to the east, but at nightfall a ship came into sight which bore up in chase and it became clear that the *Junon* had found her. Casting her prizes adrift she made all sail away, hoping to lose her pursuer in the dark. The following morning however saw the frigate still in chase. The pursuit went on all through the morning until, at about 1 o'clock in the afternoon, the French ship commenced the action with her bow-chase guns. The fire was well aimed, and the main topmast stay was shot away, which led to the main topmast going overboard. Soon after, the firing commenced in earnest, the *Junon* firing high, and within 30 minutes the rigging was reduced to shreds. Unable to escape and faced with a superior force the sloop surrendered.

Note: retaken in January 1781 by the *Regulator* privateer.
[TNA: ADM.1/5317]

2–3 October: Jamaica Hurricane

In early October a particularly strong hurricane struck Jamaica, causing widespread devastation and loss of life, '… the most terrible hurricane that ever was felt in this country, with repeated shocks of an earthquake, which has almost totally demolished every building in the parishes of Westmoreland, Hanover, part of St James's and some part of Elizabeth's and killed numbers of the white inhabitants as well as of the negroes' [letter from Major General Dalling, Governor of Jamaica, quoted in the London Gazette 30 December 1780].

Several ships were lost in the storm:

4 October PHOENIX Fifth Rate
Limehouse 1759; 856 tons; 140.9ft x 37.1ft; 44 guns
Captain Sir Hyde Parker

Caught in the tropical storm off Jamaica, she was carried by the wind and currents towards Cuba. The storm steadily increased in strength over two days, and she was driven before the wind under bare poles, with the ship rolling so much that the decks were constantly under water and the weather-side pumps were unable to function as the ship heeled so much. The mainmast was cut away to ease the ship and guns and stores were heaved overboard. A particularly heavy sea washed over the upper deck and everything movable went overboard. When she saw land ahead, she was unable to steer away and ran hard aground on the coast of Cuba about nine miles from Cape Cruz. The ship swung broadside-on to the shore, the foremast going by the board soon after. A hawser was successfully swum ashore and over the next three days the crew went ashore and worked hard to land provisions and stores from the wreck. The ship's cutter was manned and sent to Montego Bay to bring help which arrived in the shape of the sloop *Porcupine* and three local shallops. The wreck was abandoned on 12 October and set on fire.
[TNA: ADM.1/5316]

5 October STIRLING CASTLE Third Rate
Chatham 1775; 1,377 tons; 159.2ft x 44.6ft; 64 guns
Captain Robert Carkett[†]

One of the British West Indies squadron cruising off San Domingo when the area was hit by the severe tropical storm of 4/5 October, she was separated from the other ships and was driven by the storm towards Hispaniola. During the night, she was driven ashore on the Silver Keys, a reef a little to the northward of Cap François (modern Cap Haïtien) and rapidly went to pieces. Some of the men struggled ashore through the pounding surf, although another group of about twenty clung to a portion of the wreck which was swept out to sea. These latter suffered appalling hardships, the numbers slowly decreasing over the next few days as men died from starvation and exposure, some evidently going mad before they died. The survivors, one Midshipman and three men (or four, reports vary) were eventually picked up by a local vessel and taken to Cap François.
[London Gazette 30 December 1780; TNA: ADM 106/125; Beatson vol V p 86; www.britishnewspaperarchive.co.uk: Bath Chronicle 8 March 1781 p2; Leeds Intelligencer 13 March 1781 p3]

The following ships, all part of the British squadron off San Domingo disappeared during the hurricane and are presumed to have foundered with all hands:

THUNDERER Third Rate
Woolwich 1760; 1,609 tons; 166.6ft x 47.2ft; 74 guns
Captain Robert Nichols[†]

SCARBOROUGH Sixth Rate
Hull 1756; 433 tons; 107.8ft x 30.4ft; 20 guns
Captain Samuel Hood Walker[†]

VICTOR Ship Sloop
Prize 1779 (*Hunter*); 14 guns
Master and Commander George Geddes Mackenzie[†]

BARBADOES Brig Sloop
Purchased 1778; 130 tons; 12 guns
Master and Commander Ralph Milbanke†

* * *

11 October: The Great Hurricane

The West Indies were again struck by a hurricane, even more severe than the previous one, this time concentrated in the Windward Islands. St Lucia and Barbados in particular suffered, with houses flattened and crops destroyed. The storm began during the afternoon of the 10 October and by the following morning was blowing a full hurricane of great violence. 'A general convulsion of nature seemed to take place and an universal destruction ensued … every plantation and building, great and small, are thrown to the ground, the cattle and stock belonging to them are almost all destroyed: the produce of the earth torn up by the roots and not a trace left behind' (letter from Major General Vaughan, Commander in Chief of forces in the Leeward Islands, quoted in Beatson)
[London Gazette 23 December 1780; Beatson vol V p76]

Several ships were lost in the storm:

BLANCHE Fifth Rate
Prize 1779; 36 guns
Captain Samuel Uppleby†
She had sailed in company with the *Alcmene* on 10 October for Antigua but became separated in the storm and was last seen 'in great distress' and was presumed to have foundered with all hands.
[Beatson vol V p79]

ANDROMEDA Sixth Rate
Cowes 1777; 601 tons; 120.9ft × 33.8ft; 28 guns
Captain Henry Byrne†
Capsized and foundered about six leagues (18 miles) to the windward of Martinique. Several survivors were rescued by the French and were sent to St Lucia under a flag of truce.
[London Gazette 23 December 1780]

LAUREL Sixth Rate
Southampton 1779; 602 tons; 120.8ft × 33.8ft; 28 guns
Captain Thomas Lloyd†
In company with the *Andromeda* during the hurricane, she was driven ashore in Martinique where she rapidly broke up. There were only thirty-one survivors from wrecks of the *Laurel* and *Andromeda*.
[London Gazette 23 December 1780]

BEAVER'S PRIZE Ship Sloop
Prize 1777 (*Oliver Cromwell*); 264 tons; 88ft × 26.1ft; 14 guns
Master and Commander John Drummond†
On passage from St Lucia to Barbados when the hurricane struck, she was driven ashore on the island of St Lucia near the Vieux fort and broke up. There were only seventeen survivors.
[Beatson vol V p72]

* * *

12 October **CHAMELEON** Ship Sloop
Rotherhithe 1777; 308 tons; 96.10ft × 27ft; 14 guns
Master and Commander James Johnstone†
Lying at anchor in Gros Islet Bay, St Lucia when the hurricane struck the island, the force of the wind drove her across the bay, until in the early hours of the morning her cables parted, and she disappeared in a mass of flying spray. She was driven ashore and wrecked with no survivors.
[TNA: ADM.1/5318]

15 October **DEAL CASTLE** Sixth Rate
Deptford 1756; 401 tons; 107.3ft × 29.2ft; 20 guns
Captain James Hawkins
Lying at anchor in Gros Islet Bay, St Lucia in worsening weather, with strong winds which increased in strength and by the early hours of 12 October the *Deal Castle*, despite laying out another anchor, found herself being driven across the bay, along with the *Chameleon* (see above). At about 4 o'clock in the morning the anchor cables parted, and she drove out of the bay with the air full of rain and flying spray, sight of the land being lost immediately. An attempt to hoist sails was made, but they instantly shredded. All the topmasts, then the mizzen mast and jib boom went overboard within three minutes, and she was driven before the wind under bare poles. The lee gunwale was constantly under water until the mainmast was cut away which eased her movements somewhat. For the next three days, she was carried along by the storm which continued with incessant rain, neither sun, moon nor stars appearing. At 2 o'clock in the morning of the 15th, land was seen close ahead and soon afterwards she was driven ashore. Rafts were hastily assembled, and the exhausted crew members went ashore, only three men sick below being drowned. They found themselves on Puerto Rico, and all were taken by the Spanish to San Juan.
[TNA: ADM.1/5318]

31 October **ONTARIO** Snow
Carleton Island 1780; 231 tons; 77ft × 25.6ft; 22 guns
Master James Andrews†
Employed on Lake Ontario, she was carrying a company of the 34th Regiment of Foot, along with dependents,

from Fort Niagara for Oswego and Carleton Island when she was overtaken by a violent storm and disappeared. Over the next several days' wreckage, including hatchway gratings, a binnacle and clothing from the vessel was washed ashore about 30 miles east of Fort Niagara. About eighty people lost their lives, including thirty-five soldiers. The wreck of the *Ontario* was discovered in June 2008 near the southern shore of Lake Ontario.
[Malcolmson p38]

17/18 November SHARK Sixth Rate
Prize 1780 (*Hannibal*); 20 guns
Captain Howell Lloyd†

Part of the squadron under Admiral Sir George Rodney that sailed from Sandy Hook on 16 November for the West Indies, the ships were battered by gale-force winds for the next two days, and the *Shark* disappeared at this time. It was presumed that she had foundered with all hands.
[Rodney: Letter Books vol 1 pp90, 98]

22 November SENEGAL Ship Sloop
Rotherhithe 1760; 292 tons; 97ft × 26.1ft; 14 guns
Lieutenant George Croft†

The *Senegal* had been captured by the French off the American coast in 1778 (q.v.); she then served in the French Navy under the same name. On 2 November, the *Zephyr* sloop successfully engaged her off Barra Point, Gambia and recaptured her. Lieutenant Croft and twenty-two seamen were put on board from the sloop as a prize crew and sailed her to Gorée. When lying at anchor she blew up and sank with all the prize crew being killed. The cause of the explosion was not discovered.
[London Gazette 10 March 1781]

24 November HUSSAR Sixth Rate
Rotherhithe 1763; 628 tons; 103.8ft × 33.10ft; 28 guns
Captain Charles Morice Pole

Attempting to negotiate the Hell Gate passage, East River, New York, in calm weather, with little wind, she struck a submerged rock known locally as the Pot. She came free immediately, but it was discovered that she was making water very rapidly, so anchored and attempted to pump herself free. The water gained on the pumps at an alarming rate, with the ship taking an increasing list, so some guns were heaved overboard to lighten her and the anchor cable cut. She initially tried to make the Long Island shore, but as the tide was so strong, and with little wind, she was carried over to the Connecticut side of the river. Now completely waterlogged, she ran aground in shallow water. Boats were hoisted out and an attempt made to take out a kedge anchor, but she settled and soon sank up to the upper deck and was abandoned as a wreck.
[TNA: ADM.1/5316]

26 November SARTINE Sixth Rate
Prize 1778; 802 tons; 132.6ft × 35.9ft; 28 guns
Captain Robert Simonton

The British in India were at war with Hyder Ali, Sultan of Mysore, and his followers, who were backed by the French in a combined effort to drive the British from India. The Sultan maintained a small navy on the Malabar coast of India which Admiral Sir Edward Hughes determined to attack. A squadron arrived at Calicut (Kozikode) on 24 November and a distant engagement took place. As the enemy ships were moored well inshore, the *Sartine* was ordered to close them. The frigate was in only three fathoms (18ft) of water at this time, and Captain Simonton hesitated, believing that it would be dangerous for him to do so, saying when he received the order, 'I cannot tell what the Commodore would have me do, if he would give me orders to run aground, I will do so with pleasure'. Commodore Sir Edward Vernon then ordered him to lighten his ship and close the enemy. When this was not performed with the speed expected, he sent a sharp note demanding to know what prevented him from carrying out his orders. Simonton replied with an equally sharp note suggesting if he did not like it, he should come aboard himself so that the duty might be carried out to his liking. This led to the sending on board of Captain Alexander McCoy, who indicated, not unexpectedly, that Commodore Vernon was angry with Simonton and urged him to attack. By that afternoon, the *Sartine* had been lightened, and she advanced into shallow water, anchoring with a spring on the cable. Shortly after this, the frigate was found to be aground, warps having to be carried out to steady her. The following morning found her still on a sandbank and efforts went on all day to free her. Some of the guns were heaved overboard and she finally floated free late in the day. Anchoring in deeper water, she found that she was making water and a sail was slung under the stern in an effort to stop the leaks. The work continued the next day, but the water gained and at 9 o'clock that night she was abandoned as a wreck. Simonton was acquitted of any blame for her loss.
[TNA: ADM.1/5316]

30 November PLUTO Fireship
Saltash 1758 (*Tamer*); 313 tons; 96.4ft × 27.4ft; 16 guns
Master and Commander Thomas Geary†

When about 140 miles to the south-west of the Scilly Isles, during the early afternoon a ship was sighted through banks of drifting fog, but her identity could not be discovered until the stranger emerged from the mist. She could then be seen to be a large warship, so the *Pluto* cleared for action as the ship closed from ahead. As the ships passed on opposite tacks a mutual exchange of broadsides took place, in which the fireship's rigging

suffered. The enemy passed, came about, and a short chase took place. Having caught her opponent, the enemy ship stationed herself on the fireship's quarter. Unable to outrun her adversary and faced with superior force, the *Pluto* surrendered to the privateer *Duc de Chartres*, 24 guns.
[TNA: ADM.1/5317]

5 December TRUE BRITON Cutter
Purchased 1778; 188 tons; 74.6ft x 25.6ft; 10 guns
Lieutenant Hon Patrick Napier

Returning to England from the Mediterranean, she was caught in a storm off Lisbon, during which the bowsprit was lost. Her situation worsened on 2 December when, in the Bay of Biscay, a further storm dismasted her. Booms and spars were used to rig a jury mast and she bore away before the wind for Ireland. It was in this condition that she met a large French privateer, the *Bougainville*, 32 guns, and had little choice but to surrender.

Note: retaken in February 1782 by the *Arethusa*.
[TNA: ADM.1/5317]

31 December INCENDIARY Fireship
Purchased 1778; 397 tons; 110.8ft x 29.2ft; 8 guns
Master and Commander William Merrick

Bound for Spithead as a convoy escort from Plymouth, the convoy split when to the west of the Isle of Wight, the *Incendiary* heading for the Solent. The ship's Master, Charles Fea, was entrusted with the piloting of the vessel and he steered close to the Needles rocks. When only 50 yards from them, the wind died away and the current carried them towards the shore and at the same time a merchant brig, also becalmed, fell across her bows. With some difficulty, the merchant vessel was cleared, but by now she was close to the hazard and the anchor was let go, even though she was now in the surf of the rock. The boats were hoisted out to tow her clear, but it was too late. She struck the ground and started beating. The rudder was knocked off and several planks and timbers stove in. The masts were cut away and guns heaved overboard to lighten her, and the boats took out the stream anchor. The efforts to kedge her off failed when the cables were cut by the rocks. With the vessel filling quite quickly, the crew were taken off. Over the next three days the stores and provisions were taken off before she finally foundered. The Master was found to have been drunk and incapable and was disrated and ordered to serve before the mast.
[TNA: ADM.1/5317]

1781

9 January FAIRY Ship Sloop
Sheerness 1778; 300 tons; 96.7ft x 26.9ft; 14 guns
Master and Commander Joseph Brown

Cruising in the western Channel, the sloop was about 30 miles to the south-south-west of the Scilly Isles, when at first light a large ship was seen closing and by 9 o'clock it was clearly gaining on the sloop. The *Fairy* had not been supplied with the current private recognition signals so presumed the stranger was an enemy and prepared for action. When within range she fired a shot at the ship, which replied in a similar manner and the pair then commenced exchanging broadsides. The action went on for an hour, with the *Fairy* finding it increasingly difficult to fire as the water washed in through the gun ports. Unable to reply effectively, with her rigging torn, and faced with a larger opponent, the sloop surrendered to the privateer *Madame*, 32 guns.

Note: retaken on 13 January by the *Valiant*.
[TNA: ADM.1/5317]

23 January CULLODEN Third Rate
Deptford 1776; 1,659 tons; 170ft x 47.1ft; 74 guns
Captain George Balfour

On 21 January Admiral Graves, commanding the squadron off Rhode Island, was informed that a number of French warships had sailed from Newport, and he accordingly despatched three ships of the line, the *Bedford*, *Culloden* and *America*, in search of them. The weather was poor and worsened as the ships headed south, and the night of 22 January was very dark with the wind gusting to gale force. The *Culloden* tried to follow the stern light of the *Bedford* but lost her when taken aback as the ships tacked. She continued on the same course, with the wind increasing. At about 4.30am the crossjack yard was carried away and soon after this, breakers were seen ahead. All sails were thrown aback, but she struck the ground and found herself hard aground. The anchor was let go to steady her, but the ship swung broadside on to the sea. At dawn, she found that she had gone ashore on Wills Point, Portpond Bay, Long Island. The main topmast was cut away and attempts were made to take out anchors to kedge her off, but the wind and seas were too high. She continued to beat on the ground which was soft sand, and she settled further down. By the following day she had 6ft of water in the hold and was given up as a wreck. Most of her guns and stores were salvaged and the wreck was then set on fire.
[TNA: ADM.1/5317]

26 January SIREN Sixth Rate
Howden 1779; 513 tons; 114ft x 32ft; 24 guns
Captain Isaac Vaillant

Having sailed from Spithead on 25 January with an eastbound convoy, the weather worsened soon after departure, with the wind shifting round to the south-east and strengthening. In the early hours of the morning, land was discovered to be close ahead and she attempted to tack but missed stays. She then successfully wore ship but found herself close to the shore, so she wore round again and then attempted to anchor. Before the anchor could take hold, she struck the ground with seas breaking over her. The cable was then cut to allow her to drive further into the bay and hopefully deeper water, but again ran aground and started beating heavily. At first light, with the ship beginning to go to pieces, the crew abandoned the wreck, the ship having come ashore in Crookmere Haven, near Seaford. The ship's Master, John Chandler, was subsequently dismissed the service and sentenced to serve six months in the Marshalsea Prison for his 'ignorance and negligence'. Captain Vaillant was reprimanded for the mismanagement and confusion on board, and his actions were considered to be 'highly reprehensible'.
[TNA:ADM.1/5317]

26 January RACEHORSE Schooner
Purchased 1779 (*Liberty*); 111 tons; 68ft x 20.6ft; 10 guns
Lieutenant George Brissac

One of the escorts to an eastward-bound convoy that sailed from Spithead on 25 January, she followed the movements of the *Siren*, the senior officer (see above). That night the wind shifted and increased in strength until it was blowing a full easterly gale. At about 1 o'clock in the morning she discovered herself to be close to land and immediately tacked. Despite this prompt action, she was unable to clear the land and anchored. The wind was increasing, and she found herself in a precarious position, with the sea regularly breaking over her. The guns were heaved overboard in efforts to lighten her, but at 3 o'clock the anchor cable parted, and she was driven across the bay. Within five minutes she had gone ashore on the Sussex coast between Seaford and Beachy Head. The masts were cut away and boats hoisted out, but at first light her situation was clearly past assistance and the crew abandoned her as a wreck.
[TNA:ADM.1/5317]

January THUNDER Bomb
Rotherhithe 1779; 305 tons; 92ft x 27.9ft; 8 guns
Master and Commander John Wallace†

Sailed from Spithead on 6 January on a cruise, but not seen again. She was presumed to have foundered in the poor weather which affected the English Channel in late January/early February, with the loss of all hands. The pay book was closed at the end of January.
[TNA:ADM 34/769; www.britishnewspaperarchive.co.uk: Hampshire Chronicle 8 January 1781 p3]

11 February NIMBLE Cutter
Purchased 1778; 183 tons; 72.7ft x 22.2ft; 12 guns
Lieutenant William Furnival

The cutter sailed from St Helens on 5 February bound for Plymouth, but the weather steadily worsened and by 11 February it was blowing a gale with frequent squalls of rain. The land was obscured, and the cutter was regularly shipping water. At about 4 o'clock in the afternoon land was discovered ahead and they found themselves embayed in Mount's Bay. An attempt was made to stand out to sea, but the wind was now so strong that the mainsail was split, and it was clear that she could not weather the headland. Guns were heaved overboard, and she anchored. At 10pm the cable parted. Another attempt was then made to make sail but baffled by the strong winds she made little headway and then struck the Tremayne Rock, which effectively bilged her, and she foundered. Twenty-eight men were lost.
[TNA:ADM.1/5317]

13 February ECHO Brig Sloop
Prize 1780 (*Hussard*); 271 tons; 84.7ft x 28.2ft; 18 guns
Master and Commander John Manley

Ordered to sail from Plymouth to Spithead, she was very short-handed, and Captain Manley left the sloop to call on the port Admiral to request further hands. That evening the weather deteriorated and the Master, Peter Peterson, as the senior officer on board, decided to leave the anchorage in the Sound and head inshore for the shelter of the Cattewater. One anchor was weighed, and the cable was cut for the other, and under reefed mainsail and foresail and main staysail she stood towards the harbour. As she was abreast the Bear's Head at the entrance to the Cattewater, she was taken aback and drove down onto an anchored privateer. With difficulty, she cleared herself, but was now close to the shore. The sloop anchored and cut away the foremast, but she struck the rocks nearby. The mainmast was then cut away and pumping commenced but the water gained rapidly, and she was abandoned as a wreck.
[TNA:ADM.1/5317]

19 February ROMULUS Fifth Rate
Buckler's Hard 1776; 885 tons; 140ft x 37.11ft; 44 guns
Captain George Gayton

Ordered to the Chesapeake from Charleston, South Carolina, when the ship approached Cape Henry, several vessels could be seen to be at anchor which they presumed to be British as Captain Gayton had no knowledge of any French vessels on the coast. As the

Romulus neared the anchorage, the ships were observed to weigh, which raised Captain Gayton's suspicions and when the private recognition signals were not answered, he made all sail away and cleared for action. The enemy ships could be seen to be a ship of the line, two frigates and a cutter and they steadily overhauled the *Romulus*. The engagement commenced with some ineffective fire from the pursuers' bow-chase guns. The frigates were the first up, the *Gentille*, 40 guns, and *Surveillante*, 32, taking station on her starboard beam and port quarter, respectively. No shots were exchanged but when the *Éveillé*, 64, came within gunshot, the British ship had little choice but to surrender.
[TNA: ADM.1/5321]

15 March EARL OF INCHIQUIN Brig Tender
Hired 1776; 130 tons; 6 guns
Lieutenant William Robertson

When in the English Channel, she was chased by a French privateer, the *Duc de Chartres*, 24 guns, with two more privateers, the *Bougainville*, 24, and *Tartare*, 12, joining in the pursuit. Unable to outrun them, the tender surrendered when overhauled.
[TNA: ADM.1/5318]

26 March PORT ROYAL Ship Sloop
Prize 1778 (*Comte de Maurepas*); 463 tons; 18 guns
Master and Commander Timothy Kelly

On 9 March, a large Spanish force started landing near the British outpost at Pensacola, West Florida, to lay siege to the fort, the *Port Royal* being one of the two British naval vessels in the harbour. On 19 March Commander Kelly was ordered to land his guns and men to assist with the defence of the fort, and preparations were made to destroy the sloop if necessary. This latter course of action was not carried out, and instead several Spanish prisoners were placed on board the sloop '… to secure them from the fury of the Indians'. On the night of 26 March several Spanish launches ran alongside the sloop as it lay at anchor and captured her without resistance.
[TNA: ADM.1/5319]

4 April SAINT FERMIN Brig Sloop
Prize 1780; 250 tons; 90ft × 25.6ft; 16 guns
Master and Commander Jonathan Faulknor

The sloop sailed from Gibraltar for Minorca with dispatches on 3 April and that night, at about 11 o'clock, some vessels could be seen approaching. The sloop made all sail away, but the bright moonlight showed the pursuers to be two xebecs, which slowly overhauled her. At 3 o'clock in the morning the moon set and the sloop, now running at over 9 knots, hoped to escape, but the chasing ships kept up and occasionally used bow-chase guns to annoy the *St Fermin*, which replied with stern guns. Just before first light both xebecs were in gunshot range of the sloop and stationed themselves on either quarter. One yawed to fire a broadside into the brig. Overpowered and unable to escape, the *St Fermin* surrendered.
[TNA: ADM.1/5320]

14 April MENTOR Ship Sloop
Purchased 1780 (*Who's Afraid*); 220 tons; 24 guns
Captain Robert Deane

At Pensacola, West Florida, when a large Spanish force arrived in March 1781 to lay siege to the colony (see *Port Royal* above), she found herself trapped and unable to escape. Captain Deane decided to strip the ship of guns and stores and send the men ashore to bolster the garrison. This work was complete by 20 March, and the ship, with a skeleton crew left on board, was taken further inshore up the Middle River into shallow water where she grounded and on 26 March capsized. On 14 April when Spanish forces approached, the small number of men left on board set her on fire.
[TNA: ADM.1/5322]

16 April INFERNAL Fireship
Purchased 1778; 307 tons; 97.6ft × 26.11ft; 8 guns
Master and Commander Henry Darby

A small British squadron was formed under the command of Commodore George Johnstone and sailed for the Dutch colony at the Cape of Good Hope, intending to attack the settlement. As they approached the Cape Verde Islands, ships were detached to find the best place for wood and water, the *Infernal* being one of those detached to the island of Maio. The bulk of the squadron, with transports and tenders, entered and anchored in Port Praya (or Praia), Santiago Island. The *Infernal* and *Terror* bomb re-joined the little fleet later that day. Commodore Johnstone had issued orders for these smaller vessels to anchor inside the large ships, but these instructions appear never to have been received, and they anchored to the east of the larger ships. All the ships busied themselves in storing, the *Infernal* assisting the *Terror* bomb in re-rigging a damaged bowsprit. To everyone's great surprise, at about 9.30am several warships appeared off the anchorage. The *Infernal* signalled their approach to the rest of the fleet, which led to considerable confusion as crews hastily prepared for both unmooring and action, whilst shore parties attempted to re-embark. Fortunately for Johnstone the approaching French squadron under Suffren was equally surprised to see the British and although they seized the opportunity to attack, several ships were not fully ready for action. The result was a confused engagement with some of the French ships entering the Bay in an unprepared state and some not taking any real part in the fight. After an hour's fighting, the French quitted the bay having suffered badly and taken only an Indiaman and

one small victualing tender. Both the *Terror* and *Infernal* had been fired at by a French 64-gun ship, with the bomb vessel catching fire. Both vessels then cut cables and made ground out to sea, the French firing into the bomb which refused to surrender. Despite losing her bowsprit and foremast, she managed to extinguish the fire and escape. The French now concentrated on the *Infernal*, which did not have as much luck as the *Terror*. Surrounded by the French ships leaving the anchorage, she surrendered. Captain Darby, five seamen and nine soldiers of the 98th Regiment were taken out of her as prisoners. The French did not stay in command for long. The British squadron weighed from the bay and pursued the French; they overhauled the *Infernal* that same evening and recaptured her.
[TNA: ADM. 1/5319]

17 April GEORGE and MOLLY Cutter Tender
Hired 1776; 8 guns
Lieutenant Richard Saunders

Bound for Plymouth from the Isle of Wight she was about four miles south of Portland Bill when a cutter was seen at first light, approaching under British colours. She closed rapidly and when alongside, hailed the tender, calling on her to surrender. With only fifteen men and boys on board, she struck her flag. Her captor was the privateer *Victoire*, 16 guns, of Dunkirk. The owner of the cutter, Mr George Field, was on board and he pleaded with the French to ransom the vessel, rather than take it to France, offering £1,000, but his pleas were ignored.
[TNA: ADM. 1/5319]

18 April GIBRALTAR Armed Brig
Purchased 1779; 85 tons; 63ft x 21ft; 12 guns
Lieutenant William Anderson

Having sailed from Gibraltar with despatches for Minorca, the brig was about 36 miles to the south-south-west of Cape Gata when two xebecs were sighted. She made all sail away with the pair in chase. After four hours chase, one of the pursuers had gained considerably on the sloop and when in pistol-shot opened fire, which was returned by *Gibraltar*, but then the Spaniard dropped under the lee quarter of the sloop and successfully raked her. Unable to escape she surrendered, her captor proving to be the *Murciano*, 34 guns.
[TNA: ADM. 1/5322]

11 May THETIS Fifth Rate
Buckler's Hard 1773; 686 tons; 126.1ft x 35.2ft; 32 guns
Captain Robert Linzee

A large French force under the Marquis de Bouillé, supported by a naval contingent under the Comte de Grasse, attacked the island of St Lucia on 10 May, landing at three places. Captain Linzee arrived at the island by coincidence and placed his four ships at the disposal of the Governor, General St Leger, who requested that the ships be moved in the Carenage to defend the main port of the island. That afternoon as the ships entered the bay, being guided by an experienced local pilot, a gust of wind carried *Thetis* onto a submerged rock. She passed over the obstruction and continued on her way, but on sounding the well, she was found to be making water quite rapidly. A sail was spread under the hull and divers were sent down to locate the damage. They reported that a section of the keel had disappeared and there was a series of holes in the hull into which they could thrust their arms. Oakum was stuffed into the holes but with little effect, and by the following morning the water was gaining, and the enemy could be seen on the heights around the bay. It was therefore decided to run her ashore and land all the men and stores to assist the garrison. She was placed on the shore near the wreck of the *Cornwall* where she filled and sank. Efforts were made to keep her upright by the use of shores and she settled on an even keel, which enabled much of the stores to be saved. No blame was placed on the pilot or Captain Linzee, who had acted under pressure from the Governor and with great zeal to get into action.
[TNA: ADM. 1/5318]

11 May ANTIGUA Brig Sloop
Prize 1777 (*Putnam*); 100 tons; 10 guns
Master and Commander John Hutt

The sloop was lying at anchor at Port Dauphin, on the east coast of St Lucia, when the French invasion force arrived (see above), and two French frigates accompanied by two cutters stationed themselves off the port, whilst large numbers of troops were seen to be landed. The sloop prepared herself for action by placing springs on her cable, to allow herself to warp into position to defend herself. The following morning the troops were seen to be lining the banks of the creek and field pieces had been positioned to cover the sloop. These commenced firing into her and unable to engage them all, she surrendered. The French burned their prize after taking possession.
[TNA: ADM. 1/5319]

28 May ATALANTA Ship Sloop
Sheerness 1775; 300 tons; 96.7ft x 26.9ft; 14 guns
Master and Commander Sampson Edwards

On 27 May the *Atalanta* was cruising to the south-east of Nova Scotia in company with the sloop *Trepassy*, when a sail was seen, and the two sloops stood towards the stranger. By nightfall they were close enough to make her out to be a large vessel, probably a frigate. Private signals were made but not answered, which led them to believe she was an enemy. The following morning the wind had fallen away and the three were still together. The strange frigate came about and stood towards the two sloops until she was about half a mile to leeward, when she hoisted American colours and fired a broadside. The sloops returned the fire and then fell back to take up positions close alongside the enemy's stern, with the *Atalanta* on the starboard quarter, being hailed as she did so to 'strike to the American frigate *Allliance*'. The action continued for two hours, with the American being unable to reply as her guns would not bear. When the wind picked up the *Alliance* could shake herself free of the sloops and manoeuvre to bring her main armament to bear. The *Trepassy* was then disabled by the devastating broadsides and fell away. The American's fire was highly effective and crippled the *Atalanta*, shooting away the main yard, crossjack yard and jib boom. After three hours' action, with six killed and eighteen wounded she surrendered.

Note: recaptured on 7 June by the *Vulture* and *Charlestown*.
[TNA: ADM.1/5319]

28 May **TREPASSEY** Brig Sloop
Prize 1779 (*Wildcat*); 342 tons; 95ft × 26ft; 14 guns
Master and Commander James Smyth†

Consort to the *Atalanta* (see above) when the large American frigate was sighted on 27 May. When the sloops attacked in light airs, the *Trepassey* attempted to take station on the larboard quarter of the enemy. She initially overshot, going alongside the *Alliance* and allowing the enemy to fire two broadsides into the sloop. This was said to have shattered the brig, but despite this she continued the fight. After about an hour the Captain was killed, and Lieutenant James King assumed command. When the *Alliance* was able to gain steerage way and fire into the *Trepassey* effectively, she was disabled and with six killed and eleven wounded, she surrendered. After being taken over by the *Alliance*, she was disarmed by her captors and sent to Halifax with the prisoners as a cartel vessel.

Note: recaptured in October 1782 as the *Defence* by the *Jason*.
[TNA: ADM.1/5319]

30 May **CRESCENT** Sixth Rate
Bristol 1779; 611 tons; 120.8ft × 34ft; 28 guns
Captain Hon. Thomas Pakenham

In company with the *Flora*, 36 guns, the pair had successfully escorted a small convoy to Minorca, and arrived off Gibraltar on 29 May, closing the Rock to advise them of the presence of a large Spanish squadron that they had encountered the day before. That complete, they stood over to the African side of the straits, having observed two ships off Ceuta. They closed and discovered them to be large Dutch frigates, the *Castor*, 36 guns, and *Den Briel*, 36. With strong winds gusting to gale force through the straits, the British pair stood away until the wind abated. The next morning, having kept the Dutch pair in sight all night, they closed. The action began with the *Crescent* passing the *Castor*, exchanging broadsides and having her fore topsail yard shot away. She then ranged along the starboard side of *Briel* to engage her. As she did so the *Castor* moved under her quarter and successfully raked the British frigate. The *Flora* now entered the action by passing in between her consort and the *Castor* to engage the latter. The *Crescent* shot ahead of the action and fired a raking broadside into the Dutch ship but was forced to throw her sails aback, to prevent the *Briel* from running his bowsprit through the shrouds. Now alongside each other, the mutual cannonade went on for two hours, when the mainmast and mizzen of the *Crescent* were shot away, the wreckage falling over the engaged side, encumbering the guns and preventing her from firing. To make matters worse, a shot had lodged in the rudder, effectively jamming it. Unable to manoeuvre or return fire, she was helpless as the Dutch frigate fell back onto her quarter and fired several raking broadsides into her. With nine guns dismounted, and most of the others masked by wreckage and very heavy casualties – twenty-six killed and sixty-seven wounded – Captain Pakenham surrendered. The Dutch, however, were not able to take possession of their prize as the *Flora* had forced the *Castor* to surrender a short time before, and now steered towards the victorious *Den Briel*. Unable to face a fresh opponent, the Dutch were forced to abandon their prize.
[TNA: ADM.1/5318; Beatson vol V pp387–92]

4 June **FLY** Cutter
Purchased 1778; 8 guns
Master and Commander Milham Ponsonby

On 27 May Admiral Rodney received intelligence that a large French force had arrived off Tobago and had commenced landing troops. On receiving further information that the French had gained possession of the island, Rodney sailed from his anchorage off Barbados and shaped course for Tobago. As the fleet approached, the Admiral sent out two schooners and the *Fly* cutter to scout ahead, being directed to different bays with the task of both locating the main French fleet and identifying places where British troops could be landed. As the *Fly* closed the island, at 4 o'clock in the afternoon of 3 June, a large ship came into sight, which bore up for the cutter. A long pursuit developed, continuing all night. it was not until 11 o'clock in the morning, after a chase of 60 miles, that the French *Glorieux*, 74 guns, came within gunshot. Several shots were fired by the French ship, most of which went over

the *Fly*, until she was alongside, at which the cutter fired a single token broadside and then surrendered.
[TNA:ADM.1/5319; London Gazette 31 July 1781]

5 June SHELANAGIG Schooner
Purchased 1781; 16 guns
Master and Commander James Keith Shephard
One of the vessels despatched by Admiral Rodney to gain intelligence of the French at Tobago (see *Fly* above). She sighted the main French fleet at 6 o'clock in the morning and was chased and despite carrying all the canvas she could, she was overhauled and captured.
[TNA:ADM.1/5319]

7 June MOLLY Armed Ship
Hired 1780; 18 guns
Master and Commander Walter Long†
Having escorted a large troop convoy across the North Sea to the River Weser, she was detached on 25 May to return to her station at Liverpool. During the afternoon, when about five leagues (15 miles) to the south-east of the Calf of Man, a fire broke out, apparently in the bread room. Thick black smoke spread through the ship, making it difficult to fight the fire. The boats were hoisted out in readiness to abandon ship, but when flames burst up through the main hatchway, several of the crew panicked and jumped into the boats. Within 30 minutes of the alarm being raised, the ship was full of smoke and flames and the remaining crew jumped overboard. Two passing merchant brigs, the *Isabella* and *Juno,* picked up most and one boat with survivors landed at Whitehaven, but Captain Long was not amongst the survivors.
[TNA:ADM.1/5321]

13 June SNAKE Brig Sloop
Purchased 1776; 287 tons; 12 guns
Master and Commander William Jackson
Bound for England from the West Indies, when she was in latitude 50 North, she met a homeward-bound convoy, whose escort warned her of the presence of two strange ships which had been seen near the convoy. She continued independently when, that same afternoon, two ships suddenly emerged from a bank of thick drifting fog. She immediately made all sail away, with the pair in pursuit. One of them, the Massachusetts privateer *Pilgrim*, 20 guns, was within gunshot very quickly and commenced the action with a broadside of double-headed and grapeshot. When the second privateer, the *Rambler*, 14 guns, took up station on the sloop's larboard quarter, Commander Jackson surrendered.
[TNA:ADM.1/5318]

19 June CASTOR Fifth Rate
Prize 1781; 36 guns
Following the action of 30 May (see above), the Dutch prize was manned by seamen from the *Crescent* and *Flora* and proceeded towards England in company with her captors. During the morning of 19 June, when to the south-west of Ushant, two large ships were seen closing through rain squalls. Each of the British ships shaped different courses, but the *Castor* was quickly overhauled by the *Friponne*, 32 guns. She was in no condition to resist and had only thirty-six British seamen on board. A single shot was fired by the *Friponne* at which she surrendered.
[Beatson vol V pp391–2]

20 June CRESCENT Sixth Rate
Bristol 1779; 611 tons; 120.8ft × 34ft; 28 guns
Lieutenant John Bligh
In company with the *Flora* and *Castor* prize when closed by the large French frigates off Ushant (see *Castor* above). The ships were in no state to resist them, the *Crescent* now having a jury-rigged mainmast and mizzen, with only five men available for each gun. Captain Pakenham had given up the command to the First Lieutenant of the *Flora* until his conduct in the action of 30 May could be investigated. All three ships steered separate courses in an effort to escape. The French initially concentrated on taking the *Castor*, after which they chased the *Crescent*. At about 4 o'clock in the morning the *Friponne* and *Gloire* overhauled the British frigate and after an exchange of shot she surrendered.
[TNA:ADM.1/5318]

20 June PHEASANT Cutter
Purchased 1778; 149 tons; 65.8ft × 24.3ft; 10 guns
Lieutenant George Matthews†
The cutter was on her way to England from Guernsey with despatches, when a violent storm broke, with heavy rain, thunder and lightning. At about 1 o'clock in the morning the cutter was struck by a squall which the Master, Donald Trail, later described as 'a sort of whirlwind', which rolled her over onto her beam-ends and she filled with water and sank in two minutes. Only the Master, the Pilot John Bragg and two boys survived, being picked up after several hours in the water.
[TNA:ADM.1/5318]

1 August DISPATCH Armed Brig
Purchased 1780 (*Independence*); 8 guns
Lieutenant John Scott
Sailed from New York in company with the *Swallow* sloop on a cruise, but the pair became separated in thick weather. She was chased and overhauled by the American privateers, *Marquise de Lafayette*, 16 guns, and

Hunter, 18, and faced with two superior opponents, she was forced to surrender.
[TNA: ADM.1/5321; Middlebrook vol 2 p150]

2 August PELICAN Sixth Rate
Deptford 1777; 520 tons; 114.5ft × 32.2ft; 24 guns
Captain Cuthbert Collingwood

Having escorted a packet vessel from Jamaica through the Windward Passage, she was returning to Port Royal when the weather worsened, with heavy rain and strong winds which obscured the landmarks and prevented any noon sights being taken. By reckoning, Collingwood believed himself to be about 30 miles from the nearest land. It was an unpleasant surprise therefore, when at 4 o'clock in the morning, breakers were seen ahead. An attempt to wear ship was made, but before this could be completed, she struck the ground. The masts were cut away as she swung broadside-on to a reef with the ship beating heavily on the rocks. At daylight, it was discovered they were ashore on a reef about a quarter of a mile to the east of Morant Keys, to the south-east of Jamaica. Unable to free the ship, the crew abandoned her as a wreck, taking to boats and rafts. Four men were lost. The court martial concluded that an uncertain current had set them off course.
[TNA: ADM.1/5318]

16 August GREYHOUND Sixth Rate
Buckler's Hard 1773; 618 tons; 124.2ft × 33.7ft; 28 guns
Captain William Fox

Standing into the Downs to anchor, she was under reefed topsails with a fresh breeze in hazy weather, when quite unexpectedly she struck the ground. Sails were loosed to try and force her over the obstruction, but this failed. The small bower anchor was then let go, but the cable parted, and the best bower was then released. There was a large swell running and she commenced beating on the sand with increasing violence, unshipping the rudder, breaking the tiller and opening seams. Within two hours the water was gaining fast on the pumps and Captain Fox ordered most of the crew to go ashore, being assisted by boats from Deal. At 1 o'clock in the morning, at low water, she capsized and was then abandoned by the small crew remaining. It was found that she had run aground on the South Sand Head, due to the carelessness of the embarked pilots, Richard Lad Canny and William Hornsby, who were found guilty of not taking proper precautions in the hazy weather, having carried on despite having the landmarks obscured. However, as both were of previous good character, they were treated leniently, being sentenced to three months in the Marshalsea Prison.
[TNA: ADM.1/5318]

16 August SWALLOW Brig Sloop
Purchased 1779; 226 tons; 79.5ft × 26.7ft; 14 guns
Master and Commander Thomas Wells

Having arrived at New York from the West Indies on 27 July with letters from Admiral Rodney for Admiral Graves, but finding that he had sailed, she was ordered to proceed to Boston to search for him. She was diverted from her mission on 12 August when she chased and captured the American brig *Venus*, and the pair was off Long Island, still in company, when at first light a number of ships which appeared to be a squadron of American privateers appeared. Clearly outnumbered she made sail away, but was forced further inshore, and Wells eventually ran the ship, along with the prize, ashore on Fire Island, and was later burned. Her pursuers had been the privateers *Hancock*, 18 guns, *Sampson*, 18, *Randolph*, 16 and *Young Cromwell*, 10.
[TNA: ADM.1/5321; Chadwick: Graves Papers p25]

16 August HOPE Cutter
Purchased 1780; 156 tons; 67.9ft × 24.8ft; 12 guns
Lieutenant Lewis Vickers

When news that a French privateer was active off Waterford, the senior officer on station, Captain Cooper of the *Stag*, despatched the *Hope* cutter under the temporary command of his Second Lieutenant, as her commanding officer Lieutenant Rochfort was detained ashore on duty. The cutter sailed from Dublin on 12 August, and she initially cruised along the Wicklow coast, and then stood over towards the Welsh shore and off Holyhead again heard of the privateer. At first light the next morning, then being off Bardsey Island, a large cutter was seen attacking a packet vessel and the *Hope* bore up in chase. She soon overhauled her and hailed to find the identity of the stranger. No response was made and a shot to bring her to was answered by a broadside. A fierce action now commenced between the pair for about 30 minutes, until the *Hope*'s jib was shot away, and she fell aboard the privateer and the French attempted to board, but they were driven back after hand-to-hand fighting. The fighting continued for another 30 minutes or so, but the privateer used small-arms fire to reduce the upper-deck crew, Lieutenant Vickers being shot and severely wounded by a musket ball in the thigh, until only twelve men remained on deck. At this the *Hope* struck her flag. However, despite calls to cease fire, she kept firing into the British cutter until a French-speaking seaman hailed them to say they had surrendered. The victorious privateer proved to be the *Chardon*, 20 guns, from Dunkirk, commanded by an Irishman named Kelly. The crew of the *Hope* were badly treated by their captors, the surgeon being threatened with a pike as he treated the wounded and all prisoners being put in irons. It was claimed that many were Irish or Scots, and one was recognised as being a former midshipman in the Royal Navy and another as a former crew member of the *Serapis*. Lieutenant Vickers never recovered from his injuries and died later that year.

Note: retaken on 21 August by the *Stag*.
[TNA: ADM.1/5319]

21 August MINORCA Xebec
Port Mahon 1779; 388 tons; 96.9ft × 30.6ft; 20 guns
Commander Hugh Lawson

On 18 August, a large Franco-Spanish invasion force arrived off the British base at Port Mahon, Minorca, to commence a protracted siege. The *Minorca* was moved into the inner harbour under the guns of Fort St Philip on their arrival and when it became clear that she could not escape, the stores, guns and provisions were landed ashore, and she was scuttled at the entrance to the harbour.
[TNA: ADM.1/5321; Beatson vol 5 p360]

24 August SANDWICH Armed Ship
Purchased 1780 (*Margery*); 20 guns
Captain William Bett

Proceeding to Charleston independently she was off the South Carolina coast when she encountered the French fleet under de Grasse. She made sail away, but was chased and overhauled by the *Souverain*, 74 guns, which forced her to surrender without offering resistance.
[TNA: ADM.1/5319]

24 August CORMORANT Ship Sloop
Ipswich 1776; 304 tons; 96.8ft × 27ft; 16 guns
Master and Commander Robert McEvoy

The sloop sailed from Charleston on 20 August to escort the *Queen Charlotte* packet ship clear of the coast, and she was returning to port when at first light a sail was seen. Within a short time more ships became visible, and it became clear that the sloop was in contact with a fleet. Rightly guessing that it the French, she made all sail away, pursued by two ships of the line. After a three-hour chase the *Citoyen*, 74 guns, was within range and fired a single shot to bring her to. The sloop ignored this and pressed on until the 74 fired all her upper-deck guns at her. Clearly overpowered and with a second French ship, the *Glorieux*, 74, coming up fast, she surrendered. The packet vessel, with Francis, Lord Rawdon on board, was also captured.
[TNA: ADM.1/5319]

26 August ROVER Ship Sloop
Prize 1781; 276 tons; 98ft × 24ft; 20 guns
Lieutenant James Duncan

Weighed from Sandy Hook, New Jersey, on 20 August, to cruise to the southward, and apart from encountering a Loyalist privateer, the voyage was uneventful. The morning of 26 August found them about four leagues (12 miles) to the south of Sandy Hook, with the wind dropping to a light breeze. During the evening, they approached the coast and when soundings showed they were in eight fathoms, they tacked, but the ship missed stays. The strong current was setting them further inshore, directly into Shrewsbury Inlet and she grounded. Sails were furled and the boats were hoisted out to lay out kedge anchors, but efforts to haul her free failed, the ebb tide being very strong. Yards and topmasts were struck and during the night some ballast was cleared from the hold and thrown overboard and the after guns were shifted forward. At first light the *Medea* arrived and sent boats to her assistance, but all efforts to kedge her free failed. The masts were cut away and more stores thrown overboard but she would not move. Water was reported entering the hold and by early afternoon it was clear that the pumps could not cope. It was decided to abandon her, and after moving what stores they could salvage, the ship was set on fire to prevent her from falling into enemy hands. The extraordinary set of the current was blamed for the wreck.
[TNA: ADM.1/5321; ADM.52/1973]

30 August LOYALIST Ship Sloop
Purchased 1779 (*Restoration, Oliver Cromwell*); 319 tons; 99ft × 27ft; 14 guns
Master and Commander Richard Williams

On 30 August, the French fleet under the command of the Comte de Grasse entered Chesapeake Bay, where they found two British warships, *Guadeloupe*, 28 guns, and the *Loyalist* lying at anchor off Cape Henry. As the French approached, the British ships weighed and made all sail away, but although the *Guadeloupe* escaped, the *Loyalist* was chased by two large ships and was overhauled by the frigate *Aigrette*, 28, with the *Glorieux*, 74, in sight, and the sloop was forced to surrender.
[TNA: ADM.1/5319]

6 September SAVAGE Ship Sloop
Ipswich 1778; 302 tons; 96.7ft × 26.10ft; 14 guns
Master and Commander Charles Stirling

During the morning, whilst escorting a merchant ship, and then being about 10 leagues (30 miles) to the east of Charleston, South Carolina, a ship was sighted bearing down on her, which then hauled her wind to the east. Suspecting that it was an American privateer, Commander Stirling prepared to give chase, but the stranger edged down towards her. At 10.30am, the ship, which was the American privateer, *Congress*, 24 guns, opened fire with bow-chase guns and 30 minutes later she was within gunshot range and fired a broadside and a volley of musketry. After an hour's action the American fell away, raising the hopes of the sloop of escaping from her larger opponent, but with a battered hull and disabled rigging she could not get away. After apparently effecting repairs to her rigging, the *Congress* came back into the action, which continued for another hour at close range before the sloop was forced to surrender, with the mizzen mast shot away and sails and rigging destroyed. Eight men killed and twenty-five wounded.

Note: retaken on 12 September by the *Solebay*, [TNA: ADM.1/5319; www.britishnewspaperarchive.co.uk: Kentish Gazette 22 December 1781 pp2–3; Beatson vol 5 p305]

11 September RICHMOND Fifth Rate
Deptford 1757; 664 tons; 127.1ft × 34.1ft; 32 guns
Captain Charles Hudson

The *Richmond* was ordered into Chesapeake Bay by Admiral Graves with despatches for Lord Cornwallis, and then, in company with the *Iris*, to lift the anchor buoys left by the French. On the morning of 10 September, she sighted the main French fleet, but stood away and easily outpaced the ships sent to chase her. Having worked to windward, she loitered that night to gather intelligence to take to Graves. The following morning several ships were again sighted, and the *Richmond* was uncertain whether this was the approaching British fleet or the French. Having made private signals which were not answered, she stood away, was again chased and again outpaced her pursuers. Her course however had taken her further inshore, and she was eventually forced to tack and steer along the shoreline. The wind shifted round to the east at this crucial moment, forcing her to perform several short boards close inshore. The French ships, closing on the wind, manoeuvred to cut off her lines of escape. Eventually Captain Hudson tried to run past the French ships with every sail set, but the French fired accurately into the rigging, cutting it up, the mainmast being shot through. Unable to escape, she surrendered to the *Bourgogne*, 74 guns.
[TNA: ADM.1/5319]

11 September IRIS Fifth Rate
Prize 1777 (*Hancock*); 763 tons; 136.7ft × 35.2ft; 32 guns
Captain George Dawson

In company with the *Richmond* (see above), she was ordered into Chesapeake Bay with orders to lift the anchor buoys left by the French and cut the cables from them. She was so employed when she was chased by a powerful squadron under de Barras, and when overhauled had little choice but to surrender.
[TNA: ADM.1/5319]

12 September TERRIBLE Third Rate
Harwich 1762; 1,645 tons; 168.8ft × 47.3ft; 74 guns
Captain Hon. William Finch

On 5 September, the British fleet under Rear Admiral Thomas Graves met the French fleet under the Comte de Grasse off Chesapeake Bay. The action was indecisive and most of the fighting was borne by the van, where the *Terrible* lay. The end of the action saw her with badly cut-up rigging, the foremast shot through and several shots in the hull. The *Terrible* had joined the fleet from the West Indies in a poor state of repair, with the pumps working constantly in her passage. The battle damage only worsened the effect, and it was with difficulty that she was kept afloat. By 10 September, the pumps were constantly going, but were unable to stem the influx of water. Several guns were thrown overboard to lighten her, but it was clear that she was sinking. At a meeting on 11 September, it was decided to abandon her. As much of the stores and provisions as could be saved were transferred to other ships, as were the men. This task continued until the evening of the following day, when at 8.30pm she was set on fire. She continued to burn until the early hours when she blew up.
[Chadwick: Graves Papers pp72, 76–81]

22/23 September VULCAN Fireship
Purchased 1777; 296 tons; 91.6ft × 27.9ft; 8 guns
Master and Commander George Palmer

Following the action between the French and British fleets off Chesapeake Bay, de Grasse led his fleet back into the Bay. Here they were able to commence an effective blockade, co-operating with the combined French and American armies then laying siege to Yorktown. In an effort to disrupt the blockade, the *Vulcan* led a fireship attack on the night of 22/23 September. Accompanied by four hastily converted merchant sloops and schooners, the force dropped down the York River into the Bay towards the blockading French vessels, the *Vulcan* being manned by only Captain Palmer, Lieutenant Dederick Charleson, the Gunner, Bosun and four seamen. The four small vessels were set on fire prematurely, alerting the French, but the *Vulcan* pressed on until she was within pistol-shot of the enemy and could hear the French shouting orders. Captain Palmer intended laying his vessel alongside a French ship, but several boats could be seen approaching, clearly intending to tow her out of harm's way. At this, Palmer ordered the crew into the boat and accompanied by Gunner Henry Lewis set light to the fuses and trains. They then left the burning ship, with the French in some confusion, with much shouting and occasional firing, some men jumping overboard and others cutting cables and hoisting out boats to tow ships out of the way. The fireship's crew successfully escaped into the night and although no ships were burnt, they had the satisfaction in the morning of seeing two of the enemy ships aground. Palmer was commended by the court martial held in June 1782 enquiring into the loss of the *Vulcan* for his highly meritorious and gallant conduct and was promoted to Captain six months later.
[TNA: ADM.1/5320]

22 September DUCHESS of CUMBERLAND Ship Sloop
Prize 1781 (*Congress*); 287 tons; 18 guns
Master and Commander Edward Marsh
The sloop sailed from Placentia, Newfoundland on 21 September to escort a convoy to St John's. She cleared harbour with a light breeze, but the wind then fell away to a calm which did not allow her to clear the land. The following morning saw banks of very thick fog, despite a stiff breeze, which obscured the land. Breakers were reported ahead, and the sloop successfully came about and hoisted more sail in an attempt to clear the hazard, but she suddenly struck a submerged reef, which stove in planks and knocked the rudder off. The masts were cut away, but she was found to be filling with water rapidly, so the crew abandoned ship, to discover that they had gone ashore at Cape St Mary's.
[TNA:ADM.1/5321]

September DELIGHT Ship Sloop
Limehouse 1778; 306 tons; 96.7ft × 27ft; 14 guns
Master and Commander Francis Thomas Drake†
Missing, presumed foundered in the Atlantic, en-route to America from England. She was last seen on 8 September on sailing from Spithead. Her pay book was closed on 31 September.
[TNA:ADM.1/80/9; ADM.34/259; www.britishnewspaperarchive.co.uk: Hampshire Chronicle 10 September 1781 p3]

7 October HOPE Ship Sloop
Prize 1781 (*Lady Washington*); 282 tons; 91.6ft × 26.6ft; 14 guns
Master and Commander William Thomas
Sailed on 4 October from Charleston, South Carolina for New York with despatches, but a leak soon became evident. By 6 October, despite the pumps going continuously the water seemed to be gaining and it was feared that a second leak had started. The guns were heaved overboard, and the larboard anchor cut away in efforts to lighten her. A sail was slung under the hull, which seemed to work, and the pumps gained on the water. A course was steered for the shoreline where she anchored. That night the wind and the swell increased, which shifted the sail slung under the hull and the leaks again started. Having pumped and bailed all night with no sign of gaining on the water, she was run ashore on Cabretta Island, Georgia to save her from sinking. Over the next two days the crew landed, taking off the stores and provisions, before she settled into the sand.
[TNA:ADM.1/5319]

10 October CHARON Fifth Rate
Harwich 1778; 892 tons; 140.3ft × 38ft; 44 guns
Captain William Symonds
Trapped at Yorktown, Virginia, by the besieging French and American armies and the French fleet under de Grasse, it was ordered that the guns, provisions and men should be landed to support the garrison ashore. On 10 October, the French opened a battery within range of the anchorage and commenced firing, which included some red-hot shot. At about 6 o'clock in the evening a heated ball struck the *Charon*, which one of the crew on board scooped up in a tin kettle and dropped into a water butt. Shortly after this a second shot struck her in the hull and entered the sail room, setting fire to the canvas. The small crew on board tackled the blaze and men were despatched from the shore to assist. Despite all their efforts, within 30 minutes the fire had taken firm hold and the men abandoned the ship to burn out.
[TNA:ADM.1/5319]

10 October GUADELOUPE Sixth Rate
Plymouth 1763; 586 tons; 118.4ft × 33.8ft; 28 guns
Captain Hugh Robinson
Another of the vessels trapped at Yorktown, unable to escape through the French and American forces, as with the other ships, the men, guns and stores were landed to support the army. When the anchorage came under fire from shore batteries, she was moved out of range and then deliberately scuttled and allowed to sink in the York River.
[TNA:ADM.1/5319]

11 October FIREBRAND Fireship
Purchased 1777 (*Porpoise*; *Annapolis*); 402 tons; 104ft × 29.7ft; 8 guns
Master and Commander Richard Hill
Lying at anchor in the Carrick Roads, Falmouth, the Captain was ashore, leaving the Master, Samuel Garner, as the senior officer on board, when during the morning smoke was seen coming from below. The Master ordered boats to be hoisted out and commenced fighting the fire which seemed to be in the galley, but thick black smoke spread through the ship which drove back the crew. Within an hour, the ship was full of smoke and abandoned. She blew up just before 5 o'clock and the wreck eventually drove ashore where it burnt out. The cause was believed to be due to loosened brickwork around the galley fireplace, which allowed the flames to come into contact with the surrounding woodwork.
[TNA:ADM.1/5319]

12 October RATTLESNAKE Cutter
Folkestone 1777; 184 tons; 69.4ft × 10.9ft; 14 guns
Master and Commander Philip d'Auvergne

The *Rattlesnake* and *Jupiter* were ordered by Commodore Johnstone to survey the island of Trinidade in the South Atlantic to ascertain whether the island would be suitable as a base for outward-bound Indiaman, and the pair arrived off the island on 5 October. The island was barren and landing difficult, but two days later they discovered a bay in the south-east of the island which allowed a landing. Over the next few days several domesticated animals brought by *Jupiter* were landed, and work started to plant crops. On 12 October, the wind increased and by 7 o'clock it was found that the cutter was dragging her anchors, and when, two hours later a cable parted, it was determined to sail out, and the main and foresail was set, which successfully put her head to the north. At this, the remaining anchor cable was cut, and the cutter wore round and tried to stand out to sea. Unexpectedly she found the ground to be shallowing quite rapidly and suddenly struck a submerged rock. She started filling with water and to preserve the lives of the crew, the cutter was run ashore in a sandy bay. The *Jupiter* managed to close the wreck site the next day and d'Auvergne indicated that he was willing to stay on the island with his men and try to establish it as a viable colony. The *Jupiter* left them on 1 November. Commander d'Auvergne stayed on the island for 12 months, until the *Bristol*, 50 guns, escort to a convoy of Indiaman, called on the island in late December 1782 and took them off.
[TNA: ADM.1/5322; ADM.51/482]

15 October FOWEY Sixth Rate
Lepe 1749; 513 tons; 113.2ft × 32.2ft; 24 guns
Captain Peter Aplin

One of the ships trapped in the York River, Chesapeake Bay, by the combined Franco-American armies. The siege of Yorktown had opened on 30 September, and the French fleet under de Grasse blockaded the bay. With no prospect of escape, all the guns, stores and men were landed ashore to support the army and the frigate was then taken upriver, scuttled and the remains set on fire.
[TNA: ADM.1/5319]

29 October ROVER Ship Sloop
Prize 1779 (*Cumberland*); 209 tons; 76.5ft × 22.8ft; 16 guns
Master and Commander Richard Hawford[†]

Stationed in the Leeward Islands, she was reported to have capsized and been lost when struck by a 'white squall'.
[Vesey-Hamilton & Laughton p8; Schomberg vol 5 p43]

14 November CONFLAGRATION Fireship
Purchased 1781 (*Loyal Club*); 343 tons; 8 guns
Lieutenant James Duncan

The fireship sailed from Sandy Hook on 19 October in company with the fleet under Admiral Graves for the Chesapeake, but parted company a few days later. She fell in with the frigate *Aeolus* off Cape Henry and the pair continued to cruise together. Throughout this time pumping was regularly required to clear water in the hold, and work was also required to overhaul the rigging, which was in a poor state. By 9 November she was making a good deal of water, requiring the pumps to be constantly manned, and the situation was not improved by the worsening weather. On 12 November, it was blowing hard, and the foremast went overboard, followed later that evening by the mainmast, which took the mizzen mast with it when it went over the side. The ship was labouring heavily, and the next day the struggle to clear the wreckage and water went on, but it became clear that it was impossible to keep her afloat. During 14 November, all the ship's company were removed to the *Aeolus*, and before Lieutenant Duncan left her, all the ports were opened, and she was set on fire. Her position then was 37.57N 69.30W.
[TNA: ADM.52/1668; ADM.1/5319]

19 November FAIRY QUEEN Schooner Tender
From 1781; 55 tons; 8 guns
Lieutenant Edward Crofton[†]

Cruising off the mouth of the Orinoco when, at daybreak, four vessels were sighted. It was presumed at first that they were Dutch coasters, but as they altered course towards the schooner suspicions were raised that they may be hostile. By 8.30am they were within range to fire a shot at the schooner, and they could now be seen to be Spanish privateer galleys. The *Fairy Queen* made all sail away, having first given them a broadside. Later that morning the wind dropped away, enabling the galleys to catch up and with only two fathoms of water under the keel, the schooner had little choice but to fight. She successfully held them at bay for over an hour, but could not sustain the fight, having almost run out of gunpowder. In addition, the bulwarks were very frail, and the recoil of the cannon had pulled them to pieces. The galleys positioned themselves around the schooner and unable to fight them all, Lieutenant Crofton struck the flag. After the surrender, the Spanish behaved in a horrifying manner, proceeding to murder their prisoners. When Crofton attempted to present his sword to his captor, his arm was hacked by a sword, almost severing it. He fell back under the main boom where the Spanish proceeded to slash at him with swords, badly cutting his head. He reeled backwards against the bulwark where he was stabbed and then pushed overboard. As a final indignity, his body was speared by

men on one of the galleys, dragged aboard, stripped of his clothing and then thrown back into the water. Seven other members of the crew were hacked and stabbed to death with a further seven wounded. The Gunner, Thomas Watson, had his right arm almost severed and jumped overboard, hanging on to a rope with his one good hand '… until they tired of the killing'.
[TNA: ADM.1/5319]

10 December BONETTA Ship Sloop
Blackwall 1779; 307 tons; 96.9ft × 27ft; 14 guns
Master and Commander Ralph Dundas
Stationed at Yorktown during the siege by the American and French forces, she was not scuttled with the other ships (see above). Under the conditions of the surrender on 19 October, it was agreed that the sloop would be handed over to the French, but she was first to be used a cartel, taking despatches and several American Loyalists to New York, after which she returned to Yorktown and was surrendered on 10 December.
Note: recaptured in January 1782 by the *Amphion*.
[TNA: ADM.1/5319]

27 December PIGMY Cutter
Dover 1781; 181 tons; 69.4ft × 25.7ft; 10 guns
Lieutenant Thomas Dyson
After the cutter sailed from Harwich on 18 December to escort a convoy through the English Channel, the weather deteriorated, becoming overcast and with banks of thick fog. Unable to obtain observations of sun or stars, she relied on dead reckoning, which was evidently upset by the strength of the current. Early in the morning she ran aground onto a sandbank off Dunkirk. Strenuous efforts were made to free her, but she could not get off and when boats from the shore closed, full of armed men, she was forced to surrender.
Note: retaken on 22 July 1782 by the *Crown*.
[TNA: ADM.1/5319]

December NECKAR Store Ship
Prize 1781; 150 tons; 22 guns
A French armed store ship, she was chased and captured on 26 October by the *Hannibal* off the Cape of Good Hope, when she was acting as an escort to a convoy from Lorient to Mauritius. The prize was taken to the shelter of the island of St Helena, where she was refitted and manned from the *Hannibal* and sent to India to both sell the cargo and boost the strength of the British squadron there. After sailing from St Helena, she was never seen again, and was presumed to have foundered in the South Atlantic.
[Various secondary]

1782

9 January BRITANNIA Armed Store Ship
Purchased 1780; 536 tons; 114.1ft × 32.8ft; 20 guns
Lieutenant Matthew Davis[†]
Sailed from the Nore anchorage on 2 January laden with stores bound for the East Indies, the weather was poor and was soon blowing a full gale. In the strong winds, she was seen by local packet vessels to run aground on the Kentish Knock Sands, her main and mizzen masts going overboard immediately after striking the sands. The seas were running so high that no assistance could be given at the time, but they brought the news of the disaster to Harwich on 10 January, and a fishing smack and the *Kite* cutter were despatched to the scene. They found only the pilot, boatswain and nine seamen were still alive to be saved. The wreck slowly broke up over the next few days, and local craft picked up a large amount of floating naval stores and timber over the next few weeks.
[TNA: ADM.1/5319; www.britishnewspaperarchive.co.uk: Bath Chronicle 17 January 1782 p3; Ipswich Journal 19 January 1782 p3, 9 March 1782 p2]

19 January HINCHINBROOKE Sixth Rate
Prize 1778 (*Astrée*); 557 tons; 115ft × 33.3ft; 28 guns
Master and Commander John Markham
Sailed on 18 January from Port Royal, Jamaica, the ship was in poor condition and during the day leaks became evident requiring the regular use of the pumps. The following day she decided to head inshore, but the wind fell away to a calm, forcing her to rely on the currents. She headed for St Ann's Harbour, Jamaica, but when close to the shore she failed answer the helm and ran aground on a reef to the east of the harbour. An attempt was made to force her over the rocks, but this failed. Kedging was next attempted, but the cables parted, continually snagging on the rocks. Eventually a schooner came alongside, the guns and stores were taken off and finally the crew before she sank that night.
[TNA: ADM.1/5319]

21 January HANNIBAL Fourth Rate
Buckler's Hard 1779; 1,054 tons; 146.3ft × 40.8ft; 50 guns
Captain Alexander Christie
Part of Commodore Johnson's squadron, which had engaged a French squadron under Suffren at Porto Praya in April 1781, whilst most of the squadron had returned to England, the *Hannibal* was sent on to the East Indies, to boost the British squadron. When in the Bay of Bengal, she again encountered Suffren's squadron. She successfully outran them but two days later at daybreak she again sighted them. A chase developed, which continued until noon, when two of the pursuing

French ships, the *Héros*, 74 guns, and *Artésien*, 64, were within range to open fire. The *Hannibal* returned the fire but being short-handed and with other ships and frigates closing, it was clear that the fight could not be sustained, and after a 15-minute exchange of fire, she surrendered.
[TNA:ADM.1/5324]

25 January SOLEBAY Sixth Rate
Newcastle 1763; 619 tons; 124ft × 33.8ft; 28 guns
Captain Charles Everitt

On 11 January, the French fleet under de Grasse appeared before the island of St Kitts and commenced landing troops. Rear Admiral Sir Samuel Hood sailed with a British force from Barbados on 14 January and after a brief stop at Antigua, arrived off the island 10 days later. The French sailed from their anchorage that evening in preparation to meet the British the next morning. At daybreak, the fleets were to the west of the island of Nevis, the British nearest to the land, the *Solebay* stationed with the rear division of the fleet to repeat signals. Hood determined to anchor his fleet in the bay just vacated by the French and for this the fleet ran close along the coast of the island. The *Solebay* as the repeating frigate was stationed clear of the line and was thus closer to the land than most. At just after noon, she ran hard aground on a reef off the south-west point of Nevis. Despite all efforts to free the frigate, she would not move and was abandoned as a wreck that evening, being set alight before being abandoned.
[TNA:ADM.1/5319]

29 January EXPEDITION Armed Schooner
From 1781; 8 guns
Lieutenant John Brand

Attempting to enter English Harbour, Antigua, at dusk, in light and fitful winds, she was struck by a sudden gust of wind which threw her sails aback. Already close to the rocks at the mouth of the harbour, she was taken by the wind and current onto a small reef. Efforts were made to warp her off, but all failed. The following morning it was clear that she could not be moved and was already beginning to break up, so the schooner was abandoned as a wreck, the stores and provisions being removed.
[TNA:ADM.1/5320]

3 February: The Capture of Demerara
The small British colony at Demerara, British Guiana, became the target for the French in late January 1782. Intelligence of an invasion force came with the sighting of the approaching ships by the patrolling sloop *Stormont* on the afternoon of 30 January. The following morning the French force of three ships, four brigs and a cutter, led by the Comte de Kersaint in the *Iphigénie*, 32 guns, arrived at the mouth of the River Essequibo. Troops were landed and advanced towards the settlement at Demerara, with the British forces abandoning batteries in their path. Commander Tahourdin, the senior naval officer, ordered his little force of converted merchantmen to cut their cables and retreat further upriver over a sandbank. The following day the French brigs and cutter advanced after the British and despite grounding, forced Tahourdin to take his vessels even further upriver. The British position was now very precarious; the small garrison was surrounded, with dwindling supplies and the ships were penned in amongst sandbanks by larger, more powerful ships. British and French officers met the following day to discuss terms of surrender were eventually agreed. On the morning of 3 February, the French brigs advanced towards the British ships, which, agreeable to the terms of surrender, discharged all their guns and small arms and then struck their flags in surrender.
[TNA:ADM.1/314; ADM.1/5320]

The following vessels were lost:

OROONOQUE Brig Sloop
Prize 1781 (*Oronoque*); 20 guns
Master and Commander William Tahourdin

BERBUDA Ship Sloop
Prize 1780 (*Charming Sally*?); 319 tons; 18 guns
Master and Commander Francis Pender

STORMONT Brig Sloop
Prize 1781 (*Pickering*); 226 tons; 80ft × 23.7ft; 14 guns
Master and Commander Christmas Paul

SYLPH Brig Sloop
Purchased 1780 (*Active*); 224 tons; 80.4ft × 2.5ft; 18 guns
Lieutenant Lawrence Graeme

RODNEY Armed Brig
Prize 1781; 14 guns
Lieutenant John Douglas Brisbane

HENRY Armed Schooner
Purchased 1781; 6 guns
Acting Lieutenant Benjamin Rothery

★ ★ ★

6 February JANE Sloop
Prize 1781 (*General Nash*); 140 tons; 16 guns
Lieutenant Jonathan Devall Burr

Ordered to cruise between Jamaica and St Kitts, the sloop rolled deeply in heavy seas and sprung the head of the mainmast. Then being off Hispaniola, she went into the lee of the Île à Vache to effect repairs. Whilst

so employed a ship was sighted approaching, at which the sloop weighed and made sail and attempted to outdistance the stranger. The large ship soon overhauled her, firing bow-chase guns as she did so. When within range, the sloop yawed and fired a broadside at her pursuer in an effort to damage the rigging. This dismounted two of her guns, as the trucks gave way, and another pulled the securing bolts from the sloop's side. The water was also constantly washing in through the ports, the guns having to be fired with the tompions in to prevent the charges being soaked. Clearly unable to offer effective resistance the sloop surrendered, finding her captor to be the American privateer *Tartar*, 24 guns. At the later court martial it emerged that the sloop had been fitted out locally in the West Indies and had been forced to use whatever stores were available; in particular, the guns and carriages were ancient and had previously been condemned.
[TNA: ADM.1/5320]

14 February ADMIRAL SPRY Tender
Hired 1776; 12 guns
Lieutenant Nicholas Hoare
Sailed from Mount's Bay with despatches and almost immediately encountered a merchant brig which informed them that a brig in sight nearby was a French Dunkirk privateer. The tender stood back towards Mount's Bay, but the wind was against her, so she altered course for the Scilly Isles. The privateer, now accompanied by two large cutters, followed and cut off her lines of escape. The brig, which was seen to be armed with 18 guns, soon overhauled her and stationed herself on the tender's port quarter, with one of the cutters coming up on the starboard. Unable to escape, the tender surrendered.
[TNA: ADM.1/5320]

14 February CHASER Ship Sloop
Prize 1781 (*Chasseur*); 320 tons; 99ft × 28ft; 14 guns
Master and Commander Thomas Parr
On a cruise between Point Palmyra and Point Gurdawar, India, when in latitude 14 North, a sail was sighted at daybreak. The sloop steered towards the ship, making private recognition signals. As they were not answered and the stranger, which could be seen to be a frigate, did not show any colours, the sloop rightly became suspicious and hauled her wind to make all sail away. The ensuing chase continued until 4 o'clock in the afternoon, by which time the pursuing frigate was within range and opened fire with bow-chase guns. The sloop yawed and returned the fire with a broadside, and then tacked away on a different course, setting studding sails. The French frigate slowly overhauled her again, and by 5pm she commenced firing at the *Chaser*, concentrating on the rigging and reducing it to tatters. Unable to escape and to save lives, Commander Parr surrendered, finding his captor to be the *Bellone*, 36 guns.
Note: retaken on 16 January 1783 by the *Medea*.
[TNA: ADM.1/5324]

27 February MANILLA Armed Transport
Purchased 1780; 406 tons; 87ft × 29.7ft; 10 guns
Lieutenant George Pigot Almes
Sailed from England in March 1781 for India, as part of the support for Admiral Hughes in the campaign against the French in that country, arriving in October. By early 1782 the campaign on the western coast was well underway, and the *Manilla* arrived in Madras Roads 9 February but foundered when a tropical storm struck the harbour
[TNA: ADM.34/823]

(17?) March REPULSE Cutter
Purchased 1779; 136 tons; 64.5ft × 22.9ft; 12 guns
Lieutenant John Atkinson†
Based at Harwich, she sailed from that port to cruise in the North Sea on 6 March but was not seen again. She was presumed to have foundered with all hands. The pay book was ordered to be made up to this date.
[TNA: ADM.180/4; ADM.34/669]

March HEYLING Hoy
Buckler's Hard 1760; 130 tons; 66.8ft × 21.8ft
Master John Lawford
Apparently foundered in the Channel, whilst on passage from Portsmouth to Plymouth, without loss of life; no details have been found but all references to her cease after March 1782.
[TNA: ADM.36/10247; Sigwart p54]

1 April SANTA MONICA Fifth Rate
Prize 1779; 956 tons; 145ft × 35.8ft; 36 guns
Captain John Linzee
Having spent the night anchored in company with three other warships off Peter Island, Virgin Islands, they weighed early in the morning and steered through the small islands off Tortola. At a little before 8 o'clock, then being about two miles to the south-west of Norman Island, she struck a submerged, uncharted rock with some force. After hanging on the rock for some minutes, she freed herself, but found that she was making water very rapidly. Pumping and bailing commenced, but it was clear that she was sinking. It was decided to run her ashore, and at just before 9 o'clock she was run aground in Coral Bay, St John's Island, where she sank in shallow water. The rigging, with sails, yards and guns were salvaged
[TNA: ADM.1/5320; Rodney: Letter Books vol 1 pp374–5]

8 April GENERAL MONK Ship Sloop
Prize 1780 (*General Washington*); 175 tons; 130.9ft × 32.8ft; 18 guns
Master and Commander Josias Rogers
In company with the *Quebec* frigate and a Loyalist American privateer, the *Fair American*, the trio stood into Delaware Bay to attack the American shipping lying there. The *Quebec* moved further up the Bay to cut off any retreat, whilst the privateer and sloop proceeded to attack the ships. They successfully drove ashore one ship and captured a brig, when the *Fair American* ran aground whilst attempting to close another vessel, leaving the *General Monk* on her own. The sloop then pursued another ship which was seen further in the Bay, which proved to be the privateer *Hyder Ally*, 18 guns. Initially she made way from the *Monk*, cutting her boat adrift to escape. The sloop closed, firing bow-chase guns, until the American suddenly put their helm up and came athwart the bows of the sloop, a move which she hastily followed to avoid being raked. A fierce action now commenced, which soon began to go in the American's favour. The British vessel was mostly armed with carronades, and it was found that most of her shot fell short. The long guns of the privateer were used to full effect, the sloop's rigging being reduced to tatters and suffering eight killed and twenty-nine wounded. Unable to resist effectively, with the *Fair American* ashore and the *Quebec* at the head of the Bay, she surrendered.
[TNA: ADM.1/490; Beatson vol 5 pp554–5]

11 April JACKAL Armed Schooner
Purchased 1782 (*Allonet*); 150 tons; 12 guns
Lieutenant Gustavus Logie
Sailed from Jamaica on 11 March bound for the Windward Islands with despatches, on 25 March she sprung her foremast and mainmast in poor weather. After fishing and securing the masts as best they could, she continued her course, although unable to bear topsails. During the morning of 11 April, when in latitude 13 North and approaching Barbados, a sail was discovered, evidently a large ship, which bore up in chase, the schooner making sail away. The chase went on until about 7.15 o'clock when the ship commenced firing bow-chase guns, the shot going over the schooner. By 8 o'clock the ship was close enough for Lieutenant Logie to see that she was an American frigate. Shortly after this she hailed the schooner and called on her to surrender. After destroying the signals and despatches, the *Jackal* surrendered to the American frigate *Deane*, 32 guns.
[TNA: ADM.1/5320; Rodney Letter Books vol 2 pp792–3]

10 May BLONDE Fifth Rate
Prize 1760; 704 tons; 133ft × 34.10ft; 32 guns
Captain Edward Thornborough
Cruising off the eastern coast of America to the north of Boston, she successfully captured an American ship laden with masts, and commenced towing the prize towards Halifax. The weather worsened, with thick fog, which prevented any observations for two days and this, coupled with the uncertain set of the currents, led to her running hard aground on an uncharted rock near Seal Island, Nova Scotia, to the west of Cape Sable. The prize was cut free and successfully bore away for Halifax. The pumps were manned but it was clear that she was filling with water rapidly, and the boats were hoisted out and rafts made and the men, including over sixty American prisoners, were slowly moved ashore to land on Seal Island safely, only one American being lost, before she sank. They remained on the island for two days, surviving by scavenging, until rescued by the American privateers *Scammel* and *Lively*, which landed the British crew members at Yarmouth, Nova Scotia. The shoal is now known as Blonde Rock (43.20N 65.59W).
[TNA: ADM.1/5320]

6 June RAIKES Armed Transport
Purchased 1780; 384 tons; 98.4ft × 29.9ft; 10 guns
Lieutenant Matthew Buckle
On passage from Madras to Trincomalee with stores for the British fleet, at first light two ships were sighted on the lee quarter, which soon altered course to close the transport. Private recognition signals were made, but not answered, although the pair showed British colours. By 8 o'clock they were on the beam of the *Raikes* which tacked away, steering for Tranquebar (Tharangambadi). Within an hour, the ships had overhauled the transport, hoisted French colours and fired a shot at her, at which she surrendered. The two proved to be the *Artésien*, 64 guns, and the *Sphinx*, 64.
[TNA: ADM.1/5324]

10 June RESOLUTION Armed Transport
Purchased 1771 (*Marquis of Granby*); 461 tons; 110.8ft × 30.5ft; 12 guns
Lieutenant Robert Hassard
Formerly used by Captain Cook as a discovery ship in the Pacific, the *Resolution* was employed as a stores and transport ship in the East Indies. Lieutenant Hassard became ill and on the voyage from Madras to Trincomalee, the ship loaded with gunpowder and stores for the fleet, he steadily worsened, and died during the evening of 9 June. At daybreak the next morning, when north-west of Negapatam (Nagapattinam), four ships were sighted, which bore up in chase. The *Resolution*, now under the command of the Master, William McQueen, made all sail away. She was soon overhauled,

but did not surrender until noon, after all the gunpowder and usable stores had been heaved overboard to prevent the French from using them. The ex-British *Annibal*, 50 guns, and *Sphinx*, 64, took possession.
[TNA: ADM.1/5324]

26 June ALLIGATOR Ship Sloop
Liverpool 1780; 304 tons; 96.8ft × 26.10ft; 14 guns
Master and Commander John Frodsham
Returning to England from Accra on the Guinea coast, Africa, she had an uneventful voyage until the morning of 26 June when approaching the Scilly Isles. As the early morning mist cleared, a ship could be seen close by, which hauled up in chase. The pursuit went on until mid-afternoon, when the sloop, which was foul after several months abroad, was overhauled by the ship, which could now be seen to be a French 32-gun frigate. At 3 o'clock, when within pistol-shot range, the frigate opened fire on the sloop, the fire being returned. The unequal action continued for over two hours, with the rigging of the sloop suffering considerably – all the royal masts were shot away as were the fore-topmast and mizzen topmast along with the lower yards and the main topsail yard. With one midshipman and two seamen killed, and with Commander Frodsham, the Captain of Marines and ten men wounded, she surrendered to the French frigate *la Fée*.
[TNA: ADM.1/5320]

31 July POLECAT Brig Sloop
Purchased 1782 (*Navarre*); 14 guns
Master and Commander Hon Patrick Napier
Chased off the coast of Virginia by two French frigates, she was overhauled by the *Emeraude*, 36 guns, off the Chesapeake and surrendered without resistance when hailed.
[TNA: ADM.1/5321]

6 August ALLEGIANCE Armed Ship
Purchased 1779 (*King George*); 16 guns
Master and Commander David Phips
The sloop was lying at anchor in Boston Bay when ten French ships of the line under the Marquis de Vaudreuil entered and unable to escape she surrendered to the *Northumberland*, 74 guns, when hailed.
[TNA: ADM.1/5321]

16 August SWAN Brig Sloop
Purchased 1781 (*Roebuck*); 272 tons; 84ft × 28.2ft; 18 guns
Master and Commander Lewis Robertson
Sailed from Waterford, Ireland, in company with the *Artois* frigate, to convoy several troop transports to England, but soon after sailing she was ordered to close the land and round up some stragglers seen astern. The weather was windy with frequent strong squalls, and she headed back under reefed foresail and mainsail, close-reefed topsails and the fore-topmast staysail. She was running into a heavy head sea and frequently shipped water as she buried her head. When a particularly heavy sea washed over her, the man at the foresheets was knocked overboard and the upper deck was flooded with water which heeled the ship over, with much of the water spilling down the hatches. She hung precariously on her beam-ends for a while before rolling over, the ship's boat falling off the booms as she did so. Sixteen men, including the Captain, Lieutenant and Master, struggled aboard the boat and spent an uncomfortable night at sea before landing at Castletown the following morning, the only survivors.
[TNA: ADM.1/5321]

29 August ROYAL GEORGE First Rate
Woolwich 1756; 2,047 tons; 178ft × 51.9ft; 100 guns
Captain Martin Waghorn
Flagship of Admiral Richard Kempenfelt, she lay at anchor at Spithead with other ships of the Channel Fleet to take on stores and effect repairs. At 5 o'clock in the morning, the first of the victualing tenders arrived, carrying bread, which was secured at the quarter, the Marines on watch commencing the unloading. At 7 o'clock a second victualing tender arrived with beer for the ship, and waited for the first to complete her task, extra hands being turned up to clear the first tender. As this was completing, a party of dockyard plumbers and shipwrights arrived to commence work on repairing a leaking cistern pipe, which served a small hand pump to provide water for washing decks. A new pipe was to be fitted and the Carpenter requested that the ship be heeled over for this work to be done, and orders were given for the lower-deck larboard guns to be run out and the starboard guns pulled back to the combings. This did not achieve a sufficient heel, so upper-deck and three middle-deck guns were run across, and shot was rolled over to the larboard side, to give the ship a sufficient list for the shipwrights to go over the side and commence work. Meanwhile, the hands having cleared the bread tender, Captain Waghorn ordered hands to breakfast, it then being 8 o'clock, intending to bring the waiting beer tender alongside afterwards. Nothing untoward was noticed at this stage and the stores lighter was brought alongside on the larboard side, in preparation for unloading. Captain Waghorn was walking on the upper deck with the officer of the watch, Lieutenant Philip Durham, when to his astonishment, the Carpenter reappeared claiming that the ship was taking in water through her lee ports, and she was settling into the water. The Captain immediately ordered the guns to be run back in and the weather-side guns run out, to right the ship, at the same time ordering the drummer to beat to quarters. Only minutes after this the ship sank very

suddenly, laying on her larboard side, until she struck the bottom, the topsail yards being above water. Over 300 people survived, including the Captain, but a large number, including the Admiral, drowned, the numbers never accurately known because of the dockyard workers and visitors on board, but perhaps as high as 800. The subsequent court martial heard that surveys of the ship had revealed that the hull was in a poor state, with dockyard workmen testifying that she had rotten timbers and beams. The Gunner's Yeoman, who was in the gunroom, testified that he heard a 'great crack' and she started to sink. The court martial into the loss ruled that the most likely reason for her sinking was that … some material part of her frame gave way … by the general state of decay of her timbers'. That verdict was doubted by many, who believed the that an uncontrolled heel was the likely cause, with the extra stores being taken onboard adding to the list, which had brought the lower ports to water level.
[TNA:ADM.1/5321]

5 September PRINCE EDWARD Armed Brig
Prize 1780 (*Wilkes*); 140 tons; 14 guns
Lieutenant Richard Simmonds
Lying at anchor in Spear Harbour, Labrador, Lieutenant Simmonds proceeded ashore on business, leaving the Gunner and Bosun in charge of the brig. The vessel was short-handed, having sent away several men in prizes and had on board twenty-nine American seamen held as prisoners. At about 5.30pm, the Bo'sun went into the boat to check the external condition of the brig and was surprised to see an American prisoner pointing a musket at him when he attempted to return on board. The prisoners, helped by several the sloop's crew, had rushed up on deck to take control of the vessel. John Holmes, the captured Lieutenant of a privateer had started the action. Allowed on deck for exercise, he had waited for the Bosun to get into the boat and then seized a poleaxe. Somewhat surprisingly they allowed Lieutenant Simmonds back on board to take his papers and destroy the private signals. The following morning, he and the loyal members of the crew were put ashore and the sloop sailed, with about eighteen members of the crew, led by the Gunner, who joined the Americans. Simmonds was reprimanded by court martial for leaving the sloop to conduct business which could have been performed by someone else and sending so many men away in prizes.
[TNA:ADM.1/5321]

12 September RACOON Brig Sloop
Purchased 1782 (*Lovely Sally*); 14 guns
Master and Commander Edmund Nagle
Chased by two French frigates off the American coast, she was overhauled off the Capes of Delaware and forced to surrender. Her captors were the *Aigle*, 40 guns, and *Gloire*, 32. The following day they anchored off Cape Henlopen and were attacked by a British force led by the *Warwick*, 50. The American pilot of the *Racoon* was reported to have entered French service and had assisted in taking the French ships and their prizes upriver to escape capture.
[TNA:ADM.1/5321]

12 September DUKE Cutter Tender
Hired 1779; 8 guns
Lieutenant Edmund Padeson
Ordered to Ireland to raise men for the Navy, she was south of Waterford when she was chased by a French brig privateer. She altered course to run for the shore but was overhauled. The tender yawed and fired into the privateer to disable the rigging but did not succeed. The privateer ran under her stern, fired into the tender, wounding one man, and called on her to surrender. Unable to escape and outnumbered, Lieutenant Padeson did so, finding his captor to be the *Sophie*, 16 guns, from Dunkirk.
[TNA:ADM.1/5321]

(17/18) September GLORIEUX Third Rate
Prize 1782; 1,718 tons; 175ft × 47.4ft; 74 guns
Captain Hon. Thomas Cadogan†
On 25 August, Rear Admiral Graves sailed from Jamaica with several of the prize vessels captured from the French at the battle of the Saintes, accompanied by a large number of merchantmen to proceed to England. On 8 September, a strong gale struck the fleet, forcing some ships to bear away for Halifax. On 16 September when in latitude 42 North they encountered another, far stronger storm, which steadily increased in strength with hurricane-force winds from the south-east. During the morning of 17th the wind flew around to the north-north-west with very heavy driving rain and heavy seas. The storm continued for several days, and it is not known when exactly when the *Glorieux* foundered. She was last seen during the 17th without foremast, bowsprit or main topmast, although when hailed, Captain Cadogan answered that they needed no help. She was believed to have sunk with the loss of all hands soon after this.
[Beatson vol V p500]

(17/18?) September VILLE DE PARIS First Rate
Prize 1782; 2,347 tons; 185.7ft × 53.8ft; 104 guns
Captain George Wilkinson†
The former flagship of the Comte de Grasse captured at the Saintes, she sailed from Jamaica for England with the other prizes at the end of August. The hurricane which overtook the fleet in mid-September sank several merchant ships and the *Ville de Paris* disappeared. She was last seen during 17 September, when all appeared

to be well apart from the loss of her mainsail and was presumed to have foundered soon after this, but the date is uncertain. The *Hector* merchant ship later claimed she kept company with her for some time after the storm struck, parting with her on 26 September, by which time she had rolled away her main and mizzen masts and thrown overboard her upper-deck guns. A seaman, James Wilson, later came forward claiming to be the sole survivor, having been picked up from a piece of wreckage by a Danish merchant ship.
[Beatson vol V p500; www.britishnewspaperarchive.co.uk: Caledonian Mercury 9 November 1782 p1; 31 March 1783 p2]

(17/18) September CORNWALLIS Store Ship
Purchased 1781; 442 tons; 107.1ft x 30.9ft; 14 guns
Lieutenant Charles Appleby†

In the fleet from the West Indies which was struck by the storm of 16/17 September, she was reported to have been seen on 17 September, having been dismasted, but afterwards disappeared. It was presumed that she subsequently foundered with all hands. Her pay book was closed on 30 September.
[www.britishnewspaperarchive.co.uk: Manchester Mercury 8 October 1782 p4; 26 November 1782 p1; TNA: ADM.34/214; ADM.180/9]

21 September RAMILLIES Third Rate
Chatham 1763; 1,620 tons; 168.8ft x 46.11ft; 74 guns
Captain Sylverius Moriarty

The flagship of Rear Admiral Thomas Graves, in charge of the convoy heading for England from Jamaica, which was hit by the storm of 16–19 September, the morning of 17 September saw the wind suddenly shift and increase in strength. The *Ramillies* cut away her mainmast and her mizzen about halfway up, to ease the constant rolling. Despite this she continued to roll and pitch heavily, constantly shipping water and later the tiller snapped, and the foreyard broke in the slings. Pumping continued despite the chain pumps becoming choked, probably with shifting ballast. The morning of 18 September revealed several ships in a sinking condition, with the wrecks of others nearby and the bodies of those drowned floating near survivors clinging to wreckage. Captain Moriarty wrote 'Oh God, a most awful and affecting view, every species of sea-distress surrounded us, a ship under our lee side ... went down very suddenly'. The ship was rolling so much that the beams were drawing away from the clamps as she moved and the ship was taking on water constantly, so that all the officers and men were working at the pumps and bailing. All the fo'c'sle and quarterdeck guns were heaved overboard, followed soon after by some of the upper-deck guns. The ship was now frapped with cables being passed around the hull, and canvas was also nailed up along the sides below decks in efforts to stem the influx of water. By 19 September, the storm abated a little, to strong winds with squalls and a heavy swell, but the ship was in a sorry condition and overnight part of the orlop deck collapsed into the hold. Both anchors were now cut away and cables, heavy stores and more guns were heaved overboard in attempts to lighten her. These were followed the next day by the spare anchors and the remaining upper-deck guns. Bailing was still supplementing the pumping, but everyone was exhausted, and the struggle could not be kept up. During the morning of 21 September, the decision was taken to leave her. Nearby merchant ships closed and the crew were taken off by boat, Captain Moriarty setting fire to her as he left at 4 o'clock that afternoon, breaking open several casks of powder at the same time. About 30 minutes after they left the flames reached the gunpowder and she blew up with a large explosion.
[TNA: ADM.1/5322; Beatson vol V pp497–502; Mariner's Mirror vol 56 pp187–97]

24 September CENTAUR Third Rate
Prize 1759; 1,739 tons; 175.8ft x 47.5ft; 74 guns
Captain John Inglefield

Another of those ships bound for England from Jamaica affected by the Atlantic storm of mid-September, when the wind suddenly shifted and increased in strength on 17 September, she was laid on her beam-ends, with all the masts going overboard, guns coming loose, shot rolling out of lockers and men being thrown from their hammocks. She righted herself, but the tiller broke, and the rudder parted, leaving them at the mercy of the storm. She hoisted an ensign on the stump of the mizzen mast, union downwards, as a distress signal, and had hopes that the *Ville de Paris* would assist, but she lost sight of her that evening. Over the next five days the crew worked to heave overboard the guns and heavy stores, as well as pumping and bailing constantly, although the pumps were regularly choked by coals which had broken loose from the after hold. The ship continued afloat until the morning of 23 September, when it was decided that the ship would have to be abandoned. By this time the orlop deck had collapsed, the chain pumps displaced, and the fore hold full of water. Three surviving boats were hoisted out and rafts were made from spars and timbers. During the afternoon, the weather again became threatening, with rain and squalls and men started to leave the ship, the ship then being in approximate position 48.33N, 43.24W. Captain Inglefield went into a boat with the Master, John Rainey, a Midshipman and nine others. They eventually reached Fayal in the Azores after 16 days at sea, the only survivors. It was believed that the ship foundered soon after they left.
[TNA: ADM.1/5322; Beatson vol V pp504–13]

September PLACENTIA Armed Brig
Prize 1780 (*Pallas*); 140 tons; 14 guns
Lieutenant Charles Anderson†

Reported to have been lost in poor weather off the coast of Newfoundland with no survivors, but no details have been found. Her books were closed on 30 September.
[TNA: ADM.34/611; Schomberg vol V p51]

4 October HECTOR Third Rate
Prize 1782; 1,783 tons; 170.2ft × 48.2ft; 74 guns
Captain John Bourchier

The *Hector* sailed from Jamaica with other French prize ships on 16 August, bound for England, but she was not in good condition, and her upper-deck guns had been landed and masts and yards replaced with smaller, so as not to place too great a strain on the ship. Only 223 men manned the ship, and she also had on board sixty-two French and American prisoners plus seventy-three soldiers. She soon dropped astern of the other ships, unable to keep up and by 22 August was alone. During the morning of 5 September, she sighted two ships approaching, which bore up in chase. They were the French frigates *Aigle*, 40 guns, and *Gloire*, 32, which had noted that she was only partly armed and probably weakly manned and decided to attack. When they were within gunshot, one placed herself ahead, the other on the stern of *Hector*. A close action of over three hours followed with the French raking their opponent several times. The *Aigle* then tried to board but was driven back after fierce hand-to-hand fighting. Unable to force the *Hector* to surrender and believing they saw other ships approaching, the two French ships sheared off and left her. The fight had damaged her even further, with the sails and rigging in tatters, several shots in the hull, the foremast shot through in two places and there were several casualties, nine killed and thirty-three wounded, including Captain Bourchier. In this condition, she struggled on, constantly pumping and bailing. The storm of 16–19 September saw her lose all the masts, the rudder broke, and new leaks started. More of the guns were thrown overboard and sails were slung under the hull in efforts to stem the leaks, but with limited success. By the end of September all provisions were gone, and the survivors were living off rainwater alone, some of the crew had died of exhaustion and the officers had to force the men back to the pumps at the point of their swords. On the morning of 3 October, a sail was sighted, which closed and proved to be the British privateer snow *Hawke*, from Dartmouth. With some skill, the snow was brought under the stern of the *Hector* and that night took off part of the crew. The next morning Captain Bourchier and the remainder, about 200 men in all, were taken off and the *Hector* left to sink.
[Beatson vol V p520–525; TNA: ADM.1/5322]

9 December LIVELY Brig Sloop
Dover 1779; 206 tons; 78.3ft × 10.10ft; 12 guns
Lieutenant Michael Stanhope

Cruising off the coast of Florida in company with the *Jupiter*, 50 guns, the pair had taken several prizes. They parted when the sloop was ordered to investigate the islands around the Double-Headed Shot keys and Cay Sal for water. The brig had forty-four American prisoners on board from the prizes and her complement had been reduced to only forty-eight by manning prizes. Having anchored off Cay Sal, this was reduced still further by sending the Gunner and 10 men ashore to fill water casks. At 2 o'clock in the afternoon, when Lieutenant Stanhope and the Master went below for dinner, one of the Americans, named Whitmore, allowed on deck to exercise, suddenly produced a cutlass and shouted 'Now, now is the time'. This was the signal for the American prisoners below to charge up onto the upper deck, which they soon controlled, and opened an arms chest to hand out cutlasses and muskets. Stanhope found himself trapped in his cabin and the only other officer, Lieutenant James Delancy Walton, the officer of the watch, was on the fo'c'sle and soon taken prisoner. The Americans took the sloop to Havana where it was turned over to the Spanish. The court martial revealed the very lax routine on board the *Lively*. Despite the large numbers of American seamen on board, there was no extra security measures, the only crew members armed were two guards who had cutlasses. Lieutenant Walton, although on duty, had no side-arms. The arms chest plundered by the prisoners had no lock, and despite this being brought to Stanhope's attention, nothing had been done. Little was done to prevent the prisoners conversing with the crew, at least one of whom was an American, who joined them, as did two others, who were Irish. Stanhope also kept a woman on board, referred during the court martial as the 'Captain's woman', who was also apparently an American, and seems to have assisted the prisoners. Stanhope's solution to the problem of the prisoners was to maroon them on Cay Sal, and it was this plan, which is said to have sparked off the rising, the woman having tipped off the prisoners of their planned fate. In turn, Stanhope was warned that the prisoners would not allow themselves to be marooned and would take the sloop, but he chose to ignore this warning. Stanhope also showed little loyalty to his crew. After reaching Havana, the crew were kept prisoner, but Stanhope, with his female companion, obtained his freedom and returned to St Augustine. The court was not impressed with Stanhope, and he was dismissed the service for neglect and inefficiency. Lieutenant Walton, who shared his negligence and had done nothing to resist the takeover, was also dismissed the service.
[TNA: ADM.1/5323]

28 December ALBANY Ship Sloop
Prize 1775 (*Britannia*); c230 tons; 16 guns
Lieutenant Robert Vardon

Ordered to sail for New York from Boston, where she had been lying for some time serving as a prison, Lieutenant Vardon decided to proceed to the Penobscot River first to take on wood and water. Whilst attempting to exit Penobscot Bay via the Two Bush Channel, it was found that she could not weather Metinic Island. As she manoeuvred, she struck a submerged ledge of rocks. The sails were thrown aback, but she found that she was stuck fast and taking in water. The mizzen was cut away and later that afternoon the main and foremasts followed. She continued to beat on the rocks for some time, until the rudder was unshipped, and the sloop filled and sank. At the subsequent court martial, it emerged that Lieutenant Vardon had had the opportunity to take on provisions at Boston but had failed to do so. Further, he had diverted into Penobscot Bay without permission, and that when the ship struck, he had taken 30 minutes to come on deck. He was dismissed the service.

Note: although it was believed at the time that she had grounded on the Northern Triangles, modern research would suggest that she struck the Southern Triangles, another jumble of rocks about halfway between Little Green and the southern end of Metinic Island.
[TNA: ADM.1/5322; info. from Bob Brookes]

31 December FLYING FISH Sloop
Purchased 1778; 180 tons; 75ft x 25.8ft; 10 guns
Lieutenant Charles Craven

Ordered to proceed to Ostend to collect vessels for a convoy, she stood over towards the French coast under the guidance of the Master, Randall Slap. The night was dark and cloudy, when at eleven o'clock in the evening she suddenly struck the ground. Lieutenant Craven ordered the sails to be taken in, but in doing so the mainsail jammed, and she was carried further inshore. The guns were all transferred forward, and water butts emptied to lighten her, and a boat was lowered with an anchor to kedge her off. By now the tide was falling and she found much of this work to be in vain. To keep her upright, spars were put over the side to act as shores, but despite this, some of them broke, leaving her heeled over. Daybreak revealed that they had gone ashore on sandbanks between Dunkirk and Gravelines, but the area was shrouded in fog, which raised their hopes of remaining unobserved. However, when a small party went ashore, they found several fresh wheel tracks in the sand, which seemed to indicate that someone had been near the sloop. They decided to wait until high tide that evening and again attempt to kedge her off. These hopes were dashed that evening when several lights were seen approaching from different directions. They found that several companies of armed French militiamen were now surrounding them and when hailed, they surrendered.
[TNA: ADM.1/5322]

1783

7 January RAVEN Ship Sloop
Woolwich 1777 (*Ceres*); 361 tons; 108ft x 27.4ft; 18 guns
Master and Commander John Wells

On 5 January when cruising off Montserrat, West Indies, in company with the *Hercules*, 74 guns, she was ordered to chase a sail then in sight. The chase proved to be a merchantman, as did another vessel nearby. The sloop was now well to leeward of the *Hercules*, which was out of sight, and she worked to regain her position. That evening the wind fell away to a calm and it remained so the next day, with the sloop working to windward. At 10 o'clock on the morning of 7 January, two frigates were observed to be standing towards her from the direction of Guadeloupe. She initially believed these to be British and steered towards them, making the private recognition signals as she did so. They answered by repeating the signals, at which Captain Wells rightly guessed they were French. The sloop immediately bore up and made all sail away, the French frigates in chase. The pursuit went on all day until at 9 o'clock that evening the nearest was in pistol-shot distance, when it yawed and fired a broadside at the sloop. This shot away the main topgallant mast. The frigate fell away a little after this, the sloop continuing to run under all possible sail, the lee gunwales frequently under water. By 10.30, the frigate was again within range and under the lee quarter, the other closing fast. Unable to escape, the sloop surrendered, finding her captors to be the *Nymphe*, 36 guns, and the *Concorde*, 32.
[TNA: ADM.1/5322]

12 January COVENTRY Sixth Rate
Buckler's Hard 1757; 599 tons; 118.4ft x 34ft; 28 guns
Captain William Wolseley

Cruising off the Indian coast near Ganjam, the frigate was looking for several East Indiamen expected in the area, to escort them to Calcutta. Sighting several large ships at anchor off the coast in hazy weather, she presumed these to be the Indiamen, having no intelligence of any French ships being in the area. There was little wind, and the *Coventry* allowed the northerly current to set her towards the ships. Not until she was close was it realised that they were all French ships of the line. An attempt was made to tack, but she missed stays and there was insufficient wind for her to escape and she was steadily carried down by the current towards the enemy ships. The French opened fire on her, at which she surrendered.
[TNA: ADM.1/5324]

(January) CATO Fourth Rate
Gravesend 1782; 1,071 tons; 147.10ft x 40.8ft; 50 guns
Captain James Clarke†
Vice Admiral Sir Hyde Parker was appointed Commander-in-Chief in the East Indies and embarked on board the *Cato* for the passage to India. She sailed from Spithead on 13 October 1782 in company with the sloop *Hound*, stopping at Madeira 1 November and Rio de Janeiro on 4 December for fresh provisions. They sailed from that place on 12 December, intending to make the passage to India without another stop. The pair parted company on 28 December in 33.36 South and she was never seen again. It was presumed that she foundered in the Indian Ocean. Her pay book was closed on 31 December. Over the next few years there were numerous reports of supposed sightings of wreckage and reports of stores belonging to the *Cato* being seen in vessels trading in the Indian Ocean and Arabian Sea, but none were ever verified as authentic.
[Lloyd's List 15 October 1782: TNA: ADM.51/463; ADM.34/211]

10 February TICKLER Brig Sloop
Prize 1781 (*Diana*); 261 tons; 77ft x 25.3ft; 12 guns
Master and Commander Lachlan Hunter
Cruising off Punta de Maisi at the eastern end of Cuba, she had just taken and scuttled a pettiauger, when a large ship was seen approaching. The sloop found that she had little room for manoeuvring, being close under the Cape and the ship closing fast from seaward. She remained uncertain of the identity of the stranger, which could be seen to be a large warship. When it was within gunshot, the stranger fired a shot across the sloop's bows and hailed her to send a boat aboard. The Master was despatched to the ship, which he found to be the French *Triton*, 64 guns. Faced with such a large opponent, which was now lying under her quarter, the brig had no choice but to surrender.
[TNA: ADM.1/5322]

12 February PALLAS Fifth Rate
Deptford 1757; 729 tons; 128.4ft x 35.10ft; 36 guns
Captain Christopher Parker
The frigate sailed from Halifax on 24 January acting as a convoy escort to England, but several leaks became evident soon after sailing. She became separated from her charges during a gale and the high winds and heavy seas only made the leaks worse. By 5 February there was 8ft of water in the hold and despite heaving guns and heavy stores overboard, little progress was made in reducing the water level. It was decided to make for the nearest land, which was judged to be the Azores. The frigate arrived off Fayal on 10 February, but contrary winds blew her out to sea again. By now all the crew, officers and men together, were working the pumps and bailing to keep her afloat. On 12 February, with the crew exhausted by the constant employment at the pumps, she was run ashore on the island of São Jorge. For the next two weeks stores and provisions were taken out of her before the wreck was burnt. The chance was taken to examine her when ashore and it was found that her keel and garboard strake were so badly worm eaten, they hardly existed.
[TNA: ADM.1/5322]

17 February ARGO Fifth Rate
Newcastle 1781; 892 tons; 140.8ft x 38ft; 44 guns
Captain John Butchart
The *Argo* sailed from Tortola on 10 February with Sir Thomas Shirley, Governor of the Leeward Islands embarked, en route to Antigua. The winds were fitful or non-existent after sailing and the frigate made little headway. During the night of 16 February, the wind steadily increased and by the morning it was blowing a fresh gale with a heavy swell. The rolling unseated the main-topmast and the frigate hove-to and started repairs. At 10 o'clock, two vessels were seen to be bearing down on the *Argo*, which cleared for action, correctly guessing that they were French frigates. By 10.30am the *Amphitrite*, 32 guns, was within gunshot and stationed herself on the lee quarter of the British ship. The *Argo* soon found that she was unable to use her lower-deck guns, due to the heavy swell; every time the ports were opened to attempt to fire, water rushed in with some force. Relying only on her upper-deck armament, she held the *Amphitrite* at bay for an hour and a half, when the second French frigate, the *Nymphe*, 36, came up and joined the action. The British frigate decided to make a running fight, heading towards Tortola, the French ships hanging on to her quarters. By 5 o'clock that afternoon the rigging of *Argo* was in tatters, '... not a sheet, tack, brace or bowline left', all the sails were holed and the main- and mizzenmasts were shot through. With thirteen killed and several wounded, she could no longer effectively resist and surrendered,
 Note: retaken three days later by the *Invincible*.
[TNA: ADM.1/5322; ADM.52/2416; www.britishnewspaperarchive.co.uk: Norfolk Chronicle 3 May 1783 p2]

21 April CERBERUS Fifth Rate
Rotherhithe 1779; 702 tons; 126.3ft x 35.7ft; 32 guns
Lieutenant Thomas Parkinson
Ordered to cruise off the entrance to the Chesapeake, her Captain, Jacob Wheate, became seriously ill and it was decided to proceed to Castle Harbour, Bermuda, where Wheate died in February, Lieutenant Parkinson assuming the command. At 10 o'clock in the morning she got under way to resume her station, but when passing the Castle struck a submerged rock. She drove over this obstruction but almost immediately fouled another. The frigate tailed off and went aground on a reef, broadside-

on. The guns were shifted forward, water casks emptied, shot heaved overboard and anchors taken out by boats to try and heave her off. She would not move and the quarterdeck and fo'c'sle guns and carronades were next heaved overboard and finally the masts cut away to lighten her. She remained firmly held by the rocks and steadily filled with water. At this the boats commenced ferrying the crew ashore, the nearby fishing vessels doing nothing to help. Over the next five days the crew salvaged a considerable amount of the stores and provisions from the wreck. The loss was blamed on the pilot being deceived by the set of the tide, the water being much lower than expected, and the harbour was generally accepted as being unsuitable for such a large ship. Many of the survivors, including Lieutenant Parkinson, later drowned in the *Mentor* (see below).
[TNA: ADM.1/5323]

April MENTOR Ship Sloop
Prize 1781 (*Aurora*); 230 tons; 18 guns
Master and Commander Richard Tilledge†
Ordered to embark the survivors of the *Cerberus* (see above), she disappeared after sailing from Bermuda and was presumed to have foundered with all hands. Pay book closed on 30 April.
[TNA: ADM.1/490; ADM.34/516; Schomberg vol V p53]

28 June NYMPH Ship Sloop
Chatham 1778; 302 tons; 96.7ft × 26.10ft; 16 guns
Master and Commander Richard Hill
Lying at Tortola, West Indies, when, at about 10.30 at night, she was found to be on fire. Aid was sent from shore and from nearby merchant ships, but the smoke and flames defeated all their efforts, and she was abandoned to burn out. Three men died.
[TNA: ADM.1/1907]

10 October ANGELICA Sloop
Detroit 1771, hired 1776; 66 tons; 52ft × 17.6ft; swivel guns
On Lake Erie, Canada, employed in supplying the various military outposts, she ran aground six miles to the east of Cayahoga and was lost. Most of the stores were saved
[Malcolmson pp24,26; http://images.maritimehistoryofthegreatlakes.ca/37087/data?n=6]

October HOPE Schooner
Detroit 1771, hired 1776; 81 tons; 54.4ft × 18ft; swivel guns
One of the vessels on stationed on Lake Erie, she was stranded and abandoned as a wreck.
[Malcolmson p24,26; http://images.maritimehistoryofthegreatlakes.ca/37087/data?n=6]

7 November SUPERB Third Rate
Deptford 1760; 1,612 tons; 168ft × 46.10ft; 74 guns
Captain Henry Newcombe
Flagship of Vice Admiral Sir Edward Hughes, the *Superb* lay at anchor in Tellicherry Roads (Thalassery), with most of the British East Indies squadron. During 5 November, the weather worsened, with strong winds and heavy rain showers. By the early hours of 6 November, the wind was at gale force with squalls, and topmasts and yards were ordered to be struck. During the morning, the best bower cable parted, and the sheet anchor was let go, which held her after she had been driven for some distance. Now secured uncomfortably close to the *Sultan*, 74 guns, she struck a submerged object several times. This was believed to be the *Sultan*'s anchor and the blows started leaks. During the afternoon, with pumps going constantly, the yards were lowered to the gunwales, shot heaved overboard and guns moved from aft to forward in attempts to ease the ship. In the early hours of the next morning, the wind shifted round to the south-south-east and increased in intensity. Bailing was now being used to help the pumps, but the water could not be cleared from the ship. At 7 o'clock in the morning, the mizzen mast was cut away and the yards previously lowered followed it overboard. The mainmast was the next to go, but despite these measures and throwing stores over the side, she continued to settle as the water gained on the pumps. The boats were brought up to the stern and the crew commenced leaving the vessel. The foremast was cut away that afternoon, in a last effort to save the ship, but nothing more could be done. By that evening the last of the crew left. The following day, with the weather moderating, the officers returned, to find the water up to the lower deck and the orlop deck blown up by the flood. She continued to settle, so that by noon only the quarterdeck remained above the surface.
[TNA: ADM.1/5323]

30 November JERSEY Hulk
Plymouth 1736; 1,065 tons; 144ft × 41.5ft
An old Fourth Rate ship, she had been employed at New York since August 1776, initially as a hospital ship, but from October 1780 as a prison, moored in Wallabout Bay. On completion of the British evacuation of New York under the terms of the peace agreement, she was abandoned and apparently later burned.
[TNA: ADM.51/493]

10 | 1783–1793: A Period of Peace and Political Agitation

THE AMERICAN WAR SAW Great Britain lose her American colonies and left the country with a large national debt. Political reforms largely solved many of the financial difficulties, but also saw the rise of demands for social and economic reforms, encouraged by the French Revolution in 1789.

1784

9 May CROCODILE Sixth Rate
Portsmouth 1781; 516 tons; 114.3ft × 32.1ft; 24 guns
Captain John Williamson
Returning to England from India, the Scilly Isles were sighted on the evening of 8 May and a course was set to take her up Channel. The weather became increasingly hazy, and by nightfall there was thick fog. At just before 3 o'clock in the morning she ran hard aground on rocks near Prawle Point, Devonshire. The fog was so thick that when the Captain arrived on deck, he cursed the officer of the watch for colliding with another ship, 'Good God Sir, despite all my precautions you have got foul of some vessel'. When it was confirmed that they were ashore, anchors were taken out astern by boat to attempt to pull her off, the booms were heaved overboard, and water casks emptied. Finally, the masts were cut away. She would not budge and with 7ft of water in the hold and the tide ebbing, threatening to overturn her, she was abandoned. After they were ashore, one of the seamen, Patrick Crawley, proceeded to get very drunk at a grog shop in East Prawle, and struck Midshipman John Burn. For this he was ordered to be flogged, receiving 100 lashes on his bare back. At his court martial, Captain Williamson was criticised for failing to order the use of the lead-line when in known to be in restricted waters in fog, and he was warned for his future conduct.
[TNA: ADM. 1/5324]

30 July ANTELOPE Brig Sloop
Purchased 1784; 14 guns
Lieutenant Robert Causzor
One of two brigs taken up in the West Indies by Admiral Gambier for local service, the Admiralty did not approve of their purchase and ordered them to be sold. In July both sloops were taken into the King's Yard, Jamaica to be de-stored. The *Antelope* paid off on 23 July and the stores were still being removed when the island was struck by a hurricane, and the brig sank at the westernmost wharf.
[TNA: ADM. 1/243; ADM.51/51]

30 July DUKE OF RUTLAND Brig Sloop
Purchased 1784; 6 guns
Lieutenant William Brown
Another brig purchased locally by Admiral Gambier and ordered to be sold by the Admiralty. The *Duke of Rutland* was laying at anchor in Port Royal, Jamaica, having paid off 6 July, and was in the process of landing stores when the island was struck by a hurricane. She dragged her anchors and was driven ashore on the boathouse slip. She was later pulled off the ground but found to have broken her back. She was therefore sold off locally for £220.
[TNA: ADM. 1/243; ADM.36/10429]

1785

10 October RAMBLER Cutter
Purchased 1778 (*Good Intent*); 139 tons; 65.7ft × 22.6ft; 10 guns
Lieutenant Miles Lowley†
Having sailed from Sheerness, she had weathered the Knock Buoy, when the Master, Abraham Clarke, advised the Lieutenant to reduce sail. The weather was threatening, with large black clouds looming. The embarked pilot dismissed the idea, saying it would more rain than wind. The bad weather continued to close in and other vessels around them started to take in canvas, which prompted the Master to again advise reducing sail. With the cutter now heeling under the freshening winds, Lieutenant Lowley agreed, and ordered the foresail to be taken in, the pilot still arguing that she could stand the weather. As the pilot and Master argued over the sails, the cutter heeled further under strong gusts of wind until the water spilled over the gunwales. She capsized and rapidly sank. Eight members of the crew, along with the pilot and Lieutenant Lowley, were drowned. The prime cause was assessed as being the stubbornness of the pilot, refusing to take in sail.

The cutter had sunk in eight fathoms of water, with the topmast still showing, and was later successfully refloated and refitted for further service.
[TNA: ADM.1/5325]

1786

18 April CYRUS Armed Transport
Purchased 1782; 625 tons; 118.5ft x 34.8ft; 16 guns
Lieutenant John Johnson
Attempting to sail from Barbados on 17 April, she successfully left the anchorage but was baffled by fitful winds which constantly took her aback, and boats were employed to tow her clear of land. Despite this, in the light winds she found herself being taken by the strong currents back inshore and she let go the anchor to await a fresh wind. Before the anchor had brought her up, she touched the ground. She commenced the work of kedging the ship off, although hampered by the cable snagging and breaking on rocks. She finally floated free in mid-afternoon and anchored in deep water, spreading a sail under the hull to try and stop the leaks. By daylight on 18 April the water was gaining on the pumps, and she was clearly settling. Assistance came with the frigate *Latona* and the sloop *Falcon*, which towed the *Cyrus* towards the shore, but before land was reached, she foundered. The court martial to investigate the loss was critical of both Lieutenant Johnson and the Master, John Callender, who had handled the ship in an unseamanlike and unskilful manner. Johnson lost his seniority and was ordered to be placed on the bottom of the list of Lieutenants and not given a command for five years. The Master was to serve a year in the Marshalsea Prison and not serve as a Master for five years.
[TNA: ADM.1/5325]

1787

7 November TORTOISE Stores Lighter
Deptford 1780; 109 tons; 60.4ft x 20.4ft; 2 guns
Based at Plymouth, the lighter was sent into the Sound to find and recover two anchors lost by the *Scorpion* sloop. Whilst manoeuvring close inshore, she was hit by a strong squall which carried her into Bovisand Bay, where she was wrecked.
[TNA: ADM.106/1291]

1789

28 April BOUNTY Armed Ship
Purchased 1787 (*Bethia*); 215 tons; 69.11ft x 24.4ft; 4 guns
Lieutenant William Bligh
The *Bounty* was purchased especially for the task of procuring breadfruit plants in Tahiti and taking them to the West Indies for use as cheap food for slaves. Bligh was an experienced seaman, having accompanied Cook on his final voyage to the Pacific. The ship arrived at Tahiti on 26 October 1788 and having acquired and loaded her cargo, she sailed on 4 April 1789, but three weeks later she became the scene of perhaps the most famous of all shipboard mutinies, the causes of which have been argued and discussed ever since. During the morning of 28 April, the Master's Mate, Fletcher Christian, accompanied by two seamen, Matthew Quintal and Matthew Thompson, and the ship's Corporal, Charles Churchill, took over the ship. The ship's company – there were forty-three of them – proved to be divided in their loyalties. Bligh was set adrift in the ship's launch, with eighteen of the crew joining him, with at least four others who supported him being kept on board the *Bounty*. Christian then took over the ship and eventually arrived back at Tahiti, where the mutineers divided, most remaining on the island. Christian, with eight others and some islanders, sailed on to Pitcairn Island where in early 1790 the ship was burnt. Bligh meanwhile completed an epic voyage in an open boat across the Pacific to Timor, from where he reached England. Christian, along with five of the others at Pitcairn, met bloody deaths in a series of massacres after arguments and disputes with the Tahitians they had taken with them. One later died a natural death and only one, Alexander Smith, alias John Adams, survived to meet European visitors many years later. Of those staying on Tahiti, two were murdered and remaining fourteen were rounded up by the *Pandora* frigate. Ten men eventually stood trial of which three, Thomas Ellison, John Milward and Thomas Burkitt, were hanged on 24 October 1792.
[TNA: ADM.1/5328; ADM.1/5330; Schomberg vol II p193-203]

1790

19 March SIRIUS Store Ship
Purchased 1781 (*Berwick*); 512 tons; 110.5ft x 32.9ft; 4 guns
Captain John Hunter
Based in New South Wales, supporting the penal colony established in Australia, she was ordered to take 186 male and female convicts to a new settlement on Norfolk

Island, along with a detachment of Marine guards. She arrived, accompanied by the *Supply* tender, on 13 March and commenced putting ashore the Marines and prisoners. By 15 March, having completed landing personnel, she was forced out to sea by strong winds. She returned to the island on 19 March to land the supplies and provisions held on board, but had difficulty securing her anchoring place, being bothered by fitful gusts of wind and a strong current. She eventually decided to stand out to sea again but found that she could not weather the reef nearby. Attempting to tack, she missed stays and was taken aback. The anchors were let go, but before they could bring her up, she struck violently on the sharp rocks of coral. The masts were cut away and pumping started, but she was filling with water fast, although the ship itself was pinioned securely to the reef. With the surf now breaking over her, a cask with a rope attached was floated out to the ship from the shore, to which a stout hawser was eventually passed and secured. Along this the crew reached the shore, the ship being given up as a wreck.
[TNA: ADM.1/5329]

12 April GUARDIAN Fifth Rate
Limehouse 1784; 896 tons; 140ft × 38.2ft; 44 guns
Lieutenant Edward Riou

Ordered to the penal colony in New South Wales, the upper-deck guns had been landed to allow the ship to carry stores for the colony, along with several passengers and twenty-five convicts. The ship sailed from the Cape Settlement and by 24 December 1789 was in the vicinity of 44 South 41.30 East, when several large icebergs were sighted. The ship closed the largest and sent her boats to collect lumps of ice to supplement the water supply. After completing the task, she recovered the boats and, with a thick fog descending, tacked away from the iceberg. About 30 minutes later, with no warning she suddenly struck a submerged ledge of ice. Hanging on the ice, the ship swung broadside-on and started beating. The rudder was unshipped, and several planks and frames were stove in. Extra sail was set, and she successfully drove over the ice, but on gaining clear water, she found that water was pouring in. Stores, guns, provisions and finally live cattle were heaved overboard to lighten the ship, sails were slung under the hull and the pumps manned. Despite all these actions, by 7 o'clock the next morning the water was gaining, with 7ft of water in the hold and the ship was labouring in the heavy seas. Believing that the ship could not survive, the boats were hoisted out and three of them were manned with about forty men, many of whom were drunk and with little food or water; only one of these boats, with ten survivors was ever picked up. Lieutenant Riou and sixty-two men, twenty-one of them convicts, were left aboard. Despite the ship having its berth deck flooded and water washing up onto the upper deck, she did not founder. It would appear that the casks in the hold helped to keep her afloat and large amounts of the shingle ballast had fallen through the holes in the ships bottom. Pumping and bailing went on constantly, a sail was put under the hull and eventually some sail could be set, and a course steered for the Cape, which, against the odds, she reached on 21 February being ' … little more than a floating raft'. During a gale on 12 April the ship was driven onto the beach where she remained until the wreck was sold in February 1791. The convicts that survived were sent to New South Wales but following Lieutenant Riou's report of their behaviour during the wreck, fourteen were pardoned and freed.
[Schomberg vol II pp204–14]

22 August ENDYMION Fifth Rate
Limehouse 1779; 894 tons; 140ft × 38.1ft; 44 guns
Lieutenant Daniel Woodriffe

Having escorted an outward-bound West Indiaman from Jamaica through the Windward Passage, she steered towards the Turks and Caicos, to deliver some embarked stores. At about 7 o'clock in the morning the low-lying Big Sand Cay was sighted on the horizon to the north-north-east. An hour later a lead-line sounding unexpectedly showed just seven fathoms, when they expected to be in deep water, and just moments later to everyone's surprise they struck an obstruction. Every effort was used to get her off, but all proved ineffectual, and water was reported to be entering. The boats were hoisted out, the ship was lightened, and the foremast was cut away, but the wreckage damaged some of the boats in its fall. Fortunately, some two hours after the accident the schooner *New Hope* hove into sight, and they assisted in taking off the men. The following day the ship continued to settle as she filled with water, sinking by the head. Lieutenant Woodriffe stood by her, attempting to salvage what stores he could, but was eventually forced to abandon her before she sank. The rock on which she struck was not marked on any charts, and none of the local pilots were aware of its presence; it is now known as Endymion Rock (21.11N 71.17W)
[TNA: ADM.1/244; ADM.1/5330]

1791

8 July ALERT Schooner
Purchased 1790; 88 tons; 4 guns
Lieutenant John Crispo

Having sailed from Quebec, the schooner was coasting off St John's Island (modern Prince Edward Isle), when the colour of the water was seen to change. They were some three miles from the shore and no known shallows existed at this point, so Lieutenant Crispo ordered the lead-line to be heaved. In successive casts this showed the water shallowing rapidly to 5 fathoms. The helm was ordered hard to port and the mainsail lowered, but before she could come around, she struck a rock. Yards and topmasts were lowered, pumping started, and the anchor was let go to steady her. The water gained throughout the day, so that by 8 o'clock that evening the casks in the hold were seen to be floating. At this, Lieutenant Crispo ordered the men to take to the boats, he being the last the leave before she sank, and they made their way to nearby Charlottetown. A party from the *Adamant* returned to the wreck and attempted to salvage her by placing twenty-four empty casks along the hull. However, this failed, as the high seas constantly washed away the barrels, so she was abandoned as a wreck.

Note: One source indicates the *Alert* was broken up in 1799, so it may be that she was salvaged later.
[TNA: ADM.1/5329]

28 August PANDORA Sixth Rate
Deptford 1779; 524 tons; 114.7ft × 32.3ft; 24 guns
Captain Edward Edwards

In March 1790 Lieutenant Bligh returned to England bringing with him the news of the loss of the *Bounty* (see above). As it seemed likely that the mutineers were still at Tahiti or the islands nearby, the *Pandora* was despatched to the South Pacific to recover them. She arrived amongst the islands in March 1791 and within a few days had secured all the survivors on Tahiti, fourteen in all. She sailed on 8 May 1791, the prisoners being confined in a small wooden cell built on the upper deck, inevitably called 'Pandora's Box', and secured with handcuffs and chains. Edwards has been criticised for this harsh treatment, especially as some of the prisoners had been loyal to Bligh but were unable to leave the *Bounty* with him. The *Pandora* steered westward until 28 August when she was approaching the Torres Straits off north-eastern Australia and the northern end of the Great Barrier Reef. A ship's boat was lowered to commence sounding ahead of the ship and during the afternoon, an opening in the reef was discovered. During the night, the current took the *Pandora* past the opening and in the early hours she struck the reef. After failing in attempts to sail her off, topgallant-yards and topmasts were struck, and boats hoisted out to take out anchors. By now the ship was being lifted by the surf and started to pound on the reef and the sharp coral pierced the hull. Water came in at an alarming Rate and within 15 minutes of striking there was 4ft of water in the hold. Pumping commenced and just after 10 o'clock in the evening she floated free of the reef allowing her to anchor with both bowers. Some of the guns were heaved overboard as were some stores, and bailing was employed to assist the pumps. The water continued to gain, and Captain Edwards ordered all four of the ship's boats to be hoisted out and stocked with provisions as a precaution. By 6.30 the next morning it was clear that the ship was sinking, the hold was full, and the water was washing up onto the berth deck. The frigate was now settling fast, and the final moments were something of a scramble to leave. An attempt was made by the Bosun's Mate of the *Pandora* to free the prisoners as she sank and all but one did get out of the box before the ship sank. Four of the prisoners drowned as did thirty of the crew. The survivors were divided amongst the boats and eventually reached Timor. The wreck was discovered in November 1977, lying in 30m of water in position 11.23S 143.59E.
[TNA: ADM.1/5330]

November CRUIZER Cutter
Purchased 1780; 199 tons; 73.7ft × 26.3ft; 14 guns
Lieutenant Thomas Rainy†

Disappeared whilst returning to England from Gibraltar and presumed foundered with all hands. She was officially paid off on 31 November 1791
[TNA: ADM.1/80/23; ADM.35/318]

11 | 1793–1802: Revolution and War

BY THE LATE EIGHTEENTH CENTURY, the French monarchy was teetering on the edge of bankruptcy and attempts to revise the inadequate tax system were never fully implemented. The financial crisis led to the convening of a National Assembly in 1789, which soon became the seat of increasingly radical ideas and the Assembly worked to abolish many institutions and alter the established order. This revolution was initially given cautious support by libertarians in Great Britain, but the increasing level of violence as rival factions developed led to most distancing themselves from events in France, and concern mounted over the course of the uprising. The attempt to establish a constitutional monarchy failed and the arrest of the royal family in August 1792 led to conflict with Austria and their allies in Europe. The success of the revolutionary armies in resisting their enemies, their advance in the Netherlands and finally the execution of the King on 21 January 1793 led to war with Britain.

The Royal Navy was superior to the weakened and divided French Navy and could carry out a close blockade of the French naval ports and was able to briefly occupy the port of Toulon. Colonial expeditions were mounted in the West Indies, South Africa and Indian waters. The destruction of the French fleet at Aboukir Bay in 1798 cut off the French army in Egypt and removed the threat to India. The formation of a Scandinavian Armed Neutrality as a response to perceived British aggressiveness towards neutral shipping led to a British fleet attacking and largely destroying the Danish fleet at Copenhagen in 1801. The war continued until March 1802, but with the success of the French army under Napoleon Bonaparte in continental Europe, Britain was ultimately forced into recognising the French Republic.

Note: The term Master and Commander was retained for most of the eighteenth century as the official term for the rank between Captain and Lieutenant, indicating the commanding officer of a ship below the Sixth Rate, who was responsible for both commanding the ship and for the navigation. This was increasingly shortened unofficially to Commander, particularly after 1746 when sloops were allowed a specialist in navigation – the Master – in their complement. In the official listing of officer's seniority published by the Admiralty in January 1794 this was finally recognised, and they simply became a Commander. I have followed this convention.

1793

27 May HYAENA Sixth Rate
Liverpool 1778; 522 tons; 114.4ft x 32.3ft; 24 guns
Captain William Hargood
Stationed in the West Indies, she was cruising off Cape Tiburon, Hispaniola. The visibility was poor, with misty patches, and when the weather cleared during the late morning, a large frigate was sighted. Private signals were made, but they were unanswered, so the *Hyaena* made all sail away, running before the wind, but she carried away her studding sails, and fore topgallant mast in doing so, and lost a man overboard at the same time. The stranger steadily overhauled her, and eventually showed French colours. The British vessel was still manned on the peace establishment, and clearly outmatched and unable to escape. After firing a few main-deck guns, Captain Hargood surrendered when the French frigate ranged under the stern. She proved to be the *Concorde*, 40 guns, which was the advanced ship of a squadron of two ships of the line and three more frigates
Note: recaptured on 27 October 1797 by the *Indefatigable*.
[TNA: ADM.1/5330]

1 June ADVICE Schooner
Purchased 1793; 10 guns
Lieutenant Edward Tyrell
Newly purchased into service, she was ordered to Belize with despatches for the *Hound* sloop, which was then gathering ships for a convoy, sailing from Port Royal, Jamaica on 27 May. During the late afternoon of 1 June, they arrived off the Cays in the approaches to Belize, but finding no suitable place to anchor, steered for Key Bokell (modern Caye Bokel, Turneffe Islands). As they approached, they started to take in sail, preparing to anchor, but they found that there was a strong current taking them further inshore and to leeward of their intended anchorage, and were still under a partly furled mainsail and flying jib when at a little after 9 o'clock she ran aground. She was held fast, and during the night the masts were cut away to prevent her from capsizing. A survey at daybreak showed that it was clearly impossible to free her, so a raft was made from the wreckage of the masts and with the boat, the crew moved to the nearby cay. Later that day a local sloop saw them and closed to

take some of them to Belize, from where the *Hound* sloop was able to organise a rescue.
[TNA: ADM.1/245; ADM.1/5330]

20 September FLOATING BATTERY NUMBER THREE
Prize 1793; 4 guns
Lieutenant John Gourly

In August 1793, the port of Toulon was occupied by allied forces under Admiral Lord Hood, and several vessels found in the harbour were manned by British crews. The battery stationed at the north-west arm of the harbour of Toulon was used to engage the advancing Republican army, which by 19 September had set up several field gun positions and engaged the ships throughout the day. The next morning a new battery was opened which fired red-hot shot at the vessel, which was hit repeatedly, leaving her in a wrecked condition. Having received forty shots in the hull and with the rigging reduced to a shambles, during that evening she was abandoned. One man was killed and six wounded.
[O'Byrne p418; London Gazette 23 October 1793]

24 October THAMES Fifth Rate
Buckler's Hard 1758; 656 tons; 127ft × 34.4ft; 32 guns
Captain James Cotes

At 9.30 in the morning, then being to the south-west of Ushant and standing to the south, a ship was sighted, steering the same course. The weather was hazy, and sight was briefly lost until 10 o'clock, when the *Thames* altered course towards the stranger and cleared for action. At 10.30am the stranger, which could be seen to be a frigate, hoisted French national colours. The pair passed close by each other on opposite tacks, the *Thames* firing a broadside as she did. Her opponent, the *Uranie*, 40 guns, did likewise, then wore round to the same tack, and the action commenced which continued until 2.20pm, when the French frigate made sail away. The *Thames* had suffered during the action, with all masts and yards shot through, stays and shrouds in tatters, main topsail yard shot away, several shots in the hull, upper works ripped apart, a gun had been dismounted on the quarterdeck and another two on the main deck. She had lost ten men killed, with one missing presumed dead, and twenty-three wounded. Unable to pursue her opponent, who disappeared over the horizon, she lay-to repairing her damage, until at 4 o'clock that afternoon, when four vessels were sighted. These were soon seen to be frigates, which closed under British colours, before one ran under her stern and fired a broadside into her. The *Thames*, being quite unable to manoeuvre and faced with three powerful frigates and a sloop, surrendered. The *Carmagnole*, 40 guns, took possession and carried her into Brest.

Note: recaptured on 8 June 1796 by the *Santa Margaritta*.
[TNA: ADM.1/5332]

20 November SCIPION Third Rate
Prize 1793; 1,810 tons; 74 guns
Captain (Hubert?) de Goy, Seigneur de Bègues

One of the French ships turned over to the British at the occupation of Toulon in August 1793, she remained manned by the French crew although under the control of the British. Whilst lying at anchor off Livorno, at about 3 o'clock in the afternoon smoke was seen to be rising from several parts of the ship, the flames spreading rapidly to the rigging and sails. Aid was sent from other ships in the harbour, but by 4 o'clock the ship was well alight, and guns started to go off and other ships nearby weighed and cleared the anchorage. She eventually parted from her anchors when the cables burnt through, and she drifted out of the harbour. At about 8 o'clock in the evening, then being about four miles off the port, she blew up sending up a huge column of smoke. The next morning showed only wreckage and bodies.
[www.britishnewspaperarchive.co: Caledonian Mercury 21 Dec 1793 p3]

16 December PIGMY Cutter
Dover 1781; 181 tons; 69.4ft × 25.7ft; 12 guns
Lieutenant Abraham Pullibank†

Having sailed from Torbay to return to Plymouth, she approached the coast in the late afternoon, and in the gloom mistakenly entered Bigbury Bay. The mistake was realised as they neared the coast, but they found it difficult to come about, so it was decided to anchor and let go the best bower anchor, despite being close to the rocks. Guns were fired to bring assistance and lights were seen on the shore and the jolly boat was launched, but immediately capsized, throwing the occupants into the water, although all but one managed to make it to the beach through the surf. The small bower anchor was then let go, but despite having both anchors out, she found that she was being driven further inshore, until she struck the rocks, carrying the rudder and sternpost away. People were now seen on the shore, and a lead-line was successfully thrown to them, and this was made fast to a hawser. Several of the crew managed to haul themselves to safety along the rope, but Lieutenant Pullibank and ten men stayed on board. The mast was cut away, but she stayed beating on the rocks until 2.30 in the morning, when she went to pieces. All eleven men on board were washed into the sea, but only two made it to the shore.
[TNA: ADM.1/5330]

18 December: Evacuation of Toulon
In August 1793, the port of Toulon was occupied by allied forces commanded by Vice Admiral Lord Hood, the French Mediterranean fleet of over fifty ships coming under his control. By mid-December, the French Republican forces had surrounded the

city and were threatening to overrun the allied army, which was made up of a mixture of French Royalists and detachments of Spanish and Italians, apart from the British. On 17 December, the decision was taken to evacuate the town, and those French ships which could not be brought away were ordered to be destroyed. The Spanish, under Admiral Langara, undertook to dispose of those ships in the inner basin, whilst a party under Captain Sir William Sydney Smith was charged with destroying the magazines and other ships.

VULCAN Fireship
Shoreham 1783; 425 tons; 108.11ft × 29.8ft; 14 guns
Master and Commander John Hare
At 8 o'clock in the evening, the *Vulcan* started the work by being towed into the inner harbour and was placed by Commander Hare alongside a line of 74-gun ships. When the work ashore was complete, about two hours later the *Vulcan* was set on fire, although the premature explosion of some of the priming blew Commander Hare overboard. The fire communicated itself to the 74s, burning several of them.

CONFLAGRATION Fireship
Shoreham 1783; 426 tons; 108.6ft × 29.8ft; 14 guns
Master and Commander John Loring
Undergoing repairs at the time of the evacuation, she could not be got ready in time, so was stripped, abandoned and set on fire.
[James vol 1 p80]

The following French vessels, which had been commissioned into the Royal Navy during the occupation of Toulon, were also lost at the evacuation:

ALERTE Brig Sloop
Prize 1793; 248 tons; 85ft × 26.7ft; 14 guns
Master and Commander William Edge
In the inner harbour, she was not fit to go to sea, so she was set on fire, burning to the waterline.

FLOATING BATTERY NUMBER ONE
Prize 1793; 4 guns
Scuttled in the harbour.

FLOATING BATTERY NUMBER TWO
Prize 1793; 4 guns
Scuttled in the harbour.

SERPENT Gunboat
Prize 1793; 70 tons; 1 × gun
Scuttled in the harbour.

VIPERE Xebec
Prize 1793; 4 guns
Foundered in Hyères Bay during the evacuation.
[London Gazette 17 January 1794; Gold: Naval Chronicle vol 2 p283-304]

★ ★ ★

1794

7 January MOSELLE Ship Sloop
Prize 1793; 520 tons; 120ft × 31ft; 18 guns
Commander Richard Henry Alexander Bennett
Sailed from Gibraltar on 19 December 1793 with a number of other British ships, bound for Toulon with stores for the garrison and the occupying British forces under Admiral Lord Hood. The sloop lost company during a gale on 25 December, the strong winds not enabling her to carry sufficient canvas to keep up. She made her way to the port independently, arriving off Toulon on 30 December and anchoring in the outer harbour, unaware that the port had been evacuated by the British 12 days earlier. Several ships could be seen in the inner harbour, but they appeared to have the white Royalist French flag flying. The weather remained poor, with a gale blowing directly into the harbour and eventually Bennett decided to anchor closer inshore. He did so, quite close to the shore batteries, but, becoming increasingly apprehensive of the situation in the harbour, sent a boat ashore with the Second Lieutenant, who was taken prisoner before he could return with the news of the French reoccupation. The French shore batteries then commenced firing at the sloop, which could not escape due to the contrary winds. When a French sloop and several gunboats emerged from the harbour, Commander Bennett had little choice but to surrender.
[TNA: ADM.1/5333]

30 January AMPHITRITE Ship Sloop
Deptford 1778; 514 tons; 114.3ft × 32ft; 18 guns
Captain Anthony Hunt
On 29 January she sailed from Portoferraio, Elba, to escort two transport ships to Leghorn (Livorno) and proceeded under all sail, raising the land to the south of the port at first light. They steered along the coast to the north and were off Vada when without warning at 9.30am she struck a rock. All sail was set in an attempt to free the sloop, but as that produced no effect, all sail was furled and the boats were hoisted out. On sounding around, her, she found herself surrounded by shallow water. Water butts were emptied, topmasts and yards were struck down and an anchor was taken out to prepare for kedging. By late morning, the anchor cable

was hauled taut, but she was held fast. Some guns were heaved overboard to further lighten her, but she was still held fast, and the ship was now striking the ground hard, the rudder being unshipped. Work continued to lighten her, but water was now reported to be entering, at a faster rate that the pumps could cope with. At 2.30pm, with the wind getting up and shifting round to the north-west, it was decided to cut the masts away, as it was feared they would go overboard. It was now clear that she could not be freed and with the water now up to the main deck, it was decided to abandon her. The boats started to ferry the crew to the transports, which had remained nearby, and at 4.30pm Captain Hunt was the last to leave, the water then being up to the quarterdeck. The remains were subsequently burned. The shoal water was not marked on any chart carried by the sloop.
[TNA: ADM.1/5331; ADM.51/21]

8 February CONVERT Fifth Rate
Prize 1793 (*Inconstante*); 930 tons; 32 guns
Captain John Lawford
Sailed from Bluefields Bay, Jamaica, on 5 February with over thirty ships bound for Europe, they were joined the next day by other merchant ships, until the convoy consisted of fifty-five square-rigged ships for European ports with five schooners for American destinations. The convoy steered for Cape Corrientes, at the western end of Cuba, although having to wait constantly for slower sailing vessels and a schooner which was leaking. By the evening of 7 February, she had finally marshalled the convoy into order and placed herself at the head of them. Overnight the formation evidently straggled and spread, and she observed that some were stretching ahead of her. At 3 o'clock in the morning distress guns were heard and the *Convert* steered towards the sound. Breakers were heard and then seen ahead, at which she tacked, firing guns as signals as she did. Despite this a merchant ship loomed out of the darkness and ran athwart her bows. Both vessels now fell off before the wind and were carried onto the rocks. Daylight revealed seven other ships aground. The masts were cut away, the ship was lightened, but she steadily filled with water and was left as a wreck. The crew was eventually taken off by ships of the convoy. The strong northerly set of the current was blamed for taking them off course and putting them onto the reefs at the eastern end of Grand Cayman.
[TNA: ADM.1/5331]

12 February SPITFIRE Schooner
Prize 1793 (*Poulette*); 61 tons; 59.4ft x 14.8ft; 4 guns
Lieutenant Thomas Walter Rich†
Capsized and sank off the eastern end of Jamaica at about 7 o'clock in the morning, when the vessel was struck by a heavy squall before she had time to shorten sail. Four survivors were picked up by the local sloop *Saucy Tom* after being in the water for four hours.
[TNA: ADM.1/245; www.britishnewspaperarchive.co: Northampton Mercury 19 April 1794 p3]

10 March NANCY Cutter
Hired 1793; 51 tons; 6 guns
Master Henry Watson
Sent from England with despatches to the Mediterranean for Admiral Lord Hood, she went into Hyères Bay, believing the British fleet to still be there. Sighting four frigates, which put out British colours, she closed until they exchanged the colours for French and took her surrender.
[TNA: ADM.49/96; www.britishnewspaperarchive.co: Kentish Weekly Post 21 March 1794 p4]

16 March PETITE VICTOIRE Tender
Prize 1793; 2 guns
Lieutenant – Morgan
One of the prizes taken away from Toulon, she was employed as a tender to the Mediterranean Fleet. Having developed a serious leak that could not be controlled. On investigation it was found that some of her planks had opened, so she was deliberately run ashore near the village of Erbalunga, Cape Corse, Corsica.
[Nicolas vol 1 p371; Gold: Naval Chronicle vol 2 p296]

11 April PROSELYTE Floating Battery
Prize 1793; 700 tons; 32 guns
Lieutenant Walter Serocold
Part of the force gathered to attack the port of Bastia, Corsica, she was ordered to anchor close to the town and assist in the bombardment. She moved inshore, but as she came to anchor off the tower of Torga, about 1,200 yards from the town, the swell and breeze made it difficult to position herself in safety, and she came under a heavy fire from the shore. The enemy fired red-hot shot and she was hit several times, which started fires in the hold. These could not be brought under control, and as it was impossible to get her off, she was abandoned, and she burnt to water's edge.
[James vol 1 p190; Nicolas vol 1 p383]

April ARDENT Third Rate
Bursledon 1782; 1,398 tons; 160.8ft x 44.7ft; 64 guns
Captain Robert Sutton†
Detached from the Mediterranean fleet off Corsica in February, to cruise between Villa Franca (Villefranche) and Antibes, southern France, to watch the movements of French ships, she disappeared. Pay book closed 30 April. Wreckage was later found, including part of the quarterdeck, which gave all the indications of a fire and

explosion; gunlocks sticking in the beams and netting embedded into planking.
[TNA: ADM 35/57; London Gazette 11 March 1794; James vol 1 p186; Brenton vol 1. pp302–03]

8 May PLACENTIA Schooner
Newfoundland 1789; 42 tons; 44.7ft × 15ft; swivel guns
Lieutenant Alexander Shippard
Based in Newfoundland, the schooner was bound for the small port of Burin from Merasheen, in misty weather, with fitful winds. As she steered past the island of Marticot, she found herself being taken inshore by the strong current. Sweeps were employed in an attempt to row clear, but she soon found herself close to breakers on a saddleback reef. The anchors were let go, which brought her up close to the surf. The following morning saw a fresh breeze from the land, so the schooner weighed but before the second anchor could be raised, the wind died and then a sudden squall took her aback. The cable was ordered cut, but before this was done, she was taken by the swell onto the rocks. She beat heavily, the rudder being unshipped and the sternpost shattered. Filling with water rapidly, she was abandoned as a wreck.
[TNA: ADM.1/5331]

9 May CASTOR Fifth Rate
Harwich 1785; 680 tons; 126ft × 35.1ft; 32 guns
Captain Thomas Troubridge
Acting as escort to several ships bound for Newfoundland, she was joined by several ships from the Channel Islands. At nightfall, then being to the south of Rame Head, several large warships were sighted. Morning revealed these to be a French squadron, which appeared to be four ships of the line and a frigate. The French bore up in chase, and the *Castor* ordered the convoy to disperse. The French ships gradually overhauled the frigate and commenced firing, the shot initially going over the ship. With a pair of 74-gun ships on either quarter and a frigate in her wake, the *Castor* surrendered to the *Patriote*, 74. The French squadron went on to capture the bulk of the convoy.
Note: retaken on 20 May 1794 by the *Carysfort*.
[TNA: ADM.1/5331]

14 May ALERT Ship Sloop
Rotherhithe 1794; 365 tons; 105.3ft × 28.1ft; 16 guns
Commander Charles Smyth
At daybreak, when in latitude 46.35 North, 15.15 West, heading across the Atlantic with despatches for Halifax, two ships were sighted to the north. The strangers altered course towards the sloop, which edged away. Private signals were made, but not answered. At 10.45am another three ships were seen on the larboard beam, which also altered towards the sloop. Signals were observed to be made between the groups at 11.20am, after which most of the ships altered away, leaving one on the beam and another astern in chase. At noon, several ships were seen ahead of them, on the bow, and Captain Smyth decided to engage her closest pursuer and if possible, cripple her rigging, which might enable the sloop to escape. Sail was shortened and at 1.45pm the chasing frigate ranged alongside and hailed her, calling on the sloop to surrender. Smyth replied 'No, no, not until you and I try first'. Shortly after this, firing began. After 30 minutes the enemy shot ahead and engaged her over the weather bow, preparing to rake her. The sloop hauled the staysail close to the wind and successfully avoided this. By 3.30pm the sloop was in a shattered state; several shots between wind and water, all the braces and standing rigging shot away, the driver boom shot away, and all the sails riddled, the mizzen staysail having no less than thirty-nine shot holes. She had suffered three men killed and nine wounded and unable to sustain the fight further, Smyth surrendered to his larger opponent, finding it to be the *Unité*, 40 guns.
[TNA: ADM.1/5333]

9 June SPEEDY Brig Sloop
Dover 1782; 208 tons; 78.3ft × 25.9ft; 14 guns
Commander George Eyre
Ordered to join the fleet off Ventimiglia, she was approaching the bay, when three ships were seen to leeward. These were presumed to be the squadron she was in search of, and course was altered to close. As they neared, private recognition signals were made, but as these were not answered the sloop wore round and made sail away with the strangers in pursuit. The strong winds allowed only double-reefed topsails to be carried and three French frigates were soon overhauling her. By 2 o'clock in the afternoon the *Sérieuse*, 36 guns, was close alongside. She crossed the sloop's wake and fired a broadside into her, at which the *Speedy* surrendered.
Note: recaptured in March 1795 by the *Inconstant*.
[TNA: ADM.1/5333]

11 June RANGER Cutter
Purchased 1787 (Rose); 195 tons; 74.7ft × 25.7ft; 12 guns
Lieutenant Isaac Cotgrave
Cruising in the English Channel, she was chased and engaged by the French frigate *Railleuse*, 36 guns, off Ushant. After offering a token resistance, the cutter surrendered. After the capture, the crew were badly treated by their captors, being stripped and kept in the open air for the two days it took to get to Brest.
Note: recaptured on 14 October 1797 by the *Indefatigable*.
[TNA: ADM.1/5333]

28 June ROSE Sixth Rate
Sandgate 1783; 599 tons; 120.5ft × 33.7ft; 28 guns
Captain Matthew Scott
The *Rose* sailed from Port Royal, Jamaica, on 26 June and the following day on hearing from a merchant ship that Sir John Jervis's fleet was then off Basse Terre. Captain Scott altered course, hoping to rendezvous with the fleet. At 1 o'clock in the morning, with little warning, the ship ran hard aground. The night was very dark, with frequent rain showers, and this had masked the breakers until the last minute. She struck the ground heavily several times as she beat over rocks, losing the rudder and staving in planks until she eventually found herself stuck fast. Guns were heaved overboard, and the anchors, topmasts and mizzen mast were cut away to lighten the ship. Morning revealed them to be on a reef off Rocky Point, Jamaica. Despite pumping and bailing the water could not be controlled and the boats were hoisted out and rafts made of booms and spars, the last of the crew leaving on 29 June.
[TNA: ADM.1/5331]

14 July HOUND Ship Sloop
Deptford 1790; 321 tons; 100ft × 27ft; 16 guns
Commander Richard Piercy
The *Hound* sailed from Port Royal, Jamaica, on 16 May to act as an escort to a homeward-bound convoy, but on 10 June she lost contact with them in thick weather but maintained her course for England. On the morning of 14 July, then being about 30 miles to the south-west of the Scilly Isles, two vessels were sighted which altered course towards her. Signals were made which were not answered, so she correctly guessed that they were French frigates. All sail was set, and she steered away, both frigates now in chase. After a three-hour pursuit, the frigates had caught her and stationed themselves on either beam. After two broadsides had been fired, the *Hound* surrendered, finding her captors to be the *Seine*, 38 guns, and *Galathée*, 36.
[TNA: ADM.1/5332]

22 July ESPION Ship Sloop
Prize 1793 (*Robert*); 276 tons; 86.5ft × 27.3ft; 16 guns
Commander William Kittoe
Encountered and chased and overhauled by a squadron of three French frigates south of the Scilly Isles, which forced her to surrender without resistance and took her into Brest.
Note: recaptured on 3 March 1795 by the *Lively*.
[TNA: ADM. 1/5333; www.britishnewspaperarchive.co: Hull Advertiser 2 August 1794 p3]

4 August SCOUT Brig Sloop
Purchased 1780; 276 tons; 82ft × 29.6ft; 14 guns
Commander Charles Robinson
Ordered to the vicinity of the island of La Galite off the North African coast, to protect Corsican coral fishermen, she was about 45 miles to the south of Sardinia, in company with nineteen Corsican fishing vessels, when two ships and a brig were sighted closing. They continued to close and hoisted Spanish colours, at which the *Scout* made the Spanish private recognition signals, which were correctly answered. She steered towards the supposed friends, until she was within hailing distance, at which point the strangers hauled down Spanish and hoisted French colours and the nearest frigate fired a broadside into her. Quite unprepared for action, the *Scout* made efforts to get away but her sheets and much of the rigging had been shot away. With large frigates now on either side of her, she had little choice but to strike her flag in surrender, her captors being the *Vestale*, 36 guns, and *Alceste*, 36. All but one of the Corsicans escaped. The Spanish signal codes had evidently been captured by the French at the evacuation of Toulon in December 1793.
[TNA: ADM.1/5333]

29 August IMPETUEUX Third Rate
Prize 1794; 1,880 tons; 182ft × 48.7ft; 74 guns
One of the prizes taken by Admiral Lord Howe at the battle known as the Glorious First of June, she was moored in Portsmouth harbour, with the stores being removed prior to being taken into dock for repairs. At about 3 o'clock in the afternoon a fire was discovered, which spread rapidly. Boats from nearby ships and the dockyard attended her, cut her free and towed her onto mudflats where she burnt out. The fire was believed to have been caused by careless use of metal tools in the magazines, which ignited loose gunpowder.
[www.britishnewspaperarchive.co: The Hampshire Chronicle 8 September 1794 p2]

6 November ALEXANDER Third Rate
Deptford 1778; 1,621 tons; 169ft × 46.11ft; 74 guns
Captain Richard Bligh
Having escorted a Gibraltar-bound convoy to a safe latitude, the *Alexander*, was in company with the *Canada* returning to England. At 2.30 in the morning, when in latitude 48.25 North, 07.53 West, several strange ships were sighted on the weather bow. By 3 o'clock these could be seen to be six large ships, at which the *Alexander* cleared for action and altered course, so that the British pair passed the strangers at about 4.30am, the nearest being about half a mile distant, but could not make out their identity. Soon after this the strangers were seen to alter course in pursuit of them. At daybreak, the *Canada* steered a more northerly

course whilst the *Alexander* continued to stand to the north-east. The strangers divided, with two ships of the line and a frigate going in pursuit of *Canada*, whilst three ships of the line and a frigate remained in chase of *Alexander* initially showing British colours, but at 8.15am both sides mutually hoisted national colours. A stern chase now developed, with the *Alexander* firing at her pursuers when she could. An attempt by the *Canada* to join her consort was blocked by the French, which were now within gunshot of *Alexander*. By 11 o'clock the leading French ship, *Jean Bart*, 74, was alongside and a close action began and when the *Jean Bart* fell away, another 74, the *Tigre*, maintained the dispute with a third ship of the line joining later. The fight was maintained for about two hours, until with main yard, spanker boom and all topgallant yards shot away, the rigging in tatters and forty casualties, she surrendered. The *Canada* was able to make her escape.

Note: recaptured on 23 June 1795 by Bridport's squadron.
[TNA: ADM.1/5332]

26 November ACTIF Gun Brig
Prize 1794; 165 tons; 10 guns
Commander John Harvey

On passage to England from the West Indies, several leaks became evident, the pumps having to be employed constantly. A survey on 24 November revealed the midship wales and fastenings were loose, the carlings and ledges had dropped out of place, several knees were broken, and the brig was working so much that she was constantly letting in water. At 6 o'clock in the evening of 26 November she was forced to make signals of distress, the *St Albans* coming to her aid. All the men were taken off and she was allowed to founder, then being in latitude 30.09 North, 76.58 West.
[TNA: ADM.1/5332]

26 November PYLADES Ship Sloop
Rotherhithe 1794; 367 tons; 105.1ft × 28.2ft; 16 guns
Commander Thomas Twysden

Making for Norway, the sloop encountered very heavy weather when off the Shetland Isles, and a constant hard gale from the south-east prevented her making much ground. It was decided to go into the lee of the islands and ride out the storm. The embarked pilot, James Hunter, undertook to perform this, although he was not familiar with the area. As they approached land some doubt existed as to which island was in view; Hunter believed it to be Fetlar, but as they neared, it became clear that it was Balta. As the wind increased, despite having only the foresail spread, the sloop was carried further in towards the land. It was decided to try to anchor off Baltasound, and they ran in to where they thought the harbour lay, only to discover that they were embayed off Haroldswick. Both anchors were let go and the sloop prepared to ride out the storm with topmasts struck, yards lowered, and yards trimmed fore and aft. To lighten the ship, most of the guns were heaved overboard, retaining two for signals. At 8 o'clock that evening the best bower cable parted, the sheet anchor being let go. She rode at anchor all night, until at 6 o'clock in the morning the small bower anchor cable parted, and she drove for some time until the sheet anchor brought her up. She was now close to the shore and the mizzen mast was cut away to ease the ship. A cutter was successfully launched with a midshipman to go ashore, and he made the return trip with a local pilot. He advised running the sloop ashore on a nearby sandy beach to save casualties. At 10 o'clock that morning staysails were hoisted, and the cables cut, and she ran herself on shore, the false keel and rudder both being beaten off. Spars were used to try and keep her upright, but these later broke and she swung broadside on to the beach and was bilged.

Note: a local man purchased the wreck and took her to Leith where she was rebuilt. The Navy re-purchased her on 27 June 1798.
[TNA: ADM.1/5332]

1795

22 February DAPHNE Sixth Rate
Woolwich 1776; 429 tons; 108ft × 30ft; 24 guns
Captain William Cracraft

Having escorted a convoy from Oporto, she had lost touch with the other ships, and was in the western approaches to the English Channel, when at daybreak on 22 February, several sails were seen to windward. Believing these to be her convoy, she steered towards them in hazy weather. As she closed, they could be seen to be large ships, probably warships. The private recognition signals were not answered, and she tacked away, clearing for action, as a frigate could be seen to be closing, with three others not far astern. By 3 o'clock in the afternoon the nearest chasing frigate was within gunshot range on the lee quarter and opened fire, and with another stationing herself on the weather side, the *Daphne* struck her flag in surrender. Her captors proved to be the *Tamise*, 32 guns, and the *Méduse*, 40, part of the Brest fleet under Admiral Villaret Joyeuse.

Note: recaptured on 28 December 1797 by the *Anson*.
[TNA: ADM.1/5332]

7 March BERWICK Third Rate
Portsmouth 1775; 1,623 tons; 168.6ft × 47ft; 74 guns
Commander Adam Littlejohn[†]

Detained in San Fiorenzo Bay to carry out repairs to the rigging after a storm, she sailed on 7 March in company with the *Nancy* transport to re-join the fleet off Leghorn (Livorno). At about 7 o'clock in the morning, when to the north of Corsica, several ships were seen to the north. Private signals were made, but not answered, so they were supposed to be French. The *Berwick* bore up for Bastia under all possible sail. By 8.45am, when close off Cape Corse, the leading French frigate, the *Alceste*, 36 guns, was close on the larboard bow and opened the action from ahead. The frigates' ability to manoeuvre kept her ahead of the more powerful *Berwick*, avoiding her broadsides. The remainder of the French ships closed, and another two frigates, the *Minerve*, 38, and *Vestale*, 36, stationed themselves close on the quarter and two ships of the line were also seen closing from astern. The action continued with all the vessels for about an hour, when Captain Littlejohn was struck by a bar shot which took off his head, the only man killed. Command devolved on Lieutenant Nisbet Palmer, who continued the fight for another 15 minutes, until, with rigging and masts in a shattered condition, he surrendered.

Note: recaptured at Trafalgar on 21 October 1805 but wrecked.
[TNA: ADM.1/5333]

18 March ILLUSTRIOUS Third Rate
Buckler's Hard 1789; 1,616 tons; 168.2ft × 46.11ft; 74 guns
Captain Thomas Frederick

On 14 March, the British Mediterranean fleet under Vice Admiral William Hotham fought an action against the French under Rear Admiral Martin off Genoa. The *Illustrious* was hotly engaged, being in action with several French ships of the line. She suffered twenty men killed and seventy wounded and was badly battered in rigging and hull. After the battle, the British fleet bore away for Spezia, the *Illustrious* being towed by the *Meleager* frigate. During the night of 17 March, the tow parted, which could not be rerigged due to the rising sea and the strong winds. The ship was now making water through the shot holes and damaged ports which could not be secured. At daylight on 18 March, land was seen which she steered towards, but on the *Meleager* signalling that she was standing into danger, they tacked away to the east. The visibility worsened, with frequent heavy showers of rain and sight of the *Meleager* was lost during one of these in the early afternoon. Shortly after this a lower-deck gun on the larboard side went off by accident, blowing away the port lid and sill. The ship wore round to prevent the water entering through the port and just after this she sighted the Mallora sand, off Livorno. A seaman, John Elias, was sent for, being acquainted with the coast, and he claimed to know a small bay nearby which was duly steered for. By 7.30pm, with the lead-line being constantly used, the ship was running into a bay near Avenza that had surf breaking violently on the shore. The ground shoaled rapidly, so the small bower anchor was let go which brought her up in six fathoms. Just as she did so, she took the ground aft and commenced beating, albeit gently. The cable soon parted, and she drove near to the shore before the best bower could be dropped. She now started striking the ground violently, lifting and pounding with every wave. At 10 o'clock the rudder went, and the seas regularly beat over her, but she held her position. The next morning attempts were made to rig a hawser to shore, with no success. Over the next two days, other ships from the fleet arrived off the bay and between 22 and 27 March the water was pumped clear of the ship, and stores and provisions removed from her. However, further attempts to haul her off failed, the ship refusing to budge. On 28 March, after all stores and provisions had been removed, she was abandoned and set on fire, burning for two days.
[TNA: ADM.1/5332]

1 May BOYNE Second Rate
Woolwich 1790; 2,021 tons; 182ft × 50.4ft; 90 guns
Captain George Gray

Flagship of Admiral Sir John Jervis, she was laying at anchor at Spithead, with the Admiral and Captain ashore and a party of soldiers exercising on the poop, firing muskets over the quarter. At about 11.30am, smoke was seen coming from the stern galleries. It proved difficult to discover the seat of the fire, but when the Admiral's cabin door was opened, the inrush of air set off a burst of flames from within. The heat and smoke were intense and soon beat back the firefighters. Within 15 minutes, smoke had spread throughout the ship and by noon the entire after section was ablaze, fanned by a breeze from abaft. The crew now started leaving, jumping overboard to cling to spars and timbers thrown from the ship, with boats from several ships nearby being sent to their aid. Eventually the anchor cable burnt through, and the ship drifted until she grounded just short of the Horse Sand where she lay, until she blew up with a massive explosion at about 5 o'clock in the afternoon, sending a huge column of smoke into the air. The exact cause was never ascertained, and different theories were put forward; the stove funnel which passed through the Admiral's cabin may have overheated and set fire to papers or a piece of burning wadding from the soldier's muskets may have drifted into an open window and set fire to the curtains. Eleven men dead or missing.
[TNA: ADM.1/5332]

16 June FLYING FISH Schooner
Prize 1793 (*Esperanza*); 80 tons; 62.7ft × 17ft; 4 guns
Lieutenant George Seaton

Having arrived at Port-au-Prince, Hispaniola, with despatches, she sailed on 14 June to return to Jamaica in company with the *Medusa*. That night she lost touch with the frigate, so proceeded independently. At 1 o'clock in the afternoon of 16 June when between Petit Gonaïves and Petit-Anse, two schooners were sighted, which bore up in chase. The wind dropped away to little more than a light breeze and both pursuers and pursued employed sweeps. A vessel was seen on the horizon, which the *Flying Fish* believed to be the *Medusa*, but despite making signals and firing guns, she took no notice. By now a third schooner could be seen closing, under British colours. This vessel closed fast, and nearing the *Flying Fish*, substituted her colours for French and opened fire. The action continued for an hour, with the other two schooners coming up and adding their fire. Unable to escape and faced with three opponents, Lieutenant Seaton surrendered to his largest opponent, *Les Resources des Republicaines*, 10 guns, which took the prize into Léogâne. The French fired high, into the rigging, with the result that there were no casualties.

Note: recaptured on 5 May 1796 by the *Magicienne*.
[TNA: ADM.1/5333; www.britishnewspaperarchive.co: Norfolk Chronicle 19 September 1795 p1]

30 June MUSQUITO Floating Battery
Deptford 1794; 309 tons; 80.1ft × 32.2ft; 4 guns
Lieutenant William McCarthy
Stationed in the Channel Islands, she was blown out of the anchorage off the Isle St Marcou in high winds and wrecked on the northern coast of France. Five men were drowned.
[TNA: ADM.35/1135; www.britishnewspaperarchive.co: Norfolk Chronicle 18 July 1795 p4; Steel's Naval Chronologist p39]

3 August DIOMEDE Fifth Rate
Bristol 1781; 887 tons; 140.2ft × 37.1 ft; 44 guns
Captain Matthew Smith
In July 1795, a force was assembled in India under Admiral Rainier to attack the Dutch colony of Ceylon (Sri Lanka), with the *Diomede* embarking two companies of troops from the 71st and 73rd Regiments. During the afternoon of 1 August, the ships arrived off the north-east coast of the island and spent the next day working towards the harbour of Trincomalee, the *Diomede* taking a snow laden with baggage and stores in tow. At daybreak on 3 August the ships were standing south, along the coast heading towards Back Bay. At 12.30pm with the ship running at about 8 knots with the snow still in tow, with no warning she struck a submerged rock. She was then between Pigeon Island and Flagstaff Point, and the lead-line had just been thrown, to show no ground. The ship passed over the obstruction, and continued, but water was reported to be entering the ship and the pumps were manned. Two hours later she successfully anchored in Back Bay, amongst the other ships, but made signals of distress, which brought several boats of the convoy to her assistance. The troops were quickly taken off by other ships as she was clearly settling. By 3 o'clock the lower deck was under water and an hour later she was ordered to be abandoned, the ship sinking at about 4.15pm. The loss was blamed on faulty charts, the rock that she struck being shown to be half a mile from its actual position.
[TNA: ADM.1/5338; ADM.51/4437; London Gazette 8 January 1796]

7 October CENSEUR Third Rate
Prize 1795; 1,820 tons; 74 guns
Captain John Gore
One of the escorts to a large convoy of over sixty ships from the Levant to England, they were off Cape St Vincent, when at just after 8 o'clock in the morning, signals were made for strange sails in sight. These were then changed, to indicate a strange fleet in sight and by 8.30 the Commodore in the *Fortitude* signalled 'prepare for battle'. The *Censeur* was then nine miles from the convoy, having been detached to investigate a strange ship earlier. She made sail to rejoin the main body and by 11 o'clock had joined the *Fortitude* and the *Bedford*, the signal for the convoy to disperse being made shortly afterwards. Within 30 minutes of this, the nearest of the French squadron, which consisted of six ships of the line and three frigates, commenced firing. The three British ships had formed into a line to receive the French, but the *Censeur*, due to her heavy rolling, had lost her fore topmast. She now dropped apart from her companions and was engaged by the *Barras*, 74 guns. She had exchanged about six broadsides with her opponent, when the mizzen topmast was shot away with the gaff. The *Barras* then ranged ahead to engage the British frigate *Lutine,* which had fallen back to assist the *Censeur*. By 2.30pm, several French liners were firing into her, the *Victoire,* 80, the *Duquesne* and *Révolution*, both 74 guns, all lay on her quarters, shooting away her main topmast and ripping up her sails and rigging. The *Duquesne* shot away her rudder at 3.45pm, which made her fly up into the wind, taking all her sail aback. Unable to resist further, she surrendered. Six men killed and eleven wounded. The other two British warships escaped, but thirty-three ships of the convoy were captured.
[TNA: ADM.1/5333]

7 November SCOURGE Brig Sloop
Purchased 1779; 234 tons; 80.6ft × 2.11ft; 16 guns
Commander William Stapp
Heading for the Nore from Germany, having escorted several ships to the coast of Denmark, the sloop was steering along the Dutch coastline as the wind steadily increased, and during 6 November shifted around to

the north. Sail was shortened and Commander Stapp became anxious that the sloop was being taken too close to the coast. The lead-line was employed constantly, and the pilot felt that they had plenty of sea room. That night the ground started shallowing and an attempt was made to tack, but she would not come around. Stapp now tried to wear, but before she would come up on the new course, she struck the ground and was held fast. The mainmast was cut away, to ease the brig as she was being lifted by the swell and beating heavily. Daybreak revealed them to be on the sands off Friesland, about nine miles from the shore. Several fishing vessels came and stood by her and took off the crew, the bows being almost completely underwater, beaten in by the pounding.
[TNA: ADM.1/5337]

12 November FLÈCHE Brig Sloop
Prize 1794; 278 tons; 92.9ft x 26.6ft; 18 guns
Lieutenant Charles Came

The sloop sailed from Leghorn (Livorno) on 9 November bound for the fleet anchorage in San Fiorenzo Bay, Corsica, arriving during the evening of 11 November. The night was dark and the wind variable and baffling as the sloop ran into the bay under double-reefed topsails, the lead-line being cast constantly. She passed close under the stern of one ship and when she was abreast the *Argo*, she prepared to anchor. As she did so the ground suddenly and unexpectedly shallowed, from 11 to 4 fathoms and the wheel was ordered hard over. The light and baffling winds then took her aback and she was taken onto a reef which ran out from the Fernelli tower. A hawser was passed from the *Argo* and anchors carried out by boats, but although moving her, she could not be freed. The sloop was now beating on the rocks in the heavy swell and soon the rudder was beaten off and she started making water. All through the next day she attempted to lighten ship, with guns and stores being taken out, but was stuck fast. That night the men were removed into the *Ça Ira,* the following morning revealing that she had capsized over onto her starboard side, the water over the gunwales. Lieutenant Came was warned for his future conduct, as he had shown a '... great want of attention' in attempting to anchor in restricted waters at night.
[TNA: ADM.1/5333]

9 December NEMESIS Sixth Rate
Liverpool 1780; 598 tons; 120.7ft x 33.7ft; 28 guns
Captain Samuel Linzee

Having escorted several merchant ships to Salonika, the *Nemesis* made her way to Smyrna (Izmir), in Turkey, to pick up other British merchant vessels. As she entered the bay, two French warships were seen at anchor inside the harbour, but as Smyrna was a neutral port, Captain Linzee decided to continue to enter, but as a precaution would anchor under the guns of Fort St James. The wind fell away to a calm as she entered, boats being hoisted out to tow her in and she was prevented from securing her original choice of anchorage when she ran aground. Although she floated free in the early hours of the morning, she had to drop anchor about four miles from the fort. The French vessels were seen to clear the inner harbour and the morning saw them joined by a third ship, and the three stationed themselves to cut off any routes of escape for the *Nemesis*. Now worried that the French were about to attack her despite being in neutral waters, Captain Linzee sent a series of letters to the British consul ashore, seeking assurances that he would receive the protection of the Turkish Government. Mid-morning saw the French ships weigh and they stood towards the *Nemesis*, with the *Sensible*, 36 guns, anchoring close under her stern, the *Sardine*, 22, on her larboard quarter, whilst the *Rossignol*, 22, placed herself between the fort and the *Nemesis*. The French hailed her and called on her to strike her flag. Boats with the First Lieutenant and finally Linzee himself paid several visits to the *Sensible* to argue that they were in a neutral port, and it was illegal to break the laws of neutrality, but all was in vain as the French remained firm that they would open fire if he did not surrender. Just after the Captain's return, the *Sensible* opened fire into the British ship. Faced with a superior force, the flag was struck. Three of her men, seaman John Waley and marines Joseph Smith and Jasper (alias Nathan) Robinson, subsequently entered French service, but were arrested after the capture of the *Sardine* in March 1796. All three were hanged.

Note: recaptured on 9 March 1796 by the *Egmont*.
[TNA: ADM.1/5334]

11 December LEDA Fifth Rate
Rotherhithe 1783; 881 tons; 137.4ft x 38.2ft; 36 guns
Captain John Woodley†

Sailed from Cork on 26 November with a convoy of merchant ships for the West Indies. The weather was poor and worsened. During a storm, when in position 37.56N 17.30W, a gun broke from its securing tackle and went through the ship's side. She rapidly filled with water and foundered. There were only seven survivors, who had managed to scramble on board the jolly boat which had floated free and was picked up by the merchant ship *Brownlow* of Belfast.
[www.britishnewspaperarchive.co: Hampshire Chronicle 19 March 1796 p4]

30 December AMETHYST Fifth Rate
Prize 1793 (*Perle*); 1,029 tons; 150.4ft x 39.5ft; 38 guns
Captain John Affleck

In company with three other ships, she departed from off Prawle Point during the evening of 29 December,

heading for the Channel Islands. By 1 o'clock in the morning the other ships had been lost, but she continued on the same course. The officer of the watch observed blue signal lights and heard signal guns astern and informed Captain Affleck, but he did not come on deck and ordered the ship to stand on. The Master came on deck at 4 o'clock for the morning watch, and believing they had run far enough to the south, it was decided to wear ship, and they were in the process of doing so when breakers were seen close ahead. The helm was put over, but she struck heavily forward. The ship drove over a ledge of rocks and floated free and initially the well was reported dry, but a short time later water was reported to be rushing into the hold, the Carpenter reporting that he feared that the water gained so fast, that the ship could float for little more than two hours. Having initially decided to return to England to survey the damage, it was clear that the ship was too severely damaged for this to be achieved. The weather was thick, with a gale blowing, so a course was steered for the island of Alderney. The guns and bower anchors were heaved overboard to lighten ship, and just after 7 o'clock the weather cleared to reveal the Casquet rocks close ahead. The frigate was run into Braye Bay, Alderney, and the sheet anchor let go to steady her and this successfully turned her stern to the beach. The masts were cut away and the ship allowed to settle before the crew went ashore, being assisted by the local people who formed a human chain through the surf. The subsequent court martial was critical of Captain Affleck. He seemed to have given very vague orders of what occasions he should be called and no orders regarding course changes. The ship had been allowed to run 40 miles through the English Channel on a southerly course, at night, with no one asking the Captain when the course should be altered, because they had no orders to do so. On being informed of losing touch with the other ships and despite observing signals astern, which indicated that they had run ahead of her consorts, Affleck had ordered the ship to stand on. It was not until the Master came on deck at 4 o'clock, in consultation with the officer of the middle watch, they decided to wear ship, although they had no orders to do so. Affleck was ordered to be reduced to the bottom of the seniority list of Captains and received no further appointments.
[TNA: ADM.1/5335]

1796

12 February SAINT PIERRE Schooner
Prize 1795
Lieutenant Christopher Pawle
Stationed at Martinique, she was cruising off that island when Lieutenant Pawle was taken ill, and with only one other watch-keeping officer on board, Midshipman Thomas Parsons, at the end of the first watch the schooner hove-to for the night off Pointe Negro, Fort Royal Bay, and had a reliable seaman, Andrew Steward, to act as lookout for the middle watch. At just before 4 o'clock in the morning, all hands were called on deck, as the vessel was drifting closer to Pigeon Island. An attempt was made to tack, but she missed stays. Lieutenant Pawle now came on deck and ordered the anchor to be let go, but before it could bring her up, she struck the ground. The flying jib was hoisted to sail her off, but this seemed to make her swing further onto the rocks. Attempts were made to kedge her off, but she was stuck fast and with the planking being stove in, she soon filled and capsized. No blame was attached to any of the officers or crew and Steward was shown to be an experienced seaman. Pawle had been the only officer on board for several days whilst Parsons had been absent on a prize and was quite exhausted. This had been the first opportunity for an unbroken night's sleep for four days.
[TNA: ADM.1/5335]

4 April SPIDER Lugger
Hired 1795; 173 tons; 18 guns
Lieutenant James Oswald
Attached to the North Sea fleet under Admiral Duncan, she was run down and sunk by the *Ramillies*, 74 guns, at about 7 o'clock in the evening. Lieutenant Oswald was not on board at the time, having been summoned on board the *Venerable*, leaving the Master, Daniel Follara, in command. The fleet was tacking in succession at the time and the Master claimed that the wind was taken from her sails by a large ship, and she would not answer the helm.
[TNA: ADM.1/5336]

11 April ÇA IRA Third Rate
Prize 1795; 2,210 tons; 80 guns
Captain Charles Dudley Pater
The ship was at anchor in the Golfe de St Florent, Corsica, when a fire was discovered in the fore cockpit, and although the outbreak was quickly tackled, the smoke, which was '... suffocating, thick and sulphurous' drove the men back. Captain Pater was on board the *Victory* and by the time he returned the flames were bursting up through the forward hatchway. After 90

minutes the forward part of the ship was evacuated, and soon after the ship was abandoned and left to burn out. The subsequent enquiry found that the origin was most likely to have been the Carpenter's cabin. He testified that when he opened the door of the cabin, flames and smoke burst out. William Briggs, a boy employed as the Carpenter's servant, had lit a brimstone match and then set in a bottle of combustible fuel that was kept in the cabin, and had probably left it burning.
[TNA: ADM.1/5336]

10 May **SALISBURY** Fourth Rate
Chatham 1769; 1,052 tons; 146ft × 40.6ft; 50 guns
Captain William Mitchell

Bound for Jamaica from the coast of Africa, she sighted Hispaniola, and during 9 May raised the island of Alto Velo and continued to steer westwards. At 3.30 in the morning breakers were seen ahead, and the helm was promptly put over, but before she could respond, the ship struck the ground hard and then swung broadside on to a reef. The sails were clewed up, boats lowered and an anchor carried out. She was stuck fast, however, and when heaved on, the cable parted. The procedure was repeated with a second anchor, with the same result. By now the ship was making water, despite heaving overboard shot and yards and topmasts being struck to lighten her. A boat was now manned and sent away to Jamaica to bring assistance, whilst a third attempt was made at kedging her off, using the sheet anchor. The wind was increasing, the water steadily gaining on the pumps and a dangerous heel was developing. Yards were put over the side to act as shore, and preparations were made to haul on the anchor in the morning. Daylight showed that they had been joined by several small boats and schooners, all Spanish, which showed an inclination to attack her. The ship was now full of water and the timbers were working so much that the upper deck planking was coming away from the sides. It was decided to give up the struggle and the ship was surrendered to a Spanish sloop which had arrived on scene. The enquiry ruled that the ship had run aground on the Île à Vache because a strong local current had set her further inshore than expected.
[TNA: ADM.1/5337]

9 June **QUEEN CHARLOTTE** Sloop Tender
Hired 1795
Midshipman Samuel Herring

Tender to the *Royal Sovereign*, she had sailed from Spithead on 28 February, with a large fleet of transports for the West Indies but became separated from the main fleet and so made her way independently across the Atlantic. Shortly after arrival, she was ordered to carry the baggage of the 55th Regiment to St Lucia, despite the protests of Midshipman Herring that no one on board had any knowledge of the islands and he had no charts. Nevertheless, he undertook the task, taking on board seventeen men of the Regiment along with one woman and her child. Thus encumbered, he attempted to enter Choc Bay, St Lucia, but ran hard aground. Efforts were made to lay out a kedge anchor and Herring asked nearby ships for help with boats to take off the baggage and passengers but received little sympathy and no help. After struggling for some time against the rising water, the mast was cut away and signals of distress were made. This finally brought assistance, with the baggage and soldiers being taken off, but by now the sloop was full of water and was abandoned as a wreck. No blame was attached to Midshipman Herring and the disaster did not affect his career as he was promoted to Lieutenant in September 1796.
[TNA: ADM.1/5336]

10 June **ARAB** Ship Sloop
Prize 1795 (*Jean Bart*); 315 tons; 90.8ft × 29.1ft; 16 guns
Commander Stephen Seymour†

Cruising off the north-western French coast, during the afternoon of 9 June a cutter and a brig were sighted, and the *Arab* bore up in chase. The pair was lost in the night, and the morning was very hazy, with light, baffling winds. Mid-morning, land was seen on the horizon, and she came about, but as she did so, without any warning she struck a submerged rock. All sail was thrown aback, but the ship was held fast and the hull was pierced, allowing water to pour in. The guns were ordered to be heaved overboard, but only one had been disposed of before the ship started sinking. The crew hastily left by boats and rafts, the ship sinking stern first. The ship had run aground on rocks off the Glénan Isles. The Captain, Surgeon and twenty seamen were lost, the remainder being rescued by the French.
[TNA: ADM.1/5336]

13 July **ACTIVE** Fifth Rate
Northam 1780; 699 tons; 126ft × 35.7ft; 32 guns
Captain Erasmus Gower

Having embarked Lord Dorchester, the outgoing Governor-General, and his suite at Quebec, the *Active* sailed for England on 9 July. Slow but steady progress was made along the St Lawrence River, although hampered by thick fog, the land being completely obscured during 12 July. The thick fog continued, and as she failed to obtain a noon sun sighting, she was forced to rely on dead reckoning to plot her course. At 7.30am, land suddenly loomed out of the fog, and before she could tack, she struck the ground. Sails were put aback, but she was well aground. As the fog cleared it was discovered that she had run onto Anticosti Island, near North West Point. Boats were hoisted out to take out kedge anchors and she was successfully heaved off

that evening, but she could not clear the rocks, and soon struck again, this time much harder. Booms and spare yards were hoisted out to act as shores, but these broke under the weight. The mainmast was cut away and guns heaved overboard to lighten her, but she remained stuck fast. All boats were now put into the water and the crew employed in clearing the ship of stores and provisions and landing on the island. The First Lieutenant was despatched in a launch to fetch aid, which arrived initially in the form of local trading schooners, and finally the *Pearl* frigate. All efforts to pull her off the rocks failed, and she was eventually abandoned as a wreck on 30 July. Seventeen men and six marines took the opportunity in this period to desert.
[TNA: ADM.1/5337]

15 July TROMPEUSE Brig Sloop
Prize 1794; 342 tons; 91.9ft × 29.7ft; 16 guns
Commander Joshua Watson
Based at Cork, she was cruising off the southern coast of Ireland, and being off Kinsale, the opportunity was taken to send in a boat to bring back some much-needed supplies, the sloop closing during the afternoon to pick up her returning boat. As she manoeuvred in Kinsale Harbour, she missed stays. An attempt was then made to wear ship, but she was very sluggish in answering the helm and despite letting the anchor go, before it could bring her up she went aground. Dockyard craft were soon in attendance, the brig was lightened, and efforts began to re-float her. This work proved to be in vain, the ebbing tide soon leaving her stranded, and timbers and planks started giving way as she settled. Water came in and by 2 o'clock in the morning as the tide turned, she started filling with water. All the crew were landed by boats and rafts, the last leaving by 9 o'clock.
[TNA: ADM.1/5336]

31 August UNDAUNTED Fifth Rate
Prize 1793 (*Arethuse*); 1,064 tons; 152ft × 39.8ft; 38 guns
Lieutenant Robert Winthrop
With Commodore Duckworth embarked, the *Undaunted*, under the temporary command of Lieutenant Winthrop as Captain Henry Roberts was ashore sick, headed for Jamaica under reefed topsails in squally, blowing weather, the horizon frequently being obscured by rain. Land was glimpsed on the evening of 30 August which was believed to be the eastern end of the island. The bad weather had prevented any observations being made, but the sight of land reassured those on board and the frigate stood on. Winthrop came on deck at 3.30 in the morning, being called after a schooner was sighted. This turned out to be a local trading vessel, but Winthrop remained on deck talking to the officer of the watch, when, without warning, the ship struck the ground with some force. All sails were thrown aback, but she would not budge and there was some confusion as to what she had struck. The morning light revealed that she was aground on the western end of the Morant Cays, to the south-east of Jamaica. The sloop *Jamaica* and a transport vessel that had been in company, stood by her, as the frigate beat heavily on the rocks in the swell. The movement became so violent that the rudder was knocked off and several people, including Duckworth, were thrown off their feet. The water gained on the pumps so fast that she was abandoned, the crew being taken off by the *Jamaica* and the transport. The lack of a sun-sight and the poor visibility combined with a strong current and the mistaken identity of the land had combined to cause the loss.
[TNA: ADM.1/5337]

July/August SERIN Brig Sloop
Prize 1794; 267 tons; 92.5ft × 26ft; 14 guns
Commander Daniel Guerin[†]
Sailed from Jamaica on 26 July to escort a convoy into the Atlantic, but not seen again; presumed foundered with all hands. Pay book closed end-July 1796.
[TNA: ADM.1/80/23; ADM.35/1829]

17 September CORMORANT Ship Sloop
Rotherhithe 1794; 427 tons; 108.6ft × 29.8ft; 16 guns
Acting Commander Thomas Gott[†]
Newly promoted to the command of the *Cormorant*, Commander Gott had only just joined his ship at Port au Prince, Haiti, when the ship was blown apart by an internal explosion. None of the few survivors, who were reported to be only twenty-six men, could give any account of how the disaster had occurred.
[TNA: ADM.1/247; ADM.35/299; www. britishnewspaperarchive.co: Hampshire Chronicle 17 December 1796 p4]

22 September AMPHION Fifth Rate
Chatham 1780; 679 tons; 126.1ft × 35ft; 32 guns
Captain Israel Pellew
The frigate was secured alongside the sheer hulk *Yarmouth* in the Hamoaze, Plymouth, to refit a damaged bowsprit, when at about 4 o'clock in the afternoon the ship was blown apart by a massive explosion. Survivors claimed that there two explosions, the first, smaller shock made Captain Pellew stand up and move to the quarter gallery, but this was followed by a huge detonation, which an eyewitness claimed to have almost lifted her clear of the water, her masts flying upwards and scattering debris over a large area. Forty officers and men were picked up but perhaps over 200 people were lost. The casualties included many dockyard workers, in addition to the wives and friends of the crew and tradesmen who had been allowed on board. Captain Pellew was amongst the survivors. He was in his cabin

with one of his Lieutenants and Captain Swaffield, Captain of the *Overijssel*. They were thrown against the deckhead, which killed Swaffield, the other two officers managing to jump through the shattered stern windows into the water. Most of the other survivors seem to have been on the upper deck. The Bo'sun, Mr Montandon, was supervising the re-rigging of the bowsprit and was blown into the sea, remembering nothing of the incident. Surprisingly, the hulk alongside suffered hardly at all but was covered in wreckage and the gruesome remains of shattered bodies. The exact cause was never ascertained, but seemed to originate in the forward magazine, and some pointed an accusing finger at the Gunner, who was employed in sponging and cleaning the guns, which included collecting loose gunpowder. Testimony at the court martial indicated that he had drawn the keys to the magazine that morning, to stow loose powder, without the knowledge or permission of the First Lieutenant. The wreckage was partly lifted in October and during November the remains were dragged to a jetty nearby and broken up.
[TNA:ADM.1/5337; www.britishnewspaperarchive.co: Hampshire Chronicle 1 October 1796 p3]

September BERMUDA Brig Sloop
Purchased 1795; 170 tons; 80ft × 23.6ft; 16 guns
Commander Thomas Maxtone†
Sailed from Halifax, Nova Scotia, on 13 September in company with the *Lynx* sloop to cruise off the eastern seaboard of the United States, but parted company that afternoon and was not seen again. She was presumed lost with all hands.
[TNA:ADM.52/3177; Steel's Naval Chronologist p40]

3 October EXPERIMENT Lugger
Plymouth 1793; 101 tons; 72.8ft × 18.6ft; 10 guns
Lieutenant George Hayes
When off Cape de Gata, Spain, several ships were sighted, which were assumed to be a convoy under Sir Hyde Parker, which was known to be in the area. The *Experiment* had been ordered to watch for any signs of the French fleet and decided to close and obtain any new information available. A frigate was observed to detach and steer for the lugger, but no national colours were shown, and being end-on, the strength could not be determined. As it closed, Lieutenant Hayes became convinced that she was British and went below to dress, in readiness to go aboard. When he returned on deck some 30 minutes later, the frigate was very close and altered course to run parallel and to his horror, she hoisted Spanish colours. By now several of the other ships were closing and it was clear that the *Experiment* had fallen in with the main Spanish fleet. She could not escape and when the frigate *Santa Sabina*, 40 guns, fired a shot at her, she surrendered.

Note: recaptured in February 1806 but not re-commissioned.
[TNA:ADM.1/5343]

3 October NARCISSUS Sixth Rate
Plymouth 1781; 430 tons; 108ft × 30ft; 24 guns
Captain Percy Fraser
The frigate was lying at anchor off Nassau, Bahamas, with Captain Fraser ashore on duty, when the weather worsened. By the morning of 3 October, the winds were at storm force, with frequent squalls of rain, which prevented Fraser from returning, leaving Lieutenant Alexander Renny the senior officer on board. During the afternoon, a third anchor was laid out and topgallant masts and yards were struck, but by 5 o'clock the weather looked so threatening, that topmasts were struck, and all yards lowered. By 8 o'clock that evening, with all hands on deck, the anchorage was in the grip of a full hurricane, with the most violent winds and lashing rain. The small bower cable now parted, and the *Narcissus* started driving across the bay. All the masts were now cut away, but she continued to drag, beating over a reef, constantly rolling and shipping water. At 11pm the winds started dropping away until they found themselves in calm waters and a clear sky. All the water was pumped out, the masts that had been cut away quickly secured and brought alongside and jury-rigged masts constructed. The night now became very dark, the wind increased and shifted round to the north-west, until by midnight it was blowing at hurricane strength again. The *Narcissus* was carried back towards the anchorage and stranded on Sandy Cay, about five miles north of Nassau. All the crew made their way ashore.
[TNA:ADM.1/5338]

11 October MALABAR Fourth Rate
Purchased 1795 (*Royal Charlotte*); 1,252 tons; 161ft × 42.2ft; 54 guns
Captain Thomas Farr
The *Malabar* sailed from Jamaica in July with a homeward bound convoy, but she became separated in poor weather about 800 miles west of Land's End. By 5 October, the weather had deteriorated into a full Atlantic storm, the *Malabar* suffering badly. She was a former East Indiaman and was a slow, sluggish sailer, difficult to handle. She rolled very deeply, the bowsprit becoming unseated, which led to its loss and in two days all the masts had been rolled overboard, the rudder unshipped, and the tiller broken. She had been given iron knees rather than the traditional oak and these soon pulled out, allowing the beams to work loose. When the securing bolts for the carronades pulled out of the bulwarks, four of the guns came loose, crashing across the waist, smashing the booms and the boats on them, killing one man and injuring four until they were

tumbled down a hatchway. All the guns were heaved overboard after this and jury masts rigged as the winds moderated, although the ship continued to work her timbers. On 8 October, the merchant brig *Martha* of Whitby came in sight and stood by the *Malabar* until the crew could be taken off. She was abandoned three days later. Lieutenant Richard Crocombe was dismissed the service afterwards for 'reprehensible conduct', as he seemed to have spent most of the time in the wardroom getting drunk. Also criticised was the Master, James Keltie, who was seen on the quarterdeck with Lieutenant Crocombe drinking, and later, when a party of seamen went to chock the broken rudder, he was so drunk that he '… tumbled out of his cabin, almost puked … and tumbled over to leeward and disabled himself'. He was ordered to be reprimanded.
[TNA: ADM.1/5337]

21 October BELETTE Sixth Rate
Prize 1793; 580 tons; 120ft × 32ft; 20 guns
Commander John Temple
A French invasion force landed on the island of Corsica on 19 October and commenced a rapid advance on the towns of Bastia and Ajaccio, then under the control of the British. The *Belette* was lying in Ajaccio Bay, and known to be in poor condition, a survey on her having been ordered at the end of September. This showed that she was not capable of proceeding to England, so masts, yards and stores were ordered to be removed. With the news of the French advance, she was towed inshore into shallow water and set on fire.
[TNA: ADM.50/79; ADM.51/1308]

21 October POULETTE Sixth Rate
Prize 1793; c580 tons; 20 guns
Commander Jeremiah Edwards
Lying in Ajaccio Bay, with the *Belette* (see above), when news of the French invasion force was received. She had also been found to be in no fit condition to get to sea, so having been stripped and emptied of all stores, at 7 o'clock in the evening she was towed inshore by boats from the fleet, run into shallow water until she grounded, and set on fire.
[TNA: ADM.50/79; ADM.51/1308]

21 October VANNEAU Gun Brig
Prize 1793; 120 tons; 6 guns
Lieutenant John Gourly
When attempting to sail from Porto Ferrajo, Elba, at 8 o'clock in the evening, in light and baffling winds, she twice missed stays and drifted in a heavy swell and struck a submerged rock. She passed over the obstruction and the small bower anchor was ordered to be let go to secure her, but it failed to bring her up before she touched the ground again. The best bower anchor was let go, but the shank broke as it was released, and she drifted onto a rocky reef, where she bilged.
[TNA: ADM.1/5337]

26 October BERBICE Schooner
Prize 1793; 121 tons; 72.9ft × 20.6ft; 8 guns
Lieutenant Thomas Tresahar
Stationed in the West Indies, the schooner was cruising in company with the *Lacedemonian* sloop between Martinique and Dominica, but lost sight of her consort during a dark, stormy night. She continued to steer on the last known course of the sloop, but ran onto Scotsman Head, Dominica, and was wrecked.
[TNA: ADM.1/5337]

1 November CURLEW Brig Sloop
Rotherhithe 1795; 316 tons; 95.1ft × 28.1ft; 18 guns
Commander Francis Ventris Field†
In company with the *Shannon*, the sloop was ordered to escort several ships bound from the Orkney Islands to the Nore. The ships sailed on 31 October in poor weather, and conditions worsened, so that by midnight the ships were obliged to lay-to under storm staysails. The gale continued the next day and the *Shannon* lost sight of the *Curlew* during the morning, when she was seen to be standing away to the southward under a forestaysail before being lost to view in squalls of hail and a heavy sea. She was not seen again and was presumed to have foundered soon after with the loss of all on board.
[TNA: ADM.51/1174; www.britishnewspaperarchive.co: Caledonian Mercury 6 February 1797 p2]

3 November HELENA Brig Sloop
Purchased 1778; 215 tons; 76.1ft × 26.9ft; 14 guns
Commander Jermyn Symonds†
Escorting a convoy to the river Elbe in company with the *Lion*, 64 guns, she was last seen ahead of the convoy in squally weather off the Dutch coast, but in the late afternoon disappeared. Sometime later some men were seen in the water, but despite the *Lion* throwing ropes over the side, they could not be saved. The *Lion* brought to, and a search in the morning revealed a quantity of debris and bodies. It was presumed that she had capsized.
[www.britishnewspaperarchive.co: Hampshire Chronicle 24 December 1796 p4]

7 December REUNION Fifth Rate
Prize 1793; 951 tons; 144ft × 38.10ft; 36 guns
Captain Henry Bayntun
The *Reunion* weighed from the anchorage at the Nore at a little after noon, with a brig in company, and made her way to the eastward. At 5 o'clock that afternoon she ran hard aground on the Sunk Sand in the Lower Swin. Sails were put aback, boats lowered, yards hoisted

over the side to act as shores and anchors taken out for use a kedge, but the heavy swell and high winds prevented them being laid at a sufficient distance to be of any use. As the tide fell that evening the wind shifted, making her position increasingly precarious. As the water dropped the shores started to break and at 7 o'clock in the morning she rolled over onto her side. Dockyard craft arrived, as did the *Martin* sloop, but they could do little but take the crew off. Captain Bayntun was reprimanded for his want of attention, as he had left the navigation entirely to the pilots and had not checked the ship's progress. The Master, William Williams, was demoted and ordered never to serve in any position higher than Master's Mate. He had failed to acquaint the Captain of the dangerous course the ship was steering and did not question the pilots. The senior pilot, Christopher Gasgoigne, was ordered to forfeit all pay due to him, never to pilot a Navy ship again and to serve a year in the Marshalsea Prison. It was found that he had not observed the landmarks and failed to take any soundings.
[TNA: ADM.1/5337]

19 December **COURAGEUX** Third Rate
Prize 1761; 1,721 tons; 172.3ft x 48ft; 74 guns
Captain Benjamin Hallowell

The *Courageux* was lying at anchor in Gibraltar Bay with Captain Hallowell absent at a court martial, when the weather worsened, with a steadily rising easterly wind and sea, and her anchor cable parted and although another anchor was readied for letting go, the ship had been carried across to the western side of the bay and under the guns of Spanish batteries before she could be brought up. This precarious anchorage clearly had to be shifted, so, now under the command of Lieutenant John Burrows, she weighed and attempted to regain her position. This proved to be most difficult, with several other ships parting their cables and the wind freshening all the time with frequent rain squalls. Several attempts were made to regain the anchorage, all unsuccessful. The Master, John Morton, recommended that they stand out to sea and re-enter the following morning, as with night approaching and the weather worsening, the enclosed waters of the bay would be dangerous. Burrows dithered and delayed, and finally called a conference of all officers on the quarterdeck, which did little but produce contrary ideas. Burrows seemed to be most concerned about leaving the bay without orders, and if the ship suffered any disaster, he would be blamed. Further time was spent beating about the bay, never gaining the anchorage until at 4 o'clock in the morning the ship finally ran out to sea. The crew, who had been on deck throughout, now went below exhausted, leaving only a Lieutenant and a reduced watch on deck to work the ship. About two hours later land was sighted ahead, and attempts made to shorten sail and wear ship. With the small numbers on deck this was taking far too long, and the Master urged Burrows to turn up all hands, but he weakly declared that he would not disturb them, as they were fatigued and had just drawn the daily issue of wine and he himself was tired and unwell. The land loomed closer, and the manoeuvre of wearing was not complete when she struck the rocks at the foot of Apes' Hill (Monte Hacho) on the coast of Morocco, quickly swinging broadside on to the shore. Water entered at a fast rate and the mizzen and main masts went overboard, the wreck being battered by the high winds and surf. The survivors scrambled onto the rocks, where they spent several uncomfortable hours before being rescued by local villagers, but 465 men died, including Lieutenant Burrows.
[TNA: ADM.1/5338]

21 December **BOMBAY CASTLE** Third Rate
Blackwall 1782; 1,628 tons; 168.6ft x 46.10ft; 74 guns
Captain Thomas Sotheby

Steering into the River Tagus, Lisbon, in company with several other ships, the officers were unacquainted with the river, so a local pilot was embarked. They passed over the bar, when the *Camel* store ship ahead of them took the ground and broached-to, swinging across the channel. The helm was put over to port to clear her, and this, combined with the strong current, carried her near to the shore. Despite attempts to get her before the wind, she would not answer and ran aground on a sandbank. Anchors were laid out and she was kedged free, but almost immediately struck the ground again, this time so hard that the rudder and tiller were unshipped. Yards were lowered overboard to act as shores, more anchors laid out, but she would not move. The struggle to release her went on for the next week, all the stores and guns being taken out and landed by boats of the squadron. Anchors were laid out and cables heaved on, but all to no avail, the ship settling deeper into the mud. She was stripped and finally abandoned as a wreck on 27 December.
[TNA: ADM.1/5338]

27 December **HUSSAR** Sixth Rate
Sandgate 1784; 597 tons; 120.6ft x 33.8ft; 28 guns
Captain James Colnett

Part of the Channel Squadron, she was driven onto the coast of northern Brittany during a heavy storm, and during the late afternoon went ashore about 15 miles west of the Île de Batz and was wrecked, the crew being taken prisoner.
[TNA: ADM.1/5339]

December VIPER Brig Sloop
Prize 1794 (*Vipère*); 291 tons; 95.7ft × 26.5ft; 16 guns
Commander Henry Parker†
Sailed from Dublin on 15 December to escort two merchant ships bound for Cork laden with Government stores, but on 20 December encountered the French fleet, bound for southern Ireland, and the ships dispersed to try and escape capture. The area was later swept by strong gales and heavy seas, which scattered the French. The *Viper* was not seen again and was presumed to have foundered with all hands at this time. Pay book closed 31 December.
[TNA: ADM.35/2030; www.britishnewspaperarchive.co: Caledonian Mercury 12 January 1797 p3]

1797

14 January AMAZON Fifth Rate
Rotherhithe 1795; 934 tons; 143.2ft × 38.4ft; 36 guns
Captain Robert Reynolds
In December 1796, the French mounted an abortive expedition to Ireland, the move being broken up by a succession of storms which scattered the fleet, and one of these, the *Droits de l'Homme*, 74 guns, finding herself alone off the Irish coast finally turned for home on 7 January. At about 3.30 in the afternoon of 13 January, when in latitude 47.30 North, about 150 miles to the south-west of Ushant, two British frigates, the *Indefatigable*, 44 guns, and the *Amazon*, sighted the French ship through drifting patches of fog. The frigates closed and soon made her out to be a ship of the line. Soon after this she was seen to lose her fore- and main-topmasts in a squall. The *Indefatigable* stretched ahead of her consort and by 5.30pm was close enough to open fire. The *Amazon* joined her companion over an hour later, firing a broadside into the French ship's quarter. The *Droits de l'Homme* despite being larger, carrying heavier armament and more men, was hampered by her damaged rigging and the steadily rising wind and sea. She found herself rolling so much that she was unable to use her lower deck guns. At 7.30pm the British pair broke off the action to range ahead and repair damaged rigging, returning to take up positions on either bow of the French ship. The weather steadily worsened, but the action continued with the ships running to the north-east, the frigates regularly raking their opponent, the French ship replying by yawing when she could, to return the fire. The fighting went on for seven hours, with occasional breaks to repair damages, the British ships falling back to the enemy's quarter. The French ship's mainmast went overboard at 10.30pm, while the *Amazon* lost her mizzen topmast, main topsail yard and spanker boom. Much of the rigging was cut up and yards shot through. The action came to an end at 4.20 in the morning when land was seen looming ahead, making the frigates haul off. The land was at first thought to be Ushant and the pair followed the French ship at a distance, until at about 6.30am, the dawn revealed surf breaking on rocks close ahead. Both frigates tacked away, the *Indefatigable* to the south, the *Amazon* to the north. About 30 minutes later the *Amazon* struck the ground with some force, close to the shore, which was Audierne Bay. The ship started to break up quickly in the surf and high winds, but the men were well disciplined, and rafts were made from spars and yards. An attempt to reach the shore in the cutter by six men, who had taken the boat without permission, failed when the boat capsized, and all were drowned. During the morning, the crew made the shore, the last raft reaching the beach at 9 o'clock. All of them were taken prisoner. Apart from the six who drowned in the wreck, she suffered three killed and fifteen wounded in the fight. The *Indefatigable* successfully beat out of the bay; the *Droits de l'Homme* was not so fortunate and was wrecked near the *Amazon* with heavy loss of life.
[TNA: ADM, 1/5341]

January HERMES Brig Sloop
Prize 1796 (*Mercuur*); 210 tons; 16 guns
Commander William Mulso†
Stationed in the North Sea, she disappeared and was presumed to have foundered and lost with all hands, probably in the series of storms which swept the area late December/early January.
[Steel's Naval Chronologist p40]

24 February BLOOM Tender
Hired 1795
Lieutenant Andrew Congalton
Employed in conveying newly-raised men to the naval ports from Ireland, she was chased and captured in the Irish Sea, along with a number of colliers, by the frigates *Vengeance* and *Résistance*, that had just landed a force in west Wales. All of the captures were scuttled
[TNA: ADM.35/216; www.britishnewspaperarchive.co: Saunders's News-Letter 16 March 1797 p2]

30 March PORT ROYAL Schooner
Purchased 1796; 10 guns
Lieutenant Elias Mann
Cruising off the northern coast of the island of Hispaniola, the early morning light showed a schooner close under the land. Lieutenant Mann decided to close and cut out the vessel, and by 6 o'clock she was within quarter musket-shot, when she opened fire with roundshot and grape. As she manoeuvred close to the enemy the wind fell away to a calm and the current began to carry her closer to the shore, where several men could be seen to be gathering on the high cliffs.

She let go her anchor, but it failed to hold her, and she was carried inshore by the tide to run aground. The people ashore now opened fire from the cliffs down into the *Port Royal*, which could not effectively reply. Water was reported to be entering at an increasing rate and being under fire no attempt could be made to get her off the ground. In this situation Lieutenant Mann had no choice but to surrender. One man was killed, two wounded.

Note: recaptured on 18 October 1797 by the *Pelican*.
[TNA: ADM.1/5340]

1 April TARTAR Sixth Rate
Rotherhithe 1756; 587 tons; 117.10ft × 33.9ft; 28 guns
Captain Hon. Charles Elphinstone
After taking several prizes off the coast of Hispaniola, the *Tartar* anchored overnight near Puerto Plata, weighing at 7 o'clock in the morning. As the sails were loosed and the ship's head put to seaward, the wind fell away, and she was carried by a strong current onto a sandbank. Sail was clewed up and boats lowered to take out kedge anchors, but she bilged and water rapidly flooded in. Within 30 minutes of grounding the water was up to the lower deck and with a shift of wind it was decided to abandon her. The crew transferred to a prize vessel and the *Sparrow* cutter, the water being up to the main chains as the last men left. Captain Elphinstone sent back a boat's crew in the night to set fire to the wreck. Two men were later found guilty of getting drunk when she grounded – the Carpenter, Thomas Marshall was dismissed the service and Seaman William Gray was flogged.
[TNA: ADM.1/5340]

6 April LACEDEMONIAN Gun Brig
Prize 1796 (*Lacédémonienne*); 195 tons; 12 guns
Commander Matthew Wrench
Cruising for privateers in the West Indies, a sloop was sighted off Point Salines, Grenada, which was chased. The chase went on for most of the day, another sloop coming into view later, which in turn bore up in chase of the *Lacedemonian*. By 5 o'clock that afternoon the chasing sloop was overhauling her and commenced firing random shots, although at too great a distance to be effective. Wrench gave over his chase, shortened sail and finally hove-to, to await the arrival of the other vessel. No colours were displayed, and doubt existed on board as to the identity of the stranger. When within hailing distance, with the crew at quarters, her identity was asked for. The reply '*Frederick* of Fort Royal' seemed to indicate a British privateer, and when ordered to send a boat on board, they replied, in good English 'Aye, aye, directly' and later 'I will come under your larboard quarter'. The crew, now believing they had a British vessel with them, relaxed. The stranger drifted under the quarter and a boat left her side. Not until it was close alongside were suspicions raised as it was seen to be full of armed men, and several men on board the sloop could be seen to be with arms. A frantic effort was made to set sail, but before anything could be done the boatload of men was coming over the side, accompanied by a volley of small-arms fire from the sloop, which then ran its bowsprit over the stern of the brig. Resistance was quickly swept aside, and although Wrench tried to organise a fight, he was knocked down and the brig captured. He was subsequently ordered to be severely reprimanded for his lack of preparedness.
[TNA: ADM.1/5339]

27 April ALBION Floating Battery
Deptford 1763; 1,652 tons; 168ft × 47.3ft; 22 guns
Captain Henry Savage
A former 74-gun ship employed as a floating battery off Foulness at the entrance to the Thames Estuary, she weighed and under the guidance of two pilots, made sail up the Swin Channel. Under reefed topsails and staysails, she made a long stern board, before setting the foresail and fore topsails to come around. As she did, she ran hard aground on the Middle Sand. Efforts were initially made to drive her over the obstruction, but this failed, so firing distress guns, all boats were lowered and anchors laid out. On heaving taut, the cables parted. By now dockyard craft had come to her aid, as well as the frigate *Brilliant,* which assisted in taking out guns and stores. The work to free her went on for two days, but only succeeded in moving her a few feet. By now the hull was showing signs of serious hogging and the remaining guns and shot were heaved overboard, the bowsprit cut away, along with the foremast. During the fall of the latter, it fouled the mainmast shrouds and damaged them to such an extent that the mainmast had to be cut away. That carried away the mizzen in its fall. Her back was broken by pounding on the sands and, unable to be shifted, she was abandoned as a wreck on 29 April. The pilots, William Springfield and Joseph Wright, were blamed for imprudent manoeuvring and going too far astern before altering course. They were both ordered to lose all pay due to them and never serve as pilots on Navy ships again.
[TNA: ADM.1/5339]

17 May PROVIDENCE Ship Sloop
Purchased 1791; 406 tons; 107.10ft × 29.2ft; 14 guns
Commander William Broughton
Broughton was ordered in October 1793 to proceed to the North Pacific for the purposes of discovery and survey. Sailing in October 1794, he proceeded via Australia and Tahiti to the Hawaiian Islands and northwards to the north-western coasts of America. The survey took him along the Alaskan coast, across to

Japan and thence south to the Chinese city of Macao. In April 1797, now accompanied by a schooner tender, the *Prince William Henry*, he continued his surveying work amongst the Sakashima Group, to the east of the island of Taiwan. At sunset no land was in sight, and they stood on with the intention of tacking at 8pm and then plying to windward. However, at 7.30pm white water was seen ahead and very soon afterwards the ship went aground on a coral reef in position 25.02N 125.40E. She beat over the obstruction, finally coming to a halt with her head lying to the south. Topmasts were struck and the boats hoisted out. She was found to be held fast on a coral reef but was not beating and little water was being made. However, as the night progressed the wind increased and by 9 o'clock the rudder had gone and several planks stove in. The *Prince William Henry* was ordered to stand by her, which she did, anchoring nearby in 25 fathoms. The water steadily gained on the pumps and by 10.30pm water was up to the orlop deck and as she was now heeling over to one side, Broughton ordered the crew to transfer to the tender, which was accomplished by 11 o'clock. Daylight revealed that the ship had settled and was breaking up. The natives on the nearby island of Ty-Pin-San (or Miyako-Jima) treated them well and the schooner eventually reached Macao. At the subsequent court martial, Lieutenant James Vashon was ordered to be dismissed the service for failing to keep a good lookout and failing to tack immediately the breakers were seen. He was later pardoned and reinstated in the service.

Note: the schooner tender was commissioned by Broughton as a new *Providence* and completed the survey.
[TNA: ADM.1/5344; Broughton: A Voyage of Discovery pp195–9; Mariner's Mirror vol 64 p243]

1 June EARL OF DENBIGH Stores Hulk
Purchased 1788 (*Carleton*); 181 tons; 73ft × 24ft
Employed in the dockyard at Antigua as a hulk, she developed a leak, which despite pumping and bailing increased in strength, and the water gained so fast, that there was barely time to haul her clear from the wharf where she lay. She foundered very soon after, lying with her topsides awash. When attempts were made to recover her timbers for possible use in the dockyard, it was found that she was very rotten, her fastenings destroyed by the reaction of iron nails and copper sheathing.
[TNA: ADM.241/2]

15 June FORTUNE Brig Sloop
Purchased 1780; 273 tons; 85.2ft × 28.10ft; 16 guns
Commander Valentine Collard
Steering along the coast of Portugal during a dark night, with drifting patches of fog, at 10pm and with no warning she ran aground. On sounding, the bottom seemed to be soft sand and initially she attempted to sail over the obstruction, but this only drove the sloop deeper into the sands. Sail was clewed up, guns shifted from forward to aft, topmasts and yards struck, and distress guns were fired. Boats were hoisted out to lay out kedge anchors and at 11.30pm she floated free. Sail was spread but it was found that she was making water at an alarming rate, baling having to be employed as well as the pumps. It was clear that she could not be kept afloat, and the ship's head was turned towards land seen nearby, with the intention of running her ashore onto a beach. She was so waterlogged, however, that she foundered some way short of the land. All spare spars and timber were heaved overboard for the crew to cling to and make their way to safety, and local fishing vessels arrived to take other men off. Daylight revealed that they had run onto the Portuguese coast near Torreira, south of Oporto. Collard was criticised for the lack of use of the lead-line when known to be so near land but was acquitted of blame.
[TNA: ADM.1/5340]

June PANDOUR Gun Brig
Prize 1795; 231 tons; 78ft × 26.11ft; 14 guns
Lieutenant Samuel Mason†
Stationed in the North Sea under Admiral Duncan, she disappeared and was presumed to have foundered with the loss of all hands.
[TNA: ADM.35/1360; Steel's Naval Chronologist p41]

June RESOLUTION Gun Brig
Purchased 1779; 198 tons; 14 guns
Lieutenant William Huggett†
Part of the Channel Squadron, based at Portsmouth, she was cruising in the western approaches, but was not heard of after taking a privateer on 3 June off Start Point. It was presumed that she had foundered with all hands. She was paid off on 31 July 1797.
[TNA: ADM.35/1505]

(2/3) July SWIFT Ship Sloop
Portsmouth 1793; 331 tons; 100.1ft × 27.6ft; 16 guns
Commander Thomas Heyward†
Stationed in the Indian Ocean, she was sent by Admiral Rainier from Trincomalee in April with despatches for Amboyna and Macao, informing them of the outbreak of hostilities with Spain. She sailed from the latter port on 15 June with a few homeward-bound East India Company ships to return to India. The ships encountered a severe tropical storm during 2/3 July, in position 19.04N, 124.18E, and the *Swift* was not seen after this, and was presumed to have foundered with all hands. Pay book closed end July.
[TNA: ADM.35/1827; Nautical Magazine January 1839 p17]

7 July MARIE ANTOINETTE Schooner
Prize 1793 (*Convention Nationale*); 187 tons; 85.6ft × 22.8ft; 10 guns
Lieutenant John McInerheny†
Cruising in the West Indies, at about midnight a portion of the crew, led by the Quartermaster, Jackson, rose in mutiny. The Surgeon and loyal members of the crew still in their hammocks were lashed up close to the deckhead by the mutineers, so that they could emerge only with difficulty. The Lieutenant was murdered by the mutineers and the schooner was taken into Gonaïves, Haiti, and turned over to the French. One of the mutineers, William Jacobs, was hanged and gibbeted in February 1799.
[TNA: ADM.1/5348]

20 July PRINCESS ROYAL Cutter
Hired 1793; 67 tons; 8 guns
Master Richard Keys
Employed as a tender the North Sea fleet under Admiral Duncan, she was chased and captured about 13 leagues (39 miles) to the north-east of Great Yarmouth by a French brig privateer. The captors put Keys and the crew into a boat, which landed at Flamborough on 24 July.
Note: other sources, including Steel, incorrectly give the year as 1798.
[www.britishnewspaperarchive.co: Norfolk Chronicle 5 August 1797 p2]

25 July FOX Cutter
Hired 1793; 124 tons; 12 guns
Lieutenant John Gibson†
When intelligence was received by the fleet under Admiral Lord St Vincent off Cadiz of the arrival of a rich Spanish ship at Santa Cruz, Teneriffe, a force of three ships of the line, with a 50-gun ship, three frigates and the *Fox* cutter were detached under the command of Rear Admiral Sir Horatio Nelson to attempt to capture the ship. The force arrived off the island on 20 July, but it was not until the night of 24 July that a landing was attempted to secure the fort and harbour. A force of about 700 marines and seamen were embarked in boats of the fleet and were led towards the mole by the *Fox*, which had a further 180 men embarked. At 1.30am, as the *Fox* approached the mole, a heavy fire was suddenly opened, accompanied by volleys of small-arms fire. The cutter was struck several times in the hull and sank very quickly, taking most of the men with her. The landing was a disaster; Admiral Nelson was severely wounded on attempting to land, having his arm shattered, and the landing party found themselves surrounded by far superior forces. They capitulated and were allowed to return to their ships the following morning. The expedition lost 140 men dead, 97 of them in the *Fox*.
[London Gazette 29 August 1797; James's Naval History vol 2 p58]

31 July ARTOIS Fifth Rate
Rotherhithe 1794; 996 tons; 146.3ft × 39.2ft; 38 guns
Captain Sir Edmund Nagle
The *Artois* was part of the blockading squadron off the western coast of France and was detached in the early morning to close the shore observe the enemy ships reported in the Pertuis d'Antioche. At about 8 o'clock she ran aground on the Baleine shoal off the north-west of the Île de Ré. She soon lost her rudder with the pounding, and although she floated free two hours later, she was unmanageable, and her head swung inshore to strike the rocks again about two miles off the shore. It was hoped that she might float free at the next high tide, but it became clear that she was held fast by the rocks, and when it was signalled that the French squadron had sailed, it was decided to abandon her. Several boats from the blockading squadron and the *Sylph* brig closed to take off all the men, the last leaving at about 4pm. She was then set on fire. The blame for the loss was placed firmly on the 'ignorance and carelessness' of the embarked pilot, Martin Martyr, and the Master, Alexander Andrews. The Master was disrated, dismissed his ship and ordered never to serve in a rating higher than a petty officer again. The pilot was reprimanded.
[TNA: ADM.1/5341; www.britishnewspaperarchive.co: Hampshire Chronicle 19 August 1797 p2]

22 September HERMIONE Fifth Rate
Bristol 1782; 715 tons; 129ft × 35.5ft; 32 guns
Captain Hugh Pigot†
Whilst cruising off the western end of Puerto Rico, the crew rose in the bloodiest mutiny ever to occur in the Royal Navy. Captain Pigot is acknowledged to have been a cruel and oppressive man, treating his crew with contempt and flogging men on a whim. It was claimed that he threatened to flog the last men down from aloft when reefing topsails, leading to two men falling to their deaths when struggling to avoid this certain punishment. After a day of silent and sullen anger, the mutiny erupted at about 10 o'clock in the evening, by shot being rolled around the decks to catch the unwary, and a small band of seamen breaking into Pigot's cabin, having first knocked down the Marine sentinel. A short struggle ensued in which Pigot was repeatedly stabbed by four of the mutineers, who then threw him out of the stern windows. The officer of the watch, Lieutenant Henry Foreshaw, was alerted by the Marine sentinel who ran on deck shouting that they were murdering the Captain. Foreshaw ordered a man below to discover what was happening, but

met with a blunt refusal, as he did on ordering the Quartermaster to steer for the *Diligence* sloop, then in sight. He attempted to take over the wheel himself, but the mutineers arrived on the quarterdeck, stabbed him and pushed him over the side. Foreshaw managed to cling to the mizzen chains and later pulled himself back on board, only to be discovered by two seamen who despatched him with pike and axe, despite his pleas for mercy. After Pigot's murder there followed a period of horror, with the officers and their adherents being pursued through the ship, dragged from hiding places and murdered. Seamen John Fletcher and David Forrester chased a midshipman until they caught him and hacked him to death with axes. Lieutenant Archibald Douglas was dragged from his cabin and killed, being pulled up a ladder by his hair whilst seamen, led by his servant, hacked and stabbed him. The mutineers, now led by a seaman named Lawrence Cronin, who declared himself to be a republican, along with Master's Mate William Turner and Boatswain's Mates Thomas Nash and Thomas Jay then convened a meeting to decide the fate of the other officers. Cronin urged them to kill all the officers, as none should be left to be a witness. It was decided that the Master should be spared, because he had the necessary navigation skills to take them to a safe port. In addition, the Carpenter and one Midshipman were spared, as it was felt that they had also suffered under Pigot's rule. All the others were condemned to death. One by one they were brought up to the upper deck and killed; this included Lieutenant McIntosh of the Marines, who was dying of yellow fever. Altogether five commissioned officers, along with the Purser, Bo'sun, Surgeon, a midshipman and the Captain's Clerk were killed. The wife of the Bo'sun was also on board and possibly raped by one of the mutineers. The frigate was then taken by the mutineers to the port of La Guairá on the coast of Venezuela and turned over to the Spanish, claiming that they had put the officers into a boat. After being paid a bounty by the Spanish, the mutineers scattered. The Master and a number of others who had not participated in the mutiny were treated as prisoners of war and soon exchanged. The mutineers were pursued for many years, with the last court martial apparently taking place in October 1806. Some of them tried to find refuge under false identities, some in the United States, although one of the main ringleaders, Thomas Nash, was handed over to the Royal Navy by the United States government; he was hanged at the foreyard of the *Acasta* in July 1799. Several of those captured in the West Indies were ordered to be hanged and then the bodies exposed on gibbets on hills, high points and headlands. In all it would appear that twenty-four of the mutineers were hanged, although some of the ringleaders, notably Cronin, were never caught.

Note: recaptured on 25 October 1799 by the *Surprise*.
[TNA: ADM. 1/5343; 5344; 5346; 5347; 5350; 5353; 5357; 5375]

16 November TRIBUNE Fifth Rate
Prize 1796; 916 tons; 143.7ft × 38ft; 36 guns
Captain Scory Barker†

Escort to a convoy bound for Canada, they sailed from Torbay on 22 September, but became separated during a gale on 10 October. They proceeded independently and sighted the land around Halifax, Nova Scotia at first light. The Master undertook to take the vessel into harbour, as he had frequently been to the port, assisted by a seaman, John Cosey, who also knew the port. By noon it was realised that she was steering close to the Thrum Shoal, and becoming alarmed, the Master sent for the Master's Mate, who had barely come on deck when the ship struck the ground. Boats from the shore came out in response to the distress guns fired, and Captain Barker was advised that the ship was lost, but he resolved to try and save her. All the guns and much of the stores were heaved overboard and at high tide that evening, about 9pm, she floated free. Efforts were made to put her head towards the harbour, but she would not steer and was carried inshore, to anchor in Herring Cove on the south side of the channel and the pumps manned, as it was found that she was making water. All this time the wind was increasing and by 10 o'clock that evening a full gale was blowing. Despite all their efforts the water gained on the pumps and the mizzen mast was cut away to further ease the ship. It was to no avail and the increasing gale added to the problems. About this time, she took a lurch and started to sink, which she did very quickly. The fore and mainmasts remained above the water and several dozen survivors clung to the rigging, but the gale and freezing wind took their toll, with frozen men losing their grip on the ropes and falling into the sea. The collapse of the mainmast in the early hours of the morning led to more fatalities. By morning only four survivors remained, and these were rescued by boats led by a 13-year-old boy, who gallantly rowed out in a skiff to take off two of them. These, with eight that had taken to boats earlier, were the only survivors.
[Gold: Naval Chronicle vol 1 pp468–73]

25 November HOPE Lugger
Hired 1794; 130 tons; 12 guns
Master – Rolfe

Sailed from the Downs as escort for a westward-bound convoy, she was run down in the night, when off Beachy Head, by the *Belfast* West Indiaman. The lugger foundered with the loss of eleven of the crew.
[Lloyd's Marine List 28 November 1797; www.britishnewspaperarchive.co: Kentish Gazette 28 November 1797 p4]

12 December **CHARLOTTE** Brig
Purchased 1797; 8 guns
Lieutenant John Thicknesse

Cruising between Hispaniola and Cuba, the weather slowly deteriorated, with strengthening winds and high seas. At 11 o'clock in the morning of 11 December, land was sighted which was believed to be Punta de Mulas, north-eastern Cuba, but by the afternoon, with no other land visible, it was realised that this could not be so. She tacked away the weather now very thick with constant heavy rain. During the afternoon, at 3.30pm land was again seen ahead and with the ground shallowing, it was decided to anchor. At 10 o'clock that night the best bower anchor cable parted, the small bower not holding her, and she started driving. The cable was cut, sail made and after making ground to seaward she re-anchored. Topmasts and yards were struck, and she rode in her new position until hit by a strong squall at 2 o'clock in the morning, which parted her cable and drove her onto a reef. The masts were cut away, but the brig was holed and soon filled with water. All the crew made the shore, along the masts, to be rounded up by the Spanish and taken to Santiago de Cuba.
[TNA: ADM.1/5343]

21 December **GROWLER** Gun Brig
Northfleet 1797; 169 tons; 76.2ft × 22.6ft; 12 guns
Lieutenant John Hollingsworth†

Sailed from the Downs anchorage on 20 December with a fleet of merchant ships, to escort them through the English Channel, it was a dark and moonless night, when at 2 o'clock in the morning, two French privateers, the *Rusé*, 8 guns, and *Espiégle*, 10, approached the convoy. The *Growler* was at the rear of the fleet and the French at first took the brig for a merchant ship and ran close alongside and hailed her, calling on her to surrender, taking the *Growler* by surprise. The officer of the watch refused and fired a gun in defiance. The action was short and sharp, the privateers running alongside to port and starboard and attempting to board. The crew managed to cut the grapnels of one attacker, which fell off, fired a broadside and then again ran alongside, entering large numbers of men. Lieutenant Hollingsworth was killed soon after, being shot through the thigh, falling back crying 'I am a dead man!' The brig was forced to surrender and taken into Boulogne.
[TNA: ADM.1/5351]

25 December **HAMADRYAD** Fifth Rate
Prize 1797 (*Ninfa*); 890 tons; 36 guns
Captain Thomas Elphinstone

Lying at anchor in Algiers Bay when the weather worsened, and with winds steadily increasing during 23 December topgallant masts and yards were struck. The following day, with winds at gale force and high seas running, topmasts were struck, yards lowered, and preparations made for quickly releasing another anchor. This proved its worth at 8 o'clock that night, when the best bower cable parted. The sheet anchor was let go, but when this failed to hold, the spare anchor was let go, which brought her up. She was now pitching and rolling wildly but held her position until daybreak the next morning when another cable parted. Cutting the remaining cable, some sail was made and an attempt was made to make the open sea, but she found this impossible. Shipping water from the waves dashing over her, Captain Elphinstone decided to run her onto a nearby sandy beach, which he did, the masts going by the board as they struck the ground. She drove up onto the beach, shattering the rudder, the surf breaking over her. Spars and yards were lashed together and about sixty of the crew left that night on these rafts. The following morning the remainder of the crew made it to the shore, the ship breaking up on the beach.
[TNA: ADM.1/5343]

27 December **HUNTER** Ship Sloop
Purchased 1795; 336 tons; 102.9ft × 26ft; 16 guns
Commander Tudor Tucker

The sloop was approaching the coast of Virginia, steering south-west by south, sounding regularly. By 2 o'clock in the morning she was in 11 fathoms, so sail was shortened, and the ship proceeded cautiously, land being faintly visible through the gloom, as was a ship ahead of the sloop. An hour later she suddenly struck the ground. She initially attempted to sail over the obstruction, but this failed. Water butts were emptied, and sail ordered to be taken in, but the sails and rigging were stiff with ice, making the handling difficult. Pumping commenced, which kept the incoming water at bay. Daylight revealed that they were aground on a reef, close to the land. The masts were cut away and boats were hoisted out and the cutter sent inshore to bring assistance. Before this could arrive, the wind had increased, and surf was soon beating over the wreck with some violence. That afternoon the wreck was abandoned, although five men were drowned in the attempt. The subsequent court martial found that the sloop had run aground on the Machipongo shoals, off Hog Island, Virginia, the Captain and crew being quite unacquainted with the coast.
[TNA: ADM.1/5332]

1798

3 January **GEORGE** Armed Sloop
Prize or purchase from 1795; 105 tons; 6 guns
Lieutenant Michael Mackie

Having sailed from Demerara on 2 January, bound for Martinique, at daybreak the following morning, two

vessels were seen, and she altered course to investigate. As they neared, they could be seen to be a schooner and a cutter under British colours, but this was not believed, and Mackie prepared for action. When within range, the cutter fired a shot at the *George*, hauling down British and hoisting Spanish colours as she did so. The ensuing action lasted for 40 minutes, the sloop holding her own against both opponents until the helmsman was killed and she flew up into the wind. At this the cutter ran onto her bow and grappled, whilst the schooner placed herself under the starboard quarter and raked her. The first attempt at boarding was repulsed, but a second was successful and the *George* surrendered. Eight killed and sixteen wounded.
[TNA: ADM.1/5348]

3 February RAVEN Brig Sloop
Blackwall 1796; 370 tons; 96ft × 30.8ft; 18 guns
Commander John Dixon
Ordered to cruise in the North Sea, she sailed from Great Yarmouth on 27 January and three days later found herself in a storm which lasted for several days, damaging her rigging and yards. It was decided to take shelter and effect repairs, so she bore up for the river Elbe. The North Sea pilot aboard attempted to take them up the river, but as they approached became confused and admitted that he did not know where he was. They anchored and took on a local, Danish pilot, who guided them towards Cuxhaven. As they entered the river, they drove onto the middle ground sand and found themselves hard aground. Yards and topmasts were struck, spars lowered over the side to prevent her from capsizing, but before anything could be done to kedge her off, she started filling with water and then keeled over. A group of fishing vessels approached and after lines were passed, encouraged the crew to tie themselves to the ropes and be pulled onto the fishermen, however, Captain Dixon noted that 'This idea, they did not seem to like at all'. To encourage the crew, several officers and petty officers were rescued in this manner before nightfall. The following morning several small boats were employed in taking off the remainder of the crew. The ship fell over onto her beam-ends at low tide. The blame was placed on the ignorance of the local pilot.
[TNA: ADM.1/5343]

4 April PALLAS Fifth Rate
Woolwich 1793; 778 tons; 135ft × 36ft; 32 guns
Captain Hon. Henry Curzon
The frigate arrived off Plymouth during 3 April from a cruise of the coast of France, and anchored in Cawsand Bay, and the Captain went ashore on duty. The weather was poor and steadily worsened, with gale force winds from the south-west, and yards and topmasts were ordered to be struck. The ship seemed to ride comfortably until the officer of the watch noted during the night that the anchor cables seemed to be slack, and at first light, it was realised that they were driving. Slack was taken up, but it found that one anchor seemed to have broken off. The second cable parted as they heaved it taut. The sheet anchor was let go, which brought her up, but she was now close to the shore, with only four fathoms of water under the keel. She again started to drag her anchor, and despite cutting away all the masts she struck the ground between Withy Hedge and Mount Batten Point, the last anchor cable parting as she did. She swung broadside-on to the sea and started beating heavily, breaking timbers and beams. As the tide left her lines were rigged to the shore and the crew were able to leave along this lifeline. One man lost his life.
[TNA: ADM.1/5344]

13 April LIVELY Fifth Rate
Northam 1794; 806 tons; 135.3ft × 36.8ft; 32 guns
Captain James Norris
Ordered to watch the harbour of Cadiz and intercept any shipping attempting to enter or leave, she cruised off the port in company with the *Seahorse* frigate. The night of 12 April was very dark, and when land was sighted, she came about and despite sounding constantly, at 2 o'clock in the morning she ran aground off Rota Point. The *Seahorse* nearby tacked away without incident. Throughout the morning efforts were made to free her, cables being passed to the *Seahorse* in efforts to haul her off, but all failed. The ground could be seen to be very shallow all around her and the ship could not be lightened, as it would only add to the obstructions. At low water she heeled over, straining the hull further. That night a lateen sailed vessel closed her, clearly reconnoitring, and daylight on 14 April showed several enemy gunboats gathering. The shore battery at Rota commenced firing at her, some of the shot going over them, and it was decided to abandon her. The crew left in an orderly fashion, being taken to the *Seahorse* by boat, the last to leave being Captain Norris, who set the frigate on fire before he left.
[TNA: ADM.1/5344]

18 April NEPTUNE Lugger
Hired 1796; 52 tons; 6 guns
Master Richard Gormer
Listed as being lost on this date, but no official account found; according to Steel she was run down and sunk in the English Channel, off Beachy Head.
[TNA: ADM.49/96; Steel's Naval Chronologist p42]

25 May DE BRAAK Brig Sloop
Prize 1795; 255 tons; 84ft × 28.11ft; 16 guns
Commander James Drew†

Sailed from Cork to escort a convoy of merchant vessels across the Atlantic, she became separated from her charges during a storm, but continued independently, arriving in Delaware Bay. As she was entering the Delaware River under mainsail and reefed topsails, she had just lowered her boat and was preparing to anchor about a mile from Cape Henlopen lighthouse, when she was struck by a strong squall. This laid her on her beam ends, and she quickly filled with water and foundered, with the loss of Captain Drew and thirty-eight officers and men. About twenty-five men were saved by her boat and a pilot boat.

Note: the remains were discovered and raised during 1986.
[www.britishnewspaperarchive.co: Hampshire Chronicle 7 July 1798 p2]

7 June GANNET Cutter
Hired 1796; 114 tons; 12 guns
Lieutenant James Clarke

Cruising off the northern coast of Hispaniola in company with the *Diligence* sloop, she was ordered to keep between the sloop and the island. Striving to maintain her station in hazy weather during a dark night, she struck a reef. Sail was taken in, both anchors laid out and guns moved from forward to aft, as it was found that she was afloat forward. As she heaved on the anchor cables in efforts to pull her free, one cable parted and she swung round, broadside-on to the reef. Daylight showed they were close to the land, which they identified as Picolet, near Cap Francois, and a boat was manned and sent away to bring help from the *Diligence*. At 7 o'clock that morning she fell over onto her starboard side and the water was gaining on the pumps. Guns and stores were heaved overboard in efforts to lighten the cutter, but an hour later several gunboats came into view and took up threatening positions. The *Diligence* could be seen about eight miles distant, too far off to be of any help. As it was impossible to free the cutter, all serviceable stores were destroyed, and the cutter surrendered.
[TNA:ADM.1/5345]

23 June ROVER Ship Sloop
Bermuda 1798; 356 tons; 104ft × 26.11ft; 16 guns
Commander George Irving

Convoying the *Elizabeth* transport to Quebec, the way was hampered by patches of thick fog the pair encountered. A brief sight of land through the fog was believed to be Scatarie Island, and the pilot pronounced himself happy to stand on through the fog. At 6.30 that evening she sighted breakers close ahead and attempted to tack, but before she could come around, she struck the ground. The larboard anchor was cut away and boats hoisted out, the foremast and bowsprit, both shaken by the impact, were cut away. A hawser was taken to the shore but became fouled on the rocks and was rendered useless. Another line was taken to the shore by a seaman who swam to the land, and this became an escape route, as the sloop was rapidly filling with water. All the men reached the shore, and the wreck was abandoned on 26 June. The boats were manned and reached the nearby settlement of Sydney. A strong current was blamed for taking them onto Cape Breton Island.
[TNA:ADM.1/5346]

30 June PIQUE Fifth Rate
Prize 1795; 906 tons; 144.1ft × 37.9ft; 36 guns
Captain David Milne

On 29 June, in company with the *Jason*, 38 guns, and the *Mermaid*, 32, the frigates were cruising off the western coast of France, they were off the Pointe de Penmarc'h when a large ship was sighted to the south-west, which was soon seen to be a large frigate apparently heading for Lorient. The British frigates steered different courses to ensure that she could not escape, the *Pique* finding that she was the closest in chase. The pursuit went all day, and it was not until 9 o'clock that evening that the *Pique* got within gunshot of the enemy and commenced the action, firing bow-chase guns. The pair finally came alongside each other two hours later and exchanged broadsides until 1.30am, when the main topmast of the *Pique* was shot away, and she fell away, dropping astern. The *Jason* was now close nearby and overtook *Pique*. Her captain, seeing the land was now very close, hailed and urged Captain Milne to anchor, but this was not heard. As they came up with the French vessel again, all three ships ran hard aground near the Pointe du Grouin du Cou within minutes of each other, the enemy ship losing all her masts. This did not stop the fighting, which went for some time until the *Mermaid* was seen approaching and at this the French frigate, which proved to be the *Seine*, 40 guns, surrendered. Efforts now concentrated on freeing the stranded ships. Both the *Seine* and *Jason* were hauled off with the assistance of the *Mermaid*, but the *Pique* could not be moved. She had bilged and as water was reported to be entering, and with her rigging and masts severely damaged, it was decided to abandon her, setting her on fire as they left. She suffered one killed with one missing, presumed killed, and six wounded.
[London Gazette 10 July 1798; TNA:ADM.1/5345]

19 July AIGLE Fifth Rate
Prize 1782; 1,002 tons; 147.5ft × 39.3ft; 38 guns
Captain Charles Tyler

Carrying despatches for Admiral Nelson, the *Aigle* was steering eastwards along the North African coast,

the island of Galite being raised during the morning. During the afternoon land was seen to the south and identified as being Cap Farina and Plane Island, and course was set to raise Cape Bon. A further landfall at 8pm was assumed to be the expected sighting of Cape Bon, and with nightfall and the wind increasing, a new course was set, and sail reduced to the foresail and reefed topsails. Quite unexpectedly, rocks were seen ahead, and despite the helm being put over, she struck a reef when running at 10 knots. The impact was very hard, and the rudder came off almost immediately. An attempt was made to sail over the obstruction, but this seemed to drive the ship onto more rocks, before she finally shuddered to a halt with the hull pierced in several places, the foremast and main mast going overboard with the shock. The pumps were manned, but could do nothing against the inrush of water, and so Captain Tyler ordered the mizzen mast cut away, to fall onto the rocks to allow the crew to escape. This was done and all the men made it to the shore. Morning revealed that they had run onto Plane Island. A merchant brig was seen, which responded to their signals to close, although the request to take them all off the island made the Master distinctly unhappy, saying that 'The Bey of Algiers would be very angry'. This drew the reply from Captain Tyler 'That is my business, not his – you will take us on board', which was done. The wreck was blamed on an error of navigation, with more distance being allowed than had been run.
[TNA: ADM.1/5346]

24 July RESISTANCE Fifth Rate
Deptford 1782; 895 tons; 140.2ft × 38.1ft; 44 guns
Captain Edward Pakenham†
On the evening of 23 July, the *Resistance* came to anchor in the Bangka Strait off the coast of Sumatra, in company with a prize Malay sloop. At about 4 o'clock in the morning the ship blew up with a tremendous explosion – the cause of the blast was uncertain, but it was conjectured that a lightning strike might have been the cause. About twelve survivors clung to the wreckage from which a raft was assembled, the prize sloop sailing off without taking any interest in their plight. Only four of the survivors succeeded in reaching the Sumatra shore, where they remained with the local natives being generally kindly treated as soon as they were satisfied that they were not Dutch. Although separated in subsequent adventures, being sold by local headmen, all four, Alexander McCarthy, John Hutton, Joseph Scott and Thomas Scott, reached the British settlement at Malacca. About 300 people perished in the disaster.
[Gold: Naval Chronicle vol 4 pp209–19]

26 July GARLAND Sixth Rate
Buckler's Hard 1779 (*Sibyl*); 599 tons; 120.7ft × 33.7ft; 28 guns
Captain James Athol Wood
Stationed at the Cape of Good Hope, the *Garland* formed part of a squadron ordered to cruise in the Indian Ocean searching for French warships. Information was received that a large ship was anchored near Fort Dauphin, Madagascar, which was believed to be one of the enemy vessels, and the *Garland* was ordered to investigate. Some miles to the north of the fort, on the northern side of Baie de Saint-Lucie, the *Garland* closed a ship seen at anchor, but as she approached, she struck a submerged, uncharted rock. The impact was such that the tiller was unshipped, and the ship filled with water rapidly. An attempt was made to run her onto a nearby beach, but she foundered before reaching it, the boats being hoisted out before she sank. The enemy ship had run herself aground on seeing the *Garland* entering the anchorage and, determined to carry out his orders, Captain Wood pushed on in the boats for the French ship, which was found to be a large merchant vessel, and captured her. Wood and his prisoners remained encamped ashore for five months before a ship arrived to take them off.
[TNA: ADM.1/5347]

17 August LEANDER Fourth Rate
Chatham 1780; 1,052 tons; 146ft × 40.8ft; 50 guns
Captain Thomas Thompson
On 1 August Rear Admiral Sir Horatio Nelson had led the British fleet into Aboukir Bay, Egypt, to inflict a crushing defeat on the French. The *Leander* was despatched on 6 August carrying Captain Edward Berry with the Admiral's letters addressed to Earl St Vincent, Commander-in-Chief, Mediterranean. At daybreak when about 6 miles to the south-west of Crete, a large ship was seen to the south-east, evidently standing towards the *Leander*. The British vessel, seeing that the stranger was a large ship of the line, spread all canvas and steered away, but the winds were light, almost a calm, and the larger ship steadily overhauled her, showing at first Neapolitan colours and then Turkish. By 9 o'clock that morning the ship could be seen to be a French 74-gun ship. Realising that she could not outrun her opponent, the *Leander* shortened sail to await the stranger, which was the *Généreux*. The French ship opened the action by firing a shot across the bows of the *Leander*, to which the British ship replied with a broadside. The pair then moved slowly ahead on the light breeze, exchanging broadsides for 90 minutes, with the *Généreux* moving closer, evidently intending to board. During this time, the *Leander* had suffered badly in her rigging, all the sails, rigging and yards having been ripped to pieces by the French fire. The bow of the *Généreux* struck the

larboard side of *Leander* and several attempts were made to board, but all failed, being strongly resisted by the Marine detachment led by Sergeant Dair, which drove them back. A slight breeze now sprang up, which as the *Généreux* disentangled herself from the *Leander* took the French ship away. The advantage was now seized by Captain Thompson to place himself under the stern of his opponent and several raking broadsides were fired, causing considerable damage. The *Généreux* eventually came around before the wind and the mutual cannonade began again, with the *Leander* suffering badly, having all the masts shot away, the hull shot through in several places and with a growing number of casualties. By 3.30pm the French ship came ahead and placed herself across the bows of the *Leander*, gaining an advantageous position. On being hailed, the *Leander* surrendered. She had suffered thirty-five men killed and fifty-seven wounded, the latter included both Captains Thompson and Berry. This was one of the hardest-fought single-ship actions of the period, and certainly the most gallant, since the *Leander* was facing an opponent which was 900 tons larger, had over 600 more men and threw a broadside two and half times as heavy.

Note: recaptured at Corfu on 3 March 1799.
[*London Gazette* 20 November 1798; TNA: ADM.1/5347]

25 August ETRUSCO Store Ship
Purchased 1794; 919 tons; 137.8ft × 38.6ft; 16 guns
Commander George Reynolds

En-route to England from Martinique with a large convoy, the *Etrusco* was in a poor state, with numerous timbers found to be rotten, but she had been cleared by dockyard officials for the passage. A storm on 23 August dismasted her completely; the ship was already leaking and the strain of all the masts going overboard made matters worse. Deck beams and planking were coming away from the ship's side and there were several leaks and she struggled under jury rig to keep company with the other ships. A request for a survey from ships in company was refused, the senior officer giving Commander Reynolds permission to act at his own discretion. The decision was therefore taken to abandon the ship, and the morning of 25 August saw the last of the men transferred to the *Beaver* and *Assurance*, Commander Reynolds discharging three guns downwards through the bottom before he left.
[TNA: ADM.1/5345]

26 August CRASH Gunboat
Deptford 1797; 160 tons; 75.3ft × 22.1ft; 12 guns
Lieutenant Bulkeley Praed

Cruising in the North Sea in company with the *Ariadne* frigate, she parted company in strong winds and high seas during the evening of 23 August. Attempts were made to stand out to sea, but the weather seemed to worsen, with the sea constantly washing over them. The guns were heaved overboard in a vain attempt to ease the gunboat, but the hull was working badly, straining the timbers. At 3 o'clock in the morning of 26 August, land was seen ahead, and she wore round and anchored, but almost immediately found that the anchor was dragging, and she was being driven inshore. At daylight she went aground on the island of Vlieland, the surf breaking around her. The bottom was scuttled, and powder, shot and small arms were heaved overboard before the crew clambered ashore, to be taken prisoner by a detachment of Dutch soldiers. She was subsequently salvaged and commissioned by the Dutch.

Note: recaptured on 11 August 1799 by the *Pylades*.
[TNA: ADM.1/5347]

16 September MUSQUITO Schooner
Prize 1793 (*Venus*); 71 tons; 55.4ft × 16.11ft; 6 guns
Lieutenant John Whyte

Off the northern coast of Cuba escorting a small convoy, when several strange ships were sighted at daybreak, which were closing, and it became clear that they were frigates. When they failed to answer private signals, the schooner ordered her charges to stand away, while she bore up for Puerto Padre, all the strangers following her. She anchored just inside the bar of the harbour, the frigates initially heaving-to outside the bar, which led to hopes that they would escape. However, these were dashed when the enemy proceeded to cross the bar and anchor within musket shot, at which the *Musquito* surrendered. Her captors proved to be the Spanish frigates *Medea*, 44 guns, *Esmeralda*, 34 and *Santa Clara*, 34.
[TNA: ADM.1/5348]

13 October JASON Fifth Rate
Deptford 1794; 998 tons; 146.3ft × 39.3ft; 38 guns
Captain Charles Stirling

Cruising off the entrance to the port of Brest in fine weather, a small convoy of coasting vessels was sighted off the Pointe de Raz, making for Douarnenez Bay. She was quickly in chase and soon took overhauled and took three of them as prizes. The remainder had made all sail for Brest, and the *Jason* steered after them, spreading studding sails in the freshening breeze. When running at about 10 knots, to everyone's astonishment she ran onto a submerged, uncharted rock. Sail was quickly clewed up and pumping started, but the water entered at an alarming rate, and she slowly started to heel over. It was feared that she might founder there, but she suddenly floated free, although the water was gaining on the pumps. Guns were heaved overboard, and the anchors cut away to lighten her, and a course was set for the nearby French coast. She was run ashore in the Anse de Dinan, the masts were cut away and

preparations were made to burn her, but before this could be completed, French soldiers came on board to take possession of the wreck.
[TNA: ADM. 1/5348]

16 October **CHARLOTTE** Schooner
Purchased 1798; 8 guns
Lieutenant John Thicknesse

On being cleared of any blame in the wreck of the *Charlotte* brig in December 1797 (qv), Lieutenant Thicknesse was appointed to the command of a newly-purchased schooner, also to be named *Charlotte*. Ordered to cruise off Cap François, Hispaniola, they were close to the headland when at daybreak a large schooner was sighted. She steered towards the stranger and soon a second, smaller schooner and two large armed launches were seen to be astern of her. At this, she altered away, the strangers in pursuit. The chase went on until 5.30pm, when the leading pursuer was close by and the *Charlotte* altered course to bring her on the beam, within half musket-shot range, and opened fire. The action continued for an hour, until the second schooner joined, as did the launches. Her main boom topping lift was shot away, as were all the braces; one gun was dismounted, and others disabled by broken breechings. Surrounded and unable to continue, she surrendered, finding her main opponent to be the *Enfant Prodigue*, 12 guns. The French practice of firing high had resulted in the rigging being severely damaged, but only one man being wounded.

Note: recaptured on 13 April 1799 by the *Amaranthe* but not recommissioned.
[TNA: ADM. 1/5347]

3 November **MARGARET** Brig Tender
Hired 1797
Lieutenant John Pollexfen†

Carrying despatches for the squadron under Captain Home off the western coast of Ireland, she encountered heavy seas and strong winds. At the height of the storm, people ashore on the island of Innishboffin heard signal guns being fired, and just after 9 o'clock at night a brig was seen to be ashore on a ridge between the mainland and the island. The watchers ashore were unable to render any help to the vessel which went to pieces with all aboard being drowned. Wreckage recovered after the storm showed the brig to have been the *Margaret*.
[www.britishnewspaperarchive.co: Hampshire Chronicle 3 December 1798 p2]

13 November **PETEREL** Ship Sloop
Frindsbury 1794; 366 tons; 105.1ft × 28.2ft; 16 guns
Lieutenant George Long

Cruising off the island of Minorca, the *Peterel* chased a local coasting vessel, but then sighted four large ships to the north. She left off her chase and altered course towards the strangers, which by 2.30pm could be seen to be frigates. The sloop tacked and stood away, the strangers following. The *Peterel* hoisted Danish colours at first, but the chase continued, heading towards Cape Formentera, and in another attempt at a ruse, she hoisted French colours, but they still pressed on after her. At sunset three of the pursuers were within three miles of her, and by 9 o'clock they were so close that it was feared they would fire into her, so the sloop bore up and spread more sail, the leading frigate firing bow-chase guns at her as she did. The chase continued through the night until at 8 o'clock in the morning, with the frigates still very close, and they took station on each quarter of the sloop and directly astern. When they opened fire, the sloop had little choice but to surrender. Her captors proved to be the Spanish frigates *Santa Casilda*, 34 guns, *Flora*, 34 and the *Pomona*, 34.

Note: recaptured the next day by the *Argo*.
[TNA: ADM. 1/5348]

26 November **MEDUSA** Transport
Plymouth 1785; 920 tons; 140.9ft × 38.7ft; 26 guns
Commander Alexander Becher

Lying at anchor off Gibraltar, she was under orders to weigh and proceed, but the wind was variable, with shifting direction and occasional squalls. She eventually got under way and loosed the foresail and fore topsail having previously set the driver and staysails. As she tried to put her head to seaward, the wind shifted again, and this took her down towards the shore. The sails were furled, and she anchored, only to receive a testy message from Admiral Lord St Vincent, indicating that he was very displeased with the display so far, and was impatient at the delay in sailing. After signalling for assistance from the dockyard, the Master Attendant came aboard to direct the manoeuvre and under his direction topsails and staysails were loosed and the cable hove in, the intention being to swing her head to seaward. The baffling winds again defeated them, the yards having to be braced constantly to take advantage of the wind and she again failed to make headway, drifting closer inshore. All sail was thrown aback and the anchors let go, but they did not bring her up in time before she struck the ground off Rosia Bay, where she bilged and filled with water.
[TNA: ADM. 1/5350]

3 December **KINGFISHER** Brig Sloop
Purchased 1782; 370 tons; 95.1ft × 30.9ft; 18 guns
Lieutenant Frederick Maitland

Lying at anchor in the River Tagus, she was under orders to sail and escort the homeward-bound Newfoundland convoy as far north as Oporto, there being considerable anxiety about its safety, since numerous privateers were

known to be in the area. A local pilot, Francisco Antonio, was embarked and Maitland, new to the sloop, suggested that the north passage be taken rather than the south, as this seemed to be quicker. The pilot agreed and took them into the North Channel. As they entered, the pilot luffed the sloop, which lost way and was taken by the current onto nearby sands. The rudder was unshipped by the blow and the sloop heeled over as it dug into the ground. The mainmast was cut away and attempts were made to bring her head round, but she was stuck fast in the sand and water was reported entering. Despite pumping, within 20 minutes the water was up to the lower deck and boats were hoisted out and rafts made for the crew. These latter were not needed as the *Latona* and several local fishing vessels came to their assistance. One man drowned during the disembarkation. The pilot was detained by the local authorities, but they refused to release him for the subsequent court martial, which acquitted Maitland of any blame.
[TNA: ADM.1/5347]

10 December **COLOSSUS** Third Rate
Gravesend 1787; 1,717 tons; 172.3ft × 48ft; 74 guns
Captain George Murray

Returning to England from the Mediterranean, she arrived off the Scilly Isles on 7 December and anchored off St Mary's. The winds steadily increased until by 10 December it was a full gale. Topgallant masts were struck, and spare anchors were provided until, at 4 o'clock in the afternoon, the anchor cable parted. The small bower anchor was let go and brought her up after she had drifted a little way. Captain Murray became worried at the position of the ship and planned to set sail, but the pilot doubted that they could weather the rocks, so they prepared to ride out the storm. The sheet anchor was let go, topmasts struck, and yards trimmed, but she soon found that she was dragging her anchors. At about 6 o'clock she struck the ground, although quite gently at first. Any thoughts of lightening the ship had to be abandoned, because of the shoal water that surrounded them, it being feared that if guns were heaved overboard the ship would strike them. They hauled taut the anchor cable, which initially freed them, but dragging in the ebbing tide, she struck the ground again, this time very hard. Pumps were manned, but the water gained and by midnight the rudder had come away with the constant pounding on the ledge of rocks near the island of Sampson, called the Southern Wells. By daybreak, the water was up to the sills of the upper deck ports and the ship was starting to break up. Local boats attended them to take off the crew, which was accomplished by 3 o'clock in the afternoon. One man was lost, falling overboard and drowning.
[TNA: ADM.1/5348]

14 December **AMBUSCADE** Fifth Rate
Deptford 1773; 684 tons; 126.3ft × 35.1ft; 32 guns
Captain Henry Jenkins

Cruising off the western coast of France, she was off the entrance to the River Gironde, when at daybreak a vessel was seen approaching from seaward. They were expecting to be joined by the *Stag* frigate that day and it was assumed that the stranger must be her companion, and no recognition signals were made. It was not until 9 o'clock, when the stranger suddenly altered course and spread sail to get away was it realised that she was in fact a French *corvette*. Somewhat startled by this, the *Ambuscade* made all sail in chase of the stranger, which was the *Bayonnaise*, 28 guns, returning to France from Cayenne. By 11am the *Ambuscade* was close enough to be able to fire a shot from her bow-chase gun, which was returned by the French ship, who shortened sail to await the arrival of *Ambuscade*. A close action now commenced, the pair exchanging broadsides for about an hour when one of the main-deck guns of the *Ambuscade* blew up, causing several casualties. This caused some confusion, during which the French vessel made sail away, and it was some time before the British frigate could continue her pursuit. The *Bayonnaise*, smaller and with the weaker armament, had suffered badly during the action, and it was realised that a renewal of the fighting might well mean a defeat, so they decided to board the *Ambuscade*, a detachment of the Alsace Regiment being on board. As the British frigate closed, it overshot her opponent, and the helm of the French ship was put up to run on her onboard, allowing her bowsprit to run into the mizzen shrouds of the *Ambuscade*, bringing down the mizzen mast, and then dropped astern as the shrouds parted, to lie under the British frigate's stern. From here the French soldiers were able fire several destructive volleys and continued to use the bow-chase guns. In a short time, Captain Jenkins was seriously wounded, having a musket ball in his thigh; the First Lieutenant, Dawson Main, was shot dead, as was Mr Brown the Master. The only surviving sea officer, Lieutenant Joseph Briggs, came up on deck, but was shot through the head and the officer of Marines, Lieutenant James Sinclair, received musket balls through the shoulder and leg. The command now devolved upon the Purser, William Murray, who attempted to rally the men who were showing signs of wavering under the onslaught. At this crucial point, an explosion of powder occurred in the cabin below, caused by cartridges carelessly left on the rudder head during the discharge of a gun through the stern windows. This blew out part of the stern, wounded all the men around the gun, and started a small fire. At this, the men quit their quarters and fled below, and when the French boarded, the Purser had little choice but to surrender. The *Ambuscade* suffered ten killed and thirty-six wounded. The action has been criticised by British naval historians, as the *Ambuscade*, being larger and carrying a heavier armament, should have quickly overwhelmed her opponent. Some blame must be attached to Captain Jenkins, who, although acquitted at his court martial, seems to have been careless in his preparations, failing to ascertain the identity of the stranger when first seen and in action the frigate had not been handled well and he had generally failed to give any display of leadership. The court also criticised the crew for having 'not shewn that intrepidity so deservedly the characteristic of British seamen'. The French captain, Jean-Baptiste Richer, was promoted in recognition of his achievement.

Note: recaptured on 28 May 1803 by the *Victory*.
[TNA: ADM.1/5350; James vol 2 pp242–9]

14 December COQUILLE Fifth Rate
Prize 1798; c900 tons; 36 guns
Captured by a British squadron off Ireland, the *Coquille* lay in the Hamoaze, Plymouth, being de-stored prior to being surveyed for service in the Royal Navy. At about 4 o'clock in the afternoon a fire was discovered on board. The blaze appeared to start aft near the gun room and, with no crew on board, only parties to remove stores, the fire spread rapidly, so that within 30 minutes, after an explosion, the ship was ablaze from stem to stern. Boats from the dockyard and other ships closed, and attempts were made to scuttle her, but the smoke and flames were too much, so she was cut from her mooring and towed to a mud bank at the entrance to Milbrook Lake to burn out. Unfortunately, a Scarborough collier, the *Endeavour*, was already aground in the mud nearby and her rigging caught fire and soon spread, and she was also burnt out. Three midshipmen, about ten men plus one woman and a visiting customs officer on board were lost.
[www.britishnewspaperarchive.co: Reading Mercury 17 December 1798 p4]

(?) CAROLINE tender
Hired 1798
Lieutenant (D?) Whittle
Listed by Steel as being 'Lost in the East Indies. Crew never heard of'; no further details found
[Steel's Naval Chronologist p42]

1799

2 January DUKE of YORK Lugger
Hired 1794; 57 tons; 6 guns
Master Benjamin Sparrow
Having sailed from Falmouth with despatches for the Channel fleet, she had successfully delivered them but at about 11 o'clock at night she struck a submerged rock off Ushant. Water rapidly entered and the boat was quickly hoisted out and all the crew managed to scramble on board before she foundered. They spent an uncomfortable 21 hours in the boat before being picked up by a merchant vessel from Bremen, which returned them to Falmouth.
[www.britishnewspaperarchive.co: Bath Chronicle 17 January p4]

7 January APOLLO Fifth Rate
Blackwall 1794; 994 tons; 146.3ft × 39.2ft; 32 guns
Captain Peter Halkett
Cruising off the Dutch coast, the winds were moderate, but a large swell was running as she approached Den Helder, sounding every 30 minutes. At 6.45am, quite unexpectedly, she ran aground. Sail was thrown aback, and this did move her a little, but did not free her. Some guns were thrown overboard and water and beer casks were emptied to lighten her, and the stream anchor was taken out by boat. Attempts to haul her free failed to have any effect, the ship settling and heeling as the tide ebbed. All the crew were taken off in boats to other ships that had come to her assistance, so that by 8.30pm all had safely left her. It was intended to return and either refloat her or set her on fire, but the wind was such that this proved impossible, and she was abandoned as a wreck. The court martial found that the ship had run aground on the Noorderhaak sands, caused by an error in dead reckoning, no sun sights having been made. The pilot, John Bruce, was judged to have shown a want of skill and dismissed the service.
[TNA: ADM.1/5348]

17 January ARGUS Lugger
Hired 1794; 148 tons; 14 guns
Lieutenant Richard Clark
Sailed from Jamaica in December 1798 with mail and despatches for England, but met with poor weather and lost her mainmast in a storm, which incident killed her Master, William Hall, and she was also forced to throw overboard most of her guns. When, in the Bay of Biscay, she met the French privateer *Vendémaire*, 18 guns, she could offer no resistance, and was carried into Bordeaux.
[www.britishnewspaperarchive.co: Hereford Journal 3 April 1799 p2]

18 January GRAMPUS Store Ship
Purchased 1795 (*Ceres*); 1,181 tons; 157.1ft × 41.3ft; 26 guns
Captain John Hall
Lying at anchor in the Long Reach, River Thames, she weighed at 7 o'clock in the morning, at the same time lowering two boats to assist by towing, a local pilot, Samuel Richardson, taking charge of her. At 9.30am she ran hard aground on the Barking Shelf. Kedge anchors

were taken out, but efforts to haul her free were to no avail. Spare topmasts and other spars were positioned over the starboard side to stabilise her at low tide, and at high tide in the afternoon more efforts to free her failed, and help was summoned from Woolwich Dockyard. Work went on for the next three days, off-loading stores into boats, getting down topmasts and yards and laying out anchors. She would not budge and began to settle in the mud, especially after the rising and falling of the tides had strained the ship so much, that beams and timbers started giving way. By 21 January she had 20ft of water in the hold, and it was clear that she could not be saved. The masts were cut away and derricks were rigged over the hatchways to recover the remainder of the stores before she was finally abandoned as a wreck on 31 March. During that night, the wreck caught fire, fanned by a strong easterly wind, and she burnt down to the lower-deck ports. The ignorance of the pilot was blamed for the wreck.
[TNA: ADM.1/5349; ADM.51/4452; NMM: ADM.359/19A]

19 January STROMBOLO Gunboat
Purchased 1797; 1 gun
Lieutenant William Davies

Fitted out for the use of the garrison in Gibraltar, she got under way at 4 o'clock in the afternoon, using sweeps, to cover the sailing of a convoy. She towed *Transport-55* clear of the mole and then returned to escort another. The activity had attracted the attention of the Spanish and a few gunboats and armed launches could be seen emerging from Algeçiras. Casting off the tow, she turned towards the Spanish vessels which were closing rapidly, using sail and sweeps. About eight of the boats surrounded her, fire being mutually exchanged at close range. Several of the enemy's shots hulled her, one in particular entered the larboard bow, the water flooding in and filling her. With the gunboat foundering, the crew took to the water, from where the Spanish picked them up.
[TNA: ADM.1/5348]

19 January WILKIN Gunboat
Purchased 1797; 1 gun
Lieutenant Henry Power

Another of the Gibraltar gunboats escorting a convoy clear of the colony (see above), she used sweeps to tow the merchant ship *Esther* clear of the harbour, when a number of Spanish gunboats were seen approaching. The *Wilkin* pulled towards them, finding that she was faced with about eight enemy boats and launches, which split up to surround her. An attempt was made to fire the long gun, but only the priming went off and the men were forced to resort to the use of muskets and pistols. The engagement was short and furious, the main-topmast and mizzen mast being shot away before several boats ran alongside her, at which she surrendered.
[TNA: ADM.1/5348]

1 February PROSERPINE Sixth Rate
Harwich 1777; 595 tons; 120.6ft × 33.7ft; 28 guns
Captain James Wallis

Sailed from Great Yarmouth 28 January with the Honourable Thomas Grenville and his suite, bound for Cuxhaven in Germany, from where Grenville was to proceed to Berlin on a diplomatic mission. Having embarked a pilot off Heligoland, the frigate proceeded to the mouth of the River Elbe, where she anchored near Scharhorn Island. It was now discovered that the buoys marking the channel appeared to have been removed, but the embarked pilot and the ship's Master undertook to take the ship into Cuxhaven. On the morning of 31 January, the ship weighed in company with the *Prince of Wales* packet vessel and proceeded upriver. The weather, which had started fine and clear, steadily worsened during the day and by mid-afternoon it had started to snow. By 4pm the visibility was so poor that the *Proserpine* anchored, then being about four miles from their destination. The weather continued to worsen, so that by 9 o'clock that night it was blowing a blizzard, with large floating masses of ice coming down the river. Morning saw the weather clearing, but the channels upriver were completely iced up, so the frigate weighed and stood away to seaward, Captain Wallis intending to make a port in Denmark. At about 9.30am she ran hard aground, to the surprise of the pilots, who thought themselves well clear of any danger. Spare yards and spars were lowered over the side to act as shores, and boats were hoisted out to take out anchors, but the ice surrounding the ship prevented the boats achieving anything. Guns and stores were thrown overboard to lighten her, in hopes of floating off at high water, but this failed. The wind steadily increased, with flurries of snow and the amount of ice around the ship steadily built up. The following morning revealed the ship to be aground on the Scharhorn Riff, near the island of Neuwerk, surrounded by ice, which was increasing. The timbers now started giving way under the pressure, the sternpost evidently being broken. Despite the appalling weather, it was decided that the only way of escape was to walk over the ice to the island of Neuwerk. At 1.30pm the ship's company and passengers quit the ship to walk the six miles to the land, in freezing temperatures, with regular showers of thick snow, walking across ice and through snowdrifts. Of the 187 people who set out, all but fourteen reached the island. Seven seamen, one boy, four Marines and one woman and her child died in the attempt. The survivors were well treated by the islanders and after a few days the diplomatic suite and the most of crew were taken to Cuxhaven by local fishermen.

The Master, Mr Anthony, accompanied by five others, returned to the wreck on 10 February, finding that it was almost crushed by the ice. A sudden snowstorm caught the little party on board before they could leave and the ship, still trapped in the ice, was swept out to sea and eventually taken by the tides onto Baltrum Island where she was driven onshore, Mr Anthony and his companions surviving this second shipwreck.
[TNA: ADM.1/5348; Gold: Naval Chronicle vol 1 pp332–5]

3 February NAUTILUS Ship Sloop
Itchenor 1784; 345 tons; 100.9ft × 27.7ft; 16 guns
Commander Henry Gunter
Escorting a convoy from the Baltic, the weather as she approached the English coast was appalling, with strong, biting winds and regular storms of sleet and snow. At 3 o'clock in the morning, she brought to under a mizzen staysail and fired signal guns for the convoy to do the same, it being reckoned that they were near the shore. It soon became clear that they were being carried by the wind and tide, at the rate of about three knots. A sharp lookout for land was ordered, but the snow became so thick, it was blinding. At 6am breakers were seen ahead, and attempt was made to wear ship, the fore topmast staysail being hoisted, she came around, but found breakers ahead again. Wearing ship for a second time, she failed to clear the land and struck the ground heavily, bilged and filled with water very quickly. Boats were hoisted out and rafts made for the crew to make the shore, finding they had been wrecked at Speeton cliffs, on the south side of Filey Bay, about four miles north of Flamborough Head.
[TNA: ADM.1/5348]

12 February WEAZLE Brig Sloop
Sandwich 1783; 202 tons; 78.11ft × 25ft; 14 guns
Commander Hon. Henry Grey†
In poor weather, she ran into Croyde Bay, North Devon, and during the afternoon anchored, but when the wind shifted to the north-west and increased in strength, she weighed and attempted to put to sea. Unable to make enough ground to seaward, she became embayed in Morte Bay. Firing signals of distress, she was driven aground on the Morte Rocks, near Baggy Point, where she rapidly broke up with the loss of all the crew, the Purser, who was on shore at the time, being the only survivor.
[Gold: Naval Chronicle vol 1 p256]

8 April PEGGY Lugger
Hired 1795; 61 tons; 8 guns
Master Henry Atkins
Listed as being 'taken' on this date, no details have been found, but likely to be identical to the report in Lloyds Marine List, which reproduced an extract from French newspapers, reporting captures of British vessels, which included the information that '*Peggy*, an English privateer of 8 guns, is sent into Port Malo'.
[TNA: ADM.49/96; Lloyd's List 26 April 1799]

10 April LORD MULGRAVE Armed Ship
Hired 1793; 429 tons; 20 guns
Commander Edward Hawkins
Sailed from Cork on 9 April, bound for Dublin, the Tusker Rock being raised at 8 o'clock that evening, and course was set to the north-east for the night. At just before 4 o'clock in the morning she ran hard aground in the shallow waters of the Arklow Bank. Water butts were broken open, ballast heaved overboard and more sail set in an effort to lighten the ship and sail over the obstruction, and at just before 6 o'clock she floated free. Water was found to be entering the ship at a fast rate, so a course was steered for the land, visible nearby, and two hours later she ran onto the beach near Arklow, the water then being up to the main deck.
[TNA: ADM.1/5349]

22 April BRAVE Lugger
Hired 1798; 137 tons; 12 guns
Lieutenant John Guyon
Escorting a convoy eastward through the English Channel in company with the *Harpy* sloop, when at a little after 8 o'clock in the evening, then being about six miles off Beachy Head, they encountered the merchant ship *Eclipse* steering down channel, en-route to Jersey with troops. It initially appeared that they would pass each other, when the *Eclipse* changed course and collided with the lugger, which was effectively cut in half and quickly sank. The merchant ship claimed that they believed the *Brave* had altered toward them, forcing them to alter to keep clear.
[www.britishnewspaperarchive.co: Ipswich Journal 27 April 1799 p6]

8 May FORTUNE Polacre
Prize 1798; 180 tons; 10 guns
Lieutenant Lewis Davis
Ordered by Captain Sir Sydney Smith to cruise off the coast of Syria to intercept any supplies bound for the French garrison at Acre, it was at dawn, off Jaffa, when a squadron of three ships and two brigs was seen. The *Fortune* altered towards them, the *Dame de Grâce* prize gun vessel, which was in company, following. About an hour later, the nearest of the strangers, a brig, hoisted a British red ensign. Lieutenant Davis closed to within hailing distance, when the brig, which was the French *Salamine*, 16 guns, substituted French for British colours and fired into her. The *Fortune* returned the fire, and the fighting went on for two hours, until the *Fortune* had expended all her cartridges, three guns had been

dismounted and the rigging reduced to shreds. When the *Salamine* came close onto her larboard quarter intending to board, the *Fortune* surrendered. Two men were killed and four wounded.
[James vol 2 pp336–7]

8 May DAME de GRÂCE Gun Vessel
Prize 1799 (*Vierge de Grace*); 87 tons; 4 guns
The companion of the *Fortune* in their cruise along the coast of Syria, when they fell in with the French squadron (see above), the *Dame de Grâce* gave what assistance she could to her consort, but when the *Salamine* forced the surrender of the sloop, and with three frigates and another brig approaching, she surrendered. The French took out the crew and scuttled her.
[James vol 2 pp336–7]

24 May DEUX AMIS Gun Brig
Prize 1796; 220 tons; 14 guns
Master Samuel Willson
Bound for Portsmouth from Jersey, with Viscount Gossett and Lieutenants d'Auvergne and Lemprière on board, she sailed on 23 May. The weather was thick and hazy, with a large sea running, the brig pitching and rolling a good deal, shipping water. No lead-line was held on board, although a temporary one had been made, which had proved unreliable. At 3.30am land was seen looming ahead and orders given to tack, but before she came around, she struck on a submerged rock. The rudder was unshipped, and she swung broadside-on to the sea, the waves beating right over her. An anchor was let go to steady her and it was with some difficulty that the boat was launched to carry out another anchor. Local fishing boats also came to her assistance, but despite heaving on the cables, she would not move. The water was now gaining on the pumps and Mr Willson decided to run her ashore, so at high tide the cables were cut, and the brig was allowed to go onto the beach, some of the passengers having been taken off by local boats. She had struck a sunken rock off the Great Chine, Isle of Wight. Although the local fishing vessels had helped, after she went ashore it was reported that the local population was more interested in plundering than saving, the local militia being called out to prevent this.
[TNA: ADM.1/5349]

6 June WILLIAM PITT Cutter
Hired 1796; 108 tons; 12 guns
Lieutenant Charles Payne
Carrying despatches for the Mediterranean fleet, she arrived off Gibraltar in the early hours of the morning, and four gunboats could be seen, which had stationed themselves between the cutter and the Rock. They altered course towards her, so the cutter stretched out into the straits. Another two gunboats were then seen approaching from the direction of Tenerife, so Lieutenant Payne decided to attempt to run past her nearest opponents into Gibraltar. She altered course as they neared, but the wind then fell away, allowing them to catch her, using sweeps to do so. By 9 o'clock they were close enough to fire into her, at which she surrendered. Lieutenant Payne was reprimanded by the court martial enquiring into the loss, for failing to use all his efforts to escape, no attempt having been made to lighten the cutter or to use sweeps.
[TNA: ADM.1/5349]

14 June SANDWICH Cutter
Hired 1798; 111 tons; 12 guns
Lieutenant George Lemprière
Cruising off the eastern coast of Spain near Barcelona, when a number of ships were sighted to the east-south-east, and believing this to be the expected British fleet, the cutter altered course towards them. When private signals were not answered and a lugger was seen to be detached to close her, she realised that this was the enemy fleet. She hauled her wind and set more sail, the lugger now in chase, joined by a frigate. The chase went on through the afternoon, the pursuers slowly overhauling her, until at 7 o'clock that evening the lugger opened fire with a bow-chase gun. The cutter continued on her way, now employing sweeps to help her keep her distance, but another hour saw the frigate in range to use her guns, the cutter bravely returning the fire. By 1am the frigate was within musket-shot, and the cutter surrendered to the frigate *Creole*, 44 guns.
[TNA: ADM.1/5350]

7 July PENELOPE Cutter
Hired 1794; 188 tons; 16 guns
Lieutenant David Hamline
Sailed from Gibraltar on 6 July, under orders to reconnoitre and gain intelligence of several ships seen heading through the straits, which were believed to be the French fleet. At 4 o'clock the following morning, when off Ceuta, she sighted them, and was able to count forty-three ships. She saw that two frigates and a brig were detached to chase her, at which she showed French colours and stood away, using sweeps to assist her in light winds. The enemy was gaining, so the boat was hoisted out and helped by towing her. By 7.30am they were close enough to start firing bow-chase guns at her, and with a breeze springing up, she cut her boat loose, ordering it to pull for Gibraltar, and then made all sail away for the North African shore. The chase continued until 11.30am, when a frigate was close astern, with the brig close to leeward, another frigate further off. The enemy fired, hulling her, at which she

surrendered to the nearest frigate, which proved to be the Spanish *Nuestra Señora del Carmen*, 34 guns.
[TNA: ADM.1/5350]

29 August CONTEST Gun Vessel
Deptford 1797; 159 tons; 75.3ft × 22ft; 12 guns
Lieutenant John Ides Short

In company with the squadron under Admiral Mitchell in the North Sea, with the weather worsening the ships ran for the shelter of the Dutch coast. During the evening of 21 August, the *Contest* anchored off Den Helder, but was forced to quit her position the following day, the gale being so strong. After being battered by the strong winds and high seas for four days, they returned to the coast on 26 August and anchored off Kijkduin. Here they rode uncomfortably for two days until the morning of 28 August when the anchor cable parted. The gunboat made sail and tried to stand out to sea, but at 10 o'clock that evening breakers were seen ahead, and she was forced to wear ship twice to clear the land and other ships at anchor. Clearly unable to weather the land, she anchored using a stream and a kedge anchor, where she remained until 4 o'clock in the morning, when the anchor cables parted. At this she ran herself into shallow water and was wrecked on a sandbank. Two men were drowned when attempting to make the shore.
[TNA: ADM.1/5351]

28 September BLANCHE Fifth Rate
Bursledon 1786; 722 tons; 129ft × 35.7ft; 18 guns
Commander John Ayscough

Fitted out as a troopship, the frigate was part of a convoy to the Texel and weighed in company with the other ships from her overnight anchorage in the Marsdiep during the afternoon of 27 September, the pilot having charge of the ship. At about 4 o'clock in the afternoon she went aground on the Middle Ground Sand, but drove over it, only to ground again two hours later. As it was high water, and being unable to drive her off, the yards and topgallant masts were struck, water butts emptied and preparations were made to kedge her off. The following morning, she was successfully hauled free and in a strong wind made sail down the channel, again under the guidance of the pilot, only to go hard aground on a bank known as the Dalrymple shoal. The wind was now whipping up to gale force and she commenced beating on the sands, with spray regularly washing over the decks. The mainmast was cut away, but there was still so much movement on the ship that she broached-to. In efforts to reduce the ship's motion, the mizzen mast was cut away and the boat's sails used to keep her steady. Signals of distress were made, but boats approaching were in some danger from the high seas and several turned over. By 4 o'clock in the afternoon the rudder had been beaten off and water was gaining on the pumps, when she suddenly floated free. It was decided to run her aground in shallow water nearby, which was successfully achieved, the water then being over the cable tier. The bulk of the crew were taken off and the ship later hauled into the Nieuwe Diep, where a survey revealed her to be in an irreparable condition, with the stern frame '… shook to pieces.' The blame for the loss was placed firmly on the incompetence of the local pilot.
[TNA: ADM.1/5351]

28 September FOX Schooner
Prize 1799; 150 tons; 14 guns
Lieutenant James Wooldridge

The schooner sailed from Jamaica on 5 September to land 'General' William Augustus Bowles, who was accepted as a Chief of the Creek nation, in the Gulf of Mexico, but attempts to procure a pilot failed. Despite this, she continued to Appalachee Bay, Florida, heading for St George's Sound, but as she was manoeuvring about nine miles from the shore, she was struck by a squall of wind when attempting to tack, which took her aback. She was carried down onto a coral reef, which pierced her bottom, and she rapidly filled with water and capsized over onto her larboard side. The officers and men managed to clamber into the rigging as she sank where they stayed all night, before managing to get ashore onto the reef in the morning. The crew remained for 32 days, surviving on a little pork rescued from the wreck and a little water, until the *Providence* privateer sighted them and took them all off.
[TNA: ADM.1/5351; Gold: Naval Chronicle vol 3 p235]

9 October LUTINE Fifth Rate
Prize 1793; 951 tons; 143.3ft × 38.10ft; 32 guns
Captain Lancelot Skinner†

Sailed from Yarmouth roads during the morning of 9 October, bound for Cuxhaven, to carry a large quantity of bullion bound for Hamburg on behalf of London merchants. They encountered a strong gale from the north-north-west and at about 11 o'clock at night, evidently having been driven much further to the south than they believed, she went ashore on the outer sandbanks of the Vliestroom passage. Although signal guns and rockets were fired, the wind was so violent that the *Arrow* sloop and several Dutch ships that were nearby could not assist. The frigate broke up overnight, morning revealing no sign of the vessel. Most sources state that there were no survivors, but two men were apparently picked up during the morning from the sea: one died almost immediately, but the other survived. Modern research has shown this to be Able Seaman John Rogers, who was picked up by the *Arrow*. The wreck was exposed at low ebb tides, lying midway

between the islands of Terschelling and Vlieland and much work went on throughout the nineteenth century at the wreck site to recover the treasure, and although much was brought to the surface, most has never been recovered.
[Gold: Naval Chronicle vol 2 p441; 535; Martin 'History of Lloyd's' pp183–209; http://www.cii.co.uk/media/581215/weerdt.pdf]

12 October **TRINCOMALEE** Ship Sloop
Purchased 1799; 315 tons; 16 guns
Commander John Rowe†

The sloop was cruising in the Gulf of Oman in company with the schooner *Comet*, 8 guns, belonging to the Honourable East India Company, when they fell in with the French privateer *Iphigénie*, 22 guns, and her prize, the *Pearl* merchantman, near the Quoins (As Salamah). It was then just before midnight, and after hailing the *Pearl* and receiving no satisfactory answer, the sloop fired at her. At this the privateer and her prize put about and made sail away. The following morning the French vessel and the *Pearl* were seen hull down to leeward, and the British pair steered towards them, with the *Trincomalee* chasing the privateer whilst the *Comet* tackled the prize. In light breezes it was not until 11 o'clock in the forenoon before shots could be exchanged, at some distance. The light and baffling winds prevented any close action until after sunset when a breeze sprang up, and at about 10 o'clock at night, in bright moonlight, when the sloop manoeuvred close alongside the privateer. The mutual cannonade went on for some two hours, when the sloop suddenly blew up with a large explosion. As the *Iphigénie* was close alongside, she took the force of the blast, the main and mizzen masts both going overboard and the sides being beaten in. The privateer was so severely damaged that she later foundered, with about thirty of the crew being picked up by the *Comet* and *Pearl* which stopped fighting to send boats to the aid of the survivors. Only two men, one English seaman and one Lascar, survived from the *Trincomalee*, being landed at Muscat.
[www.britishnewspaperarchive.co: Madras Courier 25 December 1799 p2; Gold: Naval Chronicle vol 4 pp319–20]

18 October **IMPREGNABLE** Second Rate
Deptford 1786; 1,886 tons; 177.7ft x 49.3ft; 98 guns
Captain Jonathan Faulknor

Heading for the fleet anchorage of St Helens, in company with several ships from Lisbon, land identified as Dunnose on the Isle of Wight was raised at 6 o'clock in the evening and she confidently stood on under the guidance of the Master, Michael Jenking. Sail was shortened, the lead-line was being cast constantly and at 7.30pm, the Master ordered the best bower anchor to be let go. Only minutes later, with only a third of the cable out, she struck the ground heavily, her rudder coming off almost immediately. The launch was hoisted out to take out a kedge anchor, but the ship was already labouring and beating quite alarmingly. The efforts to kedge her off failed, and at 9.30pm the masts were cut away to ease the movement, and this did help. The ship was lightened, stores being heaved overboard, and first light revealed that she had gone aground on the Chichester shoals and had driven over the flats during the night. Assistance arrived from Portsmouth Dockyard, the rescuers taking out the guns and other stores and helping in laying out anchors. At the afternoon high tide an effort was made to haul her off, but she would not move. The work was repeated the following morning and this time she did shift and was pulled into shallow water. As she did so water came in at a fast rate, but despite pumping and bailing, she could not free herself and was eventually abandoned as a wreck. The Master was guilty of negligence, having run beyond the proper distance before he altered course for St Helens, and failing to anchor in time, although it was accepted that he had been deceived by confused reporting of soundings. He was dismissed the service.
[TNA: ADM.1/5350]

25 October **NASSAU** Third Rate
Bristol 1785; 1,384 tons; 160.1ft x 44.5ft; 32 guns
Captain George Tripp

Fitted out as a troopship, she was ordered to the Dutch coast with stores and sailed from the Downs anchorage during 20 October and in strong winds stood on and off the shoreline until she steered for Den Helder, under the guidance of the pilots. Soon after midnight on 24 October she struck the North Haak sand off the Texel. A boat was hoisted out to take out an anchor, but it immediately overset, throwing the occupants into the sea. The ship found herself beating heavily on the sands, the seas regularly breaking over her, the wind increasing to gale force. Signal guns were fired, and at first light these brought assistance from other ships. The ship was now in a poor way, settling into the sand, the water having defeated the pumps, being up to the spar deck, the ship heeling over so that the starboard gun ports were under water. The merchant brig *Jalouse* closed and another attempt to hoist out a boat was made. This also overset, all the men being drowned, and the brig was unable to close until late afternoon when the winds had dropped away, and she took off over 200 men. Forty-two men were lost in the disaster. The court martial enquiring into the loss found that the wreck was due to the negligence and incompetence of Captain Tripp in the course he ordered to be set. The previous evening, he had apparently argued with the pilots on board, William Moody and Edward Wilson. The Master, George Prowse, was also blameable and

was severely reprimanded. The court also heard that the Captain, far from setting an example of leadership during the crisis, had retired to his cabin and proceeded to get very drunk. The Master testified that when he went to his cabin in the early hours of the morning, he found him sitting with several bottles in front of him; 'I could not make out what was wanted of me, his speech was altered, and he was not able to stand'. The First Lieutenant, George Harris, stated that Tripp was extremely intoxicated, so that his orders were unintelligible. During the morning they lay on the sands, beating and filling with water, and discipline had partly broken down, with some of the crew following the Captain's example, breaking into the spirit store and officers' cabins to steal alcohol and get very drunk. Captain George Tripp was dismissed the service. Two seamen were flogged for their behaviour, Roger Lake receiving 200 lashes, James Brookes 50.
[TNA: ADM.1/5351]

25 October AMARANTHE Brig Sloop
Prize 1796; 290 tons; 86.1ft × 28.2ft; 14 guns
Commander George Blake
Cruising off the North American coast, no land had been sighted during the day, but a sun-sight had been obtained at noon and it was estimated that they were about 40 leagues (120 miles) from the coast of Florida. They steered westward, heading towards the coast during the day, but no land had been sighted by sunset. At just before 9 o'clock that evening, with little warning, she went aground and within five minutes had bilged. The masts were cut away, boats hoisted out and rafts ordered to be made. By 11 o'clock she was almost full of water and beginning to break up. The crew left by the boats and rafts, the last men having to swim ashore as the wreck fell apart. Morning revealed that they had gone ashore near Cape Canaveral, twenty-two men having drowned in the attempt at getting shore. The survivors walked for 13 days along the shoreline until they reached the Spanish settlement at Matanzas. Commander Blake was reckoned to be blameable, for running to the west at too high a speed after dark and failing to order the frequent use of the lead-line. One seaman, Daniel Day, was found to have prevaricated in his evidence. The court, exasperated at his irrelevant, shifting evidence, ordered that he spend a month in jail.
[TNA: ADM.1/5351]

30 October SOMERSET Prison Hulk
From 1797
Lieutenant William Adams
Employed as a prison, she accommodated 150 French prisoners of war and was moored at St George's, Bermuda, with a small naval crew and an army guard. At 7 o'clock in the morning the Sergeant of the guard came to Lieutenant Adams' cabin somewhat alarmed, claiming that the ship was sinking. The Lieutenant hastily dressed and went below, to discover the hold full of water. The ensign was hoisted upside down as a distress signal and a musket fired at regular intervals to draw the attention of the dockyard. Boats came from the shore and all the prisoners were taken off. That done, the cables were cut and the iron bolts securing the moorings were driven out, which allowed her to drift towards the shallows. She ran aground short of the beach and foundered. The court heard that the hulk was infested with rats, and although these had caused damage previously, they considered it possible but unlikely that they had damaged the floor timbers sufficiently for the ship to be endangered. Lieutenant Adams was convinced that the prisoners had smuggled tools on board and drilled holes in the bottom, his suspicions being aroused in the first minutes of the incident, on finding that the prisoners were all packed and prepared to go ashore.
[TNA: ADM.1/5352]

5 November ORESTES Ship Sloop
Prize 1781 (*Mars*); 396 tons; 100.1ft × 30.4ft; 16 guns
Commander William Haggit†
The *Orestes* sailed from Bombay 31 October to cruise in the Persian Gulf and was last seen on 4 November. The next day a strong tropical storm swept through the area, after which she was never heard or seen again, and was presumed to have been lost with all hands on or about this date.
[www.britishnewspaperarchive.co: Hampshire Telegraph 2 Feb 1801 p5]

5 November SCEPTRE Third Rate
Rotherhithe 1781; 1,398 tons; 159.9ft × 44.9ft; 64 guns
Captain Valentine Edwards†
Laying at anchor in Table Bay, South Africa, as the wind freshened during the morning, topmasts were struck, and the yards trimmed into the wind. The weather steadily deteriorated, and at just before noon the best bower anchor cable parted in winds which were now at gale force, the sheet anchor being let go which brought her up, but four hours later the cable parted. The spare anchor was now readied and let go, but the cable immediately parted. She was now held by the small bower anchor only and dragging nearer the shore. A stream anchor was prepared with a 9-pounder cannon attached, and this was let go at 6.30pm. She remained riding in this situation for just an hour when the small bower cable parted, and she started driving across the bay. The remaining cable was cut, and an attempt made to spread sail, but before any headway could be made, she struck the ground and swung broadside on to the sea. The main and mizzen masts were cut away, upper-deck guns heaved overboard, but she pounded heavily

on the ground and the surf broke over her constantly. It soon became impossible to use the pumps and at about 10 o'clock she started to break up in the pounding surf. Within an hour she had entirely gone to pieces with wreckage and bodies strewn along the beach. About 290 men died.
[TNA:ADM.1/5351]

17 November ESPION Fifth Rate
Prize 1794 (*Atalante*); 983 tons; 148.9ft × 39.2ft; 18 guns
Commander Jonas Rose
Fitted out as a troopship, she was carrying Russian troops from Den Helder and heading for the Downs anchorage, the North Foreland being sighted during the evening of 16 November. At 1.30am, with no warning, she struck the ground. All sail was thrown aback, but she would not move, and boats were hoisted out to lay out anchors, and distress guns were fired. Efforts were made to kedge her off, but she seemed to be stuck fast. After this, topgallant masts and topmasts and yards were struck, and stores heaved overboard to lighten her. Spare yards and spars were lowered over the side to act as shores, to prevent her heeling over as the tide ebbed. Daylight saw the *Roebuck* troopship and several local fishing boats coming to her aid. The troops were disembarked, more stores transferred and further attempts made at heaving her off, but water was entering and gaining on the pumps, and she was settling into the sand. Later that day she was abandoned as a wreck. The court martial decided that she had run aground in a channel through the Goodwin Sands due to the incompetence and drunkenness of the pilot, James Gough. He was ordered to lose all pay due, serve six months in the Marshalsea Prison, and never serve as a pilot again. The Gunner, Archibald Freeborn, who had been the officer of the watch when she grounded, had been inattentive and failed to acquaint the Captain of a course change made by the pilot. He was severely reprimanded.
[TNA:ADM.1/5351]

25 December ETHALION Fifth Rate
Harwich 1797; 992 tons; 146.1ft × 39.2ft; 38 guns
Captain John Earle
One of several cruisers stationed off the north-eastern French coast, watching for any movement of the Brest fleet, a hard gale on 18 December had driven them from the coast and Captain Searle was anxious to resume his station off the entrance to Brest roads. She regained her position during the afternoon of 24 December, the wind falling away to a calm, the ship manoeuvring to keep the light at Pointe de Sainte-Mathieu in sight. At 8 o'clock, with the light bearing east by north, about nine miles distant, she headed south under reefed topsails and a staysail. At a little after 3 o'clock in the morning rocks were discovered close ahead and an attempt was made to wear ship, but with so little wind the ship would not answer, and she struck the ground. All hands were turned up, pumping started, and boats were hoisted out, water butts emptied and some upper-deck guns heaved overboard. She was found to be held firmly on the rocks and as the tide fell, she commenced beating, the rudder and sternpost being shattered. At 6 o'clock she capsized over to starboard, the rocks piercing her in several places, and the starboard side being quite beaten in. At daylight, several ships and cutters from the blockading squadron closed to send their boats and commenced taking off the men, the last of the men off being the Captain, First Lieutenant and the Master's Mate. Before they left, they set fire to the ship, having previously cut away the masts. The cause was believed to be the lack of wind coupled with a strong current, which had carried the ship further inshore than reckoned, and put her on the rocks off the western edge of the Île de Sein.
[TNA:ADM.1/5351; Gold: Naval Chronicle vol 3 pp74–5]

1800

5 January MASTIFF Gunboat
Purchased 1797 (*Herald*); 163 tons; 71.7ft × 23ft; 12 guns
Lieutenant James Watson
Having sailed from Great Yarmouth, she had rounded the Cockle Buoy when the wind shifted and dropped away to a calm. It being a strong ebb tide, with a heavy swell she was carried down onto the Cockle Sands where she ran aground and was held fast. A boat was hoisted out but was stove in by the heavy surf that was now breaking over her and she filled with water. Distress guns were fired, and this brought some local fishing boats to the scene, but they could not get close to her. Another boat was launched, and this managed to carry some men to the waiting boats but could not return. The remainder were forced to spend the night on the wreck, clinging to the rigging. With the sea moderating in the morning, the survivors were taken off by local craft. Seven men died in the wreck. Two fishermen from Winterton, Abel King and William Pile, were later awarded 25 guineas each by the Admiralty for their exertions in rescuing the survivors.
[TNA:ADM.1/5351; www.britishnewspaperarchive.co: Newcastle Courant 12 April 1800 p4]

21 January WEYMOUTH Transport
Purchased 1795 (*Earl of Mansfield*); 1,434 tons; 175.5ft × 43.3ft; 26 guns
Commander Ambrose Crofton
Sailed from Spithead on 4 January with a number of troops embarked for Gibraltar, she suffered weather damage during the passage, and it was decided to put into Lisbon to effect repairs. As she approached the

harbour, she ran onto the bar at the entrance to the River Tagus and was wrecked. No lives were lost and most of the embarked stores were able to be saved.
[www.britishnewspaperarchive.co: Kentish Gazette 25 February 1800 p2]

26 January BRAZEN Ship Sloop
Prize 1798 (*Invincible Général Bonaparte*); 363 tons; 105.2ft × 28.1ft; 18 guns
Commander James Hanson†

The sloop sailed from Portsmouth on 18 January to cruise in the English Channel but encountered increasingly poor weather. In the early hours of the morning, it being a dark night with strong winds and rain, she struck the ground under the cliffs about two miles to the west of Newhaven. Firmly aground and being struck by large waves, the main and mizzen masts were cut away in a vain attempt to ease the ship. The force of wind and waves battered the ship constantly, and onlookers gathering on the shore, who discovered the wreck at daylight, could do little to help. Attempts were made to swim ashore or use rafts, but all came to grief. By the afternoon, the ship had gone to pieces, part of the side coming ashore near the eastern pier at Newhaven, whilst the bows remained firmly wedged on the rocks. Only one seaman, Jeremiah Hall, survived. Clinging to part of a gun carriage, he was washed ashore under the cliffs from where he was hauled to the top. Dozens of bodies were washed ashore over the next few days.
[www.britishnewspaperarchive.co: Sussex Advertiser 27 January 1800 p3; Gold: Naval Chronicle vol 3 pp147–8]

10 March REPULSE Third Rate
Cowes 1780; 1,387 tons; 159.6ft × 44.7ft; 64 guns
Captain James Alms

Cruising off Brest as part of the blockading squadron, in poor weather, during 8 March, with the ship pitching and rolling, the gangway ladder to the poop became detached, knocking down several seamen and throwing the Captain down a hatchway. This effectively disabled him, injuring his back and breaking a rib, and he was confined to his cabin by the Surgeon. The following day, with the weather still very thick, Captain Alms decided to leave his station and go to Torbay, where the ship could ride out the storm and he could go ashore to receive proper treatment. Orders to that effect were given to the Master, George Finn, and it was thus a considerable shock to Alms when, at just before midnight, the *Repulse* shuddered violently as she stuck a reef. She drove over the rocks and floated after about 45 minutes but had been holed and was filling with water at a fast rate. Hands were turned to pumping and bailing and a sail was hung under the hull. Despite these measures, by 4 o'clock in the morning the water was gaining and was 2ft above the orlop deck. She steered for the nearby shore, being very sluggish, settling further into the water all the time. At just after 5am she was run ashore on the French coast near Cléden, about nine miles north of Audierne. Three men were drowned in the efforts to go ashore. The First Lieutenant, John Rothery, declined to go ashore and with nine others took the cutter, in which they reached the Channel Islands. The court martial, in its investigation, found that the Captain and First Lieutenant were not on best terms. When Alms had been confined to his cabin, Rothery had taken a remark by the Captain that 'He should do as he felt best' when a strange sail was sighted, to mean that he was now in command. He clearly felt insulted by the Captain discussing the ship's future movements with the Master without reference to him. He therefore ordered the ship to stand over towards the French coast and look for a coastal convoy. The Master readily agreed with him, and course was altered. Rothery instructed Finn not to inform Alms of this alteration. Further to this, after going aground, the First Lieutenant had taken the boat without the permission or knowledge of the Captain. Lieutenant John Rothery and the Master, George Finn, were both dismissed the service for misconduct and disobedience.
[TNA: ADM.1/5353]

14 March DANAE Sixth Rate
Prize 1798; 507 tons; 119.2ft × 30.11ft; 20 guns
Captain Lord William Proby

Cruising off the French coast near Brest, the frigate had been busily employed chasing French merchant shipping, driving several vessels into sheltered bays. At about 9.30 in the evening, several men from the watch on deck, led by a seaman called William Jackson, the captain of the foretop, attacked the Master, who was the officer of the watch. Knocked to the deck, he regained his feet only to be knocked down again and thrown down the main hatchway. Alerted by the commotion, an attempt by Lord Proby and some of his officers to gain the deck failed, finding the way blocked, and Proby was driven below, receiving a cut on his head at the same time. The mutineers then placed the ship's boats over the hatchways, effectively preventing anyone from gaining the deck, and steered for Brest. Although about forty men below remained loyal to Proby, they could only muster ten cutlasses, four muskets and the officers' pistols between them, and could do nothing to gain the deck. The next morning the *Danae* anchored off Fort Conquet, near Brest, and a boat was sent to the French sloop *Colombe*. A French officer boarded and on being asked if he surrendered, Proby answered 'To the French nation, but not to mutineers'. All of them were taken ashore, the officers and loyal members of the crew being treated well by the French, and all were released

to England on parole by June. The mutiny seems to have been led by Jackson, assisted by an Irishman named Ignatius Feeny or Finney. Of the forty-one members of the crew who were identified as mutineers, many of them Irish or American, the majority disappeared, but three were later captured. John Marret was captured on board a French privateer the *Vengeur*; he was recognised when in prison at Plymouth by Lieutenant Neville Lake, formerly the First Lieutenant of *Danae*. He was hanged on board the *Pique* in October 1800. John MacDonald, alias Samuel Higgens, was arrested in Wapping High Street on being recognised by Lieutenant Lake. He was executed on board the *Zealand* in June 1801. The last mutineer caught was John Williams who was sentenced to be hanged in September 1801 but pardoned at the last minute as he was an American citizen.
[TNA:ADM.1/1/5353; 5354; 5356; 5358; Mariner's Mirror vol 42 pp38–53]

17 March QUEEN CHARLOTTE First Rate
Chatham 1790; 2,286 tons; 190ft x 52.5ft; 100 guns
Captain Andrew Todd†
Flagship of Admiral Lord Keith, the Admiral and some other officers went ashore at Leghorn (Livorno), Italy, the ship being despatched to survey the island of Cabrera, some way distant, in preparation for an attack. At just after 6 o'clock in the morning the cry of fire was raised, the flames spreading rapidly in the waist, the boat coverings on the booms and the mainsail soon catching fire. Efforts to fight the fire from spreading below decks were led by Lieutenant George Dundas, and these initially proved successful, the ports being opened, and stopcocks turned on, which flooded the lower decks and prevented the magazines from exploding. Nevertheless, by 10 o'clock in the morning the fire still had a firm hold amidships and was spreading through the rigging, and men started leaving the ship. Several ships had come to stand by her, picking up men from the water, although they were deterred from getting too close, due to the discharging of guns set off by the heat. Twenty officers and 144 men were saved, but over 600 men were lost. The ship burnt to the waterline. The cause of the blaze was not definitely established, but it would seem to have started in some hay lying on the half deck, a lighted match in a match-tub being kept nearby.
[TNA:ADM.1/5352; Gold; Naval Chronicle vol 3 p299]

17 May LADY JANE Cutter
Hired 1795; 53 tons; 8 guns
Commander Wyndham Bryer†
On 16/17 May the fleet blockading the north-eastern coast of France was scattered by a strong gale, with many of the ships bearing away for ports in southern England. Three vessels, *Lady Jane*, *Railleur* and *Trompeuse*, were never seen or heard from after this, and were presumed lost with all hands.
[www.britishnewspaperarchive.co: Hampshire Chronicle 21 July 1800 p4]

17 May RAILLEUR Ship Sloop
Prize 1797; 261 tons; 89.6ft x 26.2ft; 20 guns
Commander John Raynor†
Part of the blockading squadron off the north-eastern coast of France, when the area was struck by a strong gale, which scattered the ships, many of which bore up for ports in southern England. Three vessels, *Lady Jane*, *Railleur* and *Trompeuse*, were never seen or heard from after this, and were presumed lost with all hands.
[TNA:ADM.1/1116; www.britishnewspaperarchive.co: Hampshire Chronicle 21 July 1800 p4]

17 May TROMPEUSE Ship Sloop
Prize 1797; 338 tons; 103.5ft x 27.6ft; 18 guns
Commander John Parker Robinson†
Like the *Railleur* and *Lady Jane* (see above), the ship was off north-eastern France, and disappeared after the area was struck by a strong gale, which scattered the ships, many of which bore up for ports in southern England. The *Trompeuse* was never seen or heard from after this and was presumed lost with all hands.
[TNA:ADM.1/1116; www.britishnewspaperarchive.co Hampshire Chronicle 21 July 1800 p4]

20 May CORMORANT Sixth Rate
Prize 1796 (*Etna*); 565 tons; 119.4ft x 32.10ft; 20 guns
Captain Hon. Courtney Boyle
Ordered to proceed to Alexandria with important despatches destined for Sir Sidney Smith, she raised the African coast near Benghazi on 15 May. Course was made for Alexandria, steering along the North African shore. During the evening of 20 May, it was estimated that they had about 40 miles to run to their destination, and Captain Boyle retired for the night, leaving instructions to run a further 20 miles and then bring-to. It was a shock, when, a little later, at just before 11pm, she ran hard aground. Sail was taken in and topmasts struck, the ship lying easily, but stuck fast. Sounding around her, they found she was surrounded by shallow water. Morning revealed the shore about a mile and a half away, a heavy sea running from the stern setting her further into the sand. It proved impossible to launch a boat with anchors into the shallow waters; but nevertheless a raft was constructed which was used to carry out kedge anchors. She proved to be stuck fast and no amount of heaving could shift her. A town could be seen in the distance, which was later identified as Rosetta, and it became clear that she had run ashore about three miles west of Burg. As she could not be saved, preparations were made for the crew to go ashore.

More sail was set to drive her further into the sand, the intention being to make it impossible for anyone to salvage her later. The crew then landed on the beach on rafts or boats where they were taken prisoner by the French. The blame for the loss was laid on the charts of the area, and '… their great incorrectness'.
[TNA: ADM.1/5354]

2 June FULMINANTE Cutter
Prize 1798; 40 tons; 44ft × 15.2ft; 4 guns
Lieutenant Edward Morris
When off Cadiz, she was chased by a French privateer, *les Deux Frères*. A 40-minute running fight ensued before the privateer ran close alongside, entered boarders, and forced her to surrender.
  Note: recaptured soon after, circumstances uncertain.
[TNA: ADM.1/5354]

7 July COMET Fireship
Wivenhoe 1783; 424 tons; 108.10ft × 29.8ft; 14 guns
Commander Thomas Leef
A French squadron of four large frigates was blockaded in the port of Dunkirk and a British force under Captain Henry Inman was assembled to attack them in the harbour. The little squadron entered the port at midnight, and one of the enemy ships was boarded and captured. Meanwhile the fireships, led by the *Comet*, were set on fire and allowed to drift down towards their targets. Commander Leef remained on board until the last minute, and was caught in the explosion, injuring him before he escaped. The French ships all cut their cables and went close inshore to avoid the fireships.
[London Gazette 8 July 1800]

Three other fireships were burnt in the attack on Dunkirk:

FALCON fireship
Sandwich 1782; 202 tons; 78.7ft × 25ft; 14 guns
Commander Henry Butt

ROSARIO fireship
Prize 1797 (*Nuestra Señora del Rosario*); 209 tons; 89ft × 23ft; 14 guns
Commander James Carthew

WASP fireship
Purchased 1782; 207 tons; 78.8ft × 26.2ft; 14 guns
Commander John Edwards

* * *

10 August DROMEDARY Troopship
Limehouse 1778 (*Janus*); 884 tons; 140ft × 37.10ft; 24 guns
Commander Bridges Watkinson Taylor
Sailed from Grenada with soldiers of the West India Regiment embarked, bound for Trinidad, it being feared that the island was under imminent threat of a French assault. The island was sighted in the early hours of the morning, and despite fitful winds and a strong current, she pressed on as they were anxious to reach their destination. As they were negotiating the Bocas del Dragon passage, the wind failed, and the current took them down onto a reef. She beat over the rocks, the rudder being unshipped, and was driven further onto the reef, before ending on the Parasol Rocks off the island of Huevos, with the bowsprit touching the rocks. The foremast was cut away and other yards and spars laid out, which allowed 500 people to scramble onto the rocks. They remained there for 15 hours, the ship capsizing over to port and breaking in half, before they were taken off by boats sent from Port of Spain. No blame was attached to the crew, although the Master, Alexander Handasyde, was dismissed the service for being found drunk and incapable prior to the wreck, and unable to assist after she grounded.
[TNA: ADM.1/5354]

6 September STAG Fifth Rate
Chatham 1794; 792 tons; 135.11ft × 36.2ft; 32 guns
Captain Robert Winthrop
Lying at anchor in Vigo Bay, Spain, the weather worsened, with gale-force winds and high seas, and at 2.30 that afternoon the best bower cable parted. Both sheet and small bower anchors were promptly let go, but the bower cable parted soon after, and she started to drag her anchor and she drove across the anchorage, passing close to the other ships. The sheet anchor cable was cut, and she tried to make sail to clear the bay but found herself laid on her beam-ends by the wind as she did. Unable to weather Point Subrido, she struck a reef which pierced her bottom, the water flooding in. Distress signals were made, and the Carpenter of the *Renown* came on board. He found that the rudder had gone, the sternpost was a wreck and there was 4ft of water in the hold, increasing all the time. With no chance of saving her, she was abandoned as a wreck, all the crew leaving her by 8 o'clock that night. The following day the First Lieutenant, Samuel Pym, returned to take off usable stores and then set her alight, which was done, although he was injured by a premature explosion.
[TNA: ADM. 1/5354]

26 September HOUND Brig Sloop
Sandwich 1796; 315 tons; 95ft × 28.1ft; 18 guns
Commander William Turquand†
Sailed from Bressay Sound, Shetland Isles, on 25 September, escorting two local merchant ships bound for Aberdeen. The weather was poor, and that evening developed into a storm, with strong south-westerly winds with heavy rain. The ships became separated, and the *Hound* disappeared, and she was presumed to

have been lost with all hands. Over the next few days, wreckage, identified as coming from the sloop, which included a topmast and part of an arms chest, was washed ashore on the islands of Unst and Balta.
[www.britishnewspaperarchive.co: Caledonian Mercury 16 October 1800 p3]

8 October DILIGENCE Brig Sloop
Bursledon 1795; 318 tons; 95ft x 28.2ft; 18 guns
Commander Charles Ross
Cruising along the north-western coast of Cuba, she was searching for a polacre-rigged Spanish privateer reported in the area, when at 7.30 in the evening she unexpectedly struck a rocky reef. Boats were hoisted out and they sounded around her, finding shallow water all round. Water was reported to be entering at a steady Rate and efforts were forced to be concentrated on pumping and bailing, as it was feared that any attempt to lighten her by throwing stores and guns overboard would lead to her running onto new obstructions in the shallow water. The water eventually gained, making 5ft in 15 minutes and she heeled over to port. Masts were cut away and the lee guns were heaved overboard to ease her. Daylight revealed that they were about five miles from the shoreline, and boats were lowered to take off the crew, some provisions also being landed. The following day the *Thunderer* came in sight and took off all the crew, the wreck being set on fire before they left. The shoal that she had run onto, near the islet of Rio Puercos, was not laid down on her charts.
[TNA:ADM.1/5355]

9 October GALGO (alias CHANCE) Brig Sloop
Prize 1799; 398 tons; 99ft x 29ft; 16 guns
Commander George Stovin†
Whilst in latitude 21 North, latitude 61 West, to the north-east of the Leeward Islands, she was sailing with all sail set in steadily freshening breezes. The Master, Thomas Forrest, came on deck for the middle watch at just before midnight and seeing that the wind was strengthening, recommended a reduction in sail. Commander Stovin agreed, and the crew started by taking in the royals, studding sails and topgallant staysails. Before this had been completed, she was struck by a squall which rolled her over onto her beam-ends, and she rapidly filled with water and sank within five minutes. Twenty-five survivors were found clinging to floating wreckage the next morning by an American ship, the *Hunter*, which took them to New York.
Note: there is some confusion over her name: the Spanish brig *el Galgo* was captured by the *Crescent* in November 1799 and taken into British service. The court-martial enquiry into the loss refers to her throughout as *Galgo*, as do the station records and contemporary newspaper reports and Schomberg vol 5 p103. Her entries in the Progress Book (*TNA ADM.180/9*) and Dimensions Book (*TNA: ADM.180/23*) also list her under the name *Galgo*. However, in some secondary sources, such as William James and College, she is referred to as *Chance*. I suspect that it was the intention of the Admiralty to rename her *Chance*, but this had not taken effect by the time of her loss.
[TNA:ADM.1/5355;ADM.1/323]

9 October ACTIVE Cutter
Hired 1794; 71 tons; 10 guns
Master John Hamilton
After escorting ships to the mouth of the river Ems, the cutter was laying at anchor when surprised by the privateer *le Modéré*, which ran alongside and entered boarders and quickly overcame the small crew.
Note: retaken 16 May 1801.
[TNA ADM.49/96; www.britishnewspaperarchive.co: Caledonian Mercury 30 October 1800 p2]

12 October URCHIN Gun Vessel
Purchased 1797; 154 tons; 3 guns
Lieutenant Thomas Croasdale
Fitted for service at Gibraltar, she was under tow of the *Hector*, 74 guns, across Tetuan Bay with only seven of the crew on board, the remainder being on the *Hector*. At just before midnight, she 'took a sheer', started to roll heavily and shipped a large amount of water before capsizing. Boats were promptly lowered, but only two of the crew were picked up.
[TNA:ADM.1/5354]

13 October ROSE Cutter
Hired 1794; 97 tons; 10 guns
Master J – Cullen
Arrived at the mouth of the river Ems during the evening to act as escort to homeward-bound vessels, where she anchored, ready to proceed upriver the following morning to the port of Emden. At 10 o'clock that night, two enemy gun brigs, the *Voorzorg* and *Adder*, closed and attempted to board, but the cutter, prepared for action, held them off. They continued to hold the attackers at bay for over an hour, until with one killed and five wounded, they were forced to surrender when *Adder* ran alongside.
[TNA: ADM.49/96; www.britishnewspaperarchive. co:Morning Post 17 January 1801 p3; https://www. navyrecords.org.uk/magazine_posts/an-account-of-the-capture-of-the-armed-cutter-rose-13-october-1800/

October BABET Sixth Rate
Prize 1794; 511 tons; 119.1ft x 31.1ft; 20 guns
Commander Jemmett Mainwaring†
Sailed from Spithead 14 September, with Major General John Knox and his suite embarked, to take up his duties

as Governor of Jamaica. The ship arrived at Martinique on 24 October and sailed the next day to proceed to Jamaica but disappeared and was supposed to have foundered with all hands. Pay books closed 31 October.

Note: in many publications the year is incorrectly given as 1801.
[TNA: CO 245/118; ADM.35/250; www.britishnewspaperarchive.co: London Courier 5 February 1801; London Gazette 30 October 1804]

October MARTIN Ship Sloop
Woolwich 1790; 329 tons; 100.8ft × 27.2ft; 16 guns
Commander Hon. Matthew St Clair†
The sloop disappeared in the North Sea during October and was presumed to have been lost with all hands. She was paid off at the end of October.
[TNA: ADM.180/9; ADM 35/1084]

4 November MARLBOROUGH Third Rate
Deptford 1764; 1,642 tons; 168.8ft × 46.11ft; 74 guns
Captain Thomas Sotheby
Stationed off the north-west coast of France as part of the squadron blockading the port of Lorient, the weather was poor, with gale-force winds and high seas and under foresail and reefed topsails, she headed for the shelter of Quiberon Bay. By 9 o'clock that morning the weather had moderated sufficiently to allow her to set staysails, and she came about to take up her station again. An hour later a cast of the lead-line revealed that the water was shallowing, and an attempt was made to wear ship, but before this could be completed, she struck the ground, gently at first, but then repeatedly and with increasing violence. She heeled over to port before a particularly heavy sea lifted her over the obstruction, allowing her to float free, although it unshipped the rudder. She anchored, manned the pumps and took in all sail and Captain Sotheby ordered a sail prepared for slinging under the hull. Upper-deck guns were heaved overboard, and these were followed by some of the lower-deck guns. Her distress signals had brought other ships of the blockading squadron down to her aid, but the poor weather prevented them giving any immediate help, and by 5 o'clock in the evening they had been lost to sight in the darkening day and the drizzling rain. That night the anchor cable parted, and she started to drive. All the masts were cut away and more stores heaved overboard, but in the high seas she laboured, pitching and rolling constantly, the drizzle turning to driving rain, with flashes of lightning. All hands were placed in three watches at the pumps, Sotheby ordering that they be given wine and sherbet every two hours when on watch. Morning found them just two miles from the shore, but still afloat. The pumping and bailing went on constantly, although the pumps were now becoming blocked with ballast at regular intervals. The cutters *Lurcher* and *Nile* came down and stood by her during the afternoon. As it was clear that she was sinking, Captain Sotheby decided he would have to leave her, so all boats were hoisted out and all the crew was transferred in an orderly manner to the ships and cutters standing by. No blame was placed on the officers and her crew, the poor weather and strong currents having conspired to allow her to run onto the shoals of the Plateau de Birvideaux, to the west of Quiberon.
[TNA: ADM.1/5355]

9 November HAVICK Ship Sloop
Prize 1796; 365 tons; 101.10ft × 28.8ft; 16 guns
Commander Philip Bartholomew
Ordered to cruise between the Channel Islands and the Île de Batz, she anchored in St Aubyn's Bay, Jersey to acquire a local pilot, being unacquainted with the shoreline. During 3 November she parted her best bower anchor cable and had to rely on her sheet anchor to hold her. No spare anchor was carried, but a temporary one was made up from a pair of guns and iron ballast. During 9 November, a tremendous storm hit the anchorage and she parted her cable. The temporary anchor was released but failed to bring her up and she was driven ashore and bilged. All the masts were cut away and upper-deck guns heaved overboard, but she filled with water very quickly, with heavy waves breaking over her, and she started settling into the sand. When the tide ebbed, it left her high and dry, and the ship settled down even further. Several other ships suffered similarly, but efforts over the next few days refloated, all of them except the *Havick*. She was found to be so severely damaged that she was abandoned as a wreck.
[TNA: ADM.1/5355]

20 November FLORA Brig
Hired 1800; 148 tons; 14 guns
Lieutenant John Cook Carpenter
Lying in the Hamoaze, Plymouth, taking on stores for Gibraltar, she dragged her anchor, and moved a little distance, which no one on board was aware of until low water, when she tailed onto a sandbank near the Old Gun Wharf. The masts were cut away and efforts made to hold her up, but she capsized over onto her beam ends. All the crew were taken off by boats sent from the *Sylph* and *Telegraph*. The brig was successfully raised on 1 December and later refitted and re-entered service.
[TNA: ADM.1/5355]

23 November ALBANAISE Brig Sloop
Prize 1800; 238 tons; 88.7ft × 24.3ft; 14 guns
Commander Francis Newcombe
Escorting a small convoy along the North African shore from Arzeu to Gibraltar, on 22 November they fell in with a Spanish vessel which they captured, placing a

small prize crew on board and taking the Spanish crew on board as prisoners. Cape Tres Forcas was sighted to the east at sunset, and Captain Newcombe retired, but wary of the prisoners on board, and concerned that some of his crew were drawn from several Mediterranean countries, he ordered that armed sentries be posted and that officers on duty carry side arms. At about midnight, the Captain was woken by movements in his cabin and heard the clash of cutlasses and men whispering. Fearing that the Spanish prisoners might be attempting to take over the sloop, he quickly arose and asked who it was. The reply was an order to 'lay still, or you are a dead man'. At this Newcombe seized a pair of pistols and fired into the group, shooting one of them dead, after which a scuffle took place during which Newcombe ran to the upper deck. Here he discovered that about twenty of the crew had mutinied and taken over the upper deck. He shouted out 'You vagabonds, what do you mean by this' and attempted to shoot the man he identified as the ringleader, Jacob Godfrey, but was foiled when only the priming of the pistol went off. After this the mutineers knocked him down and tied him up. The Gunner, Mr Lewin, attempted to lead loyal members of the crew from below, but was shot in the leg for his troubles. All the officers and loyal members of the crew were then secured, and the mutineers took the sloop into Malaga, arriving the next day and handed her over to the Spanish. Some of the mutineers were later captured. Jacob Godfrey, the ringleader, was hanged in January 1802, as was Patrick Kennedy. Other sentences included James Marriott, seaman, 100 lashes and three months in the Marshalsea Prison: Alexander McEver, seaman, 50 lashes and three months' imprisonment. All the officers were cleared of any blame except for the Master's Mate, John Terrell (or Tyrell). He was accused of being party to the mutiny and was only prevented from taking part by being absent in the prize. He was eventually brought to trial in June 1802 but was acquitted of the charge.

[TNA: ADM.1/5356; ADM.1/5360; ADM.1/5361; ADM.1/5362; Mariner's Mirror vol 43 pp194–202]

9 December SIR THOMAS PASLEY Brig
Hired 1800; 163 tons; 16 guns
Lieutenant Charles Niven

En-route to Gibraltar from Plymouth, she was off Ceuta when a large Spanish gunboat approached, using sail and sweeps. The Spaniard kept astern of the brig and with the wind falling away to a calm, they used the sweeps to keep their position, which meant that the *Pasley* could not get her broadside to bear. Attempts were made to shift guns aft, but there was insufficient space between the carronades to allow this, and she could only reply effectively with muskets, whilst having to suffer the fire from the gunboat. After maintaining the struggle for over two hours and with Lieutenant Niven wounded in three places, the Master wounded, three killed and six others wounded, she surrendered.

[TNA: ADM.1/5358; Gold: Naval Chronicle vol 5 p179]

1801

1 January REQUIN Gun brig
Prize 1795; 166 tons; 71.2ft × 23.9ft; 10 guns
Lieutenant Samuel Fowell

Cruising off the coast of Morbihan, southern Brittany, she was keeping a look out for a convoy that was reported to be ready to sail. Manoeuvring in the entrance to Quiberon Bay, she had just tacked when a rock was sighted to leeward. Extra sail was ordered to be set, and the helm put over to avoid the obstacle, but only minutes later she struck a reef and thumped violently over it. All sail was thrown aback and she floated free, but it was found that she had been holed and water was entering. She attempted to stand out to sea, but breakers were seen ahead, and before she could avoid them, she found herself on the rocks again. She filled her sails and forced herself over the reef, floating free again in a few minutes. Water was now entering at a fast rate, and she anchored, firing distress guns and rockets. Boats were hoisted out, guns heaved overboard, and pumping and bailing commenced. The foremast and booms were next cut away in the continuing efforts to ease her. It became clear that they were fighting a losing battle and one of the boats with twenty men on board was despatched to the French coast to bring help. At 11 o'clock that night a boat from the *Excellent* arrived to give assistance and this, with other ships' boats, took the remainder of the crew off before she settled and sank. The crew of the boat sent ashore were made prisoners by the French, despite pleas from the British that they were on French soil as a result of shipwreck, not action. The haziness of the weather, which prevented any landmarks being observed, was blamed for the loss.

[TNA: ADM.1/5355]

5 January CHARMING MOLLY Cutter
Hired 1798; 71 tons; 8 guns
Master David Sheriff

Disappeared and presumed foundered with all hands in the English Channel in poor weather whilst en-route to England from the Channel Islands. The weather on this occasion was said to be dreadful '… the gale increased to a hurricane at SSW of the most tremendous kind, with a florid brassy sky … the roaring of the wind and sea so frightened many families that they actually staid up all night'.

[Gold: Naval Chronicle vol 5 p92]

5 October 1744. A ship in distress – the loss of the *Victory*. (© *National Maritime Museum, Greenwich, London*)

10 June 1772. Schooner *Gaspee* being burnt. (*Mary Evans Picture Library*)

11 October 1780. The *Andromeda* in a hurricane. (© *National Maritime Museum, Greenwich, London*)

23 September 1779. *Serapis* versus the *Bonhomme Richard*. (*Mary Evans/The Everett Collection*)

29 August 1782. *Royal George* heeling over. (*Mary Evans Picture Library*)

16 September 1782. *Centaur* in the storm. (© *National Maritime Museum, Greenwich, London*)

28 April 1789. *Bounty* mutineers cast adrift Captain Bligh. (*Mary Evans Picture Library*)

28 August 1791. *Pandora* sinking in the Torres Strait, Great Barrier Reef. (*Mary Evans Picture Library*)

29 August 1794. The burning of the *Impetueux*. (© *National Maritime Museum, Greenwich, London*)

1 May 1795. *Boyne* on fire. (© *National Maritime Museum, Greenwich, London*)

5 November 1799. Wreck of the *Sceptre* in Table Bay. (© *National Maritime Museum, Greenwich, London*)

17 August 1803. Rafts leave the wreck of the *Porpoise*. (© *National Maritime Museum, Greenwich, London*)

8 May 1804. Action between *Vincejo* and a French flotilla. (© *National Maritime Museum, Greenwich, London*)

11 April 1809. *Mediator* in the Basque Roads 1809. (© *National Maritime Museum, Greenwich, London*)

24 August 1810. Battle in the Grand Port, Mauritius. (© *National Maritime Museum, Greenwich, London*)

25 October 1812. Capture of the *Macedonian* by USS *United States*. (*Mary Evans/Classic Stock/H Armstrong Roberts*)

10 September 1813. Battle of Lake Erie. (© *National Maritime Museum, Greenwich, London*)

29 April 1814. USS *Peacock* captures the *Epervier*. (© *National Maritime Museum, Greenwich, London*)

2 October 1817. Wreck of the sloop *Julia* on Tristan da Cunha. (© *National Maritime Museum, Greenwich, London*)

20 December 1847. The loss of the steam frigate *Avenger*. (© *National Maritime Museum, Greenwich, London*)

9 January CONSTITUTION Cutter
Hired 1796; 122 tons; 12 guns
Lieutenant William Faulknor
At daybreak, whilst cruising to the east of Portland, she sighted two large cutters and made sail after them. As they neared it could be seen that they were French privateers and cleared for action. After standing out to seaward for some time, the enemy cutters tacked towards them and commenced an action, with one on each side. The fighting went on for an hour, until one of them ran onto her quarter and entered a large number of boarders, and with eight men killed or wounded, Lieutenant Faulknor surrendered. Now in French hands, she was pursued by several ships, and was recaptured later that day by the *Greyhound* revenue cutter, with the *Weasel* and *Harpy* sloops in sight.
[www.britishnewspaperarchive.co: Star (London) 12 January 1801 p3]

10 January NANCY Cutter
Hired 1793; 47 tons; 6 guns
Master Joseph Yeames
Listed by Steel as having been captured by a French privateer in the English Channel in March, and the list of hired cutters gives the date of her loss as 10 January. No further details have been found.
[TNA: ADM.49/96; Steel: Naval Chronologist p44]

15 January LURCHER Cutter
Hired 1795; 103 tons; 12 guns
Lieutenant Robert Forbes
Attached to the blockading squadron off the coast of Brittany, she was captured by a French lugger privateer of 16 guns and taken into Lorient. Lieutenant Forbes was cleared of any blame, most of his guns being unfit for service or dismounted.
[www.britishnewspaperarchive.co: Exeter Flying Post 5 March 1801 p4; The Morning Chronicle 28 May 1801 p3]

29 January FORTE Fifth Rate
Prize 1799; 1,401 tons; 170ft x 43.6ft; 44 guns
Captain Lucius Hardyman
The *Forte* was part of the squadron under Rear Admiral John Blankett in the Red Sea, with the aim of restricting the influence of the French in the region. In late January, the squadron arrived at the port of Jeddah, to confer with the Sharif, but as the officers of *Forte* were unfamiliar with the port, William Briggs, the Master of the *Leopard*, came onboard to act as a pilot for the entrance. Under his guidance, they passed the outer marks under topsails and mizzen staysail, the Master standing on the foreyard, checking for obstructions. They had passed clear of a known shoal, when a rock was seen about half a ship's length ahead and sails were ordered to be braced round and the helm put up, but she struck the rock with some force. All sail was thrown aback and she floated free of the rock but had been holed and water was reported entering the ship. The frigate stood on and at just before noon anchored, with the other ships, in the harbour. Work began to clear the fore hold to get to the source of the leak, whilst the pumps were manned, with portable pumps being sent to her from the other ships. The topmasts were struck, boats hoisted out and a sail prepared for lowering over the bows. The water steadily gained on the pumps and by noon was covering the casks in the hold and as she was settling, the ship was taken into shallow water, where she eventually capsized. Mr Briggs, who had acted as the pilot, took most of the blame. The rock was known to him, and it was seen well in time, but he failed to issue any sensible orders, Captain Hardyman eventually having to shout. 'Put the helm over, port or starboard'. Briggs was ordered to lose a year's seniority and to be more circumspect in the future.
[TNA: ADM.1/5356; ADM.51/4449]

29 January INCENDIARY Fireship
Dover 1782; 422 tons; 108.9ft x 29.7ft; 16 guns
Commander Richard Dunn
Sailed from Gibraltar to cruise in the approaches to the Straits, at daybreak two large ships were seen on the lee bow. *Incendiary* initially made ground toward them and made out that they were ships of the line, but after making private signals which were not answered, at 9am she altered away, the ships in pursuit. The chase went on until 11 o'clock at night, when she was overhauled, and surrendered to the *Indivisible*, 80 guns, one on Admiral Ganteaume's squadron. After all the crew were taken out, she was scuttled by her captors
[TNA: ADM.1/5356]

2 February LÉGÈRE Ship Sloop
Prize 1796; 453 tons; 116.2ft x 30ft; 18 guns
Commander Cornelius Quinton
Cruising off the coast of Colombia, South America, the weather steadily worsened, with high seas and the wind increasing to gale force. The sloop reduced sail down to reefed topsails, but she pitched and rolled in the heavy swell, regularly shipping water which washed over the upper deck, the pumps being constantly employed. At 2 o'clock in the morning she took a particularly heavy sea on the weather bow, which split planking, and water entered, flooding the hold. She altered course, to stand in towards the land, guns being heaved overboard, stores following them, as did one of the anchors. At 3 o'clock in the afternoon she anchored in Samba Bay, about 36 miles to the north-east of Cartagena. By now the hold was full, the storerooms filling, and the sloop was settling fast. Boats were hoisted out and the crew abandoned her, setting the ship on fire as they

did so. The boats made a six-day voyage to the Spanish settlement at Cartagena.
[TNA: ADM.1/5357]

10 February SPRIGHTLY Cutter
Dover 1778; 151 tons; 66ft × 24.4ft; 12 guns
Lieutenant Robert Jump
Heading for Gibraltar with despatches, she was 40 miles to the south-west of Cape de Gata when a number of ships were sighted and seemed to consist of seven ships of the line and two frigates. Private signals were made but not answered, and she hauled away, spreading more sail in the light winds. A ship was seen to detach from the squadron and commenced to chase her, initially showing Russian colours. As she neared the cutter, the Russian flag was hauled down, to be replaced by French. After a two-hour chase, she was overhauled and surrendered without a fight to the *Dix-Août*, 74 guns, part of the squadron of Admiral Ganteaume. The French ship scuttled their capture.
[TNA: ADM.1/5356]

13 February SUCCESS Fifth Rate
Liverpool 1781; 683 tons; 126ft × 35.2ft; 32 guns
Commander Shuldham Peard
On 9 February, the *Success* was laying at anchor off Gibraltar when the French squadron of seven ships of the line and two frigates under Admiral Ganteaume was sighted, heading through the Straits into the Mediterranean. She weighed and steered after them, to confirm their strength and destination. The French ships initially steered along the Spanish coast toward Cape de Gata but by the evening of 12 February, Captain Peard was convinced that the French ships were heading for the eastern Mediterranean. He made sail away on a fresh southerly wind, to proceed to Egypt and inform Lord Keith. She was pursued by the French squadron, the chase going on through the night. At daybreak, the leading French frigate was close astern with two ships of the line nearby. It was clear that they would soon overhaul the *Success*, so Peard deliberately reversed his course, in the hope of both retarding the progress of the French as well as meeting any pursuing British force. By mid-afternoon two of the French ships of the line were still in pursuit and were within gunshot and opened fire with bow-chase guns. The *Success* continued to flee until the French pair were within musket shot, when she surrendered, then being 14 leagues (42 miles) to the east of Cape Palos.
Note: recaptured on 2 September by the *Primrose*.
[TNA: ADM.1/5355]

(14/15) February TELEGRAPH Brig
Hired 1798; 263 tons; 14 guns
Lieutenant Caesar Corsellis†
Sailed from Plymouth on 9 February, bound for the Mediterranean to join Sir Richard Calder's squadron, after intelligence was received that part of the Brest fleet under Admiral Ganteaume had escaped. When off Cape Ortegal, northern Spain, she became separated from the squadron in poor weather and disappeared. The area was swept by a storm during 14/15 February, and it was presumed that she was lost with all hands at this time.
[TNA: ADM.49/96; www.britishnewspaperarchive.co: Hampshire Chronicle 9 March p2; Morning Post 19 March 1801 p3]

27 February BULLDOG Bomb Vessel
Dover 1782; 317 tons; 98.1ft × 27.3ft; 10 guns
Commander Barrington Dacres
Ordered to proceed to Ancona and assemble and escort ships bound for Malta, she arrived off that port during the evening, anchoring off the lighthouse. A boat with an officer was sent ashore, but when he failed to return, suspicions were aroused that all was not as expected, and Commander Dacres ordered another boat lowered and manned, with the Gunner in charge, to scout along the shoreline. Before this could be done however, two shore batteries opened fire on them, quickly hitting the bomb. With no wind to assist her, and being struck regularly by shot, she had little choice but to strike her flag in surrender. The port had been occupied by the French without their knowledge.
Note: recaptured on 16 September by the *Champion*.
[TNA: ADM.1/5356]

16 March INVINCIBLE Third Rate
Deptford 1765; 1,630 tons; 168.6ft × 47.3ft; 74 guns
Captain John Rennie†
Flagship of Rear Admiral Thomas Totty, she sailed from Great Yarmouth under the guidance of local pilots. The passed the Cockle Sands and then stood to the northward, the pilots indicating that they were happy to take the ship through the Hazeboro' Gap. At 2.30pm she struck heavily on the ground. The pilots claimed to be mystified as to what they had grounded on and assured the Admiral that it must be a new bank recently thrown up. Topmasts were struck and she lay quietly, not striking at all, to await high water, no leaks being apparent at this time. The wind freshened and by 5 o'clock the sea had got up sufficiently for the ship to start lifting and pounding, with increasing violence. At this, the main- and mizzenmasts were cut away and some stores heaved overboard to lighten her. An hour later she floated free, but it was found that she was very sluggish in her movements and the rudder had been beaten off. She anchored in 17 fathoms. Everyone was confident at this stage that all would be well, but the winds steadily increased and at flood time at 9 o'clock that night, she tailed onto a sandbank and started pounding on the ground again. A local fishing smack now appeared and informed them that they were on

Hammond's Knoll. The boats were hoisted out, and the Admiral along with some of his staff were transferred to the fishing smack, along with Midshipmen, boys and some sick, the smack remaining at anchor during the night. Daybreak showed that the *Invincible* had drifted into deeper water but was clearly settling. The fishing smack and a collier approached the wreck, which sank as they approached. Some of the crew succeeded in jumping into boats alongside, but most were forced to take to the water and cling to wreckage. In his account of the wreck, Admiral Totty wrote '… the horror of the scene and the screams of the unhappy sufferers at the moment the ship went down far exceeds all power of description, and their Lordships must make allowance for the unconnected manner of this narrative'. About 190 of the crew of 600 were saved, two men being picked up two days later. The pilots and the Master were blamed, having neglected to make allowance for the rapid tide, and the land and seamarks being in sight.
[TNA: ADM.1/5355; Gold: Naval Chronicle vol 5 p261]

24 March FULMINANTE Cutter
Prize 1798; 40 tons; 44ft × 15.2ft; 4 guns
Lieutenant Robert Corbet

Supporting the British army in Egypt under General Abercromby, during their advance on Alexandria, the cutter being stationed close inshore in Aboukir Bay. She had been firing repeatedly at French positions, but it was found that her carronades did not reach their target, so she manoeuvred closer and anchored just a cable's length (200 yards) from the shore. During the night, the wind rose and at 3 o'clock in the morning one of her anchor cables parted, probably because it chafed on rocks. She drove towards the shore, the second anchor never holding her, probably having parted at the anchor. Within minutes she had gone ashore and was wrecked.
[TNA: ADM.1/5356]

24 March BLAZER Gunboat
Deptford 1797; 161 tons; 75.1ft × 22.2ft; 12 guns
Lieutenant Jonah Tiller

Part of the large fleet commanded by Admiral Sir Hyde Parker that was sent to Copenhagen to act as a threatening military option, backing up diplomatic moves then in progress to end the Armed Neutrality of the Baltic states. The fleet arrived in the Kattegat on 18 March to be met with a heavy gale, which scattered some of the small vessels, including *Blazer*. The gunboat lost her main topgallant mast and had a boom carried away in the storm and was forced to lay-to under close reefed topsails. During 23 March it snowed heavily, but during the early hours of the following morning, land was sighted, with numerous reefs. With difficulty she managed to keep herself clear of the rocks and sighting several ships at anchor ran towards them and was able to anchor in relatively sheltered waters. The weather cleared and it was found that she was under the castle of Varberg, Sweden. A party of Swedish officers boarded her later, and took possession of the gunboat, all the crew being interned ashore. The *Blazer* was later restored by the Swedish government, the crew regaining possession on 1 August.
[TNA: ADM.52/2767]

25 March SCOUT Ship Sloop
Prize 1800 (*Venus*); 406 tons; 111ft × 29.1ft; 18 guns
Commander Henry Duncan

Ordered to proceed from Portsmouth to the northern coast of France as part of the blockade, Commander Duncan was anxious to take up his station and with a pilot embarked, decided to proceed with the wind, through the Solent into the English Channel. The sloop weighed and stood down the waterway until at 9.30 in the morning, when she struck the Shingles Bank. All sail was thrown aback, but she would not move. Work was started to lighten her, distress guns being fired at the same time, which soon brought several local boats to her assistance. With the water butts emptied, shot heaved overboard and some of the stores transferred into the boats, an attempt was made to sail her off at high tide the next morning. This failed, so anchors were laid out and she next tried to kedge herself free, but this also failed. By the afternoon of 27 March water was found to be entering the sloop, and so rapidly that it threatened to overtake the pumps. The main- and mizzenmasts were cut away in an effort to ease her, and the foremast had to follow as short time later. The water was now flooding in, so that by 5 o'clock the main deck was awash. The crew were taken off by the boats which stood by her, the last men leaving at 8 o'clock by which time the water was over the gunwales. The subsequent court-martial enquiry decided that she had drifted down onto the Shingles through the rapidity of the tide.
[TNA: ADM.1/5356]

28 March CHARLOTTE Schooner
Purchased (1795?) 1800; 6 guns
Lieutenant John Williams

Based at Jamaica, she sailed from that island for Martinique, the Île-à-Vache off Hispaniola was raised at 2 o'clock in the morning to the north-west. She altered away, losing sight of land as she did so. About two hours later land was seen again, this time very close ahead, and despite the helm being put over she struck the ground, the rudder coming off as she did so. Guns and shot were heaved overboard, boats hoisted out and water butts emptied. Kedge anchors were laid out, but all the heaving would not shift her, and it seemed that the wind and sea were taking her further onto the reef. Water was entering at a fast rate and was soon above the

ballast. The mast was cut away to ease her and rafts made from spars and yards. At first light some of the crew managed to get ashore through the surf, but further escape by this method was curtailed by the arrival of the frigate *Circe*, whose boats took off all the crew. The thickness of the weather and a strong current had taken her down onto the Île-à-Vache. Lieutenant Williams was reprimanded for failing to maintain a good lookout.
[TNA: ADM.1/5356]

9 June MELEAGER Fifth Rate
Frindsbury 1785; 682 tons; 126ft × 35.1ft; 32 guns
Captain Hon. Thomas Capel

Having sailed from Port Royal, Jamaica, on 25 May, she was cruising in the Bahia del Campeche, Gulf of Mexico, when at just before midnight, surf was seen ahead. The helm was put over, but she ran onto a reef, striking very hard. Boats were hoisted out and an anchor was laid out, but the cable snagged on rocks and then sheered when they attempted to heave in. The frigate was lightened, but further efforts at kedging her free all failed. The water gained steadily on the pumps, and it was clear that she was settling. Provisions were put into the boats and all the crew embarked before she sank. The boats reached Vera Cruz, from where the *Apollo* frigate picked up the crew in mid-July. The court martial blamed the wreck on the great error of the charts held on board, particularly Romain's, which failed to correctly show the position and extent of the Triangles Shoals (Triàngulos) on which she had been wrecked.
[TNA: ADM.1/5357]

20 June IPHIGENIA Troopship
Mistleythorn 1780; 681 tons; 126.2ft × 35ft; 16 guns
Commander Hassard Stackpoole

Anchored in the Bay of Aboukir, Egypt, loaded with firewood and broom intended for the British army ashore. At 4.30 in the morning, smoke was seen coming from a store of broom under the fo'c'sle. The magazines were flooded, and the decks scuttled in the firefighting efforts, but the fire spread to a stack of timber. By 6 o'clock the fire had a firm hold and the crew started leaving her. The ship burned for another hour, until at 7 o'clock she blew up.
[TNA: ADM.1/5356]

24 June SWIFTSURE Third Rate
Deptford 1787; 1,621 tons; 168.9ft × 47ft; 74 guns
Captain Benjamin Hallowell

Escorting a convoy of transports and cartels from Egypt to Malta, the *Swiftsure* became separated on 22 June and proceeded independently. At first light on 24 June, then being seven leagues (21 miles) to the north-east of Derna, Libya, five large ships were seen to leeward. Rightly suspecting them to be a French squadron, known to be in the area, Captain Hallowell made all sail away. The strangers closed, proving to be four ships of the line and a frigate; the signals used between them showed that they were indeed French. The strangers split into separate groups, with two ships tacking to follow in the wake of *Swiftsure*, the others continuing on the same tack. By 2 o'clock in the afternoon the ships to leeward, two ships of the line and a frigate, had forereached her and tacked to close. The *Swiftsure* tacked and attempted to run astern of the group to leeward, hoping to disable one or more of them and escape. She was foiled in this by the French ships altering towards her. The action commenced at 3.30pm, when the leeward French ships opened fire. About an hour later the two trailing liners were within range and joined the action. Her efforts to escape were foiled, as she found herself surrounded, with the *Indivisible*, 80 guns, on the larboard bow: the *Dix-Août*, 74, on the larboard quarter, with the *Jean Bart*, 74, and the *Constitution*, 74, on the starboard side and quarter. The fore yard and fore topsail yard were shot away, and all the running and standing rigging along with the sails were soon cut to pieces. Outnumbered and unable to escape, she surrendered. The French ships had fired high, into the rigging, and casualties were consequently light: two killed and eight wounded.

Note: recaptured on 21 October 1805 at Trafalgar.
[TNA: ADM.1/5357]

3 July SPEEDY Brig Sloop
Dover 1782; 208 tons; 78.3ft × 25.9ft; 14 guns
Commander Lord Thomas Cochrane

Engaged in a cruise along the coast of southern Spain, during 2 July the sloop chased some local craft inshore near Alicante and then set them on fire. At daybreak, three large ships were sighted, which could be seen to be ships of the line, evidently investigating the burning ships, and they bore up in chase. The *Speedy* made all sail away and employed sweeps to assist in her flight. By 9 o'clock the pursuers separated, taking different tacks, evidently with the intention of cutting off all avenues of escape. Guns were heaved overboard to lighten her, and studding sails set as the chase continued. By 10 o'clock the nearest of the enemy ships was within musket shot on her quarter and commenced firing at the sloop. An attempt to run between the enemy ships was blocked and even though it was clearly a large French ship of the line, Cochrane fired at his opponent, receiving broadside as a reply, which cut up his rigging and shot away his main boom. At this, *Speedy* surrendered to the *Desaix*, 74 guns, part of Admiral Linois' squadron, then being about four miles to the east of Gibraltar.
[TNA: ADM.1/5357]

5 July HANNIBAL Third Rate
Blackwall 1786; 1,685 tons; 170.10ft × 47.6ft; 74 guns
Captain Solomon Ferris

During the afternoon of 4 July, a squadron of three French ships of the line, with a large 38-gun frigate, were seen to anchor off the Spanish port of Algeçiras. The intelligence was quickly passed to Rear Admiral Sir James Saumarez commanding the ships blockading the port of Cadiz, who, with six ships of the line, stood towards the French ships. They approached the anchorage in the morning of 5 July and found them to be placed close under shore batteries, supported by a number of Spanish gunboats. The approaching ships were frustrated by light and fitful winds, which had fallen to a calm by the time the *Hannibal*, last in the line, got into action. In this situation the British ships attempted to anchor near their opponents, but not all could effectively take part, being too far away and finding their line of fire blocked. When a light breeze sprang up, Saumarez ordered the *Hannibal* to cut her cables and support the *Pompée*. However, as she was manoeuvring, the wind fell away, and the *Hannibal* drifted into shoal water and went aground. She now found herself in a difficult position: unable to move, close to the guns of a shore battery and with a French 80-gun ship and several gunboats nearby, to which she could not effectively reply as not all of her guns would bear. She was battered and raked constantly, although some relief came when the French ships took advantage of another fresh breeze, cut their cables, and went further inshore. At about 1.30pm the British broke off the action and made for Gibraltar, being forced to leave the grounded *Hannibal*. Captain Ferris held out for some time after this, but with all rigging and sails shattered and a large number of casualties, she surrendered, signalling her surrender by hoisting the ensign upside down. The *Formidable* took possession of the prize. Seventy-five men were killed, six missing and sixty-two wounded.
[TNA: ADM.1/5358]

7 July AUGUSTUS Gun Vessel
Purchased 1796; 3 guns
Lieutenant James Scott

Based at Plymouth, she weighed from the Cattewater and made sail for Stonehouse Pool. At 8 o'clock, when she was close to the Hoe, she attempted to tack, but missed stays and found herself being taken down towards the shore. An anchor was quickly let go, but found that she was driving, the cable stoppers breaking as she did so. In a short time, she had struck the rocks at the western end of the Hoe, the rudder being unshipped and the counter giving way, allowing water to flood in. Boats were hoisted out and one was despatched to the Barbican to bring assistance. In the meantime, guns, shot and stores were heaved overboard and pumping commenced. A dockyard launch was soon alongside, followed by boats from ships nearby. They attempted to haul her off but failed, and during the night she started to break up, the crew being taken off. The following day dockyard craft did succeed in hauling her off the rocks and towed her into the Cattewater, but she was declared a total loss.
[TNA: ADM.1/5357]

9 July AMBUSCADE Fifth Rate
Prize 1799 (*Embuscade*); 770 tons; 127ft × 37.5ft; 32 guns
Captain W- van Voss

A Dutch-manned frigate under British control, she weighed from Sheerness at 8 o'clock in the morning en route for the Downs. Little more than an hour later, when near the Middle Sand she heeled over, a plank in the bottom apparently having given way. Several women on the lower deck discovered water flooding into the ship through the hawse holes and raised the alarm. In less than five minutes she had rolled over onto her beam-ends and was almost entirely under water. Local tenders and boats went to the frigate's aid and all but about eight men were rescued. The wreck was salvaged on 13 July and towed alongside the *Drochterland* hulk. The *Ambuscade* was refitted, but only to serve as a hulk, being renamed *Helder* in 1803.
[www.britishnewspaperarchive.co: Morning Post 11 July 1801 p2]

24 July JASON Fifth Rate
Bursledon 1800; 1,053 tons; 150.2ft × 39.8ft; 36 guns
Captain Hon. John Murray

Cruising off St Malo as part of the blockade, watching for any movement by frigates known to be in that port. When she was to the west of Île Césambre, with no warning she struck a submerged rock and after striking several times, beat over it, only to run hard aground again on a second obstruction. Water flooded in at a fast rate, and within 10 minutes there was 5ft of water in the hold and half an hour after striking, the magazines were flooded. The boats were hoisted out and several local fishing vessels came to their assistance, all the crew being rescued. The pilot was a Frenchman, apparently named Omness, who, clearly fearing that he would take the blame, disappeared. There were various reports of his whereabouts, one stating that he was seen to climb into a local fishing vessel, then cut off his hair and put on fisherman's clothes. In the event the court martial investigating the loss decided that no blame should be placed on the pilot or crew, the rock being uncharted. The wreck was later blown up by boats from other ships of the blockading squadron.
[TNA: ADM.1/5357]

11 August **LOWESTOFFE** Fifth Rate
Deptford 1761; 717 tons; 130.6ft × 35.3ft; 32 guns
Captain Robert Plampin
Acting as an escort to a homeward-bound convoy from the West Indies, she sailed from Kingston, Jamaica, on 22 July. The convoy assembled off Port Antonio and got underway on 27 July. Cape St Nicholas Mole was raised on 8 August, and course was set for the Caicos passage. Land was sighted two days later, which was identified as Great Inagua. It was noted that the current was strong, and the set was different from that previously noted. That night, at just after 10 o'clock, the ground was found to be shallowing and very soon she sounded in 15 fathoms. Breakers were then seen to leeward and although the ship's head was set to clear them by some distance, she was found to be drifting down onto the rocks, broadside-on. The helm was put over and an attempt made to tack, but she missed stays. Luffing up into the wind, she anchored, the surf beating only a short distance from the stern. Before the anchor could bring her up, she struck the ground aft. The rudder and tiller were both unshipped immediately, and the ship started pounding on the rocks. The mizzen- and mainmasts were cut away as she continued to drive over the rocks before she finally brought up filling with water. Guns were heaved overboard, the foremast cut away and pumping and bailing started. Daybreak revealed that they had run ashore on Little Inagua island, and five of the convoy had suffered a similar fate. Boats were hoisted out, but little work could be done to heave her off as the water was up to the coamings of the main deck. Other ships from the convoy came to their aid and by mid-afternoon all the crew had been taken off, five men being drowned when one boat capsized in the surf. The cause was determined to be the sudden and unexpected change of current.
[TNA: ADM.1/5358]

21 August **SPITFIRE** Schooner
Prize 1798; 64 tons; 6 guns
Lieutenant ... Campbell
Carrying despatches from Bombay to the Red Sea, at just after 5 o'clock in the morning, going at about four knots under her fore topsail, she ran hard aground. The grounding came as a shock as no reef was known in the area and the lead-line had shown 20 fathoms only a short time before. The masts were cut away to ease the schooner and she was carried by the surf over the rocks into shallow water where she went aground. The crew were able to land on the small atoll, taking stores and provisions with them. A small party led by Lieutenant Campbell left in the ship's boat six days later and reached the settlement at Mahé, from where a rescue was organised. It was found that she had grounded on the African Banks to the north of the Amirante Islands, part of the Seychelles Group.
[www.britishnewspaperarchive.co: Madras Courier 7 October 1801 p2; Gold: Naval Chronicle vol 7 p357]

4 September **PROSELYTE** Fifth Rate
Prize 1796 (Jason); 748 tons; 133.1ft × 35.8ft; 32 guns
Captain George Fowke
With Captain Fowke ashore, the ship was under the command of Lieutenant Henry Whitby as she entered the Great Bay, Saint Martin, in the Leeward Islands. The Master, Luke Winter, had charge of the ship and he guided her in and had just given orders to bring-to, when she struck the ground. All sail was thrown aback, but she was stuck fast. The boats were hoisted out, which carried out an anchor astern, but it was already too late. Within six minutes the water had flooded the orlop deck and she started to heel over to starboard. The guns were heaved over the side and all masts cut away, but all was in vain. She capsized over to starboard, the water flooding in through the ports as she lay on her beam-ends. Other ships despatched boats to her aid and picked up all the crew. It emerged at the subsequent court-martial that they had run onto the Man-o'-War shoal, the position of which was well known and the bearings to be observed on entering the harbour were specified in local Standing Orders. These had evidently been ignored by the Master. There had been no discussion between Master and Lieutenant Whitby about the entrance, Whitby being entirely happy to leave it entirely to Winter. Further, no anchors were prepared for letting go. Lieutenant Whitby was reprimanded for his want of attention. Master Luke Winters was dismissed the service for his carelessness.
[TNA: ADM.1/5359]

25 October **BONETTA** Ship Sloop
Prize 1798 (les Huits Amis); 348 tons; 103.1ft × 27.8ft; 18 guns
Commander Thomas New
During the night she ran hard aground on a reef at the eastern end of the Jardines de la Reina, south of Cuba, where she subsequently capsized and was lost. The officer of the watch, Lieutenant John Goakman, was found guilty of the charges of sleeping on watch and disobeying orders he had received from Commander New. He was ordered to forfeit all pay due, suffer two years' imprisonment, and was dismissed the service.
[TNA: ADM.1/5360]

October **FLY** Ship Sloop
Sheerness 1776; 302 tons; 96.7ft × 26.10ft; 14 guns
Commander Thomas Duvall†
Sailed from Spithead on 16 September with a convoy for Newfoundland but became separated during

poor weather and not seen again. Presumed to have foundered with all hands
[www.britishnewspaperarchive.co: *Salisbury & Winchester Journal* 28 December 1801 p2]

1 November COCKCHAFER Lugger
Hired 1793; 37 tons; 8 guns
Master … Philpott
Foundered at anchor in Guernsey Roads in gale-force winds. All the crew were saved.
[TNA: ADM.49/96; www.britishnewspaperarchive.co: *Morning Post* 24 November 1801 p3]

2 November FRIENDSHIP Gun Vessel
Purchased 1796; 2 guns
Lieutenant James Ashley
Stationed at Guernsey, she was driven out of the anchorage off the island in gale-force winds during the night of 1/2 November. Carried before the wind, she was driven on to the coast of Brittany near St Malo and wrecked. At first light the crew managed to scramble ashore onto the rocks, having to wade ashore through waist-deep water. They were well treated by the local populace and were repatriated some days later.
[www.britishnewspaperarchive.co: *Morning Post* 25 November 1801 p2]

2 November POLLY Brig Tender
Hired 1796; 130 tons; 4 guns
Lieutenant John Brown
Returning to Plymouth after carrying released prisoners of war to Morlaix, she anchored in the Sound during 31 October. The weather worsened, and during 2 November she weighed and ran into Mill Bay for shelter and re-anchored, putting out two anchors. During the afternoon, the wind rose to gale force and one anchor cable parted, so she weighed and made ground into the Sound and anchored again, but almost immediately she parted the cable and was driven inshore and onto rocks at Withyhedge. With waves beating over her, she was soon full of water and abandoned. Over the next few days, with dockyard assistance, the stores were salvaged, and she was eventually hauled clear and taken into the dockyard but discharged from service.
[TNA: ADM.51/4031]

4 November WILLIAM AND LUCY Gun Vessel
Purchased 1795; 2 guns
Lieutenant William Lydiard
Stationed at Guernsey, Channel Islands, her condition was assessed to be so poor that she was ordered to return to Plymouth for repairs. The initial attempt by the *Grappler* gun brig to tow her across the Channel had to be abandoned because of poor weather, and she anchored off Castle Cornel. The anchor was of poor quality, with a loose stock and it failed to hold her. Driving across the bay, she fired distress guns as she was taken inshore. The *Aggressor* gun brig came to her aid, passing a line which was used to secure her to the brig. She stayed secured to the *Aggressor* while efforts were made to obtain a new anchor and cable, but before they could be brought on board, the heavy swell and high winds made the vessels pitch and roll, and the securing hawsers started to chafe. The *William and Lucy* was now seen as a danger to both herself and other ships and the crew was taken off, the ropes cut, and she was allowed to drive out of the harbour and founder.
[TNA: ADM.1/5360]

November SCOUT Ship Sloop
Prize 1801 (*Premier Consul*); 448 tons; 113.8ft × 30.3ft; 18 guns
Captain Henry Duncan
Sailed from Portsmouth 20 October en-route for Newfoundland and disappeared in the Atlantic. Presumed to have foundered with all hands.
[www.britishnewspaperarchive.co: *Morning Post* 22 October 1801 p3]

November UTILE Brig Sloop
Prize 1799; 279 tons; 89.6ft × 26.7ft; 16 guns
Commander Edward Jekyll Canes†
Sailed from Gibraltar on 5 November, bound for Minorca and Malta, and never seen again. Believed to have foundered with all hands in poor weather off Gibraltar. Pay Book closed 30 November 1801.
[TNA: ADM.35/1959; www.britishnewspaperarchive.co: *Morning Post* 8 February 1802 p2]

1802

3 March SENSIBLE Fifth Rate
Prize 1798; 946 tons; 146.3ft × 38.8ft; 36 guns
Captain Robert Sauce
Sailing from her anchorage in the River Hugli on 17 February, she steered south along the eastern seaboard of India, heading for Trincomalee, being joined on 28 February by the *Victorious*. At 2 o'clock in the morning breakers were observed close ahead. The helm was put over to starboard and sail was ordered to be taken in, but she took the ground soon after, the land looming nearby with surf crashing around them. Captain Sauce arrived on deck to curse the helmsman, 'Dorman, you villain, did you not see the land before you?' All hands were turned up and topmasts were struck, and boats hoisted out. An anchor was taken out astern, in an attempt kedge her free, but she would not move. Water was reported to be entering at a fast rate, the ship lifting and pounding on the ground and spare

yards were lowered over the side to try and stop her capsizing. Pumping continued, but water was soon up to the lower deck beams, the rudder was unshipped and after 16 hours of work she was finally abandoned as a wreck. One man was drowned, but all the remainder of the crew successfully made it to the shore in the boats or rafts. It was found that she had run onto a shoal off Mullaitivu through the erroneous and negligent manner of navigation employed on board. None of the Midshipmen or Master's Mates were required to keep any reckoning, and no one on board was capable of lunar observations, relying and on a noon sun-sight and dead reckoning. The Captain had been warned by Captain Malcolm of the *Victorious* shortly before the wreck that his reckoning was more than 40 miles out. Sauce was severely reprimanded and placed on the bottom of the seniority list. The Master, James O'Connor, was dismissed the service.
[TNA:ADM.1/5361;ADM.51/4498]

29 March **ASSISTANCE** Fourth Rate
Liverpool 1781; 1,053 tons; 145.1ft × 40.8ft; 50 guns
Captain Richard Lee

Sailed from Great Yarmouth on 28 March bound for Spithead, and the ship ran south all through the night. At first light the next morning, land was seen ahead which was identified as the French coast in the vicinity of Dunkirk. In strong winds and heavy seas, she tacked twice to head westwards, sounding constantly. At 10 o'clock she struck the ground, hitting a sandbank situated between Gravelines and Dunkirk. Anchors were let go and efforts were made to lighten the ship, with shot and stores being heaved overboard. She successfully floated free, but with the tide going out, she found herself surrounded by breakers and sandbanks and she soon ran aground again. Signal guns of distress were fired, which brought out two French pilots under whose guidance she was again freed, and an attempt made to reach open water, but at 3.30pm, she grounded for a third time. This time she could not be freed, and with the rudder unshipped and several leaks now evident, the pumps were fully employed. When one of the pumps broke, the water gained rapidly, and it became clear that she was settling. The crew took refuge in the pilot boat which took them to Dunkirk. By the following morning, the ship had disappeared beneath the water. The subsequent court martial decided that Captain Lee had placed far too much faith in his pilots, who had allowed the ship to run too far to the south. Lee was admonished to take more care in who he placed his confidence. Pilots Edmund Coleman and Watson Richards were both mulcted of all pay due and sentenced to six months' confinement in the Marshalsea Prison.
[TNA:ADM.1/5361]

12 | 1803–1815: World War

THE TREATY OF AMIENS which ended the conflict of 1793–1802 had created an uneasy peace. Both sides were irritated by perceived failures to abide by the Treaty: Napoleon's annexing of Piedmont and occupation of Switzerland alarmed many and added to the anxiety about the growing power of the French state. The failure of the British to evacuate Malta caused further friction. Negotiations between the powers failed, and war was declared in May 1803.

For the Royal Navy it meant the imposition of a blockade of French ports and a campaign against French colonial possessions. The alliance of France with Spain brought that latter country into the war during 1804. The immediate threat of an invasion of Great Britain was ended with the victory over the combined Franco-Spanish fleet off Cape Trafalgar in 1805, but this was matched by the continued success on land of the French army which dominated western Europe.

The imposition by Napoleon of the Continental System, a trade embargo on British goods, expanded the threat. The need to maintain trade with the Baltic states and the prospect of the Danish fleet coming under French control led to action against Denmark. Support for the efforts of the Portuguese to eject the French led to increasing British assistance for what became known as the Peninsular War.

The British blockade of French-controlled ports caused considerable resentment in the United States, and this was exacerbated by impressment of American seamen, leading to the conflict known as the War of 1812. The British, fully occupied in Europe, were initially on the defensive in North America, but steadily increased the blockading of American ports and expanded the war onto the Great Lakes.

1803

26 March DETERMINÉE Sixth Rate
Prize 1799; 545 tons; 124.5ft x 31.5ft; 20 guns
Captain Alexander Becher
Ordered to proceed to Jersey from Spithead with a detachment of the 81st Regiment on board, along with their families. Before sailing, efforts were made at Portsmouth, Cowes and Yarmouth to obtain a Jersey pilot, but none were available. She eventually sailed in company with the *Aurora*, hoping to pick up a pilot off the Channel Islands. This also proved a vain hope, so Captain Becher decided to follow in the wake of the *Aurora*. The ships commenced working into St Helier, but at 4.30 in the afternoon, tacking to follow her consort, she unexpectedly struck a rock. In less than three minutes the water was up to the lower deck. The anchors were let go to hold the ship steady and sail was taken in. The soldiers and their accompanying families were now in state of some panic, and when a cutter was launched, a large number tried to crowd into the boat, which promptly overset. With the ship settling fast, pleas from Captain Becher and their officers to stay calm and allow the women and children into the boats fell on deaf ears. Soon after this the ship fell over onto her side, throwing many people into the sea. Over the next three hours the *Aurora* and local boats took off the survivors who were clinging to the rigging and masts which were still above water. Two seamen, ten soldiers, four women and three children were drowned.
[TNA: ADM.1/5363; Gold: Naval Chronicle vol 9 pp326–7]

31 May RESISTANCE Fifth Rate
Bursledon 1801; 975 tons; 146.1ft x 38.9ft; 36 guns
Captain Philip Wodehouse
The ship was steering south, along the coast of Portugal in poor weather, thick fog and little wind, when at 6.30 in the morning, breaking surf was first heard and then seen close ahead. An attempt was made to tack, but before she came around, the frigate struck the ground. Boats were hoisted out and pumping commenced, and efforts to lighten ship got under way with upper-deck guns and some provisions being heaved overboard. It was clear that she was firmly aground on rocks and a spare topmast was hoisted over the side to act as a shore and prevent her falling over. All the masts were cut away, but the ship continued to fill and settle deeper. When it was clear that she could not be saved, rafts were constructed to augment the boats and the crew went ashore, several taking the opportunity to desert. She had run onto the shore to the north of Cape St Vincent because of an ill-judged course ordered by the Master, James Ross, and the failure to maintain a good lookout by the morning watch. Mr Ross was dismissed the service and the officer of the watch Lieutenant John Southcott was severely reprimanded.
[TNA: ADM.1/5363]

23 June SURINAM Ship Sloop
Prize 1799 (*Hussard*); 417 tons; 105.2ft × 30.2ft; 18 guns
Commander Robert Tucker

After suffering storm damage, with her fore topmast sprung, the sloop put into the Dutch colonial harbour at Curaçao to effect repairs. Whilst so engaged a prize schooner commanded by Lieutenant Thomas Forrest arrived, bringing news of the outbreak of war. Unable to immediately sail, Commander Tucker employed himself in making plans of the harbour and its defences, which he successfully despatched to Admiral Sir John Duckworth. One set of letters was intercepted by the Dutch authorities, and Tucker was summoned by the Governor, to arrest him and take over the sloop. Tucker subsequently spent four months in close confinement in a dungeon before being released. The capture of the *Surinam* and Tucker's conduct were the subject of considerable rumour and gossip on the station, some of which seems to have been picked up by the historian William James. In his usually reliable *Naval History*, he claims that Tucker had 'imprudently' gone ashore to demand the surrender of the garrison on hearing of the outbreak of hostilities, and the Dutch had taken '… his word, his sword and his ship and all on board of her'. Tucker strongly denied he had acted improperly, and the court-martial enquiry believed the evidence produced by Tucker to show that he could not sail and acquitted him of any blame for the loss. However, he was found guilty of un-officer like conduct in his various transactions with the Dutch authorities, particularly by his signing an agreement with the Governor to 'be obedient to him'. He was ordered to be placed on the bottom of the seniority list of Commanders and he was not subsequently employed. It is noteworthy that the scurrilous rumours were brought to the attention of the court, who added a footnote to their proceedings, that they were '… indignant at the malicious and groundless charges made against Tucker'.
[TNA: ADM.1/5365; O'Byrne p1208; Marshall vol 3 pt2 p385]

3 July MINERVE Fifth Rate
Prize 1795; 1,102 tons; 154.4ft × 39.11ft; 38 guns
Captain Jahleel Brenton

One of the squadron blockading the port of Cherbourg, during the evening of 2 July a number of ships were seen through patches of drifting fog. Course was set for them, the pilot assuring Captain Brenton that he might steer straight for them. As the frigate closed, she ran hard aground, the fog lifting a little at the same time revealing that they had grounded by the Western Cone Head, a stone-filled cone marking the entrance to the harbour breakwater. They were clearly in sight of two forts, both of which opened fire on the stranded vessel, as did two gun brigs, the *Chiffonne* and *Terrible*. Boats were hoisted out to take out an anchor, but Captain Brenton's decision that the larger, bower anchors would be used as kedge anchors meant that the ship's boats proved to be too small. A lugger was seen moored near one of the forts was therefore attacked by the boats and brought back alongside. Work now commenced on clearing the lugger of the cargo of stone found on board, whilst the upper-deck guns of the frigate were run forward to lighten her aft. It was now after midnight, with bright moonlight, and the work continued under constant harassing fire from the forts and brigs, which had stationed themselves ahead of the *Minerve* to rake her. The anchor was laid out in difficult circumstances, the lugger being raked regularly by one of the gun brigs until she was finally dismasted. Despite this, by 5 o'clock in the morning the ship was hauled off the obstruction and a land breeze filled the sails and seemed to be taking them out of the harbour. This hope was dashed when the breeze fell away to a calm and the incoming tide took her further into the harbour, where she again took the ground. Now being raked regularly by the *Chiffone* and *Terrible*, her rigging destroyed, the *Minerve* surrendered. Eleven killed and sixteen wounded.
[TNA: ADM.1/5379]

21 July SEINE Fifth Rate
Prize 1798; 1,146 tons; 156.9ft × 40.6ft; 38 guns
Captain David Milne

Steering north-east along the Dutch coast, she was attempting to regain her station as part of the blockade off the River Elbe. The light on Terschelling Island was raised at just after 8 o'clock that night and Captain Milne became anxious and urged the pilots not to get any closer to the land, at which they assured him that all was well. Just 40 minutes later the ship struck the ground and after beating over the obstruction for some minutes, stuck fast. An anchor was let go to hold her steady, and yards were hoisted overboard to act as shores and distress guns were fired. The latter signals brought two merchant ships to their aid and the initial attempts to free her concentrated on passing hawsers to the ships nearby and hauling her off. When this failed, guns and stores were heaved overboard, and anchors were taken out to act as kedge anchors. All of this took up most of the night and the following morning saw her still stuck fast, labouring and pounding on the sands, which worked the timbers and frames to such an extent that the leaks became uncontrollable. By 11.30pm the water was over the cockpit, and she was settling fast. The crew was removed into the merchant vessels and the frigate was abandoned, the ship being set on fire as the last men left. The pilots onboard, Horsburgh and Waite, were both judged guilty of ignorance and negligence

and were sentenced to lose all pay due and to serve two years in the Marshalsea Prison.
[TNA: ADM.1/5363]

30 July CALYPSO Ship Sloop
Limehouse 1783; 342 tons; 101.6ft × 27.9ft; 16 guns
Commander William Venour†
After sailing from Jamaica on 17 June to act as escort to a large homeward-bound convoy, the ships encountered poor weather, during which the *Calypso* disappeared. Subsequently the 406-ton *Dale* merchant ship reported that she had collided with an unknown ship which foundered very quickly, not allowing any rescue. It was believed that this was the *Calypso*, which was lost with all hands.
[www.britishnewspaperarchive.co: Star (London) 23 August 1803 p3]

4 August REDBRIDGE Schooner
Purchased 1798; 148 tons; 80ft × 22.2ft; 12 guns
Lieutenant George Lempriere
Sailed from Malta on 6 July carrying a number of supernumeraries for the British fleet under Lord Nelson in the western Mediterranean. She searched along the coast of southern France, but could find no sign of the fleet, and with no news of Nelson, Lieutenant Lempriere decided to go to Gibraltar. Before she did so, on 3 August she closed the port of Toulon to observe the shipping there, and as she left the coast, she encountered a British sloop, the *Cameleon*, which informed her that the British fleet was indeed nearby, but further to the west. That evening a frigate was seen to the west and was observed to heave-to with her head to the northward. From the smartness of the manoeuvre, it was supposed that the ship was British, and this proved to be the case, as during the early hours she was close enough to identify herself as the *Phoebe*. At first light, four ships could be seen further to the west, which *Redbridge* assumed to be other ships of the British fleet, but Captain Capel of *Phoebe* hailed and said the strangers were probably French and advised them to make all sail away. As the British pair altered away the ships on the horizon were seen to make sail to follow. The *Phoebe* soon outpaced her companion, and the strangers steadily overhauled the schooner. When the frigate *Cornélie*, 40 guns, came with gunshot and fired a broadside, the *Redbridge* surrendered. Lieutenant Lempriere was later unfortunately drowned when a boat carrying him ashore at Toulon capsized.
[TNA: ADM.1/5444]

17 August PORPOISE Store Ship
Prize 1799 (*Infanta Amelia*); 308 tons; 93ft × 27.11ft; 10 guns
Lieutenant Robert Fowler
Having completed a voyage to New South Wales, the *Porpoise* sailed from Port Jackson on 10 August in company with two merchant ships, the *Cato* and *Bridgwater*, for Batavia (Jakarta). On board she carried as a passenger Lieutenant Matthew Flinders of the *Investigator* sloop, who had been employed surveying the Australian coast. During the afternoon, whilst steering north along the east coast of Australia, shallow sandbanks were seen, and that evening at about 9.30pm, breakers were seen ahead. Before any action could be taken, she ran hard aground. Her companions attempted to tack away, but nearly collided, and by giving way, the *Cato* also ran aground. The *Bridgewater* meanwhile avoided the reef and stood away and disappeared into the night. The *Porpoise* rolled over onto its broadside, the surf breaking over the ship, but all the crew were able to take to the boats and made it safely to a low sandbank visible nearby. When it became clear that the *Bridgewater* was not returning, the cutter of the *Porpoise* was used by Lieutenant Flinders and twelve men to successfully return to Port Jackson, from where the sloop *Rolla* sailed to take off the survivors. The site of the wreck is now known as Wreck Reef (22.19S 155.35E)
[TNA: ADM.1/5366; Gold: Naval Chronicle vol 32 pp184–5]

10 November GARLAND Sixth Rate
Prize 1800 (*Mars*); 529 tons; 124.4ft × 31.5ft; 24 guns
Commander Frederick Cotterell
Cruising with a squadron off the northern coast of San Domingo (Hispaniola) in the West Indies, when ordered to chase a sail seen to windward. She tacked and stood towards the stranger, but in light winds made little headway. By 8 o'clock that evening the ship was close to the land and it was found that they were being taken by a strong current further inshore. They tacked away, but hardly had the manoeuvre been completed before she struck the ground. All sail was thrown aback, the boats hoisted out and some stores thrown overboard to lighten her. These efforts were of little use as it was found that water was gushing in, the after hold and magazines being flooded within 20 minutes. At this, the main- and mizzenmasts were ordered to be cut away, and soon after the ship capsized over to starboard to lay on her beam-ends. Her situation was seen by other ships of the squadron, which closed and took off all the crew, all being removed by 3 o'clock in the morning. The following day the stores and provisions that could be reached were taken out and the ship was then set on fire. The wreck was blamed on the strong currents which had taken the frigate down onto a reef off Caracol, near Cape François.
[TNA: ADM.1/5364]

17 November CIRCE Sixth Rate
Dover 1785; 600 tons; 120.6ft × 33.7ft; 28 guns
Captain Charles Feilding

Stationed off the northern coast of France as part of the blockade, strong winds had blown her off station into the southern North Sea. The morning of 16 November saw the ship standing to the south under a press of sail to regain her station. At 3 o'clock in the afternoon she struck a sandbank, later identified as the Leman and Ower, beating over the obstruction, but striking heavily on the ground several times. Although the ship was now clear of the bank, she had lost her rudder and was making water. Pumping and bailing was started, and a sail was prepared for lowering over the side. By 2 o'clock the next morning the water was found to be shoaling to 11 fathoms, so they anchored. Daylight showed the Norfolk coastline, and several Yarmouth fishing vessels came down to her aid. At 11 o'clock that morning she weighed and with two of the fishing vessels in tow, the skippers on board to act as pilots, the frigate turned to head for the shore. The weather was still poor and in the choppy seas the tow lines parted, and several large seas were shipped over the bows. The water was still gaining on the pumps and the ship was settling, and as the men were exhausted by the constant work, it was decided to abandon the ship. All hands were removed by 7 o'clock that evening and taken into the fishing smacks, the ship sinking some two hours later. The inaccuracy of the charts held onboard were blamed for the wreck.
[TNA: ADM.1/5364]

5 December AVENGER Ship Sloop
Purchased 1803 (*Elizabeth*); 263 tons; 96.6ft × 25.4ft; 14 guns
Commander Francis Snell

Stationed in the North Sea off the coast of Germany, to enforce a blockade of the River Elbe, the sloop embarked a local pilot from Heligoland. At 2 o'clock in the morning, with the ship steering south, the light on Wangerooge Island was raised, but the pilot recommended standing on to the south. The soundings showed the water shallowing, but the pilot confidently assured them that they could continue their course. At 4 o'clock in the morning, she struck a sandbank. Sail was taken in and distress guns were fired. Despite heaving on the warps laid out, the ship would not move, and water was reported to be entering. Pumping was started, but soon had to stop when the pumps became choked with sand. The main- and mizzenmasts were cut away to ease her, but she was settling into the sands. Several local fishing vessels came to her aid and all the crew were taken off, being landed at the local harbour of Minsen. The blame for the wreck was placed squarely on the pilot, who had disappeared soon after the landing.
[TNA: ADM.1/5365]

10 December SHANNON Fifth Rate
Frindsbury 1803; 881 tons; 137.1ft × 38.2ft; 36 guns
Captain Edward Leveson Gower

Blockading the port of Le Havre, the *Shannon* had been blown out of Seine Bay by bad weather, and with the winds moderating, the ship stood southwards to regain her station. The embarked pilot had been loaned to the *Pluto*, and Captain Gower and the Master relied on their own knowledge and experience as they neared the land. The French coast was sighted at noon on 10 December and course was altered to the west, shortening sail down to a reefed foresail and mizzen staysail as the weather worsened again, with heavy seas and high winds. The aim was to raise the light at Cap Barfleur and then alter course again. At 8.30pm, with little warning, the ship ran onto a reef. The sails were loosed to try and force her over the obstruction, but she was held fast by the rocks. Boats were hoisted out and an anchor carried out in preparation to kedge her free, an at the same time the ship was lightened by heaving overboard shot, stores, several upper-deck guns and the anchors. Finally, the mizzenmast was cut away. Her plight had been observed from the shore and a nearby battery commenced firing at her and was soon hitting with every shot. Daylight revealed that she had run aground on Tatihou Island between Cap Barfleur and La Hougue, and troops could be seen gathering, bringing with them field guns to further annoy her. Work went on to pull her off and she finally floated free, but found herself low in the water, having several shot holes in the hull. Although an attempt was made to put her head to seaward, she again ran aground, and it was clear that she could not escape. By this time over sixty shot had struck the ship, shattering the rigging, both the fore- and mainmasts were shot through, and the hull riddled. At 8.30 that evening she struck her flag in surrender. Three men killed and eight wounded. The *Merlin* sloop went to the site six days later and set fire to the wreck.
[TNA: ADM.1/5379]

17 December CUMBERLAND Schooner
Purchased 1803; 29 tons
Commander Matthew Flinders

Having survived the wreck of the *Porpoise* (q.v.), Flinders was given the *Cumberland* at Port Jackson to return to England. After sailing from Coupang, Timor, the upper works became increasingly leaky, and the pumps were employed constantly. Unaware that hostilities had recommenced with France, Flinders steered for Mauritius, arriving on 16 December. The French Governor, General Decaen, detained the schooner and took the crew prisoner, despite Flinders having a passport from the French government to travel

freely on voyages of exploration. Flinders remained imprisoned for a further seven years.
[Flinders vol 2 pp334–59]

25 December **SUFFISANTE** Brig Sloop
Prize 1795; 286 tons; 86.1ft × 28.3ft; 14 guns
Commander Gilbert Heathcote

Laying at anchor in Cork harbour, Ireland, awaiting a chance to sail as soon as wind and weather would allow. A local pilot came aboard and moved the sloop further inshore near Spike Island to allow her to ride more comfortably and on completion of the move was allowed to go onshore by Commander Heathcote, the local man undertaking to return in the morning. At just after 5 o'clock that afternoon the brig was felt to touch the ground, gently at first, but then began to strike alarmingly. Distress guns were fired which brought boats from ships nearby, but no anchors or cables could be laid out due to the choppy seas. Water was found entering the sloop, but pumping was able to keep it at bay until sand clogged the pumps. After this she filled quickly. The cutter, stowed on the booms, was ordered to be hoisted out and this had hardly been achieved before she capsized over onto her beam-ends and sank. The officers of the sloop tried to place the blame entirely on the local pilot, for placing them in an unsafe position, but the court heard testimony that the sloop was poorly managed that afternoon. Lieutenant John Forbes, who should have had the first dog watch, when the trouble became apparent, had not taken over the watch and remained below, allowing a young Midshipman to take charge. The Master, John Coleman, had left the manoeuvring entirely to the local man and went below for his Christmas dinner, although he later claimed he had never been informed that the pilot had been given permission to go ashore. Captain Heathcote had been dining in the wardroom with his officers when the disaster happened, and was found to be partially to blame for the loss in allowing such a state of affairs, but he did not suffer any punishment. Forbes was sentenced to lose one year's seniority and Coleman was reprimanded.
[TNA: ADM.1/5365]

31 December **GRAPPLER** Gun Boat
Northfleet 1797; 169 tons; 76.1ft × 22.7ft; 12 guns
Lieutenant Abel Wantner Thomas

Sailed from Guernsey on 22 December to land former prisoners of war at Granville in France under a flag of truce, but strong winds and high seas prevented them proceeding, and the gunboat anchored off the Îles Chausey until 26 December, when Lieutenant Thomas decided to land the prisoners on the islands. On 30 December, the weather had moderated sufficiently for them to proceed, and they prepared to weigh, spreading topsails in readiness. As they were hauling upon a hawser acting as a spring to heave her head round, it parted, and a sudden squall of wind filled the topsails. Before she could be brought under control, she struck a rock and found herself held fast. Attempts were made to lighten her and haul her off, but it was soon evident that her back was broken, the vessel hanging on the rock under the main chains. It was decided to send to Jersey for assistance, so the boats were hoisted out and manned, the cutter being despatched to the Channel Islands, the remainder taking the crew to the nearby Maître Island. The crew secured the island and waited for help to arrive. The following morning two vessels could be seen approaching from the east and it was determined to capture them. The boats were manned and pulled towards the strangers, but as they did so, other vessels came into sight, and soon five chasse-marées were visible. Thomas pressed on, and came under fire, not only from the closing French vessels but from people on the nearby islands. The Lieutenant ordered the boats to retire but was hit in the face by a musket shot as he did so. Gravely wounded, he ordered the boat's crew to leave him in the boat and make their own escape back to the island. The chasse-marées soon worked their way into the bay, rounded up all the crew and captured the *Grappler,* which was then burnt as they could not free her. Lieutenant Thomas was very severely injured, the bullet that struck him having knocked out several teeth, severed his tongue and lacerated his lips, leaving him permanently scarred and unable to speak clearly. He served 11 years as a prisoner in France before returning to face a court martial for the loss of his vessel, but he was acquitted of any blame for the loss and praised for his bravery. In recognition of his gallantry, he was promoted to Commander on 15 June 1814 and in December 1815 awarded a pension of £150 per annum by the Patriotic Fund.
[TNA: ADM.1/5443; O'Byrne p1167]

1804

January **YORK** Third Rate
Purchased 1796 (*Royal Admiral*); 1,433 tons; 174.3ft × 43.3ft; 64 guns
Captain Henry Mitford†

Stationed in the North Sea as part of the squadron blockading the Dutch coast, she parted company with the other ships in poor weather on 26 December and was not seen again. It would seem likely that she was blown further north and foundered sometime later with the loss of all onboard. During February wreckage identified as coming from the *York*, which included the lid of a box with Captain Mitford's name, a sprit-sail yard and topsail yard with the name of the ship, were

washed ashore between Peterhead and Fraserburgh. Pay books closed 31 December 1803.
[TNA:ADM.35/2070; www.britishnewspaperarchive.co: Morning Chronicle 16 February 1804 pp3 & 27 February 1804 p3]

3 January **CREOLE** Fifth Rate
Prize 1803; c1,070 tons; 38 guns
Captain Austin Bissell

A French frigate captured in the West Indies in July 1803, she sailed from Jamaica on 1 December 1803 as part of a large convoy for England, with a prize crew embarked and several French prisoners. The ship was not in a good condition, and on 26 December, when to the north of Bermuda, a leak was discovered. This caused the pumps to be employed constantly, but the water level steadily increased and by 30 December she was making 2ft of water an hour. On investigation it became clear that more than one leak was evident, one forward under the fore-chains and a second aft in the hold. Some guns were heaved overboard, and these were soon followed by iron ballast and stores. The water continued to increase, which led to all the guns and shot being thrown over the side, and a sail was prepared and slung under the hull. This initially helped to stem the flow, but by 2 January the water was again gaining on the pumps. The crew, British and French, who had been working alongside each other to save the ship, were exhausted and could no longer keep to the pumps. It was decided to abandon her, the *Cumberland* coming close by to take all the men off. The last of them left during the afternoon of 3 January, and she sank later that day, her position then being 40.42N 51.24W.
[TNA:ADM.1/5365]

6 January **RAVEN** Brig Sloop
Prize 1799 (*Arethuse*); 390 tons; 107.7ft x 29.4ft; 18 guns
Commander Spelman Swaine

Sailed from Malta on 4 January to escort the merchant brig *Dolphin* to Naples. Course was set along the southern coast of Sicily, aiming to sail between the islands of Favignana and Maretimo. Nothing was judged amiss until 11 o'clock in the evening of the following day when she ran aground. Sails were thrown aback, but she would not move. The sloop was lightened and efforts to free her went on through the night and into the next morning. By 2 o'clock in the afternoon, the water had so defeated the pumps that it had flooded the lower deck and she was abandoned, the crew being taken off by the *Dolphin*. The Master's Mate, Robert Incledon, had the watch when the sloop grounded, and had sighted a faint shape ahead of the ship through the gloom of the moonless night and had taken it for a sail. Only later did it become clear that it was actually a tower on the cliffs near the town of Mazara del Vallo, Sicily. The Master, Henry Lawrence, was reprimanded for setting a course too near the coast.
[TNA:ADM.1/5365]

20 January **FEARLESS** Gun Brig
Gravesend 1794; 149 tons; 75.1ft x 21.2ft; 12 guns
Lieutenant Richard Williams

Ordered to escort a small convoy of merchant ships to the Channel Islands, the weather was poor, and the brig anchored in Cawsand Bay to wait for it to clear. The conditions worsened, the brig lowering topmasts and yards, bracing lower yards into the wind and laying out a second anchor. Despite her precautions, during the afternoon the best bower anchor broke in the shank, and she started to drive across the bay. She had little chance to do much to save herself, apart from firing a distress gun, before she struck the rocky shore at Redding Point, swinging broadside-on. All the crew, apart from one man, managed to reach the shore, helped by the local people.
[TNA:ADM.1/5365]

8 February **HUSSAR** Fifth Rate
Woolwich 1799; 1,043 tons; 150.3ft x 39.6ft; 38 guns
Captain Philip Wilkinson

Carrying despatches for Admiral Cornwallis and the blockading squadron off Brest, she sailed from Ferrol on 6 February. The noon observation the next day showed them to be to the south-west of Ushant and course was laid accordingly. At 11 o'clock that night, with little warning, she ran onto a reef near the Île de Sein. An hour later, on the flood tide, she floated free of the obstruction, but found that she was surrounded by rocks and breaking surf. Unable to find a way out, she anchored. As the tide ebbed, she again grounded, spars and yards being lowered over the side to prevent her keeling over. Daylight revealed that she was jammed amongst the rocks, and the rising water from several leaks was defeating the pumps. A landing party commanded by the Lieutenant of Marines went onto the island and soon secured the place, which was occupied by a few fishing families. Unable to free the ship, all the crew was landed over the next two days, the frigate being set on fire on 10 February. Despite the protests of the islanders, local fishing boats were taken over and the crew set off for England. Some of them were taken inshore and captured, but the *Sirius* frigate picked some up, including Captain Wilkinson. At the subsequent court martial, Wilkinson was severely reprimanded for the loss. He was judged to have set a course that took them too close inshore and failed to order soundings to be regularly taken. The ship's Master, Adam Weymouth, was dismissed his ship, having failed

to advise the Captain of the danger of the course and not having soundings taken.
[TNA: ADM.1/5400]

20 February CERBÈRE Gunboat
Prize 1800; 138 tons; 79.6ft × 19.8ft; 10 guns
Lieutenant John Patey

Heading for Plymouth from Guernsey, the onset of poor weather made her to run for shelter and anchor in Torbay. She rode at anchor for five days before weighing and started to work out of the bay. Little headway could be made against the wind and sea, and she was forced to anchor again during the afternoon of 14 February off Brixham. A local boat was hired to assist with laying out anchors to enable her to warp out and this work continued until the morning of 20 February when she attempted to make sail. She was baffled by the shifting winds and when she missed stays found herself taken down onto Berry Head. A particularly strong wave lifted her onto rocks which pierced the hull, and the ship filled with water within minutes. All the crew managed to land safely on shore.
[TNA: ADM.1/5365]

1 March WEAZLE Brig Sloop
Purchased 1799; 214 tons; 77ft × 26.1ft; 12 guns
Lieutenant William Layman

Off Gibraltar to cover the arrival of a convoy, she cruised in the Straits in deteriorating weather. During the afternoon of 29 February, a thick fog arose, which became so dense that the men on the quarterdeck could not see the jib boom. Just before midnight, rocks were seen looming out of the gloom, and before any action could be taken, she ran aground. Anchors were let go to hold her steady, whilst boats were lowered and then the masts cut away. It was found that the hull had been pierced and she filled with water very quickly. The sloop was abandoned, all the men managing to make the shore. It was judged that a strong current, coupled with the thick fog, had led her to run onto Cabrita Point, opposite Gibraltar.
[TNA: ADM.1/5365]

24 March WOLVERINE Gun Brig
Purchased 1798 (*Rattler*); 286 tons; 98ft × 27.6ft; 14 guns
Commander Henry Gordon

During the morning, when in position 48.15N 23.15W, with a convoy of merchant ships bound for Newfoundland, two vessels were sighted approaching. By early afternoon, the pair could be seen to be frigates, and when they did not respond to private recognition signals it became clear that they were French. The *Wolverine* ordered the convoy to proceed independently, and then placed herself between the convoy and the oncoming French ships. One of the strangers stood after the fleeing merchant ships, whilst the larger ship closed the sloop. By 4pm the *Wolverine* was within pistol shot range of the stranger, which was the privateer *Blonde*, 30 guns. The privateer fired a broadside into the sloop and then wore round, attempting to rake her opponent, but this was frustrated by the sloop's manoeuvring. The pair then hove-to and commenced a mutual exchange of broadsides, which soon went the way of the more powerful privateer. By 5 o'clock the *Wolverine* had all her rigging and sails cut to tatters, her wheel shot away and numerous shots in the hull and she struck her flag in surrender. The sloop was found to be making water and the French captors had to hastily remove all the crew before she foundered. Five men killed and ten wounded.
[TNA: ADM.1/5420]

25 March MAGNIFICENT Third Rate
Deptford 1766; 1,613 tons; 168.6ft × 46.10ft; 74 guns
Captain William Henry Ricketts Jervis

Stationed off Brest as part of the blockading squadron, during the early hours of the morning several vessels had been observed inshore, and the ship closed and anchored, with the intention of manning boats for an attack. As the weather worsened, the attack was abandoned, and at 8 o'clock the ship weighed and stood out to sea. As she rounded the reef known as the Black Rocks (Pierres Noires), she unexpectedly struck an obstruction which brought her up. Sail was thrown aback, and the ship floated free, but she swung round, bringing her head to the wind as she did so. Boats were hoisted out, pumps manned and guns were fired as signals of distress. This brought several ships of the blockading squadron down to her aid. The water entered rapidly. In less than an hour it was up to her orlop deck. and two hours after striking she was abandoned, the ship rolling over and sinking as the crew left her. All the crew were rescued, although her cutter was carried inshore, and the occupants taken prisoner. It was found that she had struck the Roche du Boufouloc, the position of which not accurately laid down in any of the charts held on board, which included the French publication *Neptune Français*.
[TNA: ADM.1/5365]

2 April APOLLO Fifth Rate
Deptford 1799; 943 tons; 145ft × 38.4ft; 36 guns
Captain John William Taylor Dixon†

Sailed from Cork on 26 March as escort to a convoy of sixty-nine ships, most bound for the West Indies, but others for Madeira. Poor weather affected the convoy in the voyage south, and on 1 April the frigate shortened sail down to foresail, with main- and mizzen-staysails. In the early hours of the following morning at 3.30am, to everyone's surprise, she struck the ground. The ship beat heavily on a shoal, damaging the bottom and she

started taking in water. The pumps were ordered to be manned, but within 10 minutes she had beaten over the shallows and floated free, only to run aground again, this time with a considerable shock. She beat violently on the ground, unshipping the rudder and casting some guns loose, which added to the confusion. The main- and mizzenmasts were quickly cut away, but the ship continued to beat heavily, driving further onto the shore until she fell over onto her starboard side, the surf beating over her. Morning revealed that they had gone ashore about nine miles south of Cape Mondego, Portugal on a long sandy beach, the land being about two cables (400 yards) distant, and many of the convoy were also ashore. The wreck was lashed by strong winds and a heavy swell, the waves constantly breaking over her. The crew all moved forward to cling to the bowsprit and foremast, and several attempted to swim to the shore, but many drowned. The ordeal lasted for two days, with some making it to the shore, but others being lost in the attempt or falling from the mast from exhaustion. On the afternoon of 4 April, the weather had moderated sufficiently for boats to be launched from the shore, which took off the survivors. At least twenty-nine merchant ships had followed the *Apollo* onto the beach, with many lost; '... Dead bodies were every day floating ashore, and pieces of wreck covered the beach upwards of ten miles' (Gold: *Naval Chronicle*). Sixty-two of *Apollo*'s men died. The loss was ascribed to an error in her reckoning.
[TNA:ADM.1/5366; Gold: *Naval Chronicle* vol 11 pp392–6]

2 April HINDOSTAN Store Ship
Purchased 1795; 1,249 tons; 160.3ft × 42.2ft; 26 guns
Captain John le Gros
Laden with stores for the Mediterranean fleet, she was steering along the south-eastern coast of Spain under courses and reefed topsails, when at just before 7 o'clock in the morning, smoke was seen rising from the orlop deck. The smoke spread through the ship, and it proved difficult to locate the source. Engines were manned, scuttles opened, and strenuous efforts made to fight the fire, but the thick choking smoke constantly defeated the work. The boats were hoisted out, in case the ship should have to be abandoned, and the Marines paraded with loaded muskets to prevent any precipitate flight. As the source could not be reached, an attempt was made to seal off part of the ship, hatches being battened down and sealed. At the same time, the gunpowder that could be reached was either heaved overboard or damped down. At noon smoke and flames burst up through the main hatchway, and it was decided to run the ship ashore, course being set for the nearest point of land in the Golfo de Rosas. At about 4pm she struck the ground just over half a mile from the shore to the north of the town of La Escala. The crew left in an orderly manner by boats and rafts, only three men being lost. The ship continued to burn until she blew up at about 9.30 that evening. The seat of the blaze seemed to be on the starboard side of the orlop deck, perhaps by combustion of materials released by the breaking of stored medicine chests in poor weather.
[TNA:ADM.1/5365]

3 April SWIFT Cutter
Hired 1803; 77 tons; 8 guns
Lieutenant William Thomas Martin Leake†
Carrying despatches from England and Gibraltar for the Mediterranean fleet, she was off Palma, when during the morning a vessel was sighted, which steadily closed the cutter. As the craft closed, it could be seen to be lateen rigged, and only a few men were visible on deck, which led Lieutenant Leake to conclude that the stranger was a local trading vessel. This was proved to be false when the stranger, which was the French xebec privateer *Esperance*, 8 guns, suddenly altered course to run alongside, and a large number of men appeared from below decks. As the enemy boarded the cutter, Leake ran below for the despatches, but was shot and killed as he tried to throw them overboard. He was the only casualty before the boarders gained control of the cutter, which was taken into Barcelona.
[www.britishnewspaperarchive.co: *Morning Chronicle* 12 May 1804 p3]

8 May VINCEJO Brig Sloop
Prize 1799 (*Vencejo*); 276 tons; 91.5ft × 25.2ft; 18 guns
Commander John Wesley Wright
Employed on the coast of France, between the Loire and Lorient, overtly employed in harrying coastal shipping, it served as a cover for Commander Wright to make night-time expeditions to the mainland to contact French royalist groups. On the evening of 7 May, Wright went ashore on the Île Houat in Quiberon Bay, to land a small party of royalists. After he returned onboard the brig weighed but could make little headway as the wind fell away to a calm and the strong tidal current took them toward the Teignouse rocks. Commander Wright anchored and then used kedge anchors and tried to pull the sloop into clear water, and then weighed and again tried to stand out to sea. The light and baffling winds and strong currents were against her, so sweeps were employed to get her free of the enemy coast. The dawn revealed her plight and several gun brigs and gunboats emerged from Quiberon, so that by 8.30am the *Vincejo* was being fired on. Still attempting to pull her way out of the bay, she returned the fire, but with the attacking force being joined by a number of other gunboats and luggers, until they totalled seventeen vessels. She was unable to engage them all, as most lay off, at a range outside that of the sloop's carronades, and maintained a

heavy and accurate fire. The combat was sustained for two hours, before the *Vincejo* was forced to surrender. By that time, the rigging had been destroyed, sails ripped up, the gaff boom shot away, three guns disabled, and she had suffered two men killed and twelve wounded. Wright was imprisoned in the Temple prison, Paris, where he died the following year, amidst rumours of his being murdered.

Note: recaptured on 30 November 1811 by the *Rover* but not returned to service.
[TNA: ADM.1/5439; London Gazette 18 September 1813]

23 June FORT DIAMOND Sloop Tender
From 1804; 6 guns
Lieutenant Benjamin Westcott

Employed as a tender to the *Diamond Rock* off Martinique, she was ordered to proceed to St Lucia to obtain supplies and after arriving in Roseau Bay the crew were busily employed cutting wood and filling barrels. Completing the task at about 7 o'clock that evening the men were sent below for dinner, with only two men remaining on deck, plus Lieutenant Westcott, who amused himself by fishing over the stern. Two boats were observed closing from the land, and as they seemed to be pulling towards the sloop, Westcott hailed them. On the second hail they replied, 'A boat from the land' and continued to close. Westcott hailed them again, asking who was on board. The reply was a volley of musket fire. At this the Lieutenant shouted an alarm and ran below to seize a cutlass, the men from the boats boarding as he did so. Having armed himself, Westcott paused, and then said, 'It's no use, it's too late', and threw down the sword, telling his small crew to surrender. At his court martial for the loss, Lieutenant Westcott was found guilty of an offence under the Tenth Article of War, in that he failed to be prepared for an engagement and did not encourage the inferior officers and men to fight. He was dismissed the service.
[TNA: ADM.1/5367]

14 July DRAKE Brig Sloop
Prize 1798 (*Tigre*); 212 tons; 79ft × 23.9ft; 14 guns
Commander William King

After escorting a convoy clear of the islands, the *Drake*, in company with the *Pandour* frigate, was cruising off the island of Nevis, in the West Indies. The brig was in a poor state, with several leaks apparent, and poor weather had damaged the rigging, masts and yards. As they turned to windward, about half a mile from the island, without any warning she struck the ground. She bumped over the obstruction but then struck again and came to a sudden halt. All sail was thrown aback, but she would not move and the bottom, already in a poor state, had clearly been holed, with water reported to be entering the hold at an alarming rate. The masts were cut away, the brig capsizing over onto her beam-ends as they did so. Within 12 minutes of hitting the bank she had sunk up to her gunwales. The *Pandour* launched boats, which picked up all the crew. The shoal she had struck was not known to any of the officers of either ship, although they were experienced in those waters.
[TNA: ADM.1/5366]

14 July DEMERARA Schooner
Purchased 1804 (*Anna*); 106 tons; 72.8ft × 18.8ft; 10 guns
Lieutenant Thomas Dutton

Cruising off the South American coast of Demerara, at daylight a ship was seen, anchored close under the land. The stranger weighed and stood towards the schooner, and could be seen to be a large, well-armed privateer. The schooner made all sail away, but within an hour she had been overhauled and when within gunshot, the privateer fired a broadside, followed by volleys of small-arms fire. The broadside cut up the rigging, the backstays being shot away, leaving her unmanageable and 10 minutes after the action commenced, she surrendered to the *Grand Décidée*, 22 guns. One man was killed and nine wounded.
[TNA: ADM.1/5367]

15 July LILY Ship Sloop
Purchased 1794 (*Sir Charles Grey*); 201 tons; 92.6ft × 22.11ft; 16 guns
Commander William Compton†

Cruising off the eastern coast of the South Carolina, to the north of Charleston, during the afternoon of 14 July, two ships were seen to windward, and the sloop bore up in chase. They appeared to be an armed vessel and a smaller ship which seemed to be her prize. The following morning the pair were still in sight, the larger ship towing the other, although as the sloop closed, the tow was cast off and the stranger made towards the *Lily*. At 10.20am the enemy ranged up on the weather quarter and opened fire with bow-chase guns. The enemy ship was the privateer *Dame Ambert*, 16 guns, which managed to drop astern and kept up a heavy fire, raking the *Lily* which could not bring her guns to bear, her braces, bowlines and running rigging being cut to pieces, and soon after the engagement began Commander Compton was killed. Lieutenant Samuel Fowler assumed the command and continued the fight. By 12 o'clock the British sloop was in a poor state, with the rigging in shreds and casualties mounting. The privateer then closed, which gave the *Lily* the first opportunity to fire a broadside at her opponent. When it was clear that the French ship was about to board, Lieutenant Fowler wished to surrender, but was dissuaded from this by the warrant officers, but was killed soon after this. After firing another raking broadside into *Lily*, the privateer ran alongside and attempted to enter

boarders. This resulted in hand-to-hand fighting, and several attempts were made, each driven back, before the *Dame Ambert* finally succeeded in putting a large number of men onto the deck of the sloop and forcing her to surrender. Two men killed and sixteen wounded. The crew were put into a prize merchant vessel and made their way to Hampton Roads, where several took the opportunity to desert.
[TNA: ADM.1/5367]

26 August **CONSTITUTION** Cutter
Hired 1804; 120 tons; 10 guns
Lieutenant James Dennis

Part of the flotilla stationed at Dover watching the French coast, particularly the port of Boulogne. During the afternoon, a number of French gunboats and other vessels were seen to set sail from the harbour, evidently bound for Ambleteuse, and they were attacked by the frigate *Immortalité*, accompanied by three smaller vessels, including the *Constitution*. The French ships kept close inshore, where they received the protection of several shore batteries, which joined in the engagement, keeping up a steady fire of shot and shell. At about 5pm the *Constitution* was hit by a large shell fired from the shore, which went through the deck and penetrated the bottom without exploding. Water entered at a fast rate and as she heeled over, the cutter was abandoned, all the crew being picked up by boats from the ships in company.
[www.britishnewspaperarchive.co: Morning Post 29 August 1804 p2; James vol 3 p230]

3 September **DE RUYTER** Store/Prison Ship
Prize 1799; 1,264 tons; 151.2ft × 44ft.
Lieutenant Joseph Beckett

A former Third Rate ship of the line, from 1802 she was employed as a store ship on the Jamaica station. The ship was in poor condition and after taking troops to Antigua, it was decided to employ her as a prison. She sailed from Falmouth, Antigua, with the *Serapis* store ship in tow, to take up station in Deep Bay. This turned into a protracted operation, due to the poor weather, with the wind steadily increasing. The tow parted and some time was spent reconnecting it and at one stage the *Serapis* fell aboard the *De Ruyter*, damaging her only bower anchor. After a struggle, she finally parted and left the store ship anchored off Five Islands and proceeded to stand into Deep Bay. The weather was now deteriorating rapidly, with strong winds and all the signs of an imminent hurricane. During 2 September, the heavy swell began to lift her to such an extent that she began to strike the ground with increasing violence. The rudder was unshipped, and the boats were smashed on the booms by waves breaking over her. During the early hours of 3 September, the anchor cable parted, and efforts were made to try and put her head to the wind. The ship was labouring in the storm and broke her back amidships, with the forward part of the ship visibly drooping. She was now steered for a nearby sandbank and deliberately run ashore, in order '… to hold her together' for a little longer. Rafts were constructed for the crew, and with hurricane-force winds, incessant driving rain and the seas breaking over them, they left the wreck. Lieutenant Beckett was the last to leave, jumping into the sea clutching his wife in his arms. All but one member of the crew made it to the shore.
[TNA: ADM.1/5367]

25 September **GEORGIANA** Cutter
Hired 1803 (*King George*); 129 tons; 12 guns
Lieutenant Joshua Kneeshaw

One of the blockading vessels off the northern coast of France, when a small convoy was seen to leave from Le Havre and make for Honfleur. The cutter was ordered to chase, and she singled out a sloop from the group and forced her so close inshore that the enemy vessel ran aground. Boats were hoisted out and manned with the intention of boarding the coaster, and the cutter tacked away from the land, but before she had completed the manoeuvre, she went aground on the western extremity of the Ratier Bank. Efforts began to free her, but she was approached by three enemy luggers, accompanied by several boats. With the tide ebbing and the cutter heeling over, she was abandoned and set on fire, the crew taking to the boats, in which they were able to pull towards British ships waiting offshore. They were pursued by the enemy, who kept up a constant harassing fire, although surprisingly there were no casualties. The gun brig *Locust* stood in and covered their escape and took them all on board. The cutter continued to burn until at 6 o'clock that night she blew up.
[TNA: ADM.1/5367]

2–3 October: Fireship attack on Boulogne
A large number of vessels had been assembled by the French at northern ports for the planned invasion of England. Several plans were formed to disrupt or destroy them, one of these involved a combined attack of fire-vessels and catamarans. These latter were cylindrical objects, about 21ft long, packed with gunpowder, which was set off by a clockwork timing device after being towed into position by boat. An attack by fire vessels and catamarans was made on Boulogne on the night of 2 October, using purchased fishing smacks as fireships.

PEGGY Fire Vessel
Purchased 1804; 27 tons

The *Peggy* was towed by an armed launch toward a line of anchored French ships, then, with sail set and combustibles lit, she was left to drift down onto them.

The French were alerted and at just after 10.30pm, when she reached the lines, she drifted harmlessly through, the French having warped vessels out of her path. The catamarans which were floated down later achieved little, apart from exploding noisily.

DEVONSHIRE Fire Vessel
Purchased 1804; 35 tons
Towed into action and released, she entered the line of vessels at about 1 o'clock in the morning, and exploded, causing damage to craft near her.

PROVIDENCE Fire Vessel
Purchased 1804; 51 tons
The *Providence* was the first to be released near the lines of French vessels, reaching the line at about 10.15pm, when she exploded, damaging two gunboats nearby.

AMITY Fire Vessel
Purchased 1804; 56 tons
The last into action, she was towed into the line and released close to the prame *Ville de Mayenne*. At just after 1 o'clock in the morning she exploded near her target, causing superficial damage.
[James vol 3 pp231–3; Gold: Naval Chronicle vol 12 pp313, 329–31]

* * *

8 October SPEEDY Schooner
Kingston, Ontario 1798; 44 tons
Lieutenant Thomas Paxton (Provincial Marine)†
Based on Lake Ontario, the schooner sailed from York (Toronto) on 7 October for Newcastle District, carrying a prisoner for trial, along with several court officials and witnesses. The weather was poor and worsened, with strong winds and regular flurries of snow. At dusk on 8 October the schooner was seen off Presqu'ile Point, and a large fire was lit to act as a guide, but the schooner was not seen again, and was presumed lost with all onboard. Articles identified as belonging to *Speedy* were later washed ashore nearby.
[Gold: Naval Chronicle vol 13 pp58–9]

13 October FIREBRAND Fire Vessel
Purchased 1804 (*Waller*); 140 tons; 80.2ft × 20.1ft
Lieutenant William McLean
Laden with ordnance stores, after spending some time laying at anchor in the Downs, she weighed during the late afternoon to proceed into Dover harbour. The weather was poor, with a freshening wind and regular squalls of rain which obscured the land. At just before midnight, she struck the ground near North Pier Head and found herself held fast. Signals of distress were made which brought a local pilot on board, who assisted in an attempt to kedge her off the obstruction. This failed and it became clear that the brig's back was broken, and water was reported to be entering. The pumps were employed, only to find that they became choked with sand and mud within five minutes and water was over the ballast in 15 minutes. Boats were hoisted out, and she was abandoned, with some of the crew jumping into the sea as they left the wreck, which broke up. During the passage, no pilot had been embarked and it was believed that lights on shore had been mistaken for ships at anchor and those marking the end of Dover pier. Lieutenant MacLean had spent some time in the water before being picked up and this may have contributed to his early death, three weeks after the wreck.
[TNA: ADM.1/5367]

24 October CONFLICT Gun Brig
Deptford 1801; 180 tons; 80.1ft × 22.7ft; 12 guns
Lieutenant Charles Cutts Ormsby
One of a flotilla of gun brigs assembled off Ostend to blockade the port, during the afternoon of 23 October a convoy of eighteen schuyts escorted by two ship-rigged praams were seen to emerge from the harbour. The *Conflict* closed to engage the leading vessel, assisted by the *Cruizer*, the action continuing for some time until three of her gun breechings were carried away. Having repaired these, the *Conflict* again looked to close the enemy. As she did so, it was realised that they were now close to the shore, but on looking for the pilot for advice, he was nowhere to be seen. Soundings were taken and found only three fathoms of water. The helm was put over, but she ran aground before she came around. The convoy were within range and the brig continued to engage the enemy as they passed. Efforts were made to free her, everything practicable being heaved overboard to lighten her, but without effect. As it was found that the water was leaving her, as the tide was ebbing, and more enemy vessels, having seen her plight, were approaching, Lieutenant Ormsby ordered his people into the boats and pulled for the nearby *Cruizer* to obtain help to free her. The *Admiral Mitchell* cutter closed the brig to cover the return of the boats, but they discovered that she was now high and dry on a sandbank, and in possession of the enemy. At high tide, a determined effort was made to attack and destroy the stranded vessel, but it was found that the French had hauled her further inshore, with her position covered by several field guns. Lieutenant Ormsby was praised for his spirited action, but the pilot, William Millbank, was found to have quitted his station. For this he was mulcted of all pay due, ordered never to take charge of any of HM ships again, and to serve six months in the Marshalsea Prison.
[TNA: ADM.1/5367]

19 November ROMNEY Fourth Rate
Woolwich 1762; 1,047 tons; 146ft x 40.4ft; 50 guns
Captain John Colville

Part of the North Sea fleet, the *Romney* sailed from Great Yarmouth on 18 November to join the squadron of Admiral Russell off the Dutch coast. The ship ran south through the day under double-reefed topsails and fore-topmast staysail, the weather closing in as she did, with drifting banks of thick fog. Sounding with the lead-line seemed to show that they were on the Broad Fourteen sands and the pilots recommended standing on southwards. At 8 o'clock that evening a large ship was seen looming ahead, apparently at anchor, and course was altered to steer towards her. When closer in they discovered her to be an American merchant ship, which was hard aground. The *Romney* instantly tacked away, but before the manoeuvre was complete, she struck the ground. Sail was taken in and topmasts struck, and the pumps ordered to be manned. Shot and provisions were heaved overboard to lighten her, distress guns fired, and the boats were hoisted out, one of which overset, throwing the occupants into the water, drowning all eleven men. At 4 o'clock in the morning she floated free and was able to move into deeper water, where she anchored and worked to pump the ship clear of water. Daylight revealed that they had run onto the south-west part of the Zuiderhaak Sand, and that she had broken her back, the water constantly defeating the pumps. A number of Dutch schuyts approached, and when called upon to surrender, Captain Colville had little choice but to submit. The guns and shot were all ordered to be heaved overboard before the ship was handed over to their Dutch captors. At a later court martial, the two embarked pilots, Thomas Cork and Richard Turner, were both found guilty of negligence and ignorance, and both were ordered to by mulcted of all pay due and never to serve as pilots in HM ships again. Cork was imprisoned for one year, Turner for six months.
[TNA: ADM.1/5367]

24 November HANNIBAL Armed Ship
Hired 1804; 16 guns
Commander Richard James Lawrence O'Connor

Laying at anchor in the Downs, the winds increased to gale force from the north-east, and at about 9 o'clock in the evening she parted her cables and was driven on shore to the north of Sandown Castle, Deal. Two merchant ships that had been anchored nearby shared the same fate.
[www.britishnewspaperarchive.co: Star (London) 26 November 1804]

24 November VENERABLE Third Rate
Blackwall 1784; 1,669 tons; 170ft x 47.2ft; 74 guns
Captain John Hunter

The Channel fleet were at anchor in Torbay in worsening weather, with strong winds and regular rains showers. At 4.30pm the fleet was ordered to weigh and proceed to sea. As the *Venerable* was catting her anchor, a seaman fell overboard. A boat was ordered away, but in the haste to lower it, one of the falls was let go too soon, spilling the occupants into the sea. A second boat was launched to pick up the men struggling in the water. All of this took time, and the ship had fallen off to leeward, close to Brixham. As it was clear that she could not weather Berry Head, she tacked and stood to the north. It was now dusk, the bay full of ships on different tacks making their way to sea and *Venerable* twice had to tack to avoid ships looming out of the gloom. The wind became fitful and baffling, with frequent strong squalls accompanied by rain. The night was very dark, with the moon obscured by thick cloud. As she manoeuvred close to the shore near Roundham Head, she touched the ground, gently at first and then more firmly. All sail was taken in, and topmasts and yards were ordered to be struck. She soon found herself being lifted by the waves and started to pound quite heavy and all the masts were ordered to be cut away to ease the movement of the ship. Distress guns were fired and attracted the attention of the *Impétueux* and the *Goliath*, which closed, to stand by her, as did the *Frisk* cutter. Water entered at an uncontrollable rate and the waves broke over her constantly. The boats from the other ships stood by her all night and took off the men, although hampered by the high seas and the rain, which turned to sleet. She finally rolled over onto her beam-ends and broke up. Eight seamen were drowned. One Marine, David Evans, was found guilty of being drunk and disobedient and plundering officers' baggage. He was ordered to be flogged around the fleet, receiving 200 lashes.
[TNA: ADM.1/5367]

25 November DUKE OF CLARENCE Cutter
Hired 1804; 65 tons; 6 guns
Lieutenant Nicholas Brent Clements

Ordered to cruise to the south of Jersey, between the Minquiers rocks and the Îles Chausey, to pick up a boat that was bringing intelligence from the French coast, a large lugger was sighted and chased, the *Albion* cutter joining in the pursuit. The lugger was seen to run herself on shore on the French coast near Granville, and the *Duke of Clarence* followed and sent a boat to board her, finding her to be a coaster loaded with oysters and cider. As the cutter manoeuvred offshore, awaiting the return of her boat, she unexpectedly struck a submerged rock. She came off the obstruction but had been holed and water flooded in rapidly. Efforts to free the prize lugger

were abandoned and the *Albion* closed to take off the crew before the cutter sank.
[TNA: ADM.1/5367]

6 December MORNE FORTUNÉE Schooner
Prize 1803; 106 tons; 65.6ft × 21ft; 6 guns
Lieutenant John Dale

Carrying despatches for Jamaica, she was to the north-east of the Bahamas, heading south-by-east under easy sail, when at 3 o'clock in the morning breakers were seen ahead. The helm was put over, but she struck a reef extremely hard and water began entering at a fast rate. The masts were cut away to ease her, the vessel was lightened, and the anchor let go to hold her steady, as it was feared that she might slide off into deep water. Morning revealed that she was on Attwood's Key, off Crooked Island, Bahamas. She was settling and all the crew took to the boats and went onto the barren island. One of the boats was despatched to Crooked Island and they were rescued two days later. An error in reckoning, coupled with a strong current, was blamed for the loss.
[TNA: ADM.1/5367]

8 December SUSANNAH Fire Vessel
Purchased 1804; 43 tons

A further attempt using explosive catamarans and a fire vessel was made on ships gathering for a French invasion, this time on the port of Calais. The target was Fort Rouge at the entrance to the harbour, and at 2 o'clock in the morning the *Susannah* was guided into place by Lieutenant Hew Steuart of the *Monarch* and was able to place the smack amongst piles near the Fort before setting her on fire. She burnt and then exploded, but little damage was caused. Neither of the catamarans that were released worked.
[London Gazette 11 December 1804]

17 December GERTRUDE Schooner
Hired 1804 (*Flying Fish*); 147 tons; 12 guns
Lieutenant George Broad

Ordered to join the blockading squadron off Brest, when off Ushant she sighted and closed the frigate *Aigle*, to speak to her. As the pair manoeuvred close to each other, the schooner fell under the frigate's bows and was struck amidships. The schooner was rolled over, the masts going overboard and the *Aigle* sailed right over her. *Aigle* quickly hoisted out her boats, and it was with some difficulty that all the men were picked up.
[TNA: ADM.1/5367; ADM.51/1522]

20 December TARTARUS Bomb Vessel
Purchased 1797 (*Charles Jackson*); 344 tons; 94.6ft × 28.6ft; 6 guns
Commander Thomas Withers

Laying at anchor in the Downs, riding out an easterly gale, when at about 6 o'clock in the evening the anchor cable parted, having apparently chafed through during the storm. No one noticed the mishap or that she was drifting inshore until a short time later when she struck a sandbank off Margate. An attempt was then made to sail her off, but without success. As she lay without labouring at all and no water was entering, it was decided to wait until high tide the next morning and then make another attempt. However, the wind shifted and increased, and by midnight she was pounding on the sands with some violence. Distress guns were fired, and local fishing boats came to her aid and with some difficulty some sick crew members were transferred, one man being drowned when a boat overturned. At low water, the sea drained away from the ship, leaving her high and dry, settling into the sands and heeling over. At high water, the sea entered rapidly, and all the crew were taken off, the ship disappearing underwater, with only the masts showing. The office of the watch, Lieutenant Charles Squarey, was admonished to be more careful in his actions in the future, having left the deck during his watch. The Master's Mate, William Tozer, was criticised for his inattention during his watch and ordered to be reprimanded and to lose six months' seniority.
[TNA: ADM.1/5367]

21 December SEVERN Fifth Rate
Bristol 1786; 904 tons; 140.2ft × 38.5ft; 44 guns
Captain Philip D'Auvergne

At anchor in Grouville Bay, Jersey, Captain D'Auvergne was ashore, the command devolving on his half-brother, Lieutenant Corbet D'Auvergne. During 18 December, the weather worsened, with increasing winds from the north-east, until it was at storm force. The poor weather continued, and during the early hours of 20 December both anchor cables parted, and she drove inshore, into shallow water. The sheet anchor was let go and main- and mizzenmasts were cut away. The bulk of the crew were taken off with the assistance of boats from the *Alcmene*. She remained in this position until the following morning when the sheet anchor cable parted. The ship was being carried inshore, so she was deliberately run onto the shore to save lives, being assisted by local people and solders.
[TNA: ADM.1/5369]

24 December MALLARD Gun Brig
Deptford 1801; 178 tons; 80ft × 22.6ft; 12 guns
Lieutenant John William Miles

Ordered to cruise off the French coast between Calais and Boulogne, the brig sailed from the Downs on 24 December in company with the *Starling* brig. As the pair stood across the Channel the weather became increasingly thick and hazy, and contact with her consort was lost during the afternoon. Lieutenant Miles suggested to the pilot, James Ayles, that they should

shorten sail, which Ayles agreed to, but only with some reluctance. As the weather continued to close in, a further suggestion of reduce down to storm staysails met with a stony silence from the pilot. Miles then ordered the lead-line be prepared for heaving, which provoked Ayles to testily exclaim that there was no need, '… as he knew perfectly well where they were', at which Miles withdrew the order. The pilot then claimed that they could continue on their present course for a further two hours before altering. One hour later the brig ran hard aground on the French coast near Calais. Efforts were made to free her, but the tide was ebbing, leaving her high and dry, and as the fog lifted, she attracted the attention of a nearby fort. She became the target for volleys of musketry, followed by roundshot and grape. The main boom was shot away, as was the rudder head, and the rigging was cut to pieces, but Lieutenant Miles persisted in trying to free her. Ballast and shot were heaved overboard to lighten her, and fire was returned when possible. At low tide, the brig capsized over onto her beam-ends and with troops approaching, they surrendered. The crew spent the next 10 years as prisoners in France, with both Lieutenant Miles and pilot Ayles dying in prison at Verdun during 1807. The court martial held on the survivors in 1814 ruled that the obstinacy and ignorance of James Ayles was the main cause, with Lieutenant Miles guilty of neglect in failing to order the constant use of the lead-line.
[TNA: ADM.1/5443]

24 December STARLING Gun Brig

Buckler's Hard 1801; 185 tons; 80.1ft x 23ft; 12 guns
Lieutenant George Skottowe
Sailed on 24 December from the Downs anchorage in company with *Mallard*, to take station off Calais. Contact with her companion was lost in the mist during the afternoon, but they were able to take the bearing of North Foreland at 4 o'clock that afternoon. This achieved, the brig steered south-by-east in thickening weather under reefed topsails and foresail. At just after 5 o'clock, as she was steering through a particularly thick bank of fog, she was ordered to be put about, but before this could be achieved, land was seen close ahead through the mist. The helm was put over and sail thrown aback, but she ran hard aground. Boats were lowered to lay out anchors to kedge her off at the next high tide, and at the same time they investigated the shore, finding themselves in Wissant Bay, near Cap Griz Nez. Skottowe ordered the Marines to be armed and prepared to resist any attempt to board whilst preparations were made to save the brig, and then ordered most of the crew into the boats to stand off and return at high tide. The wait over, the boats returned, and as the French had evidently not discovered them, work started to haul her free, with shot and provisions being heaved overboard to lighten her. She would not move however, having sunk into the sand, so at dawn they left her, setting fire to the ship as they did, All the boats made the journey across the Channel without incident. The embarked pilot, George Fearne, was subsequently found guilty of taking the brig too far to the south and failing use the lead-line. Because of his previous good character, he was cautioned to be more careful in his actions in the future.
[TNA: ADM.1/5367]

December ALTHORPE Cutter

Hired 1804; 164 tons; 14 guns
Lieutenant William Scott†
Sailed from Plymouth on 7 November with despatches for Sir John Orde's squadron off Cadiz, but not seen again, and presumed lost with all hands.
[TNA: ADM.49/97; www.britishnewspaperarchive.co: Exeter Flying Post 8 November 1804 p4]

December HAWK Ship Sloop

Prize 1803 (*Atalante*); 320 tons; 90.11ft x 27.11ft; 18 guns
Commander James Tippett†
Stationed off Brest as part of the blockading squadron, she was in company with the *Boadicea* when she was detached on 1 December to chase a strange sail then in sight. She was not seen again and was presumed to have been lost with all hands. Pay book closed on 31 December 1804.
[TNA: ADM.35/782; Leyland vol 2 p193]

December MARY Cutter

Hired 1803; 100 tons; 8 guns
Lieutenant Thomas Pacey†
Sailed from Plymouth in mid-December with despatches for Admiral Cornwallis, commanding the ships off Brest. She was not seen again and was presumed to have foundered with all hands.
[Leyland vol 2 p193]

December SEAGULL Brig Sloop

Deptford 1795; 317 tons; 95.3ft x 28.1ft; 16 guns
Commander Henry Burke†
Sailed from Plymouth at the end of December for a cruise in the English Channel, but was not seen again. Presumed foundered with all hands, perhaps in the storms which affected the Channel. The pay books were closed on 31 December 1804 and the name deleted from the Disposition of Ships List in February 1805.
[TNA: ADM.35/1723; ADM.8/89; www.britishnewspaperarchive.co: Exeter Flying Post 11 April 1805 p4]

1805

8 January SHEERNESS Fifth Rate
Buckler's Hard 1787; 906 tons; 140.3ft × 38.5ft; 44 guns
Captain Lord George Stuart

Anchored in the inner harbour, Trincomalee, Captain Stuart went ashore for the afternoon to dine with friends, leaving Lieutenant Abraham Hawkins in command. The weather steadily deteriorated during the day, and with the wind getting up to gale force, the topmasts and yards were struck in preparation for the storm. At about 5 o'clock that afternoon the small bower anchor cable parted, the sheet anchor was let go, which, with the best bower held her. At 6.30pm the sheet anchor cable parted and 30 minutes later, in winds which were now approaching hurricane force, the best bower cable parted. She was driven across the anchorage and went aground on the south-west end of York Island. Water entered at a fast rate, the pumps being unable to cope with the flow. The mizzen- and mainmasts were cut away and everything moveable was heaved overboard. Despite these measures she settled fast, and the water was soon level with the gunwales. Over the next few days most of the stores were salvaged, soldiers being drafted in to help in the work.
[TNA: ADM.1/5369]

13 January DORIS Fifth Rate
Gravesend 1795; 915 tons; 142.6ft × 38.1ft; 36 guns
Captain Patrick Campbell

Sent to reconnoitre the French squadron off the Île d'Aix, Rochefort, she observed that they were preparing to leave, and sailed to take the news to Admiral Graves and the blockading squadron. Arriving off Quiberon Bay on 11 January she found no sign of the British squadron. She anchored overnight and weighed the following morning in search of the Admiral, being advised by an American merchant ship that the main fleet was off Belle Isle. The wind shifted to the south, and it was decided to gain an anchorage for the night. At 6 o'clock that afternoon as she was going through the Béniguet passage into Quiberon Bay, she struck a submerged object. She rode over it easily, but the bottom was severely damaged, and water entered at a fast rate. Pumps were manned, guns and shot heaved overboard and a sail prepared to be slung underneath her. The measures seemed to work, as by 8 o'clock the following morning the ship was nearly clear of water, and she anchored. The *Felix* schooner joined her during the afternoon, with the news that the Rochefort squadron had indeed sailed. Judging that it was now imperative that this news be taken to the blockading squadron, Captain Campbell decided to sail, even though repairs were not complete. At 1.30pm she sailed, but as she attempted to work out of Quiberon Bay, she laboured in the heavy sea, the leaks opened, and water started to gain on the pumps. She clearly could not keep the sea, so her head was turned inshore, and she anchored, then being about eight miles north of Croisic and hoisted out her boats. The *Felix* had stayed in company, and the passing American schooner *Lydia* also joined to assist, and they took off all the crew. Captain Campbell set fire to the frigate before leaving. The pilot, Jean le Gall, was later judged to have been unskilful and was reprimanded. One seaman, Woodford Simms, was found guilty of insolent and improper language to the Bosun and was ordered to be flogged, 200 lashes on his bare back.
[TNA: ADM.1/5368; Leyland vol 2 pp163–6]

17 January COMMERCE Brig Tender
Hired 1803; 117 tons; 4 guns
Lieutenant Duncan Menzies

Based at Limerick, she sailed from Plymouth to return to her station. The weather was poor, with a constant gale from the east, which prevented her from entering the river Shannon. Loop Head was sighted on 15 January, and Lieutenant Menzies ordered the vessel to heave to for the night. At 2 o'clock in the morning breakers were seen ahead, and she was forced to haul out to seaward again. Closing the coast, the following day in abysmal weather, with strong winds, high seas and frequent heavy showers of snow, Loop Head was seen again, and she steered north along the coast. In the early hours of the morning of 17 January breakers were seen close ahead and before she could haul off, she struck the ground. After the initial impact, the waves lifted her over the rock and then forced her with great violence onto a reef. The bowsprit and fore topmast went overboard with the shock and the waves crashed over her smashing the stern cabin windows and carrying away the main boom and the boats. The waves again lifted her over the obstruction, and she found herself floating in free water, but filling fast. The head was set for the shore, and she was run aground in Roundstone Bay to save the lives of the crew. The wreck soon attracted the attention of the local populace, including the Sea Fencibles, all of whom seemed to be more interested in plundering the wreck than saving the men. Two men were drowned in the efforts to reach safety. Lieutenant Menzies was found to have placed too much trust in the skills of the Master and admonished to be more careful in the future. The Master, William Fry, was found to have taken no precautions for approaching the coast during a storm and generally to have been of little assistance. He was ordered to lose all pay due and never to serve as a Master again.
[TNA: ADM.1/5369]

19 January ARTHUR Cutter
Hired 1803 (*Venus*); 71 tons; 6 guns
Lieutenant Robert Baron Cooban

Sailed from Falmouth at the end of December with despatches for Admiral Lord Nelson in the Mediterranean, she was captured off Mahon by a French squadron from Toulon, surrendering to the *Neptune*, 90 guns. Lieutenant Cooban managed to throw the despatches overboard before the capture.
[TNA: ADM.49/97; www.britishnewspaperarchive.co: London Courier 21 March 1805 p3]

24 January JULIA Schooner
Hired 1804 (*Lord Nelson*); 157 tons; 12 guns
Lieutenant James Harley

Steering down the English Channel in poor weather, the schooner laboured in the sea, pitching and rolling heavily. Some of the shrouds parted and the timbers showed signs of the strain. Lieutenant Harley decided to head for a sheltered anchorage and made for Dartmouth. Arriving off the haven in the evening, the Master, Luke Smithett, said he felt confident to take her in, despite the late hour. When in the narrows, the wind became fitful and squally and it was decided to anchor, but before she could be brought up, the schooner struck the Castle rocks. Distress guns were fired as the vessel pounded heavily on the shore, the rudder coming off and the stern frame starting to come apart. About 20 minutes after striking, a large wave lifted her off the rocks and she floated into clear water. Filling quickly, she foundered within minutes, all the crew being picked up from the water. Lieutenant Harley was later judged to have exaggerated the damage and was reprimanded and admonished to be more careful in his actions in the future. Luke Smithett the Master was blamed for the loss, in taking a vessel into a harbour with which he was unacquainted in the dark and in poor weather. He was dismissed the service.
[TNA: ADM.1/5369; ADM.49/97; Lloyd's List 29 January 1805]

30 January RAVEN Brig Sloop
Blackwall 1804; 384 tons; 100.2ft x 30.6ft; 18 guns
Commander William Layman

Ordered to Gibraltar with despatches for Admiral Sir John Orde, the *Raven* arrived at the entrance to the Straits on 29 January, to find poor weather and no sign of the squadron. Sail was reduced to treble-reefed topsails and she hove-to for the night. During the night, the weather cleared a little and lights were seen which were taken to be ships, but it later became clear that they were the lights of Cadiz, and the sloop was evidently drifting closer to them. Reefs were shaken out and sail made, and she stood out to sea, beating over a shoal as she did so. Morning revealed that she was off the Spanish coast near Rota, and when the main yard parted in the slings, she anchored to effect repairs. Several gunboats could be seen hovering nearby, but they did not approach. The weather worsened during the day, being very dark with regular squalls of rain. At 7 o'clock that evening the anchor cable parted and she found herself being taken inshore. Sail was made, but the contrary winds baffled her attempts to clear the land. She struck the ground extremely hard, being bilged in three places as she drove onto rocks. Clearly unable to free the brig, she was abandoned, and all but two of the crew made it safely to the shore. Both Commander Layman and the Master, John Edwards, were criticised for their actions. Edwards was adjudged guilty of neglect, in failing to sound regularly and failing to appreciate the movement of the sloop. He was ordered to be ineligible for promotion to Lieutenant for two years after completing his time. Commander Layman was found to have shown a great want of caution in his actions in approaching the Straits. He was severely reprimanded and placed on the bottom of the seniority list. The minutes of the court martial are noted by an Admiralty official 'Their Lordships are of the opinion that Captain Layman is not a fit person to be entrusted with the command of one of H.M's ships'. He was never again employed.
[TNA: ADM.1/5369]

4 February ACHERON Bomb Vessel
Purchased 1803 (*New Grove*); 388 tons; 108.3ft x 29.2ft; 8 guns
Commander Arthur Farquhar

One of a pair of escorts to a convoy from Malta, bound for England, at daylight of 3 February, when the convoy was coasting along the North African shore, two ships were sighted astern, hull down. The *Acheron* was ordered to close the strangers to identify them, and by 11.30am had established that the pair were large frigates, and probably French. An hour later saw the *Acheron* returning to the convoy under all sail, the strangers not having answered signals. The *Arrow* sloop joined the bomb vessel and ordered the merchant ships to make sail away, while the escorts remained between them and the closing frigates. All the ships continued steering to the west under all sail, in light and fitful winds, the strangers slowly closing, with the land to the east of Ténès on the North African coast being visible about 30 miles away. At just after 4 o'clock in the morning the leading frigate, which was the French *Hortense*, 40 guns, passed close to the British pair, hailing as she did so. When the French ship came up with the *Acheron*, she fired a broadside into her, which ripped up the sails and rigging, shooting away the main topgallant-yard and cutting the main-yard in half. The *Acheron* returned the fire, hauling around to fire the opposite broadside into her opponent, who stood away to the

west. The *Acheron* then took the opportunity to fire into the second frigate, the *Incorruptible*, 38 guns, as she passed. There followed a lull in the action until daylight, which showed the convoy about four miles to the west, crowding sail to escape, the French frigates to the south. The frigates determined to dispose of the escorts and made sail towards the *Acheron* and *Arrow*, and after firing into the sloop, the *Incorruptible* came alongside the bomb vessel and a mutual exchange of fire commenced. All four ships soon became heavily engaged, the *Acheron* manoeuvring to assist her consort. At 8.30am the *Arrow* surrendered, at which the bomb attempted to make sail to escape, but her rigging was too damaged, and she was quickly overhauled by the *Hortense* and forced to surrender. The bomb was found to be in such a shattered condition that the French removed the crew and burnt her. She had three killed and eight wounded. Commander Farquhar was promoted to Captain as a reward for his bravery.
[TNA: ADM.1/5369; London Gazette 19 March 1805]

4 February ARROW Ship Sloop
Redbridge 1796; 386 tons; 128.8ft × 30ft; 18 guns
Commander Richard Budd Vincent

The second escort to the convoy attached by the frigates *Hortense* and *Incorruptible* off the North African coast (see *Acheron*). During the first exchange of fire in the early morning, the *Arrow* had successfully raked one of the French ships and she repeated the action when the fighting was renewed later. The sloop bore the brunt of the fight against the French pair, engaging them both for over an hour, until with her masts shot through, rigging cut to pieces, rudder disabled, several shots in the hull and mounting casualties, she surrendered. The French removed the crew only just in time, the ship rolling over onto her beam-ends and sinking. All but three ships of the convoy escaped. Commander Vincent was promoted to Captain in recognition of his bravery.
[TNA: ADM.1/5370; London Gazette 19 March 1805]

17 February CLEOPATRA Fifth Rate
Bristol 1779; 689 tons; 126.5ft × 35.2ft; 32 guns
Captain Robert Lawrie

At daybreak of 16 February when to the south-east of Bermuda, a ship was seen, which the *Cleopatra* altered course to chase. The stranger spread more sail, and the *Cleopatra* followed suit, both ships running to the north-east under all sail. The stranger could be seen to be a large frigate and the *Cleopatra* attempted to make her shorten sail by hoisting American colours, but the chase continued. At daybreak the following morning, the pair were only four miles apart, with the British frigate slowly gaining. At noon, both ships hoisted national colours, the stranger showing French. At 2.30pm, then being in position 29.24N 64.30W, the *Cleopatra* commenced the action by firing her bow-chase guns, then being about 100 yards on the weather quarter of the stranger, which was the French ship *Ville de Milan*, 40 guns. The French ship then luffed and fired two broadsides at her opponent, which was returned in kind. A close action then commenced which continued until about 5 o'clock in the afternoon when the French frigate's main yard was shot away. This so retarded her sailing that the British frigate, despite having her rigging damaged, with her mainstay and most of the halliards shot away, moved ahead. Captain Lawrie determined to take the advantage and rake his opponent, but as he did so a shot took away the wheel, the broken spokes jamming it. The rudder itself was also jammed by the rudder head filling with splinters and a dislodged set of pistols, The *Cleopatra* could no longer manoeuvre, and a few moments later the *Ville de Milan* ran her bowsprit over the quarterdeck between the main- and mizzen-shrouds. The French took advantage of this by attempting to board but were driven back. Volleys of small-arms fire from the tops of the French ship cleared the decks of the *Cleopatra*, and attempts led by the First Lieutenant, William Balfour, to spread staysails and spritsail were defeated when the men were shot. The French now boarded for a second time and with little resistance being offered captured the *Cleopatra*. Shortly after the surrender both fore- and mainmasts went overboard, taking the bowsprit with them, the *Ville de Milan* losing her main- and mizzenmasts later that day. The musketry of the French had been particularly effective, the British having twenty-two men killed and thirty-six wounded.

Note: recaptured, along with the *Ville de Milan*, on 23 February by the *Leander*.
[TNA: ADM.1/5369]

21 February BOUNCER Gun Brig
Newcastle 1804; 177 tons; 80.2ft × 22.7ft; 12 guns
Lieutenant Samuel Bassan

The brig sailed from Portsmouth on 17 February to cruise on the northern coast of France, but in poor weather ran hard aground on a sandbank between Dieppe and Boulogne. She pounded heavily causing uncontrollable leaks. All the crew were taken prisoner. The brig was later hauled off and taken into French service.
[www.britishnewspaperarchive.co: Morning Post 13 April 1805 p3; Demerliac 5 no. 928]

26 February REDBRIDGE Schooner
Prize 1803 (*Oiseau*); 170 tons; 81ft × 21ft; 12 guns
Lieutenant Francis Blower Gibbes

Laying at anchor in Pedro Bay, Jamaica, on sounding the well at 7 o'clock in the morning, water was found to be entering. The pumps were ordered to be manned,

but the water gained, and the rate became so rapid that bailing soon had to be used. A kedge anchor was taken out, and after heaving overboard some stores to lighten her, work commenced on heaving the schooner further inshore. The vessel was settling all the time, and at 9 o'clock she foundered quite quickly. All the crew were rescued. The inquiry heard that the schooner was in a poor condition, being very leaky.
[TNA:ADM.1/5369]

8 March FLY Ship Sloop
Bursledon 1804; 369 tons; 106ft × 28.2ft; 16 guns
Commander Pownall Bastard Pellew

Sailed from the Bay of Honduras on 22 February with a small convoy of merchant ships bound for England. On 8 March, the noon sun sighting and by dead reckoning indicated that they were well clear of any danger, and it was therefore a surprise when at just before midnight one of the convoy was heard to make signals of distress. A sounding was taken, which indicated 20 fathoms. The helm was ordered to be put over, but before this was completed, the ship struck a reef with considerable violence and was brought up, still striking heavily. Guns were fired as signals of warning to the other ships and efforts were made to launch a boat to carry out an anchor, but with the ship thumping hard on the rocks this proved impossible. Daylight revealed that two ships of the convoy were also on the reef and to their utter astonishment, they realised that they were on the Carysfort Reef, close to the Florida shore, Key Largo being five miles to the north. The topmasts and mizzenmast were cut away, all guns along with shot and stores were heaved overboard to lighten her. By 8 o'clock that evening, however, the constant pounding had taken effect, with the stern frame falling apart and several timbers stove in. With 4ft of water in the hold, she was abandoned, the crew being taken off by the other ships of the convoy. The wreck attracted the attention of several wrecking vessels, which attended to strip the remains of anything useful. The court martial found that the cause was a major error in the chart published by Hamilton-Moore.
[TNA:ADM.1/5369; www.britishnewspaperarchive.co: Hampshire Chronicle 10 June 1805 p1]

12 March IMOGEN Ship Sloop
Prize 1800 (*Diable a Quatre*); 399 tons; 108.2ft × 29.4ft; 18 guns
Commander Henry Vaughan

Ordered to proceed to England from Barbados, she sailed as escort to a convoy on 27 January. On 11 February, when about 900 miles north of Barbados, a leak became evident, and pumping started. This initially seemed to work, as the following day the well was found to be dry. Later that day however, water was found to be entering again and from then on the pumps were manned constantly, supplemented regularly by bailing. Efforts were made to find the source of the leak, but it could not be found, although the stern seemed to be the culprit. The sloop had iron knees and fastenings, and these seemed to be suffering from iron-sickness, being very loose. Oakum, spare hammocks and bedding were used to pack the sides of storerooms in an effort to stem the leaks, pumping continuing, an extra pump being passed to the sloop from a merchant ship in company. A sail was spread under the hull which helped for some time, but by 11 March the water was gaining on the pumps, being over the ballast and casks in the hold, the crew exhausted by the constant work. Guns and stores had been heaved overboard and it was clear that they were fighting a losing battle. Early the following morning the boats were hoisted out and ships in the convoy stood by whilst the crew abandoned her. The last known position was 43.46N 28.07W.
[TNA:ADM.1/5369]

12 May CYANE Ship Sloop
Frindsbury 1796; 423 tons; 111.9ft × 29.7ft; 18 guns
Commander Hon. George Cadogan

Cruising in the West Indies, between Barbados and Martinique, when she fell in with the French fleet under Admiral Villeneuve. Sail was made away, but two frigates, *Hortense* and *Hermione*, were detached from the fleet to chase the sloop, and when overhauled, faced with such overwhelming force, she struck her flag in surrender, being taken into Martinique.
[TNA:ADM.1/5370]

2 June DIAMOND ROCK 'Sloop'
Commissioned 1804; 5 guns
Commander James Maurice

A small island lying to the south-west of Martinique which, being in an ideal position to harass shipping approaching or leaving that island, was occupied and fortified by a party from the *Centaur* and commissioned as a sloop of war. The *Diamond Rock* was used with great success, firing at every ship passing, to the great annoyance of the French. When Admiral Villeneuve's fleet arrived in the West Indies in May 1805, it was determined to put an end to this harassment. An expedition of 400 troops was landed from a force of two ships of the line, a frigate, a brig, a schooner and eleven gunboats. The French force arrived off the island on 31 May and a mutual cannonade commenced. The lower gun batteries were abandoned later that same day, and the defence concentrated on the summit. The fighting went on until the afternoon of 2 June, when Commander Maurice surrendered, having exhausted his supply of gunpowder, and having little fresh water left. Two men killed and one wounded.
[TNA:ADM.1/5370]

11 July ORESTES Ship Sloop
Purchased 1803; 280 tons; 101ft x 27ft; 14 guns
Commander Thomas Brown

Ordered to reconnoitre the harbour of Dunkirk, the sloop closed the port, and having completed her task, at 12.45pm wore ship to stand out to sea, having sounded in four fathoms. This move had hardly been completed when she struck the ground. The sloop was lightened, and distress guns fired, which brought down the *Cruizer* sloop and two gun brigs. An attempt was made to sail free of the obstruction by spreading all available canvas, but this failed. Sail was taken in, and yards and spars were hoisted over the side to act as shores, the tide being on the ebb. It was found that she was settling into the mud, which was drying all around her. Several gunboats could be seen getting under way from the harbour, and as it was clear that she could not defend herself properly, the sloop was abandoned, the crew taking to the boats, Commander Brown setting fire to the ship as he left.
[TNA: ADM.1/5370]

16 July PLUMPER Gun Brig
Deptford 1804; 177 tons; 80.1ft x 22.6ft; 12 guns
Lieutenant James Henry Garrety

One of the vessels blockading the northern French coast, the brig was stationed off Granville, in company with the *Teazer* gun brig, when the wind fell away to a calm. Concerned that the tide might carry the brigs onto the French coast, during the afternoon the pair anchored off the Îles Chausey and were soon enveloped in a thick fog. The following morning, at about 2.30am, several French gunboats were seen looming out of the darkness and mist, and the *Plumper* weighed in an attempt to close the *Teazer*, anchored some distance away. The French force could now be seen to be six gun brigs, a schooner and a ketch, and fire was opened on the *Plumper*. Within 30 minutes her rigging had been reduced to a wreck. Fire was returned, but it proved difficult to engage so many opponents, which stayed at long range. After suffering an hour of battering, in which Lieutenant Garrety was severely wounded, losing an arm and his leg crippled by grapeshot, and his chest lacerated by a piece of langrage, and with four other men wounded, she surrendered. Sub-Lieutenant William Richards, who assumed the command after Lieutenant Garrety had been taken below, was later accused by some of the crew of striking the flag too early.
[TNA: ADM.1/5396]

16 July TEAZER Gun Brig
Deptford 1804; 178 tons; 80.1ft x 22.6ft; 12 guns
Lieutenant George Lewis Kerr

Consort to the *Plumper* (see above), she anchored off the Chausey Islands, at some distance from her companion. When the French attacked in the early hours of the morning, she was too far distant to give her any support and the lack of wind did not allow her to sail. Dawn showed the *Plumper* to be in the hands of the enemy, surrounded by gunboats at anchor. At 6am the French weighed and pulled towards the *Teazer* and commenced a sharp fire. Within 30 minutes she was being hit regularly and she cut her anchor cables just before 9 o'clock, in an attempt to pull away using sweeps. The sweeps were shot away, and the lack of wind did not enable her to make sail. Unable to escape, surrounded, the rigging in tatters and with nine shots in the hull, the *Teazer* surrendered.

Note: recaptured on 25 August 1811 by the *Diana*.
[TNA: ADM.1/5446]

19 July BLANCHE Fifth Rate
Deptford 1800; 951 tons; 145.1ft x 38.3ft; 36 guns
Captain Zachary Mudge

At daybreak, when in position 20.20N 66.44W, bound for Barbados with despatches, three ships and a brig were sighted. They were at first believed to be a British convoy known to be in the area, and the *Blanche* continued towards them. When the private recognition signals were not answered, it was suspected that they were French, and she altered away. The strangers came around in chase, showing British colours, although this last act tended to confirm Captain Mudge's suspicions that they were French as the colours were the wrong shade. The *Blanche* was in poor condition, and now found herself being chased by all four vessels, which soon began to overhaul her. After a short chase, the leading French ship, the frigate *Topaze*, 40 guns, came up on the starboard side of *Blanche* and a mutual exchange of broadsides commenced. The *Topaze* was joined by the *Département-des-Landes*, 22, which, with the *Torche*, 18, hung on the stern and quarter of the British ship annoying her with fire from bow-chase guns and occasional broadsides. A fourth sloop, the *Faune*, 16, remained at some distance astern. After 30 minutes, the *Blanche* attempted to get under the bows of *Topaze* and rake her, but sharp manoeuvring by the French captain in luffing, allowed her to get under the stern of *Blanche* as she passed. She then successfully raked the British frigate. The action came to an end after two hours, with the rigging and spanker boom shot away and several shots through the masts and in the hull. The *Blanche* was found to have 6ft of water in the hold by her captors who set her on fire after removing the crew and some stores. She burned for some time until sinking that evening. Eight men killed and fifteen wounded.
[TNA: ADM.1/5370; London Gazette 20 August 1805]

19 July RANGER Ship Sloop
Limehouse 1794; 367 tons; 105.3ft × 28.2ft; 16 guns
Commander Charles Coote

Cruising in the western approaches to the English Channel for the protection of trade, during 13 July she sighted and chased two French privateer schooners. The chase went on for two days, when she finally gave over the pursuit then being to the south-west of Cape Finisterre. She turned north and commenced working to windward to regain her station. At 3 o'clock in the afternoon of 19 July, then being in position 46.10N 09.21W, a sail was sighted right ahead. A little later a second vessel was seen, which seemed to be in chase of the first. The *Ranger* continued to close the pair, making the private recognition signals, which were not answered. More ships then came into sight, and it became clear that she was in contact with an enemy squadron, the ships in sight evidently being a frigate in chase of a merchant ship. All sail was made away, the frigate leaving the merchant ship to pursue the *Ranger*, and a little later a second frigate was seen to detach from the main body of the squadron and join the chase. Boats, booms and anchors were cut away to lighted the sloop, but she was steadily overhauled. By 8 o'clock that evening one of the frigates was on her lee beam, the second in her wake, and they opened fire, the shot initially going over her. Unable to escape, she struck her flag in surrender, finding her pursuers were the *Armide*, 44 guns, and the *Gloire*, 22, part of the Rochefort squadron commanded by Rear Admiral Allemande.
[TNA: ADM.1/5430]

5 August DOVE Cutter
Purchased 1805; 103 tons; 68ft × 19.4ft; 4 guns
Lieutenant Alexander Boyack

Employed as a despatch vessel, the *Dove* sailed for the Mediterranean, and was in the Bay of Biscay when at 3 o'clock in the morning a vessel was seen right ahead. An extremely high sea was running, with strong winds, and when the cutter attempted to tack away, she twice missed stays and the vessel refused to come around. She therefore wore ship, and tried to run to leeward, one seaman being lost overboard as she did so. The stranger was soon in chase and commenced an occasional fire from bow-chase guns. When within range, the enemy vessel, which could now be seen to be a sloop, fired several times and was preparing to fire a broadside, when the *Dove* surrendered. Lieutenant Boyack managed to throw the despatches he was carrying overboard before the enemy took possession of the cutter. Her captor proved to be the *Gloire*, 22 guns.
[TNA: ADM.1/5443]

10 August PIGMY Cutter
Prize 1779 (*Mutine*); 215 tons; 79.11ft × 26.2ft; 14 guns
Lieutenant William Smith

Sailed from her anchorage in St Aubin's Bay, Jersey, to cruise on the northern coast of France, but just an hour later, at 10.30 in the morning, she ran hard aground on a submerged reef. Several attempts were made to free her, which included all the crew crowding onto the fo'c'sle and bowsprit to lift the stern. With the tide now ebbing, yards were placed over the side to prevent her falling over, and the boats were hoisted out to lay out anchors in readiness the kedge her off at high tide. Distress signals were made which brought boats from other ships nearby, and guns, shot and stores were taken out and finally the mast was cut away. At flood tide, the work to pull her free failed and she started filling with water. All the crew left her and by 4 o'clock that afternoon she had disappeared. It was found that she had run onto the Sillette Reef, south of Noirmont Point, the pilot Nicholas Delaree being found at fault, for recommending the course to be steered. He was reprimanded.
[TNA: ADM.1/5370]

26 September CALCUTTA Fourth Rate
Purchased 1795 (*Warley*); 1,176 tons; 156.11ft × 41.3ft; 54 guns
Captain Daniel Woodriffe

Acting as an escort to homeward-bound ships from St Helena, the convoy being composed of a mixture of East India Company ships and whalers. The little convoy had arrived in the English Channel, to the south-west of the Scilly Isles, when during the afternoon of 25 September, a number of ships were seen, but were too far distant to make out their identity. The *Calcutta* placed herself between the convoy and the strangers, but progress was slow, due to the sluggish sailing of one of her charges. Dawn showed thirteen strange ships, all now considerably closer. By 11am they were close enough for the *Calcutta* to make the private recognition signals, which were ignored, This added to the suspicion that they were French, and at noon made the signal for 'enemy in sight' and ordered the *Indus* Indiaman to take charge of the convoy and make all sail away. The enemy ships could now be seen to be five ships of the line, the remainder being frigates and sloops. After making sure that her convoy was making all sail away, the *Calcutta* steered for the nearest enemy ship, a frigate, which was leading the pursuit of the convoy. At 3 o'clock *Calcutta* fired a broadside at the *Armide*, 40 guns, but found that she was out of range. The frigate initially replied with stern-chase guns, but after a while shortened sail to await the *Calcutta*. The British ship kept up an intermittent fire, edging away to the south, away from the fleeing convoy and keeping her distance from the French frigate. The

contest went on for over an hour, until the *Armide* hauled out of gunshot and ceased firing. The aim of Captain Woodriffe had been to deflect the enemy away from his convoy, and he had succeeded. The fighting had brought down the rest of the squadron, except for one brig, which captured the sluggish sailer that had so held back the convoy. At 5 o'clock, the leading ship of the French squadron, the *Magnanime*, 74 guns, was in range and the *Calcutta* very bravely turned to engage the larger opponent. The unequal contest went on for 45 minutes, until with rigging disabled and the rest of the French squadron closing, she surrendered. Six men killed and six wounded.
[TNA: ADM.1/5385]

30 September FLYING FISH Schooner
Bermuda 1804; 71 tons; 55.2ft × 18ft; 4 guns
Lieutenant Clement Ives

Laying at anchor in St George's Harbour, Bermuda, she was being used to accommodate fifteen French seamen, prisoners from the privateer *Mathilde*, recently captured. A guard of a corporal and six soldiers from the 7th Regiment, the Royal Fusiliers, was also on board. The captain of the privateer had been allowed some freedom, under parole, being permitted to be on the upper deck and also to go ashore. The prisoners were regularly employed in small numbers to fetch stores and water from the shore to the schooner. Lieutenant Ives went ashore during the afternoon to dine with a local shipbuilder, Mr Goodrich, and in his absence, prisoners returning from a storing trip and led by their captain, took over the ship. They weighed and sailed her out of the harbour, passing several unsuspecting British warships and a shore battery as she did so. This audacious move was evidently made easier as the schooner had earlier prepared to sail in search of a missing ship from a convoy,

Note: recaptured on 5 April 1808 by the *Pheasant* but not taken back into service.
[TNA: ADM.1/5372]

September PAPILLON Gun Brig
Prize 1803; 145 tons; 64ft × 22.6ft; 10 guns
Lieutenant William Wolsey†

Sailed from Port Royal, Jamaica, in company with the *Vanguard*, as escort to a homeward-bound convoy on 28 July. The brig parted company with the other ships in poor weather on 25 September and was not seen again. It was presumed that she was lost with all hands soon after this.
[www.britishnewspaperarchive.co: Morning Chronicle 16 October 1805 p2]

September SEAFORTH Gun Brig
Prize 1805 (*Dame Ernouf*); 215 tons; 14 guns
Lieutenant George Steel†

Sailed from Antigua to convoy the *Island* packet ship clear of the Leeward Islands at the beginning of September and not heard from afterwards. Presumed lost with all hands. Pay book closed 30 September 1805.
[TNA: ADM.1/326; ADM.35/2470]

3 October BARRACOUTA Schooner
Bermuda 1804; 71 tons; 55.2ft × 18ft; 4 guns
Lieutenant Joel Orchard

The schooner sailed from Grand Cayman in company with the *Pique* and *Port Mahon* and headed north in deteriorating weather. During 1 October it blew a full gale and the schooner struck topmasts and shortened sail to ride out the storm. That night, in poor visibility, with no moon, she lost sight of her companions. The following day the weather moderated, and she continued to steer north-east until land was raised, which was identified as Cabo Cruz, Cuba. Lieutenant Orchard had believed himself to be much further to the west, so altered course to steer west-north-west in hope of regaining contact with the other ships. At 2.30 the next morning, with little warning, she found herself amongst breakers and ran hard aground. Sail was taken in and the boats hoisted out to lay out a kedge anchor. It was found that a strong current was running, which defeated the efforts of the board and anchor. Efforts were now made to lighten her, with stores, provisions and then the ballast being thrown over the side. The lightened vessel now lifted with each wave and was pounded with increasing violence on the rocks, starting uncontrollable leaks. As she was now flooding with water the schooner was abandoned, the masts being first cut away. The crew spent several days on the nearby keys salvaging stores before the wreck broke up. The crew's adventures continued. Leaving the small island in two open boats, intending to navigate back to the Cayman Islands, they encountered a Spanish schooner, which they boarded and captured. Their luck did not last, however. Two Spanish privateers found them on 23 October and took them back to Cuba as prisoners. The subsequent court martial found that the schooner had been wrecked in the Jardines del Reina, on 'Padro Keys' (Cayo Piedra?) due to the poor weather and the strong current.
[TNA: ADM.1/5377]

11 October SQUIB Fire Vessel
Purchased 1804 (*Diligent*)

Laying at anchor in the Downs, at about 5 o'clock in the morning in strong winds, she dragged her anchors and struck the ground. The cables were cut, and she was

driven on the beach at Deal, where she capsized. all the crew were saved and most of her stores.
[www.britishnewspaperarchive.co: Morning Post 14 October 1805 p3; Kentish Weekly Post 15 October 1805 p4]

7 November **ORQUIXO** Ship Sloop
Prize 1805 (*Orquijo*); 384 tons; 18 guns
Lieutenant John Bassett Balderston

Having embarked a detachment of soldiers from the 60th Regiment, she was in company with the *Penguin* sloop off Port Antonio, Jamaica, when Lieutenant Balderston was ordered aboard the *Penguin*. Lieutenant Anthony Stanton assumed the command and when a merchant ship was sighted, he altered course to speak with her. As they closed, a squall was seen approaching and orders were given to shorten sail, but before this could be completed the squall struck her and rolled the sloop over onto her beam-ends. Guns and stores broke loose and some of the carronades smashed through the side, causing her to fill and sink very quickly. Thirty-nine men were picked up by the *Penguin*, but about 100 men lost their lives.
[TNA: ADM.1/5370]

10 November **BITER** Gun Brig
Blackwall 1804; 177 tons; 80ft x 22.6ft; 12 guns
Lieutenant George Thomas Wingate

Ordered to cruise off the northern coast of France in the region of Étaples, at 4 o'clock in the morning during a particularly dark and gloomy night, she ran hard aground near St Valery-sur-Somme. Stores were heaved overboard to lighten the brig and the cutter was hoisted out to carry out an anchor, with the intention of kedging her off. This proved successful and soon after daybreak she pulled herself free. However, she had been seen, and her plight brought down a body of troops who commenced a harassing fire of musketry, but fire was smartly returned, to keep them at bay. A shore battery now joined in the action, firing shot and shell at the brig as she slowly moved off the beach. One shell struck her forward, going right through the deck and penetrating the bottom without exploding. Water gushed in through the shell hole and she was forced to run herself aground to avoid sinking, where she surrendered.
[TNA: ADM.1/5443]

13 November **WOODLARK** Gun Brig
Leith 1805; 182 tons; 80.7ft x 22.9ft; 12 guns
Lieutenant Thomas Innes

Sailed from Lowestoft on 13 November to take newly raised men to Portsmouth, running south during the day in thick and hazy weather. At 8.30 that evening, with little warning, she ran aground. The pilot, John Steadman, thought they had run onto the Goodwin Sands, so distress guns were fired and lights shown. The brig was being lifted by the waves and pounded heavily on the sands, which prevented them from launching a boat, and efforts were concentrated on lightening her. At 11 o'clock, lights were seen astern and soon after, a shot was fired at the brig. Completely baffled, a boat was ordered to be hoisted out, despite the high seas. Shots were now being fired regularly, and she was being hit every time. The boat pulled away towards the attackers and were taken prisoner, discovering that the brig was on the French shore near Calais. All the crew were then ferried ashore by the boat to surrender. The brig, when left by the crew, was in a poor state, with her forefoot and cutwater knocked off, sternpost badly shaken and loose and the rudder unshipped. Lieutenant Innes was ruled to have ordered too much sail to be carried and was admonished to be more careful in the future. Pilot John Steadman was found to have run too far to the south and to have misjudged the distance run. As he had been held a prisoner in France for nine years, he was dealt with leniently, and only admonished to have more caution in the future.
[TNA: ADM.1/5443]

30 November **PIGEON** Schooner
Purchased 1805 (*Fanny*); 75 tons; 57.7ft x 17.6ft; 4 guns
Lieutenant John Luckraft

Sailed on 27 November from Great Yarmouth for Bremen, with a King's Messenger embarked, carrying despatches for General Sir George Don, commanding British forces in Hanover. They ran south and then east, but in poor weather ran aground on a sandbank off the Texel. Unable to be freed, she surrendered to the Dutch when they approached the ship. The pilot, Robert Barrett, was found to have been in charge of the vessel at the time, despite being unfamiliar with that part of the coast. He was ordered to lose all pay due and to be severely reprimanded. The most severe criticism was reserved for Lieutenant Luckraft. His actions before and after the wreck were so incompetent that the court martial enquiring into the loss ruled that he was criminally negligent. He had embarked and given responsibility to Barrett even though warned that he was inexperienced and had failed to exercise '… the usual and most necessary precautions generally taken' when steering close to a hostile shore. Finally, he was found to be drunk when the wreck occurred and was unable to issue any sensible orders. He was ordered to be dismissed the service and be imprisoned in the Marshalsea Prison for two months.
[TNA: ADM.1/5372]

22 December MANLY Gun Brig
Deptford 1804; 178 tons; 80.1ft × 22.6ft; 12 guns
Lieutenant Martin White
On 20 December, whilst investigating the entrance to the River Ems, the brig ran hard aground on a sandbank, about three-quarters of a mile off Rysum. After making some effort to free the brig, Lieutenant White went in a boat to supervise the laying out of anchors to pull her off. Whilst so engaged, the boat was approached by a Dutch armed schuyt, which detained White and the boat's crew, despite White's protestation that they were in neutral waters. On 22 December, a Dutch force of three armed galleys approached the brig and called upon them to surrender. The Master, William Golding, replied that they would comply, and the Dutch took possession. This action was deemed to be highly unbecoming of an officer and Golding was subsequently disrated from his position of Master and ordered to serve as a seaman for two years. Lieutenant White was reprimanded for failing to lighten the brig before attempting to kedge her free.

Note: the date of her capture is obscure in British records: it is not mentioned in the court-martial proceedings. The account above is from court testimony and secondary sources. Continental newspapers, quoted in British journals, reported the detention of Lieutenant White on 31 December, and the capture of the brig on 7 January.

Note: recaptured on 1 January 1809 by the *Onyx*.
[TNA: ADM.1/5372; www.britishnewspaperarchive.co: Hampshire Telegraph 13 January 1806 p3; London Courier 31 January 1806 p2; https://en.wikipedia.org/wiki/HMS_Manly_(1804)]

1806

6 January FAVOURITE Ship Sloop
Rotherhithe 1794; 427 tons; 108.5ft × 29.9ft; 16 guns
Commander John Davie
Having escorted a convoy to the Île de Gorée, west Africa, the sloop remained in the area, and had taken a French prize. At 1.30 in the morning, the Captain was woken by the officer of the watch with the news that a number of ships were in sight to windward. The ship was then to the south-east of the Cape Verde Islands, with the prize vessel in tow. The tow was cast off and the sloop attempted to work to windward of the strangers. Sight of them was lost in the night, but at dawn were they again sighted, apparently three ships and a brig, still to windward and steering towards the sloop. The strangers were end-on to the *Favourite* and it was difficult to make out their identity, but as they closed it was believed that they could be a convoy of East Indiaman with a brig-sloop escort. Not until they were fairly close was it realised that all four were warships, a line of battle ship with two frigates and a brig-sloop. All sail was made away, with two of the ships in chase. A large frigate harried the sloop with constant fire and the liner yawed occasionally to fire at her. At 11am, with the two-decked ship on her beam and frigate on the quarter, the *Favourite* surrendered, finding her captors were the *Régulus*, 80 guns, and *Président*, 44.

Note: recaptured on 27 January 1807 by the *Jason*.
[TNA: ADM.1/5373]

10 January UNIQUE Schooner
Prize 1804 (*Harmonie*); 120 tons; 74ft × 20.8ft; 12 guns
Lieutenant George Rowley Brand†
Stationed in the Leeward Islands, she was engaged by a large French 16-gun privateer. She maintained a stout resistance until she was overwhelmed by repeated volleys of musketry, which killed or wounded the men on the upper deck including all of her officers, and she was left in a foundering state. The schooner sank after surrendering. Eighteen men killed.
[TNA: ADM.1/326]

31 January VENUS Cutter
Hired 1803; 51 tons; 10 guns
Lieutenant Nicholas Wray
Captured in the Bay of Quiberon by the French privateer lugger *l'Ami Nationale* from Nantes.
[TNA: ADM.49/97; www.britishnewspaperarchive.co: Oracle & Daily Advertiser 10 March 1806 p2]

16 March ANT Cutter
Hired 1803; 27 tons; 4 guns
Master John Vautier
Noted as being lost by capture, but no further details found.
[TNA: ADM.49/97]

25 March AGNES Lugger
Hired 1804 (*Venus*); 67 tons; 6 guns
Lieutenant William Morgan
Stationed in the North Sea, she ran aground on the Haak Sand and went to pieces. The crew were all rescued by Dutch boats.
[TNA: ADM.49/97; www.britishnewspaperarchive.co: Morning Post 25 April 1806 p3]

12 April BRAVE Third Rate
Prize 1806; 1,890 tons; 74 guns
Commander Edmund Boger
As part of a French squadron, she had been captured in February off San Domingo by Sir John Duckworth. During the action she had suffered considerable damage, mainly in the hull, with many of the knees supporting the beams shot away. With temporary repairs

effected, she was ordered to sail to England, and with a small crew onboard and a number of French prisoners, she sailed from Jamaica with several other ships. Leaks became evident almost immediately and by 9 April she had both chain pumps and a hand pump constantly employed to keep the water at bay, the ship working and labouring heavily. The following day the French prisoners were released to assist with the work at the pumps and several of the gundeck guns were heaved overboard. During 11 April total chaos reigned for a time, after the shot lockers burst open, spilling out their contents, which smashed much of the ship's furniture and put one of the pumps out of action. The last of 800 shot was finally heaved overboard that evening. The ship was now in an extremely poor state, low in the water and rolling heavily. The following day the mainmast was rolled away, taking the mizzen-topmast with it. This also ripped up the deck planking, crushed gunwales and boats and sent wreckage everywhere, and 30 minutes later the fore topmast went overboard to add to the confusion. Distress guns were fired, and the *Donegal* came to her aid and started taking off the men, although this was a hazardous and difficult manoeuvre in the high seas. At nightfall, the evacuation stopped, and the following morning, with the ship settling all the time, distress signals were made, and the ensign hoisted upside down. All available boats were sent to her to take off the last of the men and she was abandoned to her fate. Her last known position was 38.16N 56.06W.
[TNA:ADM.1/5374]

21 May DOMINICA Schooner
Purchased 1805; 85 tons; 6 guns
Lieutenant William Dean
Laying at anchor off Roseau, Dominica, Lieutenant Dean went ashore to collect despatches for Admiral Cochrane, leaving the schooner in the roadstead under the command of the Master, Richard Osborne. At 9.30 that evening, George Farrington, a seaman, approached the Master on the upper deck, produced a cutlass and struck him. A struggle ensued, in which the Master disarmed his opponent and demanded to know what was going on, to which he received a defiant answer that the crew wanted liberty. A group of seamen now came up and overpowered Osborne, who was sent below with other loyal members of the crew and secured below hatches, before weighing anchor. The following morning the schooner arrived at Basse Terre, Guadeloupe, where she was handed over to the French. Her new owners promptly commissioned her as a privateer and several of the crew remained on board. She was recaptured three days later by the *Wasp*. Sixteen of the mutineers were arrested, one of them being the leader of the mutiny, the Bosun's Mate, William Proctor, also known as Henry Proctor. In his defence he claimed he was an American citizen and produced a certificate of citizenship showing he was from Salem, Massachusetts. Further, he had harmed no one in the mutiny and had destroyed the confidential signals before handing the schooner over to the French. This cut no ice with the court martial, and he was hanged with the rest. One man who did escape was the cook, Naiad Suarie, who was sentenced to death, but given a Royal Pardon on hearing evidence that he was a negro from Martinique and had been in fear of Proctor, who had threatened him with a cutlass.
[TNA:ADM.1/5374]

24 May BERBICE Schooner
Prize 1805 (*Serpent*); 78 tons; 4 guns
Lieutenant James Gooding
Stationed in the River Demerara, she was unseaworthy, and had been condemned as being in a rotten and decayed condition when she foundered at her anchors. She was not thought worth weighing.
[TNA:ADM.1/327]

June HEUREUX Sixth Rate
Prize 1799; 598 tons; 127.8ft x 33.2ft; 22 guns
Captain John Morrison†
Sailed from Antigua for Halifax on 5 June, for much needed repairs. She captured a Spanish letter-of-marque ship on 11 June, and the pair parted company in poor weather on 15 June, in position 37.40N 62.56W, but she was not seen again. Presumed foundered with all hands. Pay book closed end-June.
[TNA:ADM.1/327;ADM.35/2268]

3 July KINGFISH Schooner
From 1805
Lieutenant Charles Newton Hunter
Employed as a despatch vessel in the West Indies, the schooner was near the island of St Kitts, when at daylight ships were seen. hull down on the horizon. The schooner stood towards them and as she approached became convinced that they were a British squadron. The paintwork, with yellow strakes and black gun ports, gave a chequered appearance that was identical to that seen recently in Admiral Cochrane's ships. The *Kingfish* closed the largest of them to hail, and it was not until they were alongside, was it realised that they were French. At that, a desperate attempt was made to flee. Initially she tried to tack, but missed stays, so attempted to wear instead. In doing so, she fell alongside the *Foudroyant*, 80 guns, and when called upon to strike her flag, she complied. The schooner was taken to the Dutch island of St Maarten, where some of the crew behaved in an unruly and insubordinate fashion towards Lieutenant Hunter. One of them, Timothy Sankey, was frequently drunk and attempted to desert and become

a soldier. He was sentenced to be flogged around the fleet, receiving 300 lashes on his bare back with a cat-of-nine-tails.
[TNA: ADM.1/5374]

12 August BELEM Schooner
Prize 1806; 88 tons; 4 guns
Lieutenant James Groves
A prize taken at the capture of Buenos Aires in June and manned from the *Diadem* to support British operations in the River Plate. In August, the Spanish mounted an effective counter-attack, and when the *Belem* could not be worked out of the harbour, she was abandoned to the enemy.
[TNA: ADM.1/58]

20 August DOVER Barracks
Bursledon 1786; 905 tons; 140ft × 38.6ft
A former 44-gun ship, the *Dover* had been fitted out as a barracks ship for the Woolwich Division of the Royal Marines, and lay in that dockyard, with about 120 men with wives and children on board. At about half past midnight, the sentinel on the quarterdeck raised the cry of 'Fire'. Within 30 minutes she was burning from end to end and by 3am she had been burnt to the waterline. All but one of the occupants escaped, albeit in some confusion: '... such a scene of distress has been seldom witnessed, men seen dragging their wives out of the port holes, while mothers were heard screaming for their children; others, half burnt, were seen leaping from the ship to the shore. A serjeant's wife threw her infant out of a port hole and jumped after it herself into the mud; both are saved' (*Gold: Naval Chronicle*).
[Gold: Naval Chronicle vol 16 pp160-1]

31 August PREVOST Schooner
From 1805; 145 tons; 10 guns
Lieutenant Samuel Stout
Employed as a despatch vessel, the *Prevost* sailed on 8 August from Coro, Venezuela, for the Leeward Islands, but experienced bad weather which lasted for several days. During this time, she heaved overboard four of her guns and suffered damage to her rigging. At daylight on 31 August, when about 50 miles to the east of Martinique, a brig and a schooner were sighted, which were joined a little later by a sloop. The strangers bore up in chase of the *Prevost* and by noon the nearest of the pursuers was close in her wake. With no prospect of escaping, Lieutenant Stout decided to fight and shortened sail to await them. At 1.30pm he tacked across the bows of the brig, firing a raking broadside into her as he did so, then came about and repeated the move. A close action then began with the brig, the sloop and schooner also joining in the battle. After an hour, with the rigging and sails in tatters, three killed and seven wounded, she struck her flag. The brig proved to be a French privateer, the *Austerlitz*, 18 guns, which conducted her prize to Guadeloupe.
[TNA: ADM.1/5376]

(26/27) August SERPENT Ship Sloop
Plymouth 1789; 321 tons; 100ft × 27ft; 16 guns
Commander John Waller†
Sailed from Port Royal, Jamaica on 4 August to escort the *Duke of Marlborough* packet ship into the Atlantic, and when that task was completed, she was to cruise in the Mona Passage, between Puerto Rico and Hispaniola. After leaving the packet, she was not seen again, and was presumed to have foundered with all hands. The Mona Passage area was affected by a hurricane on 26/27 August and is likely to have been responsible for her loss. Pay Book closed end-August
[TNA: ADM.1/256; ADM.35/2476]

August MARTIN Ship Sloop
Dartmouth 1805; 368 tons; 106ft × 28.1ft; 16 guns
Commander Thomas Prouse†
Ordered to the Leeward Islands, she arrived in Barbados during early August. She was subsequently ordered to cruise in the vicinity of Guadeloupe, but nothing more was seen or heard of her and was presumed to have foundered with all hands. A hurricane passed over Dominica on 8/9 September, which may have been responsible. The pay books were closed on 31 August 1806
[TNA: ADM.1/327; ADM.35/2334]

4 September WOLF Ship Sloop
Dartmouth 1804; 367 tons; 105.10ft × 28.1ft; 16 guns
Commander George MacKenzie
Cruising to the north of Hispaniola, she was informed of a ship seen nearby in a dismasted condition, believed to be a French ship of the line. The *Wolf* proceeded to search the area, sighting the South-east Point of Great Inagua at 4 o'clock in the afternoon. It was decided to check the western side of the island and course was set accordingly to take them around the island. At 9 o'clock that night, white water was seen ahead, at which the wheel was put over, but before she could come around, the sloop struck the ground. A kedge anchor was laid out, but this failed to move her, the cable being cut by sharp rocks. A second attempt using a bower anchor also failed, it being found that the sloop had swung to sit broadside-on to the rocks and was filling with water. At 2 o'clock in the morning she fell over to port onto her beam-ends, the masts being cut away shortly afterwards. Daylight revealed land close by, and the crew were all landed safely. Several days were spent stripping the wreck, before being taken off by merchant ships, several of the crew taking the opportunity to desert. It

was found that she had been wrecked on a reef about a mile and half from the south-west point of Great Inagua, due to a combination of a strong current and inaccurate charts.
[TNA:ADM.1/5375]

September FLIGHT Cutter
Purchased 1805 (*Ariadne*); 187 tons; 4 guns
Lieutenant John Wells†
Missing, supposed foundered with all hands, in the English Channel. Pay book closed 30 September.
[TNA: 180/13; ADM.35/4118]

12 October CONSTANCE Sixth Rate
Prize 1797; 532 tons; 121.8ft x 31.1ft; 22 guns
Commander Alexander Saunderson Burrowes†
On 9 September, the *Constance*, in company with two brigs, chased a French store ship, the *Salamandre*, 26 guns, into a sheltered bay near St Malo. After waiting for some time, the British retired, believing their quarry to have been wrecked. However, the *Salamandre* extricated herself from her difficult position and resumed her voyage on 12 October, only to encounter the *Constance* again. At 8 o'clock in the morning, when off Cape Fréhel, now in company with three brigs and a cutter from the blockading squadron, the *Constance* sighted the French ship and immediately chased. By noon, the French ship had run into a rocky bay near the town of Erquy, laid out springs and had the support of some troops ashore with field guns. By 1.45pm, the British ships were within gunshot range, and opened fire, the *Constance* working in close to anchor near the *Salamandre*. A close action now commenced, which lasted for over an hour, when the French ship struck her colours. At the height of the action, Captain Burrowes was killed when struck by grapeshot. After taking possession of her prize, the action continued with the shore batteries, and at 5 o'clock the ship's anchor cables were shot away. With a freshening wind which had shifted round to blow from seaward, she drifted inshore, the troops taking heart at this, and commenced firing roundshot and grape as well as a destructive small-arms fire. *Constance* ran aground, and unable to mount any attempt to haul her off under fire, the crew quit her, leaving the wounded behind. Nine men killed and sixteen wounded, eight of whom later died of their injuries. At high tide that night a party returned to attempt to float her off, but all thirty-eight officers and men were captured.
[TNA:ADM.1/5375]

20 October ATHENIENNE Third Rate
Prize 1799; 1,412 tons; 163ft x 44.6ft; 64 guns
Captain Robert Raynsford†
Sailed from Gibraltar for Malta, carrying 10,000 dollars as payment for troops on the island. During the afternoon of 20 October Sardinia was sighted, and course set for Malta. At 9.30 that night she ran hard aground without warning on a submerged reef, with some violence. The ship rapidly started filling with water and heeled over to starboard. Efforts were made to lighten the ship, including cutting away all the masts and this served to bring her upright. Within 30 minutes the sea had taken her further onto the rocks and she fell over onto her larboard beam-ends. Boats were hoisted out and rafts ordered to be constructed, but the barge, loaded with men capsized, and a further two boats disappeared into the dark after being lowered. The one surviving boat, the launch, was successfully lowered with ninety survivors, and despite being very overcrowded, survived the night to be found in the morning by a Danish merchant brig, others being picked up by local fishermen; in all 121 men and two women survived but 353 people perished. It was found that she had run onto the Esquirques rocks in the Skerki Channel, which were wrongly laid down in charts held onboard, although it was also felt that the ship had steered too close to the shore for safety.
[TNA:ADM.1/5376]

25 October HANNAH Gunboat
Gibraltar 1805; 44 tons; 50.7ft x 14ft; 1 gun
Lieutenant John Foote
Locally fitted out and manned by detachments from the *Royal George* and *Queen*, the gunboat was ordered to cover the passage of a convoy through the Straits of Gibraltar. When off Cabrita Point, a lateen-rigged Spanish privateer was seen, towing a captured British merchant ship towards the Spanish shore. Lieutenant Foote headed towards them, with the intention of re-taking the merchant ship, but as he approached, the privateer cast off the tow, and altered towards the *Hannah*, showing herself to be a large, well-armed vessel. Efforts were made to get away, but the privateer soon overhauled the smaller craft and commenced a harassing fire. Foote decided that the only way out was to board, and he ran the gunboat alongside his opponent. Fierce hand-to-hand fighting went on for about 10 minutes, before the Spanish gained control of the upper deck and Lieutenant Foote surrendered. Eight men killed and eleven wounded.
[London Gazette 22 November 1806; O'Byrne p368]

28 October TOBAGO Schooner
Purchased 1805; 127 tons; 10 guns
Lieutenant John Salmon
Having taken on fresh water in Dominica, the schooner sailed just before first light, to proceed to Antigua. Soon after sailing a brig was sighted and a little later a schooner and a sloop were seen to join her. They stood towards the *Tobago* which cleared for action and steered away, the strangers in pursuit. By 8.30am, the

enemy sloop and schooner were close by and opened the action by firing broadsides and volleys of musketry. The pair then attempted to board, but this was repulsed. Lieutenant Salmon attempted to work the ship to leeward, but found himself cut off by the brig, which at 9.30am ran her jibboom over the taffrail of the *Tobago* and raked the decks with small-arms fire. Lieutenant Salmon was shot and wounded at this point and Sub-Lieutenant Nicholas Gould assumed command. About 30 minutes later, unable to sustain the fight, and with one dead and fifteen wounded, she surrendered to the *Général Ernouf* privateer, 16 guns.
[TNA: ADM.1/5379]

30 October ZENOBIA Schooner
Bermuda 1804; 111 tons; 68.2ft × 20.4ft; 10 guns
Lieutenant Archibald Hamilton
Sailing from Bermuda on 22 October bound for Norfolk, Virginia, she sighted the American coast during 29 October. A local pilot, John Dart of Baltimore, came aboard that afternoon to guide them into Norfolk. At 4 o'clock in the morning a light was seen, which Dart identified as Cape Henry light, and course was set accordingly. Thirty minutes later breakers were seen ahead, and the helm put over and three attempts were then made to tack, but she failed to come around on each occasion and then took the ground, striking heavily. All sail was taken in and a boat hoisted out to carry out a kedge anchor. At the same time another boat was despatched to the shore to bring help. Daylight revealed that they were aground on the shore about 20 miles south of Cape Henry, the pilot having mistaken a fisherman's light on False Cape Henry. Yards were struck and put over the side to act as shore and over the next few days several attempts were made to re-float her, with assistance from shore and from other ships nearby, but all failed. The work was hampered by the crew taking every opportunity to desert – eighteen out of a crew of twenty-four disappearing ashore. Lieutenant Hamilton with his small band of survivors finally abandoned the schooner as a wreck on 6 December.
[TNA: ADM.1/5379]

4 November REDBRIDGE Schooner
Purchased 1804 (*Union*); 131 tons; 12 guns
Lieutenant Edward Burt
Sailed from New Providence, Bahamas, in company with the *Gipsy* schooner, but when the latter sprang a leak soon after leaving it was decided that they should return to Nassau. At 4 o'clock that afternoon she anchored, using the only bower anchor available, the small bower having been slipped and left on a buoy that morning, a small, spare anchor being used in its place. A boat was hoisted out to recover the anchor and Lieutenant Burt went ashore to speak to the Governor. A local pilot then came onboard, to assist the Master in shifting the schooner to a better berth as they were on foul ground. As they veered the anchor cable, the rope became snagged on rocks and parted. With the spare anchor unable to hold her, sail was ordered to be set, and an attempt made to wear the schooner. As they did so the mainsail sheet unrove, and before control could be regained, she struck a rock, which punctured the hull and she rolled over to starboard. The masts were cut away and distress guns fired. Lieutenant Burt hastily returned, but little could be done that night but take off the crew. The following morning, she had sunk up to her gunwales and was abandoned as a wreck.
[TNA: ADM.1/5377]

(23–24) November CLINKER Gun Brig
Northfleet 1804; 178 tons; 80ft × 22.7ft; 12 guns
Lieutenant John Salmon†
Sailed from Portsmouth on 22 November to resume her station off Le Havre as part of the blockading squadron, after which she disappeared and was presumed lost with all hands. There were strong gales that affected the Channel during the next few days, and it was presumed that she was lost at this time. Pay book closed 30 November.
[TNA: ADM.35/2179; www.britishnewspaperarchive.co: Hampshire Chronicle 24 November 1806 p4; Royal Cornwall Gazette 17 January 1807 p4]

9 December ADDER Gun Brig
Topsham 1805; 181 tons; 84ft × 22ft; 12 guns
Lieutenant Molyneaux Shuldham
Part of the blockading squadron off the northern coast of Brittany, she was lying-to off l'Aber-Wrac'h for the night, with the main-topsail against the mast. At 4 o'clock in the morning, the midshipman who was officer of the watch discovered breakers ahead on the lee bow. The brig wore round, but more breakers were seen ahead. The small bower anchor was let go, but within minutes the cable was cut by rocks and the brig soon found herself in breaking surf. She beat over a reef, and finding herself free, let go the best bower anchor, which brought her up in five fathoms. She rode quietly at anchor until daybreak when they found they were just a quarter of a mile from the shore and surrounded by rocks. The jolly boat was hoisted out to sound around the brig, but when it went to investigate a cove nearby was captured. No way could be seen through the rocks to seaward, and at 9.30am, at flood tide, the cable was cut, and with Lieutenant Shuldham at the fore topmast guiding them, the brig carefully steered for the cove. Having run through the network of rocks, the brig was taken into the haven and then run onto the beach, all the crew being taken prisoner. Lieutenant Shuldham spent the next eight years as a prisoner of war, and

although found by a court martial on his release to be blameable for the loss in failing to order the regular use of the lead-line, he was merely admonished to be more careful in his actions in the future.
[TNA.ADM.1/5442]

9 December UNITED BROTHERS Tender
Hired 1803; 143 tons; 4 guns
Lieutenant William MacKenzie†
Engaged in the impress service, the tender was carrying newly-raised men to Plymouth from Bristol and was 12 miles to the south-west of the Lizard when, at first light, a ketch was seen ahead of them. The stranger was lost for a time in the gloom and haze, and then reappeared close on the weather quarter. Lieutenant MacKenzie quickly ordered the vessel to be cleared for action and when the ketch opened fire on her, she was able to reply. A running battle went on for the next 40 minutes, when the Lieutenant was killed and the Master, Francis Hernaman assumed command. After another 40 minutes a second sail was seen, which seemed to be approaching, and which was believed to be another privateer. By now the fore topsail and fore-and-aft mainsail were riddled with holes, and with tackles and halliards shot away she surrendered. Two men were killed and one wounded. Her captor was the *Glaneur* privateer, 14 guns, which took her prize into Perros, Brittany.
[TNA:ADM.1/5443]

17 December NETLEY Gun Brig
Purchased 1798; 177 tons; 86.6ft × 21.8ft; 16 guns
Lieutenant William Carr
Stationed in the West Indies, she was off Guadeloupe, when two vessels were seen at daybreak, which the brig bore up to investigate. The pair were low on the horizon and difficult to identify, and although the *Netley* showed her colours as she closed, there was no response from the strangers. The pair could be made out to be a ship and a brig, with the ship in a 'slovenly condition', with unstowed studding sail booms and lines hanging loose. It was thought they were a French privateer brig with a merchant prize. The *Netley* cleared for action and edged away, the strangers coming around in chase, and as they did so it became clear that the ship was a large frigate. All sail was now made away, with the chasing pair steadily overhauling the *Netley*. When within range, the frigate opened an accurate fire, one shot hitting the hull, others smashing the boats on the booms, killing one man. Further shots went into the rigging and the enemy brig closed on the quarter to join in the action. The *Netley* found she could not effectively reply, as when she engaged, the lee guns could not be used, the ports dipping under water. She struck her flag in surrender, finding her captors to be the French *Thétis*, 44 guns, and the *Sylphe*, 18.

Note: recaptured on 23 September 1809 by the *Blonde*, but not recommissioned.
[TNA:ADM.1/5377]

December BUSY Brig Sloop
Harwich 1797; 336 tons; 96.1ft × 29ft; 16 guns
Commander Richard Keily†
Stationed at Halifax, Nova Scotia, she sailed from that port on 3 December to convoy several ships to the West Indies, but parted company with them the following day, and was not seen again. She was presumed to have foundered with the loss of all hands. Pay book closed 31 December 1806.
[TNA:ADM.1/497; ADM.35/2144]

1807

4 January NAUTILUS Ship Sloop
Milford 1804; 438 tons; 112ft × 29.6ft; 18 guns
Commander Edward Palmer†
Sailed from the Dardanelles bound for Malta with despatches, she was steering between the islands of Kithera and Antikithera, during a dark and stormy night, when at about 4 o'clock in the morning breakers were seen ahead. There was no time for any action to be taken before the ship struck heavily on a reef and started to lift and pound on the rocks. She rapidly filled with water, which soon covered the orlop deck. It was soon clear that the ship could not be saved, but a small boat was hoisted out, with a small number of men, and despite the storm-force winds and high seas, the boat managed to row to the island of Kithera, to summon help. The masts went overboard and most of the crew managed to scramble off the wreck onto the rocks. The survivors on the rocks suffered badly, as there was no shelter, and were constantly being lashed by breaking surf. Local fishing vessels from Kithera went to the wreck, but it was six days before the winds abated enough for them to rescue the survivors, but many had perished from exposure. Fifty-eight men died.
[TNA:ADM.1/5381; Gold: Naval Chronicle vol 23 p481]

23 January FELIX Schooner
Prize 1803; 158 tons; 90.4ft × 22.2ft; 14 guns
Lieutenant Robert Cameron†
Acting as a cartel vessel, to carry released prisoners of war, she embarked the men at Santander, Spain on 19 January, but was unable to sail due to adverse winds. Anchored under the guns of the fort, the Spanish fired at the schooner that evening, evidently to make her leave the port. Despite a heavy sea running and the wind blowing directly into the harbour Lieutenant Cameron felt that with the fort firing at the schooner at regular intervals, he had no choice but to leave. At 8 o'clock

in the morning of 20 January, he weighed anchor, but was unable to make any progress and anchored again at the entrance to the bay, out of the range of the guns, but at the mercy of the sea and wind. That evening she hauled down her cartel flag and hoisted the ensign upside down as a signal of distress, but the weather was such that no vessel could leave the harbour to come to her assistance. On the morning of 21 January, eight of the upper-deck guns were heaved overboard, with some stores, but the upper deck was now a dangerous place, with seas regularly breaking over her. The boat was washed away, as was anything moveable. The third day of her ordeal saw the bulwarks being smashed and the crew had to lash themselves to eyebolts. At midnight, the bowsprit and masts went overboard, and at 2 o'clock in the morning the anchor cables finally parted, and the schooner drove ashore, where she rapidly went to pieces. There were only three survivors from a crew of sixty.
[Annual Register 1807 pp507–08]

23 January ORPHEUS Fifth Rate
Deptford 1780; 689 tons; 126.4ft × 35.2ft; 36 guns
Captain Thomas Briggs

Arriving off Jamaica from England during the evening of 22 January, Captain Briggs decided to try and enter Port Royal that night. His anxiety to do so was occasioned by having only one usable butt of water left after 13 weeks at sea, and the wind was favourable for him to do so. The frigate manoeuvred around the outer reefs and then altered course towards the harbour. As she did so, at about midnight, she struck a reef. More sail was set to try and force the ship over the obstruction, but it was found that she was hard aground. Sail was taken in, topmasts and yards struck, and boats hoisted out to carry out a kedge anchor. The swell was lifting the ship, and she started to pound on the rocks and by 2 o'clock water was reported entering the hold. To lighten her, all the starboard guns and the shot were heaved overboard, but the water continued to gain, and as she beat on the reef, more timbers gave way. The mizzenmast was cut away, followed later by the foremast in further attempts to ease the ship, but by first light the water was up to the main deck, at which the crew were ordered into the boats, and she was abandoned as a wreck. Captain Briggs was reprimanded for failing to call for a pilot before he entered harbour, although this was tempered by the fact that the chart by Heather held onboard did not accurately show the Middle Ground she had struck.
[TNA: ADM.1/5377]

(1/2) February BLENHEIM Third Rate
Woolwich 1761; 1,827 tons; 176.1ft × 49.1ft; 74 guns
Captain Austin Bissell†

In April 1805 Rear Admiral Sir Thomas Troubridge was appointed to the command of the ships and vessels in the Indian Ocean and in April 1806 to the post of Commander-in-Chief at the Cape of Good Hope. After completing operations against Dutch settlements in the Java Sea, in December 1806 he embarked in the *Blenheim*, to sail from Madras for the Cape. When in the vicinity of Rodrigues Island, to the east of Mauritius, a hard gale overtook the little squadron, with winds increasing to hurricane force. The sloop *Harrier* was the last to see the *Blenheim* during the afternoon of 1 February, when she lost sight of her during a heavy squall of rain. For the next two days the area was subjected to extreme weather conditions – the *Harrier* survived the storm, although she lost sails and spars, boats and booms and '… shipped a great sea which filled the waist and waterlogged the brig for some minutes'. It was presumed that the *Blenheim* foundered at this time, with the loss of all onboard.
[TNA: ADM.51/1825]

(1/2) February JAVA Fifth Rate
Prize 1806 (*Maria Reijersbergen*); 850 tons; 32 guns
Captain George Pigot†

In company with the *Blenheim*, she was last seen by the *Harrier* in heavy seas and high winds during the afternoon of 1 February. That night the winds reached hurricane force, and the *Java* was not seen again. She was presumed to have foundered in the storm that night with the loss of all hands.
[TNA: ADM.51/1825]

12 February ATALANTE Brig Sloop
Prize 1797; 310 tons; 99ft × 27.3ft; 16 guns
Lieutenant John Bowker

Ordered to watch the movements of enemy ships in Rochefort, the brig took station to the south-west of the Île de Ré, when at 10 o'clock at night, she ran onto a reef. A heavy surf was running around them, and the rudder was soon knocked off and timber gave way allowing water to flood in. Boats were hoisted out to take out an anchor, the pumps were manned, and spars hoisted overboard to support her. As the sloop was lightened, with stores and ballast being heaved over the side, she lifted and pounded even more, until it became difficult to stand upright on the upper deck. The masts were cut away to try and ease the movement of the brig and distress guns were fired at regular intervals with the ensign hoisted upside down. At daybreak, the *Nile* cutter approached, with the *Penelope* and *Pomone* frigates joining later in the morning, and these lifted off the men, coming under fire from a shore battery as they did so. During the night, two of the boats left the ship without permission; the cutter with twenty-two men embarked made the shore, to be taken prisoner, whilst the jolly boat, with the Gunner and six men, was taken out to sea where they were picked up by a ship

of the blockade. The subsequent court martial into the loss heard that although a French pilot, Jean Legall, was embarked, he was borne in an advisory capacity and was not allowed to direct the ship. The officer of the watch had been the Gunner, John Brockman, who clearly had a low opinion of M Legall, having asked what the pilot was doing on board, if he could not direct the ship's course. Just before the wreck, Legall had advised the Gunner to come about, but Brockman had stubbornly said 'Hold your tongue, don't make such a noise'. He had also ceased heaving the lead-line, although ordered to employ it constantly, and had done himself little good by leaving the ship in the jolly boat without permission. He tried, unsuccessfully, to shift the blame onto Legall and claimed the pilot had told him it would be safe to stand into seven fathoms of water, which was irrelevant, as the Captain's night orders had specifically ordered that the sloop should go into less than 11 fathoms. Brockman was dismissed from his position of Gunner and ordered to serve before the mast as a seaman.
[TNA: ADM.1/5379]

13 February WOODCOCK Schooner
Great Yarmouth 1806; 75 tons; 56.2ft × 18.3ft; 4 guns
Lieutenant Isaac Charles Smith Collett
Laying at anchor off Vila Franca, São Miguel, Azores, in a rising storm, the topmasts and yards were struck, and lower yards trimmed into the wind. At 4 o'clock in the afternoon, at the height of the gale, the best bower anchor cable parted, and she started to drive. The second anchor brought her up occasionally, only to start driving again. An hour later the second cable parted, leaving her adrift. An attempt was made to put some sail on her, a jib being hoisted, and this gave her some control of her movements. Unable to keep the sea, and with water constantly washing over her, she was run ashore in order to save the lives of the crew. Lines were passed to the shore, and all made it to the land before the schooner broke up.
[TNA: ADM.1/5382]

13 February WAGTAIL Schooner
Great Yarmouth 1806; 75 tons; 56.4ft × 18.3ft; 4 guns
Lieutenant William Cullis
The schooner arrived at the anchorage off Vila Franca, Azores, during the morning of 13 February, to anchor near to her sister, the *Woodcock*. As the wind increased, she witnessed the other schooner part her cables and drive ashore. Her own cables held until 8 o'clock that evening, when both parted in quick succession, and with waves breaking over her, she drove ashore near the wreck of the *Woodcock*. One man was lost, but all the remainder made the shore.
[TNA: ADM.1/5382]

14 February AJAX Third Rate
Rotherhithe 1798; 1,953 tons; 182.5ft × 49.6ft; 74 guns
Captain Henry Blackwood
Part of the force sent to the northern Aegean under Admiral Duckworth to confront the Turks, who it was feared were about to declare war on Russia, the *Ajax* was laying at anchor off the island of Tenedos (Bozcaada). At 9 o'clock in the evening, a cry of fire was raised from aft, the seat of the blaze seeming to be the after cockpit. The ship beat to quarters, and the crew mustered to fight the fire, but thick smoke spread through the ship, driving the men back. After an hour, flames burst up the main hatchway, at which men started to leave the ship, jumping overboard. The fire had prevented the boats being hoisted out, apart from the jolly boat, and the ship's company were forced to cling to spars and drifting wood and await the arrival of boats from ships in company. The ship burned throughout the night until she drifted inshore and ran aground on the island, blowing up with a tremendous explosion at about 5 o'clock in the morning. About 150 men died. Various theories were advanced as to the cause, the most likely being a spark falling into some hay stowed in the cockpit, although spontaneous combustion of some coal held onboard was also suggested.
[TNA: ADM.1/5380]

16 February JACKDAW Schooner
Newcastle 1806; 76 tons; 56.2ft × 18.3ft; 4 guns
Lieutenant Nathaniel Brice
Despatched by Admiral Collingwood to take letters to England from the Mediterranean, the schooner steered north along the coast of Portugal. At daybreak on 15 February, in the vicinity of 41.20N 10.30W, three vessels were sighted, which later altered towards her, the largest of which could be seen to be a lateen-rigged vessel. This soon outpaced the others, and a stern chase developed, the *Jackdaw* holding her own through the day, spreading every sail she had including studding sails. The following morning the lateen-rigged stranger was still in chase, about five miles astern and used sweeps to narrow the gap. At 9 o'clock the *Jackdaw* fired a shot at the stranger, who ignored the challenge and continued to close at a fast pace, moving to her quarter. About five or six shots were fired by the schooner, before the stranger took up a raking position on her quarter and returned the fire, hoisting Spanish colours as she did so. Lieutenant Brice and the Mate, John Edwards, then consulted and convinced each other that any resistance would be useless, having only two guns mounted and only seventeen men borne. They therefore surrendered the schooner. After being taken prisoner, some of the crew became drunk and abusive, which later led to charges by Brice and Edwards of insubordination. This seems to have led two of the crew to testify against their

officers, accusing them of too readily surrendering the schooner. Lieutenant Brice was found guilty of giving up his ship without offering a fight, and Mr Edwards was found guilty of discouraging his Captain to fight. Both were dismissed the service, but on appeal were later reinstated. Two of the crew, John Driscoll and John Ward, were found guilty of misconduct in getting drunk after the action and were sentenced to lose all pay due.

Note: recaptured the following day by the *Minerva*.
[TNA: ADM.1/5381]

Storm of 18/19 February 1807

The south coast of England was struck by a storm during the early hours of 18 February, with high winds accompanied by sleet and snow, the poor weather continuing for some days. The south-east of the country was the worst affected, with dozens of ships lost or forced from their anchors, and the shoreline of Kent was reported to be strewn with wreckage and bodies.

> The day and evening of Tuesday last was marked by a peculiar and uncommon mildness of the atmosphere, the morning of Wednesday by a storm of wind and snow, as violent and severe as any in the most wintry period ... the whole of the Coast from the Nore to South Foreland, from its exposed situation appears to have suffered most, on this coast several vessels have been wrecked ... there are 13 sail of vessels driven on shore on the beach from Deal to Walmer, eight vessels in the Downs have cut away their masts ...
> (*Kentish Gazette* 20 February 1807)

The storm was responsible for numerous marine casualties, including many of the small vessels involved in blockading the northern coast of France.

18 February GRIPER Gun Brig
King's Lynn 1804; 179 tons; 80.2ft × 22.7ft; 12 guns
Lieutenant Edward Morris†

After sailing from the Downs anchorage on 21 January to take up her station on the French-controlled coast near the port of Ostend, the brig disappeared and was presumed to have been lost with all hands, probably during the storm.
[TNA: ADM.35/2255; www.britishnewspaperarchive.co: *Kentish Gazette* 23 January 1807 p4; *Steel's Navy List*]

18 February INVETERATE Gun Brig
Bridport 1805; 182 tons; 84ft × 22.2ft; 12 guns
Lieutenant George Newton

Cruising off Étaples, northern France, during the early hours of the morning the wind steadily increased and by mid-morning the brig found herself in a violent storm. Several sails were split and when all efforts to furl others failed, they were cut loose or allowed to blow away. By nightfall, under storm staysails only, she found herself being carried further inshore and could make little ground to seaward. The best bower anchor was let go, but this failed to bring her up, although the release of the second bower did hold her. However, they discovered that the brig was driving, and the sheet anchor was let go, which held her for a time, before she began to drive once more. With no prospect of making an escape to sea, and getting closer to the shore all the time, it was judged prudent to cut cables and run the brig ashore to save lives. Just before midnight she went ashore near St Valéry-en-Caux. Four men were drowned in the struggle to gain the beach from the wreck.
[TNA: ADM.1/5442]

18 February MAGPIE Schooner
Newcastle 1806; 76 tons; 56.2ft × 18.3ft; 4 guns
Lieutenant Edward Johnson

Sailed from Plymouth on 15 February, she found herself caught in the storm which swept the English Channel. During 17 February in strong winds and rains, she shortened sail to storm staysails and struck her topmasts. That night the wind increased to storm force, and she was compelled to run before the wind under bare poles. Morning showed the coast of Brittany, and an attempt was made to anchor off les Sept Îles, but this proved impossible, and she eventually ran into a sheltered bay near Perros. Having anchored, she found herself aground and troops could be seen on the shore. When boats full of armed troops approached, she had little choice but to surrender.
[TNA: ADM.1/5443]

18 February PROSPERO Bomb Vessel
Purchased 1804 (*Albion*); 400 tons; 107ft × 30.5ft; 8 guns
Commander William King

Sailed from the Downs anchorage on 14 February, she was caught in the storm and driven inshore and stranded near Dieppe with the loss of seven of the crew.
[www.britishnewspaperarchive.co: *Morning Post* 14 March 1807 p4]

18 February SPEEDWELL Gun Brig
Purchased 1780; 193 tons; 75.3ft × 25.10ft; 14 guns
Lieutenant William Robertson†

Sailed on 29 January from off Deal to take up blockading duties off Dieppe, she disappeared and was presumed to have foundered, with no survivors. Pay book closed end-January.
[*Steel's Navy List*; TNA: ADM.35/3144]

19 February IGNITION Fire Vessel
Purchase 1804 (*Jeany*); 130 tons; 69.3ft × 2.1ft.
Lieutenant Philip Griffin†
Sailed from the Downs 14 February, she was reported to have been wrecked on the French coast near Dieppe, with just four survivors.
[www.britishnewspaperarchive.co: Morning Post 14 March 1807 p4]

★ ★ ★

4 March BLANCHE Fifth Rate
Prize 1804 (*Amfitrite*); 1,037 tons; 150.1ft × 39.11ft; 38 guns
Captain Sir Thomas Lavie
Sailed from Spithead on 3 March to join the squadron of Sir James Saumarez off Ushant. By sunset that night, the wind was increasing in strength and the frigate shortened sail to reefed topsails and foresail. Captain Lavie intended to close the French coast and then alter course to take the ship six leagues (18 miles) west of Ushant. At 11 o'clock that evening, having run the distance, the foresail was ordered to be taken in and the ship prepared to tack, but the ship had not completed the manoeuvre when breakers were seen ahead and then she struck the ground, beating over an obstruction. The ship wore round and let go both bower anchors, being surrounded by rocks and breaking surf. An inspection of the well found she was making water. The masts were cut away, which eased the movement of the ship, and she rode quietly for some time, which raised hopes of their escaping. In the early hours of the morning, however, she tailed onto a reef, and started to strike violently. The anchor cables were cut by the rocks and the ship pounded and rolled over onto the rocks, breaking up as she did, sweeping several men into the sea. The survivors remained on board until first light, when they started to scramble ashore. They were taken prisoner, although some of those that had reached the shore died of exposure having become extremely drunk. About forty-two men died in all. The ship had been wrecked near l'Aber-Wrac'h, which was several miles to the east of where they had believed themselves to be. The blame for this was placed on the extensive ironwork in the ship, which had iron knees and standards supporting the poop and quarterdeck. In addition, a large quantity of small arms had been stowed between the beams under the poop, all of which would have fatally affected the compasses held on board.
[TNA: ADM.1/5443]

5 March PIGMY Gun Brig
Purchased 1806 (*Ranger*); 217 tons; 79ft × 26ft; 14 guns
Lieutenant George Montagu Higginson
Ordered to the Île de Ré to observe the movements of a French squadron at Rochefort, she arrived during the evening of 4 March to find the *Pomone* frigate already on station. The brig was short-manned, and with the Master ill in his bed, Lieutenant Higginson had been constantly on deck for several days and was exhausted. A request to the *Pomone* for permission to anchor for night was refused, so the brig reduced sail and lay-to for the night off the Île d'Oleron in the Pertuis d'Antioche. At 3.30am, in a dark and cold morning with strong winds and frequent squalls, she went aground on the island. The brig touched the ground gently at first, then after trailing through the shallows for several minutes, came to a shuddering halt. When Lieutenant Higginson came on deck, he found the brig heeling over to port, the sails shaking in the wind. The yards were braced around and an attempt made to sail off, but after bouncing over the ground for two or three minutes, she again stopped and heeled over to port. All sail was taken in and the boats hoisted out, but the tide was on the ebb, and little could be done before she rolled over onto her beam ends and bilged. Daylight revealed their position to a nearby fort, which opened fire, several shots striking her hull. Unable to escape, all the crew were ferried ashore by the boats to be taken prisoner. After being held as a prisoner of war for seven years, Higginson was court-martialled for the loss and was admonished to be more circumspect in the future, having placed too much faith in the pilot, and not going on deck when warned by the watch on deck that the bearings of the shore lights showed they were in danger.
[TNA: ADM.1/5443]

9 March CRAFTY Schooner
Prize 1803 (*Renard*); 146 tons; 76.5ft × 19.10ft; 12 guns
Lieutenant Richard Spencer
Bound for England with despatches, the schooner sailed from Gibraltar on 7 March. The gun brig *Confounder* was ordered to accompany her clear of the Straits, but the pair did not co-ordinate their actions, consequently the *Crafty* carried too much sail, the *Confounder* too little, and the pair soon became separated. The schooner stood over towards the Barbary coast and the following day anchored in a small bay to the north of Tetuan to await a favourable wind. During the afternoon of 9 March, three lateen-rigged vessels were seen off the bay heading towards the schooner. Fearing that they were hostile, she cleared for action and when they closed, she cut her anchor cables and moved out to meet her opponents, which were the Spanish feluccas *Generalissimo*, 4 guns, *Huron*, 4, and *Pastora*, 4. A brisk action commenced, until both fore and main yards were shot away, the wreckage falling over the starboard side. Unable to manoeuvre, she could not prevent one of the feluccas closing her stern and hooking a grapnel on to the rudder pendant, which held her fast. The other two ran alongside, one on the bow and the other on the

quarter, and both entered a large number of boarders. The initial attack was repulsed, but a second attempt succeeded, and Lieutenant Spencer surrendered. Three men were killed and fourteen wounded. Lieutenant Spencer was subsequently reprimanded for failing to make greater efforts to keep company with the *Confounder*, and for staying too long at anchor in the bay.
[TNA: ADM.1/5380]

18 March PIKE Schooner
Bermuda 1804; 85 tons; 58ft × 18.6ft; 4 guns
Lieutenant John Otley

Sailed from Jamaica on 10 March with despatches and raised the land around Tiburon, Haiti. four days later. That same day a schooner was seen, which closed her, but after a brief exchange of fire, sheered off and stood into the land. The following day a second schooner was seen, which again suffered an exchange of fire before retiring, and was seen to join her opponent of the previous day, which was still loitering some way off. The *Pike* made all sail away, the pair following her in chase, but the British schooner outpaced them. The two persisted however, and in the early hours of 17 March the larger of the pair could be seen astern, slowly gaining on the *Pike*. The chase went on through the day, until by dusk the stranger was in gunshot range. There was sporadic firing between the pair during the night, employing bow- and stern-chase guns. At daylight on 18 March her opponent was within musket-shot range and a mutual exchange of fire commenced. The action lasted 45 minutes, until the enemy vessel took up a raking position aft, and with the rigging in pieces, the gaff shot away, all the masts and yards shot through, and with the second schooner closing fast, Lieutenant Otley surrendered, finding his captor was a French privateer, the *Impérial*, 8 guns. One man killed and five wounded. Lieutenant Otley complained that some of the crew, who had been put on board only shortly before the schooner sailed, had left their quarters during the action, and had to be forced back, the Bosun using a boarding pike to drive one man back into his place. The court-martial enquiry felt that the action could have been better conducted, and Lieutenant Otley was warned to be more circumspect in the future, although it was recognised that the crew were raw and inexperienced.

Note: recaptured on September 1808 by the *Moselle*.
[TNA: ADM.1/5381]

29 March SAINT LUCIA Gun Brig
Prize 1803 (*Enfant Prodigue*); 183 tons; 85.6ft × 23ft; 14 guns
Commander Charles Gordon

At daylight, then being off the western end of Guadeloupe, two French schooners were seen close inshore. Commander Gordon determined to attack them, and by 7am was within a quarter of a mile of his enemy. The French pair got under way as he approached, taking advantage of a fresh breeze from the land. Now within gunshot range, the *St Lucia* fired a broadside, but in doing so, three of the 18-pounder carronades pulled the breeching bolts out of the side timbers, rendering them useless. When the fourth broadside was fired, another carronade was disabled in a similar manner. The French schooners wore round, and Commander Gordon matched their move, happy to engage with the other broadside. However, this also proved disastrous, as two of the carronades were put out of action when the timbers gave way, the bulwarks caving in with the recoil. Now outgunned, she continued the action for another two hours, until the pair closed to board her, at which the brig surrendered. Her opponents proved to be the *Vengeance*, 12 guns, and the *Friponne*, 5. Seven men killed and eight wounded.
[TNA: ADM.1/5381]

31 March FERRETER Gun Brig
Blackwall 1801; 184 tons; 80.1ft × 23ft; 12 guns
Lieutenant Henry Weir

Part of the force in the North Sea ordered to blockade the River Ems, she anchored close inshore at the entrance to the river, near the King's Buoy, to ride out a snowstorm. In the morning, the snow cleared, revealing seven sloop-rigged gunboats under Dutch colours closing her. The brig was hastily cleared for action, cutting her anchor cables, and fired a broadside at her opponents, but the range was too great, the shot from her carronades falling short. A sharp action commenced, with the gunboats keeping their range, and were able to shoot her rigging to pieces and the sails shot through so much they resembled a sieve. When she grounded, two of the gunboats ran alongside to board the brig, at which she surrendered. With her opponents firing high, into the rigging, there were no casualties. Lieutenant Weir reported that the crew had behaved well during the action, except for the German pilot, who after warning that she would take the ground, retired below, out of the action.
[TNA: ADM.1/5380]

April MOUCHERON Brig Sloop
Prize 1801; 286 tons; 93ft × 26.7ft; 16 guns
Commander James Hawes†

Sent from England with despatches for Admiral Lord Collingwood in the Mediterranean, the sloop was reported to have arrived at Malta on 10 February. She subsequently sailed to join the main fleet in the Dardanelles but was not seen again. Her pay books were closed end-April 1807
[TNA: ADM.35/2317; www.britishnewspaperarchive.co: Hampshire Chronicle 13 April 1807 p3; Morning Chronicle 15 October 1807 p2]

16 May DAUNTLESS Ship Sloop
Hull 1805; 427 tons; 117.4ft × 28.2ft; 20 guns
Commander Christopher Strachey
Part of the British Baltic squadron that was attempting to support the Prussian garrison at Danzig (Gdansk), during the siege of the place by the French army. The *Dauntless* tried to break the siege and supply the garrison with 600 barrels of gunpowder. She ran up the river Vistula engaging enemy shore positions as she did so. As the river narrowed and turned, manoeuvring became more difficult, and as the wind dropped, she found herself being raked by shore batteries. Her halliards were shot away and she drifted inshore and ran onto a sandbank off Holm Island, where she surrendered
[TNA: ADM.1/5442; www.britishnewspaperarchive.co: Sun (London) 16 June 1807 p2]

30 May JACKAL Gun Brig
Blackwall 1801; 186 tons; 80ft × 23.1ft; 12 guns
Lieutenant Charles Stewart
Cruising in the southern North Sea, a French lugger privateer was sighted on 29 May and the *Jackal* chased her towards the Dutch coast. After a long chase, the lugger finally escaped into Dunkirk that evening. By now the weather was worsening, with large black clouds looming to the north-east, and at 10.30pm the brig altered around to the north, intending to take shelter in the Downs anchorage. By midnight it was blowing a strong gale with heavy rain, and when the leadsman reported the water shoaling, she wore round to find deeper water. Thirty minutes later, with no warning, she took the ground. The rudder was unshipped immediately, and the brig swung round beam-on to the wind and sea before coming to a halt, the surf breaking over them. All believed themselves to be on the Goodwin Sands, so decided to pump constantly to keep her free of water and await the dawn. They were therefore astonished at daybreak to discover themselves on the French coast, about three miles from Calais. The brig had pounded on the ground during the night, which had opened several leaks, and at 5 o'clock that morning, with high water, she filled and sank, the crew taking to the rigging. Three hours later the water had ebbed sufficiently for them to climb out of the rigging and go ashore, where they were taken prisoner by waiting troops.
[TNA: ADM.1/5443]

13 August CASSANDRA Cutter
Bermuda 1806; 111 tons; 68.2ft × 20.4ft; 10 guns
Lieutenant George le Blanc
Ordered to carry despatches to the squadron blockading the French port of Bordeaux, she joined the *Naiad* frigate during the morning. Later that day Lieutenant le Blanc left the cutter to deliver the despatches, with the crew busy shortening sail. The weather was poor, with dank, drizzling rain and a heavy swell, but little wind. As sail was being reduced, she was struck by a squall which rolled her over onto her beam-ends. Sails were let fly and the helm put over, and despite having shipped a large amount of water, she started to right herself. However, she was then struck by another gust of wind, which heeled her over again, and the belly of the mainsail filled with water, which capsized her completely. She sank rapidly, stern first. Eleven men, one woman and her child were drowned.
[TNA: ADM.1/5383]

(17–19) August BACCHUS Cutter
Bermuda 1806; 111 tons; 68.2ft × 20.4ft; 10 guns
Lieutenant George Skinner[†]
Having escorted a packet vessel from the island of Tortola to the northwards, she subsequently disappeared and was presumed to have foundered with the loss of all hands. A hurricane affected the area in mid-August, and it was thought likely to have been responsible for her loss.
[TNA: ADM.1/328]

10 September EXPLOSION Bomb Vessel
Purchased 1797 (*Gloster*); 368 tons; 99.9ft × 28.10ft; 6 guns
Commander Edward Ellicot
Sailed from Great Yarmouth on 3 September to carry despatches to Admiral Russel's squadron off the German coast. She initially steered south to gain a landfall, which was achieved on the Dutch coast at 9 o'clock the following morning. Just two hours later she ran aground on the Haak sands off the Texel, but by spreading more sail, she was forced over the obstruction. Course was set for Heligoland, which was sighted two days later. As the bomb vessel steered towards the anchorage, she struck the ground. Boats were hoisted out and together with the assistance of boats from the fleet, two hours later she was hauled free. The groundings had taken their toll, and she was found to be making water. Taken into the anchorage by a local pilot, pumping and bailing commenced, and stores and provisions were taken off. She could not be cleared of water and after off-loading all her stores, she was deliberately run aground on a beach on Sandy Island (Dűne) and abandoned as a wreck. The performance of the pilot, John Parkinson, came in for considerable criticism. The running onto the Haak sands he blamed on exhaustion, having been up all the previous night. The Heligoland grounding was through his admitted ignorance of the extent of the local reefs. He was sentenced to serve six months in the Marshalsea Prison, be mulcted of all pay due and ordered never to serve as a pilot in a Royal Navy ship again.
[TNA: ADM.1/5383]

15 September BARBARA Schooner
Bermuda 1806; 111 tons; 68.2ft × 20.4ft; 10 guns
Lieutenant Edward D'Arcy

Returning to Demerara from Devil's Island, having watered, the schooner was steering along the coast of Guiana when, on 14 September, a brig was sighted which altered course towards her. Recognition signals not being answered, she assumed the stranger to be a French privateer and made sail away and successfully kept her distance until nightfall. The following morning the brig was still in sight, some nine miles to windward and still in chase. When it became clear that she could not escape, the *Barbara* altered towards the brig, until by 3 o'clock in the afternoon the pair were within gunshot of each other. The schooner fired into the brig, which returned the fire and a sharp contest of 30 minutes followed, until the brig ran her bowsprit over the larboard quarter of the *Barbara* and entered a large number of boarders. A short struggle followed before she surrendered, her captor being the *Général Ernouf*, 14 guns. Four men killed and six wounded, two of whom died later of their wounds. The schooner was taken into Cayenne.

Note: recaptured on 17 July 1808 by the *Guerriére*.
[TNA:ADM.1/ 5385]

(1–5) September ELIZABETH Schooner
Prize 1805 (*Elizabet*); 110 tons; 10 guns
Lieutenant John Sedley†

Stationed in the Leeward Islands, the schooner disappeared and was presumed to have been lost with all hands. A hurricane passed through the area during the first days of September and was believed likely to have been responsible for her loss.
[TNA:ADM.1/328]

(1–5) September MARIA Schooner
Prize 1805 (*Constanze*); 130 tons; 72ft × 20.1ft; 12 guns
Lieutenant John Henderson†

As with *Elizabeth* (see above), stationed in the Leeward Islands, and disappeared at this time. Presumed to have foundered in the hurricane of early September and lost with all hands.
[TNA:ADM.1/328]

16 October PERT Brig Sloop
Prize 1804 (*Bonaparte*); 206 tons; 84.6ft × 23ft; 14 guns
Commander Donald Campbell

Cruising off the coast of what is now Venezuela, on 14 October she sighted and chased a ship. The sloop quickly overhauled the ship off the island of Margarita and forced her to surrender. The ship proved to be a Spanish packet ship, the *Alarma*, 40 days out from Ferrol, for the Spanish Main and Havana. In an effort to save the despatches she carried, a boat had been sent to the island, but this was observed, and Commander Campbell sent a boat in pursuit to recover the letters. The crew of the prize was put into boats and under a flag of truce was sent to the town of Cumana, the *Pert* anchoring off Margarita Island to await the return of her boat. The weather became squally, with a steadily rising wind and swell. By the morning of 16 October, it was blowing a full gale, shifting to the south as it increased in strength. At noon, the small bower anchor cable parted, and 10 minutes later the best bower cable gave way, and she was carried inshore onto the island, running onto rocks which bilged her. The brig swung broadside-on to the sea, and careened over, having 9ft of water in the hold in a few minutes. The crew hastily left the sloop as it built up, struggling through the surf to the island. Ten men were lost. The survivors were taken off by the prize packet the following morning when the weather abated.
[TNA:ADM.1/5383]

26 October SUBTLE Schooner
Prize 1806 (*Imperiale*); 102 tons; 8 guns
Lieutenant William Dowers

Bound for Barbados from the Capes of Delaware, Lieutenant Dowers decided to head for Bermuda, as the schooner was short of water and an annoying leak had developed in the bread room. She stood into St George's Channel, sounding constantly during the night of 25 October. At 1 o'clock in the morning she touched the ground, hitting gently at first and then striking violently, swinging bodily onto a reef of sunken rocks. A boat was hoisted out which found deep water nearby and an anchor was laid out to heave her off, shot and stores being heaved overboard to lighten her. However, she continued to pound heavily on the ground and within three minutes the sternpost gave way allowing water to flood in. The masts were cut away but soon afterwards she fell over onto her beam-ends. The schooner had run aground on a reef eight miles north-north-west of Somerset Island, which was 20 miles from where they believed themselves to be. A strong current was blamed for the error.
[TNA:ADM.1/5384]

11 November LEVERET Brig Sloop
Dover 1806; 384 tons; 100ft × 30.7ft; 18 guns
Commander Richard James Lawrence O'Connor

Sailed from the Nore for the Downs anchorage on 10 November in company with the *Waldemar*, a captured Danish ship. The weather was poor as the pair beat out into the North Sea, and the *Waldemar* decided to anchor for the night near the Long Sands. The *Leveret* prepared to do the same but struck the ground before she could do so. The rudder was knocked off as she beat over the sands, striking regularly, until she found herself floating

free in seven fathoms, and she quickly anchored. Guns and stores were heaved overboard, distress guns were fired and pumps manned. The morning saw the wind still strong and a high sea running. The anchor cables were cut, and she tried to set sail and stand towards vessels seen to the north-east, near the Essex shore. At 11 o'clock she passed the Sunk light vessel, and two hours later a fishing smack, the *Samuel* of Ipswich, came alongside. The smack took the brig in tow and headed towards the shore, but it was found to be an increasingly difficult task, as the sloop was settling, and pumping and bailing could not clear the water. The boats were hoisted out to shift the crew to the *Samuel*, which took them into nearby Harwich, the sloop foundering later that day. Commander O'Connor was later court-martialled not only for the loss of the sloop but also for failing to assist another ship aground on the sands and in distress at the same time as the *Leveret*. He was acquitted of blame on both charges.
[TNA:ADM.1/5384]

11 November **WILLIAM** Store Ship
Purchased 1798; 374 tons; 99.8ft × 29.1ft; 4 guns
Master John Foxten
Having sailed from Halifax, in poor weather she went ashore near Cape Canso, Nova Scotia. It was initially hoped that she could be saved, and the sloop *Emulous* and craft from the dockyard were sent to her assistance. With their help she was re-floated on the 15th, with minimal damage. That same night however, in high winds she was driven back onto the rocks where she bilged.
[TNA:ADM.1/497]

17 November **FIREFLY** Schooner
Prize 1803 (*Poisson Volant*); 150 tons; 78.8ft × 21.7ft;
12 guns
Lieutenant Thomas Price†
Stationed at Jamaica, she was carrying despatches to Curaçao, but in gale force winds was driven onto a reef off the island and wrecked. The Surgeon and three men were the only survivors.
[TNA:ADM.1/257]

21 November **BOLINA** Brig Tender
Hired 1803; 181 tons; 6 guns
Lieutenant Edward Claributt
Ordered to Liverpool, she sailed from Plymouth during the afternoon of 20 November in poor weather, which deteriorated as she headed into the Bristol Channel. At about midnight she was struck by a strong squall which almost rolled her over. She shortened sail to double-reefed topsails and staysails. By 2 o'clock in the morning the wind was blowing at gale force, with a very heavy sea, and at 3am it began snowing. When the wind backed to the north-north-west, she turned into the land, which was sighted at daybreak. As she did so she shipped a particularly heavy sea, which swept a Marine overboard who was drowned. Now in sight of Padstow, north Cornwall, she stood to the south under storm sails, with another heavy sea hitting her at about 1.30 in the afternoon, which carried away the best bower anchor and the cathead. It became clear that she could not weather the Man and His Man rocks, and with the brig in a poor condition, the head was put to the southward, and she was deliberately run ashore on a sandy beach near Perranporth.
[TNA:ADM.1/5385]

28 November **BOREAS** Sixth Rate
Great Yarmouth 1806; 526 tons; 118ft × 31.7ft; 22 guns
Captain Robert Scott†
Approaching the island of Guernsey from the west, she manoeuvred in strong northerly winds to secure a pilot boat alongside, which had been blown offshore. When attempting to tack away from the land she struck a submerged rock, part of les Hanois reef. After hanging on the obstruction for some time, she came free, but found herself swinging round and then struck again and this time was held fast. The pilot boat promptly cut the painter and made off, leaving the ship to its fate. Sail was taken in and the pumps manned to stem the water which gushed into the hold. Boats were hoisted out and spars and yards were lowered over the side to act as shores, as the ship started heeling over on the ebbing tide. The task of shoring proved difficult in the heavy seas and with no solid bottom for the spars. One of the masts was cut away at about 7 o'clock that evening which helped for a while in keeping her upright. At 11 o'clock Captain Scott ordered the crew to abandon ship, and they started to take to the boats, landing at Hanois Point. The ship was heeling over and settling, the crew leaving the pumps to take refuge in the rigging. The boats that had gone to the shore returned to the ship but found it difficult to get alongside in the high seas. By 5am the ship had disappeared beneath the water, leaving the masts remaining above the waves. Several vessels were despatched by Admiral Saumarez and at daylight thirty men were taken off the wreck. Over 100 men lost their lives – the numbers are somewhat obscure, as it was known that at least twenty-six of the survivors took the opportunity to desert.
[TNA:ADM.1/5384]

29 December **ANSON** Fifth Rate
Plymouth 1781; 1,375 tons; 159.6ft × 44.5ft; 44 guns
Captain Charles Lydiard†
The frigate sailed from Plymouth on 24 December to take station with the blockading squadron off Brest but was baffled by contrary winds and unable to make

ground to the west. During 27 December they raised the Île de Batz off the northern coast of Brittany, but with the wind increasing to gale force, the following day Captain Lydiard decided to return to port until the weather was more favourable. During the afternoon land was sighted, but not positively identified. The frigate wore round but soon after land was again seen ahead, which was recognised as the Lizard; they now realised that were embayed in Mount's Bay. She attempted to tack, but was unable to clear the land, so anchored at 5pm in 25 fathoms. The wind and sea increased, and at 4 o'clock in the morning, the anchor cable parted. The small bower anchor was let go, which successfully brought her up and held her until 8 o'clock, when it too parted. It was decided that in order to save lives, the frigate should be run ashore in a controlled manner, so the fore topsail was set and she was run towards a beach at Loe Bar, about three miles from Helston. As she struck the ground, the ship swung broadside-on to the beach and the mainmast went by the board, which was used by many to reach the shore. The seas were beating over the wreck constantly, and despite all the efforts of those onshore, many men drowned in their attempts to reach safety, including Captain Lydiard. By 3 o'clock in the afternoon the frigate had gone to pieces. About 126 men were believed to have been lost.
[TNA: ADM.1/5385: www.britishnewspaperarchive. co:Gloucester Journal 18 January 1808]

1808

11 January LORD KEITH Cutter
Hired 1804 (*Active*); 72 tons; 10 guns
Lieutenant Mitchell Roberts
Blown from her anchors when stationed off Heligoland, and driven by strong winds to the south, she took shelter in the harbour of Cuxhaven, where all the crew were taken prisoner, except her commander, who happened to be on shore on Heligoland at the time.
[www.britishnewspaperarchive.co: Morning Chronicle 28 January 1808 p4]

14 January SPARKLER Gun Brig
Brightlingsea 1804; 179 tons; 80.3ft × 22.7ft; 12 guns
Lieutenant James Samuel Aked Dennis
Ordered from Great Yarmouth to cruise off the Dutch coast, she took up her station between Texel and Terschelling Islands. A heavy gale commenced on 9 January, which continued until 12 January, when the wind shifted to the north-north-west, setting her further inshore. At 1.30 in the morning, she struck the ground to the south-west of Terschelling. An attempt was made to hoist out a boat, but it was immediately swamped, and a second attempt with the jolly boat astern saw it

washed away into the night. Within 45 minutes she was completely flooded, and the crew was forced to take to the rigging to save their lives. The brig settled into the sands and by morning only the masts remained above the water. Local fishermen came to their aid and took off the survivors, who were exhausted and suffering from frostbite. Fourteen men died.
[TNA: ADM.1/5387]

19 January FLORA Fifth Rate
Deptford 1780; 869 tons; 137ft × 38ft; 36 guns
Captain Loftus Otway Bland
Having escorted a cartel vessel with released prisoners to Holland, the frigate remained off the Dutch coast, closing the Texel on 17 January to reconnoitre the ships in the Maasdiep. That completed, she opened the shore again and was informed by the Dutch pilot of an American merchant ship that the cartel ship was now at Harlingen, waiting to return to Great Yarmouth. The frigate ran north along the coast, to wait off the port. At noon on 18 January, as she steered north-east off the island of Terschelling under all sail, she ran aground. Sail was taken in, topmasts were struck, and spare yards were lowered over the side to act as shores. A boat was hoisted out to take out the stream anchor with the intention of hauling her off at high tide. As she waited, stores and shot were heaved overboard to lighten her. At 9 o'clock that evening, on the high tide, they commenced heaving in on the anchor cable, and the ship lifted and moved and came off the sandbank, to float in deep water. As she freed herself, the rudder became unshipped, and several leaks became evident. Pumping and baling commenced, and a sail was slung under the hull to stem the inrush, but the water steadily gained on them. Guns and heavy stores were heaved overboard, but the frigate slowly settled in the water. The main- and mizzenmasts were cut away, and a course was steered for the shore. The following morning, in black and threatening weather, she was run ashore on Schelling Strand, all sail being set on the foremast in an effort to force her well up onto the beach. The crew left the ship in boats, rafts or clinging to spars, the water being bitterly cold, snow beginning to fall as they did so. Nine men died in the attempt. Captain Bland was cleared of any blame for the loss but criticised for failing to order the constant use of the lead-line. The pilots were admonished to have more care in the future, and not place such implicit confidence in their knowledge of the shoreline.
[TNA: ADM.1/5389]

24 January CARRIER Cutter
Purchased 1805 (*Frisk*); 54 tons; 47.8ft × 17.2ft; 10 guns
Lieutenant William Milne
Sailed from Spithead on 23 January, bound for Great Yarmouth, by 8 o'clock that evening she was abreast of

Beachy Head. Sail was reduced for the night, Lieutenant Milne leaving orders to be called when Dungeness Light was seen, or at 11pm, whichever was soonest. At 2 o'clock in the morning Milne was woken with the news that Dungeness Light was visible – he was understandably annoyed at not being called earlier, but worse was to follow, as when he came on deck, he realised that the light in sight could not possibly be Dungeness. The cutter was luffed, but she struck the ground, then swung to lie beam-on to the sea and heeled over onto her side in the surf. A boat was hoisted out to carry out an anchor, but all attempts to kedge her off proved fruitless, the tide being on the ebb. By daylight it became clear that she was on the French shore, near Étaples and nearby shore batteries opened fire on her as the crew left the cutter to gain the shore and safety. An attempt was made to set her on fire, but the flames went out and she was taken by French troops. After spending six years as a prisoner of war, Lieutenant Milne was cleared of blame for the loss at his court martial. It emerged that the pilot, John Hughes, who had the watch on deck, had left the upper deck, claiming he felt ill, handing over to the Master's Mate, William Williams. The cutter steered on through the night, without the Captain being called as he had ordered and Williams mistaking the light at Boulogne for Dungeness. The Master's Mate was blamed for the loss, although he had died in captivity in France and was unable to defend himself. Pilot John Hughes was also judged partly to blame, but as he had served so long as a prisoner of war, and 'showed signs of madness', he was only admonished.
[TNA:ADM.1/5443]

31 January DELIGHT Brig Sloop
Fremington 1806; 285 tons; 93ft x 26.6ft; 16 guns
Commander Philip Cosby Handfield†
Part of the British squadron based at Palermo, when intelligence was received that the French had captured four Sicilian gunboats and taken them to Reggio de Calabria. Sail was made and the sloop steered for that port and when she arrived, the gunboats were sighted in the harbour. She cleared for action and also prepared an anchor for letting go. As she ran towards the gunboats under mainsail and jib, she found a strong current was affecting her, setting the brig further inshore than expected. On sounding, 35 fathoms were found, but soon after this she struck the ground. An anchor was let go and the boats launched to lay out a second anchor to pull her off, the boats of the *Glatton* coming to her aid, with Captain Thomas Seccombe joining from that ship. They were now coming under an increasingly heavy fire from the shore, using small arms as well as cannon fire. She returned the fire, using grape and canister shot, but casualties started to mount, with Commander Handfield being killed and Captain Seccombe severely wounded. The crew continued to try and shift her, but she would not move, and they were under constant fire from the shore. To save further lives, the crew were ordered into the boats and the flag was struck, but not all had left before the French came on board to take possession.
[TNA:ADM.1/5385]

31 January LEDA Fifth Rate
Chatham 1800; 1,071 tons; 150.2ft x 39.11ft; 38 guns
Captain Robert Honeyman
Sailed from Cork on 24 January to cruise in the western approaches to the English Channel in poor weather, which steadily worsened, until it was blowing a full westerly gale, which whipped up high seas. The headrail was carried away and the bumkins damaged; the rudder coat was torn off and boats were stove in on the beams. Captain Honeyman decided to make for a sheltered anchorage and the ship steered for the coast of south Wales and the port of Milford Haven. In poor visibility, with regular showers of rain, the frigate attempted to enter the harbour, but ran hard aground. A boat was hoisted out to take out a stream anchor to try and pull her off, and the masts were cut away to try and ease her rolling, but she was stuck fast. The waves were beating over her constantly and when the local quarantine master managed to come aboard, at considerable risk to himself, it was to advise them to leave. All the crew were taken off, the last leaving in the early hours of the next morning. The court-martial enquiry into the loss heard that the pilot, James Garrety, had mistaken Thorn Island for the Stack Rocks and so laid a wrong course, taking the ship into West Angle Bay. The court cleared him of any blame, because of the bad weather and poor visibility.
[TNA:ADM.1/5386]

3 February SUSSEX OAK Ketch
Hired 1804; 124 tons.
Master George Thomas
Employed as a store vessel, she was loaded with hemp and copper sheets, and bound for Chatham from Portsmouth, when she became detached from her convoy and fell astern of the other ships. She then became a target for the French lugger privateer *Rodeur* of Calais, which overhauled the ketch off Dover, and with only six men and one boy onboard, had little choice but to surrender.
[www.britishnewspaperarchive.co: Morning Chronicle 5 February 1808 p3; Lloyd's List 8 February 1808]

15 February RAPOSA Gun Brig
Prize 1806; 173 tons; 10 guns
Lieutenant James Violett
Cruising off the coast of South America, in the vicinity of Cartagena, she was about 50 miles to the west of

that city when four vessels were sighted. She altered towards them, and a chase was soon under way, with the brig pursuing a schooner and three sloops. The vessels steered towards the Islas del Rosario, and anchored close inshore in line abreast. The *Raposa* stood towards them, sounding constantly. At 3.30pm the leadsman shouted, 'Shallow water', and minutes later she struck a sandbank and went aground. The sails were filled, and an anchor was taken out by boat in an attempt to free her, but she was stuck fast. The enemy vessels, realising that she was in trouble, weighed and used sweeps to approach her, taking up raking positions ahead from which she could not effectively reply. At dusk they anchored, again in line abreast, ahead of the grounded brig. By now the rudder had come off and pieces of the false keel could be seen floating up alongside. Some of the guns were heaved overboard and throughout the night the crew persisted in their efforts to pull her free of the obstruction but failed. At 5 o'clock in the morning the enemy was seen to be preparing to close again, at which she surrendered, the crew taking to the boats and setting the brig on fire. The court-martial enquiry cleared Lieutenant Violett of any blame for the loss and praised his zealous conduct.
[TNA: ADM.1/5386]

23 February HIRONDELLE Gun Brig
Prize 1804; 210 tons; 14 guns
Lieutenant Joseph Kidd†

Sailed from Malta for Tunis with despatches, the land around Cape Bon was raised and course was set to run towards the port. At 10.30 that night breakers were seen close ahead. The starboard anchor was quickly let go to bring her up, but she was already in the surf and ran aground. An attempt was made to hoist out a boat, but it was swamped soon after it was launched, the men being swept away into the breaking waves. Soon after this the brig capsized, the crew having to fight their way through the surf. Only four men were still alive by the morning, and they were able to walk to a nearby village. The court martial enquiring into the wreck decided the most probable cause was the brig steering a wrong course, which had taken her onto the North African shore about two leagues (six miles) to the east of Cape Bon.
[TNA: ADM.1/5390]

February TANG Schooner
Bermuda 1807; 71 tons; 55.2ft × 18ft; 4 guns
Lieutenant Joseph Derby†

Newly built, she completed her fitting out in Bermuda in January 1808, and sailed for England on 8 February with a small crew but was never seen again. It was presumed that she had foundered with all hands. The pay book was closed on 29 February.
[TNA: ADM.1/498; ADM.35/3181]

23 March ASTRAEA Fifth Rate
Cowes 1781; 703 tons; 126ft × 35.7ft; 32 guns
Captain Edmund Heywood

Sailed from Jamaica with the *Prince Edward* packet, which the frigate convoyed through the Mona Passage into the Atlantic. After parting company, the weather became very hazy, and she passed several days without being able to take an observation of the sun. During 23 March land was sighted, which they believed to be Puerto Rico, the Master declaring that '… it could be no other land', and they stood on until 8 o'clock that evening, when it was decided to tack. As she was preparing to do so, she ran hard aground. The frigate beat heavily on rocks, the keel being unshipped and within 30 minutes water was entering at an alarming rate. A boat was lowered to take out an anchor, the masts were cut away, and stores were thrown overboard in attempts to lighten her, but without effect. Guns were fired as signals of distress, but unfortunately one burst, killing two men. The Carpenter reported that the ship had broken her back amidships and could not be saved, indeed if she were hauled off the rocks, she would sink. Daylight revealed that they were on the Horseshoe Reef, off the island of Anegada in the Virgin Islands, and the men started leaving the ship in boats and rafts. Captain Heywood was one of the last to leave, and all but two men made it to safety on the nearby shore. The *St Christopher* sloop arrived later that morning and rescued all the survivors. It was judged that lack of observations coupled with an extraordinary current, which had taken them further to the west than they had realised, and the failure to identify the land correctly, were to blame. One seaman, George Wright, was charged with using 'riotous and mutinous language' during the wreck. He had verbally abused Captain Heywood, calling him a rascal, blaming him for the wreck and saying he would take his sword and '… give him the contents'. He was found guilty and hanged.
[TNA: ADM.1/5387]

24 March MUROS Sixth Rate
Prize 1806 (*Alcide*); 444 tons; 107.11ft × 30.6ft; 22 guns
Captain Archibald Duff

After convoying a fleet of merchant ships to Halifax, the *Muros* was returning to Jamaica, when intelligence was received that the Spanish were erecting fortifications around Bahia Honda, Cuba. It was decided to attack and if possible, destroy them, a Providence privateer, the *Tambourine*, joining her and sending aboard John Fleming to act as a pilot. The pair approached the bay just before dusk, and when about 1½ miles from their object, the privateer shouted a warning to 'Starboard your helm'. Shortly afterwards she ran aground on a sandbank. The *Tambourine* closed and attempted to pull her off but failed, as did an attempt to kedge

her off with anchors laid out by boats. Stores were transferred or heaved overboard, and pumping started to deal with the water entering the hold. The pumps could not cope with the inrush, and when she fell over to starboard with the ports under water, she was abandoned as a wreck. Only one man was lost, '… a French black who fell victim to his inebriety'. The blame was placed on the acting pilot, John Fleming, the man loaned from the privateer, but no punishment was inflicted, as he had volunteered his services in order to attack the enemy.
[TNA:ADM.1/5386]

25 March **ELECTRA** Brig Sloop
Mistleythorn 1806; 285 tons; 93.2ft × 26.6ft; 16 guns
Commander George Barnes Trollope
Ordered to Augusta, Sicily, carrying money for the troops on the island. At just after 8 o'clock in the morning, as she worked into the bay, the brig struck the outer edge of a reef. After initial hopes that she might beat over it, the sails were furled, boats hoisted out and preparations made to heave her off. Several boats joined her from the port to give assistance and shot and stores were off loaded to lighten her. Efforts to haul her off the reef proved fruitless, and the pumps were manned when water was found to be entering. During the day, the wind increased, and she was soon lifting and pounding on the rocks, with the result that the rudder was unshipped and the sternpost badly shaken. Water flooded over the casks in the hold until by 2pm, having settled deep into the water, she was abandoned as a wreck. Commander Trollope was judged to have been at fault, by entering a port with which he was not familiar without signalling for a pilot and for failing to use the lead-line. He was ordered to be placed at the bottom of the seniority list of Commanders. Lieutenant Richard Connelly was reprimanded for leaving the deck during her time on the reef.
[TNA:ADM.1/5388]

25 March **MILBROOK** Schooner
Redbridge 1798; 148 tons; 81.8ft × 33ft; 12 guns
Lieutenant James Leach
Bound for Lisbon, the schooner arrived off the Islas Berlingas during 24 March and decided to anchor. That evening, both the bower and stream anchor cables were seen to be chafing on rocks and it was decided to shift anchorage to a safer position. She weighed and the stream anchor was then carried out to warp her to a new position, which she had nearly reached when a strong squall struck her, throwing her head towards the shore. The best bower anchor was let go, but she was driven down onto a reef before the anchors could bring her up. It was decided to try and haul her off and the stream anchor was again laid out, but it was slow work

and the wind increased, building up a contrary sea. A gale was looming, and it became imperative that she be moved. A hawser was taken to a nearby rock, and by hauling on this she was successfully warped off into clear water. Here she rode for the night as the wind and waves steadily increased. At 8 o'clock the next morning the cable fasteners gave way and she was carried onto the rocks and bilged. She fell over onto her beam-ends and was lost.
[TNA:ADM.1/5386]

20 April **WIDGEON** Schooner
Brixham 1806; 75 tons; 56.3ft × 18.3ft; 4 guns
Lieutenant George Elliott
Off the coast of Scotland assembling a convoy for America, the schooner was ordered to Banff to inform the ships there of its imminent departure. Arriving off the port on 18 April, she lay-to in a hard gale of wind, with occasional showers of snow. The following day, as the weather cleared and the wind shifted round to the south, the opportunity was taken to send in a boat to the harbour, the schooner remaining four to five miles off the port to await the return of the boat. At 2.30 in the morning, she struck the ground heavily and was soon being lifted by the swell to pound on rocks. Shot and stores were ordered to be heaved overboard and a boat hoisted out to lay out a kedge anchor. Water butts were emptied, the pumps manned, and distress guns fired, but the water was flooding in fast, and all the crew was soon ordered into the boats as she foundered. The pilot, Alexander Layell, had been ordered to maintain a distance of at least four miles from the shore during the night, but this he had failed to do, leaving the deck that night in the charge of a Bo'sun's Mate. In consequence the schooner had drifted inshore where she was wrecked at Blackpots. Layell was ordered to be confined in the Marshalsea Prison for six months and to lose all pay due to him.
[TNA:ADM.1/5387]

22 April **BERMUDA** Ship Sloop
Bermuda 1806; 399 tons; 107ft × 29.11ft; 18 guns
Commander William Henry Byam
Cruising off the Grand Bahamas in search of enemy merchant ships, particularly for a rich Portuguese ship reported in the area, at 2 o'clock in the morning, in dark, hazy weather, the lookout reported a rock on the lee bow. The helm was put over and all hands turned up to spread more sail. She successfully tacked, only to discover breakers ahead of her. She wore ship, but 15 minutes later rocks were again seen ahead. A further attempt was made to come about, but at 2.30am she ran aground. The ship started to fill with water immediately. Pumping and bailing commenced, and the masts were cut away. Daylight revealed another ship aground about

five miles away, and it was discovered that it was the sought-after Portuguese ship. The boats were lowered and sounded around her, but it was found that the sloop was resting on a ridge of rocks from which she could not escape. The Portuguese ship, however, was seen to free herself, and the boats pulled towards her, boarded and quickly secured her without a fight. Abandoning *Bermuda*, except for a Lieutenant, a Midshipman and six seamen to safeguard the stores, the remainder of the crew transferred to the captured ship, the *Concepcion*, apart from five men who stole the jolly boat and deserted. Repaired with the rudder from the *Bermuda*, the *Concepcion* sailed on 26 April, arriving at New Providence on 4 May, to organise vessels to return to the wreck and take off the stores. The party left onboard had kept a number of wrecking vessels at bay until the ships from Providence arrived, After removing what stores they could, the ship was abandoned as a wreck on 3 June. The court-martial enquiry blamed an excessively strong current for setting her onto the Memory Rock in the Little Bahama Bank.
[TNA: ADM.1/5388]

18 May RAPID Gun Brig
Topsham 1804; 179 tons; 80ft × 22.6ft; 12 guns
Lieutenant Henry Baugh

Cruising off Cape St Vincent in company with the *Primrose* sloop, the pair saw and chased two feluccas which took shelter in Sagres Bay. Despite their quarry anchoring close under a gun battery, it was decided to attack them, the *Rapid* leading her consort into the bay. As they neared the feluccas, the shore battery opened an accurate fire on the advancing vessels, and two large shot struck the bows of *Rapid*. She filled with water very quickly and despite pumps being manned, she settled until at 7.30 that evening the sloop came alongside to take off the crew before she foundered. Lieutenant Baugh was commended for his zeal and gallantry.
[TNA: ADM.1/5387]

4 June TICKLER Gun Brig
Brightlingsea 1804; 179 tons; 80.3ft × 22.7ft; 12 guns
Lieutenant John Watson Skinner†

Part of the British fleet in the Baltic, she was cruising in the Great Belt, off the northern end of Langeland during the afternoon of 3 June, when two Danish gunboats were sighted. They mutually closed and when within gunshot, an exchange of fire began, which lasted for 45 minutes, after which the Danish pair broke off the engagement. The next morning the gunboats could be seen close under the land, and a further four gunboats were in sight off Lolland, rowing towards her. There was almost no wind, leaving her little chance to manoeuvre, and the gunboats were able to take station ahead of the brig. The pair from the previous day were seen to be closing to join them. At 2.45pm, the gunboats opened their fire, the *Tickler* responding with bow-chase guns. Soon after the engagement began, Lieutenant Skinner was killed, struck on the head with grapeshot. Sub-Lieutenant James Sheppheard assumed the command and the fight. In an attempt to bring the broadside to bear, a kedge anchor was streamed astern, with a spring attached to it and efforts were made to haul the brig round to bring the broadside to bear, sweeps being used to aid the attempt. In the event, she failed to achieve a full broadside, the sweeps being shot away. At 7.15pm, after maintaining the fight for over four hours, she surrendered, the hull being riddled with shot holes, and the sails and rigging reduced to tatters. One man killed and seven wounded.
[TNA: ADM.1/5388]

9 June TURBULENT Gun Brig
Dartmouth 1805; 181 tons; 84.2ft × 22.1ft; 12 guns
Lieutenant George Wood

One of the escorts, along with gun brigs *Charger* and *Piercer* and bomb vessel *Thunder*, to a large convoy for England that sailed from Malmö, Sweden. The ships attracted the attention of the Danes, and when the convoy was to the south of the island of Saltholm, and as the wind fell away to a calm, over twenty gunboats and mortar boats emerged from the harbour of Dragør to attack the rear of the convoy. As the *Turbulent* was stationed astern of the ships, she bore the brunt of the attack, the *Charger* and *Piercer* at the head of the convoy being unable to assist. The only other escort, the *Thunder* bomb, tried to help by firing shell and grapeshot from her mortar, but with little success. Within 15 minutes of opening the engagement the *Turbulent* had her fore topsail yard and main topmast shot away and her foremast shot through. At 8 o'clock, after a two-hour fight, finding herself surrounded by fifteen gunboats, she struck her flag in surrender. Three men wounded.
[TNA: ADM.1/5388]

19 June SEAGULL Brig Sloop
Dover 1806; 282 tons; 93ft × 26.5ft; 16 guns
Commander Robert Cathcart

Cruising in the Skaggerak, when a brig was sighted running to the east, and chase was given. By 4.30 in the afternoon, now close to the coast of Norway, she was within gunshot range, and when the *Seagull* hoisted her colours, the brig showed a Danish flag, and opened fire. The *Seagull* used sweeps to move inshore to cut the Dane off from the shoreline and returned the fire. After 20 minutes, six gunboats were seen closing under sail and oar from the nearby harbour at Kristiansand. The gunboats took up position around the sloop, with the Danish brig remaining on the larboard bow. With the wind falling away to a dead calm, the *Seagull* was

unable to escape, her sweeps being shot away when she attempted to use them. She was raked repeatedly, the rigging reduced to shreds, the hull shot through in several places, and five of her carronades were dismounted. At 7.30pm, unable to resist any further, she surrendered. She found her main opponent was the *Lougen*, 20 guns; the gunboats mounted two guns each. Soon after the Danes took possession of the sloop, she filled with water, and foundered. Eight men were killed and twenty wounded. Commander Cathcart was praised at his court martial for his determined resistance and courage and promoted to Captain. Lieutenant Villiers Hatton was likewise singled out for praise, having remained at his post, encouraging the men, despite being dangerously wounded. He was promoted to Commander.
[TNA:ADM.1/5390]

28 June CAPELIN Schooner
Bermuda 1804; 70 tons; 55.2ft × 18ft; 4 guns
Lieutenant Josias Bray

Part of the blockading squadron off Brest, at 4 o'clock in the morning she was ordered to close and reconnoitre the port, with several other small vessels. Bray retired to his cabin, leaving the Gunner's Mate, Thomas Cole, in charge of the watch. At 7 o'clock, as she manoeuvred off the entrance to the port, she struck the Parquette rock. A boat was swiftly hoisted out to take out an anchor, and other cutters and schooners of the squadron closed. When the attempt to kedge her free failed, a hawser was passed to the *Adrian* cutter, which tried to pull her off, and when this failed, the schooner *Whiting* made a similar attempt, also in vain. By now the tide was on the ebb and the schooner was left stranded, hanging on the rock. The activity had attracted the attention of the French and several ships could be seen preparing to sail from the roads. In one final effort to free her, the *Entrepenante* cutter took the hawser, and this time she was pulled free of the rock. However, no sooner had she floated free than the water gushed in, and she settled and sank very quickly, stern first, the crew being taken off by the attendant craft. Lieutenant Bray was reprimanded for not remaining on deck when she approached the harbour. Cole was reprimanded for failing to call Bray when he lost sight of the light at Pointe de St Matthieu in the haze.
[TNA:ADM.1/5388]

10 July NETLEY Gun Brig
Prize (*Déterminée*); 173 tons; 14 guns
Lieutenant Charles Burman†

Cruising in the vicinity of Barbados, at about 9 o'clock in the evening she was struck by a strong squall which rolled her over before she could reduce sail, and she quickly sank. Only one Midshipman and eight seamen were rescued the following morning by the schooner *Julia*, having spent five hours in the water clinging to floating wreckage. Fifty-six men died.
[TNA:ADM.1/329]

27 July PICKLE Schooner
Purchased 1800 (*Sting*); 127 tons; 73ft × 20.7ft; 8 guns
Lieutenant Moses Cannadey

Carrying despatches from England for Admiral Lord Collingwood at Cadiz, Cape Santa Maria was sighted at 6 o'clock in the evening of 26 July and a course set accordingly. At just after midnight, broken water was seen ahead, and the helm put over to port. Despite this, she struck the ground. All hands were turned up, and the cutter lowered to take out a kedge anchor, but before any work could be done, she was found to be filling with water extremely fast, and the schooner started to heel over to port. All the boats were quickly hoisted out and the crew abandoned her before she foundered. The following morning Lieutenant Cannadey returned to the wreck, but found that she was on the Chipiona Shoal with her bottom beaten in. All the crew landed on the Spanish coast nearby. Lieutenant Cannadey was reprimanded and warned to be more careful in the future, the cause apparently being an unaccountable error in the reckoning of the distance travelled. The despatches were reported to have been recovered by a Maltese diver who worked for three days to salvage them.
[TNA:ADM.1/5388]

30 July MELEAGER Fifth Rate
Chatham 1806; 875 tons; 137ft × 38.1ft; 36 guns
Captain Frederick Warren

After sailing during the afternoon from Port Royal, Jamaica in strong breezes, the Master fixed land he identified as Portland Point at 6 o'clock that evening and laid a course to take them clear of the land. Less than 30 minutes later broken water was sighted ahead, and despite the helm being put over, she struck the ground. More sail was spread in an effort to force the ship over the obstruction, but when this failed, all sail was taken in, and preparations made to haul her off. It was now realised that the was on Barebush Cay, and with the strong wind whipping up a heavy swell, the frigate started pounding on the rocks. Pumps were manned as water was reported to be entering, but it was found that much of the bottom had been pushed up and water was flooding into the hold at an uncontrollable rate. During the night, the masts were cut away and rafts made, so that at daylight work was concentrated on getting the crew ashore. A line was successfully passed to the shore by veering out a hawser secured to one of the rafts which was floated through the surf. All but three of the crew made it safely to the shore, the last leaving at 3 o'clock

in the afternoon. By this time, the frigate's back had been broken. Work went on for several days afterwards on the wreck, recovering the guns and a large amount of the stores. The cause of the wreck appeared to be the Master's wrongly identifying Bazaletto Hill as Portland Point, which had led to the fateful course being set. Both Captain Warren and the Master were warned to be more careful in their actions in the future and pay closer attention to the courses steered and distances run.
[TNA: ADM.1/5388]

2 August TIGRESS Gun Brig
Deptford 1804; 177 tons; 80.1ft × 22.6ft; 12 guns
Lieutenant Edward Nathaniel Greensword
Carrying despatches for Admiral Saumarez in the Baltic, the brig anchored in calm weather off the north-western end of Langeland in the Great Belt. At 10 o'clock that night a breeze sprang up, so the brig prepared to weigh, but as they did so several Danish gunboats were observed approaching from Agersø. The anchor cable was hastily cut, and they cleared for action, but when sixteen vessels were counted, she was put before the wind and headed for the position of the *Edgar*, laying at anchor some miles off. When the breeze died away, the gunboats gained on the brig using sweeps, firing as they did so. The cutter was lowered and sent ahead to tow the brig, but achieved little, a brisk action soon being underway. Surrounded by gunboats, being regularly hulled by shot, and with casualties mounting, she surrendered after one hour. Two men killed and eight wounded.
[TNA: ADM.1/5390]

4 August DELPHINEN Brig Sloop
Prize 1807; 306 tons; 98.7ft × 27.4ft; 16 guns
Commander Richard Harward
Cruising off the coast of Holland to enforce the blockade, the brig hove-to at dusk on the evening of 3 August, Commander Harward leaving instructions that she be kept 12 miles from the shore. The Master, Thomas Fleetwood, had the middle watch, and apparently came on deck, instructed the watch to keep a good lookout and then lay down on an arms chest, wrapped himself in an ensign and went to sleep. At 3 o'clock in the morning, land was seen close ahead, and soon after this she went aground. An attempt was made sail her off and she bumped across a sandbank, striking all the time, before she was brought up. The boats were hoisted out, but as they were in danger of being swamped by the surf no anchors could be laid out. Water was reported to be entering, which soon defeated the pumps. With waves constantly washing over them and the vessel settling all the time, she was abandoned, all the crew taking to the boats and the sloop being set on fire as they did so. Harward hoped to pull away from the land, but the tide pushed them back inshore, where they landed, to be taken prisoner. The court martial ruled that she had gone ashore on the south-eastern end of the island of Vlieland through the gross negligence of the Master, who was unable to defend himself, having died in prison at Harlingen.
[TNA: ADM.1/5389]

18 August ROOK Schooner
Ringmore 1806; 75 tons; 56.3ft × 18.3ft; 4 guns
Lieutenant James Lawrence†
Having successfully delivered despatches from England to Jamaica, the schooner sailed on 13 August to make the return trip, carrying $27,000 plus the mail and some passengers. On the morning of 18 August at daylight, when off Cape St Nicholas Mole, Hispaniola, two schooners were seen closing. The largest of them, carrying 10 guns, approached under British colours until within gunshot, when French colours were shown. The action then began, with Lieutenant Lawrence shooting the Captain of the nearest opponent. After an hour's exchange of fire, the enemy schooners ran alongside and boarded, Lieutenant Lawrence being mortally wounded by a musket shot. The French mistreated the crew after the capture, kicking the body of Lieutenant Lawrence, stabbing to death a wounded Sergeant of the Royal Artillery, and throwing overboard some of the wounded. After looting the schooner, the survivors were turned into an open boat, which reached the nearby land. Three men killed and eleven wounded.
[TNA: ADM.1/5390]

August JASEUR Brig
Prize 1807; 12 guns
Lieutenant Thomas Laugharne†
Sailed from Calcutta on 8 August with despatches for Admiral Drury at Prince of Wales Island (Penang), in company with a local brig that was bound for the island and Macao. A few days later they were overtaken by a tropical storm, and the brig was last seen, apparently in some distress, low in the water and with her fore topsail 'flying about'. The country ship was unable to render assistance due to the high winds and heavy seas. It was presumed that she foundered soon after this with all hands.
[www.britishnewspaperarchive.co: Public Ledger 9 August 1809 p2]

12 September LAUREL Sixth Rate
Bridport 1806; 526 tons; 118ft × 31.8ft; 22 guns
Commander John Charles Woolcombe
Cruising off the French island of Mauritius, during the day the *Laurel* sighted and chased a ship close into the shore, before discovering her to be a cartel ship, with released prisoners of war. Wearing ship, she sighted another ship to the south-south-west and made sail

towards the stranger, until it could be seen to be a large frigate. When it became clear that she could not flee from the larger ship, Captain Woolcombe decided to lay his opponent as close as possible. She came across the frigate's bow, and when the latter attempted to wear ship, the *Laurel* fired a destructive broadside into her. The pair then fell alongside, and a mutual exchange of fire went on for 90 minutes, when, with the gaff shot away, all the rigging cut to pieces and the mizzen mast shot through, the *Laurel* surrendered. The French frigate, which was the *Cannoniére*, 40 guns, had fired high, with the resulting casualties being low: one man killed and eight wounded.

Note: recaptured on 12 April 1810 by the *Unicorn*, she was recommissioned as *Laurestinus*.
[TNA: ADM.1/5403]

28 September SEAFLOWER Gun Brig
Purchased 1782 (*Swiftsure*); 203 tons; 72.5ft × 25.11ft; 16 guns
Lieutenant William FitzWilliam Owen

Sailed from the East India Companies port at Bencoolen (Bengkulu), Sumatra, on 24 September to return to India. During the morning of 27 September, a ship was seen closing the brig, which being end-on made it difficult to identify. As a precaution, the *Seaflower* cleared for action, and by 10 o'clock the stranger could be seen to be a frigate, at which the brig made all sail away. Sweeps were used to speed their flight, but by 11 o'clock the frigate was about a mile astern and commenced a harassing fire from a bow-chase gun. The *Seaflower* replied occasionally as the pursuit went on through the afternoon. The wind fell away and by using sweeps, the brig found herself gaining on her opponent, and by 7 o'clock that evening she was able to take advantage of a breeze and close the land. The frigate kept up the pressure through the night, with the brig using her sweeps to keep her distance. At first light the following day, stores, shot and finally most of the guns were heaved overboard in attempts to lighten the brig, retaining only two 6-pounders. All the time the sweeps were kept working, but the frigate steadily overhauled her, until by noon she was just a cable's length astern. The crew were exhausted by their efforts, the tropical heat adding to their fatigue, and several collapsed. The *Seaflower* therefore struck her flag in surrender to the French frigate la *Manche*, 40 guns. Several of the crew took the opportunity to desert to the French.
[TNA: ADM.1/5408]

29 September MARIA Gun Brig
Purchased 1808; 172 tons; 14 guns
Lieutenant James Bennett†

Cruising off Guadeloupe, West Indies, at daybreak a ship was seen close in with the land and believing it to be a merchant ship or letter of marque, the *Maria* shook out reefs and made sail to close her. As they approached, she could be seen to be a large vessel, but her strength could not be determined. Just before 7 o'clock a squall of wind took them aback, and whilst in this position the stranger hoisted French colours and fired a shot at the brig. She then hauled up her ports, revealing that she was a powerful corvette, and fired a destructive broadside into the *Maria*. The brig would not come around, so sweeps were manned to pull her broadside to face her opponent, but before this could be completed, a further two raking broadsides had been fired into her. In the last broadside Lieutenant Bennett was struck by grapeshot and killed. The Master, Joseph Dyason, assumed command and fought the French ship for some time, until, with the sails and rigging cut to pieces and several shots in the hull, the flag was struck. Her captor proved to be the *Département des Landes*, 22 guns, which ran the brig on the shore later that day to prevent her sinking. Six men killed and nine wounded.
[TNA: ADM.1/5397]

3 October CARNATION Brig Sloop
Bideford 1807; 383 tons; 100.1ft × 30.6ft; 18 guns
Commander Charles Marshall Gregory†

When to the north-east of the island of Martinique, a brig was sighted and chased, proving to be the French sloop *Palinure*, 16 guns. On overhauling the brig, a close action commenced, with lasted for over an hour, when, with all the filled powder expended and the rigging badly cut up, the *Carnation* fell aboard the French brig. By this time Commander Gregory was dead and they had suffered a large number of casualties, including both Lieutenants and the Master. The Bosun, William Triplet, took command and attempted to lead a boarding party, but he was not supported, and the Sergeant of Marines, John Chapman, fled below, being followed by several of the crew. The *Palinure* then boarded, and with little resistance, the *Carnation* surrendered. Ten men were killed and thirty wounded. In subsequent courts martial thirty-two members of the crew were found guilty of cowardice and ordered to be transported to Botany Bay for 14 years, although it is uncertain whether this was carried out. Sergeant Chapman was sentenced to death and was hanged from the main yard of the *Ulysses*.
[TNA: ADM.1/5392; ADM.1/5394]

11 October GREYHOUND Fifth Rate
Mistleythorn 1783; 682 tons; 126ft × 35.1ft; 32 guns
Captain Hon. William Pakenham

Part of a small squadron assembled at Madras under the command of Vice Admiral Drury, she was ordered to proceed to Macao and assist with the occupation of that place. She was steering along the coast of Luzon, Philippines, sounding regularly, and at 4 o'clock in the

afternoon the lead-line showed no bottom at 35 fathoms, but 30 minutes later breakers were seen ahead. The helm was put over, but before the frigate could come around, she struck a submerged reef. The ship thumped heavily over the rocks, losing the rudder, before coming to a standstill. The boats were hoisted out, but water was reported to be entering at an alarming rate, and within 10 minutes the lower deck was flooded. The masts were cut away, and the crew were ordered to abandon ship. All but one man made it to the shore, which was about five miles to the north-west of Capones Point. They were all taken prisoner and taken to Manilla.
[TNA: ADM.1/5405]

23 October VOLADOR Brig Sloop
Prize 1807; 270 tons; 87.6ft × 25.6ft; 16 guns
Commander Francis George Dickens
Sailed from Curaçao on 22 October to search for a privateer reported to be in the area of Maracaibo. As she steered west along the coast, at 1 o'clock in the morning, without warning she ran aground, bumping over rocks until coming to a stop, losing her rudder and heeling over as she did so. The masts were cut away, the guns thrown overboard to lighten her, and the pumps manned to keep the water in check. She lay in this position for the rest of the night, beating on the rocks and being lashed by the strong surf and regular heavy squalls of rain. Daybreak revealed that they were ashore about five or six miles south of Cape Areekala, in the Gulf of Coro, with a Spanish schooner nearby, which was not only also aground but breaking up. The boats were hoisted out and the crew started to leave the brig. Despite their own troubles, a boat was sent over to assist the schooner, but this unfortunately capsized, drowning one man. They persisted, however, and all of the schooner's crew were taken off, to join the men of the brig on the shore A party was sent along the coast to the town of Coro to bring help, which arrived four days later in the shape of the packet ship *Honduras*. The blame for the loss was placed on the charts published by David Steel, which were described as grossly inaccurate.
[TNA: ADM.1/5390]

26 October CRANE Schooner
Great Yarmouth 1806; 75 tons; 56.2ft × 18.3ft; 4 guns
Lieutenant Joseph Tinsdale
Laying at anchor at Plymouth, between Drake's Island and the Hoe, in poor weather, with frequent heavy squalls of rain. At 7.30pm, it was discovered that she was dragging her anchor, and a second anchor was let go, which brought her up. At 4 o'clock in the morning it was found that she was again driving, and by 7am she was getting dangerously close to the shore. She weighed, with the intention of standing out into the Sound to re-anchor but found herself constantly baffled by strong squalls. She was carried down onto the western end of the Hoe, where she struck a rock. Her guns of distress brought several boats from the dockyard to her aid, and she was hauled off the rock, only to fill with water and founder very quickly. All the crew were picked up from the water.
[TNA: ADM.1/5390]

29 October BANTERER Sixth Rate
South Shields 1807; 538 tons; 118ft × 32ft; 22 guns
Commander Alexander Shippard
Sailed from Halifax bound for Quebec, the ship embarked a pilot off the island of Bic and commenced her passage of the St Lawrence. At 4 o'clock in the morning, believing themselves to be near to the northern shore, the ship was tacked, but as they did so the ship ran aground. Land, later identified as Point Mille Vache, was visible some distance away, the ship having run aground on a shoal. Sail was taken in and the boats hoisted out to lay our anchors to kedge her off, but the steadily increasing wind prevented them going far enough away. Efforts were made to haul her off, but without success, and by midday she was striking heavily on the sand, with waves frequently breaking over her. The topmasts were struck and attempts made to use spars as shores, but the motion of the ship was too great. That evening, with the water gaining on the pumps, it was decided to commence leaving her, the sick, boys and Marines being landed by boat. The remainder of the crew threw overboard all but two of the guns, along with shot and provisions and continued efforts to sail or kedge her off the sandbank. All failed, and morning saw sand coming up in the pumps. Over the next three days all the crew were landed ashore, the Captain being the last to leave on the morning of 1 November. A boat was despatched to bring help, but the weather deteriorated into snowstorms, and it was a week before it returned, and not until 25 November that the crew could be embarked on a schooner sent from Quebec to take to Halifax. The subsequent court martial placed the blame for the loss on the neglect shown by Robert Clegram, the Master, and Lieutenant Stephen McCurdy, officer of the middle watch. The Master had failed to ensure the lead-line was constantly used or that the leadsman was being relieved every 30 minutes. McCurdy had not only allowed the pilot to leave the deck but quitted it himself to spend time in the gunroom, drinking grog. The Master was severely reprimanded, and Lieutenant McCurdy was dismissed the service.
[TNA: ADM.1/5391]

(end) October CRICKET Ketch
Hired 1806; 97 tons; 8 guns
Lieutenant John Graham Douglas[†]
Sailed from Corunna, northern Spain, for Lisbon on 25 October, with despatches for Sir Charles Cotton, but

failed to arrive. She was last seen on 28 October off Cape Finisterre and was presumed to have foundered soon after this. The *Lively* frigate searched the area, but without result.
[www.britishnewspaperarchive.co: Morning Chronicle 26 November 1808 p2]

5 December PROSELYTE Bomb Vessel
Purchased 1804 (*Ramillies*); 404 tons; 107.6ft × 29.6ft; 4 guns
Commander Henry James Lyford

Equipped with lights, in October she took up station off Anholt in the Kattegat, to mark the position of the island. The night of 4 December was bitterly cold, and ice was seen building around the ship. By the early hours of the following morning, she was completely iced in and was being pushed by the ice field down onto the island. Unable to move, her port side struck a rock and she canted over, losing her rudder, the sternpost badly shaken. By 8 o'clock that morning the ice was crushing her against the reef, and the ship was abandoned, Captain Lyford leading his crew across the ice to safety on the island.
[TNA:ADM.1/5391]

6 December CRESCENT Fifth Rate
Bursledon 1784; 888 tons; 137.2ft × 38.5ft; 36 guns
Captain John Temple†

Sailed from Great Yarmouth on 29 November for the Baltic, she sighted the coast of Denmark during the afternoon of 5 December. The pilots advised that the frigate should continue to steer east-south-east, sounding with the lead-line constantly. At 2 o'clock in the morning course was altered to the south and sail shortened, the weather being poor, with thick rolling black clouds, rain and strong winds. The water was found to be shallowing and land could be made out, but the pilots recommended that the ship stand on. At 10 o'clock that evening she suddenly struck the ground. Sail was taken in and a boat lowered to commence sounding around the ship. Anchors were also put into boats, ready to be taken out for kedging, but the strong winds, strong currents and high seas made this impossible, and the boats were swept away into the surf beating on the land visible nearby. The best bower anchor was let go to hold the ship, guns heaved overboard and pumping commenced. During the night, the anchor cable parted, and she started pounding heavily, opening more leaks. At daybreak, the fore- and mizzenmasts were cut away, which eased the ship somewhat, and a double issue of grog was issued to the crew, who were exhausted by constant pumping. By midday, the water was gaining rapidly, and hands were employed in constructing rafts. The first raft was manned by Lieutenant John Weaver, Royal Marines, with Midshipmen Mason and Lavender and about twenty men. The raft successfully made the perilous journey to the shore, some two miles away, despite being half under water and having freezing water constantly washing over them; three men subsequently died of exposure. A second raft proved impossible to use, and only the jolly boat, with eighteen men made the shore in safety. During the night, the wreck broke up. Two hundred and twenty-two people died, including six women and one child. The court-martial enquiry found that the ship had been wrecked at Rubjerg Knude due to the ignorance and negligence of the pilots, but as both had died, they were unable to defend themselves; it is likely that the pilots mistakenly believed that the Skaw (Skagen) had been passed.
[TNA:ADM.1/5394]

10 December JUPITER Fourth Rate
Rotherhithe 1778; 1,061 tons; 146.1ft × 40.10ft; 50 guns
Captain Henry Edward Baker

Sailed from Spithead on 3 December for Spain, she arrived off Vigo Bay during the early hours of 10 December and spent the day tacking into the shore. Captain Baker decided, although the daylight was fading, to anchor as close to the harbour as possible before dark, to allow an early entrance the next morning. Working into the bay, by 8 o'clock, she was close by the northern shore and had just tacked, when she struck a submerged reef. All sail was put aback, but she would not move. The boats were hoisted out, and on sounding around her, found that she had no more than five fathoms of water. Guns were fired as signals of distress, and this brought boats from other ships, and pumping was started, as water was reported to be entering the hold. At half-past midnight, the ship heeled over to starboard, and stores and shot were heaved overboard, followed by some of the guns, but so much water was entering, this had little effect, and it was feared that if she were hauled off, she would founder. At first light on 11 December most of the crew were taken off, and work was concentrated on saving stores, until during the evening of 12 December, when she fell over onto her larboard side and was abandoned as a wreck. Captain Baker was admonished to act with more caution in the future.
[TNA.ADM.1/5391; ADM.51/1829]

15 December FLYING FISH Schooner
Purchased 1806 (*Revenge*); 151 tons; 78.8ft × 21.7ft; 12 guns
Lieutenant John Glassford Gooding

Returning to Port Royal, Jamaica, with a French schooner prize in tow, she was working along the south coast of Hispaniola in worsening weather. The swell became so high, the tow was in danger of being swamped, so Lieutenant Gooding altered course to close the land. When she was close to the land, about six

miles to the east of Punta Salinas, she tried to tack, but missed stays and a second attempt also failed. Breakers were seen ahead, and she next tried to wear, but the schooner was slow in coming around, and struck the ground. The impact was quite gentle, and everyone was confident that she could be freed, but there were shouts from below that '… the vessel is full'. Water was flooding in, and within minutes the gunroom and other compartments on the starboard side were full, and she fell over onto her beam-ends. The prize schooner came as near as she could and took off the crew. The Master, Fowler Shute, was subsequently reprimanded for failing to keep the lead-line going as they neared the shore. Lieutenant Gooding was adjudged to have stood too close to the shore and was admonished to be more careful in the future.
[TNA: ADM.1/5391]

23 December FAMA Brig Sloop
Prize 1807; 315 tons; 82.10ft × 21.6ft; 18 guns
Lieutenant Charles Topping†

Sailed from Karlskrona, Sweden, on 22 December in company with several ships to escort a convoy to England. The weather was poor and soon worsened, with strong winds and heavy falls of sleet. At 1.30 in the morning, with no warning she ran hard aground on the north-eastern point of Bornholm Island. Lieutenant Topping came on deck immediately, wearing only his shirt, and ordered the mainmast cut away, but before this could be done the brig started beating over the rocks with increasing violence, being lifted by the heavy swell. Little could be done, as the storm worsened, with showers of snow and one seaman, one woman and the ill-clad Topping died of exposure. At daybreak numerous local people came down to their aid, passing lines to the brig and assisting the crew ashore, although four men and one woman died in their attempts to reach the land. It was found that William Affleck, the Master, was guilty of improper conduct, by altering the course of the sloop without informing Lieutenant Topping; further he had failed to maintain a good lookout during his watch, thereby losing sight of the *Salsette* frigate. Because of his previous good character, he was only reprimanded.
[TNA: ADM.1/5394]

23 December SALORMAN Cutter
Prize 1808 (*Søornen*); 121 tons; 10 guns
Lieutenant Andrew Duncan

Another of the escorts to the convoy from Karlskrona, (see *Fama* above), the cutter became separated from her charges in poor weather, pitching and rolling deeply in high winds and heavy seas. One man was washed overboard and lost, and the foresail and storm jib split, before Lieutenant Duncan decided to make for shelter, and the cutter bore up and steered for Ystad in southern Sweden. Land was sighted, but then lost in a blinding snowstorm. At just before 4 o'clock in the morning she ran hard aground, about half a mile to the east of Ystad. The rudder came off and several pieces of the false keel could be seen floating nearby. She lay on the shore all night, firing distress guns, and at first light several boats came to her aid from the nearby port. Guns and provisions were taken off, but efforts to pull her off failed, and when night fell, she was abandoned. On returning to her the following morning, she was found to have bilged and had sunk up to the gunwales.
[TNA: ADM.1/5396]

26 December BUSTLER Gun Brig
Topsham 1805; 181 tons; 84ft × 22ft; 12 guns
Lieutenant Richard Welch

Stationed off the northern coast of France as part of the blockade, the weather was poor, with thick cloud, when, just before dawn, in the act of tacking, she ran aground. The tide was falling and soon after grounding she fell over onto her side. With daylight and the weather clearing, it was found that she was on the shore just a few hundred yards from Cap Griz Nez. The boats were put into the water to pull her off, but before they could achieve anything, a shore battery commenced firing on the brig. The fire was accurate, and the brig was soon being hit regularly, cutting up the rigging and piercing the hull. Quite unable to do anything, the crew were ordered into the boats which pulled away at 8 o'clock. Lieutenant Welch and a small party remained on board to set fire to the wreck. The *Nymph* cutter saw the brig on shore and closed to pick them up. However, the fire seemed to go out, and the *Nymph* attempted to return, but several luggers and gunboats could be seen closing from Calais and Boulogne and the shore battery was still firing at them, so they gave over the attempt and left her to the French. The blame for the loss was placed on the pilot, William Sanders, and the Master, Richard Fearne, who were found guilty of neglect. They had ceased using the lead-line during the morning watch, despite being close to the shore in poor visibility, and had shown a lack of awareness. Both men were dismissed the service, mulcted of all pay due and imprisoned for one year.
[TNA: ADM.1/5391]

1809

5 January PIGEON Schooner
Great Yarmouth 1806; 75 tons; 56.2ft × 42.4ft; 4 guns
Lieutenant Richard Cox

Cruising in the North Sea in company with the *Calliope*, the weather was poor and worsened, until by the morning of 4 January it was blowing an easterly gale

with showers of snow. Contact with her consort was lost in the night, and the following day she decided to make for shelter and headed for the Downs anchorage. The poor weather meant that no observations of the sun or stars could be made, forcing them to rely on dead reckoning and the constant use of the lead-line. The soundings led them to believe that they were close to the Galloper Sand and course was shaped for the North Foreland. At 8 o'clock that night a light was seen ahead which was thought to be the North Sand Head light, but 40 minutes later she ran hard aground at Kingsgate, near Margate. The rudder parted as she struck, and she was bilged. Within minutes the hold was flooded, and she started to sink, the crew taking to the rigging. Here they remained all night, two of the crew dying from exposure. The following morning the local people and the Sea Fencibles came to their aid and took off the survivors.
[TNA: ADM.1/5391]

9 January MORNE FORTUNÉE Gun Brig
Prize 1804 (*Regulus*); 184 tons; 12 guns
Lieutenant John Brown†
While employed in the blockade of Martinique, she capsized during the evening, when struck by a strong squall. Seven men were picked up clinging to floating wreckage by the brig's boat, which was serving as a guard boat, and one man managed to swim ashore, to be taken prisoner. Forty-one men died.
[TNA: ADM.1/330]

11 January MAGNET Brig Sloop
Northam 1807; 382 tons; 100ft × 30.6ft; 18 guns
Commander George Morris
Another of the escorts to the ill-fated Baltic convoy which sailed from Karlskrona, Sweden, on 22 December (see *Fama* above). The weather was poor, being cold with strong winds and showers of sleet and snow. The convoy anchored off Falsterbo on 25 December, where they remained until 6 January, when the weather cleared sufficiently for them to weigh and attempt to reach Malmö. The entrance to the harbour was found to be blocked with ice, and during 7 January the Swedish warship *Camilla* and six ships of the convoy went aground. Soon after this, surrounded by ice, the *Magnet* found herself grounding on the Saltholm shoal with three ships of the convoy. She remained there until 9 January, when the ice cleared sufficiently for the sloop to be pulled clear of the shoal and she was able to anchor in clear water. During 10 January, she weighed, but found a strong current was taking her inshore, so anchored again. During that night ice formed around them, and by morning a large field of ice, about four miles wide, was visible, being carried down towards them by the current. She tried to weigh, but the ice prevented this, so the cables were cut, and sweeps manned to mover her away from danger. Strong currents foiled her efforts, and she was carried into shoal water where she again anchored. Cables were carried out by boats and work began to warp her into Malmö Bay, but the ice increased, and she was steadily pushed inshore, dragging her anchors, until she struck the Halk Sand. The pressure from the ice continued and within 15 minutes she was on her beam-ends, the rudder hanging on one pintle and several leaks started. Boats were hoisted out and her they pulled her head round to face the nearby shore. Sail was spread and she was deliberately run onto the shore about four miles to the west of Malmö and abandoned as a wreck.
[TNA: ADM.1/5395]

20 January CLAUDIA Cutter
Bermuda 1806; 111 tons; 68.2ft × 20.4ft; 10 guns
Lieutenant Anthony Bliss William Lord
Ordered to the Baltic with despatches, the island of Flekkerøy, off Kristiansand, was raised during 18 January, and a new course was laid to the south-east. The weather worsened, with strong northerly winds accompanied by showers of snow. The following day they could make little progress and found themselves among floating floes of ice and altered round to try and make ground to the west, constantly frustrated by large ice fields. At 2 o'clock in the morning breakers were seen ahead and very soon after this the cutter struck a reef near the Naze of Norway (Lindesnes). She thumped over the rocks, several of the crew leaping off the deck onto the reef as she did so before they found themselves in clear water. The bows had been holed and the bottom damaged in the grounding, and water poured in at an extremely fast rate. The boats were ordered to be hoisted out, but only the jolly boat was lowered and manned before the cutter sank, the mast still above the water. The men remaining on board took to the rigging, although some, including Lieutenant Lord, jumped into the freezing water to swim to the nearby reef. There they spent a miserable night, wet and bitterly cold, and several men died of the cold. The following morning several local boats approached the wreck, but could not get close enough to help, at which Lord again took to the water, swimming to one of the boats by which a line was passed. The survivors were then pulled on board the rescue boats. Fourteen men died.
[TNA: ADM.1/5397]

22 January PRIMROSE Brig Sloop
Fowey 1807; 384 tons; 100.2ft × 30.6ft; 18 guns
Commander James Mein†
Sailed from Spithead on 14 January in company with the *Fisgard* and *Niobe*, to escort a large convoy of troop transports bound for Spain, the ships met hard weather,

and several took shelter. The *Primrose* was driven by the gale onto the Manacle rocks off Helston, Cornwall, in the early hours of the morning. Lashed by strong winds and beating surf, little could be done for the wreck, which at noon capsized over onto her side. Several local men risked their lives attempting to help the crew, but from a crew of 120, only one boy, John Meaghan, was rescued alive.
[*Gold: Naval Chronicle vol 21 pp62–3*]

28 February PROSERPINE Fifth Rate
Paul 1807; 922 tons; 144.3ft × 37.8ft; 32 guns
Captain Charles Otter
Stationed off the port of Toulon to watch the movements of the French fleet, she was laying off Cape Sicié, when at 4 o'clock in the morning two darkened ships were made out approaching from the land. More sail was hastily made, and the ship's head put to seaward, but the strangers were soon alongside, the only reply to Captain Otter's hail being a shot from one of the ships, which could now be seen to be large frigates. The *Proserpine* was still beating to quarters when the first frigate, the *Pénélope*, 40 guns, fired a broadside into her, followed shortly after by similar treatment from the *Pauline*, 40, on the opposite side. Faced with a large opponent on each side and largely unprepared, the fight was not a long one. In less than an hour the *Proserpine* had her rigging cut to pieces, with the main topsail yard shot away, foremast shot through, shrouds reduced to shreds and all braces and bowlines cut. When the French prepared to board, Captain Otter surrendered. One man killed and ten wounded.
[*TNA: ADM.1/5442*]

February VIPER Schooner
Purchased 1807 (*Princess Charlotte*); 81 tons; 57.10ft × 18.7ft; 4 guns
Lieutenant William Sidney Smith Towning†
Reported to have sailed from Cadiz on 18 February for Gibraltar, with Mr Robert Arbuthnot, former Chief Secretary to the government of Ceylon being carried as a passenger, but not heard from again and presumed lost with all hands.
[*www.britishnewspaperarchive.co: Kentish Gazette 16 February 1810 p4; Scots Magazine 1 March 1810 p79*]

26 March CACAFUEGO Gunboat
Gibraltar 1805 (*Gunboat – ?*); 44 tons; 50.7ft × 14ft; 2 guns
Lieutenant Richard Cull
Sailed from Cadiz for Tangier with despatches, she arrived on 25 March to deliver them, and then picked up mail for the Rear Admiral at Cadiz. She sailed that same evening in fresh, blowing weather, but found it difficult to work out to the west. Morning saw her to the south-east of Gibraltar, and she steadily worked up to Europa Point, intending to gain the bay. By 9 o'clock the land was just 100 yards away from the point, and as she attempted to tack, a squall of wind laid her aback. Sweeps were hastily manned, but it was far too late and within five minutes she struck the rocks and was bilged. All the crew made it safely to the shore.
[*TNA: ADM.1/5391*]

March HARRIER Brig Sloop
Deptford 1804; 383 tons; 100ft × 30.6ft; 18 guns
Commander John James Ridge†
Bound for the Cape of Good Hope from India, in company with the *Terpsichore*, the *Culloden* and a number of homeward-bound East Indiamen, the brig parted company on 10 March, in poor weather, when in the vicinity of the Île Bourbon (Réunion) and not seen again. It was presumed that she foundered with all hands. Her pay book was closed 31 March 1809.
[*TNA: ADM.35/2851; www.britishnewspaperarchive.co: Madras Courier 5 July 1809 p5; Public Ledger 20 December 1809 p2*]

11 April: The Attack on the Basque Roads
Admiral Lord Gambier was in command of a squadron blockading the Basque Roads, at the approaches to the River Charente. The situation of the French ships in the Roads was such that it was decided that an attack by fireships might succeed in destroying them. To this end, the Admiralty sent Captain Lord Cochrane in the *Imperieuse* frigate to direct such an attack. A number of transport ships were despatched from England, and a further eight ships serving with Gambier's squadron were fitted out as fire and explosion vessels for the assault. Finally, the *Mediator* store ship was ordered to be fitted out in a similar manner. During 11 April preparations were made for the attack; cutters armed with Congreve's rockets and a bomb vessel took up positions to carry out a bombardment, with sloops and gun brigs stationed to guide in the fireships. At about 8.30pm, the night being dark and moonless, eighteen fireships and three explosion vessels cut their anchor cables and drifted down towards the French ships, with Lord Cochrane being aboard one of the small vessels laden with gunpowder and shells. The *Mediator* was the largest of the little fleet and took the lead, striking the boom spread across the river, breaking it, and allowing through the smaller craft. Fires were then lit, and crews took to the boats, although several men were injured by premature explosions. As the fireships and explosive ships burnt, the bomb and rocket vessels started their bombardment, ' ... dark as was the night the sky soon became illuminated by the glare of so many vast fires, and, what with the flashes of the guns from the forts and ships the flight of shells and rockets ... and the reflection of the light from the sides of the French ships, a scene

was formed peculiarly awful and sublime'(*James's Naval History*). The French were thrown into confusion, and morning revealed that although no enemy ships had been burnt, several ships were aground on nearby mudbanks. Subsequent accusations that Admiral Gambier had failed to follow up his advantage and take the opportunity to destroy some of the grounded ships, led to a very public argument between Gambier and Lord Cochrane.

The following were expended in the attack:

MEDIATOR Store ship
Purchased 1804 (*Ann and Amelia*); 689 tons; 134.8ft × 34.5ft; 22 guns
Commander James Wooldridge

ADVENTURE Brig
Hired 1809; 144 tons

AGENORIA Brig
Hired 1809; 223 tons

ALICIA Ship
Hired 1809; 222 tons

CERES Bark
Hired 1809; 288 tons

GEORGE Snow
Hired 1809; 275 tons

HARMONY Brig
Hired 1809; 242 tons

HERCULES Ship
Hired 1809; 270 tons

MARY Brig
Hired 1809; 100 tons

MERCHANT Brig
Hired 1809; 266 tons

OCEAN Brig
Hired 1809; 213 tons

SALLY (1) Snow
Hired 1809; 222 tons

SALLY (2) Snow
Hired 1809; 138 tons

SISTERS Ship
Hired 1809; 316 tons

SOPHIA Ship
Hired 1809; 308 tons

THOMAS Brig
Hired 1809; 250 tons

TIBER Snow
Hired 1809; 254 tons

TRIPTOLEMUS Snow
Hired 1809; 224 tons

WILLIAM Brig
Hired 1809; 238 tons

ZEPHYR Snow
Hired 1809; 308 tons
[*London Gazette* 21 April 1809; *James's Naval History* vol 5 pp106–10; TNA: ADM.1/5398; ADM 108/174]

★ ★ ★

13 April **AENEAS** Brig
Hired 1809; 276 tons
A follow-up attack on grounded ships in the Basque Roads was planned to take place on 13 April, and three more transport ships were fitted out as fireships. In the event, the prepared ships were not used. As the *Aeneas* was working out of the roads to re-join the fleet, she ran aground on a bank off the Île d'Aix and was abandoned.
[*James's Naval History* vol 5 p117; ADM 108/174]

30 April **ALCMENE** Fifth Rate
Harwich 1794; 803 tons; 135.3ft × 36.7ft; 32 guns
Captain William Henry Brown Tremlett
In company with the *Amelia* frigate, during the afternoon the pair stood in towards the mouth of the River Loire to reconnoitre the anchorage. The weather was hazy, making identification of the landmarks difficult. At about 4 o'clock she struck the Trois-Pierres rocks on les Blanches reef and found herself held firmly by the obstruction. Spars were lowered over the side to act as shores, and some guns were thrown overboard, but as the tide ebbed, she settled further down onto the rock and bilged. By 10 o'clock water had flooded the lower decks and she was abandoned, the *Amelia* taking all the men onboard. Over the next few days *Amelia* worked at the site, removing as much of the provisions and stores as they could, before setting the wreck on fire on 6 May. The pilot, André Claro, was cautioned to be more careful in his actions in the future.
[TNA: ADM.1/5396; ADM.51/2114]

31 May UNIQUE Gun Brig
Prize 1807 (*Duquesne*); 177 tons; 86.6ft × 21.8ft; 12 guns
Lieutenant William Fellowes

Part of the squadron in the West Indies blockading the island of Guadeloupe, she had been engaged in regular bombardments of the enemy's land batteries, which had shaken the hull and she had become very leaky. When two French frigates, the *Félicité* and the *Furieuse*, laden with stores for the garrison on the island were chased into Basse Terre roads, the senior officer of the squadron decided to convert the brig into a fireship for an attack on the pair. The assault was carried during the evening of 11 May, but without result, it being a squally day, and a change in wind caused her to luff, and she ran aground a short distance from one of the frigates. Having no alternative, Lieutenant Fellowes had to abandon her, setting fire to the brig as he left.
[O'Byrne p351; Marshall: Supplement pt.2 p317]

16 June AGAMEMNON Third Rate
Buckler's Hard 1781; 1,384 tons; 160.2ft × 44.5ft; 64 guns
Captain Jonas Rose

Part of a squadron based at Rio de Janeiro the *Agamemnon* was ordered to proceed to the River Plate in company with other ships of the squadron. They arrived off Maldonado Bay during the evening of 15 June, intending to enter the following day. The next morning, they proceeded with caution, a Spanish chart being used for navigation. When the water started shoaling as expected, she let go the bower anchor, but as she did so, without warning she took the ground. Boats were hoisted out and laid out a kedge anchor, and on heaving on the hawser, she moved a little, and encouraged by this, the stream anchor was laid out, but she would shift no further. It was now found that she was making water and the pumps were manned, and the schooner *Mistletoe* was ordered to close and give assistance. Work started to offload stores, commencing with the sails and cordage from the Bosun's store, but as the store was cleared, it was found that water flooded in. The water gained on the pumps, and was soon up to the hatch coamings, and by 10.30 that evening she had 9ft of water in the hold and had developed a heavy list to starboard. The following morning it was clear that she could not be saved, and after more stores were removed and the men were taken off, the ship was left to settle. It was found that she had run onto an unmarked shoal, and then probably sat on her bower anchor. Captain Rose claimed that she could have been hauled off, had it not been for her poor state, with many knees, beams and timbers in a state of decay.
[TNA: ADM.1/5399; ADM.51/1934]

18 June SEALARK Schooner
Brixham 1806; 76 tons; 56.4ft × 18.4ft; 4 guns
Lieutenant James Proctor†

In company with the *Blake* and *Britomart* in the North Sea, at 10 o'clock in the morning, when about three to four miles from her companions, she was seen attempting to wear, but then disappeared after she capsized when struck on the broadside by a particularly heavy sea. Both *Blake* and *Britomart* hoisted out boats to search the area, but there was only one survivor, found clinging to a spar.
[TNA: ADM.51/1927; ADM.51/1935]

11 July SOLEBAY Fifth Rate
Deptford 1785; 683 tons; 126.3ft × 35ft; 32 guns
Captain Edward Henry Columbine

Part of the force covering an attack on the French settlement at Gorée, West Africa. Captain Columbine and a proportion of the crew were landed to assist the Royal Africa Corps in their attack, all the boats being taken for this purpose. The *Solebay* and *Derwent* frigates were ordered to close the fort at Babagué to bombard it, and under the command of the Master, Daniel Lye, the *Solebay* moved near the fort to commence the action. After sunset, Mr Lye decided to shift her berth further out, fearing a boat attack from the shore, and not entirely trusting the 'insubordinate soldiers' he still had onboard. The frigate weighed, but the strong currents initially took her down onto the *Derwent*, which was cleared with some difficulty, and it was then found difficult to bring her head round, the current forcing her back inshore. The anchor was let go, which brought her up, but at 9 o'clock she was felt to bump on the ground. She was lightened by heaving overboard some of the ballast and shot, and when a light breeze sprang up, the anchor cable was cut, and an attempt made to sail out. Before she could reach deeper water, the breeze fell away and she was again taken by the current further inshore. Despite letting the anchors go, she again grounded, and this time started pounding. Stores were shifted and heaved overboard, but no anchor could be taken out as no boats were available, and the *Derwent* had only one jolly boat to help her. At first light, shore batteries opened fire on her and were soon hitting her. By early afternoon, the foreyard had been shot away, all the masts shot through, the rigging cut up and with fourteen shots in the hull, she was given up as a wreck. Over the next few days most of the stores were taken off, but with no hope of hauling her off she was finally abandoned on 17 July, the water then being up to the orlop deck. Whilst she was lying on the sandbank, several of the crew refused to obey orders and got very drunk. Four men were subsequently punished: Michael Grace received 150 lashes; Thomas Jones 100, whilst Claus Neleus and Robert Storks each had 50 lashes.
[TNA: ADM.1/5399]

3 August DOMINICA Gun Brig
Prize 1807 (Tape-à-l'œil); 153 tons; 10 guns
Lieutenant Charles Welsh†
Disappeared in the vicinity of Tortola, Virgin Islands after escorting the *Prince Adolphus* packet clear of the Leeward Islands and believed to have foundered during a storm with the loss of all hands on or about this date.
[TNA: ADM.1/330; www.britishnewspaperarchive.co: Barbados Mercury 19 August 1809]

3 August LARK Ship Sloop
Northfleet 1794; 429 tons; 108.7ft x 29.9ft; 18 guns
Commander Robert Nicholas†
Laying at anchor off Punta Palenque, San Domingo, when a strong north-easterly gale blew up with the winds steadily increasing through the night. In order to clear the land, the anchor cables were cut at daybreak, and she stood out to sea under reefed topsails and foresail. When clear of the land, she was in the process of shortening sail to storm staysails, when she was hit by a strong squall. All the sails were split, and the sloop was rolled over onto her beam-ends. She lay in this state for several minutes, but before she could recover a heavy sea struck her, after which she filled rapidly with water and sank within 15 minutes. Several men survived, clinging to floating wreckage, but when the sloop *Moselle* arrived in the area that evening, only three remained alive to be picked up.
[TNA: ADM.1/5399]

5 August LORD NELSON Cutter
Hired 1807; 69 tons; 8 guns
Master John Wood
Part of the force supporting the expedition to Walcheren, the cutter ran aground in shallow water near Flushing and, when it proved impossible to free her, was abandoned as a wreck.
[TNA: ADM.49/97; www.britishnewspaperarchive.co: Morning Advertiser 9 August 1809 p3]

10 August ALAART Brig Sloop
Prize 1807; 306 tons; 94.7ft x 27.3ft; 18 guns
Commander James Tillard
Cruising off the coast of Norway, the brig chased two merchant ships close under the land, which made for the harbour of Fredricksvern. The wind fell away, and the ships successfully escaped into the port, where the *Alaart* observed two brigs of war – the *Lougen* and *Seagull* – at anchor, with several gunboats. All the Danish vessels slipped on sighting the British sloop and rowed out of harbour towards her. The brig manned her sweeps and she made off as best she could, but the gunboats, fifteen in all, divided into three divisions and steadily overhauled her. After a three-hour chase, the gunboats were spread out astern and abeam of the *Alaart*, and at a little after 12.00 noon, they opened fire with roundshot and grape. The fire was returned, and the fight went on for the next two hours, until with the mainmast shot through, main-topmast, bowsprit gammoning, part of the standing rigging and all the running rigging shot away, she surrendered. One man killed and three wounded.
[TNA: ADM.1/5400]

August FOXHOUND Brig Sloop
Dover 1806; 384 tons; 100ft x 30.7ft; 18 guns
Commander James MacKenzie†
Sailed from Quebec 10 August to escort a large convoy to England, she parted company with the convoy on 20 August in poor weather and was not seen again. Presumed foundered with all hands.
[www.britishnewspaperarchive.co: Morning Advertiser 21 September 1809 p2]

August CONTEST Gun Brig
Chester 1804; 178 tons; 80.1ft x 22.6ft; 12 guns
Lieutenant John Gregory†
Arrived in the Chesapeake with despatches 29 July, she sailed to return to England a few days later, but was not seen again. Presumed foundered with all hands. Pay book closed 31 August.
[TNA: ADM.35/2697; www.britishnewspaperarchive.co: Morning Post 15 February 1810 p3]

2 September MINX Gun Brig
Northfleet 1801; 180 tons; 80.1ft x 22.8ft; 12 guns
Lieutenant George LeBlanc
The brig was stationed off the Skaw (Skagen), northern Denmark, acting as a light vessel, and during the morning, several vessels were observed gathering close to the shore. By 10am, six gunboats could be seen rowing towards her, at which the brig weighed anchor and made sail. By 4 o'clock in the afternoon the wind had dropped away to a calm, and even though she was using sweeps, the gunboats steadily overhauled the *Minx*. Half an hour later the gunboats formed up in a line on the quarters and stern of the brig and opened fire. After returning fire with stern-chase guns, she used her sweeps to pull herself round to employ the broadside. The engagement went on for over two hours, at a range of 400 to 500 yards, the *Minx* suffering badly, with damaged rigging, the mainsail gaff shot away, and three guns disabled. When the gunboats closed to board her, the brig surrendered. Two men killed and nine wounded.
[TNA: ADM.1/5400]

22 September CURIEUX Brig Sloop
Prize 1804; 329 tons; 97ft × 28.6ft; 18 guns
Lieutenant Henry Gorges Moysey

After taking on water at St Louis, Marie Galante, the sloop weighed and proceeded towards Grand Terre, Guadeloupe. Lieutenant Moysey left night orders for the brig to come about and shorten sail at 1 o'clock in the morning and was therefore surprised when he was woken at 3.30am with the sloop running aground. A bower and the stream anchor were laid out by the boats but heaving on them had no effect. At first light they discovered that they were on Petite Terre, to the south-east of Guadeloupe. Later that day the *Hazard* sloop came to her aid, and after off-loading most of the stores and the guns, a hawser was passed. The *Hazard* started heaving, and the brig moved, and slid off the reef very quickly. No sooner was she free, however, that the cable parted, and she swung back onto the rocks and bilged, quickly filling with water. The officer of the watch, Lieutenant John Fulton, was found to have been disobedient and negligent in failing to carry out the night orders and had further failed to inform the Captain or act promptly when the danger was realised. He was dismissed the service. The Master, John Wood, was admonished to be more careful in the future, as he had not clearly stated the position of the brig to Fulton.
[TNA: ADM.1/5400]

24 October GLOMMEN Brig Sloop
Prize 1807; 303 tons; 94.2ft × 27.1ft; 16 guns
Commander Charles Pickford

Laying at anchor at Bridgetown, Barbados, the Master Attendant of the yard came onboard to assist in mooring her, in preparation for a looming storm. Topmasts were struck, an anchor laid out to seaward, and a hawser passed to the *Dart* sloop nearby. Commander Pickford was ashore that evening when, at about 9.30pm, the anchor cable parted. Distress guns were fired but the brig swung round before another anchor could be let go, to be carried rapidly towards the nearby shore where she went aground. With the surf beating over her, she bilged, rapidly filled with water and sank very quickly.
[TNA: ADM.1/5400]

2 November VICTOR Brig Sloop
Prize 1808 (*Jena*); 400 tons; 18 guns
Commander Edward Stopford

Cruising in the Bay of Bengal, during the afternoon a large frigate was seen, which bore up in chase of the sloop. Clearly outmatched, the *Victor* made all sail away, the pursuit going on until early evening, with the frigate slowly overhauling the brig. Exchanges of fire between stern- and bow-chase guns went on for some time, until the frigate was able to bring her broadside to bear. At 10 o'clock, with her rigging cut to pieces and both masts shot through, she surrendered to the French frigate *Bellone*, 40 guns. Two men were wounded.
[TNA: ADM.1/5403]

12 November GIBRALTAR Gunboat
Gibraltar 1805 (*Gunboat-14*); 44 tons; 50.7ft × 14ft; 2 guns
Lieutenant Thomas Spence†

Attached to the *San Juan* hulk at Gibraltar, she sailed on 11 November bound for Cadiz with despatches for Admiral Purvis at that port. The next morning, when off Sancti Petri island, the gunboat was hit by a strong squall, which capsized the vessel, throwing all the crew into the sea. Only one man was still alive later that day, when he was found, clinging to the binnacle, by a passing merchant ship. Eleven men were lost.
[www.britishnewspaperarchive.co: Public Ledger 15 December 1809 p2; TNA: ADM.51/2801]

12 November HADDOCK Schooner
Bermuda 1803; 71 tons; 55.2ft × 18ft; 4 guns
Lieutenant Henry Edwards

Bound for England from Jamaica with despatches from Vice Admiral Rowley, at 1.30pm, then being in position 49.45N 18W, a brig was sighted on the weather quarter. The brig was evidently in chase of the schooner, and was overhauling, and when no response was made to private recognition signals, the *Haddock* made all sail away. The chasing brig showed British colours, but these were not believed. By 6 o'clock, with the brig closing rapidly on the schooner, Lieutenant Edwards altered course and attempted to cross her bows, but the brig matched her movements carefully. The enemy vessel was now using her bow-chase guns at regular intervals, and in an effort to outpace her, the *Haddock* heaved overboard her guns, shot and some stores. The lightened schooner did increase the distance slightly, but the brig was soon steadily closing again. By 8.30pm she was 2 cables (400 yards) astern, with shot from the bow-chase guns going through the rigging. The signals and despatches were heaved overboard, and when the brig fired a volley of musketry, the *Haddock* surrendered, finding her captor was the French *Génie*, 18 guns.
[TNA: ADM.1/5399]

7 December HARLEQUIN Ship Sloop
Hired 1804; 185 tons; 18 guns
Lieutenant Philip Charles Anstruther

Sailed from Plymouth on 5 December to escort a convoy of more than twenty ships eastward through the English Channel. The convoy proceeded uneventfully until at 4 o'clock in the morning, with little warning they ran hard aground. With surf breaking over them, the masts were cut away and guns fired, and blue lights burnt. Despite these actions, another six ships of the convoy also went ashore. The darkness of the night,

coupled with the belief that they had weathered Beachy Head, had led to a premature alteration of course, and the subsequent wreck to the west of Seaford. Two men were lost attempting to get to the shore.
[Gold: Naval Chronicle vol 23 p111]

13 December JUNON Fifth Rate
Prize 1809; 1,102 tons; 154.8ft × 40ft; 38 guns
Captain John Shortland†

In the early afternoon, in position 17.18N 57W, the *Junon* was in company with the sloop *Observateur*, searching an American merchant ship they had stopped, when four strange ships were seen to the north. Leaving the American, the British pair made sail in the direction of the strangers, and by 4 o'clock they could be seen to be frigates. The *Junon* made the private recognition signals as she approached, which was answered by the ships hoisting Spanish colours. At this, the *Junon* made the private signals for Spanish warships, and the largest of the ships made the correct answer. Now confident that they were a Spanish squadron, the *Junon* and her consort closed, shortening sail as they neared. When about a quarter of a mile distant, the largest frigate, which was actually the French *Renomée*, 40 guns, hauled down the Spanish colours and replaced them with French, then ran down to the *Junon* and fired a broadside into her. Captain Shortland attempted to get under the stern of his opponent, but found the second frigate, the *Clorinde*, 40, in his path, and there was an exchange of broadsides for 10 minutes, until the *Renomée* re-joined the fray by running onto the British ship's larboard side. The other French ships, the *Loire*, 20, and the *Seine*, 20, both added to the distress of the *Junon* by laying off her quarter and firing into her when they could. The *Junon* also found herself hampered in returning fire, as being a prize capture herself, she had not yet been fitted with gunlocks, and still relied on matches, which were of poor quality and constantly going out. At 6 o'clock Captain Shortland had his legs shattered by grapeshot, but Lieutenant Samuel Deecker maintained the struggle. The French attempted to board but were driven back by the detachment of Royal Marines, led by Lieutenant John Green. After a further 30 minutes of this unequal struggle, a second attempt at boarding was successful, and the *Junon* surrendered. The *Observateur* sloop made her escape while the French concentrated on her larger companion. The French removed the crew from their prize and burnt her. Twenty men killed and forty wounded. The subsequent court-martial enquiry into the loss drew the attention of the Admiral commanding the station to the conduct of the Master's Mate, James Edwards, who was found to be drunk after the action, and to Midshipman Frederick Whitehurst, who had used expressions 'injurious to the service'.
[TNA:ADM. 1/5402]

14 December DEFENDER Gun Brig
Chester 1804; 179 tons; 80.1ft × 22.7ft; 12 guns
Lieutenant John George Nops

Running from the Downs anchorage for Spithead in worsening weather, as she coasted along the Sussex shore, it became clear that she would not weather Dungeness. The brig headed for Folkestone and during the afternoon of 13 December she anchored, intending to wait for more favourable weather. In the early hours of the next morning the anchor cable parted. Another anchor was let go, which brought her up, but 30 minutes later, this also parted. The strong winds forced down onto the shore, at Copt Point, to the east of the town. The local Sea Fencibles came to her aid, and most of the stores were saved, but the brig's bottom was beaten in, and she was abandoned as a wreck.
[TNA:ADM.1/5400]

1810

7 February ACHATES Brig Sloop
Rotherhithe 1808; 238 tons; 90.2ft × 24.7ft; 10 guns
Commander Thomas Pinto

Ordered to cruise in company with the *Freya* frigate in the vicinity of Englishman's Head, Guadeloupe, the sloop was standing in for the island in late afternoon. Commander Pinto was exhausted after being up for most of the preceding night and dropped off to sleep as he sat on the starboard gangway. The officer of the watch, Lieutenant Edward Cotgrave, confidently stood on towards the shore, having been accustomed in the recent past to do so until the breakers were seen, when they would alter course. A strong lee current took them into the land far quicker than he realised, and no warnings came from his slumbering Captain. When the breakers were seen, they were close ahead, and although the helm was put over, it was too late, and she ran hard aground on a reef. All sail was thrown aback, but she was held fast and would not move. Boats were hoisted out to carry out an anchor, but the brig capsized over to port before this could be done. The main- and foremasts were cut away to steady the vessel and the crew were employed during the night in making rafts. The following morning several boats from Guadeloupe approached and lifted the crew off. Commander Pinto was severely reprimanded for failing to give orders to officers regarding the precautions to take when approaching the land; he was not subsequently employed. Lieutenant Cotgrave was criticised for failing to use the lead-line or log. He was admonished to be more careful in the future.
[TNA:ADM.1/5402]

15 February WILD BOAR Brig Sloop
Frindsbury 1808; 238 tons; 90ft × 24.8ft; 10 guns
Commander Thomas Burton

Bound for Cork from Falmouth, the sloop was negotiating the passage between the Scilly Isles and the mainland, when at 4 o'clock in the afternoon, in fine weather and running at 8 knots, she struck the Runnel Stone, off Gwennap, Cornwall. She hung on the obstruction for about two minutes, before slipping off, water gushing in. Within five minutes the lower deck was flooded and although attempts were made to hoist out the boats, and guns of distress were fired, most of the crew were forced to jump into the water. The *Earl of Uxbridge* merchant ship was fortunately in sight and came to their aid, but twelve men drowned. About 15 minutes after striking the rock she was seen to '... take a lurch' and foundered. The Master, John Elder, was blamed for the loss through his incompetence – the rock was a well-known and marked obstruction. His actions after the wreck were described as highly reprehensible, as he had jumped into the jolly boat being towed astern when she struck and made off. He was let off surprisingly lightly, being disrated from his position as Master and ordered to serve in the future only as a seaman.
[TNA: ADM. 1/5402]

March PELTER Gun Brig
Deptford 1804; 178 tons; 80.1ft × 22.6ft; 12 guns
Lieutenant William Evelyn†

Stationed in the West Indies, she successfully escorted a convoy to Halifax, Nova Scotia, in December 1809. She sailed on 3 March to return to her station but was not seen again. Presumed to have foundered with all hands. Pay book closed 31 March 1810.
[TNA: ADM. 35/3020]

6 April CUCKOO Schooner
Great Yarmouth 1806; 76 tons; 56.3ft × 18.3ft; 4 guns
Lieutenant Silas Hiscutt Paddon

Ordered to the Dutch coast, to circulate new orders regarding the detention of foreign fishing vessels to ships of the blockade, the weather was poor and worsened. During the night of 3 April, the main boom was carried away by the rising storm. The following evening, soundings showed the water shallowing, and she was ordered to wear. Scarcely had she done so when she struck the ground. Pumping was started and stores thrown overboard to lighten her, but the water steadily gained on the pumps. At 1 o'clock in the morning the boats were hoisted out and some of the crew were sent ashore, the remainder being forced into the rigging as the schooner settled. Those left onboard spent several uncomfortable hours clinging to spars and ropes before the cutter could return. All but two were rescued, one man and a boy – the latter being Lieutenant Paddon's son – dying of exposure, and Paddon was injured by a falling spar, which broke his shoulder and two ribs. All were taken to the Texel where they were detained as prisoners. The blame for running the schooner onto the Haak Sands off Calantzoog was placed on the pilot, Joseph Delaby, through his negligence and ignorance. He seems to have suspected the outcome of the court martial, as he deserted before the trial. Lieutenant Paddon was admonished to be more careful in the future, having placed too much confidence in Delaby.
[TNA: ADM. 1/5405]

13 April GRINDER Tender
From 1810; 41 tons; 2 guns
Master's Mate Thomas Hester

A vessel fitted out on the island of Anholt, occupied by the British during 1809, to act as a tender to the garrison on the island, the opportunity was taken to act offensively, and interrupt Danish shipping. On 13 April, the tender chased a small convoy near Randers Fjord. As the tender closed, several gunboats that had been concealed behind the convoy emerged, at which the *Grinder* made all sail away. The gunboats chased the tender for 90 minutes, firing regularly, until she was overhauled and surrendered. One man was killed.

Note: recaptured on 5 July 1811 by the *Sheldrake*.
[TNA: ADM. 1/10]

24 May FLÈCHE Ship Sloop
Prize 1798 (*Caroline*); 278 tons; 92ft × 26.6ft; 18 guns
Commander George Hewson

Ordered to the River Elbe, the sloop picked up two pilots from Heligoland during 23 May, and stood south-east until that evening, when she anchored. At 3.30 the following morning, she weighed and 45 minutes later raised the beacon on the island of Scharhorn. The ship stood on, sounding constantly until 5.30am, when the water started shoaling, and despite a confused attempt to wear ship, she ran aground on the sands between Scharhorn and Neuwerk. An initial attempt to sail off failed, after which all sail was taken in and topgallant masts and yards were struck. Spars were lowered over the side to act as shores, but the sloop settled, and when several rotten timbers gave way, she capsized and started to fill with water. Distress guns brought the *Pincher* and *Exertion* gun brigs to her aid. By 9 o'clock the water was over the lower deck and the crew started to leave the ship. This proved a long process; by early afternoon, the vessel had disappeared, apart from the poop and masts, and several survivors were forced to cling to them. The last men were taken off at 2 o'clock. The blame for the loss was placed on the pilots, Martin Hoas and Andreas Hornsmoor, and they were mulcted of all pay due.
[TNA: ADM. 1/5406]

1 June BLACK JOKE Lugger
Hired 1808; 109 tons; 10 guns
Lieutenant Moses Cannadey

Carrying mail and despatches from Malta for Gibraltar and Cadiz, she was chased and captured by two large privateers off the North African coast and taken into Algiers.
[TNA: ADM.49/97; www.britishnewspaperarchive.co: Hampshire Chronicle 20 August 1810 p1]

4 June IDAS (2) Cutter
Hired 1809; 102 tons; 10 guns
Lieutenant James Rayson

Part of a force off the Scheldt, during the afternoon the cutter was manoeuvring off the entrance to the river, when she ran aground on the Elleborg reef. The falling tide and the proximity of land forces meant that if she were to be freed it would have to be done quickly. An anchor was laid out astern and a party from the *Drake* sloop was sent onboard to destroy her if she could not be freed. The party was led by an officer dressed in a plain blue jacket with no marks of rank and his authoritative manner led everyone to believe he was senior to Lieutenant Rayson, who himself believed it was Commander Maxwell of the *Drake*. The officer was actually Lieutenant Samuel Langley, who was two years' junior to Rayson, and after stating that they were attempting the impossible to pull the cutter off stern-first on a falling tide, he ordered everyone to leave, since he was about to blow the cutter up. Lieutenant Rayson did not question this, but promptly joined his crew in taking to the boats, leaving Lieutenant Langley and his small party from the *Drake* onboard. The cutter was now coming under harassing fire from the shore, field guns and musketry being used. Only one boat was left, and after ordering his own party to leave, Lieutenant Langley decided to join them, without setting fire to the cutter, apparently intending to return after putting his men onto ships nearby. That achieved, Langley found it impossible to return, due to the rapidity of the current and the fire from the shore, and the cutter was given up to the French. Langley was later reprimanded for his actions.
[TNA: ADM.1/5406]

4 June PORGEY Schooner
Bermuda 1807; 71 tons; 55.2ft × 18ft; 4 guns
Lieutenant Hugh Gould

Off the River Scheldt, she observed the cutter *Idas (2)*, run ashore and was one of the vessels ordered to stand by her (see above). The jolly boat was hoisted out to go to the aid of the cutter, but at 4 o'clock, the boats were seen to pull away from her. The *Porgey* was manoeuvring nearby and in order to receive her boat she attempted to luff up into the wind. She refused to do so, however, and the current took her down onto a sandbank, near the stricken *Idas*. An attempt to carry out a kedge anchor was abandoned, as the tide was ebbing fast, and she was left high and dry. The troops ashore now had a second target to engage, and field guns were soon hitting her. Lieutenant Gould ordered all the men into the boats and set fire to the schooner before he left.
[TNA: ADM.1/5406]

10 August LIVELY Fifth Rate
Woolwich 1804; 1,076 tons; 154.1ft × 39.6ft; 38 guns
Captain George McKinley

Escorting a small convoy to Malta, the island of Gozo was sighted during the evening of 9 August and a course was laid which would allow them to pass within three miles of Valletta. The intention was to close to about 12 miles from the island, lie-to overnight and enter the following morning. At 2 o'clock in the morning, the Master brought her to, much closer to the land than ordered, her head to the shore, but did not inform the Captain that he had done so. She was slowly taken inshore by a strong current until breakers were seen ahead. Despite an attempt to tack, she ran hard aground. Boats were hoisted out and the masts were cut away to fall onto the shore, the men all being ordered off the ship. Morning revealed that they had had gone ashore near Coura Point (Qawra), in St Paul's Bay, and were surrounded by rocks. All the stores and provisions were taken out of her, and dockyard workmen were despatched to the scene, strenuous efforts being made to haul her off. The work continued until the end of September, when she was abandoned as a wreck, anything useful being stripped from her. The Master, Michael Richard, was found to have brought the ship too close to the shore, and was dismissed his ship and disrated, being ordered to serve before the mast. The officer of the watch, Lieutenant Hon. Augustus Fitzharding Berkeley, had failed to acquaint the Captain of the position of the ship, and failed to realise the danger the ship was in. He was admonished to be more careful in the future.
[TNA: ADM.1/5410]

23–25 August: Action at Mauritius
The summer of 1810 saw a campaign against the French Indian Ocean possessions: the Île de Bourbon (Réunion) was captured in July. In August attention was turned to Mauritius, and a force of four frigates, *Nereide*, *Sirius*, *Magicienne* and *Iphigenia* with the *Staunch* gun brig was assembled off the island under the command of Captain Pym of the *Sirius*. Two of the frigates were stationed on the west coast of the island, blockading Port Louis, whilst the other ships were brought to the other side of the island to blockade Grand Port. This latter force captured an outlying island on 13 August,

and parties of men were landed to man gun batteries. All proceeded smoothly and the *Sirius* sailed to join the force off Port Louis, leaving the *Nereide* and *Staunch* to maintain the blockade of Grand Port. On 20 August, a French squadron arrived off Grand Port, comprising two large 40-gun frigates, the *Bellone* and *Minerve*, and the 18-gun corvette *Victor* with two East Indiamen prizes. The French squadron entered the port, exchanging fire with the *Nereide* as they did so, only one of the Indiamen prizes sheering off. Captain Pym learned of the arrival of the French force and took all three frigates to join *Nereide*. They arrived off the Grand Port during 22 August and Pym determined to act quickly, reasoning that his force of four frigates were stronger than the two French ships. During the late afternoon of 23 August, the *Nereide*, the only ship to have a pilot on board, led the way, threading their way through coral reefs and took up her station. The ships following failed to negotiate the entrance and ran hard aground.

The resulting action proved to be a costly defeat for the British, with the loss of all four frigates and the deaths of over 100 men.

24 August NÉRÉIDE Fifth Rate
Prize 1797; 892 tons; 142.5ft × 37.6ft; 36 guns
Captain Nisbet Josiah Willoughby

Captain Willoughby, leading the column of frigates into Grand Port with a pilot embarked, was able to enter the harbour and took up his assigned position close to the *Bellone*, 40 guns, but with the failure of his consorts to join, found himself facing the enemy squadron alone. A fierce action began, initially with some success for the British, the former British East Indiaman striking her flag and running ashore. At 6.30pm, her main opponent, the *Minerve*, had her anchor cable shot away, and drifted a short distance before she ran aground. The other French frigate, *Bellone*, being fouled by both ships, cut her anchor cables to free herself and was soon aground as well. After this, the advantage swung away from the British. The *Nereide* had her spring cable shot away, and she swung round to present her stern to the *Bellone*, which raked her repeatedly, causing many casualties. These included Captain Willoughby, a splinter lacerating his cheek and taking out an eye. The First Lieutenant, John Burns, was killed and most of the other officers wounded. As the gun duel continued, the more powerful armament of the French ships gained over the British, the *Nereide*, being the nearest, suffering the most. By 10 o'clock that evening most of her guns had been dismounted or disabled and she could no longer offer any effective reply. A boat was sent to the *Sirius* for assistance, but that ship could do little except to request Willoughby to leave the ship, which was declined. The boat then attempted to reach the *Bellone*, to say that they would surrender, but failed to reach her, the boat being in a sinking condition. All the crew were now ordered to take shelter below, as the fire continued to pour into her from the French vessels. The mainmast went overboard at midnight and fires were started, all of which were put out. Finally, at 1.50 in the morning after being hailed repeatedly, the French ceased firing. Daylight brought a return of their misery, with the enemy again opening fire. In desperation, French tricolours were hoisted, but the fire continued. It was then realised that a Union flag was still flying from the mizzen topgallant masthead; unable to lower it, the mast was cut away, at which the firing stopped. At 2 o'clock in the afternoon a boat from the *Bellone* came alongside to take possession. The casualties taken by the *Nereide* during the action were frightful: 92 men killed and 137 wounded from a complement of 281. The subsequent court martial on Captain Willoughby praised him for his bravery but was critical of his overconfidence which had led him to signal during the morning that the 'Enemy is of inferior force', which was judged injudicious.

Note: recaptured on 3 December 1810 by a British squadron, still in the harbour, but in such a poor state that she was broken up locally
[TNA: ADM. 1/5411]

24 August SIRIUS Fifth Rate
Deptford 1797; 1,034 tons; 148.10ft × 39.7ft; 36 guns
Captain Samuel Pym

Second in the column of British frigates entering Grand Port, *Sirius* followed the *Nereide*, but touched the ground. Having freed herself, she touched again at 5 o'clock. Still going ahead and with shallow water visible ahead, both bower anchors were let go which brought her up, although she found herself on a coral reef as she did so. She was now grounded about half a mile from the action, and could do little but fire occasionally in support, whilst work went on to try and free her. Every effort to kedge her off failed and the next morning she sent parties to help the *Iphigenia* to warp out of the harbour, whilst engaging shore batteries as and when she could. Firmly aground, making water, and unable to be freed, Captain Pym ordered stores and provisions to be transferred to *Iphigenia*, and after this was complete, the men were removed. The last of the crew left her during 25 August, setting fire to the frigate as they did so, the ship burning until she exploded at about 11 o'clock that night.
[TNA: ADM. 1/5411]

24 August MAGICIENNE Fifth Rate
Prize 1781; 968 tons; 143.9ft × 39.2ft; 32 guns
Captain Lucius Curtis

Followed the *Sirius* into Grand Port, and when that ship went aground for a second time, steered well clear to head

for the harbour. At 5.15pm, when heading for her station between the *Minerve* and the captured East Indiaman, *Ceylon*, she ran aground. She was then about 400 yards from her allotted position and could only fire from her foremost guns. All efforts through the night to free her proved fruitless, the morning of 24 August seeing her still hard aground. She resumed her fire to try and support the stricken *Nereide*, but after that ship had surrendered and the *Iphigenia* had warped out of the anchorage, she took the full force of the French fire. Unable to effectively reply, being regularly hulled by the enemy fire and stuck fast in the mud, it was decided to abandon her. The crew were transferred to the *Sirius* and Captain Curtis set her on fire when he left the ship at 11 o'clock that evening. Eight men killed and twenty wounded.
[TNA: ADM.1/5411]

28 August IPHIGENIA Fifth Rate
Chatham 1808; 876 tons; 137ft × 38.2ft; 36 guns
Captain Henry Lambert
The only survivor of the attack on the Grand Port, she had avoided following the *Sirius* and *Magicienne* but finding herself in six fathoms of water, anchored some distance from the action. She began warping herself out of the harbour during 25 August, being assisted by the *Sirius*, taking onboard the crew from that ship. By early morning she was out of range of the French guns, but found it hard going, having to warp all the way. At 4 o'clock in the morning of 26 August, on hauling in the cable from the bower anchor to recommence warping, it was found that the anchor had broken, and they had to resort to using a cannon as a kedge anchor to continue their progress. By 8 o'clock that evening, she was in 13 fathoms, about three-quarters of a mile from the small island of Île de la Passe, which was in the hands of the British. There being insufficient water to sail, the work of kedging and warping continued the next morning, when three frigates were sighted closing from seaward. They were seen to exchange signals with a French brig off the harbour, and Captain Lambert correctly surmised that these were yet more enemy ships. The French frigates in the harbour were also observed to be afloat, making the position of the *Iphigenia* very precarious. The men taken off the stranded vessels were landed on the island, and Lambert cleared his ship for action as the newcomers closed. They were the *Astrée*, 40 guns, *Vénus*, 40, and the *Manche*, 40, and at 1 o'clock in the afternoon of 27 August they sent a message to *Iphigenia* to surrender. This was refused and the work to warp her clear continued. The following morning several boats carrying flags of truce shuttled between the British and French, discussing terms of surrender. The *Iphigenia* was in no position to dictate terms, and low on ammunition and supplies and faced with overwhelming superiority, during 28 August, Captain Lambert agreed to surrender his ship and the island.

Note: recaptured on 3 December 1810 by a British squadron.
[TNA: ADM.1/5411]

★ ★ ★

12 September ALBAN Cutter
Bermuda 1806; 111 tons; 68.2ft × 20.4ft; 10 guns
Lieutenant Samuel Thomas†
Off Læsø Island in the Kattegat, in calm and hazy weather, when six Danish gunboats were seen to be pulling towards her from the land. With no wind, the cutter manned her own sweeps and attempted to open the range, but the gunboats steadily closed her. By 2.15 in the afternoon, they were close enough to open fire, which was promptly returned by the cutter. The action was continued for three hours, when Lieutenant Thomas was killed, being struck by a roundshot, and the command devolved on Midshipman Alexander Hutchinson. He continued to fight for another hour, when with the sails and rigging in tatters, the gaff shot away, seven shots in the hull and surrounded by gunboats preparing to board, she surrendered. Two men killed and three wounded.

Note: recaptured on 11 May 1811 by the *Rifleman*.
[TNA: ADM.1/5409]

13 October AFRICAINE Fifth Rate
Prize 1801; 1,085 tons; 153.10ft × 39.11ft; 38 guns
Captain Robert Corbett†
During the morning of 12 October, the *Africaine* arrived off the Île de Bourbon (Réunion), and observed two frigates at anchor, which were identified as French. The pair weighed and made sail away, and soon after a British frigate, the *Boadicea*, accompanied by two gun brigs, came into sight. The *Africaine*, after embarking soldiers of the 86th Regiment from the British forces on the island, made sail to join the *Boadicea* and pursue the French. By 6.30 that evening, she had stretched ahead and lost sight of the other British ships, but was closing rapidly on the French pair, which were the *Astrée*, 40 guns, and the former British frigate *Iphigénie*, 36. Night closed in with the *Africaine* staying astern of the French, burning blue lights and firing signal rockets at regular intervals, to keep the *Boadicea* in touch. At 2 o'clock in the morning, the French altered course, evidently heading for Port Louis, Mauritius, and Captain Corbett decided he must act to prevent this. Accordingly, the frigate closed and fired a broadside into the *Astrée*, which was returned. Captain Corbett was mortally wounded by the second broadside from the French ship, his right leg being struck by a cannon ball, taking off his foot. Lieutenant Joseph Tullidge assumed command and continued the fight. The *Astrée*, having her rigging damaged and jib boom shot away, ranged ahead, whilst the *Iphigénie* now

joined in, on the opposite beam. Now engaged with two opponents, the *Africaine* fought them both, hoping that the *Boadicea* would soon join, which she was unable to do, being some five miles astern, with the wind dropping away to a calm. After an hour, the fore topmast of the *Africaine* was shot away, followed by the mizzen topmast. Casualties were mounting, with Lieutenant Tullidge severely wounded, as was Lieutenant Robert Forder and the Master, Samuel Parker, was killed. At just before 5am, being unable to offer any more resistance, the *Africaine* surrendered. All her masts went overboard during the day, leaving her a hulk. Captain Corbett died of his wounds shortly after the surrender. The casualties were extremely high: 49 killed and 114 wounded. Later that afternoon the *Boadicea* came up with the crippled *Africaine* and recaptured her without a fight.
[TNA: ADM.1/5415]

18 October CEYLON Fifth Rate
Purchased 1805 (*Bombay*); 672 tons; 130ft × 34.8ft; 32 guns
Captain Charles Gordon
Despatched from Madras to join the Indian Ocean squadron, the frigate arrived off Mauritius on 17 September, but was surprised to find no sign of the British force, only French ships at anchor. Sail was made for the Île de Bourbon, with two French ships weighing anchor and pursuing her. The chase went on until midnight, when the leading French ship, the *Vénus*, 40 guns, was close astern. The *Ceylon* shortened sail to await her arrival, which was signalled by the fire of the French frigate's bow-chase guns and a volley of musketry. The pair exchanged fire for over an hour, when the *Vénus* dropped astern, allowing the *Ceylon* to repair damage and attempt to escape. The *Vénus*, however, after conducting her own repairs, was soon in chase again, and at 2.15am, firing was again resumed. Close action continued for a further two hours, during which the British ship lost all her topmasts, and the rigging and sails were torn to shreds, the *Vénus* suffering in a similar manner. By 4.30am the pair fell apart, but by now the second French ship, the corvette *Victor*, 18 guns, had arrived, and stationed herself on the bows of the *Ceylon*. Believing this to be a second large frigate, Captain Gordon surrendered. Ten men killed and thirty-one wounded. During the morning, the *Boadicea* frigate arrived on the scene, with two gun brigs, and recaptured the *Ceylon*.
[TNA: ADM.1/5411]

28 October RACER Cutter
Sandgate 1810; 203 tons; 75ft × 26.1ft; 10 guns
Lieutenant Daniel Miller
Ordered to cruise off the North Foreland to annoy the enemy and to protect local trade, during 27 October, *Racer* sighted and chased a French lugger privateer over to the French coast, which escaped into Calais. Having lost her quarry, the cutter looked for other prey, and when two brigs were seen hauled up on shore a little to the east of the port, Lieutenant Miller determined to attack them. The boats were hoisted out, and a successful attack was mounted, setting one brig on fire. The cutter was then manoeuvring offshore, with the leadsman calling out depths between six and eight fathoms, and when five fathoms was called, the cutter tacked, intending to put her head to seaward, but as she came round, so she took the ground, and swung around, head to the shore. Boats were used to take out an anchor and sound around them, and to Lieutenant Miller's dismay, he found them to be in little more than three fathoms and must have been in shallow water for some time. They could not pull her free on the ebbing tide, so they patiently waited for high water, but at 2 o'clock in the morning, she heeled over to starboard. At daybreak she was approached by several troops who opened fire, the cutter responding when they could. By the afternoon she was still high and dry, with her gunwale in the sand, and troops were now gathering in strength. Unable to do more, Lieutenant Miller surrendered. It was later ruled at the court martial that Seaman John Perry, the leadsman, must have deliberately given false depths to cause her wreck, although he was unable to defend himself, having disappeared.
[TNA: ADM.1/5443]

28 October CAMPERDOWN Gunboat
Gibraltar 1805 (*Gunboat-2*); 44 tons; 50.7ft × 14ft; 2 guns
Lieutenant William Style
Part of a small flotilla assembling at Cadiz from Gibraltar, she ran aground on Los Corrales reef between Cadiz and Puntales and was wrecked. One midshipman and fourteen men were drowned.
[O'Byrne p1140; Marshall Supplement 2 p323]

9 November CONFLICT Gun Brig
Topsham 1805; 182 tons; 84ft × 22.1ft; 12 guns
Lieutenant Joseph Bainbrigg Batt[†]
Sailed from Plymouth on 2 November for Corunna, arriving at that place on 8 November, and then sailed to cruise off the northern coast of Spain. She was last seen on that date by the *Arethusa*, '… in great distress' in gale force winds, and was presumed to have foundered soon after with all hands.
[www.britishnewspaperarchive.co: Ipswich Journal 26 January 1811 p21]

9 December MANDARIN Gun Brig
Prize 1810 (*Madurense*); 178 tons; 12 guns
Lieutenant Charles Jefferis
In February 1810, the British had captured the Dutch outpost of Amboyna (Ambon) in the Moluccas, and one of the Dutch vessels found in the harbour was

commissioned as the *Mandarin*. After refitting, the brig was ordered to Penang, to carry despatches from Captain Tucker of the *Dover*, and to procure stores and provisions. The brig sailed on 2 November, and by 8 December was off Singapore and the following day commenced beating through the Straits, although no reliable chart was held. As they steered along the shore, they ran hard aground. Efforts were made to free her, but as the tide left her, she was in danger of capsizing, and the masts were cut away, and as she thumped heavily on the rocks, she bilged and started to fill with water. The boats were hoisted out to start carrying supplies to the nearby island, later identified as 'Red Island' (Pulau Pelampong) and during the day the crew, except for four Lascar seamen who were drunk, were safely landed on the island. The following day the frigate *Chiffone*, escorting a convoy of Indiamen from China, sighted the wreck, and was able to rescue them all, apart from one man, who was reported to have drowned.
[Gold: Naval Chronicle vol 26 p209; TNA: ADM.54/335]

18 December **NYMPHE** Fifth Rate
Prize 1780; 938 tons; 141.5ft × 38.3ft; 36 guns
Captain Edward Sneyd Clay

Returning from a cruise off the coast of Norway, the land around Aberdeen was raised at daylight on 18 December. The frigate altered course to the south and later that day sighted Bell Rock. Course was then set for May Island, the light of which was just in sight. The light was then lost in the gloom, but by continuing the same course, a light was seen, which both pilot and Master agreed must be the May Island light. At about 9.45pm land was discovered close ahead, the helm being hastily put over, but shortly after she ran onto a reef, the rocks piercing her bottom. The water rapidly flooded in, and she soon had a pronounced list to starboard. Masts were cut away and distress guns fired, but little could be done, and the crew were ordered to make their way to the shore, clambering over the wreckage of the masts. Morning showed her to be full of water, and although an effort was made to save the stores, little could be secured. The ship had gone ashore at Torness near Dunbar, impaled on a rock known as the Devil's Ark. Both the pilot, Christopher Gascoigne, and the Master George Scott were severely reprimanded for being '... incautious in asserting in such a positive manner the light seen was the May Island light'. The lights seen were lime-burners working at Broxmouth.
[TNA: ADM.1/5412]

18 December **PALLAS** Fifth Rate
Plymouth 1804; 665 tons; 127.1ft × 34.2ft; 32 guns
Captain George Paris Monke

As with the *Nymphe* (see above), she was returning from a cruise off the coast of Norway. Buchan Ness was sighted on 16 December and the ship altered to the south, intending to enter Leith. The visibility was poor, with frequent showers of cold rain, and when nothing could be seen of the Bell Rock light, Captain Monke became increasingly anxious and ordered extra lookouts to be posted. During the night of 17 December, a light was observed, which was identified as Arbroath pier, and when another light was seen ahead, the Master claimed that it must be the expected Bell Rock light. Course was altered to allow them to make the next landmark, the May Island light. During the early hours of 18 December, a light was seen ahead, which was taken for May Island. Soon after this, with little warning, she ran hard aground. The ship was immediately bilged, and within minutes had 12ft of water inside her. Fore- and main-masts were cut away, falling towards the land now visible in the light of the rising moon. As the frigate heeled over to starboard and settled, the crew were ordered to leave, some jumping overboard to attempt to swim, others making their way over the wreckage of the masts to the shore. Others remained onboard, to be rescued later that morning by boats from the shore, although one capsized doing so, with the loss of nine men. A total of fourteen men were lost. It was found that she had run onto the Scottish coast at Barns Ness near Dunbar. Like the *Nymphe*, the officers of the *Pallas* had mistaken the lights of lime-burning kilns at Broxmouth for the May Island light. Captain Monke and the pilot James Burgess were both severely reprimanded for the loss, with the Master, David Glegg, being dismissed his ship and demoted, being ordered never to serve as a Master again.
[TNA: ADM.1/5412]

19 December **SATELLITE** Brig Sloop
Sandwich 1806; 289 tons; 93.2ft 26.8ft; 16 guns
Commander Hon. Willoughby Bertie[†]

Sailed from Spithead on 17 December to join the ships blockading the northern coast of France in the vicinity of Cap de la Hague. She was last seen at about 6 o'clock in the evening of 19 December by the *Vautour*, in a hard gale of wind, with regular strong squalls of rain. The following morning *Vautour* picked up wreckage, including spars and a boat from the *Satellite*, and it was presumed that she had foundered with the loss of all hands.
[www.britishnewspaperarchive.co: Star (London) 31 December 1810]

22 December **MINOTAUR** Third Rate
Woolwich 1793; 1,718 tons; 172.1ft × 48ft; 74 guns
Captain John Barrett[†]

Sailed on 15 December from Gothenburg in company with the *Plantagenet* to escort a convoy to Great Yarmouth, the weather was poor, with strong winds

and rain. During the evening of 22 December, her companion was seen to haul round to the westward, but the pilots onboard indicated that they might stand on for some time yet. At just before midnight the pilots advised they wear ship, but as they were doing so, the ship struck the ground with some violence. All believed themselves to be on Smith's Knoll (actually 60 miles away), and all sail was thrown aback in an effort to free her, but she was held fast. Distress guns were fired, but an attempt to launch a boat failed, the ship lifting and pounding so heavily that the men had difficulty in gaining the upper deck. It soon became evident that she had bilged, and the water was defeating the pumps; by 2.30am the water was up to the gundeck. The masts were cut away to try and ease the movement of the ship, but she still laboured in the high seas and a tremendous surf broke over the ship constantly. Daylight showed that they were on the Haak Sands off the Texel, and the ship now showed signs of breaking up, so renewed efforts were made to launch the boats, the gunwale being cut away to do so. The Gunner, Joseph Bones, volunteered to lead a party of thirty men in the yawl and try and gain the shore, which they achieved, and although the boat overset as they made the beach, drowning one man, all the others reached safety. Encouraged by this, the launch, led by Lieutenant Robert Snell, also made the hazardous journey with another party. A third attempt with the second yawl with the Captain onboard failed, the boat capsizing in the surf, drowning all the occupants. At 2 o'clock in the afternoon the ship broke in half, with the after part rolling bottom up. About 400 men were drowned, with 140 men saved, who made their way to the nearest village of De Koog, where they were taken prisoner. The Gunner eventually escaped from prison at Valenciennes, made his way to the coast and reached England by bribing the captain of a smuggling lugger. The cause of the wreck was believed to be an error in reckoning, with the ship being many miles to the south-east of their estimated position.
[TNA: ADM.1/5442]

25 December **MONKEY** Gun Brig
Rochester 1801; 188 tons; 80.2ft x 23.1ft; 12 guns
Lieutenant Thomas Fitzgerald†
Part of the blockading force off the port of Lorient, she was battered by heavy gales for several days. She finally headed towards Belle-Île on Christmas Eve, intending to take shelter in Quiberon Bay. As they approached the island, the wind was a strong north-westerly, with showers of sleet and snow. At 4 o'clock in the morning, as they prepared to anchor, they were hit by a squall, and the sails were either split or blown out, and with the ground shoaling to 13 fathoms, they let go both anchors. One anchor cable parted almost immediately, and the other failed to hold her, and, unmanageable, she drove down towards the island. At just before 5am, she struck the ground, beating violently on rocks which pierced the bottom and she rapidly filled with water. The crew initially took to the rigging, before jumping into the sea for the short swim to the land. Two men drowned in the attempt, one being Lieutenant Fitzgerald, who was nearly ashore when the brig lurched forward on a big wave, and he disappeared.
[TNA: ADM.1/5442]

29 December **FLEUR DE LA MER** Schooner
Purchased 1807; 117 tons; 72.3ft x 19.4ft; 10 guns
Lieutenant John Alexander
Escorting the merchant ship *Cassius* to Jamaica in poor weather, during the morning of 28 December she was struck by a particularly heavy sea, which broke over her fore-and-aft and swept the upper deck clear of anything moveable. The water flooded down the hatchways, and it was with some difficulty that the schooner was cleared by pumping and bailing. Lieutenant Alexander decided to run for the shelter of the land and bore up for Maracaibo. That evening it was noticed that the deck was sagging, and it was discovered that the main beam was broken. Pumping was continuing and it became clear that the schooner also had a leak. Shot and stores were heaved overboard, followed that night by four of the guns. At about 10.30pm another sea broke over her, but she survived. Boats and spars were heaved overboard at midnight, but the vessel was clearly settling. Marines and landsmen were transferred to the *Cassius* by boat in the early hours of 29 December, the remainder of the crew following later, and all were clear by 3 o'clock. By daylight she was seen to be quite waterlogged, and just before 11 o'clock she sank, her position then being 15.15N 71.02W.
[TNA: ADM.1/5412]

1811

13 February **PANDORA** Brig Sloop
Great Yarmouth 1806; 384 tons; 100ft x 30.6ft; 18 guns
Commander John McPherson Ferguson
Laying at anchor off the Skaw (Skagen), in company with the *Venus* frigate, the weather was poor, with strong winds and regular showers of snow. During the morning, the weather cleared, and a brig was sighted close inshore. The boats were manned, and the *Venus* ordered *Pandora* to weigh and support an attack on the brig by the boats. As the boats closed the vessel, it was discovered to be a wreck and they pulled back to the *Pandora*. As the sloop manoeuvred off the shore awaiting the return of the boats, the weather closed in, and sight of the land, the boats and the *Venus* was lost in a thick downfall of snow. She hove-to and then anchored. In

a brief lull in the weather, she was able to recover her boats, and then weighed to close the *Venus*, but with the daylight now fading fast, and the snow resuming, she was again lost to view. As she was feeling her way cautiously forward, breakers loomed out of the dark and an attempt was made to wear ship, but she struck the ground. The rudder was unshipped as she bumped over rocks and water flooded in. Distress guns were fired and the masts cut away, but scarcely had this been completed when she rolled over onto her beam-ends. The sloop remained laying on the rocks all through the night, and dawn brought no relief. It remained bitterly cold, with regular flurries of snow, surf beating over the wreck constantly, and the crew were unable to launch any boats. They remained in this state all the next day, and not until the morning of the 15th did the weather abate and several local fishing boats came to their aid, taking off the survivors. Twenty-seven men died of exposure during their ordeal. It was found that she had run onto the Skagen Reef, and Commander Ferguson and the pilot, William Farnie, were both severely reprimanded, for failing to carry sufficient sail and not using the lead-line constantly.
[TNA:ADM.1/5416]

16 February AMETHYST Fifth Rate
Deptford 1799; 1,046 tons; 150ft × 39.7ft; 36 guns
Captain Jacob Walton
At anchor in Plymouth Sound, she had been ordered to join the blockading squadron off Brest with provisions, which included a consignment of live bullocks. During 15 February Captain Walton went ashore to expedite the loading, leaving orders for the frigate to be fully prepared for sailing early the next morning. In readiness for this, one anchor was weighed, leaving her secured to the best bower only – this being approved by the Captain on his return from shore. That evening the weather became increasingly windy, with frequent squalls of rain, but it was not until midnight that it was realised that she was dragging her anchor. Orders were hastily given to let go another anchor, but before it could bring her up, she tailed onto the ground near Cony Cliff rocks, Mount Batten. Her starboard quarter struck first, then she swung broadside-on to the rocks and was bilged. Distress guns were fired, which brought several craft to her assistance from the dockyard and a number of men were lifted off. Ropes were passed to the shore, by means of which more of the crew were hauled to safety, although eight men died in the attempt. Over the next few days, the hull was stripped of stores and provisions, and by 10 March the hull had broken up by the constant pounding of the waves. Both Captain Walton and the Master, Robert Owen, were severely reprimanded for allowing the ship to ride so close to the shore at single anchor. The Master was also ordered not to serve in anything larger that a Sixth-Rate ship for the next year.
[TNA:ADM.1/5414]

25 February SHAMROCK Schooner
Bermuda 1808; 150 tons; 78.8ft × 21.7ft; 10 guns
Lieutenant Wentworth Parson Croke
Cruising to the south-east of Cape St Vincent in search of Sir Thomas Williams' squadron, she was steering north to resume her station after chasing two merchant vessels. Thinking themselves well clear of land, it came as a considerable shock when at 10.30pm, with little warning, she ran aground. Boats were hoisted out and an attempt made to lay out an anchor to haul her off, but this proved impossible in the high seas. Surf was breaking over her and the constant pounding started several leaks. Within an hour she was almost filled with water. The masts were cut away, falling towards the shore, along which the crew managed to reach safety apart from two men who were drowned in the wreck. Daylight showed that they were on shore about 1½ miles north of Cape Santa Maria, Portugal. An error in the reckoning and a strong current had combined to carry her further north than they had realised, although the officers were blameable, for failing to take any precautions, when known to be approaching land. Lieutenant Croke was admonished to be more careful in the future.
[TNA:ADM.1/5414]

2 March OLYMPIA Cutter
Bermuda 1806; 111 tons; 68.2ft × 20.4ft; 10 guns
Lieutenant Henry Taylor
Sailed from the Downs anchorage on 1 March to take station off Dieppe. At 2 o'clock that afternoon, five luggers were seen running along the French coast and the *Olympia* steered towards them, but as she closed, so they dispersed and ran inshore and by nightfall were effectively lost. The following morning, one of the luggers was sighted and the cutter bore up in chase. The day was hazy, with patches of mist, and as she closed her quarry, several more luggers emerged from the haze, until thirteen vessels were in sight. At this, she altered course and made all sail away, the luggers coming around in chase. By 2 o'clock in the afternoon the nearest enemy vessel was close enough to open fire, and a running action commenced, with the cutter hampered by the water constantly washing in through the gun ports. Another two of the luggers closed and ran alongside and attempted to board her, but they were repulsed, the vessels retiring to join the others, which now surrounded her. The firing went on for over an hour, when the rigging and sails had been destroyed, the bulwarks stove in, and Lieutenant Taylor wounded.

When the luggers again closed, she surrendered. Two men wounded.

Note: recaptured on 29 November by the *Quebec*.
[TNA: ADM.1/5443]

6 March THISTLE Schooner
Bermuda 1808; 150 tons; 78.8ft × 21.7ft; 10 guns
Lieutenant George McPherson
Ordered to Sandy Hook, New Jersey, with despatches, she closed the American coast in deteriorating weather, with high winds and regular showers of snow. Soon after darkness fell, the water was found to be shoaling, and at 7 o'clock, Lieutenant McPherson determined to come about. Before he could do so, breakers were seen ahead which was a surprise, as the schooner was believed to be at least seven miles from the shore. The vessel thumped over a bar into clear water, losing the rudder as she did so and found herself about two cables (400 yards) distant from the shore. Before an anchor could be let go, she was taken down onto the beach and capsized over onto her beam-ends, throwing two men into the sea. The surf was breaking all around them, but despite this, several of the crew attempted to swim through the surf, but after one drowned, McPherson ordered them to stop further attempts. A line was heaved to those ashore and using this, the others were pulled to the beach. A local farmer took them in, and over the next few days some of the stores were salvaged and sold. The wreck of the schooner was sold on 13 March to a local man for 135 dollars, which was used to pay local people for goods provided. The subsequent inquiry found that she had been wrecked on Manasquan Beach, about 30 miles south of Sandy Hook, due to the inaccuracy of the chart, which showed incorrect soundings. In all, four men died in the wreck.
[TNA: ADM.1/5442]

12 March CHALLENGER Brig Sloop
Blackwall 1806; 285 tons; 96.2ft × 25.11ft; 16 guns
Commander Goddard Blennerhasset
Off the Île de Batz, Brittany, in company with the *Firm* gun brig, other ships of the blockading squadron were in sight, hull-down on the horizon. At 3 o'clock in the afternoon, two vessels were seen to windward, which were soon made out to be large frigates, probably French. The *Firm* was ordered to proceed to the nearest British port to carry the news, whilst the *Challenger* attempted to shape a course towards the blockading ships, hoping to carry the French ships with her. The French, however, steered to cut her off and forced the sloop to steer further to the west. All sail was set by the *Challenger* in hopes of outpacing her pursuers, but the main topmast was carried away, which retarded her sailing. By 4 o'clock the frigates were in range to open fire, and a running fight commenced, which lasted for three hours, until with the frigates on either side, the sloop surrendered. Her captors proved to be the *Prégel*, 38 guns, and the *Revanche*, 44, which avoided the blockading ships to take their prize into Conquet. Two men were killed, one being lost when the topmast went overboard.
[TNA: ADM.1/5442]

27 March GUNBOAT 23 Gunboat
Built 1806; 44 tons; 50.7ft × 14ft; 2 guns
Lieutenant William Hollanby Hull
Stationed at Cadiz, the gunboat was one of a number secured alongside the *St Albans*. The weather was poor, with strong winds and a heavy swell, and during the afternoon she was swamped and foundered. All the crew were rescued. She was salvaged on 2 April and repaired.
[TNA: ADM.51/2828; www.britishnewspaperarchive.co: Globe 23 April 1811 p4]

25 April SWAN Cutter
Hired 1807; 119 tons; 10 guns
Lieutenant Edward Mourilyan
In company with the *Hero* cutter, the pair were cruising in the Kattegat, and during the evening of 24 April came anchor off Kongsham, Norway. At 3 o'clock in the morning, three boats were seen to be closing, evidently part of a squadron of Danish vessels which had been concealed inshore, behind rocks. Both British vessels cut their anchor cables and made sail, trying to gain sea room. By 4am the Danes were within range to open fire, with some accuracy, and three shots struck the hull of the *Swan*, one penetrating the magazine, damaging the powder. The breeze fell away, and the gunboats concentrated on the *Swan*, which was unable to make headway. In 30 minutes, her sails were riddled with holes, the rigging shot away, and the hull holed in several places. In a sinking state, with two men killed and one wounded, she surrendered. Shortly after the Danes took possession, she foundered.
[TNA: ADM.1/5412]

2 May DOVER Fifth Rate
Purchased 1805 (*Duncan*); 990 tons; 130ft × 35ft; 38 guns
Captain Edward Tucker
Laying at anchor off Madras, the frigate was largely unrigged, with topmasts struck and the foreyard lowered, whilst undergoing a refit. During 1 May the wind steadily freshened, and the surf built up, until by the early hours of 2 May it was blowing a full gale. Captain Tucker was ashore at the time, and command devolved on Lieutenant Charles Jefferis. A second anchor was let go and the sheet anchor prepared for use as the weather continued to worsen, with a very heavy swell and regular showers of rain. At 3 o'clock in the afternoon the best bower anchor cable parted, but the

sheet anchor was let go, and she continued to ride easily. At 11 o'clock that evening she was struck by a strong squall which parted the small bower cable, and she found herself driving. The remaining anchor cable was cut, and an attempt was made to hoist staysails, but these were blown out as soon as they were spread. Carried rapidly inshore by the wind and waves, she struck the north-east corner of Fort St George, '… with a dreadful shock', which bilged her. Despite the fore- and mainmasts being cut away to ease the movement of the ship, she was battered against the walls of the fort until she sank. Two men were drowned.
[TNA: ADM.1/5428]

3 May CHICHESTER Store Ship
Prize 1809 (Var); 777 tons; 140.10ft × 35ft; 18 guns
Master William Kirby

Laying at anchor off Madras, during 1 May the wind steadily increased, and topmasts were struck in preparation for a storm. By the afternoon of the following day, the anchorage was being lashed by gale force winds and a heavy swell, and several ships parted their anchor cables, but *Chichester* rode well. During the afternoon of the 3rd, the wind was at hurricane force, and waves were breaking over her. At about 9.30pm both anchor cables parted. The sheet anchor was let go, but could not hold her, and she went ashore, the ship striking very heavily. The masts went overboard, and she started to break up. The storm moderated during the night, and in the morning the crew were able to gain the beach. Three men died.
[TNA: ADM.1/1183]

26 May ALACRITY Brig Sloop
Newcastle 1806; 382 tons; 99.10ft × 30.6ft; 18 guns
Commander Nesbit Palmer†

Cruising off the island of Corsica, when at daybreak a brig was sighted closing from leeward, and the *Alacrity* altered course towards, spreading topgallants and occasionally using sweeps to close. As they bore down, the stranger, which was the French corvette *Abeille*, 20 guns, shortened sail and hoisted French colours. The pair closed on opposite tacks and exchanged broadsides as they passed, after which the *Alacrity* wore round to run alongside the French brig. Soon after the action began, Commander Palmer was wounded, being struck on the hand by a splinter, which severed his index and second fingers, and he left the deck to have the wound dressed, Lieutenant Thomas Rees assuming command, until he was killed. The Master, David Laing, then took over the quarterdeck and inexplicably ordered the helm to be put over, by which means the *Abeille* was able to lay herself on the quarters of the *Alacrity* and fire several destructive raking broadsides, with only partial replies from the *Alacrity*. Her position was relieved slightly when, due to her damaged rigging, she fell back, which allowed her to reply in full. At this point the Master was shot in the thigh and forced below, the Bosun, James Flaxman, stepping forward to assume command. He threw all sail aback and attempted to get under the stern of the French ship, but this was skilfully avoided. The *Alacrity*, now with damaged rigging and sails, fell away, to be raked again by *Abeille*. At this point a seaman appeared from below saying he had been sent to strike the flag. Flaxman's response was to order the man away, with the comment that he would '… blow the brains out of anyone who attempted to do so'. Despite this threat, some minutes later the Gunner appeared on the upper deck and quietly hauled down the ensign in surrender, after an action of 45 minutes. The *Alacrity* suffered four men killed and eighteen wounded, four of them fatally. Considerable criticism was subsequently levelled at Commander Palmer. The brig was not well handled in the fight, and he had shown a lack of leadership. After having his wound dressed, he had retired to his cabin and had failed to return to the upper deck, except to stand in the hatchway and weakly ask the Bosun 'What more was to be done?' and express his fears that all was not going well. It was he who had sent the seaman and later the Gunner to surrender. Palmer died on 22 June from an infection in his wounded hand, probably tetanus, and perhaps fortunately did not face a court martial. The Bosun was praised for his courage and zeal. The French commanding officer, Ange-Reneé de Mackau, was deservedly promoted to Captain in recognition of his seamanship and bravery.
[TNA: ADM.1/5442]

29 June FIRM Gun Brig
Frindsbury 1804; 180 tons; 80.1ft × 22.7ft; 12 guns
Lieutenant John Little

The *Firm* was part of the squadron blockading the coast of northern France, and during 27 June, in company with the *Fylla* frigate, chased two brigs into Cancale Bay, where they were seen to run aground. The following day the British pair returned to the brigs, to find them both afloat and underway. They chased the pair, driving them into a sheltered bay near St Jean-le-Thomas, where they were seen to anchor. It was decided to mount a boat attack that night: the *Firm* would enter the bay to support the operation. The boats were manned and pulled away from the ships at 9.30pm, the *Firm* following to enter the bay afterwards. To their disappointment it was found that the French vessels had been taken further inshore, and the attack was accordingly abandoned and the boats recovered. In the early hours, as the brig manoeuvred to leave the bay, she ran aground on a mudbank. Stores and shot were heaved overboard, and a kedge anchor taken out, but the tide was on the ebb, and she was soon left high and

dry. Unable to free her, and with the light beginning to break, she was abandoned and set on fire.
[TNA: ADM.1/5417]

29 June SAFEGUARD Gun Brig
Topsham 1804; 178 tons; 80ft × 22.6ft; 12 guns
Lieutenant Thomas England

Cruising in the Kattegat, the brig was about 12 miles to the east of Fornaes when at 7.30 in the evening, a group of four vessels were sighted to the westward, under the land. She altered course towards them and by 8.30pm they could be seen to be gunboats. In light winds she tacked away to gain some sea room, but the breeze dropped away to a calm, and the gunboats employed sweeps to come up with her. An action commenced, with the gunboats able to manoeuvre to avoid a broadside, and the brig suffered badly, with the sails and rigging cut up and several shots in the hull. With mounting casualties and 4ft of water in the hold, she surrendered. One man killed and fourteen wounded.
[TNA: ADM.1/13]

7 July GUACHAPIN Brig Sloop
Prize 1801; 176 tons; 80.5ft × 23.1ft; 16 guns
Lieutenant Michael Jenkins

Laying at anchor off Antigua when the area was struck by a hurricane. The brig was secured by two anchors, but one of the anchor cables parted at 1 o'clock in the afternoon at the height of the storm, and just 30 minutes later the second cable parted, and she commenced driving across the anchorage. The stream anchor was let go, and this held her for some time, but it was soon found to be dragging. A little later she went ashore at Rat Island, bilged and soon started breaking up. Most of the stores were saved.
[TNA: ADM.1/5418]

14 July SNAPPER Schooner
Bermuda 1805; 70 tons; 55.2ft × 18ft; 4 guns
Lieutenant Henry Thrakston

Off Les Sables d'Olonne, western France, tasked with interrupting coastal shipping, at daybreak several coasters were seen near the harbour, which the schooner steered to intercept. As she closed, several other vessels were seen to join them, and it became clear that they were armed: a large 7-gun lugger, a 4-gun brig and four large pinnaces armed with swivels and full of men. Outnumbered and outgunned, the schooner hauled her wind, with the enemy now in chase. At 9.30am the schooner commenced firing on her pursuers with a stern-chase gun, the fire being returned sporadically. The pinnaces pulled ahead of the others and closed the *Snapper*, evidently intent on boarding, and by 10 o'clock a close action had started. Well aimed-fire from the schooner dismasted two of the pinnaces, and all of them then fell back, allowing the *Snapper* to pull away from the enemy flotilla. By 11 o'clock, however, the wind had fallen away to a calm and the French, using sweeps, steadily gained on the schooner and firing recommenced. The action became heavy, and in a short time the rigging and sails of the schooner were cut to pieces and the fore topmast shot away. When the pinnaces again closed to board on both sides, Lieutenant Thrakston surrendered to the lugger *Rapace*. No casualties.
[TNA: ADM.1/5443]

18 August TARTAR Fifth Rate
Frindsbury 1801; 895 tons; 142ft × 37.8ft; 32 guns
Captain Joseph Baker

Stationed in the Baltic, the frigate headed for the island of Dago (Hiiumaa), intending to anchor and take on wood and water. She approached a sheltered bay, sounding constantly, and when the water shallowed to five fathoms the helm was put over. The water continued to shallow however, and she gently took the ground forward. All sail was thrown aback, which promptly freed her, but she almost immediately went aground again. The yards were braced round, and she successfully sailed off the obstruction. The impacts had been so gentle that the Purser, working in his office below, did not realise that the ship had twice been aground. The ship anchored and to everyone's surprise it was reported that she was making water. The pumps were manned, and it was determined that the leak was between the sternpost and the step of the mizzen mast. The storerooms were cleared to allow the Carpenter to find the leak, but as they were emptied, the water entered with increasing force. A sail was thrummed and passed under the hull, and divers sent down to examine the bottom. They found that the garboard strake on the starboard side had been holed. To tackle this, a spar was covered with canvas and wood and placed over the hole, but with little effect. Next, oakum, canvas and bedding were thrust into the gap, and this seemed to work, the flow of water noticeably decreasing. The next morning (19 August) saw the vessel steadily settle down, with the leak gaining on the pumps. Stores and provisions were landed on the island, and the pumping and bailing continued, but after three days' work, it was clear that they were fighting a losing battle. During 21 August she was deliberately run ashore on a small island between Dago and Worms (Vormsi), where she was later set on fire. They were rescued some days later by the *Ethalion*. One man, Marine Thomas Browne, was punished when ashore with thirty-six lashes for 'insolent and blasphemous language' to Lieutenant Butler of the Royal Marines. He continued to be insolent to the Lieutenant after the punishment and was later sentenced to 150 lashes by court martial.
[TNA: ADM.1/5419]

2 September MANLY Gun Brig
Deptford 1804; 178 tons; 80.1ft x 22.6ft; 12 guns
Lieutenant Richard Simmonds
Cruising off the southern coast of Norway in company with the *Chanticleer* sloop, in the early hours of the morning three brigs were sighted. They mutually closed until at 3.30am, the *Chanticleer* was close enough to hail the first brig, which was the Danish *Samsø*, 18 guns. The reply was a broadside, and a mutual exchange of gunfire began. The *Manly* was some way astern and unable to assist her consort, who was now being engaged by the other two brigs, also Danish warships, the *Låland*, 18, and the *Ålsen*, 18. The *Chanticleer* promptly made sail to escape from her opponents, and succeeded in distancing herself from them, who seeing the *Manly* had become separated, turned their attentions to her. The *Låland* commenced the action, being joined later by the remainder of the Danish squadron. By 6 o'clock, the British vessel was surrounded, with the *Samsø* on the larboard bow, the *Låland* on the starboard quarter and the *Ålsen* on the starboard bow. In this situation, with all the rigging cut to pieces, the sails in tatters and four guns dismounted, she surrendered. One man killed and three wounded. The *Chanticleer* made her escape.

Note: recaptured in March 1813 by the *Redbreast*.
[TNA:ADM.1/5422]

14 October POMONE Fifth Rate
Frindsbury 1805; 1,076 tons; 150.2ft x 40.2ft; 38 guns
Captain Robert Barrie
Returning to England from the Mediterranean with Sir Harford Jones, late Ambassador to the Persian court, on board as a passenger. Portland was sighted during the afternoon of 14 October and course was set to the east, intending to anchor in Yarmouth Roads for the night, the Master, James Sturrock, being quite confident that he could take the ship in at night. At 6 o'clock that evening, the light on Hurst Castle was sighted and the bearing was such that Captain Barrie became concerned that they were too far to the south. He went forward and clearly saw the land looming ahead. A warning was shouted, and the helm was put over, but it was too late, and the ship struck a submerged rock, two cables' length (400 yards) from the Needles Rocks. She ran over the obstruction, losing the rudder as she did so, and ripping several holes in the bottom. Filling with water, the ship became very sluggish and difficult to manoeuvre, and the wind and tide took her down onto the Needles. The boats were hoisted out and the masts were cut away before she foundered. All the men were picked up by local boats who were quickly on scene. The Master was severely reprimanded for his conduct: he had not taken accurate bearings of landmarks and had not heeded the concerns expressed by Captain Barrie. One Marine, Bernard Lowry, was ordered to receive fifty lashes for being found drunk as the ship was abandoned, but was recommended for a pardon, because of his previous good character.
[TNA:ADM.1/5419]

21 October GROUPER Schooner
Bermuda 1804; 70 tons; 55.2ft x 18ft; 4 guns
Lieutenant James Atkins
Having completed watering and storing at Antigua, the schooner sailed on 20 October for Guadeloupe under easy sail, before lying-to off the island with her head to the wind for the night. At 5 o'clock in the morning she ran aground on a reef three miles north-west of Ilet Caret, Guadeloupe. She thumped hard on the rocks, the sternpost quickly separating from the frame. An attempt was made to launch a boat but it was immediately swamped in the surf. The masts were cut away, and with the schooner starting to break up, rafts were ordered to be made. Just after daylight the quarterdeck separated from the wreck and was washed ashore with several men clinging to it. After this the crew commenced leaving the schooner on rafts, one Marine being drowned in the attempt. Midshipman James MacLeod, who had the morning watch, was found to have been inattentive, since he had no lookouts posted and had kept the schooner off the wind, rather than lying-to as ordered. MacLeod, along with the quartermaster of the morning watch, had deserted when the survivors were landed at Point-a-Pitre. Lieutenant Atkins was reprimanded for allowing the vessel to lie too close to land.
[TNA:ADM.1/5423]

(30/31) October FANCY Gun Brig
Great Yarmouth 1806; 181 tons; 84.1ft x 22.1ft; 12 guns
Lieutenant Alexander Sinclair†
Sailed Wingo Sound (Vinga Sund), Gothenburg, on 25 October as one of the escorts to a homeward-bound convoy, but the ships were affected over the next few days by gale-force winds, accompanied by frequent squalls of snow. *Fancy* was ordered to take charge of those vessels bound for Dundee, but several of these were lost in the storm. *Fancy* was last seen on 30 October off Montrose, endeavouring to clear the land, in gale-force winds. It is presumed that she was lost soon after this. Pay books closed 31 October.
[TNA:ADM.1/694; ADM.35/2807]

4 December SALDANHA Fifth Rate
South Shields 1809; 951 tons; 144.8ft x 38.4ft; 36 guns
Captain Hon. William Pakenham†
Sailed from Cork on 19 November to take station in northern Ireland at Lough Swilly, and after arriving sailed on 30 November in company with the *Talbot* sloop, with the intention of cruising off that place. The weather worsened after they sailed until by the early

hours of 4 December there was a strong north-westerly gale blowing. The *Saldanha* evidently attempted to return to the shelter of her anchorage, as at 10 o'clock that night lookouts on a signal tower at the entrance to the lough saw the lights of a ship being carried very rapidly into the harbour. It is likely that she then struck rocks, before being driven ashore in Ballymastocker Bay and wrecked. Morning revealed a large amount of wreckage and dozens of bodies strewn along the shore. It was reported that one man was hauled ashore alive, but died later. Several weeks after the wreck a parrot was shot nearby and found to have a collar with Captain Pakenham's name on it. Two hundred and fifty-three men died.
[Gold: Naval Chronicle vol 27 pp42–3; Annual Register 1811 pp139–40]

24 December SAINT GEORGE Second Rate
Portsmouth 1785; 1,950 tons; 177.6ft × 50.3ft; 90 guns
Captain Daniel Oliver Guion†
Flagship of Rear Admiral Robert Reynolds, *St George* was part of the Baltic fleet which weighed anchor and sailed from their anchorage off Matvik, southern Sweden on 1 November, intending to return to England, with a large convoy. The weather was poor, with strong winds and a heavy swell, and little progress was made, the ships frequently having to anchor. On 15 December whilst anchored off Nysted, during a gale, a merchant ship was driven from her anchors and fell aboard the *St George*. This parted her cable, and she was driven inshore, where she grounded, losing her rudder and having to cut away her masts. She was hauled off, repairs made and jury masts rigged and was able to proceed to Gothenburg a few days later, where she again anchored. They sailed again on 17 December, accompanied by the *Defence*, 74 guns, and the *Cressy*, 74, passing Skagen on 22 December. The little squadron stood to the westward, but during 23 December the weather worsened, with strong winds and heavy seas, and they made little progress. The morning of 24 December saw the wind increase and shift round to the north-north-west. During the day attempts were made to wear ship and stand to the west, but a succession of sails was blown out by the gale. It was decided to try to club haul the ship – forcing the head round by anchoring and then cutting the cable as the ship swung round. The ship anchored off the Danish coast between Thorsminde and Ringkøbing, with the sea breaking over them, but the attempt to club haul failed, when the ship was driven over the cable before it could be cut, and the hawser caught under the temporary rudder and unshipped it. Unable to bring the ship around, their only option was to anchor and both bower anchors were let go, but failed to bring her up, and she struck the ground. The masts were cut away, but she pounded heavily in the surf, making water so fast that the pumps could not cope. During the night, the ship started to break up and by the morning of 25 December, only the stern remained in one piece. Attempts were made by the little band of survivors to make rafts or use spars to reach safety, but only eleven men made the shore alive. About 850 men died.
[TNA: ADM.1/5425; Annual Register 1812 pp283–4]

24 December DEFENCE Third Rate
Plymouth 1763; 1,603 tons; 168ft × 46.9ft; 74 guns
Captain David Atkins†
In company with the *St George* (see above) during the voyage from the Baltic to England. They suffered in a similar manner during the storms of 23 December and were forced to reduce to storm staysails. At 9.30pm, the *Cressy* was seen to successfully wear ship and stand away to the south-west, and although preparations were made to follow her, Captain Atkins would not do so until the Admiral in the *St George* did, saying he would not leave her. The wind seemed to increase during the early hours, two of the three staysails hoisted being split or blown away and they lay to under a storm mizzen. At about 4.30am they decided to try and wear ship, but as they attempted to do so, she struck the ground, gently at first and then violently. The main and mizzen masts went overboard within minutes and the ship swung round onto the shore, heeling over, and five minutes later the foremast followed the others. The sea broke over her and the ship pounded heavily on the ground, casting guns loose, smashing the boats and flooding down the hatchways. She rapidly broke up, with just five survivors from a ship's company of 530, with the shore a little to the north of Thorsminde being strewn with wreckage and bodies.
[TNA: ADM.1/5425; Annual Register 1812 pp283–4]

24 December HERO Third Rate
Blackwall 1803; 1,746 tons; 175ft × 47.9ft; 74 guns
Captain James Newman†
Another of the Baltic squadron returning to England, the *Hero* had sailed from Gothenburg on 18 December, escorting a large convoy. During the subsequent gales and poor weather, the convoy was scattered, and the *Hero* proceeded with just the *Grasshopper* sloop and a few ships of the convoy in company. During the night of 24 December, she ran onto the Noorderhaaks sands off the Texel, losing her masts as she did. The following morning, she was seen to be lying on her larboard beam ends with the crew gathered on the poop and foc's'le but being constantly battered by heavy seas which were washing over her. The ship broke up during the day with no survivors from a crew of 530.
[Annual Register 1812 pp285–6]

24 December GRASSHOPPER Brig Sloop
Hythe 1806; 383 tons; 100ft x 30.6ft; 12 guns
Commander Henry Fanshawe

Returning to England from the Baltic, she was in company with the *Hero* when they sailed from Gothenburg on 18 December with a large convoy. The storms of 23–24 December scattered the convoy, the *Grasshopper* finding herself in company with the *Hero* and eighteen ships, mainly transports. During the morning of 23 December, *Hero* indicated that they believed themselves to be in the region known as the Silver Pits, to the east of Spurn Head, and the ships subsequently steered to the south-west. At about 10 o'clock in the evening the *Hero* made the night signal to alter course two points to port, which the *Grasshopper* complied with. The weather continued to be extremely poor, with frequent showers of snow, during which she lost sight of the other ships. At 3.30am, she found herself in broken water and soon after ran hard aground. The pilots thought themselves to be on Smith's Knoll off the coast of Norfolk, and it was hoped to free her by sailing off. The brig bumped several times, but then found herself free in three fathoms, at which she quickly let go an anchor. Another ship was visible in the gloom, believed to be the *Hero*, which was firing guns of distress and burning blue lights. The sloop remained at anchor until daylight, when it was discovered that they were on the Haak sands, off Texel. The *Hero* could be seen some distance away, laying on her beam-ends, with the sea beating over her, the crew gathered on the poop, and one of the transports was wrecked nearby. Distress signals were made, and several boats came to them from the shore, but because of the high seas they could not get near enough to take men off. Guns and stores were thrown overboard to lighten her, and the Master courageously took the jolly boat out in the high seas to sound around the sloop. He found that they were surrounded by sands, with no channel to seaward. At sunset, with the wind moderating a little, the cable was cut, and she ran down to a Dutch dogger and surrendered, the Dutch guiding her into the Texel. All the crew except the pilot were saved.
[TNA: ADM.1/5442; Annual Register 1812 pp285–6]

26 December EPHIRA Brig Sloop
Upnor 1808; 237 tons; 90.2ft x 24.7ft; 18 guns
Commander Thomas Everard

Ordered to escort two transports from Cadiz to Tarifa, she weighed at 1 o'clock in the morning. About 90 minutes later, believing the brig well clear of the land, the Master altered course to the east, then left the deck. The wind fell away to a calm after this, but when it picked up a little later, the brig stood onwards. At just after 4am she ran onto the Cochinos reef in Cadiz Bay. All sail was thrown aback, but she was held fast, and water was found to be pouring in. Distress guns were fired, anchors let go and the boats hoisted out. Shortly after this she capsized over to port and started settling, sinking up to the gunwales. Boats from the British squadron in the bay attended and stood by her until daylight, when stores were unloaded, and the men disembarked, with the sloop being abandoned as a wreck. The sloop had probably altered course too early, and the period of calm had allowed her to drift inshore. The Master, Samuel Mabson, was blamed for the loss. The court-martial enquiry judged him to have been inefficient and ignorant, and he was demoted, being ordered to serve before the mast as a seaman, and not be eligible for promotion for two years. Commander Everard was admonished to be more careful in the future, having placed too much trust in the Master, having left him in charge of the brig.
[TNA: ADM.1/5421]

A note on a phantom loss:

STAUNCH gun brig – reported in the contemporary press (i.e., *Caledonian Mercury* 15 August 1811 and *Morning Post* 30 September 1811) as well as more reliable sources, such as Clowes (*vol 5 p553*) as being lost in the Indian Ocean in 1811. No trace can be found of an account of this loss and her pay book (*TNA: ADM.35/4301*) shows *Staunch* in service until paying off on 18 November 1811. A letter from Rear Admiral Sir Robert Stopford, commanding the Cape of Good Hope station, in November 1811 (*TNA: ADM.1/64*), stated that the *Staunch* was in no fit state to go to sea, and was so defective that she was being paid off and sold locally.

1812

26 January CARLOTTA Brig
Prize 1810; c.200 tons; 8 guns
Lieutenant James Oliver

Driven by a violent south-easterly gale, coupled with a strong current, onto Cape Passaro, Sicily and wrecked. Lieutenant Oliver exhausted himself over the next few days salvaging stores and specie, losing the sight of an eye in the process.
[TNA: ADM.1/5425; O'Byrne p834]

28 January MANILLA Fifth Rate
Woolwich 1809; 947 tons; 145ft x 38.3ft; 36 guns
Captain John Joyce

Cruising in the North Sea, the weather was poor, with strong winds from the south-west. Her estimated noon position was 53.15N 02.52E, and a southerly course was steered to make landfall on the Dutch coast, the lead-line

being heaved every hour. At 7 o'clock in the evening they found themselves in smooth water and soon after struck the ground. The sails were thrown aback, and the ship did fall back a little before coming to a halt, held fast. An anchor was let go, boats hoisted out, water butts emptied, and shot and stores heaved overboard to lighten her. The stream anchor was laid out by the boats, at some risk to themselves due to the strong current. All efforts to heave her free during the night failed, as the tide was on the ebb. The mainmast was cut away and further stores and some guns heaved overboard, but the rising tide lifted the lightened ship and she started to pound on the sand, starting several leaks. At daylight, the Dutch coast was visible, and it became clear that they had run onto the Noorderhaak sands off Texel. Guns were fired and the ensign hoisted upside down as signals of distress, which brought several boats from the shore to their aid. The seas were now running so high, with a surf beating over the wreck, that despite several attempts, the boats could not close her. The men were employed making rafts, and at 11 o'clock that morning, Master's Mate John Gowdie led a party of thirty-five men onto the first raft, which was veered away by a hawser towards a schuyt which had approached closer than the rest. The surf and currents meant that the raft could not be brought near to her would-be rescuer, but Gowdie jumped into the sea and swam to the schuyt carrying a line, by which the raft was pulled to safety. Unable to keep their position, the Dutch boat was forced to run for shelter and the crew of the *Manilla* were busing in making more rafts and pumping. Signal rockets were fired during the evening, although at midnight, due to the carelessness of one drunken seaman, sparks from a signal rocket fell into cartridge boxes on the fo'c'sle, setting off a large explosion which destroyed part of the upper deck, killing eight men and wounding another eight. The morning of 30 January saw the weather moderating sufficiently for several boats to reach her and lift off all the survivors, the last man off being Captain Joyce. The subsequent court martial ruled that the ship had continued too long on the same tack and Captain Joyce had not heeded the warnings of the pilots when advised to alter course. He was reprimanded and warned to be more careful in his future actions. The pilots, Joseph Spendle and Thomas Paul, had allowed the ship to stand on a southerly course too long, and had not sufficiently stressed the dangers of not altering course. Both were severely reprimanded.
[TNA: ADM.1/5443]

31 January LAUREL Fifth Rate
Prize 1809 (*Fidèle*); 1,104 tons; 152.1ft × 40.5ft; 38 guns
Captain Samuel Campbell Rowley
Ordered to join the blockading squadron off the western coast of France, the *Laurel* arrived in Quiberon Bay during 30 January. The following morning, she weighed and proceeded with the frigates *Rota* and *Rhin*, the weather being blustery with regular squalls of rain. The squadron steered through the narrow Teigneuse Passage, between the mainland and Houat Island. Captain Rowley was unfamiliar with the passage and followed in the wake of the *Rota*, the *Rhin* astern of them. As they entered the passage the rain obscured the landmarks, but it was a shock when the frigate struck a submerged object, then travelling at about seven knots. Pieces of the false keel were seen floating up alongside and water was reported entering the ship at a fast rate, with 6ft of water in the hold in 10 minutes. The *Rhin*, astern of her, did touch the ground, but got off immediately. *Laurel* slid off the rock into deep water and promptly let go an anchor, but the cable snagged on rocks and parted. Another anchor was let go to hold her steady, whilst pumping and bailing began. The water gained rapidly, and the ship was visibly settling. The cable was therefore cut, sail set, and she was run onto a ridge of rocks called les Trois Peres, about a mile from the shore at Quiberon Point. The boats were hoisted out and the fore- and mizzenmasts were cut away after she grounded, the crew preparing to leave. A shore battery commenced firing on the ship, striking her repeatedly as boats from the other ships closed the wreck. Seventy-eight men were landed on the shore by the ship's boats, all being taken prisoner, but the French would not allow the boats to return to the wreck. Boats from the other ships lifted off the remainder. It was found that the ship had run onto the Govivas Rock, a known hazard, but no blame was levelled at the officers of the *Laurel*, who were unfamiliar with the area and the landmarks were obscured by haze.
[TNA: ADM.1/5423; Gold: Naval Chronicle vol 27 pp228–9]

19 February GUNBOAT 11 Gunboat
Built 1806; 44 tons; 50.7ft × 14ft; 2 guns
Midshipman John Lloyd
Based at Cadiz, the gunboat was ordered to weigh and close the *St Albans* to take on victuals. All hands were turned up at 7 o'clock in the morning and she set off into the bay in bright weather, with patches of drifting fog. Suddenly a wreck was seen, looming out of a fogbank close ahead. The helm was put over, but she struck the wreck. The sails were taken in and sweeps manned, but she was caught fast. An attempt was made to heave the forward gun overboard, but this failed. By now a shore battery at Fort Napoleon, Matagorda, was firing at them and other gunboats came to their assistance. *Gunboat 8* passed a line and attempted to haul her off the wreck, but she failed to move. With enemy shot now passing close to them, it was decided to abandon the boat and the other gunboats lifted off the crew.
[TNA: ADM.1/5423]

28 February FLY Brig Sloop
Bridport 1805; 286 tons; 96.4ft × 25.11ft; 16 guns
Commander Henry Higman
Part of a British squadron standing to the north-east in the Kattegat, the island of Anholt was sighted during the morning. The bearings of the lighthouse on the island made Commander Higman concerned for the safety of the sloop, but both embarked pilots assured him that they were well clear of any danger. The sloop stood on until 1 o'clock in the afternoon when she was ordered to tack and follow the *Pyramus*. She was in the act of doing so when she ran aground on the Knoben reef, to the east of Anholt. Boats were hoisted out to lay out an anchor, but these attempts were frustrated by a heavy swell. An attempt to sail off the obstruction also failed. The sails were furled, and she was anchored to hold her steady, as the wind was increasing. Topmasts were cut away and stores and shot heaved overboard, but all efforts to move her failed. During the night, the wind continued to increase, and the temperature dropped, becoming bitterly cold. The upper deck, masts and rigging became covered in ice making it difficult to work. During the early hours, the rudder came off, and soon after this the anchor cable parted, and the sloop swung around to present her stern to the sea. She was lifted by the swell and pounded heavily on the ground until at 2 o'clock in the afternoon of 29 February, when she suddenly floated free and was carried into deep water. Icy water flooded into the numerous leaks that had started, and she started to settle at a fast rate. All the crew were taken off by boats from the squadron, Commander Higman setting her on fire as he left. Both pilots carried, James Burness and John Mafham, were severely reprimanded and were ordered to be mulcted of all pay due.
[TNA:ADM.1/55425]

3 May SKYLARK Brig Sloop
Newcastle 1806; 283 tons; 93.1ft × 26.5ft; 16 guns
Commander James Boxer
Part of the blockading squadron off the northern coast of France, the *Skylark* was patrolling between Cap Gris Nez and Étaples in company with the *Apelles* sloop. Thick fog descended at about 3 o'clock in the morning, and 45 minutes later she ran aground. All sails were thrown aback, but she would not move. Work started to lighten the brig, heaving overboard the anchors, guns and shot, but the water ebbed away to leave them high and dry. The boats had been lowered, and with daylight, a shore battery commenced firing at the sloop and troops could be seen gathering nearby. The crew was ordered into the boats and Commander Boxer set fire to the sloop as he left. The blame for the loss was shared by the Master and the pilot. It was found that they had steered too close to the shore, failed to use the lead-line, and failed to acquaint the captain of the fog. Master William Turner was found guilty of neglect and inattention and was demoted. Pilot John Norris lost all pay due and was sentenced to three months' confinement in the Marshalsea Prison.
[TNA:ADM.1/5426]

3 May APELLES Brig Sloop
Woolwich 1808; 251 tons; 92ft × 25.6ft; 16 guns
Commander Frederick Hoffman
Consort to the *Skylark* brig (see above), as the pair felt their way along the French coast in thick fog, the *Apelles* following the movements of the *Skylark*. At 4 o'clock in the morning, the brig went aground and found herself held fast. The tide was ebbing, and she could do little but wait for high water. Daylight revealed the *Skylark* onshore near her, and the sandhills of the French coast north of Boulogne. Boats were hoisted out when the depth of water was enough and preparations were made to haul her off, shot and stores being heaved overboard. A shore battery nearby opened fire as they did so, and troops could be seen gathering. Efforts went on to free her went on, with booms being lowered over the side to prevent her capsizing. By 5.30am, the troops had advanced close enough to open a fire of musketry on the brig, and field guns were also brought up. The fire was returned by the brig's Royal Marines, but by 6am the rigging was badly cut up and both masts shot through. The boats were ordered away by Commander Hoffman, but there were not enough places for all the crew and several men were left onboard. Commander Boxer of the *Skylark* came alongside and appealed to Hoffman to leave, but he refused as long as any of his men remained onboard. Thirty minutes later, however, with more troops and field guns arriving, the brig surrendered by hoisting a white flag. She was re-floated later that day by the French but was retaken the following day by a boat attack from the sloop *Bermuda*.
[TNA:ADM.1/5427]

8 July EXERTION Gun Brig
Great Yarmouth 1805; 180 tons; 84ft × 22ft; 12 guns
Lieutenant James Murray
Anchored at the mouth of the River Elbe at Cuxhaven, the brig weighed to proceed to sea during the morning, under the guidance of local pilots. With no warning, at 1 o'clock in the afternoon, when off Scharhörn Island, she ran aground. Boats were hoisted out, shot and stores were heaved overboard or transferred to the boats and topgallant masts were struck. A stream and a kedge anchor were laid out, and at high tide that evening she heaved on the cables and successfully moved some distance but was still on the sandbank. As the tide ebbed away, she found herself held fast and anchored to prevent her being taken further onto the bank by the current. In the early hours of 9 July several enemy

gunboats could be seen approaching and it was decided to abandon her. The *Redbreast* sloop had come to her aid and lifted off all the crew, the brig being set on fire as they left. The court-martial enquiry apportioned no blame as it was deemed that she had struck a shifting bank of sand unknown to any of the pilots.
[TNA: ADM.1/5429]

8 July WHITING Schooner
Bermuda 1805; 70 tons; 55.2ft × 18ft; 4 guns
Lieutenant Lewis Maxey
Sailed from Portsmouth on 8 May carrying a King's Messenger with despatches for America, the schooner arrived in Hampton Roads on 8 July, unaware that hostilities had broken out. A pilot was embarked to take the vessel up to Annapolis, and Lieutenant Maxey took the opportunity to go ashore to obtain fresh provisions. They were thus quite unprepared when the privateer *Dash* ran alongside and called on them to surrender, and the crew had little choice but to comply. The US Prize Court declined to condemn the schooner as a legal prize, as she had been engaged on a diplomatic mission. She was restored to Lieutenant Maxey on 12 August.
[www.britishnewspaperarchive.co: London Courier 11 September 1812 p2]

11 July ENCOUNTER Gun Brig
Northam 1805; 185 tons; 84.3ft × 22.4ft; 12 guns
Commander James Hugh Talbot
Cruising off Cadiz in company with the *Tuscan* sloop, the pair chased two privateers inshore, which then took shelter under a two-gun battery near San Lucar. During the afternoon, the British pair closed the anchorage and engaged the shore battery, which was silenced with several well-directed broadsides. Attention was now turned to the privateers, and the boats were launched and manned and successfully boarded and captured both vessels. As they prepared to take the prizes out of the anchorage, they came under a steady fire from the shore. One of the privateers was successfully taken out, but all the shore fire was now directed at the remaining vessel and casualties started to mount. After a jolly boat was taken inshore by the current and captured, the *Encounter* closed the prize to provide covering support, but as she did so, she ran aground. A heavy fire was now directed at the brig, which was returned, but this hampered efforts to free her. The shore battery which they had silenced earlier had now been repaired and joined the bombardment, hitting the brig several times. Unable to free her, Lieutenant Talbot ordered the crew to leave the brig and the boats started to take men to the *Tuscan*. The enemy ashore, seeing the brig being abandoned, mounted a boat attack and with only Lieutenant Talbot and fourteen men left onboard, they easily captured her. One man killed and fourteen wounded.
[TNA: ADM.1/5428]

2 August EMULOUS Brig Sloop
Newcastle 1806; 383 tons; 100.1ft × 30.6ft; 18 guns
Commander William Mulcaster
Cruising off the coast of Nova Scotia, *Emulous* had successfully chased and captured the American privateer *Gossamer* on 30 July, and during the morning of 2 August was joined by the sloop *Colibri*, with news of another privateer sheltering on the coast nearby. The pair decided to seek out the vessel and steered towards the coast under all sail. As the day progressed, the weather worsened, with gloomy, cloudy conditions and sail was shortened as the course was altered to the west-north-west to pick up the coastline. At 1pm, breakers loomed ahead on the lee bow. The helm was put over, but as the *Emulous* came up into the wind, she struck the ground. All sail was thrown aback in an attempt to force her off, but she would not move. The small bower anchor was let go to hold her steady, while the sails were clewed up and preparations made to haul her off. This proved difficult, as she was being lifted by the sea and pounded heavily on the rocks. The rudder was soon unshipped, and several leaks started. The brig was lightened by throwing stores overboard and a boat was hoisted out to carry out a kedge anchor astern but on heaving on the hawser the cable parted. The masts were cut away to further ease her as the *Colibri* closed to give assistance, passing her stream anchor over to act as a kedge. The prisoners held on board, together with all non-essential crew members, were taken off by the *Colibri*, while the stream anchor was laid out ahead. Before any further work could be done, the brig fell over onto her beam-ends, ending all attempts to free her. Her position was found to be 19 miles south-east of Cape Sable. Commander Mulcaster was admonished to be more careful in the future. Lieutenant Thomas Fowle was reprimanded for having been remiss in his duty as officer of the watch, when he failed to send for the pilot on finding that they were in shallow water. Finally, the Master, John Wilson, was severely reprimanded for failing to heave the lead-line constantly during his watch.
[TNA: ADM.1/5431]

13 August ALERT Ship Sloop
Purchased 1804 (*Oxford*); 393 tons; 105ft × 29.4ft; 16 guns
Commander Thomas Lamb Poulden Laugharne
Cruising off Newfoundland, she was in search of the American sloop *Hornet*, reported as being in the area, when in position 41N 35.24W, they sighted a ship to leeward. A course was steered to intercept the stranger, which seemed to be a merchant ship, and preparations made to engage. At 11.30am the *Alert* was on the stranger's larboard quarter, which hoisted American colours. The *Alert* fired a broadside at the enemy, which attempted to wear round to present her broadside. This

was avoided by the *Alert*, which now realised that her opponent was an American 32-gun frigate and made efforts to escape. The frigate pursued the sloop and despite all attempts to manoeuvre out of range, the American was able to rake her as she tried to wear ship. The frigate then placed herself within pistol shot of the sloop, which surrendered, finding her captor was the *Essex*. Three men were wounded. At the later court martial, it was found that the sloop's First Lieutenant, Andrew Duncan, had given Commander Laugharne no support and had urged him to strike the flag. He was dismissed the service.
[TNA: ADM.1/5431]

14 August CHUB Schooner
Bermuda 1807; 70 tons; 55.2ft × 18ft; 4 guns
Lieutenant Samuel Nesbitt[†]
Stationed at Halifax, Nova Scotia, she sailed on 14 August to search the area, following reports of an American privateer being active in the area. That same night, in gale-force winds, she was driven ashore on the reef known as the Sisters, two miles from Sambro Light, and was wrecked. There were no survivors.
[TNA: ADM.1/502]

19 August GUERRIÈRE Fifth Rate
Prize 1806; 1,092 tons; 155.9ft × 39.9ft; 38 guns
Captain James Richard Dacres
Cruising to the south of Newfoundland in position 40.20N 55W, when at 2 o'clock in the afternoon, a ship was sighted to the north-west steering towards her. Another hour saw the ship close enough for it to be seen to be a large warship under all sail, clearly in chase. As the stranger neared, the *Guerrière* backed her main topsail to await her opponent, which shorted sail preparatory to the action. The *Guerrière* hoisted her colours at just after 4pm, and fired a broadside at the stranger, which was the *Constitution*, 44 guns, then wore ship and fired the other broadside. The shot either fell short or did little damage. The *Guerrière* then wore ship several times to avoid being raked by the American's broadside, this manoeuvring going on for 45 minutes, until the *Constitution* was able to run under her opponent's larboard quarter, from where she was able to fire a raking broadside. The ships then steered alongside each other, exchanging broadsides. The American's heavier weight of shot began to tell, the mizzen mast of the *Guerrière* being shot away at 5.20pm, which led to the *Constitution* to shoot ahead, from where she lay on the larboard bow of the *Guerrière* and fired several raking broadsides into her. The American then attempted to board, dropping nearer and sweeping the British frigate's upper deck with small-arms fire and grapeshot. The British repulsed the attempt to board and the frigates fell apart, the foremast of the *Guerrière* falling overboard as they did so, apparently from the shock of the disentanglement. The foremast brought down the mainmast in its fall, leaving her quite disabled. This allowed the *Constitution* to range ahead to repair her damage, returning in about half an hour to renew the fight. The *Guerrière* was in a hopeless position, with no masts, even the jury-rigged mast falling over, the ship rolling heavily in the seas, with her main-deck guns being swamped, and in this state, she had little choice but to surrender. The Americans found her in a shattered condition, with dozens of shot holes in the hull and the upper works wrecked. At daylight, the next day all the crew were removed, and she was set on fire at 3 o'clock in the afternoon, burning until she blew up. Fifteen men were killed and sixty-three wounded.
[TNA: ADM.1/5431]

19 August ATTACK Gun Brig
Southampton 1804; 180 tons; 80.1ft × 22.8ft; 12 guns
Lieutenant Richard William Simmons
Sailed from the entrance to the Randers Fjord, Denmark, having picked up boats from the British squadron and headed back to re-join the fleet. At 11 o'clock in the evening of 18 August, when about six miles off Fornaes, two gunboats were observed to be closing them from the land. The *Attack* cleared for action and about 20 minutes later the pair of closing gunboats opened fire, it soon becoming clear that these were just the leading vessels of a division of twelve Danish gunboats. An action was maintained for over two hours, when the Danes broke off the action. The *Attack* now steered for the *Wrangler* gun brig, which could be seen some way off, also engaged with several enemy gun vessels. However, the lack of wind, the strong current and the damage sustained by the *Attack* conspired to defeat this object, and the *Wrangler* was soon lost to view. The crew set about repairing the damage, the main boom having been shot away, the foremast and bowsprit shot through, and three guns dismounted. At a little after 2 o'clock in the morning, a large number of gunboats were seen, apparently drawn up in a crescent, laying along the larboard side. The enemy closed and recommenced the action, which lasted until 3.20am, when, with all the rigging cut to pieces and the hull shot through in several places, she surrendered. Two men killed and fourteen wounded.
[TNA: ADM.1/5430]

22 August WHITING Schooner
Bermuda 1805; 70 tons; 55.2ft × 18ft; 4 guns
Lieutenant Lewis Maxey
After her capture in July (see above), the schooner was restored on 12 August and later escorted out of Hampton Roads by the *Gallatin* revenue cutter. She sailed for England but had not cleared the coast when

she encountered the French brig privateer *Diligent*, 18 guns, and after a running fight of an hour and a half, was forced to surrender.
[www.britishnewspaperarchive.co : Public Ledger 27 October 1812]

8 September LAURA Cutter
Bermuda 1806; 111 tons; 68.2ft × 20.4ft; 12 guns
Lieutenant Charles Newton Hunter
Stationed off the eastern seaboard of the United States, she was off the Capes of Delaware, stopping merchant shipping, who warned Lieutenant Hunter of the presence of a large French privateer in the area. During the afternoon, having manned three prize vessels, a brig was sighted to leeward, which was suspected to be the privateer. The *Laura* bore up for the stranger and in less than an hour was near enough to fire a round from the bow-chase gun. The reply was a full broadside from the brig, which was answered by the *Laura*. After 30 minutes of exchanging fire, the brig, which was the French privateer *Diligent*, 18 guns, tried to set more sail and tack, the move being matched by the *Laura*. However, both vessels missed stays and the pair now fell close alongside each other, yardarm to yardarm. After a further exchange of fire, the French brig fell astern, the cutter not matching the move, being unable to spare men to both work the sails and serve the guns. The manoeuvre by the *Diligent* took the wind from her opponent's sails and she followed this by running her bowsprit over the starboard quarter of the *Laura*, impaling the mainsail as she did so. An attempt was now made to board the British vessel, but this was repulsed. At this critical moment, Lieutenant Hunter was shot through the head and seriously wounded. The only other officer onboard was a Midshipman, John Griffiths, who was also wounded. The crew thus found themselves leaderless, and when a second boarding attempt was made by the French, it succeeded. A total of fifteen men were killed or wounded. One seaman, James Cooper, was found to have quit his station at one of the guns and taken shelter behind a boat during the action. For this he was sentenced to death, but this was commuted to transportation to Botany Bay for seven years, when it was submitted that he was of unsound mind.

Note: recaptured in April 1813 by the *Unicorn*, but not recommissioned.
[TNA: ADM.1/5431]

(11?) September MAGNET Brig Sloop
Prize 1809 (*St Joseph*); 286 tons; 90.5ft × 27.10ft; 16 guns
Commander Ferdinand Moore Maurice†
Sailed from Spithead on 14 August for America with the squadron under Admiral Sir John Borlase Warren, in the *San Domingo*. During the afternoon of 11 September, in position 41.43N 41.08W the *Magnet* parted company and was not seen again. The weather was poor at the time, with gale-force winds and a heavy sea. It was presumed that she foundered with all hands soon after parting company. Pay book closed 31 September.
[TNA: ADM.51/2694; ADM 35/3585]

21 September GUNBOAT 10 Gunboat
Built 1806; 44 tons; 50.7ft × 14ft; 2 guns
Lieutenant Henry Lyon
Ordered to Gibraltar with despatches, she sailed from Cadiz on 13 September, only to encounter strong winds and heavy seas. The gunboat regularly shipped water, and when a leak developed, her head was turned inshore to take shelter. Early in the morning of 16 September she was beached near Pointe Pedro, to prevent her foundering. The leaks and damaged rigging were repaired, and with the weather moderating, she was re-launched on the 18th to recommence her journey. The following day the weather again worsened, with the wind freshening from the east, and that afternoon she again ran for shelter, anchoring close to the shore in five fathoms. She remained at the anchorage, with heavy seas regularly breaking over her and the leaks re-opened during the evening of 20 September. At 4 o'clock the following morning the pump broke, after which the water from the leaks steadily gained. By mid-morning it was clear she must soon founder, so the cables were cut, and she was run ashore, then being about nine miles north-west of Cape Trafalgar, where she soon went to pieces.
[TNA: ADM.1/5431]

27 September BARBADOES Sixth Rate
Prize 1804 (*Brave*); 775 tons; 139.8ft × 35.2ft; 28 guns
Captain Thomas Huskisson
Sailed from Bermuda on 15 September, to escort a small convoy to Halifax, Nova Scotia, and during the evening of 27 September they assessed themselves to be in the vicinity of Sable Island. This seemed to be confirmed by the soundings, which appeared to indicate that they were to the south of the island, and the sloop altered to the south-east to gain deeper water. At 9.15pm, when they believed themselves to be at least 10 miles clear of land, they ran hard aground on the north-eastern point of the island. Strong winds and high seas constantly frustrated efforts to free her, and morning revealed a sloop and a schooner from the convoy were also ashore nearby, with surf breaking over them. Unable to be re-floated and with water from leaks gaining on the pumps, she was abandoned during the day, one man drowning in the attempts to reach the shore. Before leaving the wreck, 60,300 dollars being carried onboard was lowered into the water near the wreck, secured to buoys to mark the position for their later recovery. A strong current was blamed for setting the ship to the west and onto the island.
[TNA: ADM.1/5431]

6 October NIMBLE Cutter
Cowes 1811; 144 tons; 63.3ft × 23.5ft; 10 guns
Lieutenant John Reynolds

In the Kattegat and heading for Gothenburg, the island of Marstrand was raised during the evening of 5 October. The cutter continued to stand on and off the land during the night until at 1.30am, the Gunner's Mate, then acting as the officer of the watch, woke the Captain and the pilot to inform them that he had just been forced to tack off the land which had loomed very close. Neither came on deck but gave orders to continue as before. About 30 minutes later breakers were seen close under the lee bow. An attempt was made to tack but she ran aground and found herself held fast by rocks. Stores and shot were heaved overboard to lighten her, and in an effort to free her, men were sent out onto the bowsprit to lift the stern, but all failed to move her. Several leaks had been started, and water was soon flooding in and could barely be kept in check. Distress guns were fired and blue lights burnt through the night, which attracted the attention of several Swedish fishing vessels, which came to her aid at first light. All the men were taken off, the cutter being full of water by this time. It was reckoned that a strong current had carried them inshore and put them on the shore six miles south-west of the beacon on the island of Salo. Lieutenant Reynolds was reprimanded for not coming on deck after being warned of the nearness of the land at 1.30am. The pilot, John Pyle, had also failed to respond to the warning and had not issued any new instructions after she had tacked. He was reprimanded and ordered to forfeit three months' pay.
[TNA: ADM.1/5431]

8 October AVENGER Ship Sloop
Purchased 1804 (*Thames*); 390 tons; 14 guns
Commander Urry Johnson

Sailed from St Johns, Newfoundland, on 6 October to cruise off that port, but the weather proved to be so bad that the sloop ran for shelter, arriving off St Johns during the evening of 8 October. It was decided to enter that night, and at 9pm she entered the narrows, keeping to the north shore. As she did so she was taken aback by a gust of wind which put her onto the shore near the Chain Rock. All sails were clewed up and boats hoisted out, which initially took out a hawser to the south shore opposite. Efforts to haul her off failed when the line parted at the first attempt. Distress guns were fired as boats were despatched into the harbour to bring assistance, whilst a kedge anchor was laid out, and the vessel was lightened by heaving overboard stores and shot. Heaving on the kedge anchor also failed to move her and by midnight the rising swell was lifting the sloop, making her pound on the rocks and opening several leaks. The pumps were manned throughout the night, but by 6 o'clock in the morning the water was up to the lower-deck beams. The foremast was cut away and hawsers rigged to the north shore to prevent her from heeling over, but by 8 o'clock she was settling fast. Several boats from St Johns were now alongside and all the crew were taken off, the evacuation being complete by 9 o'clock.
[TNA: ADM.1/5434]

9 October DETROIT Brig
Prize 1812 (*Adams*); 125 tons; 6 guns
Lieutenant Charles Frédéric Rolette (Provincial Marine)

Anchored in the mouth of the Niagara River, Lake Erie, having just convoyed the North-west Company's brig *Caledonia*, laden with furs, from Amherstburg to Fort Erie. The arrival was noted by the Americans at Buffalo, and that night two boats with about 100 men embarked set off to attack them. At about 3 o'clock in the morning they ran alongside both of the vessels, boarded and captured them. As the Americans attempted to run their prizes past the shore batteries at Fort Erie, an exchange of fire between the brig and the shore damaged the vessel. She then drifted ashore on Squaw Island, where she was abandoned. A party of British troops attempted to regain possession of the brig but were driven away by fire from the American shore. She lay grounded on the island throughout the day, wrecked by shots from both sides, until she was finally boarded by a party from the American shore and burnt.
[Dudley vol 1 pp328–33]

10 October SENTINEL Gun Brig
Purchased 1804 (*Friendship*); 194 tons; 80.10ft × 24ft; 12 guns
Lieutenant William Elletson King

Sailed from Hanö, Sweden to act as one of the escorts to a large homeward-bound convoy of ships from the eastern Baltic, they steered west along the north German shore, in poor visibility. During the afternoon of 10 October, the fog was so thick that all sight of the convoy had been lost and the brig was brought-to under reefed topsails, their position estimated to be 18 miles north-east of the island of Rügen. Glimpses of the other ships of the convoy were seen through the mist, and at 5 o'clock that evening a succession of gun signals were heard, ordering the convoy to lay-to on the larboard tack, which was done. At 9 o'clock it was decided to alter course, as they feared that the lack of wind and a strong current was taking the brig closer to the island, but they almost collided with a ship that loomed out of the fog. They manoeuvred clear and attempted to wear ship, but as they did so breakers were heard and then land was discovered close by, the brig running aground on the north-eastern end of Rügen soon after. Sails were thrown aback, but this had no effect. The cutter was hoisted out to take

out anchors and some stores and guns were thrown overboard to lighten her. The brig was now pounding heavily forward and with water entering, she started to settle, the pumps unable to cope with the inrush. To add to their troubles, troops could be seen gathering on the cliffs above them and they opened a sporadic fire on them. The brig remained in this situation until the morning, the fog clearing a little, revealing two other ships on shore nearby. The masts were cut away to ease the pounding, but it was clear that she could not be saved, the water being up to the lower deck. Men were seen on the cliffs above and were engaged with small-arms and signal rockets, the latter causing some confusion amongst them. Having silenced the enemy above, the crew took to the boats and were rescued by the *Neptune* brig, the *Sentinel* being set on fire as they left.
[TNA: ADM.1/5431]

18 October FROLIC Brig Sloop
Bridport 1806; 384 tons; 100ft × 30.7ft; 18 guns
Commander Thomas Whinyates

Escorting home a convoy from the West Indies, the sloop became separated from the other ships during a gale on 16 October, when to the north of Bermuda. The storm also carried away her main yard and sprung the main topmast. The following day she started to round up her scattered charges, and by the morning of 18 October six of the vessels had re-joined her. At daybreak, a strange ship was seen closing them; the *Frolic* hoisted Spanish colours and dropped astern of the merchant ships to allow them to escape, whilst placing themselves in the way of the threat. The stranger closed to within 60 yards of the *Frolic* before Whinyates ordered the British flag to be substituted for the Spanish, and fired a broadside into the stranger, which was the American sloop *Wasp*, 18 guns. The *Wasp* returned the fire, and a close action began. Within 10 minutes, the American had lost her main topmast and mizzen topgallant mast. The *Frolic*, already without her main yard, had the head and gaff braces shot away in the same time period. The brig-rigged British vessel thus found herself disabled, whilst the ship-rigged American, although damaged, could still manoeuvre. The advantage was taken, and the *Wasp* stationed herself ahead and fired several raking broadsides into her opponent. The American then wore and allowed herself to fall onboard the *Frolic*, the latter's bowsprit going between the main and mizzen masts. After clearing the upper deck with grapeshot and musketry, the *Wasp* boarded and captured the British sloop. Both *Frolic*'s masts went overboard after the surrender. Later that day the British 74-gun ship *Poictiers* arrived on the scene and captured both the *Wasp* and the *Frolic*. Fifteen men killed and forty-three wounded.
[TNA: ADM.1/5434]

25 October MACEDONIAN Fifth Rate
Woolwich 1810; 1,081 tons; 154.6ft × 39.6ft; 38 guns
Captain John Surman Carden

A short time after daybreak, then being in position 29N 29.30W, a sail was seen on the lee beam. Course was shaped towards the stranger, which by 7.30am could be seen to be a large American frigate. Preparations were made for action, the American initially edging away, until at about 8.30am she came about and 30 minutes later the ships passed on opposite tacks. The pair exchanged broadsides, with little effect, the *Macedonian* then wore round and closed the American ship, which was the *United States*, 44 guns, on the larboard quarter. The mizzen topmast of the British frigate was shot away, as was the American's mizzen topgallant mast. The wreckage of the mizzen rigging in the *Macedonian* fouled the maintop and impeded her sailing to the extent that the *United States* was able to keep her distance from the *Macedonian*. The more powerful 24-pounder guns of the American were used to great effect for the next hour, ripping the British frigate's rigging to shreds and shattering her hull. At just after 10 o'clock, the *United States* closed the *Macedonian* to maintain a close action for another hour, during which the mizzen mast, fore- and main-topmasts of the British frigate were shot away, all but two of the upper deck guns dismounted and two of the main deck guns disabled. She had received dozens of shot in the hull and a large number of the crew were killed or wounded. An attempt was now made to board the American, the bows of the *Macedonian* being run between the main- and mizzen masts of the *United States*. However, at this point the fore braces were shot away and she flew up into the wind. The American, after laying off for a short while to repair rigging, returned to lay herself under the stern of the *Macedonian* and prepared to rake her opponent. At this point, further resistance being useless, Captain Carden surrendered. The long action produced extremely high casualties: thirty-six men killed and sixty-eight wounded.
[TNA: ADM.1/5436]

24 November BELETTE Brig Sloop
Dover 1806; 384 tons; 100ft × 30.7ft; 18 guns
Commander David Sloane†

Bound for Gothenburg, as she headed into the Kattegat the weather became increasingly thick and hazy, and by 8 o'clock in the evening of 23 November the fog was so thick that she was forced to anchor, no land being in sight. The following day the fog showed no signs of lifting, and at just before midday she weighed and proceeded under reefed topsails, sounding constantly. At 10 o'clock that evening the water started shoaling, from 15 down to 12 fathoms, and 30 minutes later, without warning, she struck the Fannot rock, or Johns Knold, to the north-

west of the island of Læso. The rocks ripped open her bottom and she rapidly filled with water, the crew being forced to take to the rigging. By midnight, the ship had broken in half, and the survivors in the rigging faced a long night in freezing temperatures. Dozens of men died from exposure or lost their grip and fell into the sea, and by daylight it was a small band of men who saw land nearby. A boat was discovered to have floated off the booms, and Commander Sloane led an attempt to gain the boat, but as the men tried to pull themselves on board in a heavy swell, it capsized, drowning them all. Some men now trusted themselves to pieces of wreckage and allowed the tide to take them to the shore, but only two survived the ordeal. Local fishermen arrived during the morning and found another four men still alive in the rigging. One hundred and sixteen men died.
[TNA; ADM.1/5434]

27 November SOUTHAMPTON Fifth Rate
Rotherhithe 1757; 653 tons; 124.4ft × 34.8ft; 32 guns
Captain James Lucas Yeo
On 22 November, the *Southampton* captured the American brig-sloop *Vixen* off the eastern coast of the United States, and in company with her prize headed south for Jamaica. During 27 November, the pair were heading for the Crooked Island Passage in the Bahamas, and before midday land was sighted, which was identified as the small island of Conception and a course ordered which would take them clear of the shoals shown on the charts. All seemed well, when breakers were unexpectedly seen nearby and on sounding, only eight fathoms were found. Before another cast of the lead-line could be made she ran aground on a reef, then being about four miles from the island. The rocks tore a hole in the bottom, and she quickly filled, the pumps being quite unable to cope with the inrush. The prize brig *Vixen* also went ashore in a similar manner. All the crew left in an orderly manner and reached the island. It was subsequently found that the reef extended much further to seaward than shown on the charts held onboard. One seaman, John Ware, was later found guilty of improper conduct during the wreck. When ordered to man a boat to return to the wreck to recover stores, he made some obscene remarks to the young midshipman in charge. However, as he was of previous good character, he was only admonished to be more careful in his actions in the future. The reef is now known as Southampton Reef.
[TNA; ADM.1/5435]

30 November SUBTLE Schooner
Prize 1807; 139 tons; 76ft × 21.1ft; 12 guns
Lieutenant Charles Brown†
The schooner sailed from Basse Terre, St Kitts, and later that same day sighted and gave chase to an American privateer. The pursuit was observed from the island of Saint Barthélemy, the *Subtle* being under a press of sail, until she was overtaken by a heavy squall, still under all sail. When this cleared, she had disappeared. Boats were sent from the island, but no survivors were found, only wreckage. Secondary sources identified the privateer as *Jack's Favorite*.
[TNA: ADM.1/1334; www.britishnewspaperarchive.co: Lloyd's List 5 February 1813]

5 December PLUMPER Gun Brig
Halifax, Nova Scotia 1807; 177 tons; 80ft × 22.6ft; 12 guns
Lieutenant James Bray†
Bound for St John's, from Halifax, she arrived off the coast of New Brunswick during the evening of 4 December in poor weather, the night being dark with regular showers of snow. At 4 o'clock in the morning she struck rocks at Red Point, about a mile from Dipper Harbour, and was wrecked. Forty-two men were drowned, including all the officers. About thirty men managed to scramble onto the rocks, the only survivors. The schooner *Bream* was sent from Halifax to the scene but found that the brig had gone to pieces immediately after taking the ground.
[TNA: ADM.1/503]

8 December FEARLESS Gun Brig
Harwich 1804; 180 tons; 80.3ft × 22.7ft; 12 guns
Lieutenant Henry Richards
Sailed from Tangier on 7 December, to escort a transport ship to Cadiz, and by 6 o'clock that evening she was in soundings off Cape Trafalgar. By the early hours of the morning, San Sebastian light at the entrance to the harbour of Cadiz could be seen, so Lieutenant Richards shortened sail and hove-to for the night, leaving the deck in the charge of the Master. Richards was rudely awakened at 5.30am by water pouring into his cabin skylight, the brig shuddering amid sounds of confusion. Coming on deck he found the brig was in the breakers near to San Sebastian light and the vessel soon broached-to, swinging broadside-on to rocks. Here she capsized over onto her larboard beam-ends and started pounding heavily. The masts were cut away and distress guns were fired, but little could be done to haul her off the rocks. A seaman volunteered to swim to the nearby beach with a line, where he was pulled to safety by the local people that were gathering. A hawser was then passed to the brig, and all the men were then hauled ashore. The subsequent court martial was critical of both the Captain and the Master. Lieutenant Richards had taken the brig far too close to the land; he was severely reprimanded and ordered to lose two years' seniority. The Master, Nathaniel Judge, had disobeyed the orders of Richards in failing to tack out to seaward if he found the brig to be in less than 10 fathoms, and had failed to

notify him of a shift in the wind. He was demoted and ordered to serve before the mast as a seaman.
[TNA: ADM.1/5434]

18 December ALBAN Cutter
Bermuda 1806; 111 tons; 68.2ft × 20.4ft; 10 guns
Lieutenant William Strugnel Key†

Stationed on the Dutch coast, in poor weather she ran aground on a sandbank. She managed to free herself but was forced to cut away her mast to do so. Under jury rig she was driven back to the coast of England, until she came to anchor about half a mile off Aldeburgh, Suffolk. The weather remained poor, with a strong easterly gale, with a large swell, causing the surf to constantly break over her. At high water, the anchor cable was cut, with the intention of running the cutter onto the shore, but they struck the Inward Shoal, a sandbank about 100 yards from the shore. The vessel swung broadside-on to the sea and rolled over, throwing everyone into the sea. Just one seaman and one woman managed to survive.
[www.britishnewspaperarchive.co: Suffolk Chronicle 26 December 1812 p4]

29 December JAVA Fifth Rate
Prize 1811 (Renomée); 1,073 tons; 152.5ft × 39.11ft; 38 guns
Captain Henry Lambert†

Fitted out to carry Lieutenant-General Thomas Hislop and his staff to India, the *Java* also carried a large quantity of naval stores for ships building in Bombay. Being short of water and provisions, when the frigate arrived off the coast of Brazil, she steered for the port of San Salvador to refit and replenish. At about 8 o'clock in the morning a strange ship was seen, which the *Java* altered towards, making recognition signals. None of these were answered and by noon the ships were within four miles of each other, the stranger edging away, with all sail set. The *Java* gained on her, until by 1.30pm she was within two miles of the chase, clearly seeing her to be a large American frigate. Sail was mutually reduced, and both hoisted national colours. At just after 2 o'clock the action began when the American frigate, which proved to be the *Constitution*, 44 guns, fired her larboard broadside at the *Java*. The British frigate held off for several minutes, receiving another broadside from the Americans, before firing when within pistol shot. This had a good effect, shooting away the wheel of the *Constitution*. The American frigate then wore ship several times, the *Java* pursuing her, firing into her with some effect. The bowsprit of the *Java* was then shot away, which restricted her movements somewhat. In this situation, manoeuvring to avoid each other's broadsides and obtain the best position continued until 3 o'clock, when the pair were alongside each other, at close range. As in similar previous engagements, the heavier 24-pounder guns of the American were used to great effect, causing numerous casualties, shattering the sides of the *Java* and ripping up the rigging. Captain Lambert determined on an attempt to board his opponent, but as she approached, the foremast was shot away. The British frigate now lay helpless before the *Constitution*, which raked her with impunity for several minutes. Quite unable to move, the *Java* suffered further when the American passed down her starboard side to place herself under the quarter and rake her again. For about 45 minutes the British frigate was pounded, having her gaff and spanker boom shot away followed at about 4 o'clock by the mizzen mast. The *Constitution* now moved alongside the starboard side of the *Java* and the pair exchanged broadsides. The American fell away and lay off for some time, believing her opponent had struck her flag, during which the mainmast of the *Java* went overboard. The American, discovering the flag still flying on her opponent, again closed and took up a position on her bows, at which, with Captain Lambert seriously wounded below and in no position to resist, Lieutenant Henry Chads surrendered the ship. The *Constitution* found the *Java* so severely damaged that she could not be saved, and the survivors were taken out and the ship set on fire. Captain Lambert died later of his wounds. There was a high level of casualties – 22 men killed and 122 wounded.
[TNA: ADM.1/5442]

(28–30) December SARPEDON Brig Sloop
Eling 1809; 241 tons; 90.4ft × 24.9ft; 10 guns
Commander Thomas Parker†

Cruising in the North Sea in company with the *Clio*, the pair stopped and detained a Danish merchant vessel on 27 December, then being to the west of the Kattegat. The weather was poor, and that night the *Sarpedon* became separated from her consort and was not seen again. The weather over the next few days worsened, with strong winds, a heavy sea and frequent squalls of rain. It was presumed that she foundered during this time, with the loss of all hands. Pay book closed 31 December 1812.
[TNA: ADM.51/2186; ADM.35/3900]

1813

7 January FERRET Brig Sloop
Dartmouth 1806; 387 tons; 100.2ft × 30.8ft; 18 guns
Commander Francis Alexander Halliday

Sailed from Leith on 6 January bound for Portsmouth. The following day it was calculated that they were in the latitude of Tynemouth, and the pilot requested that they close the land to gain sight of the lights. The brig stood towards the land throughout the afternoon, in hazy

weather, the pilot in a confident mood. By 6 o'clock in the evening they were still closing, with no sight of the land. Commander Halliday was uneasy at this but was assured by the pilot that they might stand on for another two hours. Still unhappy, Halliday ordered the sloop to heave-to and sound, which showed that they were in 24 fathoms. This led to a dispute with the pilot over their position, with the Captain finally ordered the brig to come about. Before this could be achieved land loomed out of the mist and shortly afterwards the sloop ran aground at Newbiggen on the Northumbrian coast. All sail was thrown aback, but to no effect. Boats were hoisted out to carry out an anchor and shot and stores were heaved overboard, and topmasts cut away to lighten her. She could not be hauled off and with the tide ebbing the brig found herself high and dry. The Carpenter took the opportunity to examine the hull and he found that she was bilged, and her back was broken. The weather worsened, so that by midnight it was blowing hard and raining. Lieutenant McKay came onboard from the nearby signal station, and warned that they would not survive the night, and advised them to leave the brig, to return in the morning. This was done, although one boat took the opportunity to desert. The following morning Halliday and a party returned on board to discover the hold full of water. Undeterred, they bailed and pumped, and local fishermen were engaged to lay out anchors and offload stores. Work went on until 17 January, when she was finally given up for a wreck. The blame was placed on the pilot, Robert Muckle, who was ordered never to serve as a pilot again and to serve three months in the Marshalsea Prison. The Master, Charles Lupton, was criticised for failing to keep a reckoning of the sloop's position: he was ordered to lose a year's seniority. Three of the deserters were picked up by the press gang nearby – all were sentenced to receive 100 lashes on their bare backs with a cat-of-nine-tails.
[TNA:ADM.1/5434]

27 January DARING Gun Brig
Ipswich 1804; 178 tons; 80.2ft × 22.6ft; 12 guns
Lieutenant William Richard Pascoe

On passage from Gorée to Sierra Leone, West Africa, it was decided to close the Îles de Los to take on wood and water. At daybreak on 27 January, when off the western end of Tamara Island, three ships were seen to the north-west. The *Daring* altered towards them, thinking that they might be slaving ships. This view was strengthened when two of the strangers hoisted Portuguese colours, and although end-on, so that their force could not be seen, Lieutenant Pascoe was happy that they were Brazilian slaving ships. He determined to stop and question them, so continued to close and when about three miles distant, hoisted out a boat to carry the Master to board them. When the boat neared the closest of the ships, it was realised that the strangers were two large French frigates with a prize vessel. The boat tried to make off but was captured. The nearest frigate, which was the *Rubis*, 40 guns, then hoisted French colours, yawed and fired a broadside at the *Daring*. The fire fortunately did little damage and the brig quickly altered away and spread all sail to make for the shelter of Tamara Island. Unable to escape, she was deliberately run ashore and then set on fire. The crew managed to commandeer a small trading schooner, but on attempting to escape from the island, the French fired on them and launched boats, which forced the schooner inshore and then burnt it. Over a period of several days Lieutenant Pascoe and his crew escaped to Sierra Leone in a number of small trading boats, where they found the British frigate *Amelia*. The *Amelia* subsequently fought an action on 6 February against one of the French frigates, the *Aréthuse*, during which Lieutenant Pascoe was killed.
[TNA:ADM.1/5435]

21 February RHODIAN Brig Sloop
Northam 1809; 240 tons; 90.2ft × 24.8ft; 14 guns
Commander John George Boss

Returning to Jamaica from Porto Bello, the land was raised at 3.30pm, and by nightfall the brig was off Plumb Point, the south-east point of Port Royal. The brig was leaking badly, making a foot an hour, one pump being in constant use and this, combined with the sloop being short of fresh water, led to the decision to enter harbour that night. Guided by the lights of the barracks at Port Royal Point, she steered into the harbour, but struck the reef off Little Plumb Point. She then realised that the lights were not the barracks but the victualling office in the dockyard. Sails were furled, boats hoisted out and distress guns fired. An anchor was laid out astern but despite heaving on the cable, she did not move, and the line finally parted. Stores, including 400,000 dollars being carried onboard, were offloaded into boats to lighten the brig, whilst a second anchor was laid out ahead. This also failed to shift her, and further lightening went on, heaving overboard shot and the remaining water butts were emptied. Heaving on the hawser now shifted her a little, but this only seemed to increase the leaks, and the water entered so fast that she started to settle. The pumps were manned through the night, and rafts were made in preparation for the morning. At daylight, several boats from the dockyard closed the wreck and took off the crew, the brig having sunk up to her gunwales.
[TNA:ADM.1/5435]

24 February PEACOCK Brig Sloop
Ipswich 1806; 386 tons; 100.3ft × 30.7ft; 18 guns
Commander William Peake†
On a cruise off the coast of Demerara, South America, during the afternoon a ship was sighted by the *Peacock*, apparently steering for the anchorage which she had recently left, the sloop *Espiegle* still being at anchor there. She altered towards the stranger, and by 4 o'clock it could be made out to be a ship of war, and *Peacock* hoisted her colours and cleared for action when the stranger failed to respond to recognition signals. The pair passed on opposite tacks at 5.25pm, exchanging broadsides as they did so, the *Peacock* then wore round to engage with the other broadside. The enemy, which was the American *Hornet*, 20 guns, ran under the brig's starboard quarter from where she commenced a heavy and accurate fire of cannon and musketry, to which the British ship could not effectively reply. Within 15 minutes the *Peacock* had been reduced to a wreck, with the Captain killed and casualties mounting. Lieutenant Frederick Wright then struck her flag, and an ensign was hoisted upside down in the rigging as a signal of distress. Both vessels then anchored. and it soon became clear that the brig was sinking. The *Hornet* sent a party of men onboard to help try and pump her free, but the water rapidly gained, and she soon sank, taking several men with her, only the fore topmast being visible above the water. Whether or not the *Espiegle* sloop could have afforded some assistance was later disputed. The Americans stated that she was laying in the anchorage off Demerara nearby and could have intervened, whereas the *Peacock*'s evidence was that she was not visible during the engagement. The reported position of the wreck, if correct, said to be six leagues (18 miles) north-north-east from Point Spirit on the eastward side of the Demerara River, would suggest that she was not visible. Commander John Taylor of the *Espiegle* was court-martialled in 1814 on several charges, which included failing to engage the *Hornet*, but was cleared of this charge. *Peacock* suffered four men killed in the engagement, with another eight men missing, presumed killed. and thirty-three wounded, five of them fatally.
[TNA: ADM.1/503; ADM.1/5436]

25 February LINNET Gun Brig
Purchased 1806 (*Speedwell*); 197 tons; 77.9ft × 25.4ft; 14 guns
Lieutenant John Tracy
When in the western approaches to the English Channel, in poor weather, with high winds and heavy seas, a ship was seen under foresail and reefed mainsail and evidently in chase. By 1pm the stranger could be seen to be a large frigate, which did not respond to private recognition signals. The larger vessel continued to close and was alongside by 2.30pm, when she hailed the brig and called on her to surrender to the French frigate *Gloire*. Lieutenant Tracy not only refused but made sail away, passing under the frigate's bow. The French ship fired repeatedly at the brig, which was handled very skilfully, making a series of short tacks and keeping ahead of the frigate and avoiding her fire, which the larger vessel found difficult to follow. *Linnet* passed under the bows three times, once so close that she carried away the frigates flying jib boom. When this happened, the French shouted at the brig '... in a violent passion and bestowed several awkward compliments after the word English'. The chase went on for over an hour, until the *Gloire* managed to shoot away some of the brig's rigging, which at last restricted her movements. The *Linnet* tried one final tack, which took her close to the frigate's bow, forcing the *Gloire* to luff. This took the frigate alongside the brig, which at last surrendered. Lieutenant Tracy was deservedly praised by the subsequent court martial for his skill and bravery and rewarded with a promotion to Commander.
[TNA: ADM.1/5442]

22 March CAPTAIN Third Rate
Limehouse 1787; 1,639 tons; 170ft × 467.10ft
Laying in Plymouth Dock, preparing to be converted to a sheer hulk for use by the Dockyard, she was secured alongside the *San Josef*, 112 guns, in order that stores could be removed. At about 11 o'clock at night a fire was discovered in the small galley under the fo'c'sle, which soon took a firm hold. The securing lines were hastily cut, and she was towed away to a safe distance to be allowed to burn out, dockyard shipwrights going alongside to attach ring bolts to which hawsers and chains could be secured. Fearing that she might still drift down onto other ships, orders were given to sink her, and ship's launches with carronades, joined by two field guns, commenced a bombardment which went on for over an hour, more than 200 shots being fired into her. Finally, at about 4 o'clock in the morning, when nearly burnt to the water's edge, she foundered. '... The blaze illumed the hemisphere and might have been descried at a distance of thirty miles. An artificial day was created, and the roaring of the flames resembled that of a furnace' (*Gold: Naval Chronicle*). Two men died, including the cook.
[Gold: Naval Chronicle vol 35 p219]

28 April (DUKE OF) GLOUCESTER Brig
Kingston (Ontario) 1807; 165 tons; 10 guns
An American force under Commodore Isaac Chauncey raided the harbour of York, Lake Ontario, with a small fleet of ten vessels, accompanied by a force commanded by General Dearborn. The Americans landed under fire and successfully drove off the British garrison. Chauncey found the *Gloucester* under repair at the small

yard and, despite an attempt by the garrison to set her on fire, carried her back to Sacketts Harbour.
[Dudley vol 2 pp452, 455]

20 May ALGERINE Cutter
Upnor 1810; 193 tons; 82.6ft × 22.8ft; 10 guns
Lieutenant Daniel Carpenter

After covering the passage of a convoy into the Atlantic through the Crooked Island Passage, off the Bahamas the cutter parted company with the convoy on 19 May to return to Jamaica. At half past midnight, with no warning she ran aground. The pumps were manned, and the boats hoisted out, laying out an anchor to act as a kedge. However, she was held fast, and despite strenuous heaving she would not move and eventually the hawser parted. Shot, guns and stores were heaved overboard to lighten her, and the boats worked to lay out another anchor. She still refused to budge, and by 2 o'clock the Carpenter was reporting that she was filling with water. The mainmast was cut away and the work of pumping and lightening went on through the night. At daylight local vessels closed her, to inform them that she was on the Gallipagos Shoal on the Little Bahamas Bank and had little chance of survival. The cutter was abandoned, all the crew and a large quantity of stores were saved and taken to New Providence. A strong current was blamed for having set her further to the south than she had realised.
[TNA: ADM.1/5438]

26 June PERSIAN Brig Sloop
Cowes 1809; 389 tons; 100.2ft × 30.6ft; 18 guns
Commander Charles Bertram

After sailing from Port au Prince, the sloop steered round the north of the island of Hispaniola. At just after 5 o'clock in the afternoon, with little warning, she struck a submerged obstruction and found herself held fast. Efforts to free her, by throwing the sails aback failed, and shot, stores and some guns were heaved overboard to lighten her, and she eventually floated free, only for the brig to tail onto another rock. Pumps were manned, boats hoisted out and more stores heaved over the side, but she still would not move. By 7pm she was clearly settling, with 5ft of water in the hold. A raft was ordered to be constructed, and the boats were stocked with stores in preparation for abandoning her as she steadily settled. At 2 o'clock in the morning of 27 June she foundered, all the crew taking to the boats and a raft. The raft, however, soon came apart, forcing all 126 men of the crew to cram into four boats, and they set off for the land. Their ordeal lasted until the following morning, when they came ashore between Cabo Frances and Cabo Cabron. It was found that she had been wrecked on the Silver Bank (Banco de la Plata) and the loss was blamed on the strong current, which was running at four knots, which had set her further to the north than she had expected, with the position of the keys being shown incorrectly on the charts held by the sloop.
[TNA: ADM.1/5438]

2 July DAEDALUS Fifth Rate
Prize 1811 (Corona); 1,094 tons; 152.9ft × 40.3ft; 38 guns
Captain Murray Maxwell

Escort to a convoy of outward-bound East Indiamen, she sailed from Spithead on 29 January, arriving off Point de Galle, Ceylon on 1 July. Course was then laid for Madras, taking them clear of the coast and the shoal waters of the Great and Little Basses reefs. After steering north-east for some time, she altered to the north, in the belief that she was some eight miles from the land and clear of any danger. At just before 8 o'clock the following morning she ran aground. The impact was gentle, so they hoped to sail her off, but the ship was held fast, and it became clear that the sternpost had given way and water started to enter rapidly. Work started to clear the after storeroom and bread room, guns were run forward and shot heaved overboard. A sail was prepared and slung under the hull in an attempt to block the leak, but by late afternoon the water was 2ft above the orlop deck and gaining all the time. Ships in the convoy were ordered to send boats to her aid and all the men were taken off before she foundered. The subsequent court martial heard that the ship had been wrecked on the Little Basses reef, and judged that the Master, Arthur Webster, had been negligent in failing to order the constant use of the lead-line; he was severely reprimanded. One Marine, Sampson Bushell, was ordered to receive fifty lashes, for being drunk at the time of the wreck.
[TNA: ADM.1/5437]

4 July EAGLE Sloop Tender
From 1813; 1 gun
Master's Mate Henry Morris†

Fitted out by the Poictiers, 74 guns, as a tender, she was employed in the waters off Sandy Hook intercepting local coastal shipping, with a small crew of twelve men. Annoyed by this, the inhabitants of the area fitted out the fishing smack Yankee to capture her. Sailing from Sandy Hook, apparently on an innocent voyage, complete with livestock onboard, she was chased and stopped by the tender. As they came alongside, about thirty armed men burst up from where they had been concealed below and fired a volley of musketry at point-blank range into the sloop. Mr Morris and Midshipman Price with one Marine were shot dead and two seamen wounded. The tender was carried into New York.
[www.britishnewspaperarchive.co: Public Ledger 10 August 1813 p2]

28 July GUNBOAT 17 Gunboat
Built 1806; 44 tons; 50.7ft × 14ft; 2 × guns
Having been fitted out at Sheerness for service, the gunboat was being taken from the dockyard to the Nore anchorage, when at 2 o'clock in the afternoon she fouled the *Devonshire* and overset and sank very quickly. A Midshipman and two crew members were quickly rescued, but two dockyard workers and a woman were unfortunately drowned.
[www.britishnewspaperarchive.co: Kentish Weekly Post 6 August 1813 p4; TNA: ADM.51/2067]

(25?) July VAUTOUR Brig Sloop
Prize 1809; 336 tons; 95ft × 28.10ft; 16 guns
Commander Paul Lawless†
Stationed in the Leeward Islands, she sailed from off the Îles des Saintes on 18 July to relieve the *Charybdis* off Tortola, being ordered to pass to the northward of St Bartholomew and call at St Thomas en-route but failed to arrive as expected. A strong gale affected the area on 25 July, and it was thought possible that she was lost at this time with all hands. Her pay book was closed on 31 August.
[TNA: ADM.1/334; ADM.35/3983]

5 August DOMINICA Schooner
Prize 1809 (*Duc de Wagram*); 203 tons; 89.6ft × 23.1ft; 14 guns
Lieutenant George Wilmot Barette†
Escorting the *Princess Charlotte* packet from the West Indies to England, when in the vicinity of latitude 23N 67W, about 300 miles north of Hispaniola, the pair fell in with the American schooner privateer *Decatur*, 7 guns. The privateer closed with the intention of boarding the schooner, and at 2 o'clock in the afternoon, attempted to pass under the stern of *Dominica*, but the British schooner luffed, and gave her a broadside. The privateer then stood off and used her 18-pounder gun to some effect, keeping out of range of the 6-pounder cannon and 12-pounder carronades of *Dominica*. After 45 minutes of this, the privateer closed and ran her bowsprit over the quarter of the British schooner, her jib boom piercing the mainsail, and fired a destructive volley of small-arms fire and then entered a large number of boarders. A short fight took place on the upper deck before the flag was struck in surrender. The fierceness of the fighting is reflected in the casualties: nineteen men killed and forty-two wounded – only two men escaped injury.
[TNA: ADM.1/5447]

5 August GUNBOAT 23 Gunboat
Built 1806; 44 tons; 50.7ft × 14ft; 2 guns
Lieutenant John Bowie
Stationed in the River Ebro at Amposta to guard a pontoon bridge, at 5.30am the crew were alerted to a commotion ashore, and on investigation Lieutenant Bowie discovered that a large body of French troops were entering the town. As they hastily attempted to get a gun to bear, the gunboat came under musketry fire, and several men were hit. Clearly unable to sustain an unequal fight, Bowie managed to get the small boat secured at the stern alongside, into which he placed the wounded men. Holes were now knocked in the gunboat's hull to ensure that it sank. The vessel was then abandoned, the crew either using the boat or swimming to gain the opposite bank of the river, with Bowie being the last to leave, cutting the hawser securing the pontoon bridge as he did, putting it out of action and preventing any pursuit. The French later set fire to the gunboat. Three men were killed and four wounded.
[TNA: ADM.1/5437; United Services Magazine vol 46 Part III pp74–5]

22 August COLIBRI Brig Sloop
Prize 1809; 365 tons; 96.9ft × 29.5ft; 16 guns
Commander John Thompson
Blockading the American port of Savannah, Georgia, in company with the *Moselle* sloop, the pair found they had little to do at sea, there being little shipping evident. A series of boat attacks were then mounted on coastal areas between Charleston and Georgetown, with some success, and the pair then moved on to the south of Charleston. to repeat the action. The sloops entered Port Royal Sound, South Carolina, and anchored with the intention of carrying out attacks on local vessels. They were frustrated in this by the activities of the local militia, which erected shore batteries and after 'annoying' the shore positions, it was decided to leave. In poor weather, with strong winds and regular squalls of rain, the sloops weighed and made their way seaward, but as the *Colibri* followed the *Moselle*, she struck the bar at the entrance to the sound. She soon came off the obstruction and tacked away to the north to find deeper water, but then struck again. She was again freed and anchored to lower boats to sound around her. The tide was on the ebb, and the brig started bumping on the bottom as the boats reported that the sandbar seemed to be more extensive that they had believed. Shot and ballast was heaved overboard to lighten her, and she weighed and attempted to wear round to find a channel through. She ran hard aground again and thumped violently, unshipping the rudder. An attempt was made to lay out a kedge anchor, but with the sloop pounding heavily it was too late. The sternpost soon parted, and timbers and planks gave way. Filling with water she fell over to larboard, the masts hastily being cut away to ease her. All the men were taken off by the *Moselle* and the wreck was abandoned.
[TNA: ADM.1/5438]

5 September BOXER Brig Sloop
Redbridge 1812; 182 tons; 84.3ft × 22.1ft; 12 guns
Commander Samuel Blyth†

Laying at anchor off Penguin Point, to the east of Portland, Maine, when at daylight a strange brig was seen closing the anchorage. The *Boxer* weighed and hoisting three ensigns, stood towards the oncoming brig, which was the American gun brig *Enterprise*, 14 guns. The wind fell away as they closed, and it was after midday before the pair could resume their manoeuvring for the better position. The *Enterprise* initially made sail away, the *Boxer* pursuing, until at 3 o'clock the American shortened sail and steered towards the British sloop. At 3.15pm the *Boxer* opened the action by firing her starboard broadside, which was returned by the American. This first exchange of fire killed both commanding officers – Commander Blyth being struck by an 18-pound ball, whilst Lieutenant Burrowes, commanding the *Enterprise*, was hit by canister shot. After 15 minutes engagement, the American moved ahead and fired a raking broadside, which shot away the main topmast and topsail yard. For the next 15 minutes *Enterprise* kept her position ahead of *Boxer*, raking her continuously. At 3.45pm the *Boxer* surrendered. Four men killed and seventeen wounded.
[TNA: ADM.1/5440]

10 September ALPHEA Schooner
Bermuda 1806; 111 tons; 68.2ft × 20.4ft; 10 guns
Lieutenant Thomas William Jones†

Sailed from Plymouth for Guernsey on 7 September but disappeared. Some days later, the stern part of a wreck was discovered, and identified as being from *Alphea* and it was presumed that she had foundered, perhaps after being in collision with another vessel. However, later reports from France showed that she had been sunk in action. The privateer *Renard*, 14 guns, encountered the *Alphea* on 9 September off Start Point, which chased the privateer, overhauling her at 1 o'clock in the morning and opening the action by firing bow-chase guns. The pair mutually exchanged fire until *Alphea* was taken by the swell under the bows of the privateer, which attempted to board. This was repulsed with considerable loss on the part of the French. The action continued until 3.30am when the *Alphea* suddenly blew up, probably from the hand grenades being thrown onboard from *Renard*. Men were seen in the water, but the French vessel was unable to help them before they disappeared.
[www.britishnewspaperarchive.co: Public Ledger 28 September 1813 p2; James vol 6 p160]

10 September: Battle of Lake Erie
In the summer of 1813, the rival British and American forces on Lake Erie, Canada, had built up their strength by new construction and purchasing local trading vessels. The six vessels of the little British squadron were manned by some seamen sent from Halifax, with soldiers from the Newfoundland and the 41st (Welch) Regiments. They sailed from Amherstburg on 9 September for the islands north of Sandusky, hoping to find the Americans at anchor. This was accomplished, when at daylight, the American squadron of nine vessels was discovered laying at anchor in Put-In Bay, South Bass Island. The advantage was lost through the wind shifting, allowing the American vessels to weigh, and by 10 o'clock they had cleared the anchorage and the rival forces were in line of battle and steering towards each other.

DETROIT Ship Sloop
Amherstburg 1813; 305 tons; 96.2ft × 27.7ft; 19 guns
Commander Robert Barclay

The action commenced just before noon when the *Detroit* fired at the American *Lawrence*. Commander Barclay was wounded early in the action, and his Lieutenant, John Garland, then assumed command, but was soon wounded. Lieutenant George Inglis continued the fight, concentrating on the *Lawrence*, which was battered to a hulk and dropped out of line, striking her flag. The American commander was forced to shift his flag to the relatively untouched *Niagara*, 20 guns, which was able to take up a raking position on the bow of *Detroit*. The problems of the sloop increased when the next British vessel in the line, the *Queen Charlotte*, fouled her. Unable to manoeuvre, with a second American vessel now in position on the other bow, a number of guns disabled and the rigging cut to pieces, she struck her flag. The subsequent court martial heard that she had only ten experienced seamen on board, the rest being a mix of soldiers, locally recruited Canadians, and some native Americans, all of whom were unused to naval fighting. The guns could not be fired except by discharging a pistol at the touchhole and they were short of supplies. The British squadron as a whole suffered forty-one killed and ninety-four wounded.

QUEEN CHARLOTTE Ship Sloop
Amherstburg 1810; 254 tons 92.2ft × 26ft; 16 guns
Lieutenant Robert Finnis†

Lieutenant Finnis followed the *Detroit* into action and engaged the American *Niagara* and two schooners. Only a short while after the action commenced, Finnis was killed and the only other naval officer, Acting-Lieutenant Thomas Stokoe, was wounded. The command devolved upon Lieutenant Robert Irvine of the Provincial Marine, who did his best to join the *Detroit* in the attack on the American flagship *Lawrence*. This was successful as the American vessel fell out of the line, but the *Charlotte* had her rigging so badly damaged, that she fell aboard the *Detroit* and was then repeatedly raked by two American ships. Eventually falling free, she had little choice but to surrender, with a number of casualties and the rigging destroyed, every brace and stay being shot away.

(GENERAL) HUNTER Brig Sloop
Amherstburg 1807; 93 tons; 54ft × 18ft; 10 guns
Lieutenant George Bignell
Stationed astern of *Charlotte*, she initially concentrated her fire on the *Lawrence*. The arrival of the American *Caledonia*, 3 guns, with a much heavier armament of 24-pounder guns against the 6- and 4-pounder guns of the *Hunter* soon took its toll. When the *Niagara* joined in the fray, she broke the British formation and on being engaged by gunboats armed with traversing 32-pounders, the *Hunter* surrendered.

LADY PREVOST Schooner
Amherstburg 1813; 120 tons; 68ft × 18.6ft; 13 guns
Lieutenant Edward Buchan
In the wake of the *Hunter* in the little British line, she found herself opposed to the American *Caledonia* and four schooners, which soon reduced her to a wreck, her rudder shattered. She fell out of line to leeward, Lieutenant Buchan being seriously wounded, as was her second-in-command, Lieutenant Frédéric Rolette. After the *Detroit* was seen to strike her flag, the *Prevost* did likewise.

LITTLE BELT Sloop
Purchased 1813 (*Friend's Good Will*); 67 tons; 59ft × 16ft; 3 guns
Lieutenant John Breman (Provincial Marine)
Bringing up the rear of the British line, she suffered from raking fire from several American gunboats. When it became clear that the Americans had won the day, the sloop attempted to escape, in company with the *Chippeway*. They were soon overtaken by the swifter sailing American schooners, the *Trippe* and *Scorpion*, and forced to surrender.

CHIPPEWAY Schooner
Purchased 1813; 32 tons; 1 gun
Masters Mate John Campbell
Led the line of British vessels into action against Commodore Perry, the American fire was concentrated on the *Detroit* and *Queen Charlotte*, and the *Chippeway* assisted those vessels. She came under fire from several of the American squadron but was not badly damaged and later joined the *Little Belt* in the attempt to escape. The pair were overhauled by two large American schooners and surrendered.
[TNA: ADM.1/5445; ADM.1/504; ADM.1/505]

* * *

11 September WOOLWICH Troopship
Bursledon 1785; 907 tons; 140ft × 38.6ft; 24 guns
Commander Thomas Ball Sullivan
Sailed from Bermuda on 26 August for Barbados, in company with the *Vine* merchant ship. During 8 September, the weather became increasingly squally and steadily deteriorated until 11 September. By this time, it was blowing a strong gale, and topgallant masts and yards were taken down, with sail shortened to reefed topsails. During the afternoon, the wind increased from the north, with a heavy sea and driving rain. At 1 o'clock the main topsail split and the ship broached-to, swinging broadside-on to the sea. She recovered, and managed to hoist the fore staysail, but found herself being driven to leeward. The wind increased and with the driving rain and spray, the horizon was obscured. At 6 o'clock, to the '... surprise and astonishment' of every officer in the ship, land was sighted close under the bow and within minutes she had run hard aground. The rudder was unshipped, and she bilged immediately. Within minutes she had been driven further onto the rocks and then capsized over onto her beam-ends. The weather slowly cleared and by daylight the following morning they were able to gain the land, discovering it to be the island of Barbuda, and the *Vine* had also gone ashore nearby. They had believed themselves to be 90 miles from the island, but the strong current and the strength of the gale had taken her far off the planned course.
[TNA: ADM.1/5440]

24 September HIGHFLYER Schooner
Prize 1813; 144 tons; 80ft × 20ft; 8 guns
Lieutenant George Hutchinson
Cruising off the North American coast between 40N and 41N, to the south of Nantucket, when at 9.30 in the morning a large ship was seen on the weather beam. The weather was hazy, and the stranger could not be seen clearly, so the *Highflyer* bore up and made sail towards her. She had no private recognition signals but hoisted her commissioning pendant which the stranger repeated. This did not arouse any suspicions and as she closed, several people identified her as the British frigate *Tenedos*, known to be in the area, and the schooner confidently stood on. When close to the stranger sail was shortened and a boat hoisted out to take Lieutenant Hutchinson onboard. As the boat closed the ship, the stranger wore round and hoisted an American ensign. Hutchinson in his boat could do little as the frigate picked him up, before running alongside the schooner and forcing her to surrender. Her captor proved to be the *President*, 44 guns. All the schooner's papers were captured, including a signal book.
[TNA: ADM.1/5441]

27 September BOLD Gun Brig
Bursledon 1812; 182 tons; 84.4ft × 22.1ft; 12 guns
Commander John Skekel
Escorting local trading vessels along the Canadian coast, the brig had successfully taken ships to Cape Canso and Sydney before setting course for Prince Edward's Island. At sunset on 26 September the Magdalen Islands were sighted, and a course was set for them to be off North Cape of Prince Edward's at daybreak. At 3.45 the following morning she ran aground with little warning and commenced striking heavily on the ground. Guns, shot and heavy stores were heaved overboard, and the mainmast was cut away to lighten and ease her. Daylight showed the land just one cable (200 yards) away, with a heavy surf rolling on the shore. The water was nearly up to the upper deck and with the weather poor, with overcast skies and a strong wind, it was decided to abandon the brig. A boat was launched through the surf which carried a line, this being used to guide the boat in further trips between the wreck and the shore, carrying the crew. All had been landed by noon and a camp established on the shore. A party was sent overland to Charlottetown to bring assistance, the remainder of the survivors being organised to salvage what they could from the wreck. Commander Skekel and the Master, Thomas Liddle, were both subsequently reprimanded for failing to order the constant use of the lead-line. Local pilot Donald Ferguson was ordered to lose all pay due to him for failing to advise of the strength and direction of the currents.
[TNA:ADM.1/5438]

21 October LAURESTINUS Sixth Rate
Bridport 1806 (*Laurel*); 526 tons; 118ft × 31.8ft; 22 guns
Captain Thomas Graham
Part of the British force blockading the Chesapeake, she left the squadron on 17 October to return to the West Indies. The ship ran south in poor weather, but they believed themselves to be well clear of any danger, when at 11.20pm, with no warning, she ran aground. The heavy swell caused the ship to lift and pound with every wave, and water was soon discovered to be entering. Sails were furled, topgallant masts and yards were struck and at midnight the fore- and mainmasts were cut away. Pumping and bailing were started but by 2 o'clock in the morning the water was defeating the pumps and 30 minutes later she capsized over to port. Most of the crew were placed in the boats, which stood by the wreck all night with those remaining on board clinging to the rigging. At daybreak, the boats commenced ferrying men to a small island seen nearby. A camp was established, and the barge manned to be sent to New Providence, but a local schooner arrived, which informed them that they were on the Spanish Keys Reef, on the Little Bahama Bank. The schooner lifted off part of the crew that day to take them to Green Turtle Key, returning for the remainder the next day. One man died in the wreck and five men deserted from Green Turtle Key. The loss was blamed on an error in dead reckoning coupled with a strong current.
[TNA:ADM.1/5439]

5 November TWEED Ship Sloop
Littlehampton 1807; 431 tons; 109.1ft × 29.9ft; 18 guns
Commander William Mather
Sailed from Cork on 2 October to escort a convoy of fifty merchant ships to Newfoundland. One month later she found herself in soundings on the Newfoundland Banks and continued to steer to the west in fine weather. During 4 November, the weather became very foggy, but with the soundings steadily deepening as they left the bank, she stood on. By the early hours of the following morning, she was forced to heave-to, the fog now being very thick. From soundings taken it was believed that the sloop was about eight leagues (24 miles) from the shore, but at 5.30 that morning, as she was preparing to cast the lead-line again, land was seen looming out of the mist. All hands were turned up and more sail made to gain headway to tack away, but before this was complete, she struck a high rock, which stove in her starboard quarter. The sloop started filling with water and in just 30 minutes she was full and fell over to starboard. The main- and mizzen masts were cut away, but their situation seemed desperate. Just then, some men were seen on the rocks astern of them. It was discovered that these were the boat's crew of the quarter boat which had been swept away when she struck the rocks. Ropes were thrown to them, by means of which the crew started to climb or be hauled to safety on the rocks. By 7 o'clock the ship was breaking up, and soon after this, fell apart, drowning those who remained onboard. The survivors scrambled over the rocks to the land, but five men died later of the cold and injuries. In total sixty-five men died. It was found that the ship had been wrecked in Shoal Bay, near Cape Spear, Newfoundland, due to an error in the soundings shown on the chart, coupled with a strong current which had carried them further inshore than they had realised.
[TNA:ADM.1/5439]

10 November ATALANTE Ship Sloop
Bermuda 1808; 399 tons; 107ft × 29.11ft; 18 guns
Commander Frederick Hickey
Part of the blockading squadron off the North American coast, she was ordered to return to Halifax to restock on water and provisions. Cape Sable was sighted during 8 November before thick fog descended to blanket the area. The sloop proceeded carefully, sounding constantly until by the morning of 10 November they believed themselves, by distance run and depth of soundings,

to be close to Halifax. They commenced firing signal guns at regular intervals, which seemed to be answered and were taken to be the signal guns at Cape Sambro lighthouse. The sloop steered towards the sound of the guns, still sounding constantly and with extra lookouts posted, expecting the fog to clear as they neared the land. At just after 10 o'clock one of the lookouts shouted a warning and the helm was put over, but she found herself amongst breakers and within a few minutes the rudder was unshipped as she bumped over rocks. The sternpost became detached, and pieces of the keel were seen floating to the surface and water was reported to be pouring in through several leaks. The boats were hoisted out and the guns ordered to be heaved overboard, but she was filling and settling so quickly that this could not be done. The main- and fore masts were ordered to be cut away, and this was scarcely complete when the sloop started to break up. The crew managed to cram into three small boats or cling to a hastily constructed raft of spars and yards. Fortunately, a local fishing boat arrived on the scene, which guided them to a sheltered beach and safety. The enquiry established that the sloop had been wrecked on the Sisters Rocks off Sambro, at the entrance to Halifax, having mistaken the guns fired by another ship in the fog for the signal guns of the lighthouse.
[TNA: ADM.1/5439]

21 November GOSHAWK Brig Sloop
Blackwall 1806; 286 tons; 96.4ft × 25.11ft; 16 guns
Commander William John Napier
Stationed off the coast of Spain, she was ordered to disrupt the supply of provisions for the French army, and to prevent any attempt to run ships into Barcelona, stood in close the harbour. When the soundings shallowed, the brig attempted to wear ship, but in light and baffling winds this failed, and when the wind died away, she was taken inshore by the swell and ran aground about 2½ miles to the east of the mole at Barcelona. All efforts to free her failed, and at daybreak all the crew were able to take to the boats and the brig set on fire as they left.
[TNA: ADM.1/5439]

November (?) DART Cutter
Purchased 1810 (*Belerina*); 127 tons; 62.7ft × 22.5ft; 10 guns
Lieutenant Thomas Allen†
Sailed from Pernambuco, Brazil, on 27 October for England, and not seen again and presumed to have foundered with all hands. Pay book closed 31 October 1813.
[www.britishnewspaperarchive.co: Cheltenham Chronicle 1 December 1814 p2; TNA: ADM.35/3431]

1814

9 January HOLLY Schooner
Bermuda 1809; 150 tons; 78.8ft × 21.7ft; 10 guns
Lieutenant Samuel Sharpe Treacher†
Steering along the north coast of Spain, the weather became so poor, with a heavy sea and strong winds, that the schooner had to bear up for shelter in the harbour of San Sebastian. During the afternoon of 28 January, she anchored at the entrance to that port and prepared to ride out the storm. At 4.30am the anchor cable parted, and she drove across the harbour. The small bower anchor was let go, but it failed to bring her up and she went onto rocks under Monte Aguillo (Urgull). Signal guns were fired, but she started to break up immediately, pounded by the surf. Fortunately, the mainmast fell over onto the rocks, along which the crew were able to make the shore. Four men, including Lieutenant Treacher, were drowned in the attempt.
[TNA: ADM.1/5441]

14 February PICTOU Brig Sloop
Prize 1813 (*Bonne Foi*); 211 tons; 83ft × 24.8ft; 16 guns
Lieutenant Edward Stephens
Escorting the merchant ship *Lovely Ann* from Bermuda to Surinam, during the evening of 13 February a strange sail was sighted to windward. The stranger was seen to alter towards the brig and when private recognition signals were not answered, it was feared that it might be an American frigate, and Lieutenant Stephens advised the merchant ship to make all sail away. The ship slowly overhauled the pair but had not caught them by nightfall. The *Pictou* kept all sail set during the night and hoped that she had lost the stranger, but at daylight she was seen on the weather quarter, and soon captured the *Lovely Ann*. The chase recommenced, with the sloop being steadily overhauled. When within musket shot, she struck her flag in surrender, finding the vessel was the USS *Constitution*, 44 guns.
[TNA: ADM.1/5444; ADM.1/333]

February ANACREON Ship Sloop
Plymouth 1813; 427 tons; 108.9ft × 29.8ft; 16 guns
Commander John Davies†
At the end of January, the French privateer *Lion* was active off the coast of Portugal, and allowed two of her prizes, after being plundered, to proceed to Lisbon, where the *Anacreon* was stationed. The sloop promptly sailed in search of the privateer and on 1 February succeeded in retaking a Spanish vessel which had been captured by the privateer. She left her prize to continue her search but was not seen again and was presumed to have foundered with all hands. Pay book closed 28 February 1814.
[Lloyd's List no.4849: 1 March 1814; TNA: ADM.35/3268]

22 March DECOY Cutter
Fishbourne 1810; 203 tons; 75ft x 26ft; 10 guns
Lieutenant John Pearce
Cruising off Calais in thick fog, the cutter believed herself to be seven to eight miles offshore, and it was a surprise therefore when she ran aground at just after 1 o'clock in the afternoon. Anchors were laid out, stores heaved overboard to lighten her, and sails furled. All efforts to pull her free failed, the water leaving her as the tide ebbed, the cutter laying on the sands of the Waldram Flats, near Calais. Several troops were seen to be gathering nearby, who opened a harassing fire on the cutter, wounding one man. Fire was returned and by employing the great guns as well as small arms, the troops were driven off. Spars and booms were lowered over the side to act as shores to await high tide, but at 3 o'clock the shores gave way and she fell over onto her beam-ends. An hour later a large body of soldiers could be seen advancing and when a party approached under a flag of truce, offering good terms if they surrendered, Lieutenant Pearce accepted and gave up the cutter. Pearce was subsequently admonished to be more careful in his actions in the future, as it was judged that he should have ordered the constant use of the lead-line and taken other precautions when on an enemy coast in the fog. Midshipman Henry Lee, the officer of the watch, was ordered to forfeit all pay due and have no promotion for three years. The pilots, John de Wymmer and Richard Tell, lost all money due to them, for negligence. In addition, Tell was ordered to serve six months in the Marshalsea Prison.
[TNA: ADM.1/5442]

2 April GLEANER Ketch
Purchase 1809; 154 tons; 2 guns
Lieutenant Alexander Branch
Lying in the harbour at St Jean de Luz, south-west France, awaiting the arrival of an officer from the Duke of Wellington's army with despatches for England, the weather steadily worsened, until by the morning of 1 April it was blowing a full gale from the north-west. The ketch was secured by both bower anchors, yards and topmasts were struck and the jibboom taken in and she initially rode out the storm, until the morning of 2 April, when a merchant sloop drove from her anchors and fell across the bows of the *Gleaner*. With some difficulty the sloop was freed, the crew taking shelter on the ketch before their vessel foundered. The *Gleaner* now found that she was dragging her anchor, and the stream anchor was let go, which brought her up. At 10am she was again found to be dragging and was driven down onto a transport brig. She became trapped under the bows of the brig and, battered by the wind and waves, started going to pieces. By 5 o'clock in the afternoon she was little more than a '... crushed and broken wreck', and the crew, along with the survivors of the sloop, were taken onto the brig. The *Gleaner* was cut free and was swept onto the beach and disappeared in five minutes. The brig continued to ride out the storm until the following afternoon, when, unable to maintain her position, she cut her cables and steered inshore and drove onto the beach, all the survivors making the shore. Seventeen other vessels were wrecked in the storm.
[TNA: ADM.1/5442]

29 April EPERVIER Brig Sloop
Rochester 1812; 390 tons; 100.5ft x 30.8ft; 18 guns
Commander Richard Walter Wales
Escorting a ship from Havana to Bermuda, when at daylight, in position 27.47N 80W, a ship was seen closing from windward. This proved to be the American ship-sloop *Peacock*, 22 guns, which at 9.30 identified herself by hoisting several American ensigns, the *Epervier* placing herself between the merchant ship and the oncoming threat. By 10 o'clock the pair were in gunshot range, and the *Epervier* opened the action by firing the starboard broadside and then steered to run alongside the American ship. The couple exchanged fire for about 45 minutes, by which time the British brig's rigging was in tatters, with all the stays destroyed and the main topmast shot away, as was the main boom. Both bowsprit and foremast were shot through; several of her guns were disabled, both from enemy fire and defective breeching bolts, and the hull was riddled with shot holes. A vain attempt was made to board the American, but the crew refused to follow their officers, after which the flag was struck. Commander Wales later complained that the crew were of poor quality, and he had suppressed a mutiny earlier. Certainly, their standard of gunnery was abysmal – not one shot hit the hull of the *Peacock*, which suffered only a few backs stays cut and the foreyard shot through. The Bosun, Joseph Deane, was later dismissed the service for '... not showing that activity and example which an officer in his situation might'. Eight men killed and fifteen wounded.
[TNA: ADM.1/5447]

19 May HALCYON Brig Sloop
King's Lynn 1813; 384 tons; 99.11ft x 30.7ft; 18 guns
Commander John Houlton Marshall
Off the island of Jamaica, the increasing number of sick men onboard led Commander Marshall to close the settlement of Annotto Bay, to send a boat inshore to purchase fresh provisions. Returning in the afternoon to pick up the boat, she was running close along the shore when she ran onto a reef off Free Point. The stream anchor was laid out, but the cable parted on heaving in. Other anchors were also tried, but she would not move. At 5pm a large piece of the keel was seen to float up alongside and it was feared that the garboard strake had

also gone. Water steadily entered, and by the early hours of the next morning she was full of water and capsized over to port. The masts were cut away, and the crew were taken off by the boats which were then standing by her. It was later found that the charts held onboard did not show the full extent of the reef.
[TNA: ADM.1/5442]

20 June BALLAHOU Schooner
Bermuda 1804; 71 tons; 55.2ft × 18ft; 4 guns
Lieutenant Francis Little

Having been stationed at the island of St Thomas in the Virgin Islands for some time, she was ordered to Antigua to be refitted and sailed with a reduced crew for the passage. During the afternoon of 19 June, then being in the vicinity of 19N 64.26W, a vessel was discovered on the lee beam and sail was made to steer away. The following morning the stranger was still in sight and clearly in chase and at just after 10 o'clock, opened fire with bow-chase guns. The pursuit went on for the next 40 minutes, until the stranger was close enough to be engaged by the *Ballahou*'s carronades. After exchanging fire for 10 minutes, the enemy could be seen to be preparing to board, and with two guns disabled, sails and rigging cut up and with only three officers and fifteen men and boys onboard, Lieutenant Little decided that further resistance was futile and surrendered, finding her opponent was the privateer *Perry*, 5 guns. One man was wounded. The schooner was taken into Wilmington.
[TNA: ADM.1/507]

(16/17) June PEACOCK Ship Sloop
Prize 1812 (*Wasp*); 434 tons; 105.10ft × 30.10ft; 18 guns
Captain Richard Coote†

Cruising off the eastern coast of the United States in company with the frigate *Lacedemonian*, she parted company with her consort during the afternoon of 16 June in poor weather when they were to the south-east of Cape Hatteras. At about 11 o'clock that night, a terrific storm hit the area with strong winds and lightning. The *Lacedemonian* rode out the storm, and the following morning searched the area, but could find no trace of her companion. It was presumed that she had foundered with the loss of all hands. Pay books closed 30 June 1814.

Note: she was initially named locally as *Loup Cervier* and some records still refer to her by that name.
[TNA: ADM.51/2517; ADM.35/3542: *Nautical Magazine* 1833 p290]

21 June GUNBOAT 8 Gunboat
Built 1806; 44 tons; 50.7ft × 14ft; 2 guns
Stationed at Altona on the River Elbe, she was lying at anchor when she was run down by *Gunboat 5* and foundered. The *Hearty* gun brig attended the scene, and with the assistance of locally-employed vessels endeavoured to raise the gunboat. Although an anchor, the broken mast and some stores were recovered, the gunboat resisted efforts to raise her, with several hawsers and cables being broken. Work on the wreck was abandoned on 8 July.
[TNA: ADM.51/2431; ADM.51/2857]

28 June LEOPARD Troopship
Sheerness 1790; 1056 tons; 146.5ft × 40.8ft; 26 guns
Captain Edward Lowther Crofton

Sailed from Portsmouth on 11 May with 487 men of the 4th Battalion, Royal Scots Guards, for Quebec, with 248 dependents, women and children. As they entered the Gulf of St Lawrence, they encountered thick banks of fog. During the early hours of 28 June, she ran onto a reef at the eastern end of Anticosti Island. Boats were hoisted out which laid out anchors to kedge her off, but the ship was held securely by the rocks. Stores and shot were heaved overboard to lighten her, but this only served to make her lift and pound on the ground with great violence. Captain Crofton ordered the troops to be disembarked, and all were safely conveyed ashore to the island. Efforts continued to free her, but all failed, and as the tide ebbed, she was left high and dry. With the hull pierced in several places she was abandoned, all the crew landing on the island where an encampment was established. They attracted the attention of a passing merchant ship four days later, but it was several more days before the *Crocodile* sloop arrived to pick up the survivors. The subsequent enquiry established that neither Captain Crofton nor the Master, Robert Maitland, had ordered the use of the lead-line, despite being in restricted waters and in fog. Both were admonished to be more careful in the future. The Second Lieutenant, Robert William Evans, who was officer of the watch at the time, took most of the blame for the loss. The court martial heard that he had ignored the Captain's instructions to call him after the ship had run a set distance and to shorten sail. Before the ship had struck, warnings had been shouted by a lookout on the fo'c'sle of approaching breakers, but Evans had failed to react. He was dismissed the service for negligence and disobedience. Finally, the Master at Arms, Edward Macnally, was ordered to lose all pay due and to be disrated and serve before the mast as a seaman, for being found drunk at the time of the wreck.
[TNA: ADM.1/5444]

28 June REINDEER Brig Sloop
Rotherhithe 1804; 385 tons; 100ft × 30.7ft; 18 guns
Commander William Manners†

Cruising in the western approaches to the English Channel, when at daybreak a ship was seen to the south-

west. The sloop bore up in chase, but in light winds it was 2 o'clock in the afternoon before the pair were close enough to hoist colours and prepare for action. The stranger was the American ship-sloop *Wasp*, 22 guns, which was engaged on a successful commerce raiding cruise. The fight began at 3.15pm, with the *Reindeer*, then about 60 yards astern of the starboard quarter of the *Wasp*, firing a shifting carronade as a bow-chase gun. After being hulled several times, the American luffed and laid herself alongside the British sloop. A fierce exchange of fire took place for about 30 minutes, with the heavier armament of the American slowly taking its toll. The hull of the *Reindeer* was riddled with shot, the upperworks and boats all destroyed, and the rigging and sails cut to pieces. Commander Manners had been severely wounded at the start of the action, having the calves of his legs taken off by a shot, and then wounded again in the thighs. Despite this he refused to leave the upper deck and rallied his men in an attempt to board the *Wasp*. The *Reindeer* ran her bows onto the larboard quarter of the *Wasp*, but Manners was shot dead as he attempted to clamber aboard the American ship, which raked the upper deck of the British sloop with small-arms fire. A few minutes later the *Reindeer* was boarded, and the only officer remaining alive on deck, Richard Collins, the Captain's Clerk, surrendered. Twenty-five men killed and forty-two wounded. The following day the foremast of the *Reindeer* went overboard and with a breeze springing up, the sloop started filling with water. She was set on fire and abandoned that evening.
[TNA:ADM.1/5444]

12 July LANDRAIL Schooner
Ringmore 1806; 75 tons; 56.3ft × 18.3ft; 4 guns
Lieutenant Robert Daniel Lancaster

On passage to Gibraltar from England with despatches, the schooner was to the west of Ushant, when at daybreak a schooner was sighted on the quarter. The stranger was seen to alter towards the *Landrail* and when she failed to respond to private signals Lieutenant Lancaster cleared for action, rightly suspecting her to be an American privateer. At 6 o'clock the stranger hoisted American colours and fired a gun, despite being at long range. Lieutenant Lancaster tried to alter away, but the American matched her move and continued firing. As she was being steadily overhauled and the enemy shot was beginning to damage the rigging, it was decided to engage her opponent, and sail was shortened which enabled a close action to commence at 7 o'clock. For 20 minutes the pair exchanged fire before the *Landrail*, with one of her engaged carronades disabled, wore round to use the other broadside. The move was followed by the American, and the pair now lay close alongside, the muzzles of the guns were touching, and the wadding was being scattered across each other's decks. By 8 o'clock, all the small-arms ammunition had been expended, all the breechings of the guns had been carried away and the men were being forced to manhandle the guns back into position using their shoulders. Unable to sustain the fight, Lieutenant Lancaster surrendered, finding his opponent to be the privateer *Syren*, 7 guns, from Baltimore. Five men wounded.

Note: recaptured on 28 August 1814 by the *Wasp*.
[TNA:ADM.1/5449]

5 August MAGNET Brig
Purchased 1813 (*Sir Sidney Smith*); 137 tons; 74ft × 18ft; 12 guns
Acting-Lieutenant George Hawksworth

One of the small British squadron on Lake Ontario, the *Magnet* sailed from Fort York in company with the *Charwell* and the *Netley* on 4 August, to take troops and stores, including gunpowder, to Niagara. During the night, the brig lost touch with her companions and morning revealed that they were well to the west of their destination. After briefly anchoring, the brig commenced working towards Niagara, but in contrary winds, progress was slow, and was still some distance away when an American squadron came into sight. The enemy ships with the wind in their favour blocked any move to Niagara, and finding that she could not escape, Hawksworth ran the brig ashore about four miles to the west of Niagara. The embarked troops were landed and most of the gunpowder and stores were saved, but by late afternoon the American brig *Sylph* had closed and opened fire on them, which brought a halt to the work. The brig was therefore set on fire and burned until she blew up. The court-martial enquiry found that Hawksworth had ignored the advice of a pilot and steered an improper course, which led to the brig losing touch with the other vessels and being too far to leeward of her destination, which ultimately led to her destruction. He received an unusually harsh sentence, being dismissed the service. This was probably the reason that Hawksworth subsequently deserted to the Americans.
[TNA:ADM.1/5447]

14 August NANCY Schooner
Purchased 1814; 67 tons; 80ft × 22ft; 2 guns
Lieutenant Miller Worsley

Originally a merchant schooner belonging to the North West Company, she was stationed in Lake Huron, Canada, supporting Fort Mackinac when that place became a target for an American force led by the schooners *Tigress* and *Scorpion*. Lieutenant Worsley moved the *Nancy* further into Nottawasaga Bay and anchored under the guns of a blockhouse but was discovered by the enemy and attacked. When it became clear that further resistance was useless, Worsley

abandoned the schooner and set fire to both it and the blockhouse, which later blew up.
[Dudley vol 3 pp571–3]

27 August AVON Brig Sloop
Falmouth 1805; 391 tons; 100ft × 30.8ft; 18 guns
Commander Hon. James Arbuthnot

In company with the *Castillian* and *Tartarus* sloops, cruising off the coast of Portugal, when an American schooner was sighted, to which all three sloops gave chase. They became strung out, the *Tartarus* being lost to view and the *Avon* trailing some nine miles astern of the *Castillian*. That evening, at about 6.30, the American ship sloop *Wasp*, 22 guns, encountered the group, and steered for the *Avon*, trailing astern of her companions. It was 30 minutes later that *Wasp* was sighted by the *Avon*, which made the private recognition signal. This was not answered by the American and the British sloop made night signals and fired signal rockets. All of these were ignored, and the *Avon*, now suspicious of her identity, fired two shots toward her, but was still ignored. By 9 o'clock the *Wasp* was close under the port quarter of the *Avon*, who hailed the American, 'What ship is that?' The reply was another question 'What brig is that?' On the *Avon* repeating the challenge, they received the shouted reply 'Heave to, and I'll let you know who I am'. Shortly after this, the *Wasp* fired into the stern of *Avon*, and the action began, the British sloop replying with a broadside. The sloops mutually exchanged fire for the next 90 minutes, during which the heavier armament of the American took effect. The British sloop's gaff-sail boom and mainmast were shot away, rigging reduced to a shreds and guns disabled. At just before 11 o'clock the *Avon* was failing to return fire and was clearly in distress. The *Wasp* hailed her and confirmed that she had surrendered. As the American came alongside her prize to take possession, she became aware of another vessel closing. This was the returning *Castillian* with the *Tartarus* following her some way astern. The *Wasp* abandoned her prize and stood away, the *Castillian* firing a single broadside at the American before returning to the *Avon*, who was now firing guns of distress. She was found to be in a shattered state and making water fast. The men were taken out and at 1 o'clock in the morning she foundered. Ten men killed and thirty-two wounded.
[TNA: ADM.1/5446]

11 September: Battle of Lake Champlain
In the late summer of 1814, a British force under General Sir George Prevost mounted an attack on New York State, with troops moving along the western shore of Lake Champlain. The small British naval force on the lake was ordered to co-operate with Prevost in an attack on Plattsburgh. Despite being unprepared, (his newly-built flagship was still fitting out), Captain Downie sailed with four vessels, accompanied by twelve open boats, fitted with a gun and which were manned by soldiers. At daybreak, they arrived off Plattsburgh, where they discovered the American squadron of four vessels and ten gunboats anchored in a line. The British squadron, in light airs, fell down towards the anchored Americans, who at about 8 o'clock commenced firing at the advancing British force.

CONFIANCE Fifth Rate
Île-aux-Noix 1814; 831 tons; 147.5ft × 37.2ft; 36 guns
Captain George Downie†

As the British vessels advanced, the American fire was concentrated on the leading ship, the *Confiance*, which suffered badly; the port anchor was shot away and the hull and rigging cut up. Because of the damage, Downie was forced to anchor on the beam of the American flagship *Saratoga*, 26 guns. The pair began a mutually-destructive exchange of broadsides and although the American ship suffered badly, with all the guns on the engaged side being disabled, the *Confiance* also suffered. Downie was killed about 15 minutes into the action, when a shot struck and dismounted a cannon, which was thrown against him. When the *Saratoga* was seen to be warping around to bring her disengaged side to bear, the movement was copied by Lieutenant John Robertson, who had taken over the command. Unfortunately, this was not achieved, and she only succeeded in laying her head towards the American line, from where she was raked continually. With few guns able to bear and the hull and rigging shattered, she surrendered. Forty men were killed and eighty-three wounded. The cause of the failure of the British attack was the lack of support from the army under Prevost, who had urged Downie to attack, coupled with the failure of the gunboats to engage and the general unpreparedness of the squadron.
[TNA: ADM.1/5449]

LINNET Brig Sloop
Île-aux-Noix 1814; 350 tons; 82.6ft × 27ft; 16 guns
Commander Daniel Pring

Second in the British line, she steered for the American brig *Eagle*, 20 guns, and took up her allotted station and anchored. Here, she was well handled by Commander Pring, who positioned the brig so that only part of the *Eagle*'s broadside could bear and proceeded to batter his opponent. The American's rigging was shattered and when her anchor cable was shot through, the *Eagle* fell out of the American line and out of range of the guns of the *Linnet* and managed to re-anchor close to the *Saratoga*. The American flagship had been reduced to a wreck by the fire of *Confiance* but had warped round to allow her undamaged broadside to bear. When the *Confiance* surrendered, the *Linnet* remained alone, and

took the full force of all the American fire for about 10 minutes, after which she struck her flag. Ten men killed and fifteen wounded. Commander Pring was praised for his actions, and on completion of the court martial in September 1815, he was promoted to Captain.
[TNA: ADM.1/5449]

CHUB Cutter
Prize 1813 (*Growler*); 112 tons; 60ft × 20.4ft; 11 guns
Lieutenant James McGhie
Ordered to support the *Linnet* in attacking the *Eagle*, she ran down and anchored, almost untouched. As she began to engage, she had her main boom shot away and soon after, her bowsprit. When her anchor cable was shot through, she drifted into the American line where she had little choice but to surrender, the *Saratoga* taking possession. The cutter suffered three men killed and fifteen wounded. McGhie was criticised at his court martial, and severely reprimanded for failing to carry the cutter into action in a proper manner and failing to anchor in the correct position.
[TNA: ADM.1/5449]

FINCH Cutter
Prize 1813 (*Eagle*); 110 tons; 64ft × 20.4ft; 8 guns
Lieutenant William Hicks
Bringing up the rear of the little British line, and leading several of the gunboats, she was ordered to steer towards the American sloop *Preble*, 7 guns. As she neared the American line, she came under accurate fire from the schooner *Ticonderoga*, 16 guns, which shot away much of her rigging. Crippled, she fell away, to run aground on a bank extending from Crab Island. Here she came under fire from a small shore battery. Unable to reply or free herself, she struck her flag. Two men wounded.
[TNA: ADM.1/5449]

★ ★ ★

15 September HERMES Fifth Rate
Milford 1811; 512 tons; 120.1ft × 31ft; 20 guns
Captain Hon. William Henry Percy
In company with the *Carron*, *Childers* and *Sophie*, Captain Percy arrived off the south-west coast of Florida, intending to mount an attack on Fort Bowyer in Mobile Bay. A party of soldiers was landed to the east of the fort during 12 September, but contrary winds held up any attacks by the ship until the afternoon of 15 September, when the squadron proceeding inshore to anchor 'within musket shot' of the fort. *Hermes* anchored the closest, but only the sloop *Sophie* could properly support her, the other two vessels having to anchor some distance off. The *Hermes* thus drew the main fire from the shore batteries, and when her cable was cut by shot, she swung round and presented her head to the fort, which raked the ship with hot shot. She promptly cut her cable and set the spanker, which enabled her to shift position and recommence the action. The ship's fire seemed to be having little effect on the fort, and with casualties mounting, Captain Percy decided to break off the action. As the ship attempted to drop clear on an ebbing tide, she went aground on a sandbank, with her stern to the fort. Initial efforts to free her failed, and the constant harassing fire prevented the work continuing. She was therefore abandoned and set on fire. Twenty-five men killed and twenty-four wounded.
[TNA: ADM.1/5447]

(26/27) September CRANE Brig Sloop
Frindsbury 1809; 386 tons; 100ft × 30.7ft; 18 guns
Commander Robert Standly†
In mid-August, the brig sailed from Antigua with stores for Vice Admiral Sir Alexander Cochrane at Bermuda. She landed them safely and sailed at the beginning of September to return but was not seen again. A tropical storm passed across her route on 26–27 September and was believed to have been responsible for her loss with all hands. Pay book closed 30 September 1814.
[TNA: ADM.1/336; ADM.35/3398]

10 October RACER Schooner
Prize 1812 (*Independence*); 250 tons; 93.4ft × 24.10ft; 12 guns
Lieutenant Henry Freeman Young Pogson
Cruising off the east coast of the United States, the schooner was in poor condition, and it was decided to leave her station in Chesapeake Bay to return to Jamaica for repairs. At 10 o'clock in the evening of 10 October she was steering south-east in a heavy sea and fresh gales, when she unexpectedly found herself in broken water and then ran aground. She started filling with water and as it was feared that she might break up, a hawser was passed under the hull to hold her together, and the mainmast was cut away. Morning revealed shallow water all around, with small cays nearby. A boat was hoisted out and rafts were constructed which during the day transferred all the men to the nearest cay, where a tented encampment was established. On 16 October Lieutenant Pogson and four men left in the boat to proceed to Providence, the crew being busily employed in salvaging stores from the wreck. They were rescued some days later by a sloop. It was found that she had been wrecked on Walker's Cay, in the Bahamas. It was assessed that a strong unknown current had set her 100 miles to the west of her reckoning. Lieutenant Pogson was praised for his efforts to save the lives of his crew.
[TNA: ADM.1/5447; ADM.51/3407]

October ELIZABETH Schooner
Prize 1805; 141 tons; 72.8ft × 21.6ft; 12 guns
Lieutenant George Simmonds†

Stationed in the Leeward Islands, she disappeared whilst on a local cruise. It was later reported that she had capsized and foundered when hit by a squall whilst in pursuit of three American schooners off the island of Saint Barthélemy, with the loss off all hands. The schooner was paid off 31 October 1814.

Note: There is some confusion over her commanding officer at the time of her loss. This evidently stems from the contemporary Navy Lists, which show a Lieutenant J W Dwyer, but there was no officer of this name. Secondary sources, evidently trying to resolve this, cite Lieutenant Jonathan Dyer – but that officer was serving in the *Bustard* sloop at this time. The pay book confirms that it was Lieutenant Edward Furman Dwyer who was in command. However, local newspapers state that Dwyer was on shore, sick, at the time of her loss, and that Lieutenant Simmonds had been appointed to temporary command, from the *Satellite*. I have followed this information.
[TNA: ADM.1/336; ADM.35/3447; www.britishnewspaperarchive.co: Barbados Mercury 20 December 1814 p2; Public Ledger 13 Mar 1815 p2]

24 November FANTOME Brig Sloop
Prize 1810; 384 tons; 94.1ft × 30.1ft; 18 guns
Commander Thomas Sykes

Escorting a convoy to Halifax from Castine, the land at Cap la Have, Nova Scotia, was sighted during the evening of 23 November and the pilot recommended a course to be set for the Sambro light. At 2 o'clock in the morning, Commander Sykes sent orders to the officer of the watch to sound and was disturbed when told that the ship was in 35 fathoms. He ordered the ship's head to be put to the south, to gain deeper water, but an hour later, when he checked with the deck, he was annoyed to discover that the pilot had countermanded his orders and steered east-north-east. Soon after this the ship ran aground in Shag Bay, near Prospect Harbour. The boats were hoisted out and the masts cut away, but little more could be done as she filled with water very quickly. All the crew were placed in the boats in an orderly fashion, safely reaching the shore. The Captain and several of the ship's officers were criticised at the subsequent court martial. Commander Sykes was reprimanded for failing to order constant soundings and placing too much confidence in the pilot. Lieutenant John Fisher, the officer of the watch, had failed to keep the Captain aware of the situation of the ship and was admonished to be more careful in the future. The Master, Joseph Forster, was severely reprimanded for failing to order or recommend constant sounding and not raising any objection to the courses steered, even though he afterwards admitted that he thought they may take the sloop into danger. The pilot, Thomas Robinson, had recommended a course which took the vessel to close inshore, had not ordered soundings and had altered course without consulting the Captain. He was severely reprimanded and ordered to lose all pay due.
[TNA: ADM.1/5447]

A note on a phantom loss:

CUTTLE – The schooner was widely cited as being lost on the Halifax station during 1814 (*see Clowes vol 5 p555; William James etc.*), but official records show that she was paid off and laid up at Bermuda in January 1813 *[TNA ADM.37/3722]* and an Admiralty Order of 29 March 1814 ordered her to be broken up locally

1815

17 January SYLPH Ship Sloop
Bermuda 1812; 399 tons; 107ft × 29.11ft; 18 guns
Commander George Dickens†

Part of the force blockading New York, at 2 o'clock in the morning, in dark and heavily overcast weather, when standing to the north, the sloop ran onto Southampton Bar in Shinnecock Bay. She beat over the bar and then ran aground in the shallow water close to the shoreline where she lay with the surf beating over her. The crew took to the rigging, but in freezing conditions and showers of snow, many died of exposure, and no one from the shore could reach them. At about 8.30am, she capsized and broke up after being hit by a particularly heavy sea, which threw the survivors into the surf. Despite the efforts of the onlookers onshore, only six men were rescued, with 111 men dying.
[Gold: Naval Chronicle vol 33 p231 quoting the New York Gazette of 26 January 1815]

20 February CYANE Sixth Rate
Topsham 1806; 539 tons; 118.2ft × 32ft; 22 guns
Captain Gordon Thomas Falcon

Providing distant cover for the passage of a convoy from Gibraltar to England, the *Cyane* was stationed off Madeira in company with the *Levant* when at about 1 o'clock in the afternoon, a ship was sighted. The *Cyane* initially steered toward the stranger, making private recognition signals, but these were not answered and the stranger continued to stand towards the British pair. Fearing that she might be an enemy frigate, the *Cyane* made sail away to join the *Levant*, pursued by the stranger, which was the American *Constitution*, 44 guns. The British pair decided that although individually they could not tackle her, if they fought together, their combined force might be enough to

disable their larger opponent and allow the convoys to escape, especially as night was coming on. Accordingly, they remained close together, and attempted to gain the weather gage, but the *Constitution* foiled their efforts, and at 6 o'clock the British pair shortened sail to await the American. Just five minutes later the *Constitution* fired her larboard broadside at the *Cyane* at long range – about three-quarters of a mile. The *Cyane* was armed with short-range carronades, and although she returned fire, it constantly fell short, whilst the more powerful long guns of the American frigate were used to great effect. After engaging *Cyane* for about 15 minutes, the *Constitution* moved away to give the *Levant* similar treatment. The *Cyane* took this opportunity to close and attempted to run under the stern of the American, but *Constitution* rapidly manoeuvred and fired a destructive broadside at close range. She then returned to her attentions to the *Levant*, only to be again interrupted by *Cyane*, which wore ship to try and assist, and succeeded in firing a raking broadside into the American's bow. The American now returned fire and ran close alongside the British vessel. At this, the *Cyane*, with several shots in her hull, the rigging in tatters, several guns disabled, and mounting casualties, surrendered. Six men killed and twenty-nine wounded. The action did prevent the *Constitution* from intercepting the homeward convoys.
[TNA: ADM.1/5449]

20 February **LEVANT** Sixth Rate
Chester 1813; 465 tons; 116ft × 29.10ft; 20 guns
Captain Hon. George Douglas

The consort to the *Cyane* in their fight against the *Constitution*. Stationed ahead of her companion, the American initially concentrated her fire on *Cyane*, firing several broadsides at long range. The attack was then held up for some minutes by the large clouds of drifting gun smoke which obscured her object. By the time it had cleared, the *Levant* found herself close to the American who fired a broadside into her, before backing sails to engage the *Cyane* once more. The *Levant* wore round to assist her companion, but was raked twice as she did so, causing much damage to the rigging. She fell away and the *Constitution* was able to concentrate on *Cyane*. At about 8 o'clock the *Levant*, which had repaired some of her rigging, renewed the contest by steering down to the *Constitution* and her prize. The American steered towards her, the pair exchanging broadsides as they passed on opposite tacks. The *Constitution* promptly wore ship to get under the stern of the *Levant* and was able to rake her. The *Levant*, now seeing that her consort had surrendered, attempted to make all sail away, pursued by the frigate. The *Constitution* used her bow-chase guns to some effect, cutting up the smaller ship's rigging. When the American was close under the larboard quarter, the *Levant* surrendered. Six men killed and sixteen wounded.

Note: recaptured on 11 March by the *Acasta*.
[TNA: ADM.1/5449]

26 February **SAINT LAWRENCE** Schooner
Prize 1813 (*Atlas*); 244 tons; 16 guns
Lieutenant James Edward Gordon

Bound for Mobile with despatches, the schooner was to the north of Cuba, the high land around Matanzas becoming visible at daybreak. At the same time, two vessels were observed close under the land, one of which appeared to be a privateer. At about 11 o'clock that morning the stranger, which was the American privateer *Chasseur*, 14 guns, was seen to be standing towards *St Lawrence* and was soon overhauling her. Private signals were made which were not answered, and Lieutenant Gordon cleared for action. Soon after this, she carried away her fore topmast, the wreckage failing to disable the maintop, after which the stranger closed rapidly. When within range the British schooner yawed and fired a broadside, the enemy schooner luffing and returning the fire. The crews of both vessels gave loud cheers, and a close action commenced at little more than 40 yards. After several broadsides had been exchanged, the American moved ahead, which allowed Lieutenant Gordon to move under the stern of his opponent and rake her. The *Chasseur* wore round and laid herself close alongside the British schooner and opened a very destructive small-arms fire, which virtually cleared the upper deck of *St Lawrence*. When she was boarded, the *St Lawrence* was unable to maintain the contest, with all her sails reduced to tatters and the rigging shattered, she surrendered. Six men killed and eighteen wounded.
[TNA: ADM.1/5448]

27 February **STATIRA** Fifth Rate
Northam 1807; 1,085 tons; 154ft × 39.7ft; 38 guns
Captain Spelman Swaine

Escorting a convoy of four troop transports, they sailed from Bermuda on 18 February. Land identified as Great Inagua was sighted, and she steered along the southern coast under easy sail, when at just before 10 o'clock in the morning, with no warning, she ran aground. A boat was hoisted out to sound, and topgallant masts and yards were struck. The ship was held fast for about 20 minutes before she swung free, sail hastily being set to tack away from the obstruction. Water was reported to be entering, and despite thrumming a sail and slinging it under the hull, the water gained on the pumps. Bailing and pumping went on through the afternoon, but by 6 o'clock they were not gaining, and the crew were becoming exhausted, and with the swell and wind increasing it became clear that the ship could not be

saved. The transports were ordered to close and send boats, the crew leaving in good order. The frigate steadily settled and finally sank at 7 o'clock that evening. No blame was imputed to the ship's officers, as the reef that she had struck was not laid down on any known charts. The rocks are now known as the Statira Shoal.
[TNA: ADM.1/5448; ADM.51/2814]

7 March CYGNET Brig Sloop
Great Yarmouth 1804; 365 tons; 106ft × 28ft; 16 guns
Commander Robert Russell

Returning to Berbice, having escorted several merchant ships to Surinam, the brig was about 15 miles from the mouth of the River Courantyne, when with no warning she found herself aground. She initially attempted to sail over the obstruction, but failed, and found that the heavy swell was carrying her further onto a submerged sandbank. Sails were furled and the boats hoisted out to lay out a kedge anchor, but despite heaving she would not move. Shot, guns and stores were heaved overboard to lighten her, and at 10 o'clock that night she floated free. Finding herself in deep water, she quickly anchored to avoid being carried down onto the bank again. Despite this, the move had hardly been completed before she struck the ground again, this time aft. She thumped heavily on the ground, unshipping the rudder and starting several leaks. The anchor cable was ordered to be cut, and sail made which did carry her off the bank, but the water was now entering so fast it was defeating the pumps. To save the crew, the brig steered for the land, and the brig was run ashore near the mouth of the river. It was established that she had grounded on a previously unknown, shifting sandbank.
[TNA: ADM.1/5449]

23 March PENGUIN Brig Sloop
King's Lynn 1813; 387 tons; 100.5ft × 30.7ft; 18 guns
Commander James Dickinson†

Cruising in the South Atlantic in the vicinity of the island of Tristan da Cunha in search of an American privateer reported in the area, a ship was sighted off the island. The sloop bore up in pursuit, and at 1.45pm, then being about five miles to the north-east of the island, she was close enough to fire a gun to bring the chase to. The stranger, which was the American ship sloop *Hornet*, 20 guns, luffed, hoisted her colours and fired a broadside at the *Penguin*. This was returned by the British brig, the continuing with the pair steering the same course, exchanging broadsides. The standard of gunnery of the American proved to be far superior to that of the British: within 15 minutes the hull and rigging of the *Penguin* had been cut to pieces, and casualties were mounting. At this, Commander Dickinson determined to board his opponent, running the bowsprit over the starboard side of *Hornet*, but as he did so, Dickinson was shot and killed, and the crew displayed considerable reluctance to follow Lieutenant James MacDonald when he urged them to board. The pair fell apart, the bowsprit of the *Penguin* becoming entangled in the mizzen shrouds of the *Hornet* as they did so, breaking the bowsprit and wrecking the shrouds, boat davits and spanker boom of the American. The British brig, now disabled, with several guns dismounted, hung on the American's quarter, unable to return fire. As the firing ceased, the Americans understood the *Penguin* to have surrendered and the American captain, James Biddle, clambered onto the taffrail, only to be shot and wounded. This brought a fierce return of small-arms fire from the *Hornet*, before Lieutenant MacDonald hailed to surrender. The *Penguin* suffered ten men killed and twenty-eight wounded. The brig was so severely damaged that the *Hornet* took all the men out of her and scuttled her. This was the last single-ship action fought between British and American ships and showed more than any other the poor state of gunnery in many British ships. The court-martial enquiry heard that although the crew were exercised at the guns at least once a week, no shot was ever fired. The court commented that '... it was their duty to observe that the gallantry displayed by the late Commander Dickinson was not backed by the advantage which might have been expected from training the men to the use of guns by firing at marks'.
[TNA: ADM.1/5451]

1 May PENELOPE Troopship
Bursledon 1798; 1,051 tons; 150ft × 39.8ft; 18 guns
Commander James Galloway

Sailed from Spithead on 31 March bound for Quebec. The ship arrived off the coast of Canada on 24 April and steered for the St Lawrence between ice floes. The mainland at Cap des Roziers was sighted on 29 April, and a course was set upriver. The weather remained very cold, with large floes of ice visible and regular showers of snow and sleet. At 8.30pm, proceeding at about four knots and having sounded in 71 fathoms only 30 minutes before, she struck the ground. The sails were thrown aback and boats ordered to be hoisted out. The stream anchor was placed in the pinnace, which was used in attempts to kedge her free, but to no effect. The guns were now heaved overboard, the bower anchors cut away and efforts to kedge were again tried, but they again failed. The topmasts were struck and then lowered over the side to act as shores, to prevent her from falling over, using pig-iron from the ballast to anchor them. By now it was daylight and the weather worsened, being bitterly cold, with showers of snow and a strong wind. It became clear that the ship was aground on the Canadian coast near Rivière Madeleine, and was beating on rocks, the water gaining on the pumps. The provisions were ordered to be got up from

the hold to save them, but the water was found to be up to the lower deck, and little could be saved. The masts were next cut away, falling towards the shore, a short distance away. The Master, Mr Honnor, was sent away to carry a line to the shore, but the boat was swamped in the surf, although the men managed to make the shore. Another three attempts were made, with the Purser and Captain Murray, an army officer carrying despatches. They all failed, with the loss of the boats, and the men struggling through the surf to reach the land. By now it was clear that the ship was doomed. The pumps could do nothing against the incoming water; the rising sea was making her pound on the rocks, opening planks and breaking timbers. Discipline started to break down, many of the crew getting very drunk. The Captain, ill from fatigue and rheumatism, was placed into a boat in another attempt to make the shore, but this again overset, and Commander Galloway only made dry land with assistance. The gig did make one successful trip with some men, but at the next attempt it capsized, and those remaining onboard clearly saw no hope of surviving and appear to have got very drunk. Many froze to death in the sub-zero temperatures and snowstorms. The survivors on shore spent a miserable night huddled together around fires, their wet clothes freezing on them, many suffering from frostbite. At about midnight a series of loud crashes were heard by those on shore, accompanied by shouts and screams: morning revealed that the ship had broken up, the wreckage covered with snow and ice. One seaman, David Bruce, did survive from the wreck and that morning managed to make the shore. The day was spent by the survivors scouring the shoreline for provisions washed ashore from the wreck, pulling the boats ashore and repairing them as well as establishing a camp. The spirit of insubordination and indiscipline continued. A party of forty-eight men deserted, walking out of the camp having plundered trunks that had washed ashore for extra clothing. After two days, a passing trading vessel brought some relief and six days later the survivors, consisting of sixty-six men and two women took to the repaired boats and reached Douglastown, but 216 men were lost, drowned or frozen to death. The subsequent court martial determined that the cause was the poor weather, which obscured landmarks, and the set of the current. The Master, William Honnor, was blamed for failing to pay attention to the situation of the ship and was ordered to be placed on the bottom of the seniority list. Commander Galloway and the First Lieutenant, Benjamin Hooper, were both criticised for the breakdown of discipline and their '… neglecting to make proper arrangements for the safety of the crew'. Both were severely reprimanded, and neither was given any further appointments. One seaman, Walter Howell, was found guilty of insubordination, desertion and being drunk. He was sentenced to receive 500 lashes on his bare back.
[TNA:ADM.1/5449]

July THRUSH Hulk
Purchase 1806 (*Prince of Wales*); 307 tons; 96.4ft × 27ft
Employed as a powder hulk at Port Royal, Jamaica, she foundered at her anchors.
[TNA:ADM.180/12]

August DOMINICA Schooner
Prize 1809 (*Duc de Wagram*); 203 tons; 89.6ft × 23.1ft; 10 guns
Lieutenant Richard Crawford[†]
Disappeared on passage from Halifax, Nova Scotia, to Bermuda and presumed to have foundered with the loss of all hands. The pay book was closed 31 August 1815.
[TNA:ADM.180/3; ADM.35/4099]

13 | 1816–1859: Empire and Expansion

THE ENDING OF THE LONG FRENCH wars in 1815 left the British Empire as the world's major power, and although there were no wars in continental Europe, the navy worked with the French and Russian navies in the eastern Mediterranean during the Greek War of Independence (1821–32), which saw the last fleet battle under sail at Navarino in 1827. The continuing tensions and disputes within the Ottoman Empire resulted in frequent interventions in the eastern Mediterranean, such as that at Acre in 1840, in support of the Sultan. In the Far East, British expansion of control in India ensured that a large squadron was maintained in eastern waters, and enforcement of opium trading with China led to the Anglo-Chinese wars of the 1830s and 1840s. The desire to resist Russian expansion in the Black Sea led the British to join the French to support the Ottomans in the Crimean War (1854–5).

Anti-slavery patrols were vigorously carried out off the coast of West Africa and in the West Indies, until the trade was suppressed. Policing roles in various parts of the world ensured that the Navy remained fully engaged, with anti-piracy operations in the Levant, East Indies, and China.

Technology also advanced, with steam being introduced from the 1820s and from the 1840s steam vessels appeared in increasing numbers, steadily replacing sail. Iron was introduced for construction during the 1840s, but wood remained dominant through the period.

1816

20 February PHOENIX Fifth Rate
Bursledon 1783; 884 tons; 137.1ft × 38.3ft; 38 guns
Captain Charles John Austen
Cruising in the Aegean, the weather steadily worsened, and by 19 February it was raining heavily, accompanied by thunder and lightning. At 2 o'clock in the morning of 20 February she was struck by lightning, which damaged the mainmast. The weather had cleared somewhat by daybreak, but as it still appeared threatening, with black clouds and regular rumbles of distant thunder, Captain Austen decided to anchor as a precaution. She closed the coast and anchored at 11.30am in the Bay of Çeşme and prepared for the oncoming storm by striking topmasts and bracing the yards round. At 1 o'clock in the afternoon, it was discovered that she was dragging her anchor and a second anchor was let go, but this failed to bring her up. The sheet anchor was now ordered to be let go, but before this could be done, she was hit by a strong squall accompanied by snow and sleet, and she took the ground. All the masts were cut away and the boats lowered to lay out the small bower anchor. On heaving on the cable, she freed herself, but before she could re-anchor, a sudden shift of wind blowing in squalls swung her broadside-on to the shore and she struck the ground again, this time extremely hard. By 2.15pm it was clear that she had bilged, the orlop being flooded, several timbers spilt and the rudder unshipped. Spars and timbers were rigged to the shore and all the crew escaped to safety. After being stripped of all usable stores and provisions, including several sheets of copper, she was burnt to the water's edge on 2 March. The remains were sold the same day to a Mr Curatovich of Çeşme for 600 dollars, the crew leaving for Malta in the *Zodiac* transport later that day. During their stay onshore, Captain Austen had to flog several of the men for drunkenness and theft.
[TNA: ADM.51/2669; ADM.1/5454]

15 September WHITING Schooner
Prize 1812 (*Arrow*); 225 tons; 98ft × 23.7ft; 12 guns
Lieutenant John Jackson
Ordered to cruise in the Irish Sea to prevent smuggling, the schooner sailed from Falmouth on 11 September. The weather was poor and after battling with strong winds and rain and in order to gain shelter, repair damage and to gain intelligence, Lieutenant Jackson decided to head for Padstow. As they entered the harbour a gust of wind took the schooner aback and she fell off onto a sandbank. The best bower anchor was let go to hold her, the head swinging round to face the harbour entrance. Advantage was taken of this, and sail was set to try and sail out, but the baffling winds would not allow it and she ran hard aground again. All boats were hoisted out, taking a cable ashore, but despite heaving for some time, she would not move. The guns were moved aft to try and lift the bows and further attempts were made to haul her off, but she remained stubbornly in position until at length the cable parted. It was decided to leave further efforts until the next high tide, and she lay quietly on the sandbank for some hours. As the time of high water approached it was found that she was making water, so the pumps were manned, and these soon had to be supplemented by bailing as the water rose. In the

event, they were unable to control the water or haul her off and she was abandoned as a wreck. Lieutenant Jackson was criticised at his court martial for entering the harbour with no pilot embarked. His actions after the grounding were judged to be inadequate, having failed to lighten the schooner prior to attempting to haul her off. He was reprimanded and lost one year's seniority. Five seamen took the opportunity to desert at Padstow. Two were subsequently detained and each ordered to suffer fifty lashes.
[TNA: ADM.1/5455]

24 October COMUS Sixth Rate
Great Yarmouth 1806; 522 tons; 120.10ft x 31.6ft; 22 guns
Captain James John Gordon Bremer
Sailed from Fortune Bay, Newfoundland, on 22 October, and felt her way eastwards in poor weather, frequent heavy rain squalls obscuring the horizon. The noon observation on 24 October, coupled with a series of soundings, showed her to be in Placentia Bay. At nightfall, she hove to for the night, having sounded in 25 fathoms. At a quarter to midnight breakers were seen ahead, and before any action could be taken, she ran aground, swinging head to wind as she did. The yards were braced round in an effort to sail off the obstruction, but her larboard quarter struck a rock which pierced the hull. She then thumped and pounded over a ridge, starting more leaks. The best bower anchor was quickly let go to hold her still, boats were hoisted out and pumping started. Within minutes the cockpit and bread room were reported as being flooded and she took a heel to port. As the tide was ebbing, she threatened to roll over onto her beam-ends, so all the crew left the ship, the last men leaving at 3 o'clock in the morning. Daylight showed them to be on the Newfoundland shore in St Mary's Bay, near Cape Pine. Several days were spent trying to haul her off, but all failed, and she was finally abandoned on 4 November, the stores having been removed. A strong current was blamed for taking them further inshore than they had realised, nevertheless, Captain Bremer and the Master, Bateman Ainsworth, were admonished to be more careful in the future, for being over confident in the assessment of the ship's position and failing to ensure the constant use of the lead-line.
[TNA: ADM.1/5455]

5 November BRISEIS Brig Sloop
Upnor 1808; 238 tons; 90.3ft x 24.7ft; 10 guns
Commander George Dommett
Sailed on 24 October from Trinidad, Cuba, bound for Nassau in the Bahamas, on 5 November land was sighted, but could not be positively identified, and she steered inshore to establish her position. At 9 o'clock that evening she hove-to for the night, then being quite close to the land. An hour later it was realised that they were being taken inshore by the current. An attempt was made to wear the ship round, but this had not been completed before she struck the ground. She thumped hard but was still under way and it was hoped that she would escape, but she struck again, the bows swinging round to present the stern to the sea. The boats were lowered to carry out anchors, but with the sea running so high, this took some time to achieve, and the brig was pounding all the time. By the time the anchors were set, the rudder had been lost and several leaks started. Despite heaving on the anchor cables, she would not move. At just after daybreak the next day she took several heavy lurches and then fell over to starboard and filled with water. All the crew was saved, landing by boat and raft, finding that they had come ashore on Point Pedro, nine miles west of Bahia Honda on the northern coast of Cuba. The court-martial enquiry into the loss was unimpressed with the performance of the ship's officers. Commander Dommett was sentenced to lose two years' seniority for his 'great want of attention'. He had ignored a recommendation by the Master to alter course during the afternoon and had then taken the sloop far too close inshore. The Master, Joseph Oakey, should have remonstrated more strongly with the Captain over his actions. He was placed at the bottom of the list of Masters and not employed as a Master for two years.
[TNA: ADM.1/5456]

11 November TAY Sixth Rate
Buckler's Hard 1813; 455 tons; 115.8ft x 29.10ft; 20 guns
Captain Samuel Roberts
Bound for the port of Campeche, Mexico, from Havana, the ship approached the land cautiously, sounding constantly. At just after 1 o'clock in the morning breakers were reported ahead, which was a surprise as no bottom had been found only a few minutes before with a 20-fathom lead-line. The helm was put over, the yards braced round and the sails filled, but she touched the ground which caused her to fly off the wind and swing broadside-on to a coral reef. Within minutes she had struck heavily twice and then heeled over, filling with water. Distress guns were fired and with some difficulty the boats launched, and the fore- and mainmasts were cut away. Pumping went on through the night and daylight showed a rocky line of coral nearby. The boats attempted to land but were swamped, one Spanish passenger being drowned. Eventually a raft was built, and this was veered away through the surf with a hawser attached. This was used to take of all the crew, despite the line being constantly cut when snagged on the sharp coral. The following day, the surviving boats and the raft were used to carry the crew to a more substantial island nearby and stores and provisions were salvaged

from the wreck. Having established a camp, Lieutenant Henry Smethwick was sent to the mainland in the yawl to bring help. This arrived on 18 November in the shape of the guarda-costa *Valencey* and a schooner, the *Zaragozana*. Having assured themselves that all the crew were off the wreck and the food and provisions were on the island, the Spanish then took all the survivors prisoner at gunpoint and demanded that all money and specie on board be handed over. With no weapons, apart from sidearms, the crew could offer little resistance, but Captain Roberts surrendered his ship and crew 'as prisoners of war', which was accepted by the Spanish who then proceeded to plunder the ship and the men, taking about 350,000 dollars plus a large amount of the ship's stores. The men were eventually taken off the island by the schooner. The loss was blamed on a strong current which had taken them onto the Alacranes reef, Yucatan. No blame was attached to Captain Roberts and his action in surrendering was fully approved. It was revealed at the enquiry that a considerable breakdown in discipline had occurred during the stay on the reef. Fourteen seamen and marines subsequently suffered punishments ranging from 50 lashes to 200 lashes for a variety of offences, mostly for being drunk or plundering the wreck. Midshipman Hilkitch Head was found guilty of breaking into a cabin and stealing papers and money. For this he was ordered to have '... his coat taken off his back on the quarterdeck of an HM ship and then turned out of the service'. After this disgrace, he should serve six months in solitary confinement in the Marshalsea Prison.
[TNA: ADM.1/5456]

16 November BERMUDA Brig Sloop
Frindsbury 1808; 238 tons; 90ft x 24.8ft; 10 guns
Commander Jonathan Pakenham
Having completed her task of escorting some merchant ships to Campeche, Mexico, she sailed from that port on 11 November to return to Jamaica. The estimated position at noon on 16 November placed her over 150 miles to the west of Tampico and the brig stood on under no apprehension of danger. It was therefore a considerable surprise when at 10.30pm, land was sighted ahead. The officer of the watch, Lieutenant Francis Dashwood, sent a midshipman to confirm the lookout's report, and then went himself to see. Dashwood then left the deck to personally acquaint the Captain with the news. The pair then returned, and the helm was ordered to be put over, but it was too late, and she ran aground, lightly at first and then commenced pounding heavily. More sail was spread to sail off the obstruction, but this failed, and she was then pooped by a heavy sea which unshipped the rudder. A second heavy sea swung her head round to the north-west and she was firmly aground and did not move again. The boats were lowered to lay out anchors, despite the surf dashing around them. One boat capsized, drowning one man, while another was swept away and carried onto the shore. It was agreed by all the officers that little could be done to save the ship and efforts should be concentrated on saving the lives of the crew. The men were employed constructing a raft, pumping and bailing, and cutting away the foremast. By daybreak it could be seen that they were close to the Mexican shore about three miles to the south of Tampico, and it was reported that the water was gaining on the pumps, with large amounts of sand entering the sloop. The raft was veered ashore through the surf and made several trips, landing all the crew in safety. The court of enquiry decided that she had wrongly calculated her position – surprisingly, no chronometers were held on board – and this was compounded by a strong current which had forced them to the west. The court also ruled that if Lieutenant Dashwood had taken prompt action when land was first reported, she might have been saved. He was censured to be more careful in the future.
[TNA: ADM.1/5456]

14 December MISTLETOE Schooner
Bermuda 1809; 150 tons; 78.8ft x 21.7ft; 6 guns
Lieutenant Wade Blake†
Ordered to cruise between Beachy Head and the Isle of Wight against smuggling vessels, she disappeared, being last seen by the *Algerine* brig 12 miles south of the Dunnose in high winds and heavy seas on 14 December. It was presumed that she foundered soon after with all hands.
[TNA: ADM.1/1266; www.britishnewspaperarchive.co: Hampshire Telegraph 20 January 1817 p4]

1817

20 January JASPER Brig Sloop
Ipswich 1808; 237 tons; 90ft x 24.7ft; 10 guns
Commander Thomas Carew
Laying at anchor in Plymouth Sound, with both the Captain and First Lieutenant ashore, the Master, Edward Smith, was in charge of the vessel. During 19 January, the weather steadily worsened and by that night a southerly gale was blowing with great force. At just after 11 o'clock the best bower anchor cable parted, and the sheet anchor was quickly let go and the topmasts were ordered to be struck. In the early hours of the morning the small bower cable parted, and the sloop began to drive across the Sound, the sheet anchor not holding her. Smith decided to try and make the more sheltered waters of the Cattewater, and the anchor cable was cut, fore trysail and fore staysail set, and she started to make her run in. The night was 'pitchy black', the wind strong

with high seas, and she could not cast her head the right way. At attempt was made to wear, but this failed and at 4 o'clock in the morning she straight onto the Bear's Head at Mount Batten. The Master ordered the weather rigging to be cut away, to allow the masts to fall overboard, but this could not be done as the sloop was beating heavily on the rocks and started going to pieces very quickly. Only one seaman, John Bone, and Marine William Horscroft survived. Bone was in the maintop and swung off the wreck on a rope into the gig which was swept onto the rocks. Marine Horscroft was on the poop when she was wrecked and watched as she broke up with the stern section rolling over until the keel was exposed. He somehow hung onto a spar and then clambered onto the copper sheathing of the upturned hull until swept off by a wave and was deposited on the rocks near Bone. The court of enquiry ruled that the Master could have prepared for the storm earlier, by striking topmasts and lowering yards and veering more cable.
[TNA: ADM.1/5456]

20 January TELEGRAPH Schooner
Prize 1813 (*Vengeance*); 180 tons; 83.7ft × 22.6ft; 12 guns
Lieutenant Jonathan Little
Laying at anchor in Plymouth Sound, when the anchorage was struck by the storm that wrecked the *Jasper* (see above). The schooner rode out the gale quite well at first, sheltering by the western end of the newly constructed breakwater, until she started to drag her anchors at about 4 o'clock in the morning. A third anchor was then laid out, but this did not bring her up and she continued driving across the bay, burning blue lights and firing distress guns. At 5.30am she struck the ground aft, then being at the eastern end of the Hoe, within a cable's length (200 yards) of the shore. It was clear that she could not be saved, but to give the best opportunity for the crew to save themselves, the cables were cut and the fore staysail set, which set her broadside-on to the shore. In this position, she went onto the rock and soon went to pieces. One man died, being crushed between the schooner and the shore, and Surgeon Dick suffered a broken leg whilst rescuing his wife from the wreck.
[TNA: ADM.1/5456]

18 February ALCESTE Fifth Rate
Prize 1806 (*Minerve*); 1,098 tons; 152.5ft × 40ft; 46 guns
Captain Murray Maxwell
The frigate sailed from Whampoa (Huangpu), China, in January 1817 with Lord Amherst and his staff embarked, who had completed an unsuccessful diplomatic mission to the Chinese court. Heading for Batavia (Jakarta), Captain Maxwell steered a course through the Gaspar Strait, the island of Pulo Leat being sighted at daybreak on 18 February. At 7.30am, when about four miles from the island and steering to the south-east, despite having all the officers on deck and extra lookouts posted, she struck a submerged reef. The best bower anchor was let go to secure the ship and the boats manned and sounded round her, which showed that they were held on a coral reef and surrounded by deep water. All efforts to free her were fruitless, as she was firmly held on the reef and water soon started to gain on the pumps. Boats were lowered and stocked with provisions, Captain Maxwell's priority being to ensure the safety of Lord Amherst, and a boat bearing Amherst accompanied by a party of Marines and sailors was despatched to the island of Pulo Leat. The remainder of the crew were disembarked in an orderly fashion into the boats and joined the small party on the island. By 8 o'clock that evening only the Captain, First Lieutenant and a small party of seamen remained on the wreck. The following day, Maxwell organised the ferrying of more provisions from the wreck to the island and joined the party ashore later that day. Lord Amherst was despatched to Batavia that evening, with some of his staff and accompanied by two other boats, which they reached several days later without incident. Maxwell and the crew of *Alceste* left on the island worked hard over the next few days to establish a camp, stripping the wreck of stores and building a defended position. This proved its worth sometime later when a party of armed Malays arrived, who burnt the wreck and showed marked hostility towards the survivors. By 5 March, several dozen boats had gathered around the settlement, cutting off any escape and constantly threatening the little band. On 7 March the East India Company's cruiser *Ternate*, sent by Amherst, arrived off the island, and took all the party off. Murray Maxwell won praise for his actions during the ordeal; he was knighted in 1818 and awarded £1,500 by the East India Company.
[TNA: ADM.51/2105; Annual Register 1817 pp432–49]

2 June TORONTO Schooner Transport
Kingston 1817; 81 tons; 47ft × 18.6ft
Lieutenant Edward Shacklock
Employed on Lake Ontario, Canada, the schooner was carrying a cargo of stores intended for local tribes, when she went ashore near Gibraltar Point lighthouse, Kingston, Ontario, and was lost as a wreck.
[maritimehistoryofthegreatlakes.ca: Kingston Gazette 17 June 1817 – Report datelined 5 June]

2 October JULIA Brig Sloop
Ipswich 1806; 284 tons; 93.1ft × 26.6ft; 16 guns
Commander Jenkin Jones
Stationed at Ascension Island, she was despatched to Tristan da Cunha to embark wood and fresh water. Arriving on 28 September, she anchored two miles

offshore and several parties were landed to start the work, Commander Jones also going ashore to make a series of observations. The weather worsened after they had landed and by the evening of 1 October the seas were running so high that the boats could not be launched though the surf. At midnight, topgallant masts and yards were ordered to be struck and by 1.30am the brig was pitching so much that seas regularly broke over her and the jib boom was carried away. An hour later the anchor cable parted and efforts to sail out of danger were foiled by the lack of wind. The strong swell pushed her further inshore, and preparations were made to cut away the mainmast, but before this was completed, she drove onto the beach. Almost immediately she rolled over onto her beam-ends, the masts going overboard, the seas breaking over her constantly, leading to her quickly breaking up. Fifty-five men were drowned.
[TNA: ADM.1/5457]

8 December MARTIN Ship Sloop
Bermuda 1809; 399 tons; 106ft x 29.11ft; 18 guns
Commander Andrew Mitchell

The ship sailed from Killybegs Bay on 3 December to cruise off the western coast of Ireland, to prevent smuggling. The weather was unsettled and by 7 December, when they were off the Aran Islands, it was blowing a full gale. Sail was shortened down to storm staysails and the main topsail, as she steered south along the coast. At about midnight the wind increased to storm force, with driving rain and heavy seas, and the sloop found herself constantly heeling over onto her beam-ends. Guns and shot were heaved overboard to ease her as the gale blew out the sails, the sloop being driven before the wind. Daylight revealed land on the lee side, and an attempt was made to alter away, but this proved impossible. Land now loomed ahead, and it was realised that they were embayed. The best bower anchor was let go, but scarcely had it brought her up than the cable parted. Soon after this she went aground, all the masts going overboard as she did so. Lashed by the surf and rain, an attempt was made to swim a rope to the shore, but this failed, the swimmer being swept away and drowned. A boat was next tried but was instantly stove in on the ship's side. The crew could do little but wait and it was found that the ship was being driven further ashore on the beach. All but four men struggled over the wreckage of the masts through the surf to safety, finding themselves in Malbay, County Clare. The wreck attracted a large crowd of people from several miles around, intent on plundering the wreck.
[TNA: ADM.1/5458]

1818

13 January SHARK Hulk
Hull 1779; 304 tons; 96.11ft x 26.10ft
Lieutenant Charles Newton Hunter

A former sloop, the *Shark* was serving out her days as a convalescent ship at Port Royal, Jamaica. During 11 January water was found to be entering the ship, but this was not unusual, and Lieutenant Hunter ordered the pumps to be manned and a search conducted for the source. Despite pumping all day, the water could not be cleared, and the site of the leak could not be found. The following morning saw the water still rising and Hunter requested assistance from the dockyard. The Port Admiral ordered her to be moved into shallow water, and the Master Attendant supervised to laying out of anchors by which she was hauled into two fathoms of water, her keel touching the ground. During that night, shores were provided to support her and men from the dockyard assisted at the pumps. The water could not be cleared, and she slowly settled into the ground. During the morning of 13 January, the foremost shore on the starboard side gave way and she fell over onto her side, filled with water and sank.
[TNA: ADM.1/5458]

1819

1 June ERNE Sixth Rate
Dartmouth 1813; 455 tons; 115.6ft x 29.8ft; 20 guns
Commander Timothy Scriven

Approaching the Cape Verde Islands, several stellar observations were made during the evening of 31 May, and Commander Scriven was content that the ship was a few miles to the north-east of the island of Sal. At 10 o'clock that night, land was sighted, which was identified as Sal, and Scriven ordered a course which would take them along the eastern side of the island and then retired to his cabin for the night. At midnight land was sighted on the starboard bow and on being informed of this, Scriven ordered the officer of the watch to alter one point (11¼ degrees) away and to call the Master. The course change was made, but the Master failed to arrive on deck. At just before 1am, breakers were seen close ahead and an attempt was made to wear ship, but she ran aground before the move was complete. Soon after this she was struck by a heavy sea which hit her stern, demolishing the gig, carrying away the jolly boat and setting her further inshore. The surf constantly broke over her, unshipping the rudder and snapping the tiller, the fore and mainmast being cut away to try and ease the ship. After 20 minutes of lying in the surf she broached-to, her port broadside

swinging onto the beach. All the crew escaped the wreck to the shore. Scriven came in for some heavy criticism at his court martial for the loss. Having sighted the island, he had set a course which took her inshore, at night, along a coast with which he was unfamiliar. No soundings had been ordered and finally no qualified officer had the crucial middle watch – a midshipman serving as the officer of the watch. Scriven was judged to have been negligent and was severely reprimanded and his imminent promotion to Captain cancelled. The Master, John McKay, was found to have been negligent in failing to appreciate the dangerous course set and disobedient in failing to go on deck when ordered to do so. He was dismissed the service.
[TNA: ADM.1/5461]

1820

6 July CARRON Sixth Rate
Buckler's Hard 1813; 459 tons; 115.8ft × 29.9ft; 20 guns
Captain John Furneaux
Sailed from the Sandheads anchorage at the mouth of the River Hooghly on 28 June, bound for Madras, the *Carron* headed south, steering along the Indian coast. At 3 o'clock in the morning of 6 July she sighted breakers close ahead and was soon amongst them. All sail was thrown aback, but she struck the ground very heavily. Thumping violently on the ground, the masts were all cut away to try and ease her, but she continued to pound heavily in the surf, numerous leaks being started. After 20 minutes, she rolled over onto her starboard side and filled with water, the survivors swimming to the nearby shore clinging to pieces of the wreck. Nineteen men drowned. She had gone aground five miles north of the Black Pagoda, which was 20 miles north of Puri. A strong, unexpected current was blamed for the loss.
[TNA: ADM.1/5463]

1821

March BERMUDA Schooner Tender
From 1819?
Listed by Gilly and Lyon as being lost between Halifax and Bermuda, but no other references to the vessel or the loss have been found. Listed for completeness.
[Gilly p373; Lyon p295]

1822

21/22 April CONFIANCE Brig Sloop
Rochester 1813; 392 tons; 100.3ft × 30.10ft; 18 guns
Commander William Thomas Morgan†
The brig sailed from Cork on 21 April in company with the *Gannet* sloop, to cruise in search of smuggling vessels. The weather was poor and worsened and the pair became separated, with the *Gannet* putting into Kinsale. During the night of 21/22 April, the sound of gunfire was heard by people residing near Mizen Head, evidently signals from a ship in distress. Daylight revealed several bodies, and a large quantity of wreckage was washed along the shore of Dunlough Bay, identified as being from the *Confiance*. There were no survivors.
[www.britishnewspaperarchive.co: Saunders's News-Letter 30 April 1822 p2]

22 June DRAKE Brig Sloop
Ipswich 1808; 235 tons; 89.3ft × 24.7ft; 10 guns
Commander Charles Adolphus Baker†
Sailed from St Johns, Newfoundland, bound for Halifax, Nova Scotia, having delivered despatches and mail. The visibility was poor, with very thick fog, and at 7.30 in the evening, breakers were seen close ahead. An attempt was made to tack, but she went aground before this was completed, swinging broadside-on to the rocks soon after. An attempt was made to lower a boat, but it sank immediately. The Bosun, Mr Turner, finally made it to the shore in the dinghy, and, encouraged by his success, the remainder of the crew jumped overboard to struggle to a group of nearby rocks, a short distance from the ship, although some drowned in the attempt. The Bosun on the nearby shore managed to cast a line to the men on the rocks and after this was made fast, the survivors started to haul themselves to the shore, hand over hand along the rope. Over forty men made the journey before the line parted, marooning four men, including Commander Baker, on the rocks, which were soon covered by the tide, drowning them all. Baker was later praised for his coolness and bravery during the wreck, as was the high standard of discipline and orderliness shown by the crew. The wreck was blamed on the poor visibility and the set of the current which had driven her ashore near Cape Race.
[TNA: ADM.1/5465; Gilly pp251–63]

14 December RACEHORSE Brig Sloop
Hastings 1806; 385 tons; 100.1ft × 30.7ft; 18 guns
Commander William Benjamin Suckling
The sloop sailed from Holyhead, Anglesey, bound for the Isle of Man to meet the Revenue Cutter *Vigilant*. At 5 o'clock that same day, in the gloom of the early evening, the lights of the island were seen, and sail was ordered to

be shortened to double-reefed topsails. About 20 minutes later a light was observed which the pilot identified as that on Douglas Pier, and course was altered, the intention being to wait off Douglas and send in a boat with orders for the cutter. Whilst in the process of taking in canvas and preparing to launch the boat, breakers were seen ahead. The helm was put down, but she ran aground on Langness Point, striking violently. The boat was launched, and an attempt made to pass the stream anchor to act as a kedge, but the movement of the brig prevented this. Water was reported entering at a rapid rate and the brig was lifting and pounding on the rocks all the time. It was decided to abandon her, and as lights could be seen, evidently from boats approaching from the land, the boats were all hoisted out to take the crew ashore. This proved to be very hazardous, although two of the larger boats did make it to the land, two smaller craft were swamped or stove in as they were launched. At this point a boat from the shore approached, and five local men showed 'manly and intrepid conduct' in making four trips through the surf to the wreck, taking off all the men. On the final journey, with Commander Suckling embarked, the boat struck a rock and overturned, throwing all into the surf. Six men from the *Racehorse* and three of the rescuers were drowned. The blame for the loss was placed on the pilot, William Edwards, who mistook the lights and steered too close to the land, and on the Master, Henry Hodder, who had failed to keep the lead-line in constant use, although approaching the land. Edwards was severely reprimanded and mulcted of all pay due. Hodder was reprimanded and warned to be more careful in the future.
[TNA: ADM.1/5466]

1823

1 April COCKBURN Schooner Tender
Purchased 1822 (*Braganza*)
Lieutenant Richard Owen
Tender to the *Leven*, based at Cape Town, standing in to Simon's Bay in the night, she mistook the land, but finding herself in 10 fathoms, anchored. During the early hours of the morning the wind increased to gale strength and the schooner parted her cables and she went on shore on the north side of False Bay near Muizenberg.
[TNA: ADM. 51/3254; www.britishnewspaperarchive.co.uk: Morning Advertiser 16 June 1823 p2]

(11–14) December ARAB Brig Sloop
Frindsbury 1812; 390 tons; 99.7ft × 30.7ft; 18 guns
Commander William Holmes†
Stationed on the west coast of Ireland to prevent smuggling, she disappeared in the early part of the month, the exact day of her loss not being established. It was thought likely that she may have foundered near Broadhaven, County Mayo, as the weather in the area was poor with high winds and heavy seas, and between the 11th and 14th it was particularly bad. Wreckage was seen coming ashore in Broadhaven Bay on 15 December, but it was not until the 24th that wreckage, positively identified as being from the *Arab*, was found at Malinbeg.
[www.britishnewspaperarchive.co: Dublin Evening Post 30 December 1823 p3; Waterford Mail 3 January 1824 p2]

1824

25 January COLUMBINE Brig Sloop
Buckler's Hard 1806; 386 tons; 100ft × 30.8ft; 18 guns
Commander Honourable Charles Abbott
Having sailed from Corfu on 15 January, the sloop arrived off the island of Sapientza, off the Greek coast, four days later. She anchored near Port Longue (Porto Longo), to allow Commander Abbott to conduct a survey of the harbour. Secured by a single anchor, with a hawser to the shore as a mooring rope, she rode securely until the night of 24/25 January. The wind increased and a strong swell built up, with regular squalls of rain. At about 6 o'clock in the morning she was hit by a particularly strong squall, during which the anchor cable parted. Soon after this the mooring hawser also parted, and the brig started driving towards the shore. The stream anchor was hastily let go and Commander Abbott ordered the topgallant masts and yards struck. The anchor did not hold her, and the men were still working aloft when she drove onto rocks, beating for some time before she lurched heavily and went further onto the reef. Water entered rapidly and she foundered. All but two men escaped onto the island. Both Commander Abbott and the Master, James Atkins, were reprimanded at the subsequent court martial for failing to take proper precautions when the weather deteriorated. Only one anchor remained laid out, with insufficient cable veered for the weather conditions, and the vessel was not properly secured for bad weather.
[TNA: ADM.1/5468]

21 February CENTURION Hulk
Harwich 1774; 146ft × 40.5ft
Serving as a receiving ship and stores depot at Halifax, Nova Scotia, she foundered at her moorings. She was eventually raised, but broken up during 1825
[Colledge vol 1 p112; Lyon p77]

22/23 February DELIGHT Brig Sloop
Portsmouth 1819; 237 tons; 90.1ft × 24.7ft; 10 guns
Commander Robert Hay†
In January reports reached Mauritius that a French slaving brig, the *Lys*, had been wrecked on Providence

Island, north of Madagascar and the *Delight* sailed on 13 January for the island. A merchant vessel was also ordered to the scene, but when they arrived, discovered that the *Delight* had already found the wreck, and had left with the survivors, including over 100 slaves, for Mauritius. On the evening of 22 February, she was sighted standing towards Port Louis, in threatening weather, which that night worsened with strong winds and heavy seas, and she was not seen again. The next day several pieces of wreckage identified as being from *Delight* were washed ashore, but there were no survivors, apart from a few men that had been onshore when she sailed.
[TNA: ADM.35/4099; State Papers vol 12 1824–5 p337]

3 March DWARF Cutter
Sandgate 1810; 74.6ft x 26.1ft; 10 guns
Lieutenant Nicholas Gould

Lying in Kingstown Harbour, Dublin, she was secured to a mooring buoy, but as the weather looked threatening, Lieutenant Gould ordered suitable precautions to be taken. The small bower anchor was let go, bowsprit and bumkins run in, topmast struck and the square sail yard lowered. The wind steadily increased and by the early morning of 3 March it was blowing a full gale, the direction shifting round to the north. At 8 o'clock the mooring cable parted, and the best bower anchor was let go. An hour later the small bower anchor cable parted, and she started to drive towards the shore, the other anchor not holding her. Within minutes she had collided with the Eastern Pier and was thrown repeatedly against it, striking violently. Within an hour, she had been battered to pieces and foundered. One Marine died when he fell between the cutter and the pier.
[TNA: ADM.1/5468]

27 November PARTRIDGE Brig Sloop
Plymouth 1822; 237 tons; 90ft x 24.7ft; 10 guns
Lieutenant Edward Yonge

Acting as tender to the *Britannia*, she sailed on 19 November from Leith, Scotland, to return to the anchorage in the Downs. The sloop ran south under reefed topsails and foresail in dismal weather, the night of 26 November being particularly dark. Several lights were visible to the west, which were believed to be ships, and when, at 1 o'clock in the morning another light was seen ahead, this was also presumed to be a ship. The Master, Edward Pearn, initially steered towards the light, but as time passed, he became increasingly worried that they were entering shallow waters, the swell becoming shorter with broken waves. He ordered the lead-line to be cast and called for Lieutenant Yonge and the pilot to come on deck as he did. They found only 3½ fathoms of water and the helm was put over and all hands called on deck. As they anxiously strained to see through the darkness, a buoy was observed to pass down the starboard side, which prompted the pilot, Richard Smith, to say that the light must be a fisherman and the buoy must mark his nets. The Master disagreed and felt sure that it must be land. He was proved correct a few minutes later when she struck the ground and thumped heavily over a sandbank. The brig successfully beat over the obstruction and the anchor was ordered to be let go, but before this could bring her up, she ran onto a second sandbank. The rudder had been lost as she passed over the first bank and the bows were buried in the sand, the forefoot being lost. The ebbing tide soon left them high and dry, the sloop sinking further into the soft sand. Efforts went on throughout the day and into the following night to free her, but all proved fruitless, and she was abandoned during 28 November. The resulting court martial found that she had been lost on the shallows off Vlieland, to the north-east of the Texel through the inattention of the pilot. However, as Smith had a previously good character, and had been sick with asthma for much of the time, he was admonished to be more careful in the future. Lieutenant Yonge was found guilty or disobedience of printed orders and instructions, in failing to carry out regular observations or order the use of the lead-line. He had also placed too much confidence in the pilot, even though he was ill. Yonge was severely reprimanded.
[TNA: ADM.1/5469]

1825

February LADY NELSON Brig Tender
Purchased 1799; 60 tons; 52.6ft x 17.6ft
Master Samuel Johns†

Part of an expedition to survey and establish colonies on the north-eastern coast of Australia, she was despatched from Melville Island on 19 February to obtain fresh provisions from islands in the neighbourhood of Timor. She was not seen again, and the wreck of the vessel was later found near the island of Babar, and enquiries established that she had been attacked by Malay pirates and all those on board killed.
[trove.nla.gov.au: Sydney Gazette 4 May 1827]

1 August FURY Discovery Vessel
Rochester 1814; 105.8ft x 28.7ft
Commander Henry Parkyns Hoppner

Several expeditions to the Arctic region of Canada had taken place following the end of the French wars and between 1814 and 1823 the knowledge of the Baffin's Bay area was considerably expanded. In 1824 a new expedition, commanded by Captain Sir Edward Parry in the *Hecla*, accompanied by the *Fury*, set out to

complete the mapping of the northern coast of Canada and, if possible, find a passage that would lead to the Pacific. The pair encountered heavy ice as they crossed Baffin's Bay, which delayed their arrival in Lancaster Sound until mid-September. The season was now well advanced, but Parry pushed on where the ice would permit, before heading south into Prince Regent Inlet at the western end of Baffin Island to make winter camp. From October 1824 until July 1825, the ships were locked in to the ice, finally floating free on 19 July. The following day the pair set sail, heading northwards, to resume the expedition, taking advantage of several open channels of water that had appeared. Frequently these channels took them close to land and sometimes petered out, leaving them facing thick ice again. On 1 August, the *Fury* found herself in just such a channel, close to the land and whilst trying to push her way through to clear water she struck the ground. Despite being a strongly-built ship, the keel was broken by the shock and water was soon reported to be entering. The ice now closed in around them and it was decided that it might be possible to heave the vessel ashore and repair her leaks. To this end cables were run ashore and secured to blocks of ice, provisions landed and masts struck. The move was achieved on 10 August, the laborious effort of clearing a free channel and pulling her to the shoreline in such a short time being a major achievement in such adverse conditions. It soon became clear that the *Fury* was severely damaged, both by striking the ground and by the crushing effect of the ice. The keel was severely damaged, and both the sternpost and forefoot were broken. Despite all their efforts, they could not properly heave her down, having to constantly clear the place of ice, threatened by large floating icebergs and the shifting of the blocks of ice she was secured to. When the weather worsened, threatening the *Hecla*, it was decided to abandon the *Fury*, after placing all the stores back on board. The crew completed the re-stocking of the ship on 25 August, leaving her beached at the place now known as Fury Beach in Cresswell Bay, Somerset Island. The *Hecla* took on board the last of the crew of the *Fury* on 2 September and sailed to return to England. The provisions left on board proved their worth in 1832–3, when a privately-sponsored expedition under Sir John Ross was forced to abandon their ship in the Gulf of Bothnia after being trapped in the ice for nearly three years. The party reached the remains of the *Fury* and lived there until the ice allowed them to escape.
[TNA: ADM.1/5469; ADM.51/3186; ADM.55/56; ADM.101/101/5]

1826

9 January ALGERINE Brig Sloop
Deptford 1823; 230 tons; 90ft × 24.8ft; 10 guns
Commander Charles Wemyss†
In company with the *Revenge*, the pair weighed from their overnight anchorage off the island of Hydra in the Aegean and steered along the eastern side of the island under topsails and topgallants, the weather being fine. As night fell, the weather looked threatening, with lightning seen to the south. At 10 o'clock that evening the *Revenge* started to shorten sail but was still reefing canvas when they were hit by a squall with strong winds and driving rain. This heeled the larger ship over and carried away her fore yard and cross-jack yard and split every sail. The *Algerine* was then about two miles astern of her companion and after the rain cleared away, she had disappeared and was not seen again.
[TNA: ADM.51/3392; www.britishnewspaperarchive.co: Hampshire Chronicle 10 April 1826 p4]

February MARTIN Ship Sloop
Portsmouth 1821; 402 tons; 108.5ft × 28.10ft; 20 guns
Commander Thomas Wilson†
Disappeared after sailing from the Cape of Good Hope in February, bound for the East Indies, and presumed foundered with all hands. Pay book closed end-February 1826.
[www.britishnewspaperarchive.co: Morning Post 26 October 1826 p3; TNA: ADM.35/4488]

27 August MAGPIE Schooner
Jamaica 1826; 70 tons; 53.3ft × 40.8ft; 4 guns
Lieutenant Edward Smith†
Cruising off the western end of Cuba in search of pirates, at about 8 o'clock in the evening heavy clouds were observed coming off the land, and the officer of the watch ordered sail to be shortened. Before this was complete, she was struck by a strong squall, which rolled her over onto her larboard side. Water poured into the schooner through open hatchways, and she sank very quickly, leaving a handful of survivors clinging to floating spars and an upturned boat. They eventually righted the boat, and some climbed in, with others clinging to the sides as efforts to bail out the little boat commenced, but it remained full of water. In the morning, several large sharks attacked them, killing two of them, and biting Lieutenant Smith's legs, from which he expired later that evening. Over the next three days the boat drifted with the current, and with the six remaining survivors suffering from the tropical heat and lack of water. During this ordeal four men died, and only two survivors remained to be picked up by the merchant brig *Pylades*.
[TNA: ADM.1/5470; Nautical Magazine 1840 pp635–7]

1827

14 January NIMROD Brig Sloop
Ipswich 1812; 384 tons; 100ft × 30.7ft; 18 guns
Commander Samuel Sparshott

Sailed from Cork on 13 January and headed into the Irish Sea in freshening winds and rising seas. By 4 o'clock the following morning the wind had reached gale force with a heavy swell, and as a precaution the topgallant masts and yards were struck. Sail was shortened down to reefed topsails and staysails. At 10.30am she shipped a particularly heavy sea which carried away the larboard bulwarks along with the quarter boat and davits. Water filled the waist, spilling down the main hatchway and flooding the lower deck. The ship hung on her beam ends for several seconds before she slowly recovered. The wreckage was cleared and pumping and bailing commenced to clear the water, and the sloop altered course to run before the wind. It was noticeable that she was trimmed down by the head, and it was feared that the ballast had shifted. The wind increased still further, blowing the sails out, the fore trysail being the only sail remaining. In this condition, land identified as the island of Anglesey was sighted and it was decided to run for shelter off Holyhead. The weather moderated a little as they approached the island and they could anchor off Holyhead at 7 o'clock that evening, both best and small bower anchors being laid out. Topmasts and yards were struck, and she prepared to ride out the storm, the wind shifting round to the north-north-west. Two hours later the best bower anchor broke in the shank, and she found that she was dragging the remaining anchor. The sheet anchor was let go, but it failed to bring her up and she went onto a ridge of rocks with great violence. The masts were all cut away as she beat over the rocks, the rudder being unshipped, and numerous holes were torn in the hull before she stopped. An attempt was made to fire a line to the ship from the shore, using Captain Manby's Lifesaving Rocket, but the wind was so strong that it carried the lines away. By midnight, the winds had dropped, and Lieutenant Ricketts volunteered to take the dinghy through the surf to the shore with a line, which he successfully achieved. The line and boat were then used to ferry the crew ashore. Over the next few days, the wreck was cleared of stores, and she was hauled off the rocks on 12 February by the steamer *Harlequin* and taken to a dry dock at Holyhead. She was assessed as being too irreparably damaged to be worth repairing and was sold 10 days later and was eventually rebuilt for further service as a merchant vessel.
[TNA:ADM.1/5471;ADM.51/3324]

18 February DIAMOND Fifth Rate
Chatham 1816; 1,076 tons; 150ft × 40.2ft; 46 guns

Laid up in Ordinary (reserve) in Porchester Lake, Portsmouth, at about 8 o'clock in the morning a fire was discovered on board. The *Victory*, as the local flagship and guard ship, fired several guns to raise the alarm, and she sent boats, which were joined by some from the dockyard, to assist in fighting the blaze. However, with a strong easterly wind fanning the flames, the fire spread rapidly and gained a hold before it could be tackled. It was with some difficulty that the fourteen people living on board, including women and children, were taken off. The ship continued to burn through the day and was burnt to the waterline. Some criticism was levelled at the standing Warrant Officers onboard who had not kept a proper watch. It was surmised that the galley fire had not been cleared the previous night, and on raking out the fire in the morning, hot cinders got under the grate and communicated to the deck.
[www.britishnewspaperarchive.co: Public Ledger 20 February 1827 p2]

6 June CYNTHIA Packet Brig
Purchased 1826 (*Prince Regent*); 232 tons; 87.2ft × 25ft; 6 guns
Lieutenant John White

Sailed from Falmouth on 7 May with the mails for Barbados, St Vincent and Jamaica. The island of Barbados was sighted late in the afternoon of 5 June and Lieutenant White decided to lay-to for the night and shortened sail accordingly. At 1 o'clock in the morning breakers were seen ahead, and despite an attempt to wear ship, she ran aground. Boats were lowered to carry out an anchor, but attempts to kedge her off failed, despite spreading more sail and setting them aback. The Carpenter reported that she was making water and efforts were concentrated on pumping and bailing, which went on through the early hours. Daylight showed them to be ashore on a reef off Kendal Point, about two miles from the southern end of Barbados. The mails were landed by boat and several local boats were employed to take off stores in efforts to lighten her, with hopes that she could be re-floated. At 3 o'clock in the afternoon the transom broke and the stern post separated, flooding the brig and bringing an end to all thoughts of freeing her. The loss was blamed on a strong current and the hazy weather, which had obscured the land.
[TNA:ADM.1/5471]

June REDWING Brig Sloop
Brightlingsea 1806; 383 tons; 100ft × 30.6ft; 18 guns
Commander Douglas Charles Clavering†

Newly arrived on the west coast of Africa to join the anti-slavery squadron, she sailed from Freetown, Sierra Leone on 16 June for a cruise, but disappeared and was

presumed lost with all hands. Some of her spars were picked up in September on St Ann's Shoals, about 30 miles to the north of Sierra Leone. Several years later a Spanish slaver claimed that he had seen her chasing two slave ships but had been caught by a strong squall and capsized after failing to reduce canvas in time. Her pay book closed 30 June 1827.
[TNA: ADM.35/4479; www.britishnewspaperarchive.co: Morning Chronicle 21 January 1828 p3; Hampshire Chronicle 4 February 1828 p2; Grindal p321]

September HEARTY Packet Brig
Chatham 1824; 227 tons; 90.1ft × 24.8ft; 10 guns
Commander Henry Jewry†
Sailed from Falmouth on 12 September bound for Jamaica with mails and five passengers, she was last seen within a few days' sail of Barbados, but never arrived. Presumed foundered at sea with the loss of all thirty-seven crew and passengers. Pay book closed 30 September.
[TNA: ADM.35/4411; Nautical Magazine vol 3 p629]

1828

31 January CAMBRIAN Fifth Rate
Bursledon 1797; 1,148 tons; 154ft × 41ft; 48 guns
Captain Gawen William Hamilton
The *Cambrian* was one of a sizeable British squadron that was based in the eastern Mediterranean during the Greek War of Independence. The British combined with the French to attack the island of Grabousa (Gramvousa) at the western end of Crete, which was being used as a base by several pirates. The force, under the command of Sir Thomas Staines in the *Isis*, closed the harbour to attack several schooners which were at anchor under the citadel, the *Cambrian* being close astern of the *Isis*. The intention was to pass the anchorage, firing a broadside at the pirates as they did, and then come about to engage with the other broadside. The *Isis* duly fired her guns and smartly came about. The *Cambrian* attempted to keep to leeward, in between her companion and the shore, and as *Isis* came about, tried to tack to keep clear. She came about very slowly, and her noticeably light condition made her difficult to control. The *Isis*, having come about, found herself confronted by the *Cambrian* still trying to manoeuvre, but being so close she was unable to avoid a collision, the bows of the *Isis* striking the quarter of *Cambrian*. The impact carried away the stern davits complete with jolly boat, along with the spanker boom. The collision, combined with the loss of the sail caused her to miss stays, and before she could recover, she grounded. An anchor was let go to hold her still, topgallant masts and yards were struck, and the boats were hoisted out. Other ships of the squadron closed to assist, but before anything could be done, she heeled over to port and water flooded in through the open gun ports. The masts were quickly cut away, but the ship settled in shallow water. All the crew left in an orderly manner.
[TNA: ADM.1/5472]

17 March UNION Schooner
Purchased 1823 (*City of Kingston*); 84 tons; 59.9ft × 18.10ft; 3 guns
Lieutenant John Wills
Sailed from Port Royal, Jamaica, on 16 March en-route for Havana. That evening she hove to for the night under double reefed topsails and fore staysail. At just after 4 o'clock the next morning, breakers were seen astern, and the sails were ordered to be loosed. She tacked away, only to find another reef ahead. She rapidly tacked again, then dropped anchor, being brought up less than 100ft from the line of breakers. It was hoped that this would hold her, but 30 minutes later the anchor cable parted, and she was carried down onto the rocks, rolling over onto her starboard side as she did so. One boat was launched, but this was swept away in the surf which was beating all around them. The weather rigging was cut away, which allowed the masts to fall overboard, the crew using these to gain the land beyond the reef, but six men drowned in the attempt. Lieutenant Wills was found to have been negligent in carrying too much sail when close to the land, and failing to order regular soundings, which had led the schooner to go onto the Porpoise Rocks at the eastern end of Rose Island. He was dismissed the service.
[TNA: ADM.1/5472]

(14–16) April ACORN Ship Sloop
Chatham 1826; 465 tons; 112.1ft × 31.2ft; 18 guns
Commander Edward Gordon†
Sailed from Bermuda 10 April, in company with the *Hussar* and *Tyne*, bound for Halifax, but they were overtaken by a strong gale and parted company during 14 April and the *Acorn* was not seen again. The storm continued to affect the area over the next two days, and she was presumed to have been lost with all hands at this time. Pay book closed at end-April.
[TNA: ADM.35/4345; www.britishnewspaperarchive.co: London Evening Standard 23 June 1828 pp4 and 9 July 1828 p2]

(14–16) April CONTEST Gun Brig
Bridport 1812; 180 tons; 84.6ft × 22ft; 12 guns
Lieutenant Edward Plaggenborg†
Sailed from Halifax on 13 April, bound for Bermuda, carrying £10,000 for use by the commissariat and was not seen again. The area was swept by a storm at this

time, and the *Contest* was presumed lost with all hands. Pay book closed at end-April.
[TNA: ADM.35/4368; www.britishnewspaperarchive.co: London Standard 9 July 1828 p2; Morning Chronicle 18 August 1828 p2]

15 May **PARTHIAN** Brig Sloop
Deptford 1808; 238 tons; 90.3ft × 24.6ft; 10 guns
Commander Honourable George Frederick Hotham

Bound for Alexandria with despatches, at daybreak on 15 May the coast of Egypt was sighted, and the sloop steered east along the coast until nightfall. She shortened sail to reefed topsails, foresail and jib, and steered a course which would allow her to enter Alexandria the following morning. At 9.30pm land was seen, close ahead on the lee bow. The helm was quickly put over, but she ran aground. All sail was thrown aback, without effect. She anchored and boats were lowered to lay out a stream anchor which was used as a kedge. However, soon after heaving commenced, the cable parted and her troubles were compounded when soon after the anchor cable parted, the brig being lifted by a heavy swell. She was carried further inshore where she started pounding heavily on the ground. Daylight showed them to be high and dry on the Egyptian shore about 16 miles to the west of Marabout Island. Cables were rigged to the shore to act as a jackstay for the transfer of stores, and all the men were put ashore to set up a tented camp. Later that day the *Weazle* arrived on the scene, and she took all the crew to Alexandria. The loss was blamed on a strong southerly current which had set her further inshore and to the west than she realised and the failure to sound regularly. Both Commander Hotham and the Master, Edward Sawkins, were admonished to be more careful in the future when navigating close to the shore.
[TNA: ADM.1/5472]

August **REDPOLE** Packet Brig
Northam 1808; 239 tons; 89.11ft × 24.8ft; 6 guns
Master John Bullock†

Sailed from Rio de Janeiro on 10 August bound for Falmouth with mail and passengers, but then disappeared. It was presumed that she had foundered at sea with all hands, but rumours circulated over the following months, that she had been attacked and sunk by a pirate. It was reported in June the following year that a man accused of piracy in Brazil testified that she had been attacked off Cape Frio by the pirate *Congress* from Buenos Aires and sunk after an engagement of an hour. Pay books closed 31 August.
[TNA: ADM.35/4479; www.britishnewspaperarchive.co: London Evening Standard 22 June 1829 pp1 and 24 January 1831 p2; Caledonian Mercury 14 August 1834 p2]

11 October **JASPER** Brig Sloop
Portsmouth 1820; 237 tons; 90.1ft × 24.7ft; 10 guns
Commander Leonard Charles Rooke

Lying at Corfu, she was ordered to proceed 'with the least possible delay' to the island of Santa Maura (Lefkada) with important letters for Sir Frederick Adam, the British High Commissioner of the Ionian Islands. She sailed during the morning of 11 October and by sunset the port of Santa Maura was visible, about 16 miles distant. Being anxious to deliver the despatches, Commander Rooke decided to stand on after dark, although he was unfamiliar with the area. At 8 o'clock that night all hands were turned up to shorted sail, but as this was in progress, breakers were seen ahead. The helm was put over and she came around, the surf being close to them. Sails were clewed up and she dropped the best bower anchor, but before it could bring her up, she struck heavily on a rock, which pierced her hull near the bow. Water flooded in and bailing, and pumping commenced as the masts were cut away and several guns heaved overboard. She was settling very quickly and all further efforts to save her were abandoned as the crew went along the wreckage of the masts to the shore. Commander Rooke was admonished to be cautious in the future when approaching an unfamiliar shore.
[TNA: ADM.1/5472]

(8) December **ARIEL** Packet Brig
Deptford 1820; 236 tons; 90ft × 24.8ft; 6 guns
Lieutenant James Figg†

Employed in the packet service, she sailed from Falmouth on 10 November for Halifax and Bermuda, with mail and passengers. She was seen standing towards Sable Island on 8 December by a trading schooner from Halifax, but was not seen again, and presumed lost soon after with all hands. Pay book closed 31 December.
[TNA: ADM.35/4345; Nautical Magazine 1834 p630]

18 December **KANGAROO** Survey Brig
Purchased 1819; 204 tons; 87ft × 22.7ft
Master Anthony de Mayne

Engaged in surveying work in the West Indies, she sighted Punta de Maisi at the eastern end of Cuba during the morning of 17 December, and set her course to the north-north-east, intending to pass to the north of the island of Inagua. At just after 5 o'clock the following morning, white water was seen on the lee bow. The officer of the watch, the Gunner's Mate Henry Hubbard, ordered the helm to be put down and called down the hatchway to the Master, but she ran hard aground on a reef within minutes of the broken water being seen. The boats were hoisted out to take out a kedge anchor and the yards braced round in efforts to pull her off stern-first. This work continued for some time, with no success, water butts eventually

being emptied and pumped out, and stores ordered to be shifted from aft to forward. This took most of the morning, achieving nothing, and it was two o'clock in the afternoon before the pinnace was put into the water to take out the stream anchor. The seas were rising, and by the time all was ready, the boat could not take out the anchor as the movement of the brig was too violent. The weather continued to worsen, and during the night the gig was washed away from the stern davits, causing a considerable amount of damage. By the next morning, water was found to be over the casks in the hold and it was decided to leave her. The boats transferred all the crew to the islands nearby, one being despatched to Crooked Island to bring assistance, which arrived two days later. The subsequent court martial decided that she had been wrecked on the Hogsty Reef due to the negligence and incompetence of the ship's officers. Mr de Mayne was found to have failed to regulate the distance run during the day and thereby placed the brig in a dangerous position. He had failed to order the regular use of the lead-line, and furthermore he had allowed the Gunner's Mate to have charge of a watch when more qualified officers were on board. Finally, his measures to save the ship after running aground had been ineffectual. The Second Master, Ralph Campbell, had failed to take bearings of Punta de Maisi and failed to take the noon observations which were his duty. The Mate, John Frimley, had failed to order the use of the lead-line and had observed the water becoming smooth, indicating shallow water, during the middle watch, but had failed to take any action. All three men were dismissed the service.
[TNA:ADM.1/5473]

1829

7 February **NIGHTINGALE** Cutter
Plymouth 1825; 123 tons; 63.9ft × 22.2ft; 6 guns
Lieutenant George Wood

Sailed from Plymouth on 6 February bound for Portsmouth, carrying Lieutenant Thomas Cole, who had been invalided from the *Harpy* in the West Indies having been declared insane, and was being taken to Haslar hospital. She entered the Solent during the following afternoon under the guidance of a local pilot, Edward Haniford, with Lieutenant Wood remaining aft, allowing the pilot to take complete charge of the cutter. Haniford inexplicably took the vessel the wrong side of the buoys marking the channel and she ran aground on the Shingles sandbank. All sails were thrown aback, but she remained stuck fast. Distress guns were fired, which brought several local boats to her assistance and hopes were high that she could be hauled off, and the crew were employed in shifting ballast and preparing to sail. The wind and sea were increasing, and she started to bump heavily on the ground and as the tide ebbed, she fell over onto her larboard side before any shores could be placed to support her. At about 8 o'clock with the next flood tide the foresail was hoisted in hopes of sailing off, but she would not move, and the hatch covers were washed away, and she quickly flooded with water and was lost. The boats in attendance managed to rescue all but the poor mad Lieutenant Cole and the wife of Lieutenant Wood. The pilot took the blame for the loss but owing to his 'great age and infirmity' he was punished only with loss of all pay due and being ordered never to pilot Royal Navy vessels again. The Master, Samuel Squire, was severely reprimanded for failing to take sufficient interest in the progress of the cutter. Lieutenant Wood was dealt with sympathetically. He was an old and experienced officer, having been first commissioned in 1798, and had commanded the *Turbulent* when captured by the French in 1808 (q.v.). He was reprimanded for placing too much confidence in the pilot. Wood was retired the following March with the rank of Commander.
[TNA:ADM.1/5473]

3 April **MYRTLE** Packet Brig
Portsmouth 1825; 232 tons; 90ft × 24.7ft; 6 guns
Lieutenant Samuel Sisson

Bound for Halifax with mail and passengers, she approached the coast in thick fog, sounding constantly. As the water increased in depth, Lieutenant Sisson was confident that they had passed over the Newfoundland Bank and set a course for Sambro Light. A sun-sight was obtained which confirmed his estimated position and he ceased sounding with the lead-line. At just after 11 o'clock that night, ice and then land were seen ahead. The helm was put down and sails thrown aback, but she struck the ground heavily, being bilged straight away. Boats were lowered and the masts cut away, but little could be done as she was rapidly filling with water, and the crew were forced to take to the boats. Soon after the last man had left her, she capsized over to starboard and sank, only the fo'c'sle and port bulwark showing above the water. She had been wrecked on the western end of Ragged Island, Nova Scotia. Although the wreck was blamed on a strong current which had taken them further inshore than expected, both Sisson and the Master, Nicholas Hill, were severely reprimanded for approaching the coast without using the lead-line constantly.
[TNA:ADM.1/5473]

1830

5 December THETIS Fifth Rate
Pembroke 1817; 1,086 tons; 150.9ft × 40.2ft; 46 guns
Captain Samuel Burgess
The *Thetis* sailed from Rio de Janeiro for England carrying a large amount of gold and silver, the weather being hazy with occasional rain squalls. At noon, the position by dead reckoning placed her 40 miles from Cape Frio, no sun sight being taken due to the overcast skies. By dusk it was raining incessantly, and she continued on her course believing herself well clear of land. At 8.15pm land was seen close ahead, and very soon after she ran into a near-vertical cliff face with such violence that all the masts went overboard, covering the upper deck with wreckage and killing or injuring several men. She was found to be floating freely, and the hull evidently undamaged, so a boat sail was rigged to the stump of the mainmast, and she fended herself off the precipice using spars. Finding that she was now in a bay, she let go an anchor, but it did not bring her up before she ran aground. She thumped and pounded her way over the ridge and floated freely again before being driven into a cove. Surrounded by rocks and rapidly filling with water she foundered. Twenty-two men died, either killed by falling wreckage or drowned in the efforts to get ashore before she sank. Captain Burgess was found to have placed too much confidence in his estimated position, which was based on dead reckoning, with insufficient allowance for the wind and currents, and further regular soundings had been neglected. He was ordered to lose one years' seniority. The Master, William Gowdy, suffered a similar rebuke and lost two years' seniority. The ship had run onto Cape Frio and considerable work went on over several months to recover the money. Under the supervision of Captains Dickinson of the *Lightning* and De Ros of the *Algerine*, about two-thirds of the treasure was recovered.
[TNA: ADM.1/5476]

1831

13 May MONKEY Schooner
Jamaica 1826; 70 tons; 53.3ft × 18ft; 4 guns
Mate Thomas Downes
Acting as consort to the *Mersey* frigate, she was ordered from the river at Tampico to Havana. A local steam boat was hired to tow the schooner over the bar, with Captain Courtney of the frigate on board to observe the event. The tug was poorly handled and only succeeded in running herself aground near the bar. Courtney ordered the schooner to cut herself free of the tug, which was promptly done, and the topsail and jib were rapidly spread. However, the wind failed, and she was taken by the strong current onto the bar where she grounded. The steam boat having now freed herself, Courtney attempted to persuade the captain to come to the assistance of the stranded vessel, but to no avail. The schooner remained hard aground on the bar and was beaten to a wreck. The remains were sold locally by auction on 24 May.
[TNA: ADM.1/286]

20 December ADDER Watch Vessel
Topsham 1813; 182 tons; 84.6ft × 22.2ft
A former gun brig converted in 1826 to be used by the Coastguard as a Watch Vessel at Rye, Sussex, on 20 December the steam vessel *Confiance* arrived in the harbour to tow her to Portsmouth for a refit. At 11 o'clock the steamer got under weigh having put a small towing party of five men on board the *Adder*. The weather was poor, and worsened, with high winds, heavy seas and rain. By 8 o'clock that night it was blowing a full gale and no headway was being made. At 9.30pm the towing party hailed the *Confiance* with the news that the *Adder* was filling with water, having sprung a leak. The steamer hove-to, head to the south, and lowered a boat and using a cable, it was veered astern to remove the people on board. As it was hauled alongside the boat was swamped, and one seaman was drowned. At 9.45pm the tow was cut, and the watch vessel was swept away in a tremendous sea and storm-force winds. She was driven inshore and wrecked. The wreck was put up for sale in April 1832, then stated to be lying under Beachy Head.
[TNA: ADM.51/3112; www.britishnewspaperarchive.co: Sussex Advertiser 9 April 1832 p3]

1832

June RECRUIT Brig Sloop
Portsmouth 1829; 231 tons; 90.1ft × 24.8ft; 10 guns
Lieutenant Thomas Hodges†
Sailed from Falmouth for the North America station, she arrived at Halifax on 24 May and sailed from that port for Bermuda on 29 May but was not seen again. Presumed foundered with all hands.
[www.britishnewspaperarchive.co: Royal Cornwall Gazette 30 June 1832 p2 ; Morning Post 28 August 1832 p4]

25 November MEDWAY Store Lighter
Sheerness 1830; 167 tons; 71.11ft × 23.4ft
Lieutenant Montagu Thomas
Sailed from Portsmouth on 15 October to take up station in the West Indies, she was under the command of Lieutenant Thomas, assisted by a Midshipman, Master and a small crew. The vessel arrived off Kingston, Jamaica,

during the afternoon of 25 November and lay-to in a calm, intending to enter the following morning. At 10 o'clock that night, Midshipman Edward Noble realised that the breakers on the shore were looming closer and called all hands on deck. The anchors were let go, but before they could bring her up, she ran aground and swung broadside on to the shore. The boat was launched to try and lay out a kedge anchor, but it achieved little, the surf driving the lighter further onto the beach and she was lost. The subsequent court martial found that the vessel had been lost by being carried inshore by the strong current. Lieutenant Thomas was judged guilty of failing to have taken care in the steering and conduct of the lighter and was severely reprimanded. Master Robert Grausell was admonished, and Midshipman Noble was reprimanded for their conduct in the affair.
[TNA: ADM.1/5478]

1833

(30/31) January CALYPSO Packet Brig
Chatham 1826; 233 tons; 90.3ft × 24.7ft; 6 guns
Lieutenant Richard Peyton†
Sailed from Halifax on 29 January with mails for England and was last seen the following day by a local fishing vessel, surrounded by icebergs and apparently in distress. Because of the ice the fishermen could not near the brig, and it was presumed that she foundered soon after this. Pay book closed 31 January.
[TNA: ADM.32/300; www.britishnewspaperarchive.co: Morning Post 11 August 1834 p4]

December THAÏS Packet Brig
Pembroke 1829; 231 tons; 90ft × 24.6ft; 6 guns
Lieutenant Charles Church†
Sailed from Falmouth on 12 December for Halifax, and was last heard of on 24 December, when to the west of Ireland, in position 50N 16W, standing to the north in gale-force winds. Nothing more was seen of her, and it was presumed that she had foundered soon after. Her launch, part of the deck and other wreckage was washed ashore during March and April on the coast of Galway. Pay book closed 31 December.
[TNA: ADM.32/446; www.britishnewspaperarchive.co: Morning Post 29 March 1834 p2; Morning Post 11 August 1834 p4]

1834

4 December NIMBLE Schooner
Purchased 1826 (*Bolivar*); 168 tons; 83.7ft × 22.2ft; 5 guns
Lieutenant Charles Bolton
Engaged in the anti-slavery patrol, she cruised along the northern coast of Cuba. On 30 November, she chased and drove ashore a slaving schooner, the *Carlotta*, off Punta Garda la Vaca. The schooner closed and found that the slaver had 272 slaves packed on board. All of them were taken off and put onto the upper deck of the *Nimble*, which then proceeded along the Old Bahama Channel, heading for Havana. The night of 3 December was very dark, with frequent squalls of heavy rain. Lieutenant Bolton posted extra lookouts and ordered the lead-line to be used constantly, but found the crew were unsettled by the constant wailing and crying of the slaves, which made it difficult to hear shouted orders. At 1 o'clock in the morning, whilst preparing to cast the lead, the vessel went hard aground, soon falling over onto her beam-ends. The foremast and main topmast were cut away, the wreckage being used to make rafts, and despite the surf breaking around them, boats were launched. At daybreak, they commenced ferrying the slaves to the nearby shore, which was identified as Cay Verde in the Old Bahama Channel. This work was made difficult because of the language barrier, and when the first boats came alongside many the slaves rushed forward, capsizing the boat, and throwing all into the sea, with the result that about fifty of them were drowned. Nevertheless, the crew persisted, and the work went on through the day until all were taken off. A boat was despatched to bring help, and a tented encampment was set up to await rescue. This arrived on 8 December, a Spanish schooner taking off all the survivors to Havana. The loss was blamed on an uncertain, strong current, which was compounded by the dark night and the uncontrollable noise from the liberated slaves.
[TNA: ADM.1/5481]

1835

27 February FIREFLY Schooner
Bermuda 1828; 84 tons; 59.9ft × 18.3ft; 3 guns
Lieutenant James Julius MacDonnell
Sailed from Belize for Jamaica on 24 February and three days later, at about 9 o'clock in the evening, with no apprehension of danger, she struck a reef, breakers being seen only minutes before she grounded. Anchors were let go to hold her steady, but despite this, she pounded on the rocks, and this worsened after the best bower cable parted at 3 o'clock in the morning. The masts were struck in a further attempt to east her, but nothing could be thrown overboard, as it was feared the schooner could strike them as well. Morning saw the schooner abandoned by the crew, who took to two boats and a raft, which was to be towed by the cutter. However, the line to the raft parted, and was swept back onto the reef and the men, including Lieutenant MacDonnell, were forced to land on the reef. The gig, with eleven men on board was later found upside down,

all the occupants evidently drowned. The cutter made the shore near Belize and organised a rescue which returned to the wreck site and found only two men, the rest having abandoned the wreck in the raft, which, with Lieutenant MacDonnell, drifted ashore several miles to the north of Belize and the survivors set out to walk along the coast. MacDonnell became weak and ill and was left behind as the others continued onwards, although a later search party found him alive. The court-martial enquiry found that she had been wrecked on the Northern Triangles reef, or Banco Chinchorro, about 70 miles north of Belize in light and variable winds. The noon observation and later calculations had put the schooner some 24 miles from the reef. Much criticism was levelled at Mr Malcolm, the Clerk, who had left Lieutenant MacDonnell for dead: '… the court can but express surprise and regret that a British officer and British seamen should have left their commanding officer exposed in so helpless and melancholy state'.
[TNA: ADM.1/548; Nautical Magazine 1835 p434]

11 March JACKDAW Schooner
Chatham 1830; 109 tons; 60.9ft × 20.4ft; 4 guns
Lieutenant Edward Barnett
Sailed from Jamaica to carry out survey work in the vicinity of Old Providence (Isla de Providencia) off the coast of Honduras, and in particular to determine the longitude of various cays and reefs. On 10 March, she anchored off Cayo Serrana and having taken several observations, weighed and proceeded towards Providence. At 4.30 in the morning, without warning, she ran onto a reef to the north of that island. The masts were cut away, water butts emptied and guns thrown overboard to lighten her, and an anchor let go to steady her, but the surf lifted and pounded her through the night. A raft was constructed, and boats hoisted out and at first light the schooner was abandoned, the crew being taken to Old Providence by a local vessel. They following morning the *Gannet* arrived, which took them back to Jamaica. The court martial determined that the position of the reef was incorrectly shown on the Admiralty chart. However, the court admonished Lieutenant Barnett to be more careful in the future, as it was believed that too much canvas had been carried the preceding night in hazy weather.
[TNA: ADM.1/5481; Nautical Magazine 1835 pp435–6]

19 May CHALLENGER Sixth Rate
Pembroke 1827; 603 tons; 125.7ft × 32.8ft; 28 guns
Captain Michael Seymour
Part of the British South American squadron, she sailed from Rio de Janeiro on 1 April, bound for Talcahuano and Valparaiso. Steering north along the coast of Chile in hazy weather, sun sights were taken at irregular intervals through the cloud, but they were confident that they were well clear of land. At 9.45pm, breakers were suddenly observed close ahead. The helm was put over and an attempt made to tack, but she was already in the surf and struck the ground with some violence, the head swinging round to seaward. She pounded on the rocks and soon rolled over onto her starboard side, the vessel was carried by the surf over the rocks into shallow water, where she righted herself although embedding herself in the soft sand. Pumping kept the water at bay, although it was found that she had lost her rudder and several timbers and planks had been stove in, the gunroom and several cabins being flooded. Morning revealed a long flat beach, with a heavy surf beating, and over the next few days the crew left the ship on rafts and boats, all making it to safety except two men who drowned when a boat overturned. When the weather moderated a considerable amount of the ship's stores were landed and a defended camp established. Help was given by local ranchers, and the ship and site were finally abandoned on 8 June, when a new camp was established at the mouth of the River Lebu and parties sent overland to Concepcion to bring help. This arrived on 5 July in the shape of the *Blonde* frigate, which took off all the survivors. The loss was attributed to a powerful current which had carried her onto the shore near Punta Morguilla, although she was out of her reckoning by 40 miles.
[TNA: ADM.1/5481; Nautical Magazine 1835 pp789–96]

1836

5 February PIKE Schooner
Prize 1813 (*Dart*); 254 tons; 93ft × 24.8ft; 12 guns
Lieutenant Arthur Brooking
Whilst on passage from Kingston to Montego Bay, Jamaica, she ran hard aground on Pelican Reef, Bare Bush Key, at about 9.30pm with little warning. Distress guns were fired, which brought assistance, the merchant vessel *Hornby* going to her aid, but she was abandoned as a wreck. The subsequent court martial found that there had been neglect in keeping her reckoning and supposed herself to be much further to the south. Lieutenant Brooking was sentenced to be dismissed the service, although he was restored in May 1837. The Mate, Mr Mitchell, was found to have prevaricated in his evidence, and in consequence of some leaves being torn from the log book, was ordered to be confined in the Marshalsea Prison for three months and dismissed the service. Mr Stokes, Master's Assistant, was also dismissed the service.
[TNA: ADM.1/5482; www.britishnewspaperarchive.co; Hampshire Telegraph 13 June 1836 p4; Nautical Magazine 1836 p243]

1838

January BRISEIS Packet Brig
Deptford 1829; 230 tons; 90ft × 24.6ft; 6 guns
Lieutenant John Downey†
Sailed from Falmouth on 6 January bound for Halifax with mails, but was not heard from again, and was presumed to have foundered with all hands. Pay book closed 31 January.
[TNA: ADM.32/297; www.britishnewspaperarchive.co: *Morning Post* 9 January 1838 p4 and 17 April 1838 p4]

6 March PINCHER Schooner
Bermuda 1827; 118 tons; 62.8ft × 21.2ft; 3 guns
Lieutenant Thomas Hope†
Sailed from Chatham on 4 March in company with the *Volage* bound for Spithead, but the pair parted soon after. They met again during the afternoon of 6 March near the Owers light vessel, off Selsey Bill, and both vessels worked westwards, heading for the anchorage under a press of sail. At about 6.30pm, they were hit by a strong squall, which took the *Volage* aback, and she was in some confusion for a while, but wore round, shortened sail and recovered. It was then realised that the *Pincher* had disappeared. She searched the area for two hours but found nothing and it was presumed that she had capsized. A subsequent search found the submerged wreck, about three miles south-east of the Owers light vessel. The wreck was raised by the *Messenger* steamer on 4 June and towed back to Portsmouth, several bodies being recovered at the same time. She was not repaired, and the wreck was sold on 31 August.
[TNA: ADM.51/3702; www.britishnewspaperarchive.co: *The Morning Chronicle* 12 March 1838 p2]

12 April RAPID Brig Sloop
Portsmouth 1829; 231 tons; 90.1ft × 24.8ft; 10 guns
Lieutenant Honourable Graham Hay St Vincent de Ros Kinnaird†
Sailed from Tunis during the afternoon of 12 April to return to Malta and having set Cape Zaffan at 8 o'clock, altered course to the east-north-east. At 9 o'clock she struck the ground with some violence, shuddering for some time until she stopped. All sails were furled, an anchor was let go to hold her steady and boats lowered to sound round her and lay out an anchor. Initial attempts to haul her free failed, and a further attempt to lay out an anchor failed when the cutter carrying the bower anchor capsized. Guns were moved from forward to aft, water butts emptied and stores heaved overboard, but she would not move. The work went on through the night and the regular firing of distress guns attracted several local Tunisian vessels to their aid at first light. These assisted in taking off stores and provisions, which were landed on the shore nearby. Guns were next heaved overboard, each being buoyed for later recovery. At 11 o'clock in the morning she floated, and on heaving on the kedge anchor cable she came free, although she lost the rudder as she did so. She re-anchored, with rocks all around her, a spring being used to keep her free, whilst a boat was employed to find a channel out. At this time hopes were high that she could be saved, but during the afternoon the anchor cable parted, probably cut by the rocks, and when the spring also parted, she tailed onto the rocks again. The mainmast was cut away to ease her, but as they did so the last anchor cable parted and she swung broadside-on to the reef and was bilged, the sea beating over her. All the crew then left the wreck, setting up a tented camp on the shore and work went on for several days to land stores and provisions from the wreck. During the recovery of the guns on 20 April, a dinghy carrying Lieutenant Kinnaird capsized and he was drowned – the only casualty of the wreck. After salvaging most of the stores, the survivors left the scene on 9 May. A strong current was blamed for taking them onto a reef off Ras al Ahmar
[TNA: ADM.51/3370]

1839

29 November TRIBUNE Sixth Rate
Bursledon 1803; 884 tons; 137.1ft × 38.4ft; 26 guns
Captain Charles Hamlyn Williams
Laying at anchor off the port of Tarragona, Spain, the weather steadily worsened, and during 28 November, as the wind shifted round to the south-west and increased in strength, preparations were made for a gale, with topmasts being struck and the guns secured for bad weather. At 9.30pm, the small bower anchor cable parted, but the sheet anchor was promptly let go. The ship was pitching and rolling deeply and at 10.15pm the best bower anchor cable parted, followed minutes later by the sheet anchor and she found herself being driven across the anchorage in heavy seas, which broke over her. Attempts were made to make sail, but she could make little headway and was carried further inshore towards the beach. Some guns were heaved overboard but at midnight she grounded in shallow water. During the early hours of the morning, she continued to pound and at 2 o'clock an abandoned Spanish schooner was driven down onto her, damaging the side before it sank under her bows. At about 6 o'clock in the morning daylight revealed that she was on the beach at the head of the harbour, surrounded by wrecks and debris and during the morning steadily embedded herself in the sand. Attempts were made to haul her off, but she was

too severely damaged and over the next few days most of the stores and guns were successfully removed.
[TNA: ADM.5/13510; www.britishnewspaperarchive.co: Morning Chronicle 18 December 1839 p2]

1840

28 July BUFFALO   Store Ship
Purchased 1813 (*Hindostan*); 589 tons; 120ft x 33.6ft; 6 guns
Master James Wood

Having completing her loading of kauri wood, the *Buffalo* sailed from Mercury Bay, North Island, New Zealand on 25 July, but in thick, squally weather she was forced to return to the anchorage the following day. The weather worsened, with fresh gales and a rising swell. Yards and topmasts were struck, and extra anchors were laid out. During the early hours of 28 July, the wind increased to hurricane strength, and when two anchor cables parted, she started to drive across the anchorage towards the shore. She let go the stream anchor and this brought her up in four fathoms. The ship was being lifted and pounded by the waves and she was rolling so deeply that plans to heave the guns overboard had to be abandoned as it was too dangerous. It was hoped that she could be steered into the Mercury River, so the head sails and main trysail were set, and her head put inshore but almost immediately she ran aground. The boats were lowered and tried to make the shore through the surf, but the cutter, with a hawser in it, capsized drowning two men. Later that morning the ship worked herself free and the wind forced her over to the western side of the channel where she grounded, pieces of the keel being seen to float to the surface. She continued to be battered by the seas which washed over her. The stern was broken up by the constant beating of the sea, and a great quantity of sand was being washed into the ship. At daylight on 29 July a large number of Maori could be seen assisting those who had made it through the surf and gathering pile of wreckage. During the afternoon, it moderated somewhat and a Maori who was on board volunteered to swim ashore with a line, which was successfully achieved. This was made fast and during the afternoon and evening the ship was abandoned.
[TNA: ADM.5/13714; ADM.7/615]

27 September: Plymouth Dockyard Fire
At about 4.30am, a patrolling police officer in Devonport Dockyard saw smoke coming from the bow port holes of the *Talavera*, which was then lying 'in Ordinary' or reserve, in the Stern (or Head) Dock, Devonport. The alarm was raised, and engines were quickly deployed, but the fire had a firm hold, and within 10 minutes flames burst through the lower-deck ports. The fire rapidly spread to the roof which covered the dock and other buildings nearby causing widespread damage before it could be controlled. Several small buildings, 200 loads of stored timber and 1,000 deals were destroyed. It took a combined effort by dockyard workers, Marines, soldiers and seamen, who fought through the day to control the blaze and finally extinguished the fire in the evening. The cause was never properly ascertained, but careless disposal of combustible material in a bin of wood shavings or spontaneous combustion from a pile of shakings (unpicked shreds of old rope), were considered to be the most likely. Two ships were burnt to the waterline, the remains being broken up locally in October.
[www.britishnewspaperarchive.co: The Western Courier 30 September 1840 p2]

TALAVERA Third Rate
Woolwich 1818; 1,718 tons; 174ft x 48.3ft; 74 guns

IMOGENE Sixth Rate
Pembroke 1831; 660 tons; 125ft x 34.4ft; 28 guns

★ ★ ★

13 November FAIRY Brig Sloop
Chatham 1826; 233 tons; 90.2ft x 24.7ft; 10 guns
Captain William Hewett[†]

Employed in surveying the English east coast, she sailed from her anchorage off Orford during the evening of 12 November and was seen by Southwold fishermen the next morning in bad weather, with reefed topsails and staysails. The area was affected by gale-force winds at the time, and it was presumed that she foundered with all hands soon after this, as local fishermen reported sighting wreckage off Kessingland later that same day. Various items of wreckage, including masts and spars, identified as being from the *Fairy* were washed ashore on the Norfolk and Suffolk shore over the next few days.
[www.britishnewspaperarchive.co: Essex Standard 18 December 1840 p3; Nautical Magazine 1841 p129]

24 November SPEY Packet Brig
Pembroke 1827; 231 tons; 90ft x 24.6ft; 6 guns
Lieutenant Robert Bastard James

Sailed from Falmouth on 17 October, bound for Cuba and Mexico with mails, she arrived off Crooked Island in the Bahamas on 22 November. The following evening, she shaped a course through the Ragged Island group, steering between Raccoon Cay and Buena Vista Cay, believing the channel to be clear and well surveyed. The next morning the beacon on the highest point of Raccoon Cay could be seen and she shortened sail, and the lead-line was ordered to be used constantly. Whilst

running at about five knots, she had just sounded in nine fathoms, but before another cast could be made, she ran hard aground. Boats were hoisted out to carry out an anchor, water butts were emptied to lighten her, and in a fresh breeze more sail was set to try and drive her off the obstruction, but all failed, and that evening the guns and more stores were thrown overboard. The next day work continued to try and free her, with the masts cut away and anchors laid out to haul her free, but the ropes parted so during the afternoon a boat was sent away with the mails, and efforts were moved to set up a camp ashore and await rescue. During 27 November, to their surprise, the brig was seen to lift off the rocks of her own volition, and she was hastily boarded and steered into shallow water near the Cay. However, she was found to be full of water, beyond pumping and bailing, so she was run inshore until she grounded and lay on her larboard side. Both Lieutenant James and the Master, William Barrett, were severely reprimanded for taking the more hazardous passage, and ordered to be placed on the bottom of their respective seniority lists.
[TNA: ADM.51/3418]

2 December **ZEBRA** Brig Sloop

Bombay 1815; 385 tons; 100.3ft × 30.7ft; 18 guns
Commander Robert Fanshawe Stopford

One of the Allied squadron assembled off the coast of Syria, intervening in a dispute in the Ottoman Empire, she was anchored off Haifa, with several other ships. During 28–29 November the weather worsened, with rain, squalls and a heavy rolling sea, and topmasts were struck, and yards braced into the wind and another anchor laid out. The wind continued to increase, with frequent strong squalls, thunder and lightning. During the morning of 2 December, the wind shifted round, to blow directly into the anchorage and at 10.30am the small bower anchor cable parted, and at noon another anchor cable was lost. She was now driving, with a heavy sea breaking over her, and when, at 1 o'clock the sheet anchor cable broke she was forced to make signals of distress, hoisting the ensign upside down. Some guns were heaved overboard, and a hawser was bent to two guns which were lashed together and let go as an anchor, but they did not bring her up. The seas were now breaking over her and with the wind blowing her directly onshore it was inevitable that she would strand. That evening the remaining, useless, cables were cut and she was steered for the shoal water inside some rocks nearby. After striking several times on the bottom, she ran onto the beach in the breaking surf. Three men attempted to escape by jumping into the gig, but this promptly overset, drowning all of them, the only casualties. The crew endured the night as the ship continued to strike heavily, but at daylight a cable was successfully veered out to the shore and secured, and the foreyard placed over the gunwale which allowed all the crew to escape.
[TNA: ADM.51/3547; Nautical Magazine 1841 p94]

1841

1 June **SKIPJACK** Schooner

Bermuda 1827; 118 tons; 62.8ft × 21.2ft; 3 guns
Lieutenant Augustus Charles May

Cruising off Grand Cayman Island, she unexpectedly ran aground, and after it was found that she would not move, the Master was put on board a merchant schooner which had arrived on the scene, to reach Jamaica, and the schooner *Hornet* was despatched to render assistance. *Hornet* arrived on 14 June, to find the *Skipjack* hard aground on the South West Cays, and an inspection the following day showed that it would be impossible to get her free. The stores and guns were removed, and she was abandoned as a wreck on 16 June. It emerged that Lieutenant May had been unable to obtain any sights or observations for 24 hours, owing to heavy weather, and in consequence was 12 miles out in his reckoning. This, along with a strong current, was blamed for the wreck.
[TNA: ADM.51/3611; www.britishnewspaperarchive.co; Naval and Military Gazette 21 August 1841 p5]

21 July **LOUISA** Cutter

Purchased 1834; 83 tons
Mate Lord Amelius Wentworth Beauclerk

Sailed from Macao on 20 July in company with the *Young Hebe* schooner, with Admiral Sir James Bremer and Captain Charles Elliot embarked, after negotiations with the colonial authorities, to return to Hong Kong. The weather became dull, calm and sultry after sailing and the cutter anchored off the island of Lantau. That evening the breeze steadily freshened into a gale, with very heavy rain showers, presaging the arrival of a typhoon. By the early hours of the morning, they were experiencing strong winds and incessant rain and were being driven onto the shore. To avoid going aground the *Louisa* slipped her cables and attempted to make sail out to sea. During this manoeuvre the Master, Mr Owen, was washed overboard and drowned. The cutter twice narrowly avoided rocks before being driven ashore on a small island – variously stated to be 'Myloo' or 'Kowlan' – near Macao. All the crew and passengers safely made it to safety but were detained. On the payment of a ransom of $3,000 all were released and taken to Macao.
[www.britishnewspaperarchive.co: Morning Post 5 November 1841 p3; Nautical Magazine 1841 p859]

1842

(5/6) September VICTOR Brig Sloop
Bombay 1814; 382 tons; 100ft × 30.6ft; 18 guns
Commander Charles Cooke Otway†
Sailed from Tampico, Mexico, on 2 September, bound for Jamaica, but was never seen again. It was presumed that she foundered with all hands. A tropical storm passed through the area on 5–6 September and may have been responsible for her loss.
[www.britishnewspaperarchive.co: Hampshire Telegraph 9 January 1843 p4]

10 September SPITFIRE Steam Paddle Vessel
Woolwich 1834; 550 tons; 155ft × 27.6ft; 4 guns
Lieutenant Hay Erskine Shipley Winthrop
Having embarked several troops of the 3rd West India Regiment, with their families, bound for Belize, Honduras, she sailed from Jamaica on 5 September. At 10.40pm, five days later, breakers were reported ahead, and despite the helm being put over to starboard and the engines stopped, she ran aground. All sail was taken in and to free herself the engines were put astern, but she was held fast. Anchors were let go to hold her steady in the surf which was breaking around her, the foremast was cut away and the cutter launched, but it was swamped as soon as it reached the water. Water was reported to be entering the hold and the troops were set to work pumping and bailing, but the water slowly gained, there being 6ft of water in the hold by 4 o'clock in the morning. The ship was now thumping heavily in the surf and the mainmast was cut away in a further effort to ease her. The gig was successfully launched at daybreak and was sent away to Half Moon Key to bring assistance, the crew remaining on board to construct rafts. One of the rafts was floated through the surf to the reef visible nearby and a line secured between the shore and the ship. The raft was then used throughout the day to carry the men ashore, all having left the wreck by 6 o'clock that evening. The following day (12 September), daylight revealed that the funnel had gone, and she was breaking up. Several boats arrived during the day to take off the survivors, the wreck being abandoned on 14 September. The loss was blamed on a strong current, which took them onto the northern Two Keys reef off Belize.
[TNA: ADM.51/3739]

1843

4 March MEGAERA Steam Paddle Sloop
Sheerness 1837; 716 tons; 150ft × 32.5ft; 4 guns
Lieutenant George Oldmixon
Sailed from Port Royal, Jamaica, during the late afternoon, bound for Vera Cruz, Mexico, with the British Chargé d'Affaires on board, and only three hours later, after dropping the pilot, breakers were unexpectedly reported ahead. At the time the paddles were turning, and the foresail, mainsail and jibs were set. The helm was put over, but she ran heavily aground. Boats were lowered to sound around her and lay out anchors, but she was found to be filling with water and little could be done to save her. The Master's Assistant, Mr Loane, in charge of the cutter, succeeded in attracting the attention of a local vessel which took him back to Port Royal, from where the *Avon* steamer was despatched to the scene, which arrived the following morning. During the boat-work one boat capsized, drowning a boy, the only casualty. Distress guns were fired, and engines kept going astern, but she would not move and was abandoned as a wreck. A strong current was blamed for setting her inshore and taking her onto Bare Bush Key. Lieutenant Oldmixon was admonished to be more careful in the future, and Mr Thomas Griffiths, the Second Master, was severely reprimanded.
[TNA: ADM 51/3636; www.britishnewspaperarchive.co: London Evening Standard 21 April 1843 p3]

24 July LIZARD Steam Paddle Vessel
Woolwich 1840; 283 tons; 120ft × 22.6ft; 3 guns
Lieutenant Charles James Postle
Having sailed from Gibraltar, bound for Barcelona, the *Lizard* was steaming along the southern coast of Spain, when at just before 1 o'clock in the morning, a light was observed two points (22½ degrees) off the port bow. The distance was estimated to be about four miles, and as a precaution, course was altered to starboard. The officer of the watch, Gunner's Mate John Attwood, went onto the port paddle box to better see the light and realised that it was a ship and closer than they had thought. Mr Hall, the Second Master, came on deck at this time and was horrified to see a ship about 150 yards away. Both Attwood and Hall shouted orders to put the helm hard-a-port, but before the order could take effect the steamer was struck on the port side, demolishing the paddle box, and throwing her over onto her starboard side. The Engineer below hastily blew steam and manned the pumps, but the engine room was already flooding and was quickly evacuated. Shouted exchanges between the ships established that the stranger was the French warship *Véloce*, which was now backing away, with several of the crew of *Lizard* jumping on board as she did so. Some boats were lowered and these, with the boats of the French ship, took off most of the crew. Lieutenant Postle entertained some hopes now that the steamer might be saved, and he returned on board with the Senior Engineer to examine her and a tow line was passed. However, she was found to be filling quickly and was rolling deeply as she settled lower in the water. The towing crew left her, believing the ship was empty, but when shouts were heard they

returned, to take off the Captain's steward, who had been asleep below, unaware of the disaster. He was taken off just before she foundered, it then being 2.20am, her position being 37.08N, 01.18W. No blame was placed on any of the officers, but Midshipman Daniel Slaughter was found to have left the deck before being properly relieved and was ordered to lose two years' seniority.
[TNA: ADM 51/3627; www.britishnewspaperarchive.co: Hampshire Telegraph 18 September 1843 p3]

1844

January SOUDAN Steam Paddle Vessel
Birkenhead 1840; 249 tons; 110ft × 22ft; 1 gun
Built to support an expedition along the river Niger in West Africa, from 1842 she was based at Sierra Leone and employed as a tender to the anti-slavery squadron. Whilst proceeding up the Sierra Leone River with some detachments of troops on board, she got aground, and was written off as a wreck.
[www.britishnewspaperarchive.co: London Evening Standard 15 April 1844 p1]

1845

25 April SKYLARK Packet Brig
Pembroke 1826; 235 tons; 90ft × 24.8ft; 4 guns
Lieutenant George Morris
Sailed from Plymouth on 23 April with volunteers for the Navy, bound for Spithead, there was little wind as the brig steered up Channel, and the brig had all plain sail set, as well as royals and studding sails. Lieutenant Morris was confined to his cabin with a severe and agonizing attack of gout, and this led to the Master, William Crane, taking charge of the passage. During the morning of 25 April, she found herself in very thick fog, the men on the quarterdeck barely seeing the bowsprit. Crane did not seem concerned and continued under all sail. He did not order the lead-line to be cast and indeed, left the deck. At 10 o'clock in the morning she ran hard aground on the Coalpit ledge off Kimmeridge, on the coast of Dorset. All sail was thrown aback, but she would not move. One of the guns was hove overboard and water butts were emptied to lighten her, and boats were lowered to try and lay out an anchor, but the heavy surf made this impossible. The surf drove them further onto the ledge, the waves beating over the stern. As the ebb tide left her, it was clear that she could not be saved and she was abandoned with difficulty, assistance being given by boats from the shore. She later capsized onto her port side. The Master, William Crane, was found guilty of gross neglect and dismissed the service.
[TNA: ADM.1/5558]

1846

11 March OSPREY Brig Sloop
Portsmouth 1844; 425 tons; 101.6ft × 31.6ft; 12 guns
Commander Frederick Patten
Stationed in New Zealand, the sloop was ordered to Hokianga to give support to the local settlers, and in thick and hazy weather the land around Hokianga was raised on 10 March. She stood off from the land until the following morning, by which time the visibility had cleared. A high headland was visible and identified as Hokianga and what was thought to be the pilot's house could be seen, so the brig confidently stood on towards the entrance to the bay. It therefore came as a surprise when at 3 o'clock in the afternoon she struck the ground. It was initially believed that she had struck the sandbar, and they attempted to sail over the obstruction, but she struck again with some force with a series of violent shocks. It was now realised that she was at the entrance to Haerekino, or False Hokianga. Guns were heaved overboard and the masts cut away, which fell towards the nearby beach. The crew remained on board until the following morning, when they used the fallen masts to reach the shore. Most of the stores were salvaged over the next few days, the crew being assisted by the local Maoris. Hopes were entertained that the brig might be re-floated, but she was found to be wedged between rocks and surrounded by shallow water. The wreck was caused by mistaking the headlands of two remarkably similar bays.
[TNA: ADM.1/5558; ADM 53/2862; www.paperspast.natlib. govt.nz: Auckland New Zealander 28 March 1846 p2]

23 December DISPATCH Hulk
Purchased 1798 (*Cornwallis*); 172 tons; 77ft × 23ft
An old merchant vessel, purchased for use as a transport and stores vessel, she was hulked at Bermuda in 1820 and variously employed as a slops ship, diving bell vessel and sheer hulk. She apparently foundered at her anchors. Her remains were ordered to be broken up in February 1847.
[Sigwart p39]

1847

3 February THUNDERBOLT Steam Paddle Sloop
Portsmouth 1842; 1,056 tons; 180ft × 36ft; 7 guns
Commander Alexander Boyle
Having sailed from Simon's Bay, the steamer was steering along the coast of South Africa, but as she rounded Cape Recife to enter Algoa Bay, at about 6 o'clock in the evening she unexpectedly ran aground with considerable violence. The engine room reported

extensive flooding and within 10 minutes the floor of the engine room was submerged. Pumping and bailing was commenced but the water gained at a rapid rate. To save the crew it was decided to run the sloop ashore, which was soon accomplished, on a beach to the south of Baakens River. The crew moved ashore, and a tented encampment was set up while work went on to pump her free of water. The guns were hoisted out, stores landed and the starboard coal bunker emptied, but all was in vain, no impression being made on the level of water as she steadily settled further into the sand. Assistance was rendered by the *President* and *Eurydice* but by 21 May it was clear that her injuries were such that even if she were cleared and hauled off, she would founder. She was abandoned on 24 May. Captain Boyle and the Master, James Dundas Milne, came in for considerable criticism at the subsequent court martial. It was found that they had '… trusted to their eyes and ignored the charts and sailing instructions'. Both were ordered to be dismissed from the service, although this was tempered by a recommendation that the Admiralty might wish to reconsider this order because of their long and consistent exertions after the wreck.
[TNA: ADM.1/5586]

29 August SNAKE Brig Sloop
Limehouse 1832; 434 tons; 101.10ft × 32.4ft; 16 guns
Commander Thomas Bourmaster Brown

Part of the British anti-slavery squadron in the Indian Ocean, her cruising station was in the Mozambique Channel. Intending to return to the island of Mozambique for fresh water and provisions, she closed the coast, and land was sighted shortly after noon and course shaped to the north-east. A cast of the lead-line during the afternoon found no bottom. She stood on until about 7 o'clock that evening, when, with no warning, she ran hard aground, a cast of the lead finding 15 fathoms shortly before. An initial attempt to sail off the obstruction failed, so all sail was furled. Boats were hoisted out and preparations made to lay out anchors and heave the guns overboard. She steadily took a list to port and water was reported entering and the Carpenter reported that she had taken so much damage, that if she were hauled free of the ground, then she would undoubtedly sink. At this, preparations were made to leave and at first light the crew were taken to the nearby shore, most of the stores and provisions being saved. It was found that she had been wrecked about five miles from the Mozambique shore on a bank between Sancoul Point (Ponta Sancul) and St Jago Island (Ilha das Cobras), '… due to a lack of care and attention'. Despite steering along the coast at night, where strong currents could be expected, the constant use of the lead-line had not been ordered. Commander Brown had been confined to his cabin with a rheumatic fever but had refused to delegate sufficient responsibility to the First Lieutenant. Both Commander Brown and the Master, Peter Chown, were ordered to lose one year's seniority.
[TNA: ADM.1/5586]

20 December AVENGER Steam Paddle Frigate
Devonport 1845; 1,444 tons; 210ft × 39ft; 10 guns
Captain Charles George Elers Napier†

Steering east along the North African coast, bound for Malta, the frigate had one boiler lit and paddles turning, with foresail and double-reefed topsails spread. She was travelling at about eight knots when at 10 o'clock at night, with little warning, she violently struck the ground, the shock being followed by a heavy, lazy roll, the frigate shuddering constantly until she stopped, her head swinging round to the south to expose her beam to the sea. Minutes after she had struck, she rolled slowly over to starboard, the foremast, mainmast and funnel all going overboard. Clouds of steam poured out from below as the water rushed in to douse the boiler. Despite the difficult conditions two boats were launched and men jumped into them, although both were swamped as the ship capsized over to lay on her beam-ends. Eight of the survivors managed to right one of the boats and after staying by the wreck for most of the night, they left the scene to make for the shore visible nearby. As they approached the beach, the surf caught them and capsized the boat, drowning four men. The only four to make the beach alive, Lieutenant Francis Rooke, the Gunner, John Larcom, the Captain's Steward, and a boy were the only survivors from a crew of 270. It was found that she had been wrecked on the Sorelli (or Sorelle) Rocks, and at the time no reason could be found for the loss, a search by the *Hecate* failing to find the wreck. However, in June 1850, a French warship, the *Roberach*, commanded by Enseigne de Vaisseau Bouchet-Rivière, surveyed the area and discovered the wreck in position 37.24 N, 08.36 E. Rivière judged that Captain Napier had not allowed for a strong north-westerly current which must have taken the ship onto the reef. He continued '… her first blow must have been terrific. It took place on the south-west part of the north-west rock, leaving a huge white furrow on it; about a quarter of a cable's length further on, she struck the south-east rock, which has not more than one fathom on it, and sank, leaving a conspicuous mark.'
[TNA: ADM.1/5586; Nautical Magazine 1850 p434]

1848

The Franklin Expedition

During the century, several expeditions were mounted to explore the northern coast of Canada, and another was despatched in May 1845 under the command of Sir John Franklin. The two ships under his command crossed Baffin's Bay and Melville Bay, where they were seen by a whaling ship on 28 July, but this was the last time that they were seen by Europeans. It was later established that the pair had explored the Wellington Channel and had wintered in 1845–6 at Beechey Island in Lancaster Sound. Resuming their work in the spring of 1846 they headed west into Barrow Strait and then south around Prince of Wales Island, probably by the Peel Strait. On 12 September 1846, they were halted by thick pack ice off Cape Felix, King William Island. Here they remained for the winter of 1846–7, locked into the ice, although local sledging operations were carried out. The ice did not clear in the following spring as expected, and the ships remained frozen in during 1847, Sir John Franklin dying in June. By the spring of 1848, with the ships still in ice, the expedition was clearly facing a crisis and the last positive evidence as to their fate was discovered in a note later found in a cairn, stating that 105 men were leaving the ships on 26 April 1848. At home, no anxiety was felt for the expedition until 1848, when the first of the search parties was despatched. Several subsequent searches were mounted, with no result. Not until 1854 did news come from the Hudson's Bay Company that Dr John Rae had recovered several items from the local Inuit, including silver cutlery, identified as belonging to the Franklin expedition. In the spring of 1857, a private search party was sailed to explore King William Island and during 1858 this expedition finally found traces of Franklin and his ships, with the discovery of the note in the cairn, and a trail of objects leading south, including skeletons and the remains of one of the boats, which had evidently been used as a sledge. In more recent years, expeditions have recovered more objects from the ships and traces of the lost men. Whether all died during 1848 during a doomed attempt to try and gain the distant outposts of the Hudson's Bay Company, or whether some remained or returned to the ships is uncertain, although some native testimony could suggest that some men may have been alive during 1849. A major step was achieved in 2014 with the discovery of one of the ships, identified as the *Erebus*, and during 2016 the remains of *Terror* were located.

22 April EREBUS Discovery Ship
Pembroke 1826; 372 tons; 105ft × 28.6ft
Captain James FitzJames†
In September 2014, an expedition by Parks Canada located one of the ships with side-scan sonar and subsequent examination identified the wreck as being the *Erebus*. The ship is in good condition and lies at the bottom of the eastern end of Queen Maud Gulf, to the west of O'Reilly Island.

22 April TERROR Discovery Ship
Topsham 1813; 333 tons; 102.4ft × 27.3ft
Captain Francis Rawden Moira Crozier†
The wreck of *Terror* was discovered in September 2016 lying in Terror Bay, Nunavut, about 100km north of the *Erebus*. The remains were reported to be in good condition, with the ship showing signs of having been secured for surviving in the ice rather than in a seagoing condition.
[Various secondary sources]

★ ★ ★

21 December MUTINE Brig Sloop
Chatham 1844; 428 tons; 101.11ft × 31.10ft; 12 guns
Commander John Jervis Palmer
Ordered to Venice, northern Italy, the sloop anchored off the port on 15 December, Commander Palmer proceeding ashore the same day, leaving the First Lieutenant Alfred Curtis in command. During 20 December, the wind shifted to the east and gained in strength, until by 8 o'clock that evening it was blowing a gale. She weighed and shifted her position to anchor off Malamocco. The weather continued to worsen, the wind increasing to storm force 10, and it became bitterly cold. At three o'clock in the afternoon the best bower anchor cable parted, but the prompt release of the small bower held her fast. Topgallant yards and masts were struck, and the port waist anchor let go, secured to the remains of the best bower cable. At just before 11 o'clock the small bower cable parted, and she drove for some distance before the waist anchor brought her up. Topmasts were now struck, but whilst this was being done the waist anchor cable parted and she drove across the anchorage. The fore and mainmasts were cut away and after clearing the wreckage the stream anchor was let go, with a chain cable. This brought her up, and to secure her position, both shell guns, weighing 39cwt each, were secured to hawsers and heaved overboard to act as anchors. This makeshift arrangement held her steady in winds now gusting up to storm force eleven, with a great rolling sea. Guns were fired during the night and the colours hoisted upside down at first light as distress signals, but little could be done from the shore to help her. At 1 o'clock in the afternoon the

port shell gun hawser parted, and she started to drag her remaining anchors, and soon after this she struck the ground aft. All guns were heaved overboard, followed by the shot, which lifted her clear of the obstruction, but she drifted nearer the shore. In a final effort to save herself the hemp hawser was cut, and the chain cable slipped, and sail spread on the stumps of the masts to gain sea room. However, she could make little headway, and at 2.30pm she ran aground and started beating heavily on the rocks, little more than 200 yards from the shore, her head swinging round to the north. A jolly boat was launched and attempted to make the shore, but this capsized, drowning the Mate, George Whitby. A hawser was successfully floated ashore, where it was secured, and this was used to haul men to safety. One man was drowned when he slipped from the bowline. By nightfall, another man had died from the cold, but all had been rescued apart from five men, and this little party, which included Lieutenant Curtis, spent the night on board the wreck in freezing temperatures and with waves constantly breaking over them. Daylight found two of them dead from exposure. The rescue efforts recommenced at first light, and at 10.30am Lieutenant Curtis left the wreck, the last man to do so.
[TNA: ADM.53/2813]

1850

April ADELAIDE Schooner Tender
Purchased 1848; 140 tons
Lieutenant John Lyons MacLeod
Serving as a tender to the anti-slavery squadron based at Sierra Leone, West Africa, she was in poor condition, but was ordered to patrol near the Banana Islands. Several leaks became evident and became so dangerous that it was decided to beach the schooner for the safety of the crew. On inspection it was found that the hull was so severely affected by the Teredo shipworm that the hull was completely eaten through in several places, and she was abandoned as a wreck.
[www.britishnewspaperarchive.co: Portsmouth Times 24 August 1850 p8]

22 November FLAMER Steam Paddle Gun Vessel
Limehouse 1831; 510 tons; 155.3ft x 26.5ft; 6 guns
Commander James Aldworth St Leger
Bound for Monrovia with despatches for the President of Liberia, she found the coastline obscured by fog. By 8 o'clock in the evening she believed herself to be off Cape Mesurado, which marked the entrance to the harbour and a light was observed soon after this, which was believed to be the light on the Cape. Course was therefore altered to steer towards the anchorage, but the fog again obscured the light and the shore. At 9pm, breakers were reported ahead. Engines were put full astern and all sail thrown aback, but two minutes after the sighting she struck the ground. Both anchors were let go to hold her, and guns, shot and stores were heaved overboard to lighten her. At 11.30pm the mist lifted to show the shore just 150 yards away. A boat made the hazardous trip through the surf with a hawser, and this enabled a series of boat trips through the night landing the crew. When all were safely landed, the despatches were sent overland to Monrovia, with a request for assistance. The crew set up a defended camp on the beach. Work went on for several weeks to take off more stores and to free her, but she was held fast, the final efforts being made by the French warship *Eldorado*, which, in December, unsuccessfully attempted to haul her off. The wreck was finally abandoned on 8 January 1851. On 28 November, during the stay on the beach, one of the ship's Royal Marines shot dead one of the Kroomen (native seaman), one Jim Crow, when he failed to give the correct password on returning to the camp. At the subsequent courts martial, it was accepted that the details of the Cape light laid down in sailing directions was incorrect and the light seen was not the Cape Mesurado light, but probably a fire ashore, which lead them to steer a fatal course. Commander St Leger was reprimanded for continuing to close the coast at night whilst in fog and was admonished to be more careful in the future. Marine Elam was cleared of any blame for the shooting of the Krooman.
[TNA: ADM.53/1874; www.britishnewspaperarchive.co: Morning Post 24 March 1851 p3]

1851

31 May REYNARD Steam Sloop
Deptford 1848; 516 tons; 147ft x 27.10ft; 8 guns
Commander Peter Cracroft
On 27 May the Master of the brig *Velocipede* arrived at Hong Kong to report that his vessel had been wrecked on shoals near Pratas Island (Dongsha Dao) in the South China Sea, and several of the crew were still on the desolate island. The following day the *Reynard* was despatched with the sloop *Pilot* to proceed to the area and rescue the survivors. That night the pair parted company but proceeded independently. The weather was overcast, and no observations were possible the following day, but the noon observation on 30 May showed they were 45 miles from the island. They proceeded under easy sail and steam, estimating that they would be about 25 miles from the shoals at daylight. At 4 o'clock in the morning, the watch had just changed, and she was steering east-south-east under steam and sail, when a line of dirty, oily-looking water was seen ahead and a few minutes later lookouts

shouted warnings. Engines were put astern and sail thrown aback, but this failed to stop her before she struck a reef. This proved to be the south-east corner of the Pratas Shoal. Boats were hoisted out, but not before the ship had swung broadside-on to the rocks. Kedge anchors and a stream anchor were taken out to haul her free, but the hawsers of the kedges snagged on the rocks and parted. The stream anchor cable held, but the anchor fell into deep water and could not be used for kedging. An attempt was made to use a bower anchor, but it was found that could not be carried out due to the shallowness of the water. At 9 o'clock topmasts and yards were struck, and a party was sent to the nearby island with provisions. Work continued in efforts to free her, engine work being combined with heaving on the stream anchor cable throughout the day, but to no effect. The surf was by now becoming extremely high, and the sloop started pounding heavily on the rocks. By 11am, the engines were disabled by the constant surging and 30 minutes later she bilged under the boilers on the starboard side and started filling with water. The stream anchor cable was cut which enabled her to fall back onto the rocks. Guns and heavy stores were heaved overboard to lighten her, provisions were rescued from the water and a raft was constructed. Early the next morning with the water over the lower-deck hatch combings, the crew started to move ashore, setting up a camp on the island, joining the survivors from the *Velocipede*. Later that day a heavy surf washed over the wreck, canting her over onto her beam-ends and carrying away much of the stores stowed on the upper deck. The *Pilot* arrived off the island the following day and took off all the crew, and the survivors of the *Velocipede*. A strong current was blamed for the loss, but Commander Cracroft and the Master, Henry McAusland, were found to have been guilty of an error of judgement by approaching the shoal from the south-east where it was known there was a steep rise, and not employing a leadsman. Both were deemed to be 'deserving of censure' for failing to take proper precautions.

[*Nautical Magazine* 1852 pp202–15; www.britishnewspaperarchive.co: *Hampshire Telegraph* 18 October 1851 p5]

1852

26 February BIRKENHEAD Paddle Troopship
Birkenhead 1845; 1,405 tons; 210ft × 37.6ft; 4 guns
Master Robert Salmond†
The troopship sailed from Cork on 7 January bound for South Africa with detachments of troops from several regiments, under the command of Colonel Alexander Seaton of the 74th (Highland) Regiment, along with twenty-five women and thirty-one children. After touching at Cape Town, she sailed on 25 February for Algoa Bay to land the troops. A few minutes before 2am, when travelling at about eight knots, without warning she struck an uncharted rock in False Bay. The concussion was heavy, ripping a hole under the foremast and allowing water to pour into the fore part of the ship, which probably drowned many of the soldiers asleep on the lower troop deck. Engines were stopped and the small bower anchor let go to hold the ship steady, and boats were ordered to be hoisted out. The troops were ordered to fall in, and they quietly lined up on the quarterdeck. Parties of soldiers assisted with the lowering of the boats and others commenced throwing the horses overboard. The engines were put astern to pull her free, but this only had the effect of ripping a large hole in the hull under the engine room, which started to flood. The women and children were ordered into the boats and the cutter was successfully sent away fully loaded. The ship was now breaking up, with the bows separating from the main body of the hull, the bowsprit going upwards towards the foremast and the funnel and foremast going overboard. This prevented any further efforts at lowering boats – only the two cutters and a gig being in the water. With the bows broken off, the forward part of the ship began to sink and within a few minutes it had disappeared. The troops still lined up on the upper deck were ordered to 'Stand fast' by Colonel Seaton as the ship broke up and they remained in this formation as the ship foundered. Several men then clambered onto the main topmast which remained above water, whilst others clung to the boats and sought wreckage to hold on to. The boats, overloaded with survivors, pulled for Simonstown but were picked up by the schooner *Lioness* just after daylight. The schooner proceeded to the site of the wreck and lifted off forty men found clinging to the mainmast. About sixty-five men managed to struggle ashore clinging to spars or wreckage, having to contend with several sharks attracted to the area. In all 438 men died in the disaster and 193 people survived, including all the women and children.

[*Nautical Magazine* 1852 pp277–81; www.britishnewspaperarchive.co: *Hampshire Telegraph* 8 May 1852 p7; *Hampshire Advertiser* 8 May 1852 p6]

1853

3 June INVESTIGATOR Discovery Ship
Purchased 1848; 422 tons; 118ft × 28.3ft
Captain Robert John Le Mesurier McClure
The *Investigator* was purchased to pursue the exploration of northern Canada and later participated in the efforts to discover what had happened to Sir John Franklin's expedition. She had conducted an exploratory voyage

in 1848–9 and in 1850 she was commissioned to search from the Pacific, through the Bering Strait and the Beaufort Sea. She reached the western coast of Bank's Island in the Canadian Arctic until she was surrounded by thick ice, but she managed to push on until September 1850 when she came to a halt. Here she stayed, locked into the ice, with the crew engaging in sledging expeditions, often covering large distances. In July 1851 with the thawing of the ice she resumed her efforts to head further eastward, but progress was slow, and in September she entered Mercy Bay, Bank's Island, and prepared for another winter, with more sledging expeditions. The summer of 1852 failed to free the bay of ice, and by the winter the crew were showing signs of scurvy and general debilitation. Three members of the crew died of scurvy in early 1853, and it was a considerable relief when a party from the *Resolute* arrived, having discovered notes left in a cairn by a sledging party. Only nine men were fit for duty, and Captain Kellett of the *Resolute* ordered McClure to abandon his ship, which was left in the ice on 3 June.

Note: in July 2010, a team from Parks Canada located the remains of the *Investigator* sitting upright in 11m of water in Mercy Bay.
[TNA:ADM.1/5645]

1854

12 May TIGER Steam Paddle Frigate
Chatham 1849; 1,221 tons; 205ft × 35.11ft; 16 guns
Captain Henry Wells Gifford†

Part of the Allied force blockading Sevastopol in the Crimea, on 11 May she was ordered to cruise off the port of Odessa, in company with two other steamers. By the afternoon, she was to the south of the town in poor weather, with thick fog masking both her consorts and the land. At just before midnight soundings showed her to be in 16 fathoms, and she confidently stood on, steaming at 8 knots. At 4 o'clock in the morning soundings still showed 16 fathoms, but then shallowing to 14. Concerned at this, the officer of the watch ordered another cast, which showed only 13 fathoms, and at the same time a brief gap in the fog revealed land on the starboard bow. Speed was immediately checked, and soundings ordered to be taken constantly. The casts showed a steadily shallowing bottom, from 13 down to 7 fathoms. Only minutes after the last report the ship went aground, gaps in the fog revealing that she was ashore under a steep cliff. The engines were put astern, and the gaff mainsail, spanker and inner jib were set to try and free her, but she was held fast. The sponson boats were lowered to carry out an anchor and signal guns were fired to attract the attention of her consorts. The foremost guns were moved aft, and a small bower anchor was laid out from forward to the port quarter and the combined efforts of engine and heaving on the capstan moved her, slewing her stern round over 20 degrees, but her bows were still held fast. Hopes were high that she could be freed, and Captain Gifford ordered other boats lowered to start taking out ballast, coals and shot to lighten her. As this was going on the fog lifted and a Russian soldier appeared on horseback, who fired a musket at the ship before galloping off. Soon after this more troops arrived and commenced firing at her. These were joined by two field guns which opened fire. The ship's guns had been prepared for jettisoning, but the pivot gun was employed to return the fire, whilst work to lighten her continued, with some of the guns being heaved overboard. When another four field guns joined the enemy troops, and large numbers of infantry and cavalry were seen in the area, it was clear that resistance was futile. The *Tiger* was being hulled by enemy shot regularly, with fires started and casualties mounting. Captain Gifford had his left leg shot away as he stood next to the pivot gun. The *Tiger* struck her flag in surrender, the men landing ashore to be taken prisoner. The ship had grounded about five miles south of Odessa. Total casualties were five killed and three wounded, the dead included Captain Gifford who died of his wounds on 1 June. The subsequent court martial acquitted the senior survivor, Lieutenant Alfred Royer, but found the Master, Francis Edington, guilty of a want of caution by continuing to steam on through the thick fog in shallowing water. He was severely reprimanded. Some criticism was also levelled at Captain Gifford for the measures to heave her off. The sails set did nothing to free her; the anchor laid out was poorly placed and finally the ballast, coals and shot could have been tipped overboard from the ship, not laboriously loaded into the boats.
[TNA:ADM.1/5671]

15 May JASPER Steam Paddle Packet
Acquired 1837 (*Aladdin*); 223 tons; 112.6ft × 21.4ft; 1 gun
Lieutenant Charles Gibbs Crawley

The packet sailed from Plymouth for the Downs on 14 May. At 6 o'clock the next morning, then being off the Sussex coast, the engine room requested permission to clean out the fireplaces. This was granted, but about 40 minutes later clouds of smoke issued from the after doors of the funnel casing. This was thought at first to be from loose timber stowed in the funnel wings, but the engineer discovered that the bulkhead between the engine room and boiler rooms was on fire. All hands were turned up and firefighting efforts started, stokers using a manual pump in the engine room, the seamen using buckets on the upper deck. The fire had a firm hold and the smoke drove the stokers back and soon filled the ship. Boats were ordered to be hoisted out and

one hour after the fire had been discovered the ship was abandoned. The boats stood off a little way, and when the fire seemed to diminish somewhat, Lieutenant Crawley attempted to return. As he came alongside the mainmast burst into flames and part of the upper deck collapsed, forcing him to sheer off and leave her. At 9.30 the after part of the vessel blew up with a loud explosion and the forward part sank shortly afterwards. The boats were towed into Brighton by the merchant ship *Vanguard* of Liverpool. The exact cause of the blaze could not be determined, although the proximity of the bulkhead to the boilers, just 18in, was thought to be probable.
[TNA: ADM.1/5645]

The Franklin Search Expedition 1854

In 1852 another expedition to search for the missing Sir John Franklin was despatched to the Canadian Arctic under the command of Sir Edward Belcher. The mission was divided, with the *Resolute* and *Intrepid* exploring along the Barrow Strait and Melville Island, whilst *Assistance* and *Pioneer* searched along the Wellington Channel and the *North Star* was to stay at Beechey Island as a supply base.

15 May RESOLUTE Discovery Ship
Purchased 1850 (*Ptarmigan*); 424 tons; 115ft × 28.4ft
Captain Sir Henry Kellett

The *Resolute*, with her steam tender, the *Intrepid*, explored around Melville Island and then spent the winter of 1852–3 in the ice, sending sledging parties to explore the region. During 1853 when the ice broke up, the pair moved eastwards, before being brought to a halt on 10 September by thick ice and drifted a little with the pack until early November, about 28 miles to the south-west of Cape Cockburn, Bathurst Island. In the spring of 1854, with the ice still thick, Sir Edward Belcher decided to abandon the ships, being concerned that they would not be able to break free. Captain Kellett objected, pointing out that the ships were sound and there was plenty of provisions left. On 21 April Belcher wrote to give him a direct order to abandon the *Resolute* and the tender, and they were left on 15 May, being abandoned in good order, hatches battened down, yards on deck, sails bent.

Note: she eventually floated free and was discovered in September 1855 by the American whaler *George Henry*, about 1,200 miles from where she was abandoned and eventually restored to the Royal Navy in December 1856.
[TNA: ADM.1/5645; ADM.101/105/1]

15 May INTREPID Discovery Ship
Purchased 1850 (*Free Trade*); 342 tons; 143.6ft × 32.9ft
Captain Francis Leopold McLintock

Tender to the *Resolute*, she accompanied her on her travels in the area of Melville and Bathurst Islands in the Canadian Arctic. During the 1853 sledging operations, McLintock was responsible for discovering Port Patrick Island. The ship was ordered to be abandoned by Sir Edward Belcher, and was left, in good order, on 15 May, the crews of the ships marching across the ice to the *Assistance*.
[TNA: ADM.1/5645; ADM.101/105/1]

25 August ASSISTANCE Discovery Ship
Purchased 1850 (*Baboo*); 423 tons; 117.4ft × 28.5ft; 2 guns
Commander George Henry Richards

Flagship of the expedition under Sir Edward Belcher which set out in 1852 to search for the lost ships of Sir John Franklin. Belcher, with his tender, the *Pioneer*, worked along the Wellington Channel and then spent the winter of 1852–3 iced up in the Northumberland Inlet. As on all such expeditions, parties were sent on sledges to explore the area, both mapping and to look for signs of Franklin. Teams from the *Assistance* and *Pioneer* mapped Bathurst Island and the area but failed to find any trace of the missing Franklin. During the summer of 1853, the ships moved further along the Wellington Channel before being stopped in the ice. In the spring of 1854 Belcher became concerned that the ice was not breaking up as expected and ordered the *Resolute* and *Pioneer* to be abandoned (see above). By August, the two remaining ships were still locked in the ice, some two miles south of Cape Osborn. Gunpowder was used to try and blast a passage out, but it proved too large a task. Unwilling to spend a third winter in the ice, Belcher decided to abandon the expedition, and the ships were left, the men walking over the ice to the depot ship *North Star* at Beechey Island.
[TNA: ADM.1/5645]

25 August PIONEER Discovery Ship
Purchased 1850 (*Eider*); 342 tons; 143.6ft × 32.9ft
Commander Sherard Osborn

Steam tender to the *Assistance*, she had accompanied the larger vessel until they were both iced in some 40 miles from Beechey Island. She was abandoned on the orders of Sir Edward Belcher.
[TNA: ADM.1/5645]

1855

20 January BERMUDA Schooner
Bermuda 1848; 180 tons; 80ft × 23.3ft; 3 guns
Lieutenant William Cashman
Ordered to cruise off the Caicos Islands, to watch the Caicos and Turks Passages for slaving vessels, during the afternoon East Caicos was sighted and sail was shortened, being reduced further at dusk. At 8.15pm, white water and breakers was seen on the lee bow, but before any action could be taken, she struck a reef. All sails were furled, and an anchor taken out to act as a kedge. Despite hauling on the hawser all night and lightening the ship by heaving overboard shot and five tons of water, she would not move. The following morning another attempt was made to heave her off, but the hawser parted, and she swung round to lie broadside-on to the reef. She pounded on the rocks, carrying away her false keel and rudder and it soon became clear that she had bilged. She was then abandoned, almost being full of water as the last men left. Both Lieutenant Cashman and the Master, Samuel Cooper Wayth, were admonished to be more careful in the future, having taken the schooner too far to the southward and having failed to order soundings to be taken more frequently.
[TNA: ADM.1/5671]

29 March BOURNABAT Paddle Tug
Bristol 1844, purchased 1854; 32 tons; 79ft × 13ft
Employed at Constantinople (Istanbul), she struck rocks off Scutari (Uskudar) and was run ashore to prevent her foundering. She was abandoned and sold locally for £150.
[TNA: ADM.1/5655]

3 May AETNA Floating Battery
Millwall; 1,469 tons; 172.6ft × 43.11ft
Under construction at the yard of John Scott Russell & Co. at Millwall, the battery was on the building slip ready to be launched. At about 9 o'clock at night a fire was discovered on board, and despite strenuous efforts to gather parties of men to tackle the blaze, the fire spread rapidly. By 11pm, despite pouring tons of water onto the ship, she was ablaze from stem to stern, with flames shooting high into the air. As the supporting timbers burned away, she launched herself from the slipway and burnt out on the opposite bank.
[www.britishnewspaperarchive.co: London Evening Standard 4 May 1855 p3]

(12–14) June NERBUDDA Brig Sloop
Bombay 1848; 419 tons; 100ft × 32.4ft; 16 guns
Commander Henry Ashburton Kerr†
The *Nerbudda* sailed from Algoa Bay, South Africa, on 9 June for Simon's Bay, having put in for provisions and water on her return from patrolling the Mozambique Channel. She was observed later that day beating out of the bay by the merchant vessel *Earl of Eglinton*, but not seen again. The area was swept by heavy storms for three or four days after she sailed, and it was presumed that she foundered with all hands at this time.
[TNA: ADM.123/15]

23 July JASPER Screw Gunboat
Cowes 1855; 233 tons; 106ft × 22ft; 4 guns
Lieutenant Joseph Samuel Hudson
Part of a squadron of gunboats sent into the Sea of Azov under the command of Captain Sherard Osborn to attack and harass Russian shipping. The *Jasper* was used by Osborn to reconnoitre the port of Taganrog on 18–19 July and on 23 July she was ordered to join the *Swallow* off the Crooked Spit (Krivaya). By that evening she was heading for the anchorage and Lieutenant Hudson, being exhausted by several days and nights constantly on alert, lay down on the upper deck, giving instructions to the lookout to watch for the lights of the *Swallow*, and wake him when seen. The lookouts eventually saw more than one light and were uncertain which was the expected *Swallow*. Twice Hudson was shaken, but although he mumbled 'Very well', he went back to sleep. The soundings were by now shallowing, and an anxious crew member shook the Lieutenant for the third time at which Hudson raised himself. Scarcely had he done so when the leadsman reported 13ft of water and the ship struck the ground. Engines were reversed and a boat ordered to be hoisted out. The rough seas breaking around her swamped the boat, preventing any attempt to lay out anchors. Dawn revealed her to be hard aground, about 100 yards from the shore, the *Swallow* visible a short distance away to seaward. Boats were lowered and, with the assistance of other gunboats the ship was lightened, and anchors laid out. Attempts to haul her free failed, and with many enemy troops gathering on shore and opening a fire of musketry, it was decided to abandon her. Fires were started before leaving, but this did not destroy her before the Russians boarded the wreck. Over the next few days further attempts were made to return to her, and some stores were recovered before she was burnt. Lieutenant Hudson was admonished to be more careful in the future, having been guilty of imprudence in failing to make the quartermaster and lookouts aware that the gunboat was heading into shallow water.
[TNA: ADM.1/5671]

11 August WOLVERENE Brig Sloop
Chatham 1836; 428 tons; 100.7ft × 32.4ft; 16 guns
Commander John Corbett
Heading for Greytown on the Mosquito Coast (San Juan del Norte, Nicaragua), the brig was steering south

under easy sail. A little before 10 o'clock Commander Corbett went on deck to give his night orders to the officer of the watch, only to discover that he was nowhere to be seen. He was eventually discovered fast asleep by the taffrail. Roused with difficulty, it became clear that he was drunk, and Corbett ordered him to be arrested and taken below. Turning his attention to the vessel's position, he became concerned when he discovered that she was steering 1½ points (about 16 degrees) to the west of her planned course. On looking ahead, he saw a phosphorescent glow in the water, and realising that this indicated shallow water he ordered the helm to be put over to starboard. Before it could take effect, the sloop struck a reef with a shock and bumped heavily. Sail was ordered to be thrown all aback, but before this could be done, she struck again very heavily and rolled over onto her side with the sea breaking over her. An attempt was made to launch the cutter, but it was promptly swamped. Corbett ordered sail to be furled and stores, provisions and water to be secured. Daylight showed them to be on the south-south-east corner of Courtown Cay, and with the seas now calmer, boats were lowered to ferry the provisions and crew ashore. One of the boats was dispatched to Greytown to bring assistance and the sloop *Buzzard* arrived the following night. Both Corbett and the Master, Horace Cook, were reprimanded for failing to order the constant use of the lead-line. The Mate, Anthony Maynard, who had been in a drunken sleep and allowed the ship to wander from her course, was dismissed the service.
[TNA: ADM.1/5671]

3 December TIVERE Paddle Tug
Purchased 1855
A tug employed locally at Constantinople, she ran aground in the Bosporus and was written off as a wreck. The tug was sold locally for £30.
[TNA: ADM.1/5655]

1856

29 January POLYPHEMUS Paddle Sloop
Chatham 1840; 801 tons; 164ft × 32.8ft; 4 guns
Commander Frederick Pelham Warren
Ordered to the Baltic, to cruise between Falsterbo and Rügen Island to intercept Russian shipping, she sailed from the Humber on 27 January. The morning of 29 January was dull and overcast, with banks of thick drifting fog, the ship steering east by north at seven knots. The estimated position at 8 o'clock, by dead reckoning, placed her 30 miles to the north of Hantsholm. She sounded with a short lead-line at that time, no bottom being found at 15 fathoms. At 10.30am she was felt to strike the ground and the engines were put astern and boats ordered to be prepared for hoisting out. The ship was found to be held fast and the boats were lowered, one being overset and lost, the second taking out a stream anchor. The fog cleared sufficiently now to reveal a snow-covered coastline with heavy rollers beating on the shore a short distance away. The anchor having been laid out, the boat attempted to return alongside, but capsized, with eight men, including the Master, being drowned. The ship was now lifting and pounding, and water was reporting to be entering, the engine room being evacuated when pipes began fracturing because of the heavy motion. The masts were cut away and fell towards the beach, the crew being ordered to leave by way of the wreckage. It was found that she had gone aground seven miles south of Hantsholm Light, her loss being attributed to a strong irregular current, plus the failure to slacken speed in the fog and obtain regular, accurate soundings. Commander Warren was reprimanded.
[TNA: ADM.1/5681]

August PUCK Schooner Tender
Acquired 1855; 1 gun
A schooner taken over in the Black Sea and manned as a tender to the *Oberon*. On the cessation of hostilities with Russia, she was ordered to be transferred to the Turkish Navy but foundered on passage from Balaklava to Constantinople.
[TNA: ADM.1/5655]

1857

14 April RALEIGH Fourth Rate
Chatham 1845; 1,939 tons; 180ft × 50.1ft; 50 guns
Captain Honourable Henry Keppel
Steering for Hong Kong under easy sail, she was heading through the chain of islands off the coast of China, when at 12.20pm, with no warning, she struck a submerged rock. The damage was soon found to be severe; a hole had been opened from the forefoot to the step of the foremast. Water entered at a rapid rate, and it soon became clear that she could not survive. It was decided to run her aground, so she altered course inshore. Pumping and bailing were commenced, guns run aft, and a sail was prepared for spreading under the hull, but before this could be done, at 3.30pm, with her head well down in the water, she struck the mud off Ka Ho on Coloane Island, Macau. Signal guns were fired and the ensign hoisted upside down as signs of distress. Several ships came to her assistance from Hong Kong and Macau, including the French frigate *Virginie*, flagship of the French Commander-in-Chief, Rear Admiral Guérin, and despite her distressed condition, Keppel ordered an Admiral's salute to be

fired. Efforts went on over several days to save her, but they were defeated by the monsoon and several days of incessant rain, the ship steadily settling into the mud. Most of her guns and all of her spars and running rigging was saved.
[TNA: ADM.1/5690]

10 July TRANSIT Screw Troopship
Purchased 1854; 2,570 tons; 302.6ft x 41.8ft
Commander Ennis Chambers
Having sailed from Portsmouth in April with a large contingent of troops for China, the troopship had anchored in the Bangka Straits, Sumatra, on 9 July. At 6.30 the following morning she weighed and under steam, steering a course to take her two miles clear of Cape Oelar (Tanjung Ular) at the north-western tip of Bangka. At 9.20am, steaming at eight knots, believing himself clear of any danger, Captain Chambers ordered a course change. Hardly had he done so when the ship struck the ground with some violence and then shuddered to a stop. The engines were stopped and sounding ordered to be taken and the boats hoisted out. Water was reported to be entering very quickly and within minutes, stokers in the engine room found themselves waist-deep in water. Masts and yards were struck, and all boats were lowered as the ship slowly settled. The troops were mustered on deck and over the next two hours were evacuated to the nearby shore. By noon, the stern was under water, and by early afternoon the hull had disappeared. A boat was sent to a Dutch settlement, but the crew and troops endured several uncomfortable days before being rescued. There were no casualties. It was found that Commander Chambers and the Master, John Allard, had showed a lack of judgement in steering a course which took the ship inside the five-fathom line at eight knots, with too much confidence being placed in a small-scale chart. They were both severely reprimanded.
[TNA: ADM.1/5690]

14 July DEFENCE Hulk
Chatham 1815; 1,754 tons; 174ft x 47.8ft.
Moored off Woolwich, the old liner was serving as a convict hulk, one of the last in service. At 9 o'clock in the morning, smoke was seen coming from the forward part of the hold. Investigation soon showed that the coal store was on fire. The blaze spread rapidly, and inmates were moved to the *Unité* hulk nearby. Firefighters from the dockyard, the *Fisgard* guardship and the Arsenal went on board but had difficulty in controlling the blaze, and after several hours it was decided to scuttle her. At 1 o'clock in the afternoon this was accomplished, and she sank 'with a lurch'. The cause was not ascertained but was thought to be either spontaneous combustion of coals embarked that morning, or a prisoner illegally smoking. The remains of the hulk were broken up at Woolwich Dockyard in January 1858.
[www.britishnewspaperarchive.co: Morning Chronicle 15 July 1857 p8]

1858

February SAPPHO Brig Sloop
Plymouth 1837; 428 tons; 100.6ft x 32.4ft; 16 guns
Commander Fairfax Moresby†
Sailed from the Cape of Good Hope on 8 January for Sydney, New South Wales, but never arrived. The vessel was last seen off Cape Bridgewater, on the coast of Victoria at the entrance to Bass Strait, heading east, by the crew of the brig *Yarra* on 18 February 1858. It is believed that the vessel either struck a rock or capsized during gales in the Bass Strait soon after this and sank with her entire crew of more than 100. Material which may have come from the vessel was reportedly seen, or found, on the coast of Victoria and at Flinders Island, Tasmania.
[www.trove.nla.gov.au/newspaper: Melbourne Argus 8 December 1858 p & 7 April 1859 p4; Sydney Morning Herald 28 January 1859 p4]

1859

8 February WIZARD Brig Sloop
Pembroke 1830; 231 tons; 90ft x 24.8ft; 10 guns
Lieutenant Alfred Prowse Hasler Helby
Employed as a boys' training ship, based at Cork, the brig sailed from Queenstown on 5 February for Bantry Bay. The weather worsened and by the evening of 8 February, then off Mizen Head, it was raining with strong winds. By 10 o'clock she was in Bantry Bay and steering for Roancarrigmore Light. The anchors were prepared for letting go and extra lookouts and leadsmen were posted. At just before midnight, as she prepared to anchor, she was struck by a strong squall with very heavy rain, which obscured their vision to little more than a few yards. Moments later the fo'c'sle lookouts shouted 'Port – hard to port!' Lieutenant Helby ordered the helm to be put down, but hardly had this been done when she ran aground on the south-west point of Roancarraig Beag (Seal Rock). Sail was ordered to be taken in, distress guns fired, and boats ordered to be hoisted out, but the brig was now heeling over at an alarming angle, which prevented the boats from being lowered. Guns were jettisoned overboard and eventually, at great risk, the dinghy was launched with two volunteers who succeeded in taking a line to the rocks. A hawser was passed and secured, and the crew commenced leaving the sloop. Just then a six-oared

boat from the shore came alongside, commanded by the local lighthouse keeper, Cornelius Sullivan, and despite the high seas and heavy rain, and at considerable risk to its crew, the boat made several trips between the brig and the shore, taking all the men to safety.
[TNA: ADM.1/5728]

26 February JASEUR Screw Gunboat
Blackwall 1857; 301 tons; 125ft × 23ft; 3 guns
Lieutenant John Binney Scott

Sailed from Port Royal, Jamaica, bound for Greytown on the Mosquito Coast (San Juan de Nicaragua) on 25 February, she was under all plain sail and going at about six knots, when at 10.15pm the following night, breakers were seen on the lee bow. The helm was put over and despite the ship answering quickly, she struck the ground, was held briefly, then swung round to starboard before grounding through her whole length and heeling over. Seas washed over her as sail was shortened and boats lowered. The first gig was launched successfully but the second gig and the dinghy both overturned and their crews were rescued with difficulty. The first gig was then sent to recover the swamped boats and disappeared into the night. The crew was employed in chopping away the masts, gathering provisions and preparing a raft. It was with some relief that daylight showed calmer waters and the gig could be seen towing the other two boats. The wreck was abandoned, and the crew took to the raft and the boats. The aim was to return to Jamaica, some 140 miles away. The boats separated as they progressed northward and had to endure several days alone and under the hot West Indian sun, one party landing on the island of Cuba, with the other being picked up by a merchant ship. Two men were lost in the wreck and one man, officers' cook William Gillespie, died, having gone mad and jumped overboard. The gunboat had been wrecked on the south-east corner of the Baja Nuevo shoal, having been taken inshore by a strong current.
[TNA: ADM.1/5728]

9 May HERON Brig Sloop
Chatham 1847; 481 tons; 105ft × 33.6ft; 16 guns
Lieutenant William Henderson Truscott†

Cruising off the coast of West Africa, in the vicinity of 04 N, 14.50W, the Mate, Frederick Blair, had the morning watch and was joined on the upper deck at first light by the First Lieutenant, Thomas Collingwood, who ordered the decks to be squared up and lines stowed and coiled. Blair objected to this, indicating that the weather was threatening, and a squall was in the offing. This was met with the reply of 'Oh, pooh, that will not amount to anything'. A little later, still under topgallants, topsails, and courses, she was struck on the beam by a heavy squall. Orders had been given to shorten sail just before the squall struck, but with lines stowed and coiled it took too long, and the brig was rolled over onto her beam-ends. Filling with water very quickly she sank, with the survivors struggling to the whaleboat which had floated free whilst others clung to wreckage and managed to lash together a raft. The boat was picked up after two days, but the raft drifted for some time before being found. Sixty-five men died in all, including Lieutenant Collingwood. There were two courts martial for the loss, the first, in June, based on the evidence from the whaleboat survivors, concluded that the loss was due to the failure to shorten sail before the squall struck. A second trial was held in September when more survivors were available. At this, a similar verdict was reached, but Mr Blair was reprimanded, it being ruled that he should have called the Captain on the approach of the bad weather. This was not the view of the Admiralty, and the First Naval Lord, Sir Richard Dundas, opined that Blair would have been guilty of insubordination if he had called the Captain because he believed the First Lieutenant had made an error of judgement.
[TNA: ADM.1/1/5728]

25 June: Battle of the Pei-Ho Forts
Relations between the Chinese and European governments had been increasingly tense since the signing of the Treaty of Nanking in 1842. This, among other points, opened five Chinese ports to foreign trade. A series of incidents had led to an outbreak of fighting in 1857 and the resulting Treaty of Tientsin forced further concessions on the Chinese. In early June 1859, British, French, and American officials arrived at Tientsin (Tianjin) before proceeding upriver to Peking (Beijing). The British envoys were refused permission to go any further, and it was discovered that barriers had been placed in the river. Rear Admiral Sir James Hope, in command of the British naval forces present, demanded that the obstructions be removed, or he would remove them forcibly. Having set an ultimatum of 8 o'clock on the evening of 24 June, by the following morning no answer had been received and Hope embarked in the gunboat *Plover* to lead a force of nine gunboats, a gun vessel and a sloop, to force a passage. At 2pm, the force got under way and passed through the first barrier, a line of piles, pulling out several of the obstructions. On reaching the second barrier, a boom of spars, the forts lining the shores opened fire. With the gunboats restricted in movements in the narrow waterway and outgunned by the forts, after an action which lasted for the afternoon and into the evening, the British were forced to withdraw, suffering 89 dead and 345 wounded. Three vessels were lost.
[TNA: ADM.1/5728; London Gazette 16 September 1859]

LEE Screw Gunboat
Northfleet 1857; 301 tons; 125ft x 23ft; 3 guns
Lieutenant William Henry Jones

The *Lee* returned the fire of the forts when the action commenced and maintained the fight until 6 o'clock that night, despite being hulled repeatedly by enemy shot. Making water and having suffered numerous casualties, she was ordered to withdraw. At this point, armed parties were being prepared to be landed to attack the forts and Captain Vansittart of the *Magicienne* ordered Lieutenant Jones to run the *Lee* onto the mud to give support to the landings. This was done, the opportunity being taken to try and pump her clear of water. This was found to be an impossible task and the *Haughty* gunboat came alongside to pull her off the mud. The pair had gone little more than 200 yards when water was found to be flooding into the engine room. In minutes, the fires were doused, and the stokers forced to evacuate. All the crew were taken off and she was allowed to sink at just before midnight, her masts and bowsprit showing above the water. The following day the frigate *Chesapeake* closed the wreck to destroy it with gunfire and powder charges. Twelve men were wounded,

PLOVER Screw Gunboat
Northfleet 1855; 232 tons; 106ft x 22ft; 3 guns
Lieutenant William Hector Rason†

With Rear Admiral Sir James Hope embarked, the *Plover* reached the second barrier when the Chinese forts opened fire. Fire was returned, but she soon started suffering. Lieutenant Rason was struck by a shot which cut him in two and Admiral Hope wounded. She anchored to maintain her position, but the cables were cut by shot and she drifted downriver until she came alongside the gun vessel *Cormorant*, bringing herself up by grappling the larger vessel. Hope left the *Plover* to shift his flag to *Cormorant*, Lieutenant George Douglas assuming command of the gunboat. She continued to engage the forts despite being hit repeatedly. At 9.30pm she cast loose from the *Cormorant* to steam clear of the barriers and forts. After briefly grounding, she headed downriver and sighted two gunboats ahead, which she presumed were at anchor. In fact, they were the *Haughty* attempting to pull the stricken *Lee* free from the mud, and the *Plover* ran hard aground alongside them. Engines were put full astern, but she would not move. Efforts to free her went on through the night but at first light she was abandoned. The following night a party returned, successfully pumped her free of water and raised steam, but she had settled deep into the mud and would not move. She was again abandoned and the following morning the Chinese boarded her and set fire to the wreck. Eight men killed with twenty-four wounded, one of whom died later of his injuries.

CORMORANT Screw Gunboat
Limehouse 1856; 670 tons; 180ft x 28.4ft; 3 guns
Lieutenant Armine Woodhouse

Lieutenant Woodhouse supported the attempt to pass through the river barriers and after two hours' engagement the *Plover* fell away to run alongside *Cormorant*, and Rear Admiral Sir James Hope shifted his flag on board. When the fire from the shore visibly slackened, it was determined that landing parties should be put ashore to destroy the emplacements. This happened at 7.30pm and turned into a disaster, with marines and sailors having to wade through mud under constant small-arms fire. Ordered to withdraw, the *Cormorant*, having cast off the *Plover*, sent her boats to take off the wounded. That complete, she then closed the grounded *Plover* to lend assistance, but drifted onto the northern bank of the river and also ran aground. Initial attempts to steam off failed and when an anchor was released to hold her, whilst kedge anchors were laid out, the stopper came off and anchor and cable were lost. Some shore fire was still being taken and to save further casualties, the *Opossum* came alongside and lifted off most of the crew, Admiral Hope leaving in the early hours. Despite the ship being hit repeatedly, the crew returned on board the following morning and raised steam, pumped the vessel clear and recommenced efforts to free her from the mud. For the next two days, the work continued to save her, all the time under harassing fire, but in the early hours of 28 June she was finally abandoned. One man killed with thirteen wounded, two of whom subsequently died.

Bibliography

Primary, Unpublished Papers

The National Archives (TNA) Kew:
ADM 1/1–5494	Admiralty Board: in-letters from Senior Officers 1699–1839
ADM 1/1435–2738	Admiralty Board, in-letters from Captains 1698–1839
ADM 1/5253–5485	Records of Courts Martial 1689–1839
ADM.1/5558–5728	Records of Courts Martial 1845–1959
ADM 8/1–138	Ships and Vessels in Sea Pay 1673–1859
ADM 10/15	Commissioned Officers' Service Register 1660–1685
ADM 33 series	Pay Books 1666–1773
ADM 34 series	Pay Books 1666–1785
ADM 35 series	Pay Books 1777–1832
ADM 43 series	Head Money vouchers
ADM 49/96–98	Navy Board: Hired Armed Vessels 1793–1818
ADM 51 series	Captains' logs
ADM 52 series	Masters' journals
ADM 106/281–1446	Navy Board: In letters 1658–1832
ADM 106/3120	List of Losses and Additions to the Navy 1689–1705
ADM 180/1–18	Progress Books 1703–1860
ADM 80/19–25	Dimensions Books 1699–1810
CO 245/1	Colonial Office Miscellaneous correspondence
HCA 32 series	High Court of Admiralty: Prize Court: Prize Papers
SP 29 series	Secretaries of State: State Papers Domestic, Charles II
SP 46/115–121	Papers of the Commissioners for the Admiralty and Navy 1653–1658

National Maritime Museum (NMM):
ADM 354 series	Navy Board: Out letters 1738–1809

Primary, Published Documents

Clarendon	*Calendar of the Clarendon State Papers preserved in the Bodleian Library* (5 vols) 1873–1970.
HCJ	*House of Commons Journal* 1547–1699 (12 vols) London, 1802–1803.
HCJ 1695	*House of Commons Journal*: 4 December 1695 – *A list of the men of war that have been taken, sunk, burnt or stranded since the year 1688*.
HCJ 1699	*House of Commons Journal*: 2 January 1699 – *Ships as have been lost before, and some since, the First of January 1697*.
HLJ	House of Lords Journal: Volume 18: 9 January 1708 – *A List of Her Majesty's Ships and Vessels, which have been taken by the Enemy, or destroyed, during this War; with their Force, where they have been taken or destroyed, and how*.
CSPC	*Calendar of State Papers, Colonial: North America and the West Indies 1574–1739* (41 vols.) London 1860–1994.
CSPD	*Calendar of State Papers, Domestic 1649 – 1702* (65 vols) London, 1860–1937.
CSP Venice	*Calendar of State Papers, relating to English affairs in the Archives of Venice vol 28 (1647-1652)* London, 1927.
CTB	*Calendar of Treasury Books 1660–1718* (32 vols) London, 1904–1962.
State Papers	*British & Foreign State Papers* (100+ vols) London, from 1812.
Thurloe	*A Collection of the State Papers of John Thurloe 1638–1660* (7 vols) London, 1742.

House of Commons Journals and the Calendar of State Papers and Treasury Books were accessed through British History Online, (*British History Online*, Version 5.0 <www.british-history.ac.uk>) a digital library based at the Institute for Historical Research. This resource provides a digital library with access to key historical documents.

Historical Manuscripts Commission

HMC: Dartmouth 1, *Historical Manuscripts Commission Report 11: Manuscripts of the Earl of Dartmouth volume 1* (London, 1887).
HMC: Dartmouth 3, *Historical Manuscripts Commission Report 15: Manuscripts of the Earl of Dartmouth volume 3* (London, 1896).
HMC: Finch 2, *Historical Manuscripts Commission Report 19: Manuscripts of the late Alan George Finch volume 2* (London, 1922).
HMC: Leybourne-Popham, *Historical Manuscripts Commission: Manuscripts of F W Leybourne- Popham* (Norwich, 1899).

Navy Records Society (NRS)

Anderson, R C (ed), *Journals and Narratives of the Third Dutch War* (London, 1946).
——, *The Journal of Edward Montagu, First Earl of Sandwich* (London, 1929).
——, *The Journals of Sir Thomas Allin 1660–1678* (2 vols) (London, 1939–40).
Gardiner, S, and Atkinson, C (eds), *Papers Relating to the First Dutch War* (6 vols) (London, 1898–1930).
Latham, R (ed), *Samuel Pepys and the Second Dutch War* (London, 1995).
Laughton, J K (ed), *Journal of Rear Admiral Bartholomew James* (London, 1896).
Leyland, D (ed), *Dispatches & Letters relating to the Blockade of Brest 1803–05* (2 vols) (London, 1900–01).
Perrin, W G (ed), *The Keith Papers* (vol.1) (London, 1926).
——, *The Naval Miscellany volume III* (London, 1927).
Powell, J R (ed), *The Letters of Robert Blake* (London, 1937).
——, and Timings, E K (eds), *The Rupert and Monck Letter Book 1666* (London, 1969).
Ranft, B (ed), *The Vernon Papers* (London, 1958).
Tanner, J R (ed) *A Descriptive Catalogue of the Naval Manuscripts in the Pepsyian Library at Magdalene College, Cambridge* (4 vols) (London, 1903–22).
Tunstall, B (ed), *The Byng Papers, the letters and papers of Admiral Sir George Byng and Admiral the Hon. John Byng* (3 vols) (London, 1930–3).
Vesey Hamilton, R, and Laughton, J K (eds), *Recollections of James Anthony Gardner* (London, 1906).

United States Naval History and Heritage Command (NHHC)

NDAR *Naval Documents of the American Revolution* (13 vols) (Washington, 1964 – 2019)
Dudley, William (ed), *The Naval War of 1812, A Documentary History* (3 vols) (Washington, 1985–2011).

Primary – General

Chadwick, French Ensor (ed), *The Graves Papers and Other Documents Relating to the Naval Operations of the Yorktown Campaign July to October 1781* (New York, 1916).
Flinders, Matthew, *A Voyage to Terra Australis* (2 vols) (London, 1814).
Foster, Sir William, *The English Factories in India 1668–1669* (Oxford, 1927).
Laughton, J K (ed.), *Memoirs relating to the Lord Torrington*, Camden Society (London, 1889).
Matthews, Thomas, *A Narrative of the Proceedings of His Majesty's Fleet in the Mediterranean … from 1741 to 1744* (London, 1745).
Nicolas, Sir Nicholas H (ed), *The Dispatches and Letters of Lord Nelson* (7 vols) (London, 1998).
Penn, Granville, *Memorials of the professional life and time of Sir William Penn* (2 vols) (London, 1853).
Rodney, George Lord, *Letter Books and Order Book of George, Lord Rodney 1780-1782* (2 vols) (New York, 1932).
Sainsbury, Ethel B, *A Calendar Of The Court Minutes Etc Of The East India Company – 1664-1667* (Oxford, 1925).
——, *A Calendar Of The Court Minutes Etc Of The East India Company – 1668-1670* (Oxford, 1929).
Thompson, Edward M, *Correspondence of the family of Haddock, 1657-1719* Camden Society (London, 1881).
Whitelocke, Bulstrode, *Memorials of the English Affairs from the beginning of the reign of Charles I to Charles II* (4 vols) (Oxford, 1834).

Secondary Sources

Aubrey, Philip, *The Defeat of James Stuart's Armada 1692* (Leicester, 1979).
Beatson, Robert, *Naval and Military Memoirs … 1727 to 1783* (6 vols) (London, 1804).

Brenton, Edward P, *The Naval History of Great Britain from 1783 to 1822* (2 vols) (London, 1837).
Broughton, William R, *A voyage of discovery to the north Pacific Ocean etc.* (London, 1804).
Burns, K V, *Plymouth's Ships of War* (Greenwich, 1972).
Charnock, John, *Biographia Navalis, or Impartial Memoirs of the Lives and Characters Officers of the Navy of Great Britain* (6 vols) (London, 1794–8).
Clowes, William Laird, *The Royal Navy: A History from the Earliest Times to the Present* (7 vols) (London, 1897–1903).
Colledge, J J, *Ships of the Royal Navy* (2 vols) (Newton Abbot, 1969–70)
de la Roncière, Charles, *Histoire de la Marine Française* (6 vols) (Paris, 1899–1932).
Demerliac, Alain, *Nomenclature des Vaisseau* (6 vols) (Nice, 1995–2007).
Erskine, D (ed), *Augustus Hervey's Journal* (London, 1953)
Fox, Frank L, *A Distant Storm, the Four Days' Battle of 1666* (Rotherfield, 1996).
Gilly, William O S, *Narratives of Shipwrecks of the Royal Navy 1793–1857* (London, 1857).
Gold, Joyce (publisher), *The Naval Chronicle* (40 vols) (London, 1799–1818).
Grindal, Peter, *Opposing the Slavers* (London, 2016).
Harris, Simon, *Sir Cloudesley Shovell, Stuart Admiral* (Staplehurst, 2001).
James, William, *The Naval History of Great Britain ... a new edition with additions and notes* (6 vols) (London, 1837).
Lediard, Thomas, *The Naval History of England* (2 vols) (London, 1735).
Lyon, David, *The Sailing Navy List* (London, 1993).
Maclay, Edgar S, *A History of American Privateers* (New York, 1924).
Malcomson, Robert, *Warships of the Great Lakes* (London, 2001).
Marshall, John, *Royal Naval Biography* (4 vols and 4 supplements) (London, 1823–35).
Martin, Frederick, *The History of Lloyd's* (London, 1876).
Middlebrook, Louis, *Maritime Connecticut during the American Revolution* (Salem, 1925).
Norrie, J W, *The Naval Gazeteer, Biographist and Chronologist* (London, 1827).
O'Byrne, William, *A Naval Biographical Dictionary* (London, 1849).
Owen, J H, *War at Sea under Queen Anne 1702-1708* (Cambridge, 1938).
Powell, John Rowland, *Robert Blake: General-At-Sea* (London, 1972).
Powley, Edward, *The English Navy in the Revolution of 1688* (Cambridge, 1920).
——, *The Naval Side of King William's War* (London, 1972).
Rogers, P G, *The Dutch in the Medway* (Oxford, 1970).
Sevin de Quincy, Charles, *Histoire Militaire du Règne de Louis le Grand* (etc) (7 tomes) (La Haye, 1726).
Schomberg, Isaac, *Naval Chronology or An Historical Summary of Naval and Maritime Events* (5 vols) (London, 1802).
Sigwart, E E, *Royal Fleet Auxiliary* (London, 1969).
Steel, David, *Steel's Naval Chronologist of the War etc.* (London, 1802; facsimile reprint London, 1969).
——, *Original and Correct Navy List* (London 1785–1814).
Troude, Olivier, *Batailles Navales de la France* (4 tomes) (Paris, 1867).
Vichot, Jacques, *Répertoire des Navires de Guerre Français* (Paris, 1965).
Walker, George, *The Voyages and Cruises of Commodore Walker* (London, 1928).
Walter, Richard, *Anson's Voyage round the World* (London, 1928).
Winfield, Rif, *British Warships in the Age of Sail 1603–1714* (Barnsley, 2009).
——, *British Warships in the Age of Sail 1714–1792* (Barnsley, 2007).
——, *British Warships in the Age of Sail 1793–1817* (Barnsley, 2005).
——, *British Warships in the Age of Sail 1817–1863* (Barnsley, 2014).

Periodicals

Annual Register, from 1758.
Gentleman's Magazine and Historical Chronicle, annually 1736–1833.
Lloyd's List, twice weekly from 1735.
Mariner's Mirror, Journal of the Society for Nautical Research since 1910.
Nautical Magazine, monthly from 1832.
Northern Mariner, Journal of the Canadian Nautical Research Society since 1991 (accessed at: https://www.cnrs-scrn.org/northern_mariner/on_line_content_e.html)

Nova Scotia Historical Society: collections.
The London Gazette, from 1665.
The London Magazine or Gentleman's Monthly Intelligencer, annually from 1732.
The Naval Review, quarterly since 1919.
United Services Magazine, monthly from 1829 to 1890.

Contemporary Newspapers

British and Irish newspapers have been archived and made available from the British Newspaper Archive published and managed by Findmypast, in collaboration with the British Library Board. These may be accessed at: http://www.britishnewspaperarchive.co.uk

Among the titles used were:

Aberdeen Journal	*Ipswich Journal*	*Pue's Occurences*
Bath Chronicle	*Kentish Gazette*	*Reading Mercury*
Bury & Norwich Post	*Kentish Weekly Post*	*Royal Cornwall Gazette*
Caledonian Mercury	*Leeds Intelligencer*	*Salisbury Journal*
Chester Courant	*London Standard*	*Salisbury & Winchester Journal*
Daily News	*Manchester Mercury*	*Saunders's News Letter*
Derby Journal	*Morning Chronicle*	*Scots Magazine*
Derby Mercury	*Morning Post*	*Stamford Mercury*
Essex Standard	*Newcastle Courant*	*Sussex Advertiser*
Exeter Flying Post	*Norfolk Chronicle*	*The Standard*
Hampshire Chronicle	*Northampton Mercury*	*Trewmans Exeter Flying Post*
Hampshire Telegraph	*Oxford Journal*	
Hereford Journal	*Public Ledger*	

https://trove.nla.gov.au/newspaper
Australian newspapers from 1803 have been made available by the National Library of Australia following digitisation

https://paperspast.natlib.govt.nz/newspapers
New Zealand newspapers from 1839 have been digitised and made available by the National Library of New Zealand :

Websites:

https://www.pepysdiary.com   Pepys' Diary
with daily entries between 1660 – 1669

https://www.heritagegateway.org.uk   Heritage Gateway
Managed by Historic England, details the historic environment, including shipwrecks

https://canmore.org.uk   Historic Environment Scotland
catalogue of Scotland's archaeology and heritage, including details of wreck sites

http://www.coflein.gov.uk   National Monuments Record of Wales
including maritime wreck sites

https://www.archaeology.ie/underwater-archaeology/wreck-viewer
The Sites and Monuments Records database of the Republic of Ireland, including The Wreck Inventory of Ireland Database

http://www.cii.co.uk/media/581215/weerdt.pdf
Insurance Institute: Sinking of the Lutine

https://www.navyrecords.org.uk   Navy Records Society
Publishes original documents on naval history

Alphabetical Index of Ships Lost

Name	Type	Date	Name	Type	Date
Abigail	fireship	25 July 1666	*Alice & Francis*	fireship	28 May 1672
Abram's Offering	machine	12 September 1694	*Alicia*	fireship	11 April 1809
Acadia	6th rate	September 1659	*Allegiance*	armed ship	6 August 1782
Achates	brig sloop	7 February 1810	*Allepine*	fireship	2 September 1667
Acheron	bomb	4 February 1805	*Alligator*	ship sloop	26 June 1782
Achilles	schooner	31 January 1748	*Alphea*	schooner	10 September 1813
Acorn	ship sloop	14 April 1828	*Althorpe*	cutter	December 1804
Actaeon	6th rate	29 June 1776	*Amaranthe*	brig sloop	25 October 1799
Actif	gun brig	26 November 1794	*Amazon*	5th rate	14 January 1797
Active	6th rate	1 September 1778	*Ambuscade*	5th rate	14 December 1798
Active	brig	10 April 1780	*Ambuscade*	5th rate	9 July 1801
Active	5th rate	13 July 1796	*Amethyst*	5th rate	30 December 1795
Active	cutter	9 October 1800	*Amethyst*	5th rate	16 February 1811
Adder	gun brig	9 December 1806	*Amity*	fireship	2 October 1804
Adder	watch vessel	20 December 1831	*Amphion*	5th rate	22 September 1796
Adelaide	tender	April 1850	*Amphitrite*	ship sloop	30 January 1794
Admiral Spry	tender	11 April 1780	*Anacreon*	ship sloop	February 1814
Admiral Spry	tender	14 February 1782	*Andromeda*	6th rate	11 October 1780
Adventure	5th rate	1 March 1709	*Angelica*	sloop	10 October 1783
Adventure	tender	17 September 1756	*Anglesea*	5th rate	29 March 1745
Adventure	fireship	11 April 1809	*Ann*	3rd rate	2 December 1673
Advice	5th rate	27 June 1711	*Ann*	3rd rate	6 July 1690
Advice	schooner	1 June 1793	*Ann*	cutter	20 September 1757
Adviser	pink	1 September 1655	*Ann & Judith*	fireship	28 May 1672
Aeneas	fireship	13 April 1809	*Ann Galley*	fireship	11 February 1744
Aetna	battery	3 May 1855	*Anna*	pink	20 August 1741
Africaine	5th rate	13 October 1810	*Anson*	cutter	1 April 1759
Agamemnon	3rd rate	16 June 1809	*Anson*	schooner	23 October 1761
Agenoria	fireship	11 April 1809	*Anson*	5th rate	29 December 1807
Agnes	lugger	25 March 1806	*Ant*	cutter	16 March 1806
Aigle	5th rate	19 July 1798	*Antelope*	2nd rate	30 September 1652
Ajax	3rd rate	14 February 1807	*Antelope*	3rd rate	June 1649
Alaart	brig sloop	10 August 1809	*Antelope*	brig sloop	30 July 1784
Alacrity	brig sloop	26 May 1811	*Anthony Bonaventure*	4th rate	30 November 1652
Alarm	galley	30 July 1778	*Antigua*	brig sloop	11 May 1781
Alban	cutter	12 September 1810	*Apelles*	brig sloop	3 May 1812
Alban	cutter	18 December 1812	*Apollo*	stores	13 April 1749
Albanaise	brig sloop	23 November 1800	*Apollo*	5th rate	7 January 1799
Albany	sloop	19 July 1746	*Apollo*	5th rate	2 April 1804
Albany	ship sloop	28 December 1782	*Arab*	ship sloop	10 June 1796
Albemarle	fireship	23 July 1667	*Arab*	brig sloop	11 December 1823
Albion	battery	27 April 1797	*Ardent*	3rd rate	17 August 1779
Alceste	5th rate	18 February 1817	*Ardent*	3rd rate	April 1794
Alcmene	5th rate	30 April 1809	*Arethusa*	5th rate	19 March 1779
Aldborough	ketch	9 February 1696	*Argo*	5th rate	17 February 1783
Alert	sloop	17 July 1778	*Argus*	lugger	17 January 1799
Alert	schooner	8 July 1791	*Ariel*	6th rate	10 September 1779
Alert	ship sloop	14 May 1794	*Ariel*	packet	8 December 1828
Alert	ship sloop	13 August 1812	*Arms of Holland*	5th rate	July 1656
Alerte	brig sloop	18 December 1793	*Arrogant*	4th rate	5 January 1709
Alexander	fireship	21 June 1689	*Arrow*	ship sloop	4 February 1805
Alexander	3rd rate	6 November 1794	*Arthur*	cutter	19 January 1805
Algerine	cutter	20 May 1813	*Artois*	5th rate	31 July 1797
Algerine	brig sloop	9 January 1826	*Asia*	hulk	7 April 1701
Algier	5th rate	17 July 1673	*Assistance*	4th rate	29 March 1802

Name	Type	Date	Name	Type	Date
Assistance	discovery	25 August 1854	Blackwall	4th rate	20 October 1705
Association	2nd rate	22 October 1707	Blade of Wheat	fireship	25 December 1689
Assurance	5th rate	24 April 1753	Blanche	5th rate	11 October 1780
Astraea	stores	17 January 1744	Blanche	5th rate	28 September 1799
Astraea	5th rate	23 March 1808	Blanche	5th rate	19 July 1805
Atalanta	ship sloop	28 May 1781	Blanche	5th rate	4 March 1807
Atalante	brig sloop	12 February 1807	Blandford	6th rate	28 March 1719
Atalante	ship sloop	10 November 1813	Blandford	6th rate	13 August 1755
Athenienne	3rd rate	20 October 1806	Blast	bomb	19 October 1745
Attack	gun brig	19 August 1812	Blast	fireship	27 June 1756
Augusta	3rd rate	23 October 1777	Blaze	fireship	22 May 1692
Auguste	4th rate	10 November 1716	Blaze	fireship	5 May 1697
Augustus	gun vessel	7 July 1801	Blazer	gunboat	23 March 1801
Aurora	5th rate	January 1770	Blenheim	3rd rate	1 February 1807
Avenger	ship sloop	5 December 1803	Blessing	fireship	25 July 1666
Avenger	ship sloop	8 October 1812	Blessing	fireship	11 August 1673
Avenger	paddle frigate	20 December 1847	Blonde	5th rate	10 May 1782
Avon	brig sloop	27 August 1814	Bloom	tender	24 February 1797
Babet	6th rate	October 1800	Bold	gun brig	27 September 1813
Bacchus	cutter	17 August 1807	Bolina	tender	21 November 1807
Badger	sloop	24 September 1762	Bolton	bomb	5 April 1776
Ballahou	schooner	20 June 1814	Bombay Castle	3rd rate	21 December 1796
Baltimore	hired	15 November 1745	Bonaventure	3rd rate	4 March 1653
Banterer	6th rate	29 October 1808	Bonetta	sloop	20 October 1744
Bantam	fireship	28 May 1672	Bonetta	ship sloop	10 December 1781
Barbadoes	brig sloop	4 October 1780	Bonetta	ship sloop	25 October 1801
Barbadoes	6th rate	27 September 1812	Boreas	6th rate	28 November 1807
Barbados Merchant	fireship	11 June 1667	Boston	schooner	November 1768
Barbara	schooner	15 September 1807	Bouncer	gun brig	21 February 1805
Barracouta	schooner	3 October 1805	Bounty	armed ship	28 April 1789
Basilisk	bomb	29 October 1762	Bournabat	tug	29 March 1855
Basing Galley	6th rate	5 July 1694	Boxer	brig sloop	5 September 1813
Beaver's Prize	ship sloop	11 October 1780	Boyne	2nd rate	1 May 1795
Belem	schooner	12 August 1806	Bramble	fireship	4 June 1665
Belette	6th rate	21 October 1796	Brave	lugger	22 April 1799
Belette	brig sloop	24 November 1812	Brave	3rd rate	12 April 1806
Bellona	armed ship	15 December 1779	Brazen	ship sloop	26 January 1800
Benjamin	fireship	22 August 1673	Breda	4th rate	15 August 1666
Benjamin	ketch	21 December 1705	Bredah	3rd rate	12 October 1690
Berbice	schooner	26 October 1796	Bridgewater	6th rate	18 September 1743
Berbice	schooner	24 May 1806	Bridgewater	6th rate	28 April 1758
Berbuda	ship sloop	3 February 1782	Briseis	brig sloop	5 November 1816
Bermuda	brig sloop	September 1796	Briseis	packet	January 1838
Bermuda	ship sloop	22 April 1808	Bristol	4th rate	24 April 1709
Bermuda	brig sloop	16 November 1816	Britannia	stores	9 January 1782
Bermuda	tender	March 1821	Buffalo	stores	28 July 1840
Bermuda	schooner	20 January 1855	Bulldog	bomb	27 February 1801
Berwick	3rd rate	7 March 1795	Burchett	sloop	6 February 1709
Betsey	sloop	18 May 1775	Burford	3rd rate	14 February 1719
Betty	frigate	14 April 1653	Bustler	gun brig	26 December 1808
Betty	5th rate	14 September 1695	Busy	brig sloop	December 1806
Bideford	6th rate	12 November 1699	Bute	armed ship	3 December 1777
Bideford	6th rate	18 March 1736	Ca Ira	3rd rate	11 April 1796
Bideford	6th rate	31 December 1761	Cacafuego	gunboat	25 March 1809
Birkenhead	troopship	26 February 1852	Cadiz Merchant	fireship	19 May 1692
Biter	gun brig	10 November 1805	Caesar	tender	28 November 1760
Black Bull	4th rate	4 June 1666	Calcutta	4th rate	26 September 1805
Black Joke	lugger	1 June 1810	Calypso	ship sloop	30 July 1803
Black Spread Eagle	4th rate	2 June 1666	Calypso	packet	31 January 1833

ALPHABETICAL INDEX OF SHIPS LOST 351

Name	Type	Date	Name	Type	Date
Cambrian	5th rate	31 January 1828	Cleopatra	5th rate	17 February 1805
Cambridge	3rd rate	19 February 1694	Clinker	gun brig	November 1806
Camel	fireship	23 July 1667	Clove Tree	3rd rate	4 June 1666
Camperdown	gunboat	28 October 1810	Cockburn	tender	1 April 1823
Canterbury	stores	27 November 1703	Cockchafer	lugger	1 November 1801
Capelin	schooner	28 June 1808	Colchester	5th rate	24 March 1667
Captain	3rd rate	22 March 1813	Colchester	ketch	March 1668
Carlisle	4th rate	28 January 1696	Colchester	4th rate	16 January 1704
Carlisle	4th rate	19 September 1700	Colchester	4th rate	21 October 1744
Carlotta	brig	26 January 1812	Colibri	brig sloop	22 August 1813
Carnation	brig sloop	3 October 1808	Colossus	3rd rate	10 December 1798
Caroline	tender	1798	Columbine	brig sloop	25 January 1824
Carrier	cutter	24 January 1808	Comet	bomb	10 October 1706
Carron	6th rate	6 July 1820	Comet	fireship	7 July 1800
Cassandra	cutter	13 August 1807	Commerce	tender	17 January 1805
Castor	5th rate	19 June 1781	Companion	4th rate	10 May 1667
Castor	5th rate	9 May 1794	Comus	6th rate	24 October 1816
Cat	pink	28 April 1656	Confiance	5th rate	11 September 1814
Catherine	sloop	19 December 1762	Confiance	brig sloop	21 April 1822
Cato	4th rate	1783	Conflagration	fireship	14 November 1781
Censeur	3rd rate	7 October 1795	Conflagration	fireship	18 December 1793
Centaur	3rd rate	17 September 1782	Conflict	gun brig	24 October 1804
Centurion	4th rate	25 December 1689	Conflict	gun brig	9 November 1810
Centurion	hulk	21 February 1824	Conqueror	3rd rate	26 October 1760
Cerbere	gunboat	20 February 1804	Constance	6th rate	12 October 1806
Cerberus	6th rate	5 August 1778	Constant John	fireship	11 June 1667
Cerberus	5th rate	21 April 1783	Constant Reformation	2nd rate	30 September 1651
Ceres	ship sloop	17 December 1778	Constant Warwick	4th rate	2 July 1691
Ceres	fireship	11 April 1809	Constitution	cutter	9 January 1801
Ceylon	5th rate	18 October 1810	Constitution	cutter	26 August 1804
Challenger	brig sloop	12 March 1811	Contest	gun vessel	29 August 1799
Challenger	6th rate	19 May 1835	Contest	gun brig	August 1809
Chameleon	ship sloop	12 October 1780	Contest	gun brig	14 April 1828
Charity	fireship	16 August 1652	Convert	5th rate	8 February 1794
Charity	4th rate	3 June 1665	Convertine	4th rate	4 June 1666
Charles	fireship	5 July 1695	Coquille	5th rate	14 December 1798
Charles	yacht	27 November 1678	Cormorant	ship sloop	24 August 1781
Charles & Henry	fireship	29 November 1689	Cormorant	ship sloop	17 September 1796
Charles Merchant	4th rate	1 September 1666	Cormorant	6th rate	20 May 1800
Charles V	4th rate	12 June 1667	Cormorant	gunboat	25 June 1859
Charlotte	tender	16 August 1776	Cornwall	3rd rate	30 June 1780
Charlotte	brig	12 December 1797	Cornwallis	stores	17 September 1782
Charlotte	schooner	16 October 1798	Coronation	2nd rate	3 September 1691
Charlotte	schooner	28 March 1801	Countess of Scarborough	armed ship	23 September 1779
Charming Molly	cutter	5 January 1801	Courageux	3rd rate	19 December 1796
Charon	5th rate	10 October 1781	Coureur	schooner	21 June 1780
Chaser	ship sloop	14 February 1782	Coventry	5th rate	12 January 1783
Chatham	sloop	10 February 1678	Coventry	5th rate	25 July 1666
Chester	4th rate	10 October 1707	Coventry	4th rate	24 July 1704
Chesterfield	5th rate	25 July 1762	Crafty	schooner	9 March 1807
Chestnut	pink	1665 (?)	Crane	schooner	26 October 1808
Chichester	stores	3 May 1811	Crane	brig sloop	September 1814
Child's Play	6th rate	30 August 1707	Crash	gunboat	26 August 1798
Chippewa	sloop	November 1775	Creole	5th rate	3 January 1804
Chippeway	schooner	10 September 1813	Crescent	6th rate	26 September 1649
Chub	schooner	14 August 1812	Crescent	6th rate	30 May 1781
Chub	cutter	11 September 1814	Crescent	6th rate	20 June 1781
Circe	6th rate	17 November 1803	Crescent	5th rate	5 December 1808
Claudia	cutter	20 January 1809	Cricket	ketch	31 October 1808

Name	Type	Date	Name	Type	Date
Crocodile	6th rate	9 May 1784	Diana	tender	16 June 1775
Crown	4th rate	29 January 1719	Diligence	brig sloop	8 October 1800
Crown's Prize	6th rate	9 February 1692	Diligent	schooner	15 July 1775
Cruiser	ship sloop	2 October 1776	Diligent	schooner	17 May 1777
Cruizer	6th rate	15 December 1708	Diligent	brig	7 May 1779
Cruizer	cutter	November 1791	Diomede	5th rate	2 August 1795
Cuckoo	schooner	6 April 1810	Discovery	4th rate	25 May 1655
Cullen	5th rate	18 May 1656	Dispatch	schooner	20 October 1772
Culloden	3rd rate	23 January 1781	Dispatch	schooner	14 July 1776
Cumberland	3rd rate	10 October 1707	Dispatch	ship sloop	8 December 1778
Cumberland	3rd rate	3 November 1760	Dispatch	brig	1 August 1781
Cumberland	schooner	16 December 1803	Dispatch	hulk	23 December 1846
Cupid	ship sloop	28 December 1778	Dolphin	fireship	3 June 1665
Curieux	brig sloop	22 September 1809	Dolphin	fireship	11 June 1667
Curlew	brig sloop	1 November 1796	Dolphin	sloop	11 August 1673
Cutter	sloop	21 September 1673	Dolphin	tender	10 September 1778
Cyane	ship sloop	12 May 1805	Dominica	schooner	21 May 1806
Cyane	6th rate	20 February 1815	Dominica	cutter	3 August 1809
Cygnet	fireship	20 September 1693	Dominica	schooner	5 August 1813
Cygnet	brig sloop	7 March 1815	Dominica	schooner	August 1815
Cynthia	packet	6 June 1827	Doris	5th rate	13 January 1805
Cyrus	transport	18 April 1786	Dove	dogger	24 February 1674
Daedalus	5th rate	2 July 1813	Dove	cutter	5 August 1805
Dame de Grace	gun vessel	8 May 1799	Dover	hulk	20 August 1806
Danae	6th rate	14 March 1800	Dover	5th rate	2 May 1811
Daphne	6th rate	22 February 1795	Dover Prize	prize	25 December 1689
Daring	gun brig	27 January 1813	Dragon	4th rate	26 March 1712
Dart	cutter	November 1813	Dragon Prize	sloop	12 January 1690
Dartmouth	5th rate	9 October 1690	Drake	6th rate	February 1695
Dartmouth	4th rate	4 February 1695	Drake	sloop	27 November 1742
Dartmouth	4th rate	8 October 1747	Drake	ship sloop	25 April 1778
Date Tree	5th rate	13 October 1679	Drake	brig sloop	12 July 1804
Dauntless	ship sloop	16 May 1807	Drake	brig sloop	22 June 1822
De Braak	brig sloop	15 May 1798	Dreadful	fireship	6 July 1695
De Ruyter	stores	3 September 1804	Dreadnought	3rd rate	16 October 1690
Deal Castle	6th rate	3 July 1706	Dromedary	troopship	10 August 1800
Deal Castle	6th rate	15 October 1780	Duc d'Acquitaine	3rd rate	1 January 1761
Decoy	cutter	22 March 1814	Duc de la Vaugignon	cutter	15 December 1779
Defence	3rd rate	24 December 1811	Duchess of Cumberland	ship sloop	22 September 1781
Defence	hulk	14 July 1857	Duke	fireship	16 June 1742
Defender	gun brig	14 December 1809	Duke	tender	12 September 1782
Defiance	3rd rate	6 December 1668	Duke of Clarence	cutter	25 November 1804
Defiance	3rd rate	15 February 1780	Duke of Gloucester	brig	28 April 1813
Delight	ship sloop	September 1781	Duke of Rutland	brig sloop	30 July 1784
Delight	brig sloop	31 January 1808	Duke of York	lugger	2 January 1799
Delight	brig sloop	22 February 1824	Duke William	schooner	5 October 1768
Delphinen	brig sloop	4 August 1808	Dumbarton Castle	6th rate	26 April 1708
Demerara	schooner	14 July 1804	Dunkirk's Prize	6th rate	18 October 1708
Deptford	ketch	26 August 1689	Dwarf	cutter	3 March 1824
Determinee	6th rate	26 March 1803	Eagle	fireship	3 May 1671
Detroit	brig	9 October 1812	Eagle	fireship	17 April 1673
Detroit	ship sloop	10 September 1813	Eagle	advice	27 November 1703
Deux Amis	gun brig	24 May 1799	Eagle	3rd rate	22 October 1707
Devonshire	3rd rate	10 October 1707	Eagle	tender	4 July 1813
Devonshire	fireship	2 October 1804	Eaglet	ketch	22 May 1693
Diamond	4th rate	20 September 1693	Earl of Denbigh	hulk	1 June 1797
Diamond	5th rate	18 February 1827	Earl of Inchiquin	tender	15 March 1781
Diamond Rock	sloop	2 June 1805	Earl of Loudon	sloop	22 March 1757
Diana	schooner	28 May 1775	Echo	brig sloop	13 February 1781

ALPHABETICAL INDEX OF SHIPS LOST 353

Name	Type	Date	Name	Type	Date
Edgar	3rd rate	15 October 1711	*Fearless*	gun brig	20 January 1804
Edward	tender	17 April 1776	*Fearless*	gun brig	8 December 1812
Egmont	schooner	12 July 1776	*Felix*	schooner	23 January 1807
Electra	brig sloop	25 March 1808	*Ferret*	sloop	23 May 1706
Elephant	stores	8 May 1779	*Ferret*	sloop	1 September 1718
Elias	4th rate	19 October 1664	*Ferret*	ship sloop	24 September 1757
Elizabeth	5th rate	5 June 1667	*Ferret*	ship sloop	26 August 1775
Elizabeth	3rd rate	12 November 1704	*Ferret*	galley	11 August 1778
Elizabeth	schooner	1 September 1807	*Ferret*	brig sloop	7 January 1813
Elizabeth	schooner	October 1814	*Ferreter*	gun brig	31 March 1807
Emulous	brig sloop	2 August 1812	*Feversham*	5th rate	7 October 1711
Encounter	gun brig	11 July 1812	*Finch*	cutter	11 September 1814
Endymion	5th rate	22 August 1790	*Firebrand*	fireship	22 October 1707
England	5th rate	16 February 1695	*Firebrand*	fireship	11 October 1781
Enterprise	6th rate	12 October 1707	*Firebrand*	fireship	13 October 1804
Epervier	brig sloop	29 April 1814	*Firedrake*	bomb	12 November 1689
Ephira	brig sloop	26 December 1811	*Firedrake*	bomb	12 October 1703
Ephraim	machine	1 August 1695	*Firefly*	schooner	17 November 1807
Epreuve	ship sloop	March 1764	*Firefly*	schooner	27 February 1835
Erebus	discovery	22 April 1848	*Firm*	gun brig	29 June 1811
Erne	6th rate	1 June 1819	*Flamborough*	6th rate	10 November 1705
Espion	ship sloop	22 July 1794	*Flame*	fireship	22 August 1697
Espion	5th rate	17 November 1799	*Flamer*	gun vessel	22 November 1850
Essex	3rd rate	4 June 1666	*Fleche*	brig sloop	12 November 1795
Essex	3rd rate	21 November 1759	*Fleche*	ship sloop	24 May 1810
Ethalion	5th rate	25 December 1799	*Fleur de la Mer*	schooner	29 December 1810
Etna	fireship	18 April 1697	*Flight*	cutter	September 1806
Etrusco	stores	25 August 1798	*Floating Battery 1*	battery	18 December 1793
Europa	hulk	9 April 1676	*Floating Battery 2*	battery	18 December 1793
Eurus	6th rate	20 June 1760	*Floating Battery 3*	battery	20 September 1793
Exertion	gun brig	8 July 1812	*Flora*	5th rate	5 August 1778
Expedition	schooner	29 January 1782	*Flora*	brig	20 November 1800
Experiment	4th rate	24 September 1779	*Flora*	5th rate	18 January 1808
Experiment	lugger	3 October 1796	*Fly*	dogger	26 September 1673
Explosion	bomb	10 September 1807	*Fly*	advice	22 August 1695
Extravagant	fireship	19 May 1692	*Fly*	cutter	4 June 1781
Fairfax	2nd rate	31 March 1653	*Fly*	ship sloop	October 1801
Fairfax	3rd rate	19 September 1673	*Fly*	ship sloop	8 March 1805
Fairy	ship sloop	9 January 1781	*Fly*	brig sloop	28 February 1812
Fairy	brig sloop	13 November 1840	*Flying Fish*	sloop	31 December 1782
Fairy Queen	tender	19 November 1781	*Flying Fish*	schooner	16 June 1795
Falcon	4th rate	1 May 1694	*Flying Fish*	schooner	30 September 1805
Falcon	6th rate	10 June 1695	*Flying Fish*	schooner	15 December 1808
Falcon	5th rate	29 December 1709	*Fogo*	fireship	7 December 1747
Falcon	brig sloop	28 September 1745	*Folkestone*	cutter	24 June 1778
Falcon	bomb	19 April 1759	*Foresight*	4th rate	4 July 1698
Falcon	ship sloop	5 August 1778	*Forester*	5th rate	18 November 1672
Falcon	brig sloop	27 August 1779	*Forester*	hoy	26 August 1752
Falcon	fireship	7 July 1800	*Fort Diamond*	tender	23 June 1804
Falkland's Prize	5th rate	19 December 1705	*Forte*	5th rate	29 January 1801
Falmouth	4th rate	4 August 1704	*Fortune*	fireship	25 July 1666
Fama	brig sloop	23 December 1808	*Fortune*	frigate	July 1652
Fame	fireship	3 June 1665	*Fortune*	flyboat	13 June 1667
Fame	6th rate	21 September 1710	*Fortune*	stores	15 December 1700
Fame	sloop	22 July 1745	*Fortune*	ship sloop	26 April 1780
Fancy	gun brig	30 October 1811	*Fortune*	brig sloop	15 June 1797
Fantome	brig sloop	24 November 1814	*Fortune*	polacre	8 May 1799
Farquhar	schooner	December 1759	*Fountain*	fireship	28 May 1672
Favourite	ship sloop	6 January 1806	*Fowey*	5th rate	1 August 1704

Name	Type	Date	Name	Type	Date
Fowey	5th rate	14 April 1709	*Gosport*	5th rate	28 July 1706
Fowey	5th rate	27 June 1748	*Grafton*	3rd rate	2 May 1707
Fowey	6th rate	15 October 1781	*Gramont*	ship sloop	27 June 1762
Fox	fireship	8 July 1656	*Grampus*	sloop	10 October 1742
Fox	fireship	9 August 1666	*Grampus*	sloop	30 September 1744
Fox	fireship	19 May 1692	*Grampus*	stores	11 November 1779
Fox	sloop	2 December 1699	*Grampus*	stores	19 January 1799
Fox	6th rate	14 November 1745	*Grappler*	gun boat	31 December 1803
Fox	6th rate	11 September 1751	*Grasshopper*	brig sloop	24 December 1811
Fox	6th rate	7 June 1777	*Great Gift*	fireship	25 July 1666
Fox	5th rate	11 September 1778	*Greenwich*	4th rate	20 October 1744
Fox	cutter	25 July 1797	*Greenwich*	4th rate	18 March 1757
Fox	schooner	28 September 1799	*Greenwich*	sloop	22 May 1779
Fox Prize	6th rate	28 August 1706	*Grenada*	bomb	16 July 1694
Foxhound	brig sloop	30 August 1809	*Greyhound*	5th rate	14 June 1656
Francis	6th rate	7 October 1683	*Greyhound*	fireship	4 June 1666
French Victory	5th rate	5 May 1672	*Greyhound*	4th rate	26 August 1711
Friend's Adventure	ketch	6 November 1695	*Greyhound*	6th rate	5 September 1718
Friendship	fireship	11 August 1673	*Greyhound*	6th rate	19 April 1722
Friendship	gun vessel	2 November 1801	*Greyhound*	6th rate	16 August 1781
Frolic	brig sloop	18 October 1812	*Greyhound*	5th rate	11 October 1808
Fulminante	cutter	2 June 1800	*Griffin*	6th rate	August 1664
Fulminante	cutter	24 March 1801	*Griffin*	6th rate	27 October 1761
Fury	discovery	1 August 1825	*Grinder*	tender	13 April 1810
Galgo	brig sloop	9 October 1800	*Griper*	gun brig	18 February 1807
Gannet	cutter	7 June 1798	*Grouper*	schooner	21 October 1811
Garland	3rd rate	30 November 1652	*Growler*	gun brig	21 December 1797
Garland	5th rate	29 November 1709	*Guachapin*	brig sloop	7 July 1811
Garland	6th rate	26 July 1798	*Guadeloupe*	6th rate	10 October 1781
Garland	6th rate	10 November 1803	*Guardian*	5th rate	12 April 1790
Gaspee	schooner	10 June 1772	*Guerriere*	5th rate	19 August 1812
General Clinton	tender	22 March 1776	*Gunboat 8*	gunboat	21 June 1814
General Hunter	brig sloop	10 September 1813	*Gunboat 10*	gunboat	21 September 1812
General Monk	ship sloop	8 April 1782	*Gunboat 11*	gunboat	19 February 1812
George	schooner	14 August 1756	*Gunboat 17*	gunboat	28 July 1813
George	sloop	9 September 1757	*Gunboat 23*	gunboat	27 March 1811
George	tender	26 December 1776	*Gunboat 23*	gunboat	5 August 1813
George	sloop	3 January 1798	*Haddock*	schooner	12 November 1809
George	fireship	11 April 1809	*Haerlem*	sloop	16 July 1779
George & Molly	tender	17 April 1781	*Halcyon*	brig sloop	19 May 1814
George of Bristol	hired	22 January 1666	*Half Moon*	fireship	24 May 1692
Georgiana	cutter	25 September 1804	*Half Moon Prize*	4th rate	28 September 1686
Germoon Prize	6th rate	4 July 1700	*Halifax*	snow	14 August 1756
Gertrude	schooner	17 December 1804	*Halifax*	schooner	15 February 1775
Gibraltar	brig	18 April 1781	*Hamadryad*	5th rate	25 December 1797
Gibraltar	gunboat	12 November 1809	*Hampshire*	4th rate	26 August 1697
Glasgow	6th rate	2 June 1779	*Hampton Court*	3rd rate	2 May 1707
Gleaner	ketch	2 April 1814	*Hannah*	gunboat	25 October 1806
Glommen	brig sloop	24 October 1809	*Hannibal*	4th rate	21 January 1782
Glorieux	3rd rate	17 September 1782	*Hannibal*	3rd rate	5 July 1801
Gloucester	3rd rate	6 May 1682	*Hannibal*	armed ship	24 November 1804
Gloucester	4th rate	26 October 1709	*Happy*	ketch	14 September 1766
Gloucester	4th rate	16 August 1742	*Happy Entrance*	fireship	4 June 1666
Golden Hand	fireship	7 August 1673	*Happy Entrance*	3rd rate	28 February 1658
Golden Phoenix	3rd rate	13 June 1667	*Happy Return*	4th rate	4 November 1691
Good Fortune	dogger	11 June 1667	*Happy Return*	machine	1 August 1695
Good Hope	4th rate	20 May 1665	*Hard Bargain*	dogger	8 August 1673
Goodwin Prize	6th rate	23 February 1695	*Hare*	ketch	15 December 1655
Goshawk	brig sloop	21 November 1813	*Hare*	fireship	20 February 1666

Name	Type	Date	Name	Type	Date
Harlequin	ship sloop	7 December 1809	Hope	hoy	June 1672
Harmony	fireship	11 April 1809	Hope	3rd rate	16 April 1695
Harp	ketch	17 June 1693	Hope	brig sloop	21 September 1779
Harrier	brig sloop	March 1809	Hope	tender	6 February 1780
Harry Bonaventure	hired	9 July 1653	Hope	cutter	16 August 1781
Hart	6th rate	13 August 1652	Hope	ship sloop	7 October 1781
Hart	dogger	26 July 1673	Hope	schooner	October 1783
Hart	pink	9 June 1692	Hope	lugger	25 November 1797
Harwich	3rd rate	3 September 1691	Hopewell	fireship	11 August 1673
Harwich	4th rate	6 October 1700	Hopewell	fireship	3 June 1690
Harwich	4th rate	4 October 1760	Hopewell	fireship	19 May 1692
Hastings	5th rate	10 December 1697	Hopewell	smack	1 May 1697
Hastings	5th rate	10 February 1707	Hornet	brig sloop	26 January 1747
Havick	ship sloop	9 November 1800	Horseman	flyboat	13 June 1667
Hawk	sloop	October 1739	Hotham	tender	10 October 1778
Hawk	brig sloop	9 December 1759	Hound	fireship	4 June 1666
Hawk	tender	4 April 1776	Hound	fireship	22 May 1692
Hawk	ship sloop	December 1804	Hound	ship sloop	14 July 1794
Hawke	cutter	4 October 1757	Hound	brig sloop	26 September 1800
Hazard	sloop	12 November 1714	House of Sweeds	3rd rate	13 June 1667
Hazard	brig sloop	25 November 1745	Humber	5th rate	18 September 1762
Hazardous Prize	4th rate	19 November 1706	Hunter	fireship	31 July 1653
Hearty	packet	September 1827	Hunter	6th rate	July 1661
Hector	5th rate	3 September 1665	Hunter	6th rate	23 September 1710
Hector	3rd rate	4 October 1782	Hunter	dogger	18 January 1748
Helderenburg	hospital	17 November 1688	Hunter	ship sloop	27 December 1797
Helena	schooner	16 September 1778	Hussar	6th rate	23 May 1762
Helena	brig sloop	3 November 1796	Hussar	6th rate	27 December 1796
Helverston	3rd rate	22 July 1667	Hussar	5th rate	8 February 1804
Henrietta	yacht	11 August 1673	Hussar	6th rate	24 November 1780
Henrietta	3rd rate	25 December 1689	Hyaena	6th rate	27 May 1793
Henry	2nd rate	16 May 1682	Idas	cutter	4 June 1810
Henry	schooner	3 February 1782	Ignition	fireship	19 February 1807
Henry & Jane	smack	22 September 1704	Illustrious	3rd rate	18 March 1795
Hercules	4th rate	1 December 1652	Imogen	ship sloop	12 March 1805
Hercules	fireship	11 April 1809	Imogene	6th rate	27 September 1840
Hermes	brig sloop	January 1797	Impetueux	3rd rate	29 August 1794
Hermes	5th rate	15 September 1814	Impregnable	2nd rate	18 October 1799
Hermione	5th rate	22 September 1797	Incendiary	fireship	31 December 1780
Hero	3rd rate	24 December 1811	Incendiary	fireship	29 January 1801
Heron	brig sloop	9 May 1859	Increase	6th rate	March 1650
Hestor	fireship	2 December 1673	Industry	tender	4 March 1744
Heureux	6th rate	June 1806	Infernal	fireship	16 April 1781
Heyling	hoy	March 1782	Intelligence	brigantine	3 February 1700
Highflyer	schooner	24 September 1813	Intrepid	discovery	15 May 1854
Hinchinbrook	brig sloop	10 December 1746	Investigator	discovery	3 June 1853
Hinchinbrook	brig	19 April 1778	Inveterate	gun brig	18 February 1807
Hinchinbrooke	6th rate	19 January 1782	Invincible	3rd rate	19 February 1758
Hind	ketch	11 December 1667	Invincible	3rd rate	16 March 1801
Hind	dogger	26 February 1674	Iphigenia	troopship	20 June 1801
Hind	pink	15 January 1697	Iphigenia	5th rate	28 August 1810
Hind	6th rate	16 September 1709	Iris	5th rate	11 September 1781
Hind	6th rate	29 November 1711	Islip	5th rate	24 June 1655
Hind	6th rate	7 December 1721	Jackal	cutter	5 December 1779
Hind	brig sloop	1 September 1747	Jackal	schooner	11 April 1782
Hindostan	stores	2 April 1804	Jackal	gun brig	30 May 1807
Hirondelle	gun brig	23 February 1808	Jackdaw	schooner	16 February 1807
Holly	schooner	29 January 1814	Jackdaw	schooner	11 March 1835
Hope	4th rate	25 July 1666	Jamaica	sloop	9 October 1715

Name	Type	Date	Name	Type	Date
Jamaica	brig sloop	27 January 1770	*Leopard*	3rd rate	4 March 1653
James Galley	5th rate	26 November 1694	*Leopard*	fireship	11 August 1673
Jane	sloop	6 February 1782	*Leopard*	troopship	28 June 1814
Jaseur	brig	August 1808	*Levant*	6th rate	20 February 1815
Jaseur	gunboat	26 February 1859	*Levant Merchant*	5th rate	4 March 1653
Jason	5th rate	13 October 1798	*Leveret*	brig sloop	11 November 1807
Jason	5th rate	24 July 1801	*Leviathan*	stores	27 February 1780
Jasper	brig sloop	20 January 1817	*Liberty*	2nd rate	14 October 1650
Jasper	brig sloop	11 October 1828	*Liberty*	tender	2 September 1775
Jasper	packet	15 May 1854	*Lightning*	bomb	16 June 1746
Jasper	gunboat	23 July 1855	*Lilly*	sloop	31 March 1674
Java	5th rate	1 February 1807	*Lily*	6th rate	7 September 1653
Java	5th rate	29 December 1812	*Lily*	ship sloop	15 July 1804
Jersey	4th rate	18 December 1691	*Lincoln*	4th rate	27 January 173
Jersey	hulk	30 November 1783	*Linnet*	gun brig	25 February 1813
John	4th rate	January 1652	*Linnet*	brig sloop	11 September 1814
John & Sarah	fireship	11 June 1667	*Lion*	hoy	9 January 1708
John & Sarah	hoy	4 March 1706	*Lion*	hoy	26 August 1752
Johnson	snow	1764	*Litchfield*	4th rate	29 November 1758
Joseph	fireship	26 June 1667	*Little Belt*	sloop	10 September 1813
Joseph & Betsey	tender	30 January 1771	*Little Mary*	6th rate	13 October 1666
Julia	brig sloop	2 October 1817	*Little Unicorn*	fireship	4 June 1666
Julia	schooner	24 January 185	*Little Victory*	fireship	8 May 1671
Juno	5th rate	5 August 1778	*Lively*	6th rate	9 July 1778
Junon	5th rate	13 December 1809	*Lively*	brig sloop	9 December 1782
Jupiter	4th rate	10 December 1808	*Lively*	5th rate	13 April 1798
Kangaroo	brig	18 December 1828	*Lively*	5th rate	10 August 1810
Katherine	fireship	28 May 1672	*Lively Prize*	5th rate	4 October 1689
Katherine	fireship	11 August 1673	*Liverpool*	6th rate	11 February 1778
Katherine	yacht	17 August 1673	*Lizard*	fireship	9 August 1666
Kent	4th rate	15 October 1672	*Lizard*	sloop	26 February 1674
King of Prussia	cutter	6 February 1765	*Lizard*	6th rate	23 March 1696
Kingfish	schooner	3 July 1806	*Lizard*	brig sloop	27 February 1748
Kingfisher	ship sloop	30 July 1778	*Lizard*	paddle	24 July 1843
Kingfisher	brig sloop	3 December 1798	*London*	2nd rate	7 March 1665
Kings-Fisher	ketch	23 March 1690	*London*	brig	14 August 1756
Lacedemonian	gun brig	6 April 1797	*Looe*	5th rate	30 April 1697
Lady Jane	cutter	17 May 1800	*Looe*	5th rate	12 December 1705
Lady Nelson	tender	February 1825	*Looe*	5th rate	5 February 1744
Lady Prevost	schooner	10 September 1813	*Lord Keith*	cutter	11 January 1808
Land of Promise	fireship	25 July 1666	*Lord Mulgrave*	armed ship	10 April 1799
Landrail	schooner	12 July 1814	*Lord Nelson*	cutter	5 August 1809
Lapwing	cutter	October 1764	*Louisa*	cutter	21 July 1841
Lark	hulk	20 October 1744	*Louisburg*	fireship	4 December 1746
Lark	5th rate	5 August 1778	*Lowestoffe*	6th rate	19 May 1760
Lark	ship sloop	3 August 1809	*Lowestoffe*	5th rate	11 August 1801
Laura	cutter	8 September 1812	*Loyal George*	4th rate	1 June 1666
Laurel	4th rate	30 May 1657	*Loyal London*	2nd rate	14 June 1667
Laurel	ketch	10 December 1705	*Loyalist*	ship sloop	30 August 1781
Laurel	6th rate	11 October 1780	*Loyalty*	hulk	7 April 1701
Laurel	6th rate	12 September 1808	*Lucas Galley*	sloop	22 December 1693
Laurel	5th rate	31 January 1812	*Ludlow*	5th rate	16 January 1703
Laurestinus	6th rate	21 October 1813	*Lumley Castle*	4th rate	19 February 1694
Leander	4th rate	17 August 1798	*Lurcher*	cutter	15 January 1801
Leda	5th rate	11 December 1795	*Lutine*	5th rate	9 October 1799
Leda	5th rate	31 January 1808	*Lyme*	6th rate	15 September 1747
Lee	gunboat	25 June 1859	*Lyme*	6th rate	18 October 1760
Legere	ship sloop	2 February 1801	*Macedonian*	5th rate	25 October 1812
Leicester	6th rate	13 June 1667	*Magicienne*	5th rate	24 August 1810

ALPHABETICAL INDEX OF SHIPS LOST 357

Name	Type	Date	Name	Type	Date
Magnet	brig sloop	11 January 1809	Mercury	brig sloop	14 April 1745
Magnet	brig sloop	11 September 1812	Mercury	6th rate	24 December 1777
Magnet	brig	5 August 1814	Merlin	6th rate	13 October 1665
Magnificent	3rd rate	25 March 1804	Merlin	brig sloop	19 April 1757
Magpie	schooner	18 February 1807	Merlin	ship sloop	23 October 1777
Magpie	schooner	27 August 1826	Mermaid	6th rate	8 July 1778
Maidstone	4th rate	27 June 1747	Mermaid	6th rate	6 December 1759
Malabar	4th rate	11 October 1796	Mermaid Prize	fireship	26 February 1693
Mallard	gun brig	24 December 1804	Messenger	advice	November 1701
Mandarin	gun brig	9 December 1810	Messenger	dogger	9 July 1747
Manilla	transport	27 February 1782	Michigan	sloop	28 August 1763
Manilla	5th rate	28 January 1812	Milbrook	schooner	25 March 1808
Manly	gun brig	22 December 1805	Milford	5th rate	7 July 1671
Manly	gun brig	2 September 1811	Milford	5th rate	1 December 1693
Margaret	tender	3 November 1798	Milford	5th rate	7 January 1697
Margate	6th rate	9 October 1707	Milford	5th rate	18 June 1720
Margueritta	tender	12 June 1775	Minerva	5th rate	22 August 1778
Maria	schooner	1 September 1807	Minerve	5th rate	3 July 1803
Maria	gun brig	29 September 1808	Minorca	stores	27 June 1756
Maria Sancta	4th rate	12 June 1667	Minorca	xebec	21 August 1781
Marie Antoinette	schooner	7 July 1797	Minotaur	3rd rate	22 December 1810
Marigold	fireship	10 August 1673	Minx	gun brig	2 September 1809
Marigold	4th rate	31 January 1679	Mississauga	sloop	December 1759
Marlborough	3rd rate	29 November 1762	Mistletoe	schooner	14 December 1816
Marlborough	3rd rate	4 November 1800	Mohawk	sloop	14 August 1756
Marmaduke	4th rate	12 June 1667	Mohawk	snow	1764
Mars	3rd rate	24 July 1755	Molly	armed ship	7 June 1781
Martin	ketch	30 August 1702	Monck	4th rate	24 November 1720
Martin	ship sloop	October 1800	Monkey	gun brig	25 December 1810
Martin	ship sloop	August 1806	Monkey	schooner	13 May 1831
Martin	ship sloop	8 December 1817	Montreal	5th rate	1 May 1779
Martin	ship sloop	February 1826	Mordaunt	4th rate	22 November 1693
Mary	yacht	23 May 1675	Morne Fortunee	schooner	6 December 1804
Mary	ketch	19 February 1694	Morne Fortunee	gun brig	9 January 1809
Mary	4th rate	27 November 1703	Mortar	bomb	2 December 1703
Mary	hoy	31 October 1778	Moselle	ship sloop	7 January 1794
Mary	cutter	December 1804	Moucheron	brig sloop	April 1807
Mary	fireship	11 April 1809	Muros	6th rate	24 March 1808
Mary	fireship	June 1667	Muscovia Merchant	stores	10 April 1703
Mary Frigate	sloop	18 March 1690	Musquito	battery	30 June 1795
Mary Rose	4th rate	February 1650	Musquito	schooner	16 September 1798
Mary Rose	4th rate	12 July 1691	Mutine	brig sloop	21 December 1848
Mastiff	gunboat	5 January 1800	Myrtle	packet	3 April 1829
Matthias	4th rate	12 June 1667	Nacton	cutter	30 May 1746
Mayflower	machine	1 August 1695	Namur	3rd rate	13 April 1749
Mediator	sloop	3 June 1745	Nancy	cutter	1 March 1794
Mediator	sloop	29 July 1745	Nancy	cutter	10 January 1801
Mediator	stores	11 April 1809	Nancy	schooner	14 August 1814
Mediterranean	xebec	23 September 1758	Narcissus	6th rate	3 October 1796
Medusa	transport	26 November 1798	Nassau	3rd rate	30 October 1706
Medway	stores	25 November 1832	Nassau	3rd rate	25 October 1799
Megaera	paddle sloop	4 March 1843	Nautilus	ship sloop	3 February 1799
Meleager	5th rate	9 June 1801	Nautilus	ship sloop	4 January 1807
Meleager	5th rate	30 July 1808	Neckar	6th rate	December 1781
Mentor	ship sloop	14 April 1781	Nemesis	6th rate	9 December 1795
Mentor	ship sloop	April 1783	Neptune	tender	4 March 1744
Merchant	fireship	11 April 1809	Neptune	lugger	18 April 1798
Mercury	advice	19 June 1697	Nerbudda	brig sloop	12 June 1855
Mercury	fireship	12 December 1744	Nereide	5th rate	23 August 1810

Name	Type	Date	Name	Type	Date
Netley	gun brig	17 December 1806	Parrot	ketch	2 July 1657
Netley	gun brig	10 July 1808	Parthian	brig sloop	15 May 1828
Newcastle	4th rate	27 November 173	Partridge	brig sloop	27 November 1824
Newcastle	4th rate	1 January 1761	Peacock	brig sloop	24 February 1813
Newport	6th rate	5 July 1696	Peacock	ship sloop	16 June 1814
Nightingale	5th rate	16 January 1674	Pearl	fireship	11 August 1673
Nightingale	6th rate	25 August 1707	Pearl Prize	6th rate	17 May 1694
Nightingale	cutter	7 February 1829	Pegasus	ship sloop	October 1777
Nimble	cutter	11 February 1781	Peggy	brig sloop	20 December 1770
Nimble	cutter	6 October 1812	Peggy	lugger	8 April 1799
Nimble	schooner	4 December 1834	Peggy	fireship	2 October 1804
Nimrod	brig sloop	14 January 1827	Pelican	4th rate	13 February 1656
Nonsuch	4th rate	3 December 1664	Pelican	6th rate	2 August 1781
Nonsuch	ketch	3 February 1659	Pelter	gun brig	March 1810
Nonsuch	4th rate	4 January 1695	Pembroke	5th rate	10 May 1667
North	sloop	12 December 1779	Pembroke	5th rate	24 February 1694
Northumberland	3rd rate	27 November 1703	Pembroke	hoy	6 May 1709
Northumberland	3rd rate	8 May 1744	Pembroke	4th rate	29 December 1709
Norwich	5th rate	19 June 1682	Pembroke	4th rate	7 February 1745
Norwich	4th rate	6 October 1692	Pembroke	3rd rate	13 April 1749
Nymph	ship sloop	28 June 1783	Pendennis	3rd rate	26 October 1689
Nymphe	5th rate	18 December 1810	Pendennis	4th rate	20 October 1705
Oak	4th rate	31 July 1653	Penelope	6th rate	November 1779
Ocean	fireship	11 April 1809	Penelope	cutter	7 July 1799
Olive Branch Prize	fireship	10 August 1674	Penelope	troopship	1 May 1815
Olympia	cutter	2 March 1811	Penguin	6th rate	28 March 1760
Onondaga	snow	23 August 1760	Penguin	sloop	3 November 1778
Ontario	brig	14 August 1756	Penguin	brig sloop	23 March 1815
Ontario	snow	31 October 1780	Peregrine	4th rate	4 March 1653
Orange	5th rate	22 December 1670	Peregrine Galley	sloop	January 1762
Orange Prize	fireship	4 June 1673	Persian	brig sloop	26 June 1813
Orange Tree	fireship	11 May 1673	Pert	brig sloop	16 October 1807
Orestes	ship sloop	5 November 1799	Peter	ketch	24 July 1691
Orestes	ship sloop	11 July 1805	Peterel	ship sloop	13 November 1798
Orford	3rd rate	14 February 1745	Petite Victoire	tender	16 March 1794
Orford's Prize	6th rate	27 May 1709	Phaeton	fireship	19 May 1692
Oroonoque	brig sloop	3 February 1782	Pheasant	sloop	10 October 1761
Orpheus	5th rate	5 August 1778	Pheasant	cutter	20 June 1781
Orpheus	5th rate	23 January 1807	Phoenix	4th rate	28 August 1652
Orquixo	ship sloop	7 November 1805	Phoenix	4th rate	3 December 1664
Osprey	brig sloop	11 March 1846	Phoenix	4th rate	12 April 1692
Oswego	brig	14 August 1756	Phoenix	5th rate	4 October 1780
Otter	sloop	28 July 1702	Phoenix	5th rate	20 February 1816
Otter	sloop	14 January 1742	Pickle	schooner	27 July 1808
Otter	ship sloop	25 August 1778	Pictou	brig sloop	14 February 1814
Owner's Adventure	smack	5 December 1705	Pigeon	schooner	30 November 1805
Owner's Endeavour	fireship	24 July 1667	Pigeon	schooner	5 January 1809
Owner's Goodwill	tender	September 1739	Pigmy	cutter	27 December 1781
Owner's Love	fireship	28 July 1697	Pigmy	cutter	16 December 1793
Oxford	5th rate	2 January 1669	Pigmy	cutter	10 August 1805
Pallas	5th rate	12 February 1783	Pigmy	gun brig	5 March 1807
Pallas	5th rate	4 April 1798	Pigot	galley	5 August 1778
Pallas	5th rate	18 December 1810	Pigot	galley	29 October 1778
Pandora	6th rate	28 August 1791	Pike	schooner	18 March 1807
Pandora	brig sloop	13 February 1811	Pike	schooner	5 February 1836
Pandour	gun brig	June 1797	Pincher	schooner	6 March 1838
Panther	tender	8 November 1746	Pinson	armed ship	7 August 1779
Papillon	gun brig	September 1805	Pioneer	discovery	25 August 1854
Paragon	2nd rate	13 July 1655	Pique	5th rate	30 June 1798

Name	Type	Date	Name	Type	Date
Pitt	cutter	August 1766	Providence	ship sloop	17 May 1797
Placentia	schooner	14 September 1775	Providence	fireship	2 October 1804
Placentia	brig	September 1782	Prudent Mary	fireship	11 August 1673
Placentia	schooner	8 May 1794	Puck	tender	August 1856
Plover	gunboat	25 June 1859	Pylades	ship sloop	26 November 1794
Plumper	gun brig	16 July 1805	Quebec	schooner	11 September 1775
Plumper	gun brig	5 December 1812	Quebec	5th rate	6 October 1779
Pluto	fireship	30 November 1780	Queen Charlotte	tender	9 June 1796
Plymouth	3rd rate	11 August 1705	Queen Charlotte	1st rate	17 March 1800
Plymouth's Prize	6th rate	21 December 1709	Queen Charlotte	ship sloop	10 September 1813
Polecat	brig sloop	31 July 1782	Queenborough	6th rate	1 January 1761
Polly	tender	2 November 1801	Racehorse	sloop	6 December 1776
Polyphemus	paddle sloop	29 January 1856	Racehorse	schooner	26 January 1781
Pomona	ship sloop	6 September 1776	Racehorse	brig sloop	14 December 1822
Pomone	5th rate	14 October 1811	Racer	cutter	28 October 1810
Pompey	hoy	5 January 1711	Racer	schooner	10 October 1814
Porgey	schooner	4 June 1810	Rachel	fireship	28 May 1673
Porpoise	stores	17 August 1803	Racoon	brig sloop	12 September 1782
Port Royal	ship sloop	26 March 1781	Raikes	transport	6 June 1782
Port Royal	schooner	30 March 1797	Railleur	ship sloop	17 May 1800
Portland	4th rate	12 April 1692	Raisonnable	3rd rate	7 January 1762
Portsmouth	sloop	28 July 1672	Raleigh	4th rate	14 April 1857
Portsmouth	pink	16 October 1673	Rambler	cutter	10 October 1785
Portsmouth	4th rate	9 August 1689	Ramillies	2nd rate	15 February 1760
Portsmouth	5th rate	11 October 1696	Ramillies	3rd rate	17 September 1782
Portsmouth	bomb	27 November 1703	Ranger	cutter	11 June 1794
Portsmouth	stores	3 December 1747	Ranger	ship sloop	19 July 1805
Portsmouth	stores	14 August 1758	Rapid	gun brig	18 May 1808
Portsmouth Shallop	shallop	June 1655	Rapid	brig sloop	12 April 1838
Portsmouth's Prize	6th rate	29 September 1696	Raposa	gun brig	15 February 1808
Postboy	advice	1 October 1694	Rattlesnake	cutter	12 October 1781
Postboy	advice	3 July 1695	Raven	4th rate	11 April 1654
Postboy	brigantine	30 May 1702	Raven	ship sloop	7 January 1783
Postboy	snow	21 October 1746	Raven	brig sloop	3 February 1798
Postillion Prize	6th rate	7 May 1709	Raven	ship sloop	6 January 1804
Poulette	6th rate	21 October 1796	Raven	brig sloop	30 January 1805
Precious	tender	2 March 1706	Recruit	brig sloop	June 1832
Prevost	schooner	31 August 1806	Redbridge	schooner	4 August 1803
Primrose	5th rate	13 March 1656	Redbridge	schooner	26 February 1805
Primrose	brig sloop	22 January 1809	Redbridge	schooner	4 November 1806
Prince Edward	brig	5 September 1782	Redpole	packet	August 1828
Prince George	2nd rate	13 April 1758	Redwing	brig sloop	September 1827
Prince of Wales	cutter	24 July 1760	Reindeer	brig sloop	28 June 1814
Prince William	flyboat	17 February 1666	Repulse	5th rate	December 1776
Princess Louisa	5th rate	29 December 1736	Repulse	cutter	17 March 1782
Princess Maria	4th rate	8 February 1658	Repulse	3rd rate	10 March 1800
Princess Royal	cutter	20 July 1797	Requin	gun brig	1 January 1801
Prohibition	sloop	14 August 1702	Reserve	4th rate	27 November 173
Proselyte	battery	11 April 1794	Resistance	5th rate	24 July 1798
Proselyte	5th rate	4 September 1801	Resistance	5th rate	31 May 1803
Proselyte	bomb	5 December 1808	Resolute	discovery	15 May 1854
Proserpine	fireship	27 June 1756	Resolution	3rd rate	25 July 1666
Proserpine	6th rate	1 February 1799	Resolution	3rd rate	27 November 1703
Proserpine	5th rate	28 February 1809	Resolution	3rd rate	21 March 1707
Prospero	bomb	18 February 1807	Resolution	3rd rate	10 January 1711
Prosperous	hoy	12 June 1667	Resolution	3rd rate	20 November 1759
Providence	fireship	25 July 1666	Resolution	transport	10 June 1782
Providence	fireship	21 October 1668	Resolution	gun brig	June 1797
Providence	fireship	28 May 1673	Restoration	3rd rate	27 November 1703

Name	Type	Date	Name	Type	Date
Restoration	3rd rate	09 November 1711	*Sapphire*	5th rate	11 September 1696
Reunion	5th rate	7 December 1796	*Sapphire's Prize*	sloop	15 September 1745
Reynard	steam sloop	31 May 1851	*Sappho*	brig sloop	February 1858
Rhodian	brig sloop	21 February 1813	*Sarah*	ketch	23 October 1706
Richard	fireship	9 August 1666	*Sarpedon*	brig sloop	December 1812
Richard & Martha	ketch	24 September 1689	*Sartine*	6th rate	26 November 1780
Richmond	5th rate	11 September 1781	*Satellite*	brig sloop	19 December 1810
Robert	6th rate	May 1649	*Satisfaction*	5th rate	19 September 1662
Rochester	cutter	16 June 1746	*Saudadoes*	6th rate	23 February 1696
Rodney	brig	3 February 1782	*Savage*	brig sloop	16 September 1776
Roe	ketch	22 March 1670	*Savage*	ship sloop	6 September 1781
Roe	dogger	11 August 1673	*Savannah*	armed ship	20 September 1779
Roe	ketch	30 August 1697	*Scarborough*	ketch	12 January 1693
Roebuck	6th rate	24 February 1701	*Scarborough*	5th rate	18 July 1694
Romney	4th rate	22 October 1707	*Scarborough*	5th rate	1 November 1710
Romney	4th rate	19 November 1804	*Scarborough*	6th rate	4 October 1780
Romulus	5th rate	19 February 1781	*Sceptre*	3rd rate	5 November 1799
Rook	schooner	18 August 1808	*Scipion*	3rd rate	20 November 1793
Rosario	fireship	7 July 1800	*Scorpion*	sloop	23 September 1762
Rose	fireship	3 May 1671	*Scourge*	brig sloop	7 November 1795
Rose	dogger	11 August 1673	*Scout*	brig sloop	4 August 1794
Rose	6th rate	20 September 1779	*Scout*	ship sloop	25 March 1801
Rose	6th rate	28 June 1794	*Scout*	ship sloop	November 1801
Rose	cutter	13 October 1800	*Seaflower*	gun brig	28 September 1808
Rover	ship sloop	13 September 1780	*Seaford*	6th rate	5 May 1697
Rover	ship sloop	26 August 1781	*Seaford's Prize*	sloop	12 June 1712
Rover	ship sloop	29 October 1781	*Seaforth*	gun brig	September 1805
Rover	ship sloop	23 June 1798	*Seagull*	brig sloop	December 1804
Royal Anne Galley	5th rate	10 November 1721	*Seagull*	brig sloop	19 June 1808
Royal Charles	1st rate	12 June 1667	*Seahorse*	6th rate	14 March 1704
Royal George	1st rate	29 August 1782	*Seahorse*	6th rate	29 November 1711
Royal James	2nd rate	14 June 1667	*Sealark*	schooner	18 June 1809
Royal James	1st rate	28 May 1672	*Sedgemore*	4th rate	2 January 1689
Royal Oak	2nd rate	14 June 1667	*Seine*	5th rate	21 July 1803
Royal Prince	1st rate	3 June 1666	*Senegal*	ship sloop	15 August 1778
Royal Savage	schooner	11 October 1775	*Senegal*	ship sloop	22 November 1780
Royal Sovereign	1st rate	27 January 1696	*Sensible*	5th rate	3 March 1802
Ruby	4th rate	10 October 1707	*Sentinel*	gun brig	10 October 1812
Ruzee Prize	fireship	4 July 1692	*Serapis*	5th rate	23 September 1779
Rye	6th rate	28 November 1744	*Serin*	brig sloop	August 1796
Safeguard	gun brig	29 June 1811	*Serpent*	bomb	19 February 1694
Saint Jacob	fireship	26 July 1667	*Serpent*	bomb	15 October 1703
Saldanha	5th rate	4 December 1811	*Serpent*	bomb	1 September 1748
Salisbury	4th rate	10 April 1703	*Serpent*	ship sloop	August 1806
Salisbury	5th rate	10 May 1796	*Serpent*	gunboat	18 December 1793
Sally (1)	fireship	11 April 1809	*Seven Oaks*	4th rate	1 June 1666
Sally (2)	fireship	11 April 1809	*Severn*	4th rate	19 October 1746
Salorman	cutter	23 December 1808	*Severn*	5th rate	21 December 1804
Saltash	sloop	18 April 1742	*Shamrock*	schooner	25 February 1811
Saltash	brig sloop	24 June 1746	*Shannon*	5th rate	10 December 1803
Saltash	hoy	26 August 1752	*Shark*	sloop	30 March 1703
Sampson	4th rate	18 February 1653	*Shark*	6th rate	17 November 1780
Samson	3rd rate	4 March 1653	*Shark*	hulk	13 January 1818
Samuel	fireship	9 August 1666	*Shedam*	6th rate	4 April 1684
Samuel & Anne	fireship	28 May 1673	*Sheerness*	5th rate	8 January 1805
Sandwich	armed ship	24 August 1781	*Shelanagig*	schooner	5 June 1781
Sandwich	cutter	14 June 1799	*Shoreham's Prize*	sloop	7 June 1747
Santa Monica	5th rate	1 April 1782	*Sir Thomas Pasley*	brig	9 December 1800
Sapphire	4th rate	31 March 1670	*Siren*	6th rate	6 November 1777

ALPHABETICAL INDEX OF SHIPS LOST   361

Name	Type	Date	Name	Type	Date
Siren	6th rate	26 January 1781	St Lawrence	schooner	26 June 1766
Sirius	stores	19 March 1790	St Lawrence	schooner	26 February 1815
Sirius	5th rate	25 August 1810	St Lucia	gun brig	29 March 1807
Sisters	fireship	11 April 1809	St Nicholas	machine	12 July 1694
Skipjack	schooner	1 June 1841	St Patrick	4th rate	5 February 1667
Skylark	brig sloop	3 May 1812	St Paul	4th rate	2 June 1666
Skylark	packet	25 April 1845	St Peter	galliot	15 February 1674
Snake	brig sloop	13 June 1781	St Pierre	schooner	12 February 1796
Snake	brig sloop	29 August 1847	Stag	5th rate	6 September 1800
Snapper	schooner	14 July 1811	Stanley	tender	19 July 1778
Society	fireship	11 August 1673	Star	fireship	23 July 1667
Solebay	6th rate	25 December 1709	Star	bomb	29 May 1712
Solebay	6th rate	6 August 1744	Starling	gun brig	24 December 184
Solebay	6th rate	25 January 1782	Statira	5th rate	26 February 1815
Solebay	5th rate	11 July 1809	Stirling Castle	3rd rate	27 November 1703
Somerset	3rd rate	2 November 1778	Stirling Castle	3rd rate	14 September 1762
Somerset	hulk	30 October 1799	Stirling Castle	3rd rate	5 October 1780
Sophia	fireship	11 April 1809	Stork	ship sloop	16 August 1758
Sorlings	5th rate	15 November 1667	Stormont	brig sloop	3 February 1782
Sorlings	5th rate	20 October 1705	Strombolo	gunboat	19 January 1799
Sorlings	5th rate	17 December 1717	Subtle	schooner	26 October 1807
Soudan	paddle vessel	January 1844	Subtle	schooner	30 November 1812
Southampton	5th rate	27 November 1812	Success	fireship	17 February 1673
Southsea Castle	5th rate	15 September 1697	Success	5th rate	2 December 1679
Southsea Castle	5th rate	12 November 1699	Success	sloop	13 September 1709
Southsea Castle	stores	1 October 1762	Success	sloop	11 April 1710
Sparkler	gun brig	14 January 1808	Success	5th rate	13 February 1801
Speedwell	5th rate	29 June 1676	Suffisante	brig sloop	25 December 1803
Speedwell	bomb	21 November 1720	Sun Prize	6th rate	17 June 1693
Speedwell	cutter	5 April 1761	Sun Prize	6th rate	17 January 1708
Speedwell	gun brig	18 February 1807	Sunderland	4th rate	1 January 1761
Speedy	brig sloop	9 June 1794	Superb	3rd rate	7 November 1783
Speedy	brig sloop	3 July 1801	Supply	fireship	11 August 1673
Speedy	schooner	8 October 1804	Supply	5th rate	12 January 1690
Spey	packet	24 November 1840	Supply	stores	14 June 1779
Sphinx	6th rate	10 September 1779	Surinam	ship sloop	23 June 1803
Spider	lugger	4 April 1796	Susannah	fireship	8 December 184
Spitfire	galley	30 July 1778	Sussex	4th rate	9 December 1653
Spitfire	schooner	12 February 1794	Sussex	3rd rate	19 February 1694
Spitfire	schooner	21 August 1801	Sussex Oak	ketch	3 February 1808
Spitfire	paddle	10 September 1842	Swallow	sloop	1672
Spread Eagle	fireship	2 June 1666	Swallow	4th rate	9 February 1692
Sprightly	cutter	23 December 1777	Swallow	sloop	19 April 1703
Sprightly	cutter	10 February 1801	Swallow	sloop	24 December 1744
Spy	fireship	13 January 1693	Swallow	ship sloop	December 1777
Spy	ship sloop	16 June 1778	Swallow	brig sloop	16 August 1781
Squib	fireship	11 October 1805	Swallow Prize	6th rate	22 February 1696
Squirrel	6th rate	21 September 1703	Swallow's Prize	5th rate	29 July 1711
Squirrel	6th rate	7 July 1706	Swan	5th rate	13 September 1653
St Albans	4th rate	9 December 1693	Swan	fireship	26 July 1667
St Albans	4th rate	20 October 1744	Swan	smack	29 October 1673
St Andrew	2nd rate	24 November 1666	Swan	6th rate	17 August 1707
St David	4th rate	11 November 1690	Swan	brig sloop	16 August 1782
St Fermin	brig sloop	4 April 1781	Swan	cutter	25 April 1811
St George	smack	22 September 1704	Swan Prize	5th rate	15 June 1692
St George	2nd rate	24 December 1811	Sweepstakes	5th rate	16 April 1709
St John Prize	advice	5 September 1696	Swift	advice	24 January 1698
St Katherine	dogger	1673	Swift	sloop	18 August 1702
St Lawrence	fireship	11 August 1673	Swift	brig sloop	October 1756

Name	Type	Date
Swift	cutter	30 June 1762
Swift	ship sloop	13 March 1770
Swift	ship sloop	22 November 1778
Swift	ship sloop	2 July 1797
Swift	cutter	3 April 1804
Swift	brigantine	August 1696
Swiftsure	2nd rate	1 June 1666
Swiftsure	3rd rate	24 June 1801
Sylph	brig sloop	3 February 1782
Sylph	ship sloop	17 January 1815
Talavera	3rd rate	27 September 1840
Talbot	ketch	12 July 1691
Talbot	ketch	15 December 1694
Tang	schooner	February 1808
Tapageur	cutter	22 March 1780
Tartan Prize	advice	12 January 1693
Tartar	6th rate	1 April 1797
Tartar	5th rate	18 August 1811
Tartar's Prize	5th rate	2 March 1760
Tartarus	bomb	20 December 1804
Tay	6th rate	11 November 1816
Teazer	gun brig	16 July 1805
Telegraph	brig	14 February 1801
Telegraph	schooner	20 January 1817
Temple	3rd rate	18 December 1762
Terrible	5th rate	20 September 1710
Terrible	3rd rate	12 September 1781
Terror	bomb	17 October 1704
Terror	discovery	22 April 1848
Thais	packet	December 1833
Thames	5th rate	24 October 1793
Thetis	5th rate	11 May 1781
Thetis	5th rate	5 December 1830
Thistle	schooner	6 March 1811
Thomas	fireship	11 April 1809
Thomas & Elizabeth	fireship	24 May 1692
Thomas & George	fireship	5 October 1672
Thomas & Katherine	smack	30 March 1707
Thomas & Mary	hoy	2 April 1707
Thorn	ship sloop	25 August 1779
Three Brothers	tender	17 November 1762
Thrush	hulk	July 1815
Thunder	bomb	6 April 1696
Thunder	bomb	20 October 1744
Thunder	bomb	14 August 1778
Thunder	bomb	January 1781
Thunderbolt	paddle sloop	3 February 1847
Thunderer	radeau	November 1777
Thunderer	3rd rate	4 October 1780
Tiber	fireship	11 April 1809
Tickler	brig sloop	10 February 1783
Tickler	gun brig	4 June 1808
Tiger	4th rate	13 January 1742
Tiger	paddle frigate	12 May 1854
Tiger's Whelp	frigate	September 1649
Tigress	gun brig	2 August 1808
Tilbury	4th rate	21 September 1742
Tilbury	4th rate	25 September 1757
Tivere	tug	3 December 1855
Tobago	schooner	28 October 1806
Toronto	transport	2 June 1817
Tortoise	stores	4 November 1779
Tortoise	ighter	7 November 1787
Transit	troopship	10 July 1857
Trepassy	brig sloop	28 May 1781
Tresco	5th rate	22 October 1651
Tribune	5th rate	16 November 1797
Tribune	6th rate	29 November 1839
Trincomalee	ship sloop	12 October 1799
Triptolemus	fireship	11 April 1809
Triton	6th rate	28 April 1758
Triumph	6th rate	January 1740
Trompeuse	brig sloop	17 July 1796
Trompeuse	ship sloop	17 May 1800
True Briton	cutter	5 December 1780
Truelove	fireship	11 August 1673
Tryal	schooner	14 February 1777
Tryall	sloop	4 October 1741
Tulip	sloop	16 September 1672
Turbulent	gun brig	9 June 1808
Tweed	ship sloop	5 November 1813
Undaunted	5th rate	31 July 1796
Unicorn	fireship	11 June 1667
Unicorn	6th rate	4 September 1780
Union	schooner	17 March 1828
Unique	schooner	10 January 1806
Unique	gun brig	31 May 1809
United Brothers	tender	9 December 1806
Unity	4th rate	12 June 1667
Unity	ketch	6 November 1695
Urchin	gun vessel	12 October 1800
Utile	brig sloop	November 1801
Valeur	6th rate	6 September 1710
Vanguard	2nd rate	13 June 1667
Vanguard	2nd rate	27 November 1703
Vanneau	gun brig	21 October 1796
Vautour	brig sloop	July 1813
Venerable	3rd rate	24 November 1804
Venus	cutter	31 January 1806
Vestal	6th rate	October 1777
Vesuvius	fireship	19 November 1693
Vesuvius	fireship	27 November 1703
Victor	brig sloop	2 November 1809
Victor	brig sloop	5 September 1842
Victor	ship sloop	4 October 1780
Victory	1st rate	5 October 1744
Victory	sloop	30 November 1766
Vigilant	schooner	14 August 1756
Vigo	4th rate	27 November 1703
Ville de Paris	1st rate	17 September 1782
Vincejo	brig sloop	8 May 1804
Viper	brig sloop	15 December 1779
Viper	brig sloop	December 1796
Viper	schooner	February 1809
Vipere	xebec	18 December 1793
Virgin	sloop	17 May 1760
Virginia	fireship	26 July 1667
Volador	brig sloop	23 October 1808
Vulcan	fireship	22 September 1781

ALPHABETICAL INDEX OF SHIPS LOST 363

Name	Type	Date
Vulcan	fireship	18 December 1793
Vulture	sloop	31 August 1675
Vulture	fireship	10 December 1708
Wager	6th rate	14 May 1741
Wagtail	schooner	13 February 1807
Warrington	6th rate	1 December 1693
Warwick	4th rate	11 March 1756
Wasp	fireship	7 July 1800
Weazle	ship sloop	13 January 1779
Weazle	brig sloop	12 February 1799
Weazle	brig sloop	1 March 1804
Welcome	4th rate	13 June 1667
Welcome	fireship	4 June 1673
West Florida	sloop	10 September 1779
Westergate	4th rate	August 1664
Weymouth	4th rate	16 February 1745
Weymouth	transport	21 January 1800
Whitehaven	armed vessel	8 August 1747
Whiting	schooner	8 July 1812
Whiting	schooner	22 August 1812
Whiting	schooner	15 September 1816
Widgeon	schooner	20 April 1808
Wild Boar	brig sloop	15 February 1810
Wild Prize	6th rate	18 June 1694
Wilkin	gunboat	19 January 1799
William	fireship	28 March 1667
William	ketch	19 February 1694
William	stores	11 November 1807
William	fireship	11 April 1809
William & Lucy	gun vessel	4 November 1801
William & Mary	machine	12 September 1694
William Pitt	cutter	6 June 1799
Williamson	brig	25 October 1760

Name	Type	Date
Winchelsea	6th rate	10 October 1758
Winchelsey	5th rate	6 June 1706
Winchelsey	5th rate	29 August 1707
Winchelsey	5th rate	8 February 1709
Winchester	4th rate	24 September 1695
Windsor Castle	2nd rate	28 April 1693
Wizard	brig sloop	8 February 1859
Wolf	fireship	22 May 1692
Wolf	sloop	24 June 1704
Wolf	sloop	19 June 1708
Wolf	sloop	2 March 1741
Wolf	brig sloop	29 October 1745
Wolf	brig sloop	31 December 1748
Wolf	armed ship	30 July 1780
Wolf	ship sloop	4 September 1806
Wolverine	gun brig	24 March 1804
Wolverine	brig sloop	11 August 1855
Woodcock	schooner	13 February 1807
Woodlark	gun brig	13 November 1805
Woolwich	troopship	11 September 1813
Worcester's Prize	6th rate	27 May 1708
Worcester's Prize	6th rate	6 October 1708
Wren	pink	29 March 1697
York	4th rate	22 November 1703
York	sloop	10 July 1778
York	sloop	4 July 1779
York	3rd rate	January 1804
Young Prince	fireship	2 June 1666
Zebra	ship sloop	18 October 1778
Zebra	brig sloop	2 December 1840
Zenobia	schooner	30 October 1806
Zephyr	brig sloop	23 August 1778
Zephyr	fireship	11 April 1809